ESSAYS IN HONOUR
OF
ANTON CHARLES PEGIS

ESSAYS IN HONOUR
OF
ANTON CHARLES PEGIS

Editor

J. REGINALD O'DONNELL

TORONTO
PONTIFICAL INSTITUTE OF MEDIAEVAL STUDIES
1974

ISBN 0-88844-550-4

PRINTED BY UNIVERSA — WETTEREN (BELGIUM)

CONTENTS

Ashley-Crippen

ANTON CHARLES PEGIS
ON THE OCCASION OF HIS RETIREMENT

J. Reginald O'Donnell

τοῦτ' ἀεὶ δραστέον διὰ βίου
παντὶ κατὰ δύναμιν

Plato, *Legg.* 644B.

ANTON Charles Pegis was born 24 August 1905 in Milwaukee, Wisconsin, U.S.A., the child of Costas and Euphrosyne Pegis. He received his B.A. in 1928 and his M.A. in 1929 from Marquette University in Milwaukee and his Ph.D. in Philosophy in 1931 from the University of Toronto. He was one of the first graduate students in Toronto to carry on his research in the newly-organized Institute of Mediaeval Studies where he worked under the direction of Etienne Gilson and Gerald Phelan. His doctoral dissertation, *The Problem of the Soul in the 13th Century,* was published in 1934 by the Institute in St. Michael's College *Mediaeval Studies.*

Dr. Pegis began his teaching career in the department of Philosophy, Marquette University, in 1931, transferring to Fordham University, New York in 1937. From 1964 until April 1973 he was special visiting lecturer at Marquette with which he always maintained close associations. He was honoured by Marquette with an honorary LL.D. in 1956 and with the Alumni Merit Award in 1972.

In 1944 Dr. Pegis joined the staff of the Pontifical Institute of Mediaeval Studies, Toronto, where he became professor of the History of Philosophy and the Institute's first Fellow. He became, at the same time, through St. Michael's College, professor of Philosophy in the School of Graduate Studies of the University of Toronto. Two years later, 1946, he was elected president of the Pontifical Institute of Mediaeval Studies, succeeding Gerald Phelan, and was confirmed in office by the Sacred Congregation of Seminaries and Universities on 16 August of that year.

During his presidency, the Institute expanded its professoriate, adding new professors in history and theology, and strongly promoted the auxiliary disciplines, especially Latin and palaeography. It accelerated its publication policy, and it received its cherished *decretum laudis* from

Pope Pius XII. In 1946 Dr. Pegis was president of the American Catholic Philosophical Association, and in 1950 was received into the Royal Society of Canada.

In 1952, early in his second six year term as president of the Institute, Dr. Pegis accepted the editorial directorship of the Catholic Textbook Division of Doubleday and Company which took him to New York for the next nine years. He had at this time to resign his presidency, but continued as a Fellow and as special lecturer in philosophy in the Institute. In 1961 he returned to full-time teaching at the Institute and the University where, as emeritus since 1971, he is still giving his graduate courses.

No summary of Dr. Pegis's career provides an adequate insight into the nature of his scholarly competence. Important in this context must be noted his upbringing in an intelligent Greek-speaking family, his training in the elementary school at Tropaea in Arcadia, and private tutoring in orthographic Greek, which provided him with a rare and valuable background for the study of philosophy. Subsequently, when working for his M.A. at Marquette he had the additional advantage of courses with Paul Shorey on Plato, Aristotle and Aristophanes, and with Carl Buck on ancient Greek dialects. At the end of his high school course, his prize essay on book 4 of the *Aeneid* won him a scholarship to the University of Chicago — an award which ill-health compelled him to relinquish during his first year. When Pegis undertook doctoral research in medieval philosophy under the direction of Etienne Gilson he already possessed a rare and effective academic training and the perceptive mind of a true philosopher.

Partly because of his broad but close textual familiarity with Greek philosophy, and partly because he came to realize that, for the philosopher, the history of philosophy is primarily an instrument, Pegis's first concern has always been to use the history of medieval philosophy as a tool and to be himself primarily a philosopher. To achieve this purpose his philosophical judgement has led him to a disciplined commitment to the teaching of St. Thomas Aquinas. His commitment here has been to St. Thomas the living theologian rather than to any excerpted philosophy (called Thomism) which he felt could never in any form be a complete philosophy and which at best was doomed to be a moribund theology shared by protagonists communicating mainly among themselves. Dr. Pegis has always preferred to focus scholarly tools on the problems of contemporary thought, assessing them in their often over-looked medieval origins. He deplores the fact that medieval philosophy, unlike Greek and modern philosophy, is becoming an increasingly specialized subject rather than part of the mainstream of the history or development of ideas. His dedication to scholarship — ancient, medieval, or modern — as a means to becoming a Christian thinker goes a long way towards explaining his constant fascination with the notion of a proper Christian philosophy.

From the beginning of his career Pegis has shown an enduring interest in the philosophical problems of the soul and has repeatedly focussed his attention on the unity of man, on the knowing process, and on intentionality, particularly in its contemporary ramifications. Moreover, the great divide between the formal causality of the uncreated world of Greek philosophy and the efficient causality of the created world of Christian thought has led Pegis to dwell on proofs for the existence of God and on the differences between a philosophy of form and a philosophy of being. Pegis's focus on problems, his extensive and close reading of the great philosophers, and his orderly mind have made him one of North America's finest directors of doctoral and research students, and, on the international scene, a universally respected and honoured colleague. Dr. Pegis will receive the Aquinas Medal from the American Catholic Philosophical Association in 1975.

χρόνια πολλά

PUBLICATIONS
OF
ANTON C. PEGIS

1930

1. "Experience and Truth in St. Augustine" (*Proceedings of the American Catholic Philosophical Association,* 6, 1930, pp. 96-105).

1932

2. Translation of E. Gilson, "The Problem of Christian Philosophy" (*Hound and Horn,* 5, 1932, pp. 433-451).
3. Translation of E. Gilson, "Christian Personalism" (*Hound and Horn,* 5, 1932, pp. 637-655).

1934

4. *St. Thomas and the Problem of the Soul in the Thirteenth Century* (Toronto: St. Michael's College, 1934. Pp. 213).

1935

5. "The Frontiers of Philosophy and the Limitations of Science" (*Proceedings of the American Catholic Philosophical Association,* 11, 1935, pp. 24-37).

1937

6. "Symbolism in Mediaeval Latin Poetry" (*Spirit,* 4, 1937, pp. 56-59).
7. Review: *Speculum,* 12, 1937, pp. 274-277.

1938

8. "Knowledge and the Catholic College" (*America,* 58, 1938, pp. 536-538).
9. "Scholasticism and History" (*Thought,* 13, 1938, pp. 206-225).
10. Review: *America,* 58, 1938, p. 190.
11. Correspondence: *America,* 58, 1938, pp. 65-66.

1939

12. *St. Thomas and the Greeks* (The Aquinas Lecture, 1939. Milwaukee: Marquette University Press, 1939. Pp. 107).
13. "Molina and Human Liberty" (in *Jesuit Thinkers of the Renaissance,* ed. G. Smith, S.J., Milwaukee: Marquette University Press, 1939, pp. 75-131, 239-241).
14. "The Catholic Contribution: The Role of Reason in Education for Democracy" (in *Education for Democracy,* New York: Columbia University Press, 1939, pp. 198-209).
15. "Higher Education and Irrationalism" (*Thought,* 14, 1939, pp. 113-119).
16. "An Historical Approach to Philosophy" (*Thought,* 14, 1939, pp. 120-122).
17. "The Question of an Historical Approach to Philosophy" (*Thought,* 14, 1939, pp. 306-309).
18. Reviews: *Thought,* 14, 1939, pp. 341-342, 658.

1940

19. "In Umbra Intelligentiae" (*The New Scholasticism,* 14, 1940, pp. 146-180).
20. "Mr. Adler and Teaching" (*The Commonweal,* 32, 1940, pp. 119-122).
21. "Plato and His Critics" (*America,* 63, 1940, pp. 243-244).
22. Reviews: *Thought,* 15, 1940, pp. 304-306, 349-350, 544-545, 546-548, 707-710, 743-744.

1941

23. "Necessity and Liberty: An Historical Note on St. Thomas Aquinas" (*The New Scholasticism,* 15, 1941, pp. 18-45; also in *Proceedings of the American Catholic Philosophical Association,* 16, 1940, pp. 1-27).

1941

24. "In Search of Man" (in *Conference on Science, Philosophy and Religion*, New York, 1941, pp. 350-368).
25. Reviews: *Thought*, 16, 1941, pp. 191-192, 384-385.
26. Review: *The New Scholasticism*, 15, 1941, pp. 176-183.

1942

27. "The Dilemma of Being and Unity" (in *Essays in Thomism*, ed. R. G. Brennan, O.P., New York: Sheed and Ward, 1942, pp. 151-183).
28. "St. Thomas Aquinas" (in *Dictionary of Philosophy*, ed. D. Runes, New York: The Philosophical Library, 1942, pp. 16-17).
29. "The Catholic Layman" (*America*, 67, 1942, pp. 232-234).
30. Review: *Thought*, 17, 1942, pp. 148-149.

1943

31. "Matter, Beatitude and Liberty" (*The Thomist* [Maritain Volume], 1943, pp. 265-280).
32. "Cosmogony and Knowledge, I. St. Thomas and Plato" (*Thought*, 18, 1943, pp. 643-664).
33. "La crise de l'intelligence aux Etats-Unis" (*L'Enseignement secondaire au Canada*, 23, 1943, pp. 155-171).

1944

34. "The Mind of St. Augustine" (*Mediaeval Studies*, 6, 1944, pp. 1-61).
35. "Concerning William of Ockham" (*Traditio*, 2, 1944, pp. 465-480).
36. "In Defense of St. Augustine" (*The New Scholasticism*, 18, 1944, pp. 97-122).
37. "Cosmogony and Knowledge, II. The Dilemma of Composite Essences" (*Thought*, 19, 1944, pp. 269-290).
38. "Man and the Challenge of Irrationalism" (in *Race: Nation: Person. Social Aspects of the Race Problem*, ed. G. B. O'Toole, New York: Barnes and Noble Co., 1944, pp. 69-93).
39. "Toward the Rediscovery of Man" (*Proceedings of the American Catholic Philosophical Association*, 19, 1944, pp. 8-17).
40. (Editor) *Essays in Modern Scholasticism:* In Honor of John F. McCormick, S.J. (Westminster, Md.: The Newman Bookshop, 1944. Pp. 295).
41. "Rev. John F. McCormick, S.J.: In Memoriam" (in *Essays in Modern Scholasticism*, pp. 1-4).
42. "In Defense of St. Augustine" (in *Essays in Modern Scholasticism*, pp. 90-115).

1945

43. *Basic Writings of St. Thomas Aquinas*. Translated, with Introduction and Notes. (2 vols., New York: Random House, 1945. Vol. I: pp. liii + 1097; vol. II: pp. xxxi + 1197).
44. "Cosmogony and Knowledge, III. Between Thought and Being" (*Thought,* 20, 1945, pp. 473-498).

1946

45. "The Middle Ages and Philosophy" (Presidential Address. *Proceedings of the American Catholic Philosophical Association,* 21, 1946, pp. 16-25).
46. "A Note on St. Thomas Aquinas, *Summa Theologica,* I, 44, 1-2" (*Mediaeval Studies,* 8, 1946, pp. 159-168).
47. "Gilson and Thomism" (*Thought,* 21, 1946, pp. 435-454).

1947

48. Review: *Traditio,* 5, 1947, pp. 391-393.

1948

49. *Introduction to St. Thomas Aquinas*. Translated, with Introduction and Notes. (New York: Random House, 1948. Pp. xxx + 690).
50. "*Principale Volitum.* Some Notes on a Supposed Thomistic Contradiction" (*Philosophy and Phenomenological Research,* 9, 1948, pp. 51-70).
51. "Autonomy and Necessity: A Rejoinder to Professor Lovejoy" (*Philosophy and Phenomenological Research,* 9, 1948, pp. 89-97).
52. "Postscript" (*Philosophy and Phenomenological Research,* 9, 1948, pp. 291-293).
53. "Some Recent Interpretations of Ockham" (*Speculum,* 23, 1948, pp. 452-463).

1949

54. (Editor) *The Wisdom of Catholicism,* with translations and introductions (New York: Random House, 1949. Pp. xxix + 988).
55. "Nature and Spirit: Some Reflections on the Problem of the End of Man" (*Proceedings of the American Catholic Philosophical Association,* 23, 1949, pp. 62-79).

1950

56. Introduction to John Henry Cardinal Newman, *Apologia Pro Vita Sua* (reprint of the 1864 edition. New York: Random House, 1950, pp. vii-xiv).

57. "Redeeming the Time" (*The Commonweal,* 52, 1950, pp. 407-409).
58. Review: *Speculum,* 25, 1950, pp. 261-268.

1951

59. "Man as Nature and Spirit" (*Doctor Communis,* 4, 1951, pp. 52-63).
60. "Matthew of Aquasparta and the Cognition of Non-being" (*Acta Congressus Scholastici Internationalis.* Romae: Pontificium Athenaeum Antonianum, 1951, pp. 463-480).

1952

61. "Some Permanent Contributions of Medieval Philosophy to the Notion of Man (*Transactions of the Royal Society of Canada.* Third Series, Section II, vol. 46, 1952, pp. 67-78).

1953

62. "St. Bonaventure, St. Francis and Philosophy" (*Mediaeval Studies,* 15, 1953, pp. 1-13).
63. "Catholic Education and American Society" (*National Catholic Educational Association Bulletin,* 50, 1953, pp. 52-59).
64. "The Responsibility of the Philosopher" (*Diamond Jubilee Convocation, Duquesne University,* 1953, pp. 29-40).

1954

65. "Teaching and the Freedom to Learn" (in *The McAuley Lectures,* 1953. West Hartford, Conn.: Saint Joseph College, 1954, pp. 17-28).

1955

66. "St. Thomas and the Unity of Man" (in *Progress in Philosophy,* ed. J. A. McWilliams, S.J., Milwaukee: The Bruce Publishing Co., 1955, pp. 153-173).
67. *St. Thomas Aquinas: On the Truth of the Catholic Faith,* Book One: God. Translated, with Introduction and Notes. (Garden City, New York: Doubleday and Company, Inc., 1955. Pp. 317).
68. "The Christian Citizen and His Society" (in *Roots of a Catholic College,* ed. A. F. Horrigan, Louisville, Ky.: Bellarmine College Press, 1955, pp. 56-64).

1957

69. (Editor) *A Gilson Reader,* with introductions and translations (Garden City, New York: Doubleday and Company, Inc., 1957. Pp. 358).

1959

70. Preface to the collected *McAuley Lectures,* 1953-1959 (West Hartford, Conn.: Saint Joseph College, 1960, pp. vii-viii).
71. *The Education of Intelligence in an Age of Science* (Toronto: The English Catholic Educational Association of Ontario, 1959. Pp. 15).
72. "Some Reflections on *Summa Contra Gentiles* II, 56" (in *An Etienne Gilson Tribute,* ed. C. J. O'Neil, Milwaukee: Marquette University Press, 1959, pp. 169-188).

1960

73. "Thomism as a Philosophy" (in *The McAuley Lectures,* 1960. West Hartford, Conn.: Saint Joseph College, 1960, pp. 15-30).
74. *Christian Philosophy and Intellectual Freedom* (The Gabriel Richard Lecture, 1955. Milwaukee: The Bruce Publishing Co., 1960. Pp. 89).
75. "Religion and the Catholic Elementary School Curriculum" (*National Catholic Educational Association Bulletin,* 57, 1960, pp. 343-350).

1961

76. "St. Thomas and the Origin of Creation" (in *Philosophy and the Modern Mind.* The Cardinal Mooney Lecture Series, 1960-1961. Detroit, Mich.: Sacred Heart Seminary, 1961, pp. 49-65).

1963

77. "St. Thomas and the *Nicomachean Ethics*: Some Reflections on *Summa Contra Gentiles* III, 44, 5" (*Mediaeval Studies,* 25, 1963, pp. 1-25).
78. *At the Origins of the Thomistic Notion of Man* (The Saint Augustine Lecture, 1962. New York: The Macmillan Company, 1963. Pp. 82).
79. *The Middle Ages and Philosophy* (Chicago: The Henry Regnery Company, 1963. Pp. xiv + 102).

1964

80. "Qu'est-ce que la *Summa Contra Gentiles?*" (in *L'Homme devant Dieu: Mélanges offerts au Père Henri de Lubac,* Paris: F. Aubier, 1964, vol. II, pp. 169-182).
81. *St. Thomas and Philosophy* (The Aquinas Lecture, 1964. Milwaukee: Marquette University Press, 1964. Pp. 89).

1965

82. "*Sub Ratione Dei*: A Reply to Professor Anderson" (*The New Scholasticism*, 39, 1965, pp. 141-157).
83. "Gerald Bernard Phelan" (*Mediaeval Studies*, 27, 1965, pp. i-v).
84. "Penitus Manet Ignotum" (*Mediaeval Studies*, 27, 1965, pp. 212-226).

1966

85. "St. Anselm and the Argument of the *Proslogion*" (*Mediaeval Studies*, 28, 1966, pp. 228-267).
86. "Thomism 1966" (*Proceedings of the American Catholic Philosophical Association*, 40, 1966, pp. 55-67).
87. "Catholic Intellectualism at the Crossroad" (in *The McAuley Lectures*, 1966. West Hartford, Conn.: Saint Joseph College, 1966, pp. 1-17).
88. "Thomism 1966" (reprinted in *The McAuley Lectures*, 1966. West Hartford, Conn.: Saint Joseph College, 1966, pp. 19-31). See item 86.

1967

89. "The Bonaventurean Way to God" (*Mediaeval Studies*, 29, 1967, pp. 206-242).
90. "Who Reads Aquinas?" (*Thought*, 13, 1967, pp. 488-504).

1968

91. "The Notion of Man in the Context of Renewal" (in *Theology of Renewal*, ed. L. K. Shook, New York: Herder and Herder, vol. I, pp. 250-264).
92. "Le Concept de l'homme dans le contexte du renouveau" (in *La Théologie du renouveau*, ed. L. K. Shook and G.-M. Bertrand, Montreal: Fides, 1968, vol. I, pp. 277-289).
93. "Toward a New Way to God: Henry of Ghent" (*Mediaeval Studies*, 30, 1968, pp. 226-247).

1969

94. "A New Way to God: Henry of Ghent (II)" (*Mediaeval Studies*, 31, 1969, pp. 93-116).

1970

95. "Four Medieval Ways to God" (*The Monist*, 54, 1970, pp. 317-358).
96. "Who Reads Aquinas?" (reprinted in *Christian Witness in the Secular City*, ed. E. J. Morgan, Chicago: Loyola University Press, 1970, pp. 60-75). See item 90.

1971

97. "Henry of Ghent and the New Way to God (III)" (*Mediaeval Studies*, 33, 1971, pp. 158-179).
98. "St. Thomas Aquinas" (in *Encyclopedia of Education*, New York: The Macmillan Company, 1971, vol. I, pp. 250-257).

1973

99. "Jacques Maritain: 1882-1973" (*Mediaeval Studies*, 35, 1973, pp. vii-x).
100. "St. Thomas and the Coherence of the Aristotelian Theology" (*Mediaeval Studies*, 35, 1973, pp. 67-117).

1974

101. "The Knowledge of the Separated Soul: *SCG* 11, c. 81" (in *St. Thomas Aquinas, 1274-1974: Commemorative Studies*. 2 vols., Toronto: Pontifical Institute of Mediaeval Studies, 1974, vol. 1, pp. 131-158).
102. "St. Bonaventure Revisited" (*in St. Bonaventure, 1274-1974*. 5 vols., Collegio S. Bonaventura. Grottaferrata [Roma], vol. 2, pp. 21-44).
103. "Between Immortality and Death: Some Further Reflections on the *Summa Contra Gentilkes, The Monist*, 58 (1974).

In Press

1. "The Second Conversion of St. Augustine" (in *Festschrift Wallach*, ed. Karl Bosl).

In Progress

1. *The World of the Philosophers*, vols. 1-2.
2. *St. Thomas and the Unity of Man*.

THE DEFINITION OF FAITH
ACCORDING TO A QUESTION OF MS. ASSISI 138:
STUDY AND EDITON OF TEXT

William J. Conlan, O.P.

THE early thirteenth century is of special interest and importance in the history of Catholic theology. It saw the rise of great universities, notably Paris and Oxford, and a gradual evolution in literary forms from glosses to questions independently discussed and organized. It was the time of the "third entry" of Aristotle, accompanied by Moslem and Jewish authors. Not only was it the period of proximate preparation of materials for the monumental achievements of St. Bonaventure and St. Thomas, but it was also a time of theologians illustrious in their own right.

Despite their interest, the writings of many authors of that time have not yet been studied or even published, nor have many of their doctrinal themes been systematically investigated. The valuable historical studies by Georg Englhardt[1] and M.-D. Chenu[2] on the theology of faith did not include MS. Assisi, Biblioteca Comunale 138. This manuscript has been found to contain an important collection of theological questions which were discussed in the second quarter of the thirteenth century. It was an important source for the *Summa Fratris Alexandri* in its

---

1 *Die Entwicklung der dogmatischen Glaubenspsychologie in der mittelalterlichen Scholastik vom Abaelard-streit (um 1140) bis zu Philipp dem Kanzler (gest. 1236).* Beiträge 30, 4-6 (Münster, 1933).

2 "Contribution à l'histoire du traité de la foi. Commentaire historique de IIa IIae, q. 1, a. 2," *Mélanges Thomistes* (Kain, 1923) pp. 123-140. "Pro fidei supernaturalitate illustranda," *Xenia Thomistica* (Rome, 1925) Vol. III, pp. 297-307. "La surnaturalisation des vertus," *Bulletin Thomiste*, 1 (1931-1933) 93*-96*. "L'amour dans la foi," *Bulletin Thomiste*, 1 (1931-1933) 97*-99*. "La psychologie de la foi dans la théologie du XIIIᵉ siècle. Genèse de la doctrine de S. Thomas, IIa IIae, q. 2, a. 1," *Études d'histoire doctrinale et littéraire du XIIIᵉ siècle: Deuxième Série* (Ottawa-Paris, 1932) pp. 163-191. "La théologie comme science au XIIIᵉ siècle" (Paris, 1957).

later editions and was used by St. Bonaventure, who may even have directed its composition. This article, therefore, will edit and examine the doctrine of a question from that manuscript in which definitions of faith are discussed. It is hoped thereby to contribute to our understanding of the development of this theme.

MS. Assisi, Biblioteca Comunale 138, was dated about 1250 by F. Pelster, writing in 1933.[3] In 1948, V. Doucet concurred, assigning the manuscript to the mid-thirteenth century.[4] He also said it was composed under the direction of St. Bonaventure,[5] but in 1960, the editors of Alexander's *Quaestiones Disputatae 'Antequam Esset Frater'* said that perhaps it was composed under the direction of St. Bonaventure.[6] In 1932, F. M. Henquinet said that almost half of it (ff. 137r-270r, out of a total of 293 folios) was written by one scribe under St. Bonaventure's direction and that he probably supervised the composition of the entire manuscript.[7] In 1938, Henquinet simply said it was studied and annotated by St. Bonaventure when he was preparing his commentary on the fourth book of the *Sentences*.[8] St. Bonaventure began his commentary on the *Sentences* with Book IV, either in 1249[9] or, as has been proposed more recently, in 1250.[10]

Although he dated the manuscript about 1250, Pelster said the questions it records date from before 1238, in fact from 1230 to 1238.[11] But Henquinet noticed that Guiard is referred to as of Cambrai (f. 148va) when one of the questions was discussed, and he pointed out that Guiard became bishop of Cambrai in 1238.[12]

In 1948, Doucet, in the prologue to Book III of the *Summa Fratris Alexandri*, stated that Books I and III were compiled about the years 1235-1245,[13] principally by John of La Rochelle,[14] who died in 1245, the

3 "Les 'Quaestiones' de Guiard de Laon dans 'Assise Bibl. comm. 138,'" *Recherches de Théologie ancienne et médiévale* 5 (1933) 371.

4 *Prolegomena in Librum III necnon in libros I et II "Summae Fratris Alexandri:" Doctoris Irrefragabilis Alexandri de Hales Ordinis Minorum Summa Theologica seu sic ab origine dicta "Summa Fratris Alexandri,"* Tomus IV (Quaracchi, 1948) p. 138. (Roman numerals are used for the pagination of the *Prolegomena,* but Arabic numerals will be substituted here to facilitate references.)

5 *Loc. cit.*

6 *ProlQuaest* I, 7*-8*.

7 "Un recueil de questions annoté par S. Bonaventure," *Archivum Franciscanum Historicum* 25 (1932) 554.

8 "Les questions inédites d'Alexandre de Hales sur les fins dernières," *RTAM* 10 (1938) 170-171.

9 *Prolegomena in Librum III ...,* p. 246.

10 J. G. Bougerol, *Introduction à l'étude de Saint Bonaventure* (Tournai, 1961) p. 241. Also I. C. Brady, "St. Bonaventure," *New Catholic Encyclopedia* 15 vols. New York, 1967. Vol. 2, p. 658.

11 "Les 'Quaestiones' ...," p. 387.

12 "Les écrits du Frère Guerric de Saint-Quentin, O.P.," *RTAM* 6 (1934) 302-303.

13 "Prolegomena in Librum III ...," pp. 120-121.

14 *Ibid.,* pp. 361 and 365.

same year as Alexander of Hales, but a few months earlier.[15] He granted that Assisi 138 was a possible source of later, expanded versions of
that work[16] and that it may contain questions by Stephen de Poligny.[17]
Pelster ascribed a question in this manuscript to Stephen de Poligny,
claiming that a marginal note in f. 13v reads: *his usque ad folium 111 de
pulia*.[18] As the question referred to appears in the original *Summa*, and
as Stephen became a Master in 1246 at the earliest,[19] this challenged
John of La Rochelle's authorship of the original form of the *Summa*.
The following year, Doucet, after carefully examining the manuscript
again, gave the reading of the note as "exactly and surely this: *Huc usque
et non plus*."[20] It may be concluded: 1) that the manuscript was not used
in the original version of the *Summa Fratris Alexandri*, 2) that, in fact,
because it contains other questions by Stephen de Poligny, its *terminus a
quo* is at least 1246, and 3) that, because St. Bonaventure used it when
commenting on Book IV of the *Sentences*, the *terminus ad quem* is 1249 or
1250.

For only a few of the manuscripts has an author been assigned in the
manuscript itself, but many have been identified by recent research, as
will be explained more fully in Chapter IV. The question to be edited
here is the first of a group of four or five questions on faith which are
found on folios 176vb51-180rb12. These questions and the three
following it, which cover folios 180rb13-182va16, were included by
Pelster in a list of seventy-five questions which he assigned, in 1933, to
Guiard of Laon.[21] Three years later, Henquinet showed that thirty seven
questions from that list belong to Guerric of St. Quentin.[22]

According to Pelster, all of the questions on faith form a single
group, by one author, this being clear from their dependence on other
questions, their object, titles and formulas.[23] Henquinet said that the
question on the unity of the Church, which immediately precedes the
group of questions on faith, may belong to it.[24] He did not regard the

---

15   *Ibid.*, pp. 211 and 355.
16   *Ibid.*, p. 140.
17   *Ibid.*, pp. 138-139.
18   "Magister Stephanus de Poliniaco und seine Quästionen. Eine Beitrag zur Geschichte der
Theologie vor Bonaventura und Thomas," *Scholastik* 20-24 (1949) 558.
19   *Ibid.*, p. 563. Also V. Doucet, "Autour des 'Prolegomena ad Summam fr. Alexandri," *Archivum Franciscanum Historicum* 43 (1950) 198.
20   *Ibid.*, p. 199.
21   "Les 'Quaestiones' ...," p. 377.
22   "Notes additionnelles sur les écrits de Guerric de Saint-Quentin," *RTAM* 8 (1936) 402-403.
23   "Les 'Quaestiones' ...," pp. 380 and 382.
24   "Notes additionnelles ...," p. 385.

homogeneity of the group as any more than probable.[25] There is no clear connection between the questions, and certain formulas lead one to think of a break between questions 43-46 and 47-49 in Pelster's list. Questions 47-48 have exclusively *Quod obicitur ... respondeo (responsio)* instead of *Quod obicitur ... solutio,* which is preferred in questions 43-46. Question 49 has neither set of formulas. Henquinet did not present these points as conclusive arguments, but as tending against the homogeneity of the questions.[26]

Who is the author of these questions on faith? Pelster attributed them to Guiard of Laon, partly because the formulas used in them resemble those used in questions 30-40 (as he numbered them), which he claimed to be by Guiard.[27] O. Lottin was doubtful, because the formulas do not correspond to those in the tract on faith in MS. Assisi 434.[28] Pelster attributed to Guerric of St. Quentin only two questions in the entire MS. Assisi 138, and he claimed that the formulas used exclude Guerric as author of any more.[29] But the method of formulas has proved to be treacherous. Henquinet showed that many of the questions attributed by Pelster to Guiard belong, in fact, to Guerric. He said that in all likelihood questions 29-31 belong to Guiard, but denied that questions 32-40, on the commandments, are by him.[30] P. C. Boeren, noting that what Guiard called political or cardinal virtues are called *virtutes generales* in question 37, concluded that his authorship of questions 30-40 is still more doubtful than it had been.[31] Thus, there is no reason now to assign the questions on faith to Guiard. Are they by Guerric of St. Quentin? His opinion on the definition of faith in Hebrews 11 : 1 is known from MS. Münster Univ. 257.[32] But the opinion expressed in Assisi 138, f. 177ra56-rb17, is so personal that Henquinet was sure the compiler of the Münster manuscript would certainly have recorded it if he had known it.[33] According to Henquinet, even if questions 43-49, on faith, are homogeneous, they are not by Guerric.[34] It seemed to him that they form two groups (43-46 and 47-49, as the questions were numbered by Pelster), and he thought that the groups

25   *Loc. cit.* and "Les écrits ...," p. 287.
26   "Les écrits ...," p. 287.
27   "Les 'Quaestiones' ...," pp. 377, 380 and 382.
28   Review of Pelster, "Les 'Quaestiones' ...," in *Bulletin de Théologie ancienne et médiévale* 2 (1933-1936) no. 785.
29   "Les 'Quaestiones' ...," p. 389.
30   "Notes additionnelles ...," p. 384.
31   *La vie et les œuvres de Guiard de Laon* (The Hague, 1956) p. 225.
32   Henquinet, "Les écrits ...," pp. 203-204.
33   *Ibid.,* p. 204.
34   "Notes additionnelles ...," p. 385.

are probably by two different authors,[35] both of whom remain
anonymous. In conclusion, the question edited here is of unknown
authorship.

Nor has its date been determined. The questions in the manuscript
cannot be confined to the years 1230-1238, as Pelster proposed, even
though many of them may be from those years. Not only must the
questions by Stephen de Poligny be dated after 1246, but it seems that
the questions by Guiard of Laon date from before 1230. Guiard was
born about 1170,[36] and very probably was a Master before 1210.[37]
Boeren was inclined to date his theological questions between 1222 and
1228.[38] Guiard became bishop of Cambrai in 1238,[39] and he died in
1248.[40] The present state of research on the questions in MS. Assisi 138
seems to authorize placing most of them in the quarter of a century
before it was compiled, but it does not exclude the possibility that some
were earlier, including the anonymous question on the definition of
faith.

STATE OF THE QUESTION IN THE EARLY THIRTEENTH CENTURY

Fides est substantia rerum sperandarum, argumentum non apparentium. (Heb.
11 : 1) These words have challenged and inspired many theologians in
their efforts to analyze faith. In the twelfth and thirteenth centuries
some important contributions were made to the understanding of this
definition and other traditional data on faith.

A few points should be mentioned about the legacy received from the
twelfth century. To begin with, there is the question of whether the
apostolic statement about faith is, in fact, a definition. For Hugh of St.
Victor, whose writing on faith was so influential, it was only a descrip-

---

35 "Les écrits ...," p. 287 and note 103.
36 Boeren, *Vie et œuvres,* p. 6.
37 *Ibid.,* p. 16.
38 *Ibid.,* p. 97.
39 *Ibid.,* p. 50.
40 *Ibid.,* p. 55.

tion.[1] No doubt this opinion and the new interest in Aristotle were reasons why authors in this period tried to show that it is a good definition.

An aspect of faith which was emphasized in the middle of the twelfth century was certitude.[2] Thus, *certitudo* was the operative word in Hugh's famous definition: *Si quis plenam ac generalem diffinitionem fidei signare voluerit, dicere potest fidem esse certitudinem quamdam animi de rebus absentibus supra opinionem et infra scientiam constitutam.*[3] The anonymous *Summa Sententiarum* noted that this certitude is voluntary: *Fides est voluntaria certitudo absentium supra opinionem et infra scientiam constituta.*[4]

The voluntary character of faith was one of the themes discussed in the early thirteenth century. But it was not approached from the need to give certitude or firmness to faith, a firmness which the object, because of its obscurity, cannot of itself supply. Rather, the problem was presented in reference to Peter Lombard's doctrine on the relation of charity to faith. St. Ambrose had called charity *fundamentum omnium virtutum et bonorum,*[5] and St. Jerome had written more specifically: *Cunctarum virtutum mater est caritas ...*[6] In his turn, the Master of the *Sentences* taught: *Fides autem qua creditur, si cum caritate sit, virtus est, quia 'caritas, ut ait Ambrosius, mater est omnium virtutum,' quae omnes informat, sine qua nulla vera virtus est.*[7] Indeed, for Peter Lombard, charity was the Holy Spirit himself in the soul.[8] By the end of the twelfth century, the role of charity in reference to other virtues came to be described as that of efficient, formal and final cause.[9] For Hugh of St. Victor, knowledge was the material element in faith, the formal element being love,[10] and this

1 Hugh of St. Victor, *De Sacramentis,* I, 10, 1 (PL 176.330C): "Sed quia in hac descriptione non quid sit fides, sed quid faciat fides ostenditur ..." This opinion was repeated in the anonymous *Summa Sententiarum,* I, 1 (PL 176.43B): "Sed hac diffinitione magis ostenditur effectus fidei quam quid ipsa sit."

2 M.-D. Chenu, "La psychologie de la foi dans la théologie du xiiie siècle," *Etudes d'histoire littéraire et doctrinale du xiiie siècle* 2 (1932) 165-172.

3 *De Sacramentis, loc. cit.*

4 I, 1 (PL 176.43BC).

5 St. Ambrose, *Precatio Secunda* (PL 17.756B).

6 St. Jerome, *Epistola 82, Ad Theophilum* (PL 22.742, *in fine*).

7 Peter Lombard, *Libri IV Sententiarum,* 2nd ed., 2 vols. (Quaracchi, 1916). III, 23, 3; p. 656, ll. 8-10 (PL 192.805).

8 *Ibid.* I, 17; pp. 106-117 (PL 192.564-569).

9 See Odon Lottin, *Morale Fondamentale* (Tournai, 1954), p. 388.

10 *De Sacramentis,* I, 10, 3 (PL 176.331B): "Duo sunt in quibus fides constat: cognitio et affectus, id est constantia vel firmitas credendi. In altero constat quia ipsa illud est; in altero constat quia ipsa in illo est. In affectu enim substantia fidei invenitur; in cognitione, materia. Aliud enim est fides qua creditur; et aliud quod fide creditur. In affectu invenitur fides; in cognitione id quod fide creditur."

view was commonly received.[11] The relation between the intellectual and voluntary aspects of faith would hold the attention of authors in the early thirteenth century.

The second part of the apostolic definition of faith was discussed at great length in the early thirteenth century. Here the influence of Aristotle and Boethius is apparent. No longer was it conceded, as Hugh of St. Victor had conceded, that the statement in Hebrews is not a definition. William of Auxerre, as will be seen, granted that it is neither a logical nor a physical definition, but he held that it is a theological definition, giving the special relation of faith of man's last end. For Philip it is a definition *per finem et effectum praesentem*. The solutions vary, more or less, from one author to another, but the problems discussed were much the same for all.

Therefore the discussion of the definition of faith in MS. Assisi 138 can be understood better if related to some similar discussions in that period. Four authors have been chosen for this purpose: William of Auxerre, Alexander of Hales, Philip the Chancellor and Roland of Cremona.

A. William of Auxerre (d. 1231)

The teaching of William of Auxerre is presented here from his chief work, the *Summa Aurea*,[12] to which various dates between 1215 and 1225 have been assigned.[13] In general it follows the plan of the *Sentences* of Peter Lombard, although it is not a commentary on that work.[14] Thus, William treats of faith in Book III, but in the course of a systematic treatment of the virtues, which is one of the areas in which he pioneered.[15] He also comments on the definition of faith in Hebrews in his preface to the entire work.

---

11   St. Albert, 3 *Sent.* 23.A.1 (ed. A. Borgnet [Paris, 1894] Vol. XVIII, p. 405): "Consueverunt magistri dicere, quod cognitio in fide est materialis, et affectus formalis."

12   *Summa aurea in quattuor libros sententiarum: a subtilissimo doctore Magistro Guillermo Altissiodorensi edita, quam ... magister Guillermus de quercu emendavit.* Paris: Pigouchet, 1500. Used in reprint edition: Minerva G. m. b. H., Frankfurt, 1964.

13   The *Summa Aurea* is certainly no earlier than 1215, for almost at the beginning it refers to the Fourth Lateran Council. Remarking that such a work would probably have taken five to ten years, Ottaviano suggests 1220-1225 as a *terminus ad quem* and he is inclined to the latter part of that period. See Carmelo Ottaviano, *Guglielmo d'Auxerre (+ 1231): La Vita, le opere, il pensiero* (Rome, [1931]) p. 33. Englhardt (*Die Entwicklung*, p. 283) dates it about 1225. Lottin (*Psychologie et Morale* IV, p. 846) gives 1220-1225, or (*ibid.* VI, p. 109, n. 2) "vers 1220-1225." The editors of Alexander of Hales say it was completed by 1220-1221 (*ProlGlossa* IV, 26*; *ProlQuaest* I, 36* and n. 1). Gál ("William of Auxerre," *NCE* 14, 921) says it was "written between 1215 and 1220."

14   R. M. Martineau, "Le Plan de la 'Summa Aurea' de Guillaume d'Auxerre," *Études et Recherches* 2 (1937) 79-114.

15   O. Lottin, *Psychologie et Morale aux XIIᵉ et XIIIᵉ siècles.* 3, p. 142. (Gembloux, 1942-60).

William begins his preface by quoting the definition of faith in *Hebrews* and then remarking that as God is loved above all things by true love, so by true faith one rests in the first truth above all and for itself. Therefore faith is most certain and cannot be proved. It is an argument not as a conclusion but as proving what was not proved. The meaning of this last statement is not explained by William, and it is not clear. An objection is made that masters and even the holy Fathers tried to prove the faith or articles of faith, but this would deprive faith of merit, according to the saying of Gregory the Great that faith has no merit where human reason offers proof.[16] Yet faith is shown forth by reason in three ways: 1) natural reasons increase and strengthen faith ; 2) reason defends faith against heretics ; and 3) sometimes natural reasons move the simple to true faith. For these reasons St. Peter charged prelates especially to be ready to give a reason for the faith, hope and charity that is in them.[17]

However, he who has true faith does not rely on the first truth because of those reasons but rather consents to those reasons because they give witness to the first truth. Because faith is an enlightenment of the mind to see God and divine things, the greater is one's faith, the more readily and the more clearly does one see such reasons. This is why Isaiah said, *Nisi credideritis non intelligetis.* (*Is.* 7 : 9) And it was well said by someone[18] that according to Aristotle an argument is a reason producing faith in a matter that is doubtful, but for a Christian an argument is faith producing a reason.[19]

But because of corruption due to original sin, man has weak spiritual vision and must proceed gradually to the clear, eternal vision of truth. Hence one begins with articles closer to the senses, as that the Son of God became man and that he was humble, meek and patient. In this way the intellect is cleansed, roused and strengthened to see that we are sons of God, heirs and joint heirs with Christ (*Rom.* 8 : 17), and finally to see God himself.[20]

16   St. Gregory the Great, *XL Homiliarum in Evangelia Libri Duo. Homilia 26*, n. 1 (PL 76.1197C).

17   *Summa Aurea*, Preface; fol. 2ra. The text referred to (1 Peter 3 : 15) has *hope* instead of *faith*. The word *faith* was often joined with *hope* and sometimes even replaced it, especially from the time of Abelard. See J. de Ghellinck, *Le mouvement théologique du XIIᵉ siècle*, 2nd ed. (Bruges-Brussels-Paris, 1948), pp. 279-284.

18   Simon of Tournai, *Expositio in symbolum s. Althanasii* in the introduction. The work was published anonymously in *Bibliotheca Casinensis: Florilegium*, Vol. IV (Rome, 1888), pp. 322-346. Information taken from Englhardt, p. 123. The work is included in his bibliography, p. 489, and is listed in *Repertorium Fontium Medii Aevi. I. Series Collectionum* (Rome, 1962), p. 72. The definition of *argumentum* as *ratio rei dubiae faciens fidem* is from Boethius, *De Differentiis Topicis*, I (PL 64.1174C). Cf. Boethius, *In Topica Ciceronis Commentariorum Libri Sex*, I (PL 64.1041C and 1048B).

19   *Summa Aurea*, Preface; fol. 2ra.

20   *Summa Aurea*, Preface; fol. 2rb.

William formally treats the virtue of faith in Book III. When the Apostle called the virtue of faith *the substance of things to be hoped for* he meant that it is the foundation by which they are acquired and that through it they subsist in us now through hope and will subsist in us in the future in reality. Through faith we already have a foretaste of eternal happiness.[21] The phrase *argument of things unseen* is usually held to mean that what we believe is true, because the patriarchs, prophets and apostles held it to be true, or that because the Church believes something it is not seen.[22]

There have been many objections advanced against the definition. It is said to apply to hope as well as to faith, because by hope things to be hoped for already subsist in us through a foretaste. On the other hand, it is said that the first part of the definition is sufficient, as applying to all faith and to it alone. In his reply, William makes a preliminary remark that the first part of the definition distinguishes formed faith from unformed faith.[23] The former expression refers, then as now, to the supernatural faith of one living in sanctifying grace, but the latter expression, as used by William and his contemporaries, refers, without distinction, to natural faith and to the supernatural faith of one living in mortal sin.[24] Then he explains that the second part of the definition distinguishes faith from other virtues, because only by faith does the intellect come to know unseen goods and because the principles of faith are *per se nota,* being known by God's illumination of the intellect. Thus the articles of faith are principles which no more need extrinsic proof than does the principle that the whole is greater than any one of its parts. And if there were no principles in theology, it would be neither an art nor a science.[25]

But faith, it is objected, should be defined by its first and principal end, to believe, rather than by its remote or ultimate end, things to be hoped for. William grants that this is true of other definitions, but he denies that it is true of theological ones. Logic defines through genus and specific difference (e.g., anger is an appetite in reaction to pain — *appetitus contrarii doloris*) and natural philosophy defines through matter[26] (e.g., anger is a rising of the blood around the heart), but theology

21   *Ibid.,* III, tr. 3, c. 1, q. 1; fol. 131va.

22   *Ibid.,* fol. 131va-vb.

23   *Ibid.,* fol. 131vb.

24   In the period 1200-1240 the expression "unformed faith" still included not only the supernatural faith of one in mortal sin but also natural faith "from miracles." Even an "unformed charity" was discussed. See M.-D. Chenu, "La surnaturalisation des vertus," *Bulletin Thomiste* 1 (1931-33) 95*-96*.

25   *Summa Aurea, ibid.*

26   The text has "per naturam," but "per materiam" is preferred by Englhardt, p. 426.

defines things through their proper relation to the ultimate end, namely to God.[27]

It is asked why faith should be said to be of things to be hoped for rather than of things to be believed or loved. William answers that faith tends principally to all things to be hoped for, and to them alone. It tends toward the enjoyment of God by them ; it does not tend toward all things to be believed or loved.[28] William's argument seems to be that faith should be defined in reference to those things toward which it tends, or toward which it tends principally, so as to enjoy God by them. Thus, the faithful believe in eternal punishment and love the many manifest benefits they have already received, but they do not hope for, or tend to, the former (because it is evil) nor to the latter (because they are already present and manifest).

The nature of faith is further explained in the discussion of whether it is a virtue and where it is located. Faith was said not to be a virtue because it is concerned with the true rather than with the good (virtues are concerned with good ends) or because it is in the higher part of the mind, the speculative intellect, in which are sciences and speculation about truth, rather than in the lower part of the mind, the practical intellect, in which are virtue and good action. Another argument against faith being a virtue is its position between science and opinion, both of which are purely speculative.[29]

William answers that, though faith is in the speculative intellect, it does not consist simply in a speculative knowledge about the first truth but also in an esteeming, *aestimatio*,[30] that the first truth is supremely delightful and its highest good, so that it moves toward it so as to delight and rest in it. By this act it moves toward eternal good and secondarily, through political virtues, toward good in activity. For it vivifies both the inner and the outer man. When the philosophers said that virtue is in the practical intellect, they had in mind only political virtues, for they knew little or nothing about faith. As for faith being

---

27 *Summa Aurea, ibid.*, foll. 131vb-132ra.

28 *Ibid.*

29 *Ibid.*, q. 2; fol. 132ra.

30 William's use of the word "estimatio" for the savorous judgment of faith is remarked by Chenu and Michaud-Quantin. They point out that the word "estimatio" (or "existimatio," which was regarded as its equivalent) was used by Abelard simply for the knowledge of what is not seen (*Introductio ad Theologiam* l. II, c. 3 [PL 178.1051D]), but it was taken by St. Bernard to mean skepticism (*De Consideratione* l. V, c. 3; edd. J. Leclercq and H. M. Rochais, *S. Bernardi Opera*, Vol. III [Rome, 1963] pp. 470-471; PL 182.790-791). See Chenu, "La psychologie ...," pp. 166-170. Also Pierre Michaud-Quantin, "'Aestimare' et 'Aestimatio,'" *Bulletin du Cange: Archivum Latinitatis Medii Aevi* 22 (1952) 175-177, 182; reprinted in his *Études sur le Vocabulaire Philosophique du Moyen Age avec la collaboration de Michel Lemoine.* (Lessico Intellettuale Europeo, 5) (Rome, 1970) pp. 9-24.

between science and opinion, actually it is not only above opinion but also above demonstrative science. It is above the opinion of unformed faith and beneath the "science," or evident knowledge whereby we will see God face to face.[31]

William's exposition of the definition of faith is brief, vigorous and usually clear. It emphasizes the dignity of faith and its intellectual aspect. As by charity one loves God above all things, so by faith one rests in the first truth above all things and for itself. Faith illuminates the intellect, cleansing, arousing and strengthening it to see the mysteries and preparing it for the clear, eternal vision of truth. William did not hesitate to put faith in the speculative intellect, which is higher than the practical intellect. He approved the use of natural reasons to prepare for faith and to strengthen and defend it. In fact, the articles of faith are the principles of theology. Yet faith is not mere arid speculation but a foretaste of the sweetness of eternal happiness, for the first truth is also the highest good. Moreover, faith directs activity through the political virtues, and the measure of one's insight into the mysteries is the degree of freedom from the corruption of sin.

William's insistence on the intellectuality of faith moderates the role given by others to charity. His view that faith is in the speculative intellect rather than in the practical intellect is unusual for its time.[32] And though his assertion that the articles of faith are the principles of theology was made in favor of their certitude, it helped to establish the scientific status of theology.[33] In conclusion, William made an important contribution to the discussion of the definition of faith.

B. Alexander of Hales (d. 1245)

The teaching of Alexander of Hales on the definition of faith is found in his *Glossa* and in his *Quaestiones Disputatae*.

The first of these works, his *Glossa in Quatuor Libros Sententiarum Petri Lombardi*,[34] probably consists of notes made by his students. Lottin thinks it very likely was not begun before 1225,[35] but its editors date it

---

31 *Summa Aurea, loc. cit.;* fol. 132va-vb.

32 Before St. Thomas faith was commonly assigned to the practical intellect. See M.-D. Chenu, "L'amour dans la foi," *Bulletin Thomiste* 1 (1931-33) 98*.

33 See Johannes Beumer, "Die Theologie als intellectus fidei. Dargestellt an Hand der Lehre des Wilhelm von Auxerre und Petrus von Tarantasia," *Scholastik* 17 (1942) 34-41. M. J. Congar, "Theologie," *Dictionnaire de Théologie Catholique XV,* 1 (Paris, 1946) 377. M.-D. Chenu, *La théologie comme science au XIIIᵉ siècle* (Bibliothèque Thomiste 33) 3rd ed. (Paris, 1957) pp. 58-60.

34 *Magistri Alexandri de Hales Glossa in Quatuor Libros Sententiarum Petri Lombardi nunc demum reperta atque primum edita studio et cura PP. Collegii S. Bonaventurae,* 4 vols. (Quaracchi, 1951-57).

35 Review of Vol. I of the *Glossa,* BTAM 6 (1950-53) no. 1158 and review of Vol. IV of the *Glossa,* BTAM 7 (1954-57) no. 2618.

1222-1229, assigning Book III, which includes his treatment of faith, to the years 1225-1227.[36]

There are three redactions of the *Glossa,* each named after the place of origin of the manuscript in which it is found. Redaction A (MS. Assisi, Bibl. Comunale 189) is authentic; Redaction E (MS. Erfurt Amplon. O. 68) is not authentic; the authenticity of Redaction L (MS. London, Lambeth Palace 347) is uncertain.[37] Hence when A and L agree, this study will be based on A and will refer to parallel passages or additions in L; but L will be treated separately when it differs much from A or adds much to it.[38]

The title *Quaestiones Disputatae* here refers to the questions disputed by Alexander.[39] According to their editors, they very probably should be assigned to the years 1220-1236, but the individual questions have not yet received a more precise dating.[40]

Alexander opens his discussion of the definition of faith in the *Glossa* by observing that it is the first of the theological virtues, preceding hope and charity because it refers to the true rather than, as do hope and charity, to the good. All discussions about it concern either the believer, what he believes or the intervening habit.[41]

The word *faith* refers to various things, including unformed faith (*Fides sine operibus mortua est. James* 2 : 26; *Si habuero omnem fidem ita ut montes transferam* ... 1 *Cor.* 13 : 1), formed faith (*Iustus ex fide vivit. Rom.* 1 : 17) and what is believed. For this last meaning all three redactions cite the words of the pseudo-Athanasian creed, *Fides autem Catholica haec est* ..., but L omits the reference given in A and E to *Heb.* 11 : 1.[42]

Coming to the definition, Alexander says that faith is a substance in the sense of a foundation (for which explanation the editors refer to the gloss of Lombard). Thus, it is a material disposition through which one is prepared for eternal life.[43] The word *argument* and the mention of what is hoped for refer, respectively, to truth and goodness, the two things which perfect the soul; hence both appear in the definition. Faith

---

36   *ProlGlossa* IV, 44* and *ProlGlossa* III, 32*.

37   The three manuscripts are described in *ProlGlossa* I, 77*-83*. The problem of authenticity is discussed in *ProlGlossa* III, 7*-35*, and by W. H. Principe, *Alexander of Hales' Theology of the Hypostatic Union* (Toronto, 1967) 16-20.

38   This is the method adopted by Principe, *ibid.,* p. 21.

39   *Magistri Alexandri de Hales Quaestiones Disputatae 'Antequam Esset Frater' nunc primum editae studio et cura PP. Collegii S. Bonaventurae* 3 vols. (Quaracchi, 1960).

40   *ProlQuaest* I, 36*. Lottin seems to concur in general (*Psychologie et Morale* IV, 407), although when treating one of them, "De intentione," he places it "tout proche de l'an 1225" (*ibid.* IV, 421).

41   *Glossa* III, 23, 1 (AE); p. 262; 14 (L); p. 274. L calls the true the "subject" of faith and adds that it precedes the good "in this life" ("in via").

42   *Glossa* III, 23, 3 (AE); p. 263; 16 (L); p. 274.

43   *Glossa* III, 23, 11 (AE); p. 268; 28 (L); p. 279.

is not said to be of things loved, because like hope, faith will pass away, whereas love will never pass away.[44] Although truth precedes goodness, *argument* is mentioned in the second place in the definition because it refers to things only as they will be seen, not as they are now unseen.[45] Faith is called an *argument* because by it the supreme truth illumines the mind, moving from the less noble to the more noble. And the definition applies only to formed faith.[46]

Alexander also treats the apostolic definition of faith in *Question 38* of the *Quaestiones*. He begins with objections against faith being the substance of things to be hoped for in the sense that it is a foundation. For, in authoritative authors, fortitude and humility are called foundations, as is, in fact, every virtue in so far as one merits by it.[47] He answers that faith is called a *foundation* because of its firmness, which is twofold — one according to which faith is preserved in works and another which accompanies faith and strengthens it in the practical intellect by grace. For, alluding to the statement of Augustine, *Credere nihil aliud est quam cum assensione cogitare*,[48] he remarks that to think belongs to the lower part and to consent belongs to the higher part, so that as there is greater or less elevation or assent there is greater or less firmness.[49] Nor is fortitude called the *foundation* of faith in the same way as faith is called a *foundation* when it is defined as the substance of things to be hoped for. Fortitude is in the natural order or it is a *gratia gratis data* (in contrast to living faith, which is a *gratia gratum faciens*) or, if it proceeds from a *gratia gratum faciens*, it is a complement of faith.[50] Humility is called the foundation of the virtues because it guards them or because it subjects the practical intellect to Christ. In the latter case it is the same as faith.[51] And every virtue, because its acts are meritorious, can be called the foundation of beatitude, but faith alone is so called by reason of the certitude of the expectation whereby we hope for beatitude.[52]

Even though faith will not remain with eternal life, it is correctly called its *substance* in the sense of its foundation, for the truth of what is believed will remain.[53] The Apostle's definition compares faith to the

---

44 *Glossa* III, 23, 11 (AE); p. 269; 28 (L); pp. 279-280.
45 *Glossa* III, 23, 11 (AE); p. 269.
46 *Glossa* III, 23, 11 (AE); pp. 269-270; 28 (L); p. 280.
47 *Quaest* 38, 1-4; pp. 662-663.
48 St. Augustine, *De Praedestinatione Sanctorum* c. 2, n. 5 (PL 44.963).
49 *Quaest* 38, 7; p. 664.
50 *Quaest* 38, 8; pp. 664-665.
51 *Quaest* 38, 9; p. 665.
52 *Quaest* 38, 10; pp. 665-666.
53 *Quaest* 38, 13; pp. 666-667.

foundation of a present and future spiritual edifice, perfecting the intellect as the argument of things now unseen and perfecting the will as the substance of things hoped for in the future.[54] It will be observed that this leaves the notion of faith as a foundation of the spiritual edifice quite undeveloped. One would like to know, for example, how, according to Alexander, faith is the foundation of the spiritual edifice, especially in what sense it can be called the foundation of the future spiritual edifice even though faith will pass away. One wonders also if he intends to refer the first part of the definition to faith as the foundation of the present spiritual edifice and the second part of the definition to faith as the foundation of the future spiritual edifice. Alexander's remarks naturally lead one to ask these questions but they do not provide an answer.

Augustine said that faith is of good and evil things and of past, present and future things, whereas hope is only of future things.[55] This being so, it is objected that faith is unduly limited when it is described as *the substance of things hoped for*. Alexander explains, first of all, that even though we believe in punishment as well as in eternal life, it was fitting that only things to be hoped for be mentioned in the definition of faith. Whereas in the cognitive power certitude regards both good and evil, in the affective power it regards evil only because through fear we merit the remission of punishment; for the affective power moves toward the good.[56] And although many adhere to the supreme truth in past and present things, only those whose faith is pleasing to God adhere to the supreme truth and want it as a future good. Thus faith is of things to be hoped for.[57]

It is objected that faith should not be called an *argument,* since, being a virtue, it is in the affective power rather than in the cognitive. But here the word *argument* is taken in a special sense, including both powers and looking toward the future. In this way it belongs only to the virtue of faith.[58] Faith is "of things unseen" by either sense or reason.[59] It is not to be understood as an argument in the sense of a principle or middle term or conclusion, nor as all of them together, but simply as a habit by which one believes what is unseen.[60]

Even though knowledge precedes appetite, the two parts of the

54   *Quaest* 38, 15; pp. 667-668.
55   St. Augustine, *Enchiridion* c. 8 (CCSL 46.63-64; PL 40.234-235).
56   *Quaest* 38, 19; p. 669.
57   *Quaest* 38, 21; p. 669.
58   *Quaest* 38, 22; p. 670.
59   *Quaest* 38, 24; p. 670.
60   *Quaest* 38, 25; pp. 670-671.

definition are given in correct order. In the virtue of faith what is first is the substance of things to be hoped for, although the use according to which it is the argument of things unseen precedes the use according to which it is the substance of things to be hoped for.[61]

This concludes Alexander's treatment of the definition of faith in these two works. The discussion is clear, succinct and orderly, as was William's, but it includes more and its emphasis is somewhat different. Sometimes it is more explicit. Thus, not content with observing that faith is called a *substance* in the sense of a foundation, he adds that it is a material disposition through which one is prepared for things hoped for. And again, he says that it is called a foundation because of its twofold firmness, one preserving it in works and another strengthening it in the practical intellect by grace. That he does not put faith in the speculative intellect is another point in which he differs from William. In fact, he assigns the thinking in faith to the practical intellect and the assent to the will. Thus faith is called an *argument* in a special sense, including the affective power as well as the cognitive. But this special meaning is adduced to meet the objection that faith should not be called an *argument* since as a virtue it is in the affective power rather than in the cognitive. According to other passages of both the *Gloss* and *Question 38,* the first part of the definition refers to goodness perfecting the will and the second part refers to truth perfecting the intellect. And faith is the foundation of the spiritual edifice not only now but even in the future, for, though faith will not remain, the truth of what is believed will remain. Alexander gives less emphasis than William to the intellectual aspect of faith. Thus he does not mention the threefold role of reason in regard to the faith, namely to prepare for, strengthen and defend it. And he makes no comparison of the articles of faith to the first principles of a science.

C. Philip the Chancellor (d. 1236)

The chief work of Philip the Chancellor, his *Summa Quaestionum Theologicarum,* or *Summa de Bono* as it is usually called, has never been published in its entirety. However, the tract on faith in that work is included in a doctoral dissertation by Victorius a Ceva[62] and in a published excerpt from that dissertation.[63] It is this latter work which will be used here.

---

61 *Quaest* 38, 26; p. 671.

62 *Il Trattato "De Fide" di Filippo Cancelliere (+ 1236). Introduzione, parafrasi, testo inedito (Cod. Vat. lat. 7669).* (Rome, 1960).

63 V. a Ceva, *De Fide ex Summa Philippi Cancellarii (+ 1236). Excerpta ex dissertatione ad Lauream in Facultate Theologica Pontificiae Universitatis Gregorianae.* (Rome, 1961).

The *Summa de Bono* comes from the last years of Philip's life. It is dated "about 1232" by Lottin,[64] 1229-1236 by a Ceva[65] and "between 1230 and 1236" by Wicki.[66]

Philip begins his discussion of the definition of faith with an objection that faith should not be called a *substance* because it is not a substance in any of the meanings given to that word by Aristotle, namely matter or form or both together or genus or as definition.[67] According to the objector, faith, because it will pass away, is not the matter of eternal life, whether matter *ex qua, in qua, per quam* or *circa quam.*[68] Philip answers that, even though it will not remain, faith is correctly called a substance in the sense of a foundation, for the apostolic definition is given in reference to the end of faith and to its present effect. Defined in reference to the end, it is a substance or foundation disposing the soul so that eternal life will subsist in it in the future. Defined in reference to its present effect, faith causes things which are hoped for to subsist in us now, not in their reality but as objects of hope.[69]

Faith is the foundation and matter *in qua* (or subject) of the spiritual life on earth, since it is the first habit disposing the soul in this life. Thus, even though faith will not remain, it is the foundation in this life. Moreover, it will remain in the future life as to its substance, i.e. as to its genus, which is knowledge. And it is the foundation of things to be hoped for in the same way as it is the foundation of hope, because it is the foundation of the former not as they are things but as they are to be hoped for.[70]

It is objected that hope rather than faith should be called the *substance of things to be hoped for.* Philip answers that, being the first habit, faith is called the foundation, and nothing subsists before the foundation. Nor should faith be called the *substance of things to be believed* rather than of things to be *hoped for,* because the first part of the definition refers to the end perfecting the will, and the second part refers to the end perfecting the intellect. And to call faith the *substance of things to be loved* would not indicate their absence, because what is loved may be either present or absent. The soul is perfected by goodness and truth. The absence of the former is expressed by *things to be hoped for,* and the absence of the latter is expressed by *things unseen.* Faith is called a *substance* as

---

64   *Psychologie et Morale* IV, 849.
65   *De Fide,* p. 2, note 3.
66   Nikolaus Wicki, "Philip the Chancellor," *NCE* 11 (1967) 274.
67   Aristotle, *Metaphysics* Z, 3 (1028b33-36).
68   *De Fide,* pp. 18-19, ll. 48-73.
69   *Ibid.,* pp. 19-20, ll. 74-95.
70   *Ibid.,* pp. 20-21, ll. 110-138.

establishing the mind in certain expectation of a *good*, and it is an *argument* as related to eternal *truth*, i.e. so that eternal truth may be apparent.[71]

Is faith an argument for the articles as they are known in this life or as they will be known in heaven? If faith is an argument for the articles as they are known in this life, then, it is claimed, faith must be an argument in the sense of a middle term or proposition or as the illative force expressed by the word *therefore*. It is objected that it is not an argument in the way a middle term is, for faith adheres immediately to the first truth, which, rather than faith, is the reason for assenting to the articles. Thus it is the first truth rather than faith which is an argument.[72] Philip answers that faith, rather than the first truth, is called an *argument* because the first truth argues only in so far as it is in faith.[73] He does not explain this further, but it seems to mean that outside of, or apart from, its activity in faith, the first truth does not argue, e.g. it does not argue as the exemplary, efficient and final cause in creating things. It is also objected that faith does not argue to the truth of the articles but presupposes their truth. Furthermore, if one believes something, e.g. the resurrection of the dead, because the patriarchs or apostles did so, it is only acquired faith (*fides suasa*). Nor, in that case, would faith be an argument for the first believer.[74] To all of this Philip answers that nevertheless faith is an argument, for it is a principle of proof, arguing from, not to, the truth of the articles.[75]

It is further objected that if faith, in reference to the articles believed, were ordered to eternal life, even the devils would have eternal life, because they believe. Philip explains that this could be understood in either one of two ways. It could mean that, because the devil assents to such propositions of faith that the Word became incarnate or that God is triune, he will have eternal life. The other meaning could be that because faith is in the devil as ordered to the final cause, he will have eternal life (*vel sic: fides inest isti finaliter, ergo habebit vitam aeternam*). According to this meaning, since eternal life is the final cause of faith, even the devils, because they have faith, will have eternal life. Philip answers simply that in all this there is no proof, first of all, because one can have only opinion about whether he has faith; moreover, faith is a kind of knowledge in this life, not in the next.[76]

---

71   *Ibid.*, pp. 21-22, ll. 139-183.
72   *Ibid.*, pp. 22-23, ll. 186-207; p. 24, ll. 224-232.
73   *Ibid.*, pp. 26-27, ll. 309-328.
74   *Ibid.*, p. 23, ll. 208-220.
75   *Ibid.*, p. 25, ll. 284-287; p. 27, ll. 329-339.
76   *Ibid.*, p. 24, ll. 239-258.

Then Philip moves to a more direct explanation. What is believed is an article of faith, that by which it is believed is the habit of faith, and that through which it is believed is the first truth. Thus the first truth is the principle (*principium*), because it gives the habit of faith; it is the *medium,* because through it faith adheres to the first truth; and it is the last (*extremum*) because faith adheres to it.[77] Because this passage occurs in the course of Philip's explanation of how faith is an argument, it seems that he means to compare the role of the first truth in faith to the roles of the major and minor premises of a syllogism and also to the role of the conclusion, or, perhaps, to the roles of the three terms in an argument. But he does not explicitly authorize this interpretation.

Faith is called an *argument,* not because of a complete likeness between faith and argumentation, but because of likeness in the effects which both produce. As a logical argument produces a conclusion, faith moves through affection from sign to reality. Things believed are here as in a sign — in heaven in reality.[78] It is an argument, not because it moves from doubt to certitude, but because by it things that are known in one way come to be more perfectly known.[79]

Argument in logic is intended to produce certitude about a conclusion. Thus, when discussing faith as an argument, Philip inquires about the certitude of faith. Whereas the mind accepts the first principles of reasoning because they are self-evident, it accepts the articles of faith because it is so informed by conscience. Arguments in favor of some articles, e.g. that God exists, are strong and are advanced even by those without faith. For other articles, e.g. that God became man, only weak arguments can be given to an unbeliever, but these same arguments are strong for one who believes.[80]

There is an objection that the certitude of faith is not very great, because, according to Augustine (really Hugh of St. Victor), faith is above opinion and beneath science.[81] Philip replies that faith derived from exterior hearing, i.e. naturally acquired knowledge of God, is beneath science, but faith from interior hearing is not beneath science.[82] And, according to Augustine, *Nihil homini certius est sua fide.*[83]

---

77   *Ibid.,* p. 26, ll. 292-308.
78   *Ibid.,* p. 28, ll. 370-387.
79   *Ibid.,* p. 29, ll. 407-414.
80   *Ibid.,* pp. 29-31, ll. 415-486.
81   See Hugh, *De Sacramentis,* I, 10, 1 (PL 176.330C).
82   *De Fide,* pp. 31-32, ll. 487-497; p. 33, ll. 528-537.
83   The saying was sometimes attributed to St. Augustine and sometimes to St. Gregory the Great. Its probable source is St. Augustine, *De Trinitate,* l. XIII, c. 1, n. 3 (CCSL 50A.383; PL 42.1014): "Non sic uidetur fides in corde in quo est ab eo cuius est, sed eam tenet certissima scientia clamatque conscientia." This passage from the *De Trinitate* is quoted by Peter Lombard, *Sent.* III, 23, 7; p. 659, ll. 9-10. See Englhardt, pp. 76 and 413.

Philip refers this to faith effected through light infused from above. Such faith is above science, sense, reason and intellect. Its beginning is in affection, or love, of God, much as, in ordinary love, one will not believe evil of one's beloved. Thus nothing is more certain for the man of faith than what he believes.[84]

The certitude of faith, it is claimed, is the greatest, according to the saying of Augustine, *Nihil intelligitur nisi ut est.*[85] But Philip recalls that, according to Boethius, *Omnis intelligens intelligit secundum naturam intelligentis et non secundum naturam rei intellectae.*[86] This statement, as applied to the question discussed here, means that, speaking according to nature, knowledge of the first truth is not most certain. However, says Philip, with the help of grace one can, in a way, understand even after the manner of what is understood. Thus the certitude of faith exceeds that of any naturally acquired knowledge.[87] Thus the certitude of faith is above not only the certitude of opinion; it is even above the certitude of all naturally acquired science.

It is objected that the two members of the definition are given in the wrong order, since faith is ordered first and more to the true than to the good. Philip gives two answers, of which the first is that because the definition is given in reference to the end, it should refer first to what is best and then refer to the true. This reflects the common view, shared by Philip, that the good enjoys a primacy over the true. The other answer, proposed as an alternative explanation, is that faith is first referred, through the medium of hope, to things which are hoped for, and then it is referred to things unseen in heaven. Thus it refers to the present effect of faith before referring faith to the heavenly vision into which it will pass over.[88]

Faith is called both a *substance* and an *argument*. The word *substance* can mean the first efficient principle (active substance), which is studied in metaphysics; or matter (passive substance), considered in physical science; or genus, in logic; or the first of the ten predicaments. In the definition of faith it means matter according as faith is the foundation of the spiritual edifice, which consists of good works and of what is built on faith. But because faith is a principle of knowing, it is also called an *argument.*[89]

---

84   *De Fide,* p. 32, ll. 498-500; pp. 33-34, ll. 538-570.

85   St. Augustine, *De Diversis Quaestionibus LXXXIII,* q. 32 (PL 40.22): "Non ergo potest quidquam intelligi nisi ut est."

86   Boethius, *Philosophiae Consolatio* l. V, prosa 4, n. 25 (CCSL 94, 96-97; PL 63.848C-849A): "... Omne enim quod cognoscitur non secundum sui uim sed secundum cognoscentium potius comprehenditur facultatem."

87   *De Fide,* p. 32, ll. 501-527; p. 34, ll. 571-590.

88   *Ibid.,* p. 35, ll. 591-606.

89   *Ibid.,* ll. 607-625.

The Apostle defined only faith and charity, and not hope, because
there are only two powers in the soul, namely the cognitive and the
motive, and by these two virtues in them we tend to the first good and
the first truth. Hope does not have still another end, but rather it
disposes one toward the good and the true in so far as they are supreme
or difficult to attain.[90] Again, the Apostle fittingly defines faith first as it
disposes toward the *possession* of heavenly things and then toward
knowing them; or, as the principle directing us to the supreme *good* and
to the supreme *truth*.[91]

Philip discusses other definitions of faith besides that which is given
in Hebrews. It is useful to see them because some will recur in the text
to be edited and studied in this article. First of all, St. Paul calls faith
the *signaculum iustitiae* (Rom. 4 : 11) both because it is the seal of the
Trinity and because it distinguishes the souls of those who have faith in
Christ, who is the character of the Father. (Heb. 1 : 13)[92]

Another definition of faith is by Augustine, who defines faith according to its first acts, saying: *Fidei est cogitare cum assensione ea quae ad
christianam religionem pertinent.*[93] A gloss on Rom. 1, *Iustus ex fide vivit*
(Rom. 1 : 17), gives the genus and species: *Fides est virtus qua creduntur
quae non videntur.*[94] Hugh of St. Victor, says Philip, distinguishes faith
from other habits of knowledge when he says: *Fides est voluntaria certitudo
absentium supra opinionem et infra scientiam.*[95] Faith is referred to as a habit
of knowledge but is not distinguished from science and opinion when a
gloss on Galatians 5 says: *Fides est invisibilium certitudo.*[96] Tully refers to
justice generally, not as a special virtue, when he calls faith *fundamentum
iustitiae.*[97] Augustine, referring faith to its truth, which will remain most

90   *Ibid.*, pp. 35-36, ll. 626-651.
91   *Ibid.*, p. 39, ll. 732-740.
92   *De Fide*, pp. 36-37, ll. 652-664.
93   Cf. St. Augustine, *De Praedestinatione Sanctorum*, c. 1, n. 5 (PL 44.963): "Quamquam et ipsum
credere, nihil aliud est, quam cum assensione cogitare. Non enim omnis qui cogitat, credit; cum
ideo cogitent plerique, ne credant: sed cogitat omnis qui credit, et credendo cogitat, et cogitando
credit. Quod ergo pertinet ad religionem et pietatem (de qua loquebatur Apostolus), si non sumus
idonei cogitare aliquid quasi ex nobismetipsis, sed sufficientia nostra ex Deo est ..." *De Fide*, p. 37, ll.
678-681; pp. 38-39, ll. 710-716.
94   Cf. Peter Lombard, *Collectanea in Epistolam ad Romanos* (c. 1, v. 17) (PL 191.1323D): "Est enim
fides qua creduntur quae non videntur, quae proprie dicitur fides." *De Fide*, p. 37, ll. 682-684; p. 39,
ll. 717-720.
95   The text is really from the anonymous *Summa Sententiarum* I, 1 (PL 176.43BC). *De Fide*, p. 37,
ll. 685-686; p. 39, ll. 717-720.
96   Cf. Peter Lombard, *Collectanea in Epistolam ad Galatas*, on Gal 5 : 22 (PL 192.160B): "*fides*, de in-
visibilibus certitudo." *De Fide*, p. 38, ll. 687-688; p. 39, ll. 725-727.
97   Cicero, *De Officiis* l. I, c. 7, n. 23 (ed. C. Atzert [Leipzig, 1932] p. 12): "Fundamentum autem
est iustitiae fides, id est dictorum conventorumque constantia et veritas." *De Fide*, p. 38, l. 689; p. 39,
ll. 728-731.

perfectly in heaven, defines it as *illuminatio mentis ad summam veritatem.*[98]

Dionysius defines faith in reference to the first truth considered as that through which one believes, for he said: *Fides est ratio simplex veritatis per se existentis.*[99] St. John Damascene says: *Fides est eorum que sperantur ypostasis, id est subsistentia rerum redargutio que non videntur, indistabilis et indiudicabilis species eorum que a Deo sunt nobis nuntiata.*[100] He also says: *Fides est non inquisitus consensus.*[101] These two definitions refer to faith from exterior hearing. It is called "inseparable" *(indistabilis)* because it is, as it were, mid-way between the habit of faith and the first truth, since the first truth is the principle by which the believer adheres.[102] The meaning of this statement is not clear. Faith is called "not subject to judgment" *(indiudicabilis)* and "a consent not to be searched into" *(non inquisitus consensus)* to distinguish it from the faith which is from exterior hearing. This latter faith it is not safe to believe without a reason. But of the former a *Gloss* on *Hebrews* says: *Fides non habet meritum cui humana ratio prebet experimentum.*[103] The saying of Peter of Ravenna, *Non est tutum credere sine ratione,*[104] was made either because many things can be turned to good or evil, or on account of heretics who attack the faith. And therefore the gift of science was added to faith for its defense.[105]

Philip's treatment of the definition of faith, and especially of the meaning of the word argument in that definition, is much longer than what is found in William and Alexander on the same subject. The greater Aristotelian influence is apparent from the beginning, when he recalls the various meanings of the words *substance* and *matter.* Faith is defined through the end and through its present effect. It is the foundation and matter *in qua* (or subject) of the spiritual life on earth, and it will remain as to its substance, i.e. as to its genus, knowledge.

Philip emphasizes the reference of the first member of the definition

---

98   The idea is expressed, but not in these words, by St. Augustine, *Epistola 120, ad Consentium,* nn. 8-10 (PL 33.456-457). *De Fide,* p. 38, ll. 690-692; pp. 39-40, ll. 741-747.

99   (Pseudo.) Denis the Areopagite, *De Divinis Nominibus,* c. 5. The translation closest to that given by Philip is by John the Saracen. *Dionysiaca.* Edd. Ph. Chevalier *et al.,* 1 (Bruges: Desclée De Brouwer 1937-1950). p. 409, *De Fide,* p. 38, ll. 701-702; p. 40, ll. 758-762.

100   St. John Damascene, *De Fide Orthodoxa,* c. 83 (Burgundio's translation); ed. E. Buytaert (St. Bonaventure-Louvain-Paderborn, 1955) p. 298. *De Fide,* p. 38, ll. 703-706.

101   St. John Damascene, *ibid.* c. 84; ed. E. Buytaert, p. 300. Some manuscripts have "inperscrutatus" instead of "non inquisitus." *De Fide, ibid.,* l. 707.

102   *De Fide,* p. 40, ll. 764-766: "Dicitur indistabilis quia veluti medium est inter habitum fidei et primam veritatem cum prima veritas sit ratio qua adhaeret credens ..."

103   *Glossa Ordinarai,* on Heb 10 : 20 (PL 114.661); from St. Gregory the Great, *XL Homiliarum in Evangelia Libri Duo,* l. II, hom. 26 (PL 76.1197); *De Fide,* p. 40, ll. 763-776.

104   The idea is expressed, but not in these words, by St. Peter Chrysologus, *Sermo 79* (PL 52.522-524).

105   *De Fide,* pp. 40-41, ll. 777-785.

to the role of faith as perfecting the will and the reference of the second member to its role in perfecting the intellect. Although Philip gives much attention to the meaning of *argument,* he does not exaggerate the intellectual aspect of faith. If one argued to the truth of the articles from the fact that the apostles believed them, one would arrive at no more than acquired faith (*fides suasa*). One argues from the articles of faith, not to them; in fact, it is the first truth which argues in so far as it is in faith. The first truth is the first, middle and last, for it gives the habit of faith, which, through it, adheres to the first truth.

Moreover, faith is called an *argument* in a special sense, for it moves, not from doubt to certitude, but, through affection, from sign to reality. Effected through light infused from above, faith is above science. It enjoys a certitude greater than that of naturally acquired knowledge of God, for grace helps one to understand even after the manner of what is understood. Philip puts the beginning of faith in the love of God, much as, in ordinary love, one will not believe evil of one's beloved. Whereas faith gives strong arguments for some articles (e.g. the existence of God), its arguments for other articles (e.g. the redemption) are strong only for those who have faith.

Philip defends the order of the definition of faith. The first part refers to the present effect of faith, and the second part refers to the heavenly vision which is its goal. He recalls other definitions of faith and comments on them briefly according to his exposition of the apostolic definition. Finally, it should be pointed out that, although Philip discusses the meaning of the word *argument* much more than either of the authors already presented, he is closer to Alexander than he is to William in his emphasis on the voluntary or affective aspect of faith.

D. Roland of Cremona (d 1259)

When Roland of Cremona entered the Dominican Order in 1219,[106] he already had a reputation as a teacher of philosophy.[107] Whether he was then a priest is not known. In 1229 or 1230, during the great strike, he became the first Dominican Master of Theology at the University of Paris.[108] He did not teach there long, for he soon went to Toulouse, where he taught from 1230 to 1232, when he returned to Italy.[109] He was a lector in the convent at Bologna when he died there in 1259.[110]

---

106 See Ephrem Filthaut, O.P., *Roland von Cremona O.P. und die Anfänge der Scholastik im Predigerorden* (Vechta, 1936) p. 12.

107 Filthaut, pp. 14-15.

108 According to Filthaut, *ibid.* p. 21, Roland was made a Master in 1230. Glorieux gives 1229 or 1230. See P. Glorieux, *Répertoire des Maîtres en Théologie au xiiie siècle,* Vol. I (Paris, 1933) p. 42.

109 Filthaut, pp. 22 and 25.

110 Filthaut, pp. 28-29.

Roland's *Liber Quaestionum* or *Summa*[111] has been assigned various dates. Filthaut sys it was finished before 1234,[112] but Lottin thinks it may have been a little later.[113] Stegmüller says it was completed about 1232.[114] Doucet discovered the prologue, in which Roland gave avoidance of idleness as a reason for writing it.[115] He concludes that Roland must have begun it after his period of teaching at Paris and Toulouse (to which period he assigns the years 1229-1233).[116]

According to Roland the statement in *Hebrews* is a very good theological definition.[117] To the objection that faith is not a substance in the sense of the first of the predicaments,[118] he answers that although this is true yet faith is a substance in the special sense of a support or foundation, giving a basis for hope and charity as a first coat of paint underlies a second and a third.[119] It is objected that the definition is bad because it applies to hope as well as to faith.[120] Roland replies that the definition does not apply to hope, for it calls faith an *argument* and it belongs to reason to argue, not to the irascible appetite, which is the subject of hope.[121] Moreover, hope is the formal or efficient cause in us of things to be hoped for; and hope is clearly not an argument.[122] The *magistri*[123] say that faith is a substance because it makes things to be hoped for to subsist in us now through hope and in the future through truth. And they explain *argumentum non apparentium* both in the sense that truths of faith can be established by arguing from the belief of the apostles (they believed them; therefore they are true) and in the sense that because they believed them, such truths are not apparent.[124] It is

---

111 *Summae Magistri Rolandi Cremonensis O.P. Liber Tercius.* Editio Princeps. Ed. Aloys. Cortesi (Monumenta Bergomensia, 7) (Bergamo, 1962).

112 Filthaut, p. 50.

113 Lottin, *Psychologie et Morale* IV, 171, note 3.

114 Fridericus Stegmüller, *Repertorium Commentariorum in Sententias Petri Lombardi* (Würzburg, 1947) Vol. I, p. 370.

115 Roland, *Prologue* to his *Summa*: "Huius autem laboris sollicitudinem suscipiendi haec causa fuit. Quoniam et prodesse modicum simplicibus et otium repellere cogitabam, quoniam otiositas in religione saepe vitulum nutrit;" Quoted from Victorin Doucet, "Commentaires sur les Sentences: Supplément au Répertoire de M. Frédéric Stegmueller," *Archivum Franciscanum Historicum* 47 (1954) 166.

116 Doucet, "Commentaires ...," p. 167.

117 *Summa,* l. III, q. 97, n. 11; ed. Cortesi, p. 293.

118 *Ibid.,* n. 2; p. 291.

119 *Ibid.,* n. 12; pp. 293-294.

120 *Ibid.,* n. 3; p. 291.

121 *Ibid.,* n. 8; p. 293.

122 *Ibid.,* n. 19; p. 295.

123 By *magistri* Roland means theological authors of the twelfth and thirteenth centuries. See Filthaut, *Roland ...,* p. 81.

124 *Summa,* III, 97, n. 4; pp. 291-292.

objected that faith should not be called an *argument* because, whereas an argument, according to Boethius, is a *ratio rei dubiae faciens fidem* faith cannot be used as an argument to convince unbelievers.[125] Roland replies that faith certifies the truths we believe, and that for believers it is an argument from authority.[126]

The now familiar objection is made that faith should be called *the substance of things to be believed* rather than *of things to be hoped for.*[127] But this is not true, because it does not cause all things which we believe, including even eternal punishment, to *subsist* in us. Furthermore, faith is not the foundation of things to be believed, but rather it is the formal cause of their existing in us.[128]

The definition distinguishes formed from unformed faith, because the latter does not cause things to be hoped for to exist in us now through assent and later in truth.[129] But unformed faith is a preparation for formed faith, e.g. adults are instructed in unformed faith before they are baptized, and it disposes bad Christians to receive grace more readily.[130] Thus unformed faith, it is objected, is a foundation, and the definition applies to it, for the foundation of a foundation is a foundation. Moreover, unformed faith is an argument of things unseen, for even by it many people believe the articles of faith and are ready to die for them.[131] As for the first objection, Roland holds that unformed faith is only improperly and remotely a foundation. As for the second objection, unformed faith is not an argument in the sense of causing things to be hoped for to exist in us. And, despite appearances, those with unformed faith would not die for it, or they would do so only because of obstinacy or some such motive.[132]

Faith, being distinguished from hope, is, for all the greater reason, distinguished from all other virtues.[133] And if it be objected that an authoritative text, whether of the Old Testament or of the New Testament, meets the apostolic definition of faith, Roland says that it is not *the substance of things to be hoped for* in the same way as formed faith is, but only, perhaps, in the way unformed faith is. Furthermore, he adds, the words *argument of things unseen* do not apply to such an authority, nor do they even apply to unformed faith, for an authoritative text does

---

125 *Ibid.,* nn. 5 and 6; p. 292.
126 *Ibid.,* n. 17; pp. 294-295.
127 *Ibid.,* n. 9; p. 293.
128 *Ibid.,* n. 18; p. 295.
129 *Ibid.,* n. 20; p. 295.
130 On unformed faith, see *supra,* note 24.
131 *Ibid.,* pp. 295-296.
132 *Ibid.,* n. 22; pp. 296-297.
133 *Ibid.,* n. 23; p. 297.

not cause that affective assent (*Assertionem cordis*) which formed faith causes.[134]

A final objection is made that the definition is not good because it is not through the final cause, as metaphysical and theological definitions should be. For the final cause of all virtues, and especially of faith, is God, not things to be hoped for.[135] Roland answers that the theologian should define through the immediate final cause, not through the ultimate final cause, God. Because God is the common final cause of all virtues and of everything else, to state that he is the final cause of faith would not distinguish faith from other virtues nor, indeed, from anything else.[136]

Roland's treatment of the definition of faith is clear and orderly. It is dependent on William of Auxerre, but it contains no such masterly expression as William's *acquiescere primae veritati propter se et super omnia*. Rather surprisingly, he has less than William on faith as an argument. Of the authors treated here, he is the only one who presents the objection that unformed faith is a foundation. His answer that unformed faith is only improperly and remotely a foundation leaves intact the point, which is worth noting, that natural faith can help to prepare one for baptism and that unformed faith can dispose bad Christians to receive grace more readily. He is not very helpful when he says that hope is not the substance of things to be hoped for in the same way as formed faith is, but only, perhaps, in the way unformed faith is. He is more fortunate when he defends the definition as being through the "immediate final cause," namely things to be hoped for, because simply to say that God is the final cause would not distinguish faith from anything else.

Of the four authors treated here, William and Alexander are more original. William emphasizes the intellectual aspect of faith, whereas Alexander emphasizes the voluntary aspect. Roland follows William and adds little to him. Philip not only follows Alexander but adds much to what is found in Alexander's *Gloss* and *Disputed Question 38*. Interesting and important in their own right, these authors were also preparing for the great doctrinal syntheses of St. Bonaventure and St. Thomas Aquinas; for our purpose, they help us to understand the question we now study.

134 *Ibid.*, n. 24.
135 *Ibid.*, n. 25.
136 *Ibid.*, n. 26.

The Doctrine in MS. Assisi 138

Most of the discussion of the definitions of faith in this manuscript is devoted to the apostolic definition of faith: *Fides est substantia rerum sperandarum, argumentum non apparentium.* (*Heb.* 11 : 1) But the author also treats definitions of faith from Pseudo-Denis the Areopagite and the anonymous *Summa Sententiarum,* which the author of this question attributed to Hugh of St. Victor. In addition, he mentions two other definitions, one from St. John Damascene and one which he attributes to St. Basil.

The present editor has divided the text into forty-nine paragraphs. The general structure of the question is sufficiently clear. Three parts can be discerned: a) statement of the definitions and of objections against them, b) exposition of doctrine by the author of this question (paragraphs 26, 30 and 32)[1] and c) answers to the objections. Thus, the teaching is developed especially by presenting objections against the definitions and answering them. The objections against the first part of the apostolic definition of faith are presented before those against the second part, and a similar order is observed in presenting the answers, although they do not occur in exactly the same order as the objections.

In this section, the doctrine of the author of this question will be presented first; then each definition will be given, accompanied by objections made to it and by the corresponding answers. In order to assess this question more carefully, comparisons will be made with the teaching of authors treated above. Thus it will be possible to show what views the author of this question shares with other authors of his time and what is peculiar to him.

The author introduces his explanation of the fittingness of the definition in Hebrews by referring to the familiar division of philosophy into natural, rational and moral. He states that corresponding respectively to those parts as subjects or first principles are matter, genus and faith. As matter is a universal power in reference to all forms (presumably for receiving them) and as genus is a universal power in reference to species and differences, "the universal power for every end in moral matters" is faith. But such an end, he says, is either the good or the true. Thus, because faith is a potency for the good which subsists in us, it is described as *the substance of things to be hoped for*; and because it is a potency for the true, leading to the knowledge of things unseen, it is

---

1 References to the paragraphs are given in parentheses in the course of this section, in order to facilitate comparison with the text.

described as *the argument of things unseen*. It was fitting that the Apostle describe faith in this way, for he was "the universal master and teacher of morals" (26).

This explanation of the subjects of the three disciplines is very much like the teaching of William of Auxerre.[2] But there are important differences, the chief of which is that William speaks of theology defining things through their proper relation to the ultimate end, namely to God, whereas the author of this question sees faith as directing to the twofold end of *morals,* namely the good and the true. William allows for the enjoyment of the supreme good by faith and, secondarily, for the doing of good through political virtues under the direction of faith.[3] But, throughout his explanation, William is much more interested in the speculative or intellectual aspect of faith. Alexander of Hales and Philip the Chancellor emphasized the affective aspect of faith,[4] but here it is the practical application of faith to morals which is emphasized. What is said here about the subjects of natural, rational and moral philosophy reminds one of Philip the Chancellor's explanation of the meaning of the word *substance* in metaphysics, physical science and logic.[5] But the resemblance is not close enough to require further comment.

The question is asked why only faith and charity, but not hope and other virtues, are defined by the Apostle (21). This gives rise to an interesting development of the author's emphasis on the role of faith in directing moral conduct. He tells us: "Faith is a universal potency for every end in morals, but charity is a universal act." Thus it was fitting that the Apostle, as "the universal teacher and master of morals," determine both, i.e. potency and act. "And on account of this also," he continues, "the Lord Jesus, who is the universal agent of salvation, handed down two sacraments: one according to the universal potency, i.e. faith — this is the sacrament of baptism; the other according to the universal act, i.e. charity — this is the sacrament of the Eucharist" (40). We have seen nothing corresponding to this in any of the authors treated above. Philip the Chancellor explains that the Apostle dfined only faith and charity because there are only two powers in the soul, namely the cognitive and the motive, and by these two virtues in them we tend to the first good and the first truth.[6]

But if it is fitting that the Apostle define only faith and charity, why

2 See p. 25.
3 See p. 26.
4 See pp. 31 and 34.
5 See p. 35.
6 See p. 36.

does he not define faith through its genus, which is knowledge (18)? The reason, one is not surprised to learn, is that, whereas the logician defines through genus and differences, "it belongs to the universal teacher of morals to determine his first principle as it is the universal potency or the universal act for every moral end" (44).

According to our author, morality deals with potency and act rather than with logic. Faith has to do with universal potency, and charity has to do with universal act. Thus, the Apostle, "the universal teacher of morals," fittingly determines universal potency by defining faith and universal act by defining charity.

The question is asked whether the apostolic definition is of formed or unformed faith. It is pointed out that a *Gloss* explains the words *substance of things to be hoped for* by saying, *i.e. making things to be hoped for to subsist in us*. Because unformed faith is said to do this, an objector claims that the definition is of unformed faith (16). However, along with the authors studied above,[7] the author of this question maintains that the definition is of formed faith (41), and he denies that unformed faith makes things to be hoped for to subsist in us. "For," he explains, "to make subsist is to make the flow stand still, through hope of eternal things, which belongs only to formed faith" (42). Presumably the "flow," which he emphatically calls the *fluxum influitatis,* refers to the fickle appetite of a man without hope of eternal things. If one distinguishes, within the notion of faith as the substance or foundation, the aspect of support and the complementary aspect of permanence, it is the latter which is emphasized here. It is not as explicitly present elsewhere in this question or in the authors treated above.

One other objection is presented against the definition applying to formed faith rather than to unformed faith. It is objected that the devils think with assent, even though *to think with assent* is the (Augustinian) definition of belief. Thus the question arises concerning this definition and the apostolic definition of faith, whether one is of formed faith and the other of unformed faith (17). In reply, the author distinguishes between two ways of understanding the words *to think with assent. Assent* may include movement to act toward the end or it may refer only to conceiving the truths of faith (*potest dicere in ratione conceptionis*). In the latter way assent belongs to unformed faith and thus to the demons. But the first way belongs to formed faith and therefore not to the demons, "because, even though they think, they are not moved" (43).

The two parts of the apostolic definition of faith were treated at

---

7 On the apostolic definition referring to formed faith, see: for William, p. 25; for Alexander, p. 20; for Philip, pp. 32-33; and for Roland, p. 40.

about equal length by William, Alexander and Roland, whereas Philip
gave more attention to the second part of the definition. Alewander explains that faith, being a substance in the sense of a foundation, is a
material disposition through which one is prepared for eternal life.[8]
Philip speaks of faith as the substance or foundation disposing the soul
to eternal life, but it is only when speaking of the spiritual life on earth
that he calls faith the foundation and matter *in qua* or subject.[9] But the
author of this question gives more attention to the first part. According
to him, the word substance in the definition of faith means "matter, i.e.
a material disposition disposing universally to every moral end" (30).
Thus he characteristically keeps in mind the role of faith in regulating
the moral life.

All of the authors studied above agree that the word *substance* in the
apostolic definition of faith means a *foundation*,[10] and the notion is
prominent in this question. According to its author, faith is the first
foundation (2). It is objected that faith cannot be the first foundation,
because St. Augustine called hope *the entrance to faith* (3). In reply,
without tarrying over the change of metaphors, the author recalls that,
according to a *Gloss,* the word *faith* here means the thing believed. He
concludes, "Hence hope is *the entrance to faith,* i.e. through hope one enters to the thing believed" (33). This seems to mean that one does not
enter into the virtue of faith through the virtue of hope, but that one
having faith enters, through hope, into the realities in which he
believes. The objection is not found in the authors studied.

But with the arrival of those future realities in which one now
believes, faith itself will pass away. How then, can it be called a foundation? William, Alexander and Philip, though admitting that faith will
not remain, refuse to concede that therefore it should not be called a
foundation even of the future life. Roland does not discuss the point in
his treatment of faith. According to William, faith is not only the foundation by which things to be hoped for are acquired and through which
they subsist in us now through hope, but it is also the foundation
through which they will subsist in us in the future in reality.[11] Alexander sees the apostolic definition as comparing faith to a substance
because it is the foundation of the present and future spiritual edifice,
perfecting the intellect as the argument of things now unseen and per-

8   See p. 28.
9   See p. 32.
10   On *substance* in the sense of *foundation* in the apostolic definition of faith, see: for William, p.
25; for Alexander, p. 29; for Philip, p. 32; and for Roland, p. 39.
11   See p. 25.

fecting the will as the substance of things hoped for in the future.[12] Alexander, therefore, is even more explicit than William in regarding faith as the foundation of the future, as well as of the present, spiritual edifice. Philip, in answer to an objection, expressly teaches that faith is correctly called a substance in the sense of a foundation, not only in reference to its present effect, but even in reference to the end of faith, disposing the soul so that eternal life will subsist in it in the future.[13] In our anonymous question the objector insists that faith, which passes away, should not be called a foundation, and, by mentioning that other virtues will remain, he intimates that they may have a better right to be called a foundation (4). The author answers that in this life faith remains and is the foundation of the edifice of the virtues, but that in heaven it will not be the foundation of the spiritual edifice (35). In this concession that faith is not the foundation of the future spiritual edifice, he differs from Alexander and Philip and, it would seem, from William.

It is also objected that St. Ambrose called fortitude the foundation of faith (5) and that fear is designated in the same way in a *Gloss* on the words of *Ecclesiasticus*, "The fear of God is the beginning of his love, and faith is the beginning of clinging to him." (*Ecclus [Sirach]* 25 : 16 [in some editions, 25 : 11]) (6). The author of this question explains that the *Gloss* does not refer to initial fear, which is an inside foundation, but to servile fear, which is an outside foundation (7). This seems to mean that initial fear is an internal foundation of the spiritual edifice and that servile fear is its external foundation. Thus, servile fear may be said to be outside and initial fear to be inside, because the former is not in the spiritual edifice of those having sanctifying grace, whereas the latter is in them. This limited explanation seems to be authorized by the text.

But the objector insists that the biblical text does not refer to servile fear, for servile fear is not joined to love and faith (8). The author simply offers this solution: "Faith is called a foundation by origin, fear by supporting, fortitude by completing; or, better: Faith is a universal foundation, but fear is a particular foundation from evil (*a malo*), fortitude is a particular foundation toward good (*ad bonum*)" (34). The fear in question is servile fear, not initial fear, for he has already said that the *Gloss* refers to servile fear (7), and he is now (34) answering the objector's insistence that it does not (8). He extols faith as a universal foundation, whereas fear and fortitude are only particular foundations. His thought seems to be that faith extends both to the evil (such as eter-

---

12 See pp. 29 and 30.
13 See p. 32.

nal punishment) from which fear turns and the good toward which fortitude is directed.

Another objection against faith being calles a *foundation* is that a vicious circle results from applying the word *foundation* to faith, hope, fear and fortitude (20). Perhaps because the remarks on fear and fortitude as a foundation (34) are considered to be sufficient, no special answer is given to this objection. But a variation of the objection elicits a response. The objector observes that, in order to believe, one must have the desire to believe, which desire is above the power of nature. "Therefore," he continues, "it is a grace. Therefore it belongs to one of these three: the good, the true, the difficult. Therefore it belongs to faith or hope or charity. If [it belongs] to charity, then charity is the foundation and beginning of faith, as faith is of charity, and thus there is a circle among the virtues;" The objector adds that a similar argument can be made concerning hope (20). The author of this question replies briefly: "That desire of believing before one believes is a *gratia gratis data, non gratum faciens*. Therefore it does not pertain to any of those three — the good, the true, the difficult or great, but is a preamble" (46). The objector argued that the desire to believe is a grace. As such, it must belong to the good and therefore to charity, or to the true and therefore to faith, or to the difficult and therefore to hope. Then, concentrating on the relation between faith and charity, he objects that there is a vicious circle if they are called the foundation and beginning of one another. Placing the desire to believe among the *gratiae gratis datae* effectively answers the objection by removing the desire to believe from the three virtues themselves, for they belong to the order of *gratiae gratum facientes*. This problem is not brought up in any of the discussions presented in Chapter II, although Alexander of Hales, in order to explain how fortitude is a foundation of faith, distinguishes three kinds of fortitude: one in the natural order, one which is a *gratia gratis data* and one which proceeds from a *gratia gratum faciens* and is a complement of faith.[14]

As do the authors treated above, our author explains how faith, though it will pass away, will make things to be hoped for to subsist in us at some time in reality. The teaching of all these authors is fundamentally the same, although they differ somewhat in their explanations. William of Auxerre is content to say that through faith they will subsist in us in the future in reality.[15] For Alexander of Hales, faith is a material disposition through which one is prepared for eternal

14 See p. 29.
15 See p. 25.

life.[16] According to Philip the Chancellor, faith defined in reference to its end is a substance or foundation disposing the soul so that eternal life will subsist in it in the future.[17] Roland of Cremona teaches that faith will cause things to be hoped for to exist in us later in truth.[18] Our author presents his position in answer to a final objection, namely against faith being called a *substance* or *foundation,* because it is not the "footing" (*pes*) of things to be hoped for (19). He offers the solution that, "faith is called a *foundation* or *substance* effectively, because it makes things to be hoped for to subsist in us now in hope, but at some time in reality" (45).

Having presented objections against calling faith a *substance* or *foundation,* the author concludes his treatment of the first part of the apostolic definition of faith by considering why it is said to be *of things to be hoped for* rather than *of things to be believed* (9) of *of things to be loved* (10). It is argued in favor of the last of these formulas that "opposed species are equally virtues," and the explanation is added that what is opposite is not in the notion (*ratio*) of its opposite. The author explains the principle when he defends the mention of things to be hoped for in the definition of faith (36) and then he shows why it was not fitting to mention, instead, either things to be believed (37) or things to be loved (38).

Thus the objection is raised: "What is opposite should not be in the notion (*ratio*) of its opposite. Therefore, hope should not be in the definition of faith;" He offers this solution: "What is formally opposite does not fall in the notion of its opposite, because thus they are opposed; but what is materially opposite, or the matter of one, can well be in the notion of another, for thus they are not opposed. In this way hope is [mentioned] in the definition of faith, because the matter of faith and [the matter] of hope are things to be hoped for, which are placed in the definition of faith" (36).

The meaning of the principle and the structure of the argument seem to be clear. Formally speaking, faith is about what is believed, whereas hope is about what is hoped for, and love is about what is loved. But materially speaking, what is believed can also be hoped for and loved. Faith, then, can be defined in reference to things that are hoped for or in reference to things that are loved; it need not be defined in reference to things that are to be believed. In their discussions of the definition of faith, none of the authors treated above mentions the principle that what is opposite should not be in the notion of its opposite.

16 See pp. 29-30 and 31.
17 See p. 32.
18 See p. 40.

But if faith can be defined in reference to what is believed in, hoped for or loved, it should be explained why it is said to be of things to be hoped for rather than of things to be believed or to be loved. Thus, first the question is asked why faith is not called *the substance of things to be believed* (9). Because to believe is the interior act of faith, the question would seem to be most natural. Both William and Alexander point out that faith tends only to those things which are hoped for, and Alexander mentions eternal punishment as something in which one believes although one does not hope for it.[19] Without mentioning eternal punishment, Philip answers this question by saying that the first part of the apostolic definition refers to the end perfecting the will.[20] Roland answers first that faith does not cause all things which we believe, including eternal punishment, to subsist in us. And he adds that faith is not the foundation of things to be believed, but rather is the formal cause of their existing in us.[21] The author of this question answers: "Faith makes things to be hoped for to stand or subsist in us. For through faith all things to be hoped for subsist in us now in hope, [and] at last they will subsist in us in reality, but it does not make to subsist in us all things to be believed, e.g. eternal punishment" (37). Thus, in answer to this question, our author is in basic agreement with the authors cited above, although Philip and Roland add points of their own. Eternal life will at last subsist in us in reality, but through faith it already subsists in us in hope.

As has been seen, it is also asked why faith is not called the *substance of things to be loved* (10). The questioner argues that this would be fitting because faith makes all things to be loved to subsist in us. The author answers that, unlike faith and hope, which are always of what is absent, love is sometimes of what is present. "Thus hope and faith have more in common than do love and faith. And therefore faith is defined through the matter of hope rather than through the matter of love" (38). Philip is the only author treated who touches this point. He handles it in what is basically the same way, for he points out that to call faith *the substance of things to be loved* would not indicate their absence, because what is loved may be either present or absent.[22]

The need for the second member of the apostolic definition of faith is challenged by an objection that it is superfluous because the first part, *the substance of things to be hoped for,* is convertible with faith (32). The principle that "a definition should be convertible with that which it

---

19 For William, see p. 26; for Alexander, see p. 30.
20 See p. 32.
21 See pp. 30-40.
22 See p. 32.

defines" was stated by an objector at the beginning of the author's discussion of the definition (2). William of Auxerre sees the first part of the definition as distinguishing formed faith from unformed faith; for him, the second part of the definition distinguishes faith from other virtues.[23] Alexander of Hales teaches that both parts of the definition are needed, because they refer to goodness and truth, the two things which perfect the soul.[24] Philip the Chancellor also holds that the parts refer, respectively, to the good and the true,[25] which seems to imply that both parts are needed. Faced with the objection that the second part of the definition is superfluous, our author grants that the first part of the definition differentiates faith from other virtues. "But," he continues, something is still needed through which it may be defined (*determinetur*) "as it is the universal potency toward every end in morals. Therefore the second [member], namely this, *the argument of things unseen,* was added so that the definition would be complete" (32). Faith, then, "the universal potency," is defined by the Apostle in reference to "every end in morals." Thus our author joins Alexander and Philip in seeing the two parts of the definition as required to define faith in reference to the twofold end, the good and the true.

An objection is made that the standard meanings of the word "argument" do not apply when it is used in the definition of faith (22). For, first of all, it is not taken in the sense in which it is used "at the beginning of the prophets" (*in principiis prophetarum*), which "Boethius" called "a foretaste of things to be said" (*praelibatio dicendorum*). This seems to mean the sense in which we speak of the "argument" of a play. The objection goes on to deny that the famous Boethian definition of an argument as *ratio rei dubiae faciens fidem* applies to faith, for he who doubts is not illumined by faith. The report notes that, on account of this, he (presumably the author of this question) said that the definition refers to a thing *previously* doubted. The objector insists that if yesterday one doubted about a conclusion but does not doubt today, the conclusion is not an argument, because it does not give faith about something doubtful. This objection does not receive a separate answer, whether because the report is incomplete or because the rest is thought to be sufficient.

The use of the word *argument* in the definition of faith requires explanation, because faith is above reason. It will be recalled that William of Auxerre simply says that faith is an argument not as a conclusion but as proving what was not proved.[26] A more developed explanation is

23 See p. 25.
24 See p. 28.
25 See pp. 32-33 and 35.
26 See p. 24.

found in Alexander of Hales, for whom faith is an *argument* in a special sense, including both the cognitive and the affective powers and looking toward the future.[27] Denying that faith is an argument in the sense of a principle, middle term or conclusion, or all of them together, he was content to call it a habit by which one believes what is unseen.[28] For Philip, faith is called an *argument* because, as a logical argument produces a conclusion, faith moves through affection from sign to reality; by it things that are unknown in one way come to be more perfectly known.[29] And according to Roland, for believers it is an argument from authority.[30] They do not speak of faith as an argument to unbelievers. It should be recalled, however, that William saw reason as defending faith and moving the simple to true faith.[31]

It is also objected against the second part of the definition of faith that it applies in civil matters as well, for in such matters there is argument about things not seen and not subject to proof. An example is the love of one person for another (24). The author answers that this second part of the definition does not give the whole meaning of faith, and that the first part of the definition does not apply to civil matters (49). The objection is not found in the authors treated in Chapter II.

In the question being edited here, the final objection to the second part of the apostolic definition of faith is that the word *argument* does not apply, because there cannot be argument or proof about things which are unseen and surpass reason and understanding (25). Our author answers that as an argument leads to knowledge of a conclusion, faith leads to the knowledge of things unseen (47).

The author of this question treated the second part of the definition from Hebrews much more briefly than the first part. In fact, he gives only two objections, and only one of these does he answer. This suggests that the report given in our manuscript is incomplete. The brevity of his treatment of the second part of the definition contrasts not only with the length of his treatment of the first part but also with the attention given to the second part by the authors discussed in Chapter II, especially Philip.

The author treats other definitions of faith much more briefly. To Hugh of St. Victor he attributes the definition of faith as *voluntaria certitudo supra opinionem et infra scientiam*. This gives rise to the objection that faith, being a middle habit, is not a first foundation (11). Despite its

---

27 See p. 30-31.
28 See p. 30.
29 See pp. 35.
30 See p. 40.
31 See p. 24.

form, the objection seems to be directed against Hugh's definition, as is the following objection, namely that faith, being more certain than every art and science, is above science (12). Both objections are answered together (39). The author grants that as to the order of habits faith is medium, but not as to the order of certitudes. Unfortunately, he does not explain what he means by the former expression. As to the latter, he explains that faith, being based on the first truth, is more certain than science, which is based on lower causes. In the treatments of the definition of faith examined only that by Philip mentions this definition. Also attributing it to Hugh, he observes that it distinguishes faith from other habits of knowledge.[32]

The author asks how Hugh's definition of faith can be reduced to that by the Apostle, or what is the basis of one or the other (14). According to his now familiar emphasis on morality, he explains that the Apostle, being occupied with morals and works, describes faith as it disposes the soul *in operando,* whereas Dionysius and Hugh were more concerned with contemplation (29).

The objector inquires how faith is certitude, because if there is certitude there is no faith, *cum fides non habeat meritum cui humana ratio praebet experimentum* (13). The author's answer to this misplaced appeal to the authority of St. Gregory has not been preserved in our question.

Two definitions of faith from Pseudo-Denis are presented briefly. According to the objector, he called faith *manens credentium collocatio* and *ornatrix scientia cognoscentia et cognitorum* (15). The first definition is given in the translation by John the Saracen. The second definition is cited in the reply as *Fides est ordinatrix scientia etc.* (28). The printed translation closest to it is that by John Erigena, namely *adunatrix scientia cognoscentium et cognitorum*.[33] The objector asks why "Dionysius" gives two definitions. He is informed that Dionysius defined faith as it is a disposition of the soul in operating and knowing, for he described faith as it is the universal bond of members to one another and to their head. It is clear enough that the first definition, *manens fidelium collocatio,* refers to faith as uniting believers. If the word "ordering" (*ordinatrix*) is read in the second definition, it seems to describe faith well as knowledge directing the faithful to the things they know by faith, or, as our author says, to their head. If the word "uniting" (*adunatrix*) were to be read instead, the emphasis would be not on the process of directing, but on the uniting which is its term. The words "bond" and "uniting" (*adunatrix*) go well together, but so do the words "disposition" and "ordering" (*ordinatrix*) (28). In the objection itself (15) another word, *ornatrix,* appears. However properly it may describe faith, its presence here raises doubt about the accuracy of our scribe, both because the notion of "beautifying" is not used in the reply and because the word is so similar to the word *ordinatrix,* which is used there. The doubt is confirmed by the strange use, immediately after the word *scientia,* of the word *cognoscentia,* which, it seems from the meaning of the reply, is, in fact, a mistake for *cognoscentium.* Philip gives the only Pseudo-Dionysian definition of faith quoted above, and it is different, namely, *Fides est ratio veritatis per se existentis.*[34]

Two more definitions of faith are presented, namely *Fides est eorum quae sperantur hypostasis,* and *Fides est eorum quae non videntur hypostasis.* The former is correctly attributed to John Damascene, and the latter is said to be from Basil. Presumably the reference is to St. Basil the Great, but this author has not been able to find it. The only remark made on these two definitions is that they mean nothing other than the substance of things to be hoped for (31). This seems to be sufficient, since *hypostasis* here is the same as *substantia* and to say *eorum quae sperantur* instead of *rerum sperandarum* is only to use a pronoun and relative clause instead of a noun and a gerundive, although it could have been noted that there is a shift from hoping to seeing, or rather to not seeing, when *eorum quae non videntur* (really a re-wording of *non apparentium,* from the second part of the apostolic definition) is substituted for *rerum sperandarum.* But even then there is little more than a re-wording of the Vulgate text in view of the Greek.

SUMMARY AND CONCLUSION

The anonymous author of this question on the definition of faith agrees with the authors studied above in that he devotes most of his attention to the statement on faith in *Hebrews.* He and they (unlike Hugh of St. Victor) regard it as a definition, and all agree that it refers to formed, rather than to unformed, faith. The author of our question uses much the same materials as the other authors we have studied. But some important differences between him and them should be recalled. Whereas William, Alexander and Roland treat the two parts of the apostolic definition at about equal length and Philip devotes more attention to the second part, the author of this question (as it has come down to us) devoted more attention to the first part. Most notable is his emphasis on the role of faith in directing morality. For him, St. Paul is

34 See p. 37.

"the universal master and teacher of morals" (26). And when he comes to compare the definition of faith in *Hebrews* with other definitions, he tells us: "The Apostle ... explains it as it disposes the soul in operating, because the Apostle was concerned with morals and works. Denis and Hugh were more occupied with contemplation" (29).

Peculiar to our author is his explanation of why the Apostle, by defining only faith and charity, determined all potency and act in moral matters: "Faith is the universal power for every end in morals, but charity the universal act." And he sees a parallel in the fact that "the Lord Jesus, who is the universal agent of salvation, handed down two sacraments: one according to the universal potency, i.e. faith — this is the sacrament of baptism; the other according to the universal act, i.e. charity — this is the sacrament of the Eucharist" (40).

The author of this question agrees with the authors studied in Chapter II that the apostolic definition is of formed faith (41), but he is alone in appealing to the permanence of substance as an explanation: "For to make subsist is to make the flow stand still, through hope of eternal things, which belongs only to formed faith" (42).

Our author agrees with the other four authors studied that faith is called a *substance* because it is a *foundation*. But he gives a unique development of the idea when he explains how faith can be a foundation even though the term is also given to fear and fortitude: "Faith is called a foundation by origin, fear by supporting, fortitude by completing; or, better: Faith is a universal foundation, but fear is a particular foundation from evil (*a malo*), fortitude is a particular foundation toward good (*ad bonum*)" (34).

Also, of the five tracts on faith which have been presented, this is the only one which discusses the relation between the desire to believe and the virtue of faith. The objector noted that, in order to believe, one must have the desire to believe, which desire is a grace. "Therefore it belongs to faith or hope or charity. If [it belongs] to charity, then charity is the foundation and beginning of faith, as faith is of charity, and thus there is a circle among the virtues" (20). He answers that the desire of believing before one believes is a *gratia gratis data,* a preamble to faith (46). Removed from the theological virtues, the initial desire to believe cannot be cited to argue that faith and charity are called foundations of one another.

After devoting considerable attention to the notion of faith as a substance, the author explains why it is said to be *of things to be hoped for* rather than *of things to be believed* or *of things to be loved*. It is objected that the mention of things to be hoped for in the definition of faith violates the principle that, "What is opposite should not be in the notion (*ratio*) of its opposite." Our author points out that this applies only to things which are formally opposed but that it does not prevent the matter of hope from being mentioned in the definition of faith (36).

To the question why faith is not said to be *the substance of things to be believed*, our author answers that "through faith all things to be hoped for subsist in us now in hope, [and] at last they will subsist in us in reality, but it does not make to subsist in us all things to be believed, e.g. eternal punishment" (37). Thus he gives basically the same answer as the authors studied above.

And faith is said to be *the substance of things to be hoped for* rather than *the substance of things to be loved*, because faith and hope, being always of what is absent, never of what is present, have more in common than do faith and love (38). The answer agrees with that given by Philip.

The first part of the apostolic definition of faith is seen by our author as distinguishing it from other virtues. This function was assigned to the second part by William, for whom the first part distinguishes formed faith from unformed faith. Our author holds that the second part of the definition, namely *the argument of things unseen,* is needed in order to define faith as the universal potency toward every end in morals (32), much as for Alexander and Philip the two parts are needed to define faith in reference to the twofold end, the good and the true.

An objection found only in our author is that the second part of the definition applies to civil matters as well, where an example of something unseen is the love of one person for another (24). He replies that this second part does not give the whole meaning of faith, and that the first part does not apply to civil matters (49).

Finally, it is objected against the word *argument* that there cannot be argument or proof about things which are unseen and surpass reason and understanding (25). Our author gives fundamentally the same answer as Alexander and Philip when he remarks that as an argument leads to knowledge of a conclusion, faith leads to the knowledge of things unseen (47).

The author of this question attributes to Hugh of St. Victor the definition of faith as *voluntaria certitudo supra opinionem et infra scientiam* (11). But he remarks that, as to the order of certitudes, faith is not a middle habit; being based on the first truth, it is more certain than science (39). Philip, the only one of our other authors to mention this definition in his treatment of faith, simply remarks that it distinguishes faith from other habits of knowledge. Of the five treatises on faith examined here, only that found in MS. Assisi 138 gives the two Pseudo-Dionysian definitions of faith which, according to our author, describe faith as the universal bond of members to one another and to their head (28).

In conclusion, the anonymous author of this question gives an interesting witness to the development of theological reflection on the definition of faith. Like William, Alexander, Philip and Roland, he concentrates on the definition given in Hebrews, and he uses mostly the same sources as they do. His teaching often agrees with theirs, but he also presents some explanations not found in them. Of special interest is his view that St. Paul, "the universal master and teacher of morals" (26), defined only faith and charity because they are, respectively, the universal potency in moral matters and the universal act (40).

DESCRIPTION OF THE MANUSCRIPT

MS. Assisi, Biblioteca Comunale 138, containing mostly theological questions, belongs to a collection of manuscripts formerly in the Convento di San Francesco in Assisi.[1] It was described in 1894 by Giuseppe Mazzatinti and Leto Alessandri.[2] In 1948, Doucet described it more accurately as follows:

> Parchment, mid-thirteenth century, 293 ff. (+ 58 bis) of different dimensions, namely 305 × 228 mm. (fasc. I-XXIX, ff. 1-232), 285 × 228 mm. (fasc. XXX-XXXV, ff. 233-285), 275 × 228 mm. (fasc. XXXVI, ff. 286-293). Fol. 197a-200d are to be read after f. 192. At least five scribes wrote it and, indeed, under the direction and for the use of St. Bonaventure, as is clear from many notes added in his own hand.[3]

In 1960 the Quaracchi editors of Alexander's *Quaestiones "Antequam Esset Frater"* somewhat qualified the last statement, for, though they still referred to it as once for the use of St. Bonaventure, they added, "and perhaps collected at his direction."[4] In 1932 F. M. Henquinet had said that folios 137r-270r were written by one scribe, under the supervision of St. Bonaventure, who probably supervised the composition of the entire manuscript.[5]

At the beginning is a table of contents, in slightly more than three columns. It begins: "De patientia formata, an sit virtus." Folio 1v is

1   Giuseppe Mazzatinti and Leto Alessandri, "Biblioteca del convento di S. Francesco," in G. Mazzatinti, *Inventari dei Manoscritti delle Biblioteche d'Italia* IV (Forli, 1894) p. 21. Used in reprint edition: Olschki, Florence, 1963.

2   *Ibid.*, p. 46.

3   *Prolegomena in Librum III ...*, p. 138.

4   *ProlQuaest* I, 7*-8*.

5   "Un recueil de questions annoté par S. Bonaventure," *Archivum Franciscanum Historicum* 25 (1932) 554.

blank. The true incipit (f. 2r) is: "Post hoc est quaestio de patientia, et primo de formata, secundo de informi. De formata ergo quaeritur primo an sit virtus vel non." The explicit (292v) is: "Res autem speciei est ipsa mens ex se species gignens, secundum Augustinum." At the bottom of folio 291v is the note: "In isto libro omnes quaterni sunt, et unum folium in principio et unum in fine sine aliqua scriptura." After the word "et" is written "xxxvi." This is not part of the sentence but only the number of the folio, for the first and last folio of each quire is numbered. There is a table of contents on the first folio. The writing, which is small, regular and not difficult to read, is in two columns of about sixty lines. Questions or groups of questions are numbered in the margin, approximately opposite the place where they begin. These numbers as well as thirty-five notes were written in the hand of St. Bonaventure, and Henquinet thought the initials "fB" or "FB" at the end of a marginal note in f. 266r mean "fr. Bonaventura."[6] The notes are of three kinds: 1) corrections of the text, 2) attributions (e.g. in f. 116r, "Q° guerrici") and 3) schemas of questions. Most are illegible.[7]

The manuscript is composed of disputed questions preserved in the form of a *reportatio*.[8] This type of literature has a special importance, more than the mere class notes of a student, because they were intended for public rather than for private use.[9] Referring to questions 14-21 (ff. 77c-84d), Henquinet described their *reportatio* as "hasty, not organized, still without any heading and without any learned technique."[10] He rejected the suggestion of Pelster[11] that the *reportator* of those questions was Richard Rufus, and said he remains anonymous.[12] No suggestion has been advanced for identifying the *reportator* of other questions.

There has been some discussion about whether the manuscript contains quodlibetal questions in the sense described by P. Glorieux[13] and held by P. Mandonnet to have been fashioned by St. Thomas.[14] Assisi 138 contains the expressions "Quaeritur de quodlibet" and "Quaestio

6 *Ibid.*, p. 553.

7 *Ibid.*, p. 555.

8 F. Pelster, "Cod. 152 der Bibliothek von S. Antonio in Padua und seine Quästionen," *RTAM* 9 (1937) 45; F.-M. Henquinet, "Les questions inédites d'Alexandre de Hales sur les fins dernières," *RTAM* 10 (1938) 168-169. Also, see p. 62, fn. 3.

9 M.-D. Chenu, "Maîtres et bacheliers de l'Université de Paris vers 1240. Description du manuscrit Paris, Bibl. Nat. lat. 15652," *Études d'Histoire doctrinale et littéraire du XIIIᵉ siècle* 1 (1932) 24.

10 "Les questions inédites ...," p. 169.

11 "Cod. 152 ...," p. 45, note 45.

12 "Les questions inédites ...," p. 169, note 70.

13 *La littérature quodlibétique*, Vol. I (Bibliothèque thomiste 5) (Le Saulchoir, Kain [Belgium], 1925) pp. 11-95.

14 "Saint Thomas d'Aquin, créateur de la dispute quodlibétique," *Revue des sciences philosophiques et théologiques* 15 (1926) 477-506; 16 (1927) 5-38.

de quolibet." F. Pelster, noticing the former of these expressions, included it among the examples he adduced to show that the type was too early to have been the work of St. Thomas.[15] M.-D. Chenu noted both expressions but pointed out that they do not introduce quodlibetal questions properly so called. He was not convinced by Pelster's examples in general, and he said he had not seen any true quodlibetal dispute in the many collections of questions from the period 1230-1250.[16]

Doucet divided the entire manuscript into one hundred and eighty-five questions or groups of questions.[17] Concerning authorship of the questions, he explained:

> The manuscript consists mostly of anonymous disputed questions. Only six bear the names of their authors, namely Guerric (q. 81), Guiard (q. 107), A. Exon (q. 171), R. Grosseteste (q. 172), Rufus of Cornwall (q. 173) and Walter of St. Thierry (q. 184). Many of the others have already been found to belong to Alexander of Hales, Jean de la Rochelle, Eudes Rigaud, William of Middleton, Guerric or Guiard; but very many still are of uncertain or entirely unknown authorship, even from among those certainly used as sources of the *Summa*.[18]

Although few of the questions are assigned an author in the manuscript itself, many authors have been identified. The literature on the authorship of the questions is quite extensive, and only a few of the more important points can be mentioned here.

The first citation of the manuscript was in 1923, by the Franciscan scholars at Quaracchi, who have frequently cited it since that time.[19] Writing in 1930, Pelster had found only one question certainly by Guerric, and another one probably by him.[20] In 1933, largerly on the basis of formulas which he regarded as characteristic, Pelster attributed seventy-five questions to Guiard of Laon, although he expressed doubt about the attribution of four of them.[21] But in 1934, Henquinet showed that thirty-seven of those questions certainly belong to Guerric of St. Quentin, and he was confident that further study would show that others also were by Guerric.[22] He also assigned questions to several

---

15 "Literaturgeschichtliches zur Pariser theologischen Schule aus den Jahren 1230 bis 1256," *Scholastik* 5 (1930) 64-65.

16 "Maîtres et bacheliers ...," p. 28, note 3.

17 *Prolegomena in Librum III* ..., pp. 138-141.

18 *Ibid.*, p. 138.

19 All these citations are listed in *Prolegomena in Librum III* ..., p. 138, note 9; *ProlQuaest* I, 8*; *Glossa* III, 37, 2 (AE); p. 461, note 2.

20 "Literaturgeschichtliches ...," p. 74.

21 "Les 'Quaestiones' de Guiard de Laon dans 'Assise Bibl. comm. 138,'" *RTAM* 5 (1933) 372-380. The four about which he was doubtful (23, 24, 50 and 51) were printed in brackets.

22 "Les écrits du Frère Guerric de Saint-Quentin, O.P.," *RTAM* 6 (1934) 402-403.

other authors. This left a treatise *de anima* and almost twenty-five questions not identified.[23] Two years later he assigned five more of Pelster's seventy-five questions to Guerric.[24]

The number of questions assigned to Alexander of Hales has grown considerably. In 1933, Pelster assigned twenty-one questions to him.[25] In 1948, when editing Alexander's *Summa*, Doucet assigned twenty-four questions of this manuscript to Alexander, and he thought that eight more may be by him.[26] In 1960, the editors of Alexander's *Quaestiones "Antequam Esset Frater"* recognized sixty-three that belong to him and one that may belong to him.[27]

In 1962, B.-G. Guyot published a study of a manuscript which he found in Prague.[28] Probably dating from between 1240 and 1245,[29] it contains seventy-nine questions which are also found in Assisi 138: thirty-six questions by Alexander of Hales, thirty-four by Guerric and two that may be by him, two by Guiard and one that may be by him, two by Jean de la Rochelle and two that remain anonymous.[30] The Prague MS. names Guerric as the author of two questions which the editors of Alexander's *Summa* described as probably by Guerric,[31] and one which they described as of uncertain authorship.[32] It attributes to Alexander a question which they thought was his.[33] It also confirms various attributions already made. As research continues, the authors of more questions may be identified.

The manuscript contains questions on a wide range of theological questions, although some very important topics are hardly treated at all. V. Doucet indicates the subject matter of most of the hundred and

23   *Ibid.*, pp. 286-287.

24   "Notes additionnelles sur les écrits de Guerric de Saint-Quentin," *RTAM* 8 (1936) 374-375. These included two questions (23 and 24) about which Pelster had expressed doubt. One of them (q. 23) Henquinet divided into two questions.

25   "Die Quästionen des Alexander von Hales," *Gregorianum* 14 (1933) 509-512.

26   *Prolegomena in Librum III* ..., pp. 138-141.

27   *ProlQuaest* I, 8*.

28   "Quaestiones Guerrici, Alexandri et aliorum magistrorum Parisiensium (Praha, Univ. IV. D. 13)," *Archivum Fratrum Praedicatorum* 32 (1962) 5-125.

29   *Ibid.*, p. 106.

30   This information was obtained by following Guyot's list of the Prague questions which are also found in Assisi 138 (*ibid.*, p. 122) and then checking his list of the former (*ibid.*, pp. 10-100).

31   Questions 151 and 156 in Assisi 138, which are, respectively, 67 and 235C in Guyot's list of questions in Praha, Univ. IV. D. 13. See "*Prolegomena in Librum III* ...," p. 140, and Guyot, *loc. cit.*, pp. 37-38, and p. 94.

32   Question 78 in Assisi 138, which is question 133 in Guyot's list. See *Prolegomena in Librum III* ..., p. 139, and Guyot, *loc. cit.*, p. 60.

33   A question "De virginiatate" (ff. 72va-73va) in the group of questions 47-51 in Assisi 138, which question corresponds to question 127 in the Prague MS. See *Prolegomena in Librum III* ..., p. 139, and Guyot, *loc. cit.*, p. 58.

eighty-five questions or groups of questions.[34] He does not mention the contents of forty-five questions (4-12, 28-33, 40-46, 82-96, 132-134, 152-156). The manuscript includes some philosophical questions (99, 165-172, 177, 181, 182, 185). Four questions (146-149) are canonical. All the rest are theological. A complete inventory is not necessary here, but the more important features may be mentioned. Except for a question on the divine intellect (173) and a long one on the knowledge of God (178), none would belong to a tract *De Deo uno*. There is only one question on the Trinity (164), and it is on the vestige. On Christ there are seven questions (98, 100, 101-103, 179), to which may be added a question on the star of the Magi (180). On the angels there are seven questions (39, 110, 160-163, 174). On the last things there are ten questions (53-57, 74, 80, 81, 143, 176). There is a group (97) of thirty questions on the sacraments, and a group (18) of four on sacramental character. There is one question (38) on satisfaction for sin, and there is a pair (108) of questions on contrition. There are seven questions (109, 136-141) on law, and a question (150) *de lege membrorum*. There is a question (52) on martyrdom and one (184) on the office of preaching. There is a question (142) on the need for grace, one (157) *de naturalitate virtutum*, one (129) on the cardinal virtues, and four (1, 2, 3, 37) on various moral virtues. There are four questions (34, 107, 151, 158) about sin, one (68) on divisions of sins, one (69) on the number of capital vices, and a group (117) of fifteen questions on the capital vices. The remaining questions on sins and vices (58-67, 70-73, 114-116, 118, 122, 149) include some on various capital vices and, it should be noted here, a question (73) on heresy and one (118) on infidelity.

The only theological virtue treated is faith, except that q. 156, *De denario*, really contains some points about charity, as is clear from the *incipit*.[35] There are two contiguous groups of questions on faith. Doucet describes them as follows: "*De fide* qq. 5, f. 176d-180b" and "113. *De fide iterum* qq. 3, f. 180b-182c."[36] They did not state how the division into questions should be made. Pelster had divided the first group into four questions rather than five.[37] It seems that the second question should be divided into two parts, even though the manuscript itself combines them.

34 *Prolegomena in Librum III* ..., pp. 138-141.

35 For the *incipit*, see Pelster, "Les 'Quaestiones' ...," p. 380. It is the last in the list of seventy-five questions he assigned to Guiard. Henquinet thought it was by Guerric ("Notes additionnelles ...," p. 387), and this opinion has been confirmed by the Prague MS., which explicitly attributes it to him (Guyot, *loc. cit.*, p. 94).

36 *Prolegomena in Librum III* ..., p. 140.

37 "Les 'Quaestiones' ...," p. 377.

Here is a list of the questions, with addition of the numbers which Pelster assigned to them:

1. "Quaesitum est de fide. Primo, de definitione fidei quam ponit Apostolus, Hebr. XI; scundo, de definitionibus Dionysii et Hugonis de Sancto Victore, Basilii, Damasceni. De prima sic proceditur: Ad Hebr. XI dicitur ..." *Expl.*: "non invenitur in civilibus." 176vb51-177va27 (Pelster, q. 43.)

2. "Postea quaeritur si fides informis fiat formata, aut veniente caritate cedat habitus fidei informis; secundo, si fidei subest falsum. Circa primum proceditur sic: *Fides sine operibus* ..." *Expl.*: "perseveraverit." 177va28-178rb38 (Pelster, q. 44.) It seems that this should be divided into two questions, the *explicit* of the first being: "sicut ex caecitate non fit visus" (178ra44). The second would have this *incipit*: "De secundo articulo sic quaeritur: Cum idem ..." (178ra44).

3. "Quaerebatur quid est articulus re, i.e. utrum sit res vel enunciabile; secundo, quid est definitione; tertio, quomodo artat nos ad credendum. Ad primum: Augustinus, in libro *De Trinitate* ..." *Expl.*: "vocat sanctos eos quibus scribit." 178rb38-179va57 (Pelster, q. 45.)

4. "Postea quaesitum fuit utrum fides se ipsa formetur vel alio. Et huius gratia quaesitum est quomodo caritas est forma aliarum. Circa hoc ita proceditur: Ambrosius: *Caritas est mater* ..." *Expl.*: "complementum et terminus viventium." 179va58-180rb12 (Pelster, q. 46.)

5. "Quaesita sunt tria de fide: primo, utrum diabolus habeat fidem; secundo, utrum sit idem per essentiam fides informis et formata; tertio, si adveniente gratia maneat fides informis, recedente recedat. Ad primum sic: Ro. I: *Iustitia Dei revelatur* ..." *Expl.*: "quod soli caritati convenit." 180rb13-181rb39 (Pelster, q. 47.)

6. "Quaesitum est de duabus definitionibus eius quod est credere in Deum, quarum una ponitur IIII Ro.: Super illud credidit ..." *Expl.*: "loquitur de corpore militantis, etc." 181rb40-182rb7 (Pelster, q. 48).

7. "Quaeritur de evacuatione fidei et scientiae et oboedientiae, sic: Quantum cognoscimus, tantum diligimus ..." *Expl.*: "ex cognitione Dei proveniet." 182rb8-182va16 (Pelster, q. 49.)

The next section will present the text of the first of these questions, namely ff. 176vb51-177va27, in which definitions of faith are discussed. The spelling has been regularized according to Lewis and Short's *Latin Dictionary*.[38] Thus, e.g., the spelling "definitio" is used rather than "diffinicio." The abbreviation "R°" has been expanded to "responsio" rather than to "respondeo." It occurs only once, namely in paragraph

38 Charlton T. Lewis and Charles Short, *A Latin Dictionary* (Oxford, 1966).

38, the usual word being "solutio." Additions by this editor are indicated thus: <fides>. Whenever the text has been corrected, the reader is referred to a note for the reading in the manuscript itself. Finally, the punctuation and division into paragraphs are the work of this editor.

TEXT

Assisi, Biblioteca Comunale, 138 — ff. 176vb51-177va27

1. Quaesitum est de fide. Primo de definitione fidei quam ponit Apostolus, Hebr. XI;[1] secundo de definitionibus Dionysii et Hugonis de Sancto Victore, Basilii, Damasceni.

2. De prima <definitione> sic proceditur: Ad Hebr. XI dicitur quod *fides est substantia rerum sperandarum, argumentum non apparentium.* Hoc convenit spei. Ergo non est definitio fidei, quia definitio debet esse convertibilis cum suo definito.[2] Dixit[3] quod *substantia rerum sperandarum* idem est quod fundamentum.[4] Fides autem est primum fundamentum. Spes autem non est primum fundamentum.

3. Contra, super Psalmos dicit Augustinus: *Spes est introitus fidei.*[5] Ergo per spem intratur ad fidem. Ergo fides non est primum fundamentum.

4. Item, fundamentum manet cum edificio. Fides autem evacuabitur;/aliae virtutes manent.[6] Ergo fides non est fundamentum.

5. Item, super Luc. XII, Ambrosius <dicit> quod *fortitudo est fidei fundamentum.*[7]

6. Item, Ecclesiasticus XXV: *Timor Dei initium dilectionis eius; fidei autem*

---

1   Heb. 11 : 1. For the text see paragraph 2.

2   Cf. Aristotle, *Analytica Posteriora* II, 4 (91a12-b11).

3   The word "dixit" here and the word "dicebat" in paragraphs 7 and 22 suggest that this is a "reportatio."

4   Peter Lombard, *Collectanea in Epistolas S. Pauli: In Ep. ad Hebr. 11 : 1* (PL 192.488A): "Et proprie dicitur fides substantia, quia sperandis substat, et facit ea esse in credente in alia vita. Et quia fundamentum est omnium bonorum quod nemo mutare potest sine quo non est bona aedificatio."

5   Peter Lombard, *Commentarius in Psalmos Davidicos: In Ps. 36 : 3* (PL 191.368B): "Spes enim est introitus fidei, initium salutis ..." Cf. Cassiodorus, *Expositio Psalmorum, in loco* (CCSL 97.326; PL 70.258B): "Primum siquidem commonet ut speremus in Domino; hoc introitus fidei, hoc initium salutis est."

6   1 Cor. 13 : 10, 13: "... Cum autem venerit quod perfectum est, evacuabitur quod ex parte est ... Nunc autem manent fides, spes, caritas, tria haec; maior autem horum est caritas."

7   St. Ambrose, *Expositio Evangelii secundum Lucam* l. VII, n. 118 (CCSL 14.253; *PL* 15.1817C): "... Ut fortitudinis incentivum est fides, ita fidei firmamentum est fortitudo."

initium agglutinandum est ei.[8] *Glossa: Timor est fidei fundamentum.*[9] Ergo fides non est primum fundamentum.

7. Item, quae est ratio differens: < fides > est fundamentum, et spes est fundamentum, et timor est fundamentum, et fortitudo est fundamentum? Dicebat quod super XXV Ecclesiastici sumitur timor pro timore servili. Ita enim nolebat dicere quod est initium sive fundamentum[10] intra: sic timor initialis est fundamentum. Est etiam initium sive fundamentum extra: sic timor servilis est fundamentum. De tali loquitur hic.

8. Contra, tria dicuntur in textu: timor, fides et dilectio. Sed dilectioni et fidei non agglutinatur timor servilis. Ergo ibi non sumitur timor pro timore servili.

9. Item, quare non dicitur: *Fides est substantia rerum credendarum?*

10. Item, quare non dicitur: *Fides est substantia rerum diligendarum,* cum aequaliter species oppositae virtutes sunt? Oppositum autem non cadit in ratione sui oppositi.[11]

11. Postea quaeritur de definitione Hugonis de Sancto Victore. Dicit ita: *Fides est voluntaria certitudo supra opinionem et infra scientiam.*[12] Ergo fides est medius habitus. Ergo non est primum fundamentum.

12. Item, fides est certior omni arte et scientia. Ergo est supra scientiam.

13. Item, quomodo fides est certitudo, quia si est certitudo non est fides, *cum fides non habeat meritum cum humana ratio praebet experimentum?*[13]

14. Item, quomodo reducitur ad definitionem Apostoli, aut secundum quid sumitur ista definitio, secundum quid illa?

15. Item, Dionysius ita definit: *Fides est manens credentium collocatio,*[14] vel *ornatrix scientia cognoscentia et cognitorum.*[15] Penes quid sumitur diversitas istarum definitionum?

16. Item, definitio Apostoli, *fides est substantia* etc., quaeritur utrum est

---

8 Ecclus. 25 : 16.

9 *Glossa Ordinaria* (Paris, 1590) Tomus III, col. 2103B: "Ipse [timor] est fidei fundamentum, et charitatis origo, et per ipsum sit bonum, et pervenitur ad praemium."

10 Fundatum MS.

11 Cf. Aristotle, *Topica* VI, 4 (142a22-24).

12 Cf. Hugh of St. Victor, *De Sacramentis* l. I, pars 10, c. 1 (PL 176.330C and 331A); *De Sacramentis Legis Naturalis et Scriptae Dialogus* (PL 176.36A). Also cf. the anonymous *Summa Sententiarum* Tractatus I, c. 1 (PL 176.43BC). Only in the last two works in "certitudo" modified by "voluntaria."

13 St. Gregory the Great, *XL Homiliarum in Evangelia Libri Duo: Homilia 26* n. 1 (PL 76.1197C): "... Nec fides habet meritum, cui humana ratio praebet experimentum."

14 (Pseudo.) Denis the Areopagite, *De Divinis Nominibus* c. 7 (*Dionysiaca* I, p. 409). The translation is that of John the Saracen.

15 Cf. (Pseudo.) Denis the Areopagite, *De Divinis Nominibus* c. 7 (*Dionysiaca* I, p. 410; PL 122.1156). The translation closest to this is the one by John Erigena: "adunatrix scientia cognoscentium et cognitorum."

definitio fidei formatae aut fidei informis. Videtur quod sit fidei informis, quia *Glossa* sic exponit: *rerum sperandarum substantia, id est faciens in nobis subsistere res sperandas.*[16] Sed hoc ipsum facit fides informis.

17. Item, *credere est cum assensione*[17] *cogitare.*[18] Hoc faciunt daemones. Cogitant enim cum assensione. Ergo ista est fidei informis, aut est[19] definitio Apostoli; aut si una est fidei formatae, alia informis, secundum quid sumitur utraque?

18. Item, cum fides sit cognitio, quare non definitur per cognitionem, ut per genus suum?

19. Item, cum res sperandae non habeant pro pede fidem,[20] quare[21] fides dicitur *substantia* sive fundamentum *rerum sperandarum?*

20. Item, cum fides sit fundamentum, spes similiter, timor similiter et fortitudo, utrum circulus sit in virtutibus istis sicut in naturalibus est circulus: ex aqua fit vapor, ex vapore nubes, et ex nube iterum fit aqua.[22] Eodem modo in virtutibus videtur esse circulus. Nam ut aliquis credat, habet desiderium credendi. Desiderium illud sive amor iste credendi est supra posse naturae. Ergo est gratia. Ergo est aliquod istorum trium: bonum, verum, arduum. Ergo pertinet ad fidem vel spem vel caritatem. Si ad caritatem, ergo et caritas est fundamentum et initium fidei quemadmodum fides caritatis, et ita circulus est inter virtutes. Simili modo possit ostendi de spe.

21. Item, cum fides et caritas definiantur ab Apostolo, quare non similiter aliae virtutes, ut spes et huiusmodi?

22. Item, argumentum definitur duobus modis. Uno modo, secundum

---

16 Peter Lombard, *Collectanea in Epistolas S. Pauli: In Ep. ad Hebr. 11 : 1* (PL 192.488B): "Per eam [i. e. fidem] enim futura bona quasi jam sunt in nobis, quia facit subsistere in anima nostra ea quae non videntur de quibus proprie fides est."

17 *Asscensione* MS. In this paragraph, and also in paragraph 43, the manuscript regularly has *asscensio* and *ascensio* instead of *assensio*. This may be due to similarity in pronunciation or to the general notion of seeking the things that are above (Col. 3 : 1-2). Alexander of Hales (*Quaest.* 38, 7; p. 664) has the following: "Dupliciter autem est firmitudo in fide: una ad opera, secundum quam servatur fides; et est alia firmitas quae est concomitantia fidei, secundum quod firmatur fides in intellectu practico, et haec est ex dono gratuito; quia [quod] elevatur intellectus practicus ad ea quae sunt super ipsum est ex gratia. ... Et sic est in aliquo etiam [maior et] minor firmitudo, secundum quod est maior et minor elevatio ..."

18 St. Augustine, *De Praedestinatione Sanctorum,* c. 2, n. 5 (PL 44.963): "Quamquam et ipsum credere nihil aliud est, quam cum assensione cogitare."

19 Et MS.

20 *Add.* qualitatum sive habituum (or habitum) MS. St. Isidore, *Etymologiarum Libri XX,* l. VIII, c. 2 (PL 82.296): "Spes vocata, quod sit pes progrediendi, quasi *est spes.* Unde e contrario DESPERATIO, deest enim ibi *pes,* nullaque progrediendi facultas est, quia dum quisque peccatum amat, futuram gloriam non sperat."

21 Quando MS.

22 Cf. James of Venice, *Priorum Analyticorum Aristotelis Interpretatio,* l. II, c. 13 (PL 64.754B-D); attributed to Boethius.

quod ponitur in principiis prophetarum[23] et est idem quod Boethius: *praelibatio dicendorum,*[24] et hoc modo non sumitur in definitione fidei. Alio modo est argumentum *ratio rei dubiae faciens fidem.*[25] Nec sic etiam videtur sumi in definitione fidei, quia dubitanti non est fides. Fides enim lux est. Dubitans autem non est illuminatus. Propter hoc dicebat esse sic intelligendum: *ratio faciens fidem rei* prius *dubiae.* Contra: Si heri dubitasti de aliqua conclusione et hodie non dubitas et hodie tibi concluditur, illa conclusio non est tibi argumentum, quia non fit tibi fides de re dubia.

23. Item, *Glossa* dicit super hoc, *Fides est substantia* etc.: *Dicuntur tria: praemonstratio,*[26] *certitudo, probatio.*[27] Secundum quid differunt haec tria?

24. Item, videtur quod civilia per fidem regantur quia in civilibus est argumentum rerum non apparentium non possibilium probari, quia quod diligam te non possit[28] probari, et ita in civilibus est fides.

25. Item, cum fides <est> eorum quae probari non possunt, quia est de non apparentibus super omnem rationem et intellectum, quomodo potest dici *argumentum rerum non apparentium?*

26. Solutio[29] sic: Triplex est philosophia: naturalis, rationalis et moralis.[30] Ita triplex est subiectum sive principium primum. In naturali philosophia est idem quod universalis potentia ad omnes formas. Hoc autem est materia. Primum in rationali est id quod est universalis potentia ad omnes species et differentias. Hoc est genus. Eodem modo primum in morali est id quod est universalis potentia ad omnem finem in moralibus. Hoc autem est fides. Ideo quemadmodum genus in philosophia rationali describitur ut est universalis potentia ad omnes species et differentias, et materia in naturali philosophia prout est universalis potentia ad omnes formas, ita fides in morali describitur/prout est universalis potentia ad omnem finem in moribus. Omnis finis in moribus est verum vel bonum. Ideo in morali describitur scientia ut universalis potentia ad verum. Quod enim dicitur *substantia rerum* est descriptio fidei ut est potentia ad bonum quod subsistat in

---

23 I was unable to find this reference.

24 I was unable to find this reference. However, cf. the following, from St. Bernard, *De Consideratione,* l. V, c. 3, n. 6 (ed. J. Leclercq and H. M. Rochais, *S. Bernardi Opera,* Vol. III Rome 1963 p. 471; PL 182.791A): "Fides est voluntaria quaedam et certa praelibatio necdum propalatae veritatis ..."

25 Boethius, *De Differentiis Topicis,* l. I (*PL* 64.1174C). Cf. Boethius, *In Topica Ciceronis Commentariorum Libri Sex,* l. I (PL 64.1041C and 1048B).

26 Demonstratio MS. Cf. note 27 and paragraph 48 *infra.*

27 Peter Lombard, *Collectanea in Epistolas S. Pauli: In Ep. ad Hebr.* (PL 192.488C).

28 Possi MS.

29 See paragraph 18.

30 See St. Augustine, *De Civitate Dei,* l. XI, c. 25 (PL 41.338-339; CSEL 40.548-550; CCSL 48.344-345).

nobis. Quod vero dicitur *argumentum non apparentium* descriptio est fidei ut est potentia ad verum. Ad hoc enim est fides ut inducat rerum cognitionem non apparentium. Ita Apostolus debuit fidem describere, qui erat universalis magister et instructor morum.

27. Hugo de Sancto Victore aliter describit, et Dionysius similiter. Hugo enim describit fidem prout disponit animam in cognoscendo tantum. Definit enim sic: *Fides est certitudo voluntaria < supra > opinionem et infra scientiam.*[31] Hic patet quod fidem describit prout est disponens animam in certitudine sic metata.

28. Dionysius vero sic definit fidem prout est dispositio animae in operando et cognoscendo quia describit eam prout est universale vinculum membrorum ad invicem et ad caput, quod patet. Definit enim ita: *Fides est manens credentium collocatio* et iterum: *Fides est ordinatrix scientia* etc.[32] Hic autem est universalis effectus respondens fidei prout animam disponit in operando et cognoscendo.

29. Apostolus autem describit eam prout disponit animam in operando, quia Apostolus versabatur circa mores et opera. Dionysius et Hugo magis vacabant contemplationi.

30. Ex hoc iam patet quomodo sumitur *substantia* in definitione fidei, quia sumitur prout *substantia* dicitur materia, id est materialis dispositio universaliter ad omnem finem in moribus disponens.

31. Damascenus autem et Basilius definiunt fidem sicut Apostolus, quia Damascenus dicit: *Fides est eorum quae sperantur hypostasis.*[33] Hoc nihil aliud est quam substantia sperandorum sive rerum sperandarum. Basilius dicit: *Fides est eorum quae non videntur hypostasis.*[33] Hoc nihil aliud est quam substantia sperandorum sive rerum sperandarum. Basilius dicit: *Fides est eorum quae non videntur hypostasis*[34] et hoc idem est cum praedictis.

32. Quod obicitur: 'Hoc, *substantia rerum sperandarum,* covertitur cum fide; ergo reliquum superfluit,'[35] solutio: Hoc, *Fides est substantia rerum*[36] *sperandarum,* facit fidem differre ab aliis virtutibus. Sed adhuc exigitur aliquid per quod determinetur ut est universalis potentia ad omnem finem in moribus. Per primum determinatur fides ut est potentia ad

---

31 See paragraph 11 and note 12 *supra.*

32 See paragraph 15 and notes 14 and 15 *supra.*

33 St. John Damascene, *De Fide Orthodoxa* c. 83 (Burgundio's translation, ed. E. Buytaert [St. Bonaventure-Louvain-Paderborn, 1955] p. 298): "'Est' autem rursus 'fides eorum quae speranatur hypostasis (id est subsistentia) rerum redargutio quae non videntur.' ..." Some MSS. have *substantia* instead of *subsistentia.*

34 I was unable to find this reference.

35 See paragraph 2.

36 *Add.* rerum MS.

bonum. Ideo secundum, hoc scilicet *argumentum non apparentium,* ut completa esset definitio, apponendum fuit.

33. Quod obicitur: *'Spes est introitus fidei* etc.,'[37] *Glossa* solvit quae dicit[38] quod fides sumitur pro re credita.[39] Unde spes est *introitus fidei,* id est per spem intratur ad rem creditam.[40]

34. Quod obicitur: 'Fortitudo est fundamentum, similiter timor et fides, quae differentia in istis?'[41] — solutio: Fides dicitur fundamentum origine, timor fulciendo, fortitudo consumendo; vel melius: Fides est[42] universale fundamentum, timor vero particulare est fundamentum a malo, fortitudo est particulare fundamentum ad bonum.

35. Quod obicitur: 'Fundamentum cum aedificio manet, fides autem evacuabitur,'[43] solutio: Fides est fundamentum virtutum secundum statum viae, et sic manet cum aedificio virtutum, quia fides manet in via. In patria non erit fides fundamentum spiritualis aedificii.

36. Quod obicitur: 'Oppositum non debet cadere in ratione sui oppositi; ergo spes non debet cadere in ratione fidei,'[44] solutio: Oppositum formaliter non cadit in ratione sui oppositi quia sic opponuntur, sed oppositum materialiter sive materia unius bene cadit in definitione alterius. Ita enim non opponuntur. Isto modo spes cadit in definitione fidei, quia materia fidei et spei sunt res sperandae, quae ponuntur in definitione fidei.

37. Quod obicitur: 'Quare non dicitur *rerum credendarum?*'[45] — solutio: Fides facit stare vel subsistere universaliter in[46] nobis res sperandas. Per fidem enim omnia speranda modo subsistunt in nobis in spe, tandem subsistent in re. Sed non facit in nobis subsistere universaliter omnes res credendas, verbi gratia poenas aeternas.

38. Sed tunc quaeritur: 'Fides facit subsistere in nobis omnia diligenda universaliter; quare ergo non dicitur: *Fides est substantia rerum diligendarum?*'[47] — responsio: Dilectio non semper est absentis, immo quandoque est praesentis; fides tamen modo est absentis, similiter et spes, quia spes est eorum quae non videntur. Unde plus conveniunt spes et

---

37 See paragraph 3.

38 Dicitur MS.

39 Peter Lombard, *Commentarius in Psalmos Davidicos: In Ps. 36 : 3* (PL 191.368B): "Spes enim est introitus fidei, initium salutis, quia per spem intratur ad videndum illud quod creditur: et sperare in Deo initio fidei docemur ..." See note 5 *supra*.

40 Increditam MS.

41 See paragraphs 5-7.

42 *Add.* universalem MS.

43 See paragraph 4.

44 See paragraph 10.

45 See paragraph 9.

46 *Add.* in MS.

47 See paragraph 10.

fides quam dilectio et fides. Et ideo magis definitur fides per materiam spei quam per materiam dilectionis.

39. Quod obicitur: 'Si fides est *voluntaria certitudo supra opinionem et infra scientiam*; ergo est medius habitus,'[48] solutio: Quantum ad ordinem habituum potest dici medium sed non quantum ad ordinem certitudinum, quia quantum ad certitudinem supra scientiam est uno modo. Quantum enim est de modo cognoscendi fides[49] certior est quam scientia,[50] quia quantum ad positionem animae maior est certitudo in fide quam in scientia. Ratio huius est quia anima penes id quod est fidei innititur primae veritati. Anima vero penes id de quo est scientia innititur causis inferioribus. Ideo in infinitum maior est certitudo in fide quam in scientia.

40. Quod quaeritur: 'Quare spes non definitur ab Apostolo, et aliae virtutes, sicut caritas et fides definitur?'[51] — solutio: Fides est universalis potentia ad omnem finem in moribus, caritas autem universalis actus. Nam[52] ille qui est universalis instructor et magister morum debuit utrumque determinare. Apostolus autem universalis erat morum instructor. Spes autem et aliae virtutes non sunt universalis actus aut universalis potentia. Ideo de his non debuit determinare. Propter hoc etiam Dominus Iesus, qui est universalis actor[53] salutis, duo tradidit sacramento:/unum iuxta universalem potentiam, id est fidem — hoc est sacramentum baptismi; aliud iuxta universalem actum, id est caritatem — hoc est sacramentum eucharistiae.

41. Quod quaeritur: 'Quae fides ibi describitur, *Fides est substantia* etc.?'[54] — dicimus quod fides formata.

42. Quod obicitur: 'Fides informis facit subsistere,'[55] dicimus quod falsum est. Facere enim subsistere est facere stare fluxum influitatis per spem aeternorum, quod solum convenit fidei formatae.

43. Quod obicitur: '*Cogitare cum assensione*[56] convenit daemonibus etc.,'[57] solutio: *Assensio* potest dicere in ratione motivi, et sic *cogitare cum*

---

48 See paragraphs 11 and 12.

49 Scientia MS.

50 Fides MS.

51 See paragraph 21.

52 Non MS.

53 The words *actor* (from *agere*) and *auctor* (from *augere*) were often used more or less interchangeably before the thirteenth century to designate the author of a book, but the word *actor* seems to have been used more commonly before and during the thirteenth century to designate one who produces or causes something in general. See M.-D. Chenu, "Auctor, Actor, Autor," *Bulletin du Cange: Archivum Latinitatis Medii Aevi* 3 (1927) 82-84.

54 See paragraph 16.

55 See paragraph 16.

56 *Ascensione* MS. See note 17 *supra*.

57 See paragraph 17.

assensione est fidei formatae. Sic non convenit daemonibus, quia etsi cogitant non tamen moventur. Vel potest dicere in ratione conceptionis. Sic *cogitare cum assensione* est fidei informis. Sic convenit daemonibus.

44. Quod queritur: 'Quare non definitur per cognitionem?'[58] — solutio: Universalis instructoris morum est determinare suum primum prout est universalis potentia vel universalis actus ad omnem finem in moribus. Logici autem est describere per genus et differentias.

45. Quod obicitur: 'Res sperandae non habent pro pede fidem,'[59] solutio: Effective dicitur fides *fundamentum* sive *substantia* quia facit in nobis subsistere res sperandas modo in spe, aliquando autem in re.

46. Quod quaeritur: 'Utrum in virtutibus sit circulus etc.?'[60] — solutio: Illud desiderium credendi antequam credatur·est gratia gratis data, non gratum faciens. Ideo non est pertinens ad aliquod illorum trium, verum, bonum, arduum sive magnum, sed est praeambulum.

47. Quod quaeritur: 'Quomodo dicitur *argumentum*?'[61] — solutio: Dicitur argumentum pro tanto quia ducit in cognitionem non apparentium sicut facit argumentum in cognitionem[62] conclusionis.

48. Quod quaeritur de illis tribus verbis positis in *Glossa* 'praemonstratio, certitudo, probatio:'[63] Dicendum quod fides dicitur 'praemonstratio' comparatione ad visionem quae erit in patria, 'certitudo' quantum ad statum praesentem (quia certior est omni arte et scientia in praesenti secundum quod dictum est[64]), 'probatio' quantum ad imperfectam cognitionem.

49. Quod obicitur: 'In civilibus *argumentum non apparentium* etc.; ergo fides etc.,'[65] solutio: Non sequitur, quia hoc, *argumentum non apparentium,* non dicit totam rationem fidei. Altera autem pars, scilicet *substantia rerum sperandarum,* non invenitur in civilibus.

Leonine Commission, Yale University.

---

58 See paragraphs 18 and 26.
59 See paragraph 19.
60 See paragraph 20.
61 See paragraphs 22 and 25.
62 Cognitione MS.
63 See paragraph 23.
64 In paragraph 12.
65 See paragraph 24.

FIVE LOGICAL TRACTS BY
RICHARD LAVENHAM

Paul Vincent Spade

THE five tracts edited below are items three through seven in the British Museum MS Sloane 3899, containing twenty-five works of Richard Lavenham.[1] The five are

Suppositiones, ff. 4r1-6v14 (abbreviated hereafter *Supp.*)
Consequentiae, ff. 6v15-12v20 (abbreviated *Cons.*)
Tractatus exclusivarum, ff. 12v21-14r15 (abbreviated *Excl.*)
Exceptivae, ff. 14r16-15v16 (abbreviated *Excep.*)
Tractatus qui differt et aliud nuncupatur, ff. 15v17-17v31 (abbreviated *Diff.*)

The tracts deal with the theory of reference and quantification, the theory of consequence, and the logical analysis (the "exposition") of certain kinds of propositions.

A. REFERENCE AND QUANTIFICATION

The first of the five tracts is the tract on supposition. Lavenham defines supposition in standard fashion: "Supposition is a property of an extreme, or the standing (*statio*) of a term for something in a proposition. For, for whatever some term stands (*stat*) in a proposition, for that it is said to suppose (*supponere*)."[2] Lavenham divides supposition as follows:

---

1 Cf. my "The Treatises *On Modal Propositions* and *On Hypothetical Propositions* by Richard Lavenham," *Mediaeval Studies* 35 (1973), 49-59.

2 *Supp.,* 1. (References to works edited below are to paragraph numbers.)

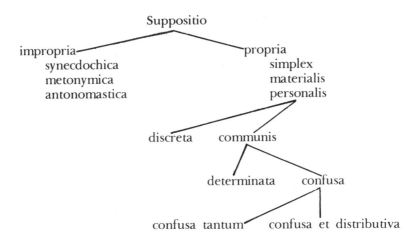

This division is essentially the same as Ockham's[3] and Albert of Saxony's,[4] and the account of the various divisions is likewise similar. Albert, however, omits any discussion of improper supposition, and Ockham mentions it, with the same three subdivisions, only at the end of his treatment.[5] On the other hand, Lavenham places it at the beginning of his tract.[6]

In *Supp.*, Lavenham does not mention Ockham's and Albert's division of confused and distributive supposition into mobile and immobile. According to Ockham,[7] confused and distributive supposition is mobile whenever it is possible to descend copulatively to *all* the singulars, and immobile whenever it is possible to descend copulatively to *some but not all* the singulars. Thus, in the exclusive proposition 'Every man besides Socrates runs', the term 'man' has immobile supposition. For it is possible to descend from that proposition as follows: Plato runs, and Cicero runs, and so on for every man *except* Socrates. Albert's account has it somewhat differently. For him,[8] confused and distributive supposition is mobile whenever it is possible to descend copulatively to all the singulars in a *uniform* way — i.e., in such a way that all the singular propositions are of the same quality (all affirmative or all negative) —

3 William Ockham; *Summa logicae* I, ca. 65-77, Philotheus Boehner, ed., ("Franciscan Institute Publications: Text Series, No. 2"; St. Bonaventure, N.Y.: The Franciscan Institute, 1957, 1962), pp. 179-214. Subsequent references are to this edition, by part, chapter and page.

4 Albert of Saxony, *Perutilis logica*, tract. 2, ca. 1-5, (Venice: Petrus Aurelius Sanutus Venetus, 1518), ff. 11ra-12vb. Subsequent references are to this edition, by tract, chapter and folio. There is a copy of this early printed edition at Paris, Bibliothèque nationale, Rés. R. 183.

5 *Op. cit.*, I, 77, 213f.

6 *Supp.*, 2-5.

7 *Op. cit.*, I, 70, 191f.

8 *Op. cit.*, 2, 5, 12ra.

and immobile whenever such a descent to singulars has to be carried out in a *non-uniform* way — i.e., the singular propositions are of different quality. Thus, in the proposition 'Every man besides Socrates runs', the term 'man' has immobile supposition, because the descent to singulars runs as follows: Socrates does *not* run, and Plato runs, and Cicero runs, etc.

But while Lavenham does not speak of mobile and immobile supposition in *Supp.*, he does use the terms in the tract *Diff.* There it is clear that he is simply identifying mobile supposition with confused and distributive supposition, and immobile supposition with merely confused supposition.[9]

Lavenham's (and Ockham's) definition of proper supposition is defective. He says[10]: "Proper supposition is when a common term does not stand otherwise from its usage in speech (*ex usu loquendi*) than it sounds (*sonat*) on account of its primary imposition."[11] But this, as it turns out, is essentially the same definition as that given for personal supposition[12]: "Personal supposition is when a term stands in a proposition for that for which it was primarily imposed to signify."[13]

In order to give a correct definition of proper supposition, one might say something like this: A term stands in proper supposition whenever it either stands in simple or material supposition, or stands for that which it was imposed to signify. Now according to Lavenham[14] and Ockham,[15] a term stands in simple supposition whenever it stands for a concept and is not taken "significatively". From the definition of being taken significatively,[16] it is clear that this reduces to: a term stands in simple supposition whenever it stands for a concept and does not stand in personal supposition. Likewise, a term stands in material supposition whenever it stands for a spoken or written expression and does not stand personally.[17] So the attempted definition of proper supposition reduces to: A term stands in proper supposition whenever it either stands for a concept and is not in personal supposition, or stands for a spoken or written expression and is not in personal supposition, or else stands in personal supposition.

9 *Diff.*, 1.

10 *Supp.*, 2.

11 Cf. Ockham, *op. cit.*, I, 77, 213: "... est suppositio propria, quando scilicet terminus supponit pro eo, quod significat proprie."

12 *Supp.*, 11.

13 Cf. Ockham, *op. cit.* I, 64, 177: "Suppositio personalis universaliter est illa, quando terminus supponit pro suo significato ..."

14 *Supp.*, 6.

15 *Op. cit.*, I, 64, 178.

16 *Supp.*, 6. Cf. Ockham, *loc. cit.*, although he does not give a strict definition.

17 *Supp.*, 10, and Ockham, *loc. cit.*

But this still does not seem to capture the distinction. For one species of *improper* supposition is the "synecdochica", which, according to Lavenham,[18] a term has whenever a part stands for the whole or a whole for the part, as in 'Christ descended into hell', which properly means 'The soul of Christ descended into hell'. Now it seems that a term may stand in this way, and yet stand in non-personal supposition for an expression. Thus, in '"Arma virumque" est poema scriptum a Vergilio', the subject term consists of the opening words of the Aeneid, and yet stands for the whole poem. It is accordingly in *improper* supposition. Yet, that term stands for an expression — namely, the whole poem — and is not in personal supposition. If it were in personal supposition, it would stand for arms and men. By the definition of material supposition, then, the term stands materially — and hence in *proper* supposition.

This is problematic only because the division of supposition into proper and improper is presumably meant to be exclusive. The trouble seems to lie with the definition of material supposition. In practice, a term-token is said to stand in material supposition whenever it stands in non-personal supposition for an *equiform* term-token (which may be itself), or whenever it is a spoken term and stands for a written term subordinated to it, or whenever it is a written term and stands for a spoken term to which it is subordinated.[19] Similarly, in practice, a term is said to stand in simple supposition whenever it stands in non-personal supposition for the concept to which it is subordinated, or, if the term is itself a concept (a mental term), whenever it stands in non-personal supposition for itself or for a "similar" concept. Hence, in order to avoid the above difficulty, and in order to head off similar difficulties that might arise over simple supposition, simple and material supposition might be defined as just above, in accordance with the actual usage of this nomenclature, and proper supposition defined as that supposition which a term has whenever it stands in simple, material or personal supposition.

Ockham[20] argues that any term in *any* proposition may be construed as having personal supposition. But a term in a proposition may have simple or material supposition only when the other extreme of the proposition is a term which is of one of certain specified sorts. Thus a

18 *Supp.*, 3.
19 On the subordination relation, cf. Ockham, *op. cit.* I, 1, 9.
20 *Ibid.*, I, 65, 179.

term may have material supposition only when the opposite extreme in the proposition is a common term signifying spoken or written expressions, and simple supposition only when the opposite extreme is a term signifying intentions in the mind.[21] When the opposite extreme is a term signifying both spoken or written expressions and intentions in the mind, it may have any one of the three kinds of proper supposition.[22] In cases where a term may have more than one kind of supposition, various senses of the proposition must be distinguished, and the proposition may change its truth-value according to the sense in which it is taken. Walter Burley[23] has a similar doctrine.

Lavenham, however, adopts a more restrictive view. For him,[24] whenever the subject of a proposition is a term of first intention and the predicate a term of second intention, the subject stands in simple supposition (not personal), and the predicate in personal supposition. Similarly,[25] whenever the subject of a proposition is a term of first imposition and the predicate of second imposition, the subject stands in material supposition (not personal), and the predicate in personal supposition.

A term of first intention is a term "through which we immediately conceive a thing outside the mind which is not an utterance".[26] Similarly, a term of first imposition is a term which is primarily imposed to signify a thing outside the mind which is not an utterance.[27] Lavenham lists 'man', 'animal', 'stone' as examples of both.[28] A term of second intention is a term through which we conceive terms of first intention. Thus, the terms 'category', 'universal', 'genus', 'species', 'difference', 'property', 'accident', 'most general genus', 'most special species', etc., are terms of second intention.[29] Terms of second imposition are terms which are primarily imposed to signify expressions. Thus 'noun', 'pronoun', 'verb', 'adverb', 'participle', 'conjunction', 'preposition', 'interjection', etc., are terms of second imposition.[30]

---

21 *Ibid.*, 180.

22 *Ibid.*, 180f.

23 Walter Burley (Burleigh), *De puritate artis logicae,* tr. longior, Philotheus Boehner, ed., ("Franciscan Institute Publications: Text Series, No. 9; St. Bonaventure, N.Y.: The Franciscan Institute, 1955), pp. 9f.

24 *Supp.*, 7.

25 *Ibid.*, 10.

26 Nor, presumably, an inscription. *Ibid.*, 7.

27 *Ibid.*, 10.

28 'Rose' is added as a further example of a term of first imposition, *ibid.*

29 *Ibid.*, 7.

30 *Ibid.*, 10.

It is not altogether clear how these distinctions are supposed to be taken. When Lavenham says that terms of first intention are distinguished from those of second intention according to what we "conceive" through them, he presumably does not mean that such terms are necessarily concepts — terms in the mental language. In fact, the context seems to indicate that he is thinking throughout only of spoken or written terms. For the discussion of terms of first and second intention occurs in the discussion of simple supposition, which is that supposition a term has when it stands for a concept and is not taken "significatively". And he says that a term is taken significatively when it stands for that which it was primarily imposed to signify. But, since, according to the usual terminology of the Middle Ages, only terms signifying *ad placitum* are *imposed* to signify anything, it seems that only conventionally signifying terms — i.e., spoken and written terms — are at stake here.

Thus, what Lavenham seems to mean is that a spoken or written term is of first intention when it is subordinated to a concept of non-linguistic things outside the mind. If this is so, then terms of first intention are just those of first imposition. This is borne out by the fact that Lavenham gives the same examples for each.

On this interpretation, terms of second intention are those terms which are subordinated to concepts of terms of first intention. Such concepts involve semantic notions. They are concepts of spoken or written terms as imposed to signify non-linguistic things outside the mind. Since imposition uniquely determines the conventional signification of a term, such concepts are concepts of spoken or written terms which conventionally signify non-linguistic things outside the mind. In short, such concepts are concepts of terms with a certain kind of semantics.

On the other hand, terms of second imposition are those subordinated to concepts of spoken or written expressions, without regard for their semantics. The examples that Lavenham gives indicate that such concepts are concepts of *syntactic* categories.

A defect of Lavenham's account is that it gives no explicit explanation of spoken or written terms which are imposed to signify concepts. The term 'concept' is not, on his criteria, a term of first intention or of first imposition, since it is imposed to signify things in the mind. But neither is it a term of second intention. For it is subordinated to the concept "concept", which is not a concept of terms of first intention. Likewise, the term 'concept' is not of second imposition, since it is not subordinated to a concept of expressions (*dictiones*).

In his discussion of confused and distributive supposition, and of merely confused supposition, Lavenham lists several words that cause the immediately following term to have the one supposition or the other. Thus, the words 'differ', 'other', 'not the same', 'to be distinguished', 'to prohibet', 'to beware of' cause the immediately following term to stand in confused and distributive supposition, as do the comparative and superlative degrees of adjectives, the affirmative and negative signs of universality, and the words 'if' and 'without'.[31] Some of these are fairly obvious, and some are discussed in the other treatises edited below. Of particular interest is the inclusion of 'if' among such words. What Lavenham seems to have in mind is a case such as 'If a man runs, then an animal runs'.[32] In such a case, there is a descent to singulars copulatively, as follows: If Socrates runs, then an animal runs, and if Plato runs, then an animal runs, etc.

Words which signify desire, appetite, promise, debt or contract cause the immediately following term to stand in merely confused supposition.[33] So too do the exclusive particles and the word 'require'.[34] The exclusive particles are discussed more fully in *Cons.* and *Excl.*

Lavenham closes his treatise with a consideration of the supposition of relative pronouns[35] and the supposition of the terms in the various positions of simple categoricals.[36] The note following the *explicit* of the treatise seems to be totally extraneous. It does not conform at all to the doctrine set out in the treatise proper.

B. CONSEQUENCE

The second of the tracts edited below is the treatise on consequences. Lavenham defines a consequence as an antecedent and a consequent which follows from the antecedent either materially or formally, together with a mark of consequence, such as 'if', 'therefore', etc.[37] Consequences are divided into two sorts: formal and material. A formal consequence is one in which "the consequent necessarily is in the understanding (*est de intellectu*) of the antecedent."[38] This definition is

---

31 *Ibid.*, 14.
32 Using the indefinite article where the Latin would have a term with no sign of quantity.
33 *Ibid.*, 16.
34 *Ibid.*, 17-18.
35 *Ibid.*, 19-20.
36 *Ibid.*, 21-27.
37 *Cons.*, 1.
38 *Ibid.*, 2.

paralleled by William Heytesbury[39]: "In omni bona consequentia et formali sic est quod consequens est de intellectu antecedentis", and Robert Fland[40]:

> Ad cognoscendum quando consequentia est formalis dantur regulae generales. Prima est ista: ubi consequens intellegitur in antecedente formaliter. Verbi gratia, ista consequentia est formalis: 'Homo est; igitur, animal est', quia hoc consequens 'animal' intellegitur in antecedente, scilicet, 'homo'.

Such a notion of formal consequence seems at first glance to be open to the charge that it introduces extraneous epistemological considerations into logic. It is quite different, for instance, from the definition given by Buridan and Albert of Saxony.[41] For them, a formal consequence was such that what the antecedent says cannot be so without its being so as the consequent says also, even when the categorematic terms are replaced by other categorematic terms. We might say that, in all possible worlds and for all substitutions of the categorematic terms, what the antecedent says is not so unless what the consequent says is so. To a modern theoretician, this has a much more appealing ring.

Nevertheless, I suggest that Lavenham's definition can be given some justification. Consider the following passages from Paul of Pergula[42]:

> Consequentiarum alia bona est illa in qua oppositum consequentis repugnat antecedenti ... Mala est illa in qua oppositum consequentis non repugnat antecedenti sive stat cum eo ...
>
> Consequentiarum bonarum alia formalis est illa in qua oppositum consequentis formaliter repugnat antecedenti ... Materialis est illa in qua oppositum consequentis materialiter repugnat antecedenti ...
>
> Illa dicuntur formaliter repugnare quae nec realiter nec conceptibiliter possunt simul stare absque contradictione manifesta ut: Te currere et non moveri.
>
> Illa autem dicuntur materialiter repugnare quae licet realiter non possint simul stare, conceptibiliter tamen possunt simul stare absque contradictione manifesta ut: Nullum Deum esse et aliquem hominem esse,

39 William Heytesbury, *De veritate et falsitate propositionis*, in *Tractatus gulielmi Hentisberi de sensu composito et diviso, Regulae ejusdem cum sophismatibus, Declaratio gaetani supra easdem, ...*, (Venice: Bonetus Locatellus for Octavianus Scotus, 1494 [Hain *8437]), ff. 183va-188rb, at f. 186ra.

40 Bruges, Bibliothèque publique de la ville, MS 497, f. 41ra.

41 Cf. E. A. Moody, *Truth and Consequence in Mediaeval Logic* ("Studies in Logic and the Foundations of Mathematics"; Amsterdam: North-Holland Publishing Company, 1953), p. 70.

42 Paul of Pergula, *Logica and Tractatus de sensu composito et diviso*, Mary Anthony Brown, ed., ("Franciscan Institute Publications: Text Series, No. 13"; St. Bonaventure, N.Y.: The Franciscan Institute, 1961), pp. 87f.

quae non possunt simul stare realiter, quia nullum Deum esse est impossibile; tamen apud intellectum non manifeste repugnat sicut apud illos
qui negant Deum esse.

The key to the interpretation here lies in the word 'manifesta'. Just
how "manifest" does the contradiction have to be? If a "manifest" conceptual contradiction is one the conceiver of which *knows* to be contradictory, then Paul's definition would have it that, given a fool dull
enough, there would be no good formal consequences whatever. Furthermore, the same consequence would be formal to one person and
material to another. On the other hand, if a manifest conceptual contradiction is one the contradiction in which is manifest, although not
necessarily to the conceiver, then to whom must it be manifest?

This is the one extreme of interpretation, the extreme which emphasizes the epistemological aspects of the definition. The opposite extreme, which I see no reason not to consider as a "benign interpretation", would minimize the importance of the word "manifest"
to the extent that it could be struck out. Then Paul's texts suddenly
become very interesting. For there is a distinction made between *real*
possibility and *conceptual* possibility. As the example shows, there are
certain conceptual possibilities that are not real possibilities.

This interpretation is strengthened by a conclusion in Paul's
discussion of ampliation[43]: "Tertia conclusio. Intelligo chimeram,
quamvis nulla chimera sit nec possit esse." This is an important text, for
it demands that the supposition of the term 'chimera' be ampliated to
(*really-*)*impossibles*.

Moreover, Paul suggests that every real possibility is also a conceptual
possibility. For there is no place in his schema for a conceptual impossibility which is nevertheless really possible. So the really-possibles
constitute a proper subclass of the conceptually-possibles.

What are we to make of this distinction? I suggest that, for Paul, a
formal consequence corresponds to what we should call an *analytically*
true conditional. A material consequence, then, does not correspond to
an analytically true conditional, but to a conditional that is nevertheless
"necessary", in some weaker sense of the word. Just what this weaker
sense is is not clear, but we know that, for one instance, there are
necessarily no chimaeras, in this weaker sense, even though it is not
analytically true that there are no chimaeras.

Now what does all this have to do with Lavenham's tract? I suggest
that we can read Lavenham's definition of formal consequence in this

---

43 *Ibid.,* tract. 2, p. 41.

sense too: a formal consequence is what we should call an analytically true conditional.

Lavenham divides the class of formal consequences into two sub-classes: the generally formal ones, and the specially formal ones. A generally formal consequence is one "a similar form of which is valid in every other matter".[44] Validity is thus not changed by substituting one matter — that is, one set of categorical terms — for another. This seems to mean that, for all *conceivable* worlds and for all substitutions of the categorematic terms, the antecedent does not hold unless the consequent holds. This would make the generally formal consequences for Lavenham the analogues of the formal consequences on Buridan's and Albert's definition, with the notion of a possible world being cashed out as the notion of a *conceptually* possible world (a *conceivable* world).

But we ought to be careful here. Paul of Pergula also has a sub-division of formal consequences, into those which are formal by their form (*de forma*) and those which are formal by their matter (*de materia*).[45] Those which are formal by their form are those "every one formally similar to which is good".[46] This sounds much like Lavenham's definition of generally formal consequence. But Paul includes such examples as 'You run; therefore, you are moved', which would *not* hold for all substitutions of the categorematic terms.

Where would Lavenham locate such consequences? Unfortunately, his text is not decisive here. All the examples he gives[47] hold for all sub-stitutions of categorematic terms. But this is only negative evidence. It seems plausible, however, that he would class such consequences as material, as we shall see. In this connection, it is noteworthy that Paul makes no mention of logical matter in his definition.

Accordingly, we shall take Lavenham's definition of generally formal consequence to be the conceivable world equivalent of Buridan's and Albert's definition of formal consequence.

A specially formal consequence, as might be expected, is one "a similar form of which is valid in some matters, but not in all".[48] His example is interesting: All A is B; therefore, all non-B is non-A. This holds for terms in one of the categories, but does not hold for tran-scendental terms, such as 'being'. For it does not follow: Every man is a being; therefore, every non-being is a non-man. Note that the point of this example demands existential import for universal affirmatives, even

---

44 *Cons.*, 3.
45 *Op. cit.*, tract. 4, p. 88.
46 *Ibid.*
47 *Cons.*, 3. A particularly suggestive remark in this connection occurs at the end of *Cons.*, 43.
48 *Ibid.*, 4.

when they contain infinite (negated) terms. Thus, a specially formal consequence corresponds to an analytically true conditional which does not hold for all substitutions of the categorematic terms. That is, for all conceivable worlds, but not for all substitutions of the categorematic terms, the antecedent does not hold unless the consequent holds. This is the analogue of Albert's definition of *simple* material consequence: one which is such that for all possible worlds, but not for all substitutions of the categorematic terms, the antecedent does not hold unless the consequent does.[49]

Lavenham divides material consequences into three subclasses[50]:

a) Those which hold "only thanks to their terms".
b) Those which hold "only by the fact that the antecedent is impossible".
c) Those which hold "only by the fact that the consequent is necessary".

Once again, there is a difficulty of interpretation. Lavenham's example of the first kind of material consequence is odd: It is true that God is; therefore, it is necessary that God is. For truth and necessity are not distinguished in God.

The necessity mentioned here is presumably not conceptual necessity, at least if we follow Paul of Pergula. And presumably also, the consequence as a whole does not correspond to an analytically true conditional. If it did, it would be formal.

But then what does it mean that the consequence holds "only thanks to its terms"? A specially formal consequence holds "thanks to its terms" too, for substitution of categorematic terms does not always preserve validity in such a case. But, presumably, specially formal consequences do not hold *only* thanks to their terms, but also thanks to a conceptual connection between the antecedent and the consequent. If this is so, then it is just this conceptual connection that is lacking in material consequences, at least of the first type.

If we look at the schema of Buridan and Albert, the third kind of consequence, for which we have as yet no analogue, is the *ut nunc* material consequence: one which for the *actual* world, but not for all possible worlds, and not for all substitutions of the categorematic terms, is such that the antecedent does not hold unless the consequent holds.[51]

49 Albert of Saxony, *op. cit.*, 4, 1, 24rb.
50 *Cons.*, 5.
51 Moody, *op. cit.*, pp. 76f.

This seems to correspond to the modern notion of a material conditional. And it seems also to fit Lavenham's example. For, on this interpretation, the consequence amounts to: Either it is not true that God is, or it is necessary that God is. And this is so, because truth and necessity are not (really) distinguished in God. So the disjunction reduces to: Either it is not true that God is, or it is true that God is, which is just a case of the Law of Excluded Middle.

What about the second and third kinds of material consequences for Lavenham? The first question to be faced is what kind of necessity and impossibility — real or conceptual — is at stake here. Lavenham gives the following example of the third type[52]: Man is or an ass is; therefore, God is. The reason is that the consequent is necessary. Again, if we follow Paul of Pergula, the consequent is only really necessary, and not conceptually so. So it seems that it is real necessity and impossibility that is in question in the second and third types of material consequence.

But if this is so, then the second and third kinds of material consequences are but special cases of the first kind. This shows that there is probably something wrong with characterizing the first kind of material consequence as corresponding exactly with the modern notion of a material conditional, although there seems to be nothing wrong with taking the class of material consequences as a whole as corresponding to the class of material conditionals.

The difficulty seems to center around the import of that recalcitrant phrase "thanks to its terms". Perhaps the most plausible interpretation is this: Material consequences of the first type depend for their validity on terms in both their antecedents and their consequents. Those of the second type depend for their validity only on the terms in their antecedents. Those of the third type depend for their validity only on the terms in their consequents. The phrase "thanks to its terms", then, can be glossed as "thanks to terms in both its antecedent and its consequent".

The remainder of *Cons.* is devoted to setting out certain rules for consequences. We shall consider only some of these here. The first rule[53] states that "whenever it cannot be as is primarily signified by the antecedent of some consequence unless it be as is primarily signified by the consequent of the same consequence, then such a consequence is good". When this is not so, the consequence does not hold.

There are a few things to notice about this rule. First, it does not stipulate that a valid consequence must be *truth*-preserving. In this

52   *Cons.*, 5.
53   *Ibid.*, 7.

respect, it conforms to Buridan's critique of the notion of consequence[54]: roughly, a valid consequence preserves correspondence with reality, but not necessarily truth.

But Buridan's own doctrine gets him into trouble. The problem arises in the case of the so-called "insolubles". Insolubles do not signify just what they seem to. The world is not as they *actually* signify, although they *seem* to say just that or something equivalent to just that. On Buridan's notion of consequence, the usual rules of consequence break down in the case of insolubles.[55] So the second point to notice here is that Lavenham does not say that it cannot be as the antecedent signifies unless it is as the consequent signifies, but rather that it cannot be as the antecedent *primarily* signifies unless it is as the consequent *primarily* signifies. Now Lavenham nowhere explains what he means by primary signification, and how it differs from any other kind of signification. But in his tract on insolubles, Paul of Pergula says that the insoluble 'Socrates speaks falsely', under the usual conditions[56]

> significat praecise quod Sortes dicit falsum, et quod ipsa est vera et non est falsa pro primo significato sed pro secundo significato.

Here the "first" significate is just what the insoluble *seems* to be saying.

It is therefore at least plausible to suggest that what Lavenham is doing here is to touch up Buridan's notion of consequence so that what is preserved is no longer correspondence in general, but rather correspondence according to *primary* signification. In non-insoluble instances, this reduces to Buridan's definition. In the insoluble ones, it allows the usual rules of consequence to continue to hold.

The second through seventh rules are standard ones for consequences.[57] The eighth rule, however, is difficult[58]: "From falsehoods, a truth; from truths, nothing but a truth". If this rule is taken as universally applicable, problems arise again in insoluble contexts. I suggest that the rule be taken to apply only to noninsoluble contexts.

Pars. 16-24 of *Cons.* set out rules for consequences in which the antecedent and consequent are propositions of certain specified sorts.

---

54 *John Buridan. Sophismata Buridani,* (Paris: Antoine Denidel and Nicole de la Barre, c. 1496-1500 [*Incunabula in American Libraries,* 3rd census, B-1295]), no folio numbers. Cf. also Theodore Kermit Scott, ed. & tr.,*John Buridan: Sophisms on Meaning and Truth,* ("Century Philosophy Sourcebooks"; New York: Appleton-Century-Crofts, 1966), pp. 180-185.

55 For a discussion, cf. my dissertation for the University of Toronto, "The Mediaeval Liar: A Study of John Buridan's Position on the Paradox, With A Catalogue of the *Insolubilia*-Literature of the Middle Ages", 1972.

56 *Op. cit.,* tract. 6, p. 137.

57 *Cons.,* 8-14.

58 *Ibid.,* 15.

Pars. 25-40 discuss consequences involving exponible terms, which we shall discuss presently.[59] Pars. 41-47 discuss rules for consequences involving hypothetical propositions.[60] There are seven such rules. The first[61] is *modus ponens*; the second[62] is a form of transposition; the third[63] is conjunction elimination; the fourth[64] is a form of De Morgan's Law; the fifth[65] posits disjunction introduction and rejects an invalid form of eliminating disjunctions; the sixth[66] is disjunctive syllogism; and the seventh[67] is a second form of De Morgan's Law.

C. LOGICAL ANALYSIS (EXPOSITION)

Cons., Excl., Excep., and *Diff.* contain an extended discussion of certain "exponible" propositions. In order to see what is going on in these tracts, some preliminary distinctions must be made. A "hypothetical" proposition is either a proposition formed from simpler propositions by means of a "mark of a hypothetical" (*nota hypotheticae*), or else the negation of such a proposition. In his fragmentary tract on hypotheticals,[68] Lavenham lists some of these "marks": 'if', 'and', 'or', 'because', 'since' (or 'when', 'although'; the Latin '*cum*'), 'before' ('*antequam*' or '*priusquam*'), 'after'. Notice that each of these "marks" is a two-place operator. It seems that all of these "marks" may be taken as logical constants, if we take a view of logic broad enough to include tense- and modal-logic, as well as a logic of causality. In general, a hypothetical proposition is any proposition in which the constant of greatest scope (other than negation signs) is such a two-place connective.

Propositions which are not hypothetical are called "categorical". In practice, for Lavenham, categorical propositions come in three kinds: there are the *simple* categoricals, exemplified by the standard singular, indefinite, and quantified propositions on the square of opposition[69]; there are the "exponibles"; and there are the negations of exponibles.

---

59 Some of the other rules involve exponible terms also.
60 On hypotheticals, cf. the reference above, n. 1.
61 *Cons.*, 41.
62 *Ibid.*, 42.
63 *Ibid.*, 43.
64 *Ibid.*, 44.
65 *Ibid.*, 45.
66 *Ibid.*, 46.
67 *Ibid.*, 47.
68 Cf. above, n. 1.
69 Although relational propositions (e.g., 'A gives B to C') are not explicitly treated in this connection, they are perhaps best considered as simple categoricals.

Even if we discount the exponibles and their negations, to which we
shall return presently, it ought to be noted that the distinction between
(simple) categorical propositions and hypothetical ones is not the same
as the modern distinction between atomic and molecular propositions.
The difference arises over negation. If k is an atomic proposition, then
its negation is molecular. But if k is a simple categorical, then its
negation will be a simple categorical too, one of opposite quality (and
quantity, if k should happen to be quantified). The mediaevals often
spoke, as Lavenham does in his treatise on hypotheticals, as though a
hypothetical were a proposition in which the operator of greatest scope
were one of the "marks of a hypothetical". But their practice betrays
them, for they in fact treated negations of such propositions as
hypotheticals too.

An exponible proposition is, to a first approximation, a proposition
which, while not itself hypothetical, is nevertheless "equivalent" to a
hypothetical. Ockham describes these propositions thus[70]:

> quaelibet categorica, ex qua sequuntur plures propositiones categoricae
> tamquam exponentes, hoc est exprimentes quid ista propositio ex forma
> sua importat, potest dici propositio aequivalens propositioni hypotheticae.

As this passage indicates, the "equivalence" in question is not merely
material equivalence. Rather, the exponents of an exponible
proposition are to express the import which the exponible proposition
has in virtue of its form. Thus, to give the exposition of an exponible
proposition is, in some sense, to give its "logical analysis".

Ockham's account differs from Lavenham's practice, however, in one
important respect. As Ockham states it in the above passage, an exponible proposition might be analyzed into a hypothetical of *any* form.
To use Lavenham's examples, discussed below, the proposition 'You
differ from a man' is - expounded by the following conjunctive
hypothetical: 'You are, and a man is, and you are not a man'. The
original proposition is false in virtue of the third conjunct of its exposition. The negation of the original proposition, namely, 'You do not
differ from a man', would then be equivalent to the following disjunction: 'You are not, or no man is, or you are a man'. Now, according to
the letter of Ockham's account, this latter proposition seems to qualify
as an exposition of the proposition 'You do not differ from a man',
since it is a disjunctive hypothetical expressing the import that the
proposition has in virtue of its form. Not so for Lavenham. He says that
such a proposition is not exponible. Rather, it has "causes of truth",

---

70 *Op. cit.*, 2, 11, 252.

namely, "either because you are not, or because nothing is which is a man, or because you are a man".[71] It is clear that this is just the former disjunctive proposition turned into a disjunction of causal clauses.

The reason that Lavenham wants to deny that such disjunctions can expound a proposition is that he wants to hold to the following rule: "From a proposition having several exponents to any of its exponents is a valid consequence".[72] This works only if the exponenible proposition is analyzed into the *conjunction* of its exponents. If Lavenham were to allow disjunctive expositions, he would have to give up this rule. As it is, by distinguishing conjunctive from disjunctive analyses, and by calling the former "expositions" and the latter (after turning them into disjunctions of causal clauses) "causes of truth", he can have both the rule mentioned and the following rule as well[73]: "By arguing from a cause of truth to the proposition of which it is the cause, there is a valid consequence".

In *Cons.*, Lavenham treats briefly the exposition of propositions of the following kinds:

1) Those formed with the words 'differ', 'other' and 'not the same'.[74]
2) Exclusive propositions, such as 'Only man runs'.[75]
3) Exceptive propositions, such as 'Every man besides Socrates runs'.[76]
4) Propositions formed with the words 'begins' or 'stops'.[77]
5) Propositions with ablative absolutes.[78]
6) Propositions with the pronoun 'who', and its various forms.[79]
7) Propositions formed with adjectives in the comparative and superlative degrees.[80]
8) Reduplicative propositions, such as '*a* insofar as it is *b*, is *c*.[81]

Propositions of types 1)-3) are discussed at greater length in the tracts which follow, edited below. Those of type 4) are discussed more fully in the thirteenth item in the MS.[82] Those of type 6) are treated in the fifteenth item in the MS.[83] Finally, those of type 7) are discussed to some

---

71   *Cons.*, 31.
72   *Ibid.*, 26.
73   *Ibid.*, 31.
74   *Ibid.*, 27-31. The expression 'not the same' is in fact never discussed very fully.
75   *Ibid.*, 32-33.
76   *Ibid.*, 34-35.
77   *Ibid.*, 36.
78   *Ibid.*, 37.
79   *Ibid.*, 38.
80   *Ibid.*, 39.
81   *Ibid.*, 40.
82   *Tractatus de incipit et desinit*, ff. 30r-40r.
83   *Tractatus relativorum* (incomplete), ff. 46r-52r.

extent in *Diff.*, and in the twelfth item in the MS.[84] We shall treat each
of these types in turn.

1. *'differ'*, *'other'*, *'not the same'*.

An affirmative proposition containing the words 'differ' or 'other'
has three exponents, two affirmative and one negative. Thus: 'You differ from a man' (*Tu differs ab homine*) has the exposition: 'You are, and a
man is, and you are not a man',[85] and is false in virtue of the third exponent.[86] 'You differ from any man' (*Tu differs a quolibet homine*) is expounded: 'You are, and any man is, and you are not any man'. Since all
the exponents are true, the original proposition is true. The third exponent is true because the negation there is outside the scope of the
quantifier. The sense is not 'Any man is such that you are not that man',
but rather 'It is not the case that you are just *any* man (but rather one
man in particular)'. 'Any' here functions like 'every'.

The term 'man' in 'You differ from every man' has merely confused
supposition. A descent can be made by disjoined extreme[87]: 'You differ
from this man or this man, etc.'. Lavenham explicitly says[88] that a
disjunctive or copulative descent cannot be made in this case — the
term does not have determinate or confused and distributive supposition. It is not clear, however, why a disjunctive descent (for determinate supposition) cannot be made in this case: 'You differ from this
man, or you differ from this man, etc.'. In another place,[89] Lavenham
observes that the terms 'differ' and 'other' are like the comparative and
superlative degrees of adjectives insofar as they cause the term
following to stand in confused and distributive supposition, *if* the term
is not governed by a sign of distribution; if the term is so governed, they
cause that term to stand *determinately* or merely confusedly. He gives no
examples.

In an affirmative proposition containing the words 'differ' or 'other',
if the ablative *follows* such a word, it is the predicate in the third exponent, as in the earlier examples. But if the ablative *precedes* the word
'differ' or 'other', it lies outside the scope of that word, and is the subject of the third exponent. Hence 'You from a man differ' (*Tu ab homine
differs*) is expounded: 'You are, and a man is, and a man is not you'.

---

84 *Diff.*, 5-6, and *Tractatus de probationibus propositionum et expositionibus earum*, ff. 29r-30r.
85 *Cons.*, 27.
86 *Ibid.*, 29.
87 *Diff.*, 1.
88 *Ibid.*
89 *Cons.*, 39.

Each conjunct is true; the third is true because there is some man who is not you.[90]

A negative proposition containing the words 'differ' or 'other' is not properly said to have an exposition, but rather to have "causes of truth", in the sense outlined above.[91]

The inference from inferior to superior on the part of the subject (*ex parte subjecti*) is valid, so long as there is no distributive sign. Thus, 'You from a man differ; therefore, you from an animal differ' is valid. But 'An ass from every man differs; therefore, an ass from every animal differs' is not. Nor is the inference from inferior to superior on the part of the predicate (*ex parte praedicati*) ever valid. Thus 'You differ from Richard; therefore, you differ from a man' is not valid.[92]

As the examples indicate, the phrase "on the part of the subject" does not pertain only to *grammatical* parts of the subject. In 'You from a man differ', the phrase 'from a man' is gramatically part of the predicate 'differ from a man', which is here broken up. This is verified in another place,[93] where Lavenham says that in 'Every proposition Thomas begins to know', the phrase 'every proposition' occurs on the part of the subject. In the Latin, it is in the accusative. What the phrase "on the part of the subject" seems to mean, then, is that the expression which is said to occur on the part of the subject occurs on the subject side of the verb — that is, preceding it. Words such as 'differ' and 'other' have a scope which extends *rightward* from the occurrence of the word. Expressions which occur to the left of such a word are outside its scope, even though they may be grammatically parts of the predicate formed from such a word.

2. Exclusives.

An exclusive proposition with the exclusive expression on the part of the subject is expounded by two propositions, one affirmative and the other negative. Thus 'Only a man runs' (*Tantum homo currit*) is expounded: 'A man runs, and nothing other than a man runs'.[94] Notice that the occurrence of 'other' in this exposition is not in a position where it can be further expounded at once. The rules for 'differ' and 'other', given in the previous section, apply only where the words occur as *predicates,* such as in 'You differ from (are other than) a man'. In the

90 *Ibid.,* 28-29.
91 *Ibid.,* 31.
92 *Ibid.,* 30. *Diff.,* 2.
93 *Cons.,* 36.
94 *Cons.,* 32. *Excl.,* 1.

present case, 'other' occurs as part of a *modifying* phrase attached to the term 'nothing'. We can put the word 'other' in predicate position by turning the phrase into a clause, so that the exposition reads: 'A man runs, and nothing which is other than a man runs'. Here the problem becomes one of expounding the term 'which', and, as we shall see, Lavenham's account of such terms applies only to cases where the antecedent is not distributed. In the end, then, Lavenham gives us no way to expound the occurrence of 'other' in the present instance.

When the exclusive expression occurs on the part of the predicate, the resulting expression is not exponible, but rather convertible with the sentence which remains when the exclusive expression is taken away. Thus 'You are only a man' is convertible with 'You are a man'.[95]

The inference from a universal (affirmative) to the corresponding exclusive with transposed terms is valid, and vice versa. Thus 'Every runner is a man; therefore, only a man runs' (*Omnis currens est homo; ergo, tantum homo currit*) is valid.[96]

Whenever the exclusive expression is added to the subject of a universal affirmative, if the subject stands for many things, then the sentence is false. Thus, 'Only every man runs' (*Tantum omnis homo currit*) is false. For it is expounded: 'Every man runs, and nothing other than every man runs'. But any individual man who runs is other than every man, since he is not every man.[97]

If an affirmative exclusive proposition has a predicate of such a kind that it cannot be verified of a whole unless it is verified of the part, then the proposition is impossible. Hence 'Only a house is white' (*Tantum domus est alba*) is false, because if a house is white, a part of the house is white. And a part of a house is not a house. So not only a house is white.[98] But this rule, attributed to a certain Hintone (Hyntone), is not without exceptions. It applies only to a heterogeneous whole, not to a homogeneous one, such as water or fire.[99]

A proposition with an exclusive expression added to a numeral on the part of the subject has two modes of exposition: one by way of 'otherness', one by way of 'plurality'. In the first way, 'Only one is' (*Tantum unum est*) is expounded: 'One is, and nothing other than one is'. In the second way, it is expounded: 'One is, and not many are' (*Unum est, et non plura sunt*).[100]

95   *Excl.*, 1.
96   *Cons.*, 18.
97   *Excl.*, 6.
98   *Ibid.*, 7.
99   *Ibid.*, 8.
100 *Ibid.*, 9.

3. *Exceptives.*

An exceptive proposition has two exponents, an affirmative one and a negative one. Thus 'Every man besides Socrates runs' (*Omnis homo praeter Sortem currit*) is expounded: 'Every man other than Socrates runs, and Socrates does not run'.[101]

An exceptive proposition is never, or at least rarely, well-formed (*propria*) unless the proposition which remains when the exceptive expression is dropped is a universal proposition. Hence 'Some man besides Socrates runs' (*Aliquis homo praeter Sortem currit*) is not well-formed.[102] This restriction probably sounded as artificial in Latin as it does in English. Presumably the rationale is something like this: In the case of 'Every man besides Socrates runs', a descent to singulars can be made as follows: 'Socrates does not run, and Plato runs, and Cicero runs, etc.'.[103] The analogous descent in the case of 'Some man besides Socrates runs' would be: 'Socrates does not run, and Plato runs or Cicero runs or, etc.'. But this is not a recognized mode of descent. This is a conjectural rationale at best. Lavenham simply gives no justification for his restriction.

4. *'begins', 'stops'.*[104]

Propositions formed from the words 'begins' and 'stops' may be expounded in two ways. In order for such a proposition to be false, it must be false under both expositions. In effect, then, the truth-condition for such a proposition is the disjunction of the truth-conditions for its two exponents.

As an example, Lavenham gives the proposition 'Socrates begins to be white'. In the first way, it is expounded: 'Socrates now is white, and immediately before this he was not white'. The second exposition is: 'Socrates now is not white, and immediately after this he will be white'. As a general rule, the first mode of exposition proceeds by an affirmative present-tense proposition and a negative past-tense proposition. The second mode proceeds by a negative present-tense proposition and an affirmative future-tense proposition.

Propositions formed from the word 'stops' are expounded in contrary fashion. Thus 'Socrates stops being white' is expounded in one way: 'Socrates now is not white, and immediately before this instant

---

101 *Cons.*, 34.
102 *Excep.*, 3.
103 Cf. the above discussion of mobile and immobile supposition, section A.
104 The whole of the following discussion is taken from *Cons.*, 36.

which is present he was white'. In the second way, we have: 'Socrates now is white, and immediately after this instant which is present he will not be white'. In general, the first mode of exposition proceeds by a negative present-tense proposition and an affirmative past-tense proposition. The second way proceeds by an affirmative present-tense proposition and a negative future-tense one.

The argument from an inferior term to a superior term on the part of the subject is valid. Thus, 'Every proposition Thomas begins to know' (*Omnem propositionem Thomas incipit scire*); 'therefore, some proposition Thomas begins to know'. It is not altogether clear how this is supposed to exemplify Lavenham's rule. But in any case, on the part of the predicate such an inference is not valid. Thus 'Thomas begins to be white; therefore, Thomas begins to be colored' is not valid.

5. *Ablative Absolutes.*[105]

Propositions with ablative absolutes have a threefold exposition. In fact, however, Lavenham combines these three expositions into one. Thus 'No one running, you are an ass' (*Nullo currente, tu es asinus*) is expounded: 'Either *because* no one runs, you are an ass, or *while (dum)* no one runs, you are an ass, or *if* no one runs, you are an ass'.

The contradictory of such a sentence is formed by prefixing a negation to the whole: 'It is not the case that, no one running, you are an ass'. Thus, the sentences 'No one running, you are an ass' and 'Someone running, you are an ass' are not contradictories.

6. *The Pronoun 'who' and Its Forms.*[106]

Propositions which contain the pronoun 'who', 'which', 'what', etc., are expounded by a copulative proposition. Thus 'Socrates runs, who is moved' (*Sortes currit, qui movetur*) is expounded: 'Socrates runs and he is moved'.

But if the word 'who' or one of its forms is preceded by the word 'differ' or 'other', then the latter "impedes" the exposition of 'who'. Hence 'You differ from an animal which is an ass' is expounded: 'You are, and an animal which is an ass is, and you are not an animal which is an ass', which is true. The point is that the exposition is *not*: 'You differ from an animal, and it is an ass'. For the first conjunct of this conjunction can be further expounded as: 'You are, and an animal is, and you are not an animal', which is false in virtue of the third exponent.

---

105 The whole of the discussion is taken from *Cons.*, 37.
106 The whole of the discussion is taken from *Cons.*, 38.

This illustrates a general rule which Lavenham lays down in *Excl.*[107]: "In omni propositione in qua ponuntur duo termini habentes vim exponendi, primus terminus habebit vim". Exposition always begins with the leftmost exponible term.

In the exposition 'You are, and an animal which is an ass is, and you are not an animal which is an ass', it is not altogether clear how the second occurrence of 'which' is to be expounded. The first occurrence poses no problem. But the term 'an animal', which is the antecedent of the second occurrence, is distributed in virtue of the negation. We cannot expound 'You are not an animal which is an ass' simply as 'You are not an animal, and it is an ass', for the first conjunct of this exposition is false. Similarly, in 'Every man who runs is moved', we cannot expound the proposition by 'Every man runs, and he is moved'. In short, Lavenham's rule for expounding 'who' applies only where the antecedent is not distributed.[108]

7. *Adjectives in the Comparative and Superlative Degrees.*[109]

Adjectives in the comparative or superlative degree, and the word 'as' (*'sicut'* in the context *'ita ... sicut'*) are like the terms 'differ' and 'other', insofar as they cause the following term to have confused and distributive supposition, if that term has a sign of universality, and to have determinate or merely confused supposition if it does not. But propositions containing such adjectives are expounded in a way different from those which contain 'differ' or 'other'. The proposition 'You are stronger than a man' (*Tu es fortior homine*) is expounded: 'You are strong, and a man is strong, and a man is not so (*ita*) strong as (*sicut*) you'. But 'You are stronger than every man' (*Tu es fortior omni homine*) is expounded: 'You are strong, and every man is strong, and not every man is so strong as you'. On this exposition, the proposition is true, as long as there is at least one man who is not so strong as you. The original proposition is not to be taken to mean 'There is no man who is as strong as you', but rather (roughly) 'You have a strength greater than the minimal strength which every man has'.

The superlative, as in 'You are the strongest of men' is expounded thus: 'You are strong, and men are strong, and no man other than you is so (*ita*) strong as (*sicut*) you.[110]

---

107 *Excl.*, 2. Cf. also *De probationibus propositionum et expositionibus earum*, the twelfth item in the MS, ff. 29r-30r, at f. 29v: "Et sciendum quod si in aliqua propositione ponantur plures termini habentes vim exponendi, prius terminus semper exercebit vim suam."

108 For a fuller discussion, cf. Ockham, *op. cit.*, 2, 15, 260f.

109 Taken from *Cons.*, 39, except where otherwise noted.

110 On the occurrence of 'other' in such a context, cf. the discussion of exclusives, above.

In the case of both the comparative and superlative degrees, then, the exposition proceeds by reduction to the positive degree in the context *ita ... sicut*. But such contexts are presumably not to be taken as absolutely primitive. For Lavenham goes on to expound 'You are as strong as a man' (*Tu est ita fortis sicut homo*) in terms of the comparative degree: 'You are strong, and a man is strong, and no man is stronger than you'.[111]

This makes it difficult to see just what is going on. It is tempting to suppose than an exposition is a reduction to canonical form. But this assumption does not square with the present examples. If the positive degree, in the context *ita ... sicut*, and the comparative degree can be expounded in terms of each other, then neither can be regarded as the primitive form to which the exposition leads. In this connection, it is perhaps instructive to observe that in the twelfth tract in the MS[112] Lavenham says "Superlativus gradus etiam probatur per suam positivum et comparativum, ut patet in *Consequentiis*." In fact, *Cons.* treats the superlative *explicitly* only in terms of the positive in the context *ita ... sicut*.

In *Diff.*,[113] Lavenham gives a different exposition of the comparative: 'Socrates is whiter than some man' (*Sortes est albior aliquo homine*) is expounded as: 'Socrates is more white than some man' (*Sortes est magis albus quam aliquis homo*). He says that "any comparative degree ought to be expounded through the terms 'more' (*magis*) and 'than' (*quam*)."

We thus have the following sequence of expositions:

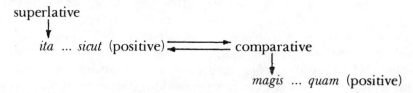

In some sense, then, we can take the context *magis ... quam*, with the positive, as primitive. For the others can be expounded in terms of it, and it is not said to be expounded in terms of anything further. It is doubtful, however, whether Lavenham thought of exposition as a kind of translation into primitive form in this sense.

111 *Cons.*, 39. *Diff.*, 5.
112 *De probationibus propositionum et expositionibus earum*, f. 11r.
113 *Diff.*, 6.

8. *Reduplicatives.*[114]

Reduplicative propositions of the form '*a* insofar as it is *b* is *c*' (*a inquantum b est c*) are expounded: '*a* is *b*, and *a* is *c*, and every *b* is *c*, and if a thing is *b*, it is *c*'. Those of the form '*a* insofar as it is *b* is not *c*' are expounded: '*a* is *b*, and *a* is not *c*, and no *b* is *c*, and if a thing is *b*, it is not *c*'. The basis for such an exposition is not altogether clear. The third exponent seems redundant in view of the others.

D. THE EDITION.[115]

The orthography of the following editions has been normalized to that of Lewis' and Short's *A Latin Dictionary*. I have inserted the folio numbers in parentheses. The titles have been supplied from the *explicits*. The MS has been examined in microfilm copy only.

< SUPPOSITIONES >

1) (4r) Suppositio est proprietas extremi seu statio termini pro aliquo in propositione. Nam pro quocumque stat aliquis terminus in propositione, pro illo dicitur supponere.

2) Et est suppositio duplex, videlicet, propria, etiam impropria. Suppositio propria est quando terminus communis non supponit aliter ex usu loquendi quam ex primaria impositione illius sonat. Suppositio impropria est quando terminus communis supponit aliter ex usu loquendi quam ex primaria impositione illius sonat. Et haec habet tres species, videlicet, synecdochicam, metonymicam et antonomasticam.

3) Suppositio synecdochica est quando pars supponit pro toto vel totum supponit pro parte, ut hic 'Christus descendit ad inferna', id est, 'Anima Christi descendit ad inferna'.

4) Suppositio metonymica est quando continens supponit pro contento, ut 'Bibe siphum', id est, liquorem contentum in sipho; 'Anglia pugnat', hoc <est> 'Gens anglicana pugnat'.

5) Suppositio antonomastica est quando terminus communis alicui causa excellentiae appropriatur, ut hoc nomen 'Philosophus' appropriatur Aristoteli, et ille terminus 'Apostolus' causa excellentiae Paulo appropriatur. Et in istis propositionibus 'Philosophus asseruit propositionem', 'Apostolus praedicavit evangelium', subjecta supponunt antonomastice. Et causa est quia cum dico 'Philosophus asseruit

---

114 Taken from *Cons.*, 40.
115 For a description of the MS, cf. the reference above, n. 1.

propositionem', nullum alium intellego quam Aristotelem, et cum dico 'Apostolus praedicavit evangelium', nullum alium intellego quam Paulum.

6) Suppositio propria dividitur tripliciter, videlicet, in suppositionem simplicem, materialem et personalem. Suppositio simplex est quando terminus supponit pro intentione vel conceptu mentis, et non tenetur significative. Et sciendum est quod terminus tenetur significative quando supponit pro illo in propositione pro quo imponebatur primarie ad significandum.

7) Sed hic notandum est pro regula quod quandocumque subjectum alicujus propositionis est terminus primae intentionis et praedicatum secundae intentionis, tunc subjectum supponit simpliciter et praedicatum personaliter. Terminus primae intentionis vocatur omnis talis terminus per quem immediate concipimus rem extra animam quae non est dictio, cujusmodi sunt isti: 'homo', 'animal', 'lapis' [et][116]. Terminus secundae intentionis vocatur ille terminus per quem concipimus terminos primae intentionis, cujusmodi sunt isti: 'praedicamentum',[117] 'universale', 'genus', 'species', 'differentia', 'proprium', 'accidens', 'genus generalissimum', 'species spe-(4v) cialissima' et sic de similibus. Unde in omnibus istis propositionibus sequentibus subjectum supponit simpliciter et praedicatum personaliter:

> Substantia est praedicamentum.
> Qualitas est praedicamentum.
> Corpus est genus.
> Homo est species.
> Animal est genus.
> Arbor est universale.
> Rationale est differentia.
> Risibile est proprium.
> Album est accidens.

Et causa est quia in omnibus istis subjectum est terminus primae intentionis et praedicatum terminus secundae intentionis.

8) Sed contra hanc regulam sic obicitur. Nam in ista propositione 'Omnis intentio animae est intentio', subjectum supponit simpliciter; et tamen non est ita quod subjectum est terminus primae intentionis et praedicatum terminus secundae intentionis; ergo, praedicta regula est insufficiens ad cognoscendum quando terminus supponit simpliciter, quando non, generaliter. Patet consequentia et minor per hoc quod idem terminus specie non est terminus primae intentionis et terminus

---

116 *MS adds* omnia praedicamenta *but del.*

117 The abbreviation is the same as that which we have read above as 'praedicatum'. So too throughout the paragraph.

secundae intentionis. Et *major*[118] probatur, quia subjectum supponit [simpliciter] pro intentione animae; ergo, illud subjectum supponit simpliciter. Patet consequentia ex hoc quod terminus supponit simpliciter quando supponit pro intentione animae.

9) Pro istis dico quod subjectum praedictae propositionis non supponit simpliciter, nec valet consequentia: 'Subjectum supponit pro intentione animae; ergo, supponit simpliciter'. Sed oportet addere quod subjectum non tenetur significative, et hoc non est verum, quia subjectum illius propositionis universalis supponit pro illo pro quo imponebatur primarie ad significandum, et ideo tenetur significative.

10) Suppositio materialis est quando terminus supponit pro voce vel pro scripto, et non tenetur significative, ut 'Homo est nomen', 'Homo est disyllabum'. Et notandum est pro regula quod quandocumque subjectum alicujus propositionis est terminus primae impositionis et praedicatum secundae impositionis, tunc subjectum < supponit > materialiter et praedicatum personaliter. Terminus primae impositionis vocatur ille terminus qui imponebatur primarie ad significandum rem extra animam quae non est dictio, quales sunt isti termini prolati vel scripti: 'homo', 'animal', 'lapis', 'rosa'. Terminus secundae impositionis vocatur ille terminus qui imponebatur primarie ad significandum dictiones, cujusmodi sunt omnes isti termini: 'nomen', 'pronomen', 'verbum', 'adverbium', 'participium', 'conjunctio', 'praepositio',[119] 'interjectio'. Exemplum patet in sequentibus (5r):

> Homo est nomen.
> Meus est pronomen.
> Diligo est verbum.
> Bene est adverbium.
> Diligens est participium.
> Si est conjunctio.
> Ad est praepositio.
> Heu est interjectio.
> Dominus est trisyllabum.
> Homo est dictio scripta.
> Homo est animal est indefinita.

Nam in omnibus istis subjectum supponit materialiter et praedicatum personaliter, et hoc pro tanto, quia in omnibus istis subjectum est terminus primae impositionis et praedicatum terminus secundae impositionis.

---

118 *MS* minor.

119 The abbreviation is the standard one for 'propositio'. The reading 'praepositio' is demanded by the example later in the paragraph, which uses the same abbreviation.

11) Suppositio personalis est quando terminus supponit pro illo in propositione pro quo imponebatur primarie ad significandum, ut hic: 'Aliquis homo currit', et hic: 'Omne nomen est pars orationis'. Sed si arguitur in contrarium sic: Subjectum illius propositionis 'Omne nomen est pars orationis' supponit pro voce vel pro scripto; ergo, supponit materialiter; et si sic, ergo non supponit personaliter, huic dico negando consequentiam. Sed oportet addere quod subjectum illius propositionis non tenetur significative, et hoc non est verum.

12) Suppositio personalis dividitur in communem et discretem. Suppositio communis est quando terminus supponit pro multis, vel natus est supponere pro multis, et tenetur significative. Suppositio communis est duplex, videlicet, determinata et confusa. Suppositio determinata est quando terminus supponit pro suppositis multis et sub eodem termino contingit descendere ad sua supposita disjunctive, ut 'Quidam homo currit; ergo, iste homo currit, et ille homo currit, et sic de singulis'. Similiter, a parte praedicati fiet descensus ad sua supposita disjunctive, ut 'Quidam homo currit; ergo, quidam homo est hoc currens, vel quidam homo est hoc currens, et sic de singulis'.

13) Suppositio confusa est duplex, videlicet, confusa et distributiva et confusa tantum. Suppositio confusa et distributiva est quando terminus supponit pro suppositis multis, vel denotatur supponere pro suppositis multis, et sub eodem termino potest fieri descensus ad sua supposita conjunctive, ut hic[120]: 'Quilibet homo currit'. Ly 'homo' supponit confuse et distributive, et sub isto termino potest fieri descensus ad sua supposita conjunctive, ut sic: 'Quilibet homo currit; ergo, iste homo currit, et iste homo currit, et sic de singulis'.

14) Et notandum est pro regula quod tales dictiones: 'differe', 'aliud', et 'non idem', 'distingui', 'prohibere', 'cavere' faciunt terminum communem immediate sequentem stare confuse et distributive. Similiter omnis comparativus gradus et superlativus, et omnia signa universalia affirmativa et negativa, et tales dictiones: 'si', 'sine' et 'sicut' faciunt terminum communem immediate sequentem stare confuse et distributive (5v). Exempla[121] patent in sequentibus, ut hic: 'Tu differs ab homine', ly 'homine' stat confuse et distributive. Item, 'Tu es aliud ab asino', ly 'asino' stat confuse et distributive. Item, hic: 'Deus prohibet furtum', 'Thomas cavebit periculum', 'Tu es fortior homine', 'Tu es fortissimus hominum', ly 'furtum', ly 'periculum', ly 'homine', ly 'hominum' stant confuse et distributive. Similiter hic: 'Tu es ita fortis sicut homo', 'Tu es magis quam homo', ly 'homo' stat confuse et distributive. Similiter, 'Si homo currit, animal currit', ly 'homo' stat confuse et distributive, et sub

---

120 Unclear in MS.
121 MS adds an illegible marginal insertion.

illo termino 'homo' potest fieri descensus ad sua supposita copulative, ut 'Si homo currit, animal currit; ergo, si iste homo currit, animal currit, et si iste homo currit, animal currit, et sic de singulis'. Similiter hic: 'Sine oculo potes tu videre', ly 'oculo' stat confuse et distributive, quia sequitur immediate hanc dictionem 'sine'.

15) Suppositio confusa tantum est quando terminus supponit pro suppositis multis, vel denotatur supponere pro suppositis multis, et sub illo termino non potest fieri descensus ad sua supposita neque copulative neque disjunctive, sed per disjunctum extremum, ut est hic: 'Quilibet homo currit', ly 'currens' supponit confuse tantum, quia sub illo termino non potest fieri descensus ad sua supposita, nec copulative nec disjunctive, quia non sequitur: 'Quilibet homo currit; ergo, quilibet homo est hoc currens, et quilibet homo est hoc currens, et sic de singulis', nec sequitur: 'Quilibet homo currit; ergo, quilibet homo est hoc currens, vel quilibet homo est hoc currens, et sic de singulis'. Sed sequitur de disjuncto praedicato, ut sic: 'Quilibet homo currit; ergo, quilibet homo est hoc currens vel hoc currens vel hoc currens, et sic de singulis'.

16) Et notandum pro regula quod omnia verba significantia desiderium, appetitum, promissionem, debitum vel contractum faciunt terminum communem immediate sive mediate[121] sequentem stare confuse tantum. Verbi gratia, 'Volo esse papa', ly 'papa' stat confuse tantum, quia sequitur verbum significans desiderium. Similiter hic: 'Appeto cibum', et hic 'Promitto tibi denarium', 'Debeo tibi aurum, lignum', 'Apparet argenteum', praedicata in his omnibus supponunt confuse tantum. Et sciendum quod nullum verborum praecedentium facit terminum communem stare confuse tantum nisi praecedat illum terminum. Nam in ista propositione: 'Denarium tibi promitto', ly 'denarium' supponit determinate et non confuse tantum, eo quod verbum significans promissionem subsequitur et non praecedit.

17) (6r) Item, dictio exclusiva[123] facit terminum communem immediate sequentem stare confuse tantum, et praedicatum stare confuse et distributive. Verbi gratia, 'Tantum homo currit', ly 'homo' supponit confuse tantum et ly 'currens' supponit confuse et distributive. Et causa est quia illa exclusiva convertitur in unam universalem talem: 'Omne currens est homo', ubi praedicti termini consimiliter supponunt.

18) Item, haec verba 'requiro, -ris' et 'exigo, -gis' faciunt terminum communem immediate sequentem stare confuse tantum, ut hic: 'Ad videndum requiritur oculus', ly 'oculus' stat confuse tantum. Item hic, 'Ad equitandum requiritur equus', ly 'equus' stat confuse tantum. Sed si

---

122 Sive mediate: interlinear.
123 Abbreviated on the line. Written out fully interlinearly.

alterum verborum subsequatur terminum communem, tunc non facit illum terminum stare confuse tantum, ut hic: 'Equus requiritur ad equitandum', ly 'equus' non supponit confuse tantum, sed determinate, quia praecedit hoc verbum 'requiro, -ris'.

19) Circa suppositionem relativorum notandum est quod nomen relativum debet eodem modo supponere sicut suum antecedens. Unde si suum antecedens supponat confuse et distributive, relativum debet sic[124] supponere. Et si antecedens supponit determinate, tunc debet relativum supponere determinate. Verbi gratia, 'Quilibet homo currit et ille est albus', ly 'ille' supponit confuse et distributive, quia sic supponit suum antecedens.

20) Sciendum est tamen quod nullum relativum habet descensum ad sua supposita, eo quod non habet suppositionem a se ipso, sed a suo antecedente. Et ideo, si quaeratur quomodo supponit ly 'ille' in ista propositione 'Quilibet homo currit et ille est albus', dicatur quod confuse et distributive. Sed si quaeratur ulterius quomodo habet descendere, dicatur quod non habet descendere, eo quod relativum caret descensu ad supposita.

21) Sciendum est quod in omni universali affirmativa subjectum supponit confuse et distributive, et praedicatum confuse tantum. Et ideo, si quaeratur quomodo supponit subjectum istius propositionis 'Quilibet homo currit', dicendum est quod confuse et distributive.

22) Notandum tamen quod si sit aliqua propositio universalis in qua ponuntur duo nomina substantiva a parte subjecti quorum utrumque est terminus communis et per signum universale distributus, tunc supponit uterque terminus confuse et distributive, ut hic: 'Quilibet homo a quolibet animali differt', ly 'homo' et ly 'animali' supponunt confuse et distributive. Sed si alter terminus sit distributus per signum et alter non, tunc supponit ille terminus qui est distributus per signum confuse et distributive, et alter terminus qui non est distributus supponit determinate, ut hic: 'Cujuslibet hominis asinus currit', ly 'hominis' supponit confuse et distributive, et ly 'asinus' supponit determinate.

23) (6v) In omni universali negativa[125] tam subjectum quam praedicatum, si sint termini communes, supponunt confuse et distributive, ut hic: 'Nullus homo est asinus', ly 'homo' et ly 'asinus' supponunt confuse et distributive.

24) In omni particulari affirmativa et indefinita affirmativa tam subjectum quam praedicatum supponunt determinate, et hoc est ubi suppositio est personalis et praedicatum est terminus communis.

25) Item, in particulari negativa et indefinita negativa subjectum sup-

---

124   Interlinear.
125   Interlinear.

ponit determinate et praedicatum, si sit terminus communis, confuse et distributive.

26) In omni singulari affirmativa subjectum supponit discrete et praedicatum determinate, si sit terminus communis. Si sit terminus discretus, supponit discrete.

27) In omni singulari negativa subjectum supponit discrete et praedicatum, si sit terminus communis, supponit confuse et distributive.

EXPLICIUNT SUPPOSITIONES COMPENDIOSE COMPILATAE PER REVERENDUM DO-CTOREM LAVENHAM ORDINIS FRATRUM DE CARMELO.

Notandum quod quando terminus stat pro accidente intrinseco, tunc supponit simpliciter; quando vero stat pro accidente extrinseco cujus est nomen vel pronomen, tunc supponit materialiter; et quando stat pro substantiis, tunc supponit personaliter.

< CONSEQUENTIAE >

1) Consequentia est antecedens et consequens ad illud formaliter vel materialiter sequens cum aliqua nota consequentiae. Notae consequentiae vocantur tales conjunctiones: 'si', 'ergo', 'ideo', 'igitur', 'itaque'. Antecedens vocatur illa propositio quae praecedit ly 'ergo', vel quae < im > mediate sequitur hanc conjunctionem 'si', ut hic: 'Homo currit; ergo, animal currit', ista propositio 'Homo currit' est antecedens. Et hic: 'Si nullum animal currit, nullus homo currit', illa propositio 'Nullum animal currit' est antecedens. Consequens vocatur illa propositio quae sequitur ly 'ergo', vel quae cum uno medio sequitur hanc conjunctionem 'si', ut 'Homo currit; ergo, animal currit', ly 'Animal currit' est consequens. Et hic: 'Si nullus homo est albus, nullus homo est coloratus', illa propositio 'Nullus homo est coloratus' est consequens.

2) Consequentia est duplex, videlicet, formalis et materialis. Consequentia formalis est quando consequens necessario est de intellectu antecedentis, sicut est in consequentia syllogistica et in multis consequentiis enthymematicis, ut hic: 'Omnis homo est animal; tu es homo; ergo, tu es animal', et hic: 'Homo currit; ergo, animal currit'.

3) Consequentia formalis est duplex, videlicet, formalis generaliter et formalis specialiter. Consequentia formalis generaliter est cujus forma consimilis valet in omni alia materia, sicut etiam forma syllogistica discursiva et forma in qua arguitur a tota copulativa < ad > alteram ejus partem, et forma illa qua arguitur ab exclusiva ad suum universale in terminis transpositis et in terminis rectis et in numero singulari, (7r)

et forma ista qua arguitur ab eodem ad idem sive ab uno convertibili ad reliquum.

4) Consequentia formalis specialiter est cujus forma consimilis valet in aliquibus materiis, licet non in omnibus, sicut haec forma est bona in terminis praedicamentalibus: 'Omnis homo currit; ergo, omne non-currens est non-homo'. Item sequitur: 'Omnis homo est animal; ergo, omne non-animal est non-homo'. Item sequitur: 'Omnis color est qualitas; ergo, omne illud quod est non-qualitas est non-color'. Sed in terminis transcendentibus haec forma non valet. Unde non sequitur: 'Omnis homo est ens; ergo, omne non-ens est non-homo', quia antecedens est verum et consequens falsum. Falsitas consequentis sic ostenditur, quia sequitur: Omne non-ens est non-homo; ergo, omne non-ens est; et si omne non-ens est, aliquod[126] non-ens est; et sic aliquid esset quod esset non-ens, quod est impossibile. Et conformiter non sequitur: 'Omnis homo vivit; ergo, omne non-vivens est non-homo', quia suppono quod nulla res sit nisi res vivens et cum hoc quod homo sit. Tunc est antecedens verum et consequens falsum.

5) Consequentia materialis est quae solum tenet gratia terminorum, vel ex hoc solum quod antecedens sit impossibile, vel ex hoc solum quod consequens est necessarium. Exemplum primi: 'Deum esse est verum; ergo, deum esse est necessarium'. Patet consequentia ex hoc quod veritas et necessitas non distinguuntur in deo. Exemplum secundi: 'Homo est asinus; ergo, quilibet homo est Romae'. Tenet consequentia solum ex hoc quod antecedens est impossibile, quia ex propositione impossibili sequitur quaelibet alia propositio. Et hanc regulam approbat Commentator 7° *Physicorum,* commento 2°,[127] ubi dicit quod duplex est consequentia, una cujus antecedens est [im]possibile et consequens est necessarium. Verbi gratia: 'Si sol ascendit in oriente, dies est'. Altera est cujus antecedens est impossibile, qua, inquit, utimur in syllogismo ducente hominem ad inconveniens. Et ponit tale exemplum: 'Si lapis volat, habet alas; sed lapidem', inquit, 'volare est impossibile'. Haec[128] Commentator. Exemplum tertii: 'Homo currit; ergo, deus est'. Tenet

126 Unclear in film.

127 Averroes, *In VII Physicorum*, tx. c. 2, Venice apud Juntas, v. 4, f. 308A-C: "Hypotheticae autem sunt duobus modis. Est enim modus in quo praecedens est possibile aut necessarium, si consecutio necessaria. Verbi gratia, 'Si sol ascendit, dies est'. Et in hoc ponitur praecedens et concluditur consequens, aut destruitur oppositum consequentis. Est alius modus, in quo praecedens est impossibile, et in hoc semper destruitur consequens et numquam ponitur antecedens. Sed talibus propositionibus utuntur in syllogismo ducente ad inconveniens. Cum igitur dixerimus quod si corpus caeleste, quod si pars ejus quieverit, totum quiescet, necessario movetur ab alio, est consecutio vera, ac si diceremus quod si lapis volat, habet alas, licet lapidem volare sit impossibile, quemadmodum corpus caeleste impossibile est ut pars ejus quiescat."

128 Unclear in MS.

consequentia ex hoc solum quod consequens est necessarium, quia regula est quod propositio necessaria sequitur ex qualibet propositione.

6) Et si quis quaerat unde istae duae regulae primitus sumpserunt originem, videlicet, quod ex impossibili sequitur quodlibet et quod necessarium sequitur ad quodlibet, dico quod ab illo dicto Boetii in *Topicis*[129]: "Si illud <quod> minus videtur inesse alieni inest eidem, et illud quod magis videtur inesse inerit eidem." Unde si iste terminus 'asinus' praedicatur de homine, multo magis iste terminus 'currens' vel 'sedens' praedicabitur de homine. Et ideo bene sequitur: 'Homo est asinus; (7v) ergo, homo currit, vel sedet'. Item, si homo vel asinus habeat esse, multo magis creator omnium habebit esse. Et ideo bene sequitur: 'Homo est vel asinus est; ergo, deus est'.

7) Consequentiarum quaedam sunt regulae generales et quaedam speciales. Prima regula generalis est haec: Quandocumque non potest esse ita sicut primarie significatur per antecedens alicujus consequentiae nisi ita sit sicut primarie significatur per consequens ejusdem consequentiae, tunc talis consequentia est bona. Et quandocumque potest esse ita sicut primarie significatur per antecedens alicujus consequentiae, quamvis non sit ita sicut primarie significatur per consequens ejusdem consequentiae, tunc talis consequentia non valet. Ideo, si quaeratur numquid talis consequentia sit bona: 'Tu curris; ergo, tu non quiescis', dicendum est quod sic. Et si quaeratur causa, respondendum est per regulam, quia nullo casu possibili postio potest esse ita sicut primarie significatur per antecedens istius, nisi ita sit sicut primarie significatur per consequens ejusdem consequentiae. Item, si quaeratur numquid haec consequentia sit bona: 'Caelum movetur; ergo, tu moveris', dicendum est quod non. Et si quaeratur causa, respondendum per regulam, quia aliquo casu possibili posito potest esse ita sicut denotatur per antecedens istius consequentiae, quamvis non sit ita sicut denotatur per consequens ejusdem consequentiae, sicut, posito quod tu non esses, tunc est antecedens verum et consequens falsum. Et per hanc regulam possumus cognoscere omnes consequentias mundi numquid valent vel non.

8) Secunda regula generalis est haec: Quandocumque contradictorium consequentis repugnat antecedenti, tunc talis consequentia est bona; et quandocumque contradictorium consequentis non repugnat antecedenti, tunc talis consequentia non valet. Et sciendum quod tales propositiones dicuntur repugnare quae non possunt simul esse verae. Unde, si quaeratur numquid ista consequentia sit bona vel non: 'Homo currit; ergo, animal currit', dicendum est quod sic. Et

---

129 Boethius, *De differentiis topicis* II, PL 64, 1191A: "Si id quod minus videtur inesse inest, id quod magis videbitur inesse inerit".

si quaeratur causa, respondendum est per regulam, quia contradictorium consequentis repugnat antecedenti. Unde ista repugnant:
'Homo currit' et 'Nullum animal currit'. Et si quaeratur quare
repugnant, dicendum est quia istae duae propositiones non possunt
simul esse verae, stante primaria significatione utriusque. Item, si
quaeratur numquid haec consequentia sit bona: 'Animal currit; ergo,
homo currit', dicendum est quod non. Et si quaeratur causa generalis
quare, quia contradictorium consequentis non repugnat antecedenti,
quia ista non repugnant: 'Animal currit' (8r) et[130] 'Nihil quod est homo
currit'. Et si quaeratur causa generalis quare non repugnant, respondendum est per regulam, quia istae duae propositiones possunt simul
esse verae.

9) Tertia regula generalis est haec in omni consequentia bona: Ubi
oppositum consequentis est et similiter antecedentis, et ex opposito consequentis sequitur oppositum antecedentis, est consequentia bona.
Unde bene sequitur: 'Tu curris; ergo, tu moveris'. Et ideo sequitur per
oppositum consequentis[131]: 'Tu non moveris; ergo, tu non curris'. Et
notandum quod, secundum Aristotelem in *Praedicamentis*,[132] quadruplex
est oppositio, scilicet, privativa, sicut oppositio inter caecitatem et
visum; relativa, sicut inter duplum et dimidium; contraria, sicut inter
album et nigrum; et contradictoria, sicut inter terminos, ut 'homo' et
'non-homo', et inter propositiones, ut 'Quilibet homo currit' et 'Aliquis
homo non currit'.

10) Quarta regula generalis est haec: In omni consequentia syllogistica discursoria ex opposito consequentis cum minori sequitur
oppositum majoris, et ex opposito consequentis cum majori sequitur
oppositum minor*is*.[133] Unde quia haec est consequentia syllogistica
discursoria: 'Omnis homo est animal; Sortes est homo; ergo, Sortes est
animal', ideo sequitur oppositum sic: 'Sortes non est animal; et omnis
homo est animal; ergo, Sortes non est homo'. Item sequitur: 'Sortes non
est animal; et Sortes est homo; ergo, non omnis homo est animal'.

11) Quinta regula generalis est haec: Quandocumque est aliqua consequentia bona, tunc quaecumque propositio potest esse antecedens ad
antecedens illius consequentiae potest esse antecedens ad consequens
illius consequentiae. Unde haec consequentia est bona: 'Homo sedet;
ergo, animal sedet'. Et ideo quaelibet propositio quae potest esse an-

---

130 *MS* ergo.
131 Interlinear.
132 Aristotle, *Categories* 10, 11b16-19, *editio composita (vulgata)*, L. Minio-Paluello, ed., (*Aristoteles
Latinus* I, 1-5, Bruges: Desclee de Brouwer, 1961), p. 69, lines 12-14: "Dicitur autem alterum alteri
opponi quadrupliciter, aut ut ad aliquid, aut ut contraria, aut ut habitus et privatio, aut ut af-
firmatio et negatio."
133 *MS* minorum.

tecedens ad illam 'Homo sedet' potest esse antecedens ad istam 'Animal sedet'. Et ideo quia sequitur: 'Johannes sedet; ergo, homo sedet', ideo etiam sequitur 'Johannes sedet; ergo, animal sedet'.

12) Sexta regula generalis est haec: Quandocumque est aliqua consequentia bona, tunc quicquid sequitur ad consequens sequitur ad antecedens. Unde quia haec consequentia est bona: 'Tu curris; ergo, tu moveris', ideo quaelibet propositio quae sequitur ad consequens sequitur ad antecedens. Et ideo quia sequitur 'Tu moveris; ergo, tu non quiescis', idem etiam sequitur 'Tu curris; ergo, tu non quiescis'.

13) Ex qua regula sequitur septima regula generalis quae est ista: Si fiant multae consequentiae enthymematicae bonae et non variatae, tunc valebit consequentia a primo ad ultimum. Verbi gratia: 'Si homo currit, animal currit; si animal currit, corpus currit; si corpus currit, substantia currit; ergo, a primo ad ultimum, si homo currit,[134] substantia currit'. Unde notandum est quod consequentiae sunt variatae quando aliquod est antecedens in posteriori consequentia quod non fuit consequens in priori consequentia, sicut est hic: 'Si nullum tempus est, dies non est; et si dies non est et aliquod tempus est, nox est; (8v) et si nox est, aliquod tempus est; ergo, a primo ad ultimum, si nullum tempus est, et aliquod tempus est'. Hic dico negando consequentiam a primo ad ultimum. Et causa est quia consequentiae sunt variatae. Nam antecedens istius conditionalis: 'Si dies non est et aliquod tempus est, nox est' non fuit consequens in conditionali praecedente. Et iste modus arguendi de consequentiis enthymematicis potest fieri in omni linea praedicamentali secundum inferius et superius. Verbi gratia, in linea praedicamentali substantiae sic: 'Asinus est; ergo, animal est. Animal est; ergo, corpus est. Corpus est; ergo, substantia est. Ergo, a primo ad ultimum, asinus est; ergo, substantia est'. Item, in linea praedicamentali qualitatis sic: 'Si albedo est, color est. Si color est, accidens est. Si accidens est, qualitas est. Ergo, a primo ad ultimum, si albedo est, qualitas est'. Item, in linea praedicamentali quantitatis sic: 'Si corpus est, linea est. Et si linea est, quantitas est. Ergo, a primo ad ultimum, si corpus est, quantitas est'.

14) Sed hic occurrit dubium de ista propositione: 'Si dico te esse asinum, dico verum'. Et videtur quod ista sit vera. Quod arguo sic, quia si dico te esse asinum, dico te esse animal. Et si dico te esse animal, dico verum. Ergo, a primo ad ultimum, si dico te esse asinum, dico verum. Patet consequentia, quia omnes consequentiae intermediae sunt bonae et non variatae; ergo, consequentia est bona. Hic dico negando primam conditionalem, et nego consequentiam a primo ad ultimum, eo quod una consequentia intermedia non <valet>, videlicet, haec: 'Si dico te

---

134 Interlinear.

esse animal, dico verum', quia ponatur quod tu non sis, et quod dicam te esse animal. Tunc est antecedens verum et consequens falsum.

15) Octava regula generalis est haec: Ex falsis verum; ex veris nil nisi verui   Hoc est dictu,[135] ex propositione falsa sequitur propositio vera in bona consequentia, sicut hic: 'Nihil est; ergo, chimaera non est', et hic: 'Homo est asinus; ergo, deus est omnipotens'. Sed ex propositione vera numquam sequitur propositio falsa in bona consequentia.

16) Jam restat ponere alias regulas speciales, et primo circa illas quae fiunt ex categoricis, et postea circa illas consequentias quae fiunt ex hypotheticis.

17) Prima regula est haec circa speciem categoricae quae est propositio universalis: Ab universali ad suam particularem vel indefinitam semper est consequentia bona, sed e contra in terminis accidentalibus non valet consequentia, ut bene sequitur: 'Quilibet homo currit; ergo, aliquis homo currit', et 'Nullus homo currit; ergo, aliquis homo non currit'. Sed e contra non sequitur, scilicet, 'Aliquis homo non currit; ergo, nullus homo currit'.

18) (9r) Secunda regula: Ab universali ad suam exclusivam de terminis transpositis in terminis rectis et in numero singulari est consequentia bona, et e contra, ut 'Omne currens est homo; ergo, tantum homo currit', et e contra.

19) Tertia regula: A superiori distributo cum constantia inferioris ad idem inferius distributum est consequentia bona. Unde bene sequitur: 'Omne animal currit[136]; et homo est; ergo, omnis homo currit'. Item sequitur: 'Nullum animal currit[137]; et homo est; ergo, nihil quod est homo currit'.

20) Jam circa secundum speciem categoricae et quartam conjunctim, quae sunt particularis, indefinita et singularis, ponuntur istae regulae: Ab inferiori ad superius a parte subjecti vel a parte praedicati sine negatione et sine distributione est consequentia bona, ut 'Homo currit; ergo, animal currit'. Hic arguitur ab inferiori ad superius a parte subjecti. Et hic: 'Tu curris; ergo, tu moveris'. Hic arguitur ab inferiori ad superius a parte praedicati.

21) Quarta regula: Ab inferiori ad superius cum negatione postposita[138] termino inferiori et termino superiori et cum constantia ejusdem inferioris est consequentia bona, ut hic[139]: 'Homo non currit; et omnis homo est animal; ergo, animal non currit'.

---

135 dictu = dicendum.
136 Interlinear.
137 Interlinear.
138 *MS may have* praeposita.
139 Interlinear.

22) Quinta regula: A superiori ad inferius a parte subjecti vel praedicati sine negatione, etiam sine distributione, non valet consequentia. Unde non sequitur: 'Animal currit; ergo, homo currit', nec sequitur: 'Tu moveris[140]; ergo, tu curris'. Et notandum quod terminus dicitur superior altero quando unus terminus significat omnia illa quae alter significat et plura, vel saltem natus est significare. Unde iste terminus 'animal' est superior quam iste terminus 'homo', quia significat omnia illa quae iste terminus 'homo' significat, etiam plura.

23) Sexta regula: Termini disparati non faciunt inferius vel superius. Termini disparati sunt tales quorum neuter vere affirmatur de reliquo mediante tali verbo 'est', quales sunt isti termini: 'asinus', 'homo', 'leo', 'capra'.

24) Septima regula: Ab uno convertibili ad suum convertibile est semper consequentia bona. Unde sciendum quod duplex est convertibilitas, scilicet, terminorum et propositionum. Convertibilitas terminorum est quando unus terminus est praedicabilis de reliquo vere universaliter et affirmative, sicut est de isto termino 'homo' et de isto termino 'animal rationale'. Unde istae praedicationes sunt verae: 'Omnis homo est animal rationale' et 'Omne animal rationale est homo'. Unde si omne quod est a est b, etiam quod est b est a, tunc a et b sunt termini convertibiles. Convertibilitas propositionum est quando a prima sequitur secunda et e contra. Unde bene sequitur: 'Omnis homo currit; ergo, omne animal rationale currit', et e contra. Et tenet utraque consequentia per hoc quod ibi arguitur ab una convertibili (9v) ad suum convertibile.

25) Jam circa illas categoricas in quibus ponuntur termini exponibiles, quales sunt isti termini: 'differt', 'aliud' et 'non idem', ponuntur istae regulae.

26) Prima regula: A propositione habente plures exponentes ad quamlibet suam exponentem est consequentia bona.

27) Secunda regula: Ab omnibus exponentibus ad propositionem cujus sunt exponentes est consequentia bona. Unde bene sequitur: 'Tu es; et asinus est; et tu non es asinus; ergo, tu differs ab asino'. Unde propositio affirmativa in qua ponitur haec dictio 'differt' vel haec dictio 'aliud' habet tres exponentes, duas primas affirmativas, et tertiam negativam. Et dicuntur exponentes intellectum propositionis. Unde ista propositio: 'Tu differs ab homine' habet istas exponentes: 'Tu es', etiam 'Homo est', et 'Tu non es homo'. Item, haec: 'Tu differs a quolibet homine' sic exponitur: 'Tu es, et quilibet homo est, et tu non [est] es quilibet homo'.

---

140   Interlinear, above a word erased on the line.

28) Sed ne circa expositionem talium propositionum error generetur propter ignorantiam, notandum est pro regula quod si ablativus casus sequatur ly 'differt', tunc nominativus casus a quo descendit ille ablativus casus est praedicatum in tertia exponente. Unde haec propositio: 'Tu differs ab animali' sic exponitur: 'Tu es, et animal est, et tu non es animal'. Sed si ablativus casus praecedat ly 'differt', tunc nominativus casus a quo descendit ille ablativus erit subjectum in tertia exponente. Unde haec propositio: 'Tu ab homine differs' sic exponitur: 'Tu es, et homo est, et homo non est tu'. Et haec propositio: 'Tu ab animali differs' eodem modo habet exponi.

29) Et si omnes exponentes sint verae, tunc est propositio vera quae exponitur per illas. Et si aliqua exponens sit falsa, tunc est propositio cujus est illa exponens falsa. Unde si quaeratur numquid haec propositio sit vera: 'Tu ab homine differs', dicendum est quod sic. Et si quaeratur causa, respondendum est per regulam, quia omnes ejus exponentes sunt verae. Unde haec est vera: 'Tu es, < et homo est, > et homo non es tu', quia ejus contradictorium est falsum, videlicet, 'Omnis homo est tu'. Item, si quaeratur numquid haec propositio sit vera: 'Tu differs ab homine', dicendum est quod non. Et si quaeratur causa, respondendum est per regulam, quia una ejus exponens est falsa, videlicet, haec: 'Tu non es homo'.

30) *Tertia*[141] regula est haec: Arguendo ab inferiori ad superius a parte subjecti cum hoc verbo 'differt' vel 'aliud' semper est consequentia bona. (10r) Unde bene sequitur: 'Tu ab homine differs; ergo, tu ab animali differs'. Et hoc si non est signum distributivum sequens.[142] Unde non sequitur: 'Asinus ab omni homine differt; ergo, asinus ab omni animali differt'. Sed arguendo ab inferiori ad superius a parte praedicati cum hoc verbo 'differt' vel 'aliud' non valet consequentia. Unde non sequitur: 'Tu differs a Ricardo; ergo, tu differs ab homine', nec sequitur: 'Tu differs ab isto homine; ergo, tu differs ab homine', nec sequitur: 'Tu differs ab isto homine; iste homo est animal; ergo, tu differs ab animali'.

31) Quarta regula: Propositio negativa in qua ponitur haec dictio 'differt' vel haec dictio 'aliud' non debet exponi, sed habebit causas veritatis, quae causae veritatis debent dari per opposita exponentium sui contradictorii praeponendo causis istas duas dictiones 'aut quia' vel 'aut quod'. Une illa propositio: 'Tu non differs ab homine' habet istas causas veritatis: aut quia tu non es, aut quia nihil quod est homo est, aut quia tu es homo. Et arguendo a causa veritatis ad propositionem

---

141 *MS* secunda.
142 Sic in MS. The sense is not altogether clear. Perhaps emend to 'praecedens' in view of the example.

cujus est causa est consequentia bona. Et e contra consequentia non valet de forma. Unde bene sequitur: 'Tu es homo; ergo, tu non differs ab homine'. Item, sequitur: 'Nullus asinus est; ergo, tu non differs ab asino'.

32) Quinta regula: A propositione exclusiva ad quamlibet suam exponentem divisim et ad omnes suas exponentes conjunctim est consequentia bona. Unde notandum quod propositio exclusiva habet tantum duas exponentes, videlicet, unam affirmativam et aliam negativam. Unde illa propositio: 'Tantum homo currit' habet istas exponentes: 'Homo currit' et 'Nihil aliud quam homo currit'. Sed haec exclusiva negativa: 'Tantum homo non currit' habet istas exponentes: 'Homo non currit' et 'Quodlibet aliud ab homine currit'. Et similiter haec: 'Tantum homo non est albus' habet istas exponentes: 'Homo non est albus' et 'Quodlibet aliud ab homine est album'. Et si omnes exponentes sint verae, tunc est propositio vera quae exponitur per illas. Et si aliqua exponens sit falsa, tunc est propositio falsa cujus est illa exponens.

33) Sexta regula: Contradictorium exclusivae debet dari praeposita negatione toti. Unde contradictorium illius exclusivae: 'Tantum homo currit' non est hoc: 'Tantum homo non currit', quia istae duae propositiones possunt simul esse falsae, quod est contra legem contradictoriarum. Unde supponamus quod Sortes currat cum equo suo, et quod Plato quiescat cum equo suo. Tunc est haec falsa, 'Tantum homo currit', quia una ejus exponens est falsa, videlicet, 'Nihil aliud ab homine currit', quia per casum equus Sortis currit, qui est aliud ab homine. Et haec propositio simpliciter est falsa: 'Tantum homo non currit', quia una sua exponens est falsa, videlicet, ista: (10v) 'Quodlibet aliud ab homine currit', quia per casum equus Platonis quiescit, qui tamen est aliud ab homine. Ideo contradictorium istius exclusivae affirmativae: 'Tantum homo currit' est hoc: 'Non tantum homo currit'. Et haec propositio: 'Non tantum homo currit' habet causas veritatis, quae causae veritatis debent dari per opposita exponentium sui contradictorii praeponendo illis causis istas duas dictiones 'aut quia' vel 'aut quod',[143] sic dicendo: 'Aut quod nihil quod est[144] homo currit, aut quia aliud ab homine currit'. Et arguendo a causa veritatis ad propositionem cujus est causa est semper consequentia bona.

34) Septima regula: A propositione exceptiva ad quamlibet suam exponentem est consequentia bona. Unde notandum quod propositio exceptiva habet tantum duas exponentes, videlicet, unam affirmativam et aliam negativam. Unde haec propositio exceptiva affirmativa: 'Omnis homo praeter Sortem currit' sic exponitur: 'Omnis homo alius a Sorte currit, et Sortes non currit'. Et haec propositio exceptiva negativa:

143 Vel 'aut quod': interlinear.
144 Interlinear.

'Nullus homo praeter Sortem currit' sic exponitur: 'Nullus homo[145] alius a Sorte currit, et Sortes currit'. Et si omnes exponentes sint verae, tunc est illa propositio vera cujus sunt exponentes. Si vero aliqua exponens sit falsa, tunc est illa propositio falsa cujus est exponens.

35) Octava regula: Contradictorium exceptivae debet dari negatione praeposita toti. Unde contradictorium istius: 'Nullus homo praeter te est asinus' non est haec: 'Aliquis homo praeter < te > est asinus', quia utraque propositio est falsa, et per consequens non mutuo contradicunt. Unde haec propositio est falsa: 'Nullus homo praeter te est asinus', quia una sua exponens, videlicet, ista: 'Tu es asinus' est falsa. Et haec propositio similiter est falsa: 'Aliquis homo praeter te est asinus', quia illa implicat quod aliquis homo est asinus. Unde contradictorium illius exceptivae: 'Nullus homo praeter te est asinus' est hoc: 'Non nullus homo praeter te est asinus'. Et si quaeratur cui haec propositio aequipollet, dico quod aequipollet huic disjunctivae: 'Aut quia aliquis homo alius a te est asinus, aut quia tu non es asinus'. Et sic illa propositio habet unam causam veritatis veram.

36) Nona regula: Propositio affirmativa in qua ponitur hoc verbum 'incipit' vel 'desinit' habet duplicem modum exponendi. Et si unus modus exponendi fuerit verus, tunc est illa propositio vera. Si vero neuter modus exponendi fuerit verus, tunc illa propositio est falsa. Unde ista propositio: 'Sortes incipit esse albus' primo modo sic exponitur: 'Sortes nunc est albus, et immediate ante hoc non fuit albus', quae exponitur per unam affirmativam de praesenti et negativam de praeterito. Secundo modo sic exponitur: 'Sortes nunc non est albus, et immediate post hoc erit albus', quae exponitur per unam negativam de praesenti et affirmativam de futuro. Sed propositio in qua ponitur hoc verbum 'desinit' debet exponi dupliciter modo contrario. Unde haec propositio: (11r) 'Sortes desinit esse albus' primo modo sic exponitur per unam negativam de praesenti et aliam affirmativam de praeterito, ut sic: 'Sortes nunc non est albus, et immediate ante hoc instans quod est praesens fuit albus'. Secundo modo exponitur per unam affirmativam de praesenti et aliam negativam de futuro, ut sic: 'Sortes nunc est albus, et immediate post hoc instans quod est praesens non erit albus'. Et notandum pro regula quod arguendo ab inferiori ad superius a parte subjecti cum hoc verbo 'incipit' vel 'desinit' est consequentia bona, ut hic: 'Omnem propositionem Thomas incipit scire; ergo, aliquam propositionem Thomas incipit scire'. Sed arguendo ab inferiori ad superius a parte praedicati cum hoc verbo 'incipit' vel 'desinit' non valet consequentia de forma. Unde non sequitur: 'Thomas incipit esse albus; ergo, Thomas incipit esse coloratus', nec sequitur: 'Thomas in-

---

145 Interlinear.

cipit videre istum hominem; et iste homo est aliquis homo; ergo, Thomas incipit videre aliquem hominem'.

37) Decima regula: Propositio affirmativa vel propositio negativa in qua ponitur ablativus casus absolutus a parte subjecti debet tripliciter exponi, videlicet, per unam conditionalem, per unam causalem, vel per unam temporalem. Unde haec propositio: 'Nullo currente, tu es asinus' sic exponitur: 'Aut quia nullus currit tu es asinus, aut dum nullus currit tu es asinus, aut si nullus currit tu es asinus'. Item, ista propositio: 'Aliquo currente, tu es asinus' sic exponitur: 'Aut si aliquis currit tu es asinus, aut quia aliquis currit tu es asinus, aut dum aliquis currit tu es asinus'. Et sic omnes exponentes sunt falsae. Et ideo utraque propositio est falsa. Ex quo sequitur quod istae duae propositiones non contradicunt: 'Aliquo currente, tu es asinus' et 'Nullo currente, tu es asinus'. Si ergo quaeratur quid sit contradictorium istius: 'Aliquo currente, tu es asinus', dicendum est quod hoc: 'Non est ita quod aliquo currente, tu es asinus'. Et si quaeratur quid sit contradictorium istius: 'Nullo currente, tu es asinus', dicendum est quod hoc: 'Non est ita quod nullo currente, tu es asinus'. Et si quis velit arguere quod praedictae duae propositiones mutuo contradicunt, quia una est universalis negativa et alia est particularis affirmativa de eisdem subjectis et praedicatis praecise et pro eisdem supponentibus, ergo stant contradictorie in figura, negatur consequentia, quia regula ista non tenet nisi in illis categoricis quae non aequipollent hypotheticis.

38) Undecima regula: Propositio categorica in qua ponitur hoc relativum 'qui' debet exponi per unam copulativam, ut ista: 'Sortes currit, qui movetur' (11v) sic exponitur: 'Sortes currit, et ille movetur'. Item: 'Thomas, qui erit albus, currit' sic exponitur: 'Thomas erit albus, et ille currit'. Notandum tamen quod si talis dictio 'differt' vel 'aliud' praecedat hujusmodi relativum, tunc impedit expositionem per nomen relativum. Unde haec propositio: 'Tu differs ab animali quod est asinus' non debet exponi per relativum, sed per hoc verbum 'differt'. Unde sic exponitur: 'Tu es, et animal quod est asinus est, et tu non es animal quod est asinus'. Ex quo sequitur quod ista consequentia non valet: 'Tu differs ab animali quod est asinus; ergo, tu differs ab animali, et illud est asinus', quia antecedens est verum et consequens falsum. Unde a propositione in qua ponitur pronomen relativum ad suas exponentes ubi nullus terminus habens vim negationis praecedit est consequentia bona. Unde bene sequitur: 'Tu, qui es albus, curris; ergo, tu es albus, et tu curris'.

39) Duodecima regula: Comparativus et superlativus gradus et iste terminus 'sicut' habent eundem vim confundendi terminum quem habet 'differt' et 'aliud'. Faciunt enim terminum communem sequentem

sine signo universali stare confuse et distributive, et[146] terminum communem sequentem cum signo universali stare determinate vel confuse
tantum. Sed habent diversum modum exponendi. Unde illa propositio:
'Tu es fortior homine' sic exponitur: 'Tu es fortis, et homo est fortis,
etiam homo non est ita fortis sicut tu'. Sed ista propositio: 'Tu es fortior
omni homine' sic exponitur: 'Tu es fortis, et omnis homo est fortis, et
non omnis homo est ita fortis sicut tu'. Et ista propositio est vera de
homine valde debili. Et similiter haec propositio est vera de obolo et de
auro: 'Hoc argentum est melius omni auro', sicut patet per exponentes
sic: 'Hoc argentum est bonum, et omne aurum est bonum, et non omne
aurum est ita bonum sicut hoc argentum'. Item, illa propositio: 'Tu es
fortissimus hominum' sic exponitur: 'Tu es fortis, et homines sunt for-
tes, et nullus homo alius a te est ita fortis sicut tu'. Item, illa propositio:
'Tu es ita fortis sicut homo' sic exponitur: 'Tu es fortis, et homo est fortis, et nullus homo est fortior te'. Sed ista propositio: 'Tu es ita fortis
sicut omnis homo' sic exponitur: 'Tu es fortis, et omnis homo est fortis,
et non omnis homo est ita fortis sicut tu'. Et notandum quod in omnibus istis, arguendo ab exponentibus ad expositum est consequentia
bona, et e contra. Unde ista consequentia est bona: 'Sortes est sapentior
omni homine; ergo, Sortes est sapiens, et omnis homo est sapiens, et non
omnis homo est ita sapiens sicut Sortes'.

40) Tertia decima regula: Propositio reduplicativa habebit quattuor
exponentes. Unde illa (12r) reduplicativa: 'a inquantum b est c' sic exponitur: 'a est b, et a est c, et omne b est c, et si b est, ipsum est c'.
Similiter ista negativa: 'a inquantum b non est c' sic exponitur: 'a est b,
et a non est c, et nullum b est c, et si b est, ipsum non est c'. Et sicut contradictorium exclusivae vel exceptivae debet dari praeposita negatione
toti, ita debet dari contradictorium reduplicativae.

41) Jam restat ponere aliquas regulas speciales circa consequentias
quae fiunt ex hypotheticis. Prima regula est haec: A tota conditionali
cum suo antecedente ad consequens ejusdem est consequentia bona, ut
'Si homo currit, animal currit; sed homo currit; ergo, animal currit'.

42) Secunda regula: A contradictorio consequentis ad contradictorium antecedentis cum tota conditionali est consequentia bona,
ut 'Si homo currit, animal currit; sed nullum animal currit; ergo, nihil
quod est homo currit'. Sed hic oritur dubium de ist<a> propositione:
'Si tu es animal, tu es asinus; sed tu es animal; ergo, tu es asinus'. Si
dicatur quod sit vera, tunc arguo sic: Si tu es animal, tu es asinus; sed tu
es animal; ergo, tu <es> asinus'. Probatur consequentia, quia hic
arguitur a tota conditionali cum suo antecedente ad consequens

---

146 Interlinear. Reading uncertain.

ejusdem. Si enim dicitur quod haec conditionalis sit falsa, contra, si tu
es animal rudibile, tu es asinus: Si tu es animal rudibile, t < u es
asinus; > ergo, < si tu es > animal, tu es asinus.[147] Hic dico negando
primam conditionalem. Et nego ultimam consequentiam. Et si obiciatur
quod hic arguitur ab inferiori ad superius sine negatione et sine
distributione, et dicatur quod non, quia illa dictio 'si' habet vim
distribuendi.

43) Tertia regula: A tota copulativa ad alteram ejus partem est semper consequentia bona de forma. Unde bene sequitur: 'Tu curris et tu
moveris; ergo, tu curris'. Sed a parte copulativae ad totam copulativam
non valet consequentia de forma. Unde non sequitur: 'Tu curris; ergo,
tu curris et tu es albus'. Et si aliquando valeat consequentia a parte
copulativae ad totam copulativam, hoc est gratia materiae, et non gratia
formae. Hoc est, talis consequentia non est formalis sed materialis, ut
hic: 'Tu curris; ergo, tu curris et tu moveris'.

44) Quarta regula: Contradictorium copulativae debet dari per unam
disjunctivam factam ex contradictoriis partium. Unde contradictorium
istius copulativae: 'Tu curris et tu moveris' est hoc: 'Tu non curris vel tu
non moveris'.

45) Quinta regula: A tota disjunctiva ad alteram ejus partem non
valet consequentia de forma. Unde non sequitur: 'Tu curris vel tu es
albus; ergo, tu curris'. Sed semper a parte disjunctivae ad totam
disjunctivam est consequentia bona. Unde bene sequitur: 'Tu curris;
ergo, tu curris (12v) vel tu es homo'.

46) Sexta regula: A tota disjunctiva cum opposito unius partis ad
alteram ejus partem est semper consequentia bona. Unde bene
sequitur: 'Tu est albus vel tu es niger; sed tu non es albus; ergo, tu es
niger'. Sed contra, videtur quod illa regula sit falsa, quia ex hac
sequitur quod tu es asinus. Probatur sic: Tu es asinus vel manus mea est
clausa; sed nulla manus mea est clausa; ergo, tu es asinus'. Si negetur
consequentia, contra: Hic arguitur a tota disjunctiva cum opposito
unius partis ad alteram ejus partem; ergo, consequentia bona. Si
negatur minor, contra: Quaelibet[148] manus mea est aperta; ergo, nulla
manus mea est clausa. Hic dico primo concedendo primam regulam et
negando totam antecedens, pro neutra parte sed pro tota copulativa,
quia antecedens est una copulativa implicans contradictionem. Unde si
sic argueretur: 'Rex sedet; et nullus rex sedet; ergo, rex sedet', ista consequentia est concedenda et antecedens est neganda, licet pro neutra

---

147 MS inserts a marg. addition after 'rudibile', but it is cut off by the edge of the folio. Only
the 't' of 'tu' and 'ergo' are legible, with some hesitation. The suggested addition is for sense. The
whole paragraph is in a rather dubious state.

148 *MS* quilibet.

parte, eo quod est una copulativa impossibilis. Et tamen prima non est
neganda, eo quod est mihi dubia; nec secunda est neganda, eo quod est
mihi dubia. Et tamen totum antecedens est negandum, eo quod est
una[149] copulativa facta ex duobus contradictoriis.

47) Septima regula: Contradictorium disjunctivae debet dari per
unam copulativam factam ex oppositis partium, ut contradictorium
istius disjunctivae: 'Tu es Oxoniis vel tu es Londoniis' est hoc: 'Tu non
es Oxoniis et tu non es Londoniis'.

EXPLICIUNT CONSEQUENTIAE COMPENDIOSE COMPILATAE PER VENERABILEM
DOCTOREM LAVENHAM ORDINIS CARMELITARUM PER MANUM CHESTREFORDE.

<   TRACTATUS EXCLUSIVARUM   >

1) Dictio exclusiva aliquando sumitur a parte subjecti, et aliquando a
parte praedicati. Quando ponitur a parte subjecti, propositio debet exponi secundum quod dictum est in *Consequentiis*.[150] Sed quando ponitur
a parte praedicati, propositio non debet exponi, sed est convertibilis
cum ista quae remanet dempta dictione exclusiva. Unde istae propositiones simpliciter convertibiles: 'Tu es tantum homo' et 'Tu es homo', 'Sortes est tantum animal' et 'Sortes est animal', quia non plus significat una quam alia.

2) Prima regula: In omni propositione in qua ponuntur duo termini
habentes vim exponendi, primus terminus habebit vim. Nam in ista:
'Tantum Sortes differt ab alio a Sorte', debet exponi per notam exclusivae, et non per notam differentiae. Unde sic exponitur: 'Sortes differt ab alio a (13r) Sorte, et nihil aliud a Sorte differt ab alio a Sorte'. Et
ista propositio est vera, quia omnes[151] exponentes sunt verae. Nam
prima exponens est vera, videlicet, 'Sortes differt ab alio a Sorte', quia
sic exponitur: 'Sortes est, et aliud a Sorte est, et Sortes non est aliud a
Sorte'. Et ista exponens similiter est vera: 'Nihil aliud a Sorte differt ab
alio a Sorte', quia ejus contradictorium est falsum, videlicet, 'Aliud
quam Sortes differt ab alio a Sorte'. Quod patet, quia haec est una indefinita cujus quaelibet[152] singularis est falsa. Nam hoc est falsum: 'Hoc
aliud a Sorte differt ab alio a Sorte', quia sic exponitur: 'Hoc aliud a
Sorte est, et aliud a Sorte est, et hoc aliud a Sorte non est aliud a Sorte',
quod est falsum. Et sic de quolibet singulari.

---

149 Interlinear.
150 *Cons.*, 32.
151 *MS* omnis.
152 Cujus quaelibet: *MS* cujuslibet.

3) Sed hic occurrit dubietas de illa[153] propositione[154] 'Tantum Sortes istorum est homo'. Et assigno duos asinos, et unum hominem, videlicet, Sortem, existentem cum eisdem in campo, et quod multi alii homines sunt in mundo. Tunc probatur prima propositio: 'Sortes istorum est homo, et nullus alius istorum quam Sortes est homo; ergo, tantum Sortes istorum est homo'. Consequentia dicitur esse bona, et totum antecedens est verum; ergo, consequens.

4) Si ergo conceditur ista propositio: 'Tantum Sortes istorum est homo', contra sequitur: 'Tantum Sortes istorum est homo; ergo, omnis homo est Sortes istorum'. Consequentia patet, quia arguitur hic ab exclusiva ad suum universalem de terminis transpositis et in terminis rectis et in numero singulari; ergo, consequentia bona.

5) Hic dico negando primam propositionem, videlicet, istam: 'Tantum Sortes istorum est homo'. Et nego consequentiam primam factam in probatione illius. Unde praedicta propositio habet sic exponi: 'Sortes istorum est homo, et nullus alius quam Sortes istorum est homo'. Et non aliter debet exponi. Minor ergo prius addita non fuit sua exponens.

6) Secunda regula: Quandocumque dictio exclusiva additur subjecto alicujus propositionis universalis affirmativae, si subjectum supponit pro multis, tunc est talis propositio falsa. Verbi gratia, 'Tantum omnis homo currit', posito tamen quod nihil currit nisi homo, ita tamen quod viginti homines currant vel centum. Tunc est illa propositio falsa: 'Tantum omnis homo currit', quia una sua exponens est falsa, videlicet, 'Nihil aliud quam omnis homo currit', quia [aliud quam omnis homo currit, quia] unus homo currit, et iste homo est aliud quam omnis homo; ergo, aliud quam omnis homo currit. Et ista exclusiva: 'Tantum omnis homo currit' convertitur in universalem talem: 'Omne currens est omnis homo', quae[155] universalis est falsa in casu isto.

7) Tertia regula: Quandocumque est aliqua propositio exclusiva affirmativa cujus praedicatum non potest verificari de aliquo toto nisi verificatur de parte illius totius, tunc est propositio falsa et impossibilis, sicut est talis propositio: 'Tantum (13v) domus est alba'. Et quod ista propositio sit impossibilis probatur, quia ex ista propositione cum veris sequuntur duo contradictoria, quia sequitur: Tantum domus est alba; ergo, domus est alba. Et sequitur: Domus est alba; ergo, pars domus est alba. Et ultra: Pars domus est alba; et omnis pars domus est aliud a domo; ergo, aliud quam domus est album. Item, sequitur ex eadem propositione: Tantum domus est alba; ergo, nihil aliud quam domus est album.

---

153 De illa: interlinear.
154 MS abbreviation seems to be 'propositioni', but unclear.
155 *MS* quod.

8) Sed ista regula, quamvis sit regula Hintone,[156] potest tamen habere multas instantias. Nam istae propositiones sunt possibiles: 'Tantum ignis est calidus' et 'Tantum aqua est frigida', et tamen calor non potest inesse toti igni nisi insit parti ignis, neque frigiditas potest inesse toti aquae nisi insit parti ejus. Hic dico quod regula Hyntone intellegitur de toto heterogeneo[157] et non de toto homogeneo. Totum homogeneum est cujus partes participant totam naturam et nomen totius, ut ignis, aer, aqua, terra. Nam quaelibet[158] pars ignis est ignis, et quaelibet[159] pars aer < is > est aer. Totum hetero[mo]geneum est cujus partes non participant naturam et nomen totius, ut homo, asinus, leo, capra. Non enim quaelibet[160] pars hominis est homo, nec quaelibet[161] pars domus est domus.

9) Quarta regula: Quando dictio exclusiva additur termino numerali a parte subjecti, illa propositio habebit duplicem modum exponendi, videlicet, ratione alietatis et ratione pluralitatis. Une illa propositio: 'Tantum unum est' sic exponitur ratione alietatis: 'Unum est, et nihil aliud quam unum est'. Sed ratione pluralitatis sic exponitur: 'Unum est, et non plura sunt'. Item, ista: 'Tantum quattuor homines sunt in claustro' sic exponitur ratione alietatis: 'Quattuor homines sunt in claustro, et nulli alii quam quattuor homines sunt in claustro'. Sed ratione pluralitatis sic exponitur: 'Quattuor homines sunt in claustro, et non plures quam quattuor sunt in claustro'. Et ista propositio: 'Tantum unum est' ratione alietatis est falsa, sed exponendo eam ratione pluralitatis est vera. Item, ista propositio: 'Tantum quattuor homines sunt in claustro' ratione alietatis est impossibilis, sed ratione pluralitatis est possibilis. Et est impossibilis alio modo, eo quo sic includit contradictoria, quia sequitur: Tantum quattuor homines sunt in claustro; ergo, duo homines sunt in claustro; sed omnes duo homines sunt alii quam quattuor; ergo, alii quam quattuor homines sunt in claustro. Et ex alio latere sequitur: Tantum quattuor homines sunt in claustro; ergo, nulli alii quam quattuor homines (14r) sunt in claustro. Et hoc exponendo eam ratione alietatis. Similiter, ista propositio: 'Tantum duodecim sunt apostoli dei' ratione alietatis est falsa; sed ratione pluralitatis est vera. Et si arguatur sic: 'Tantum duodecim sunt apostoli dei; ergo, omnes apostoli dei sunt duodecim', negatur consequentia. Sed si obiciatur quod hic arguitur ab exclusiva ad suum universale, etc., dico quod regula non tenet nisi arguatur in singulari numero.

156 Identity unknown.
157 *MS* heterogeneum. hetero-: interlinear.
158 *MS* quilibet.
159 *MS* quilibet.
160 *MS* quilibet.
161 *MS* quilibet.

10) Verumtamen potest distingui an ly 'omnis' teneatur divisive vel collective. Si divisive, negatur consequentia. Si collective, probatur consequentia et antecedens, quia tunc non plus significat nisi quod omnes apostoli simul sumpti sunt duodecim.

11) Quinta regula: Istae dictiones: 'tantum', 'tantummodo', 'solum', 'solummodo', 'praecise', 'dumtaxat' faciunt propositiones exclusivas. Unde ista propositio: 'Praecise sicut est *a* significat' est exclusiva. Et sic exponitur: 'Sicut est *a* significat, et non aliter quam sicut est *a* significat'. Et praedictae dictiones vocantur dictiones exclusivae.

12) Sciendum est etiam quod praejacens exclusivae vocatur propositio quae manet dempta dictione exclusiva. Unde praejacens illius exclusivae: 'Tantum homo currit' est haec: 'Homo currit'. Et ab exclusiva ad suum praejacens est semper consequentia bona. Unde bene sequitur: 'Tantum homo currit; ergo, homo currit'.

EXPLICIT TRACTATUS EXCLUSIVARUM PER DOCTOREM LAVENHAM CARMELITAM.

< EXCEPTIVAE >

1) Dictiones exceptivae sunt istae: 'praeter', 'praeterquam' et 'nisi'. Sciendum tamen quod ista dictio 'nisi' aliquando tenetur consecutive, et tunc facit propositionem conditionalem, sicut patet de ista: 'Thomas non potest audire nisi habeat aures' et 'Si Thomas non habeat aures, Thomas non potest audire'. Et aliquando tenetur exceptive. Sed tunc non facit propositionem conditonalem, sicut patet hic: 'Nullus homo facit nisi Thomas'. Et tunc haec dictio 'nisi' habet idem officium quod haec dictio 'praeter' habet. Unde ista propositio: 'Nullus homo currit nisi Thomas' sic exponitur: 'Thomas currit, et nullus alius a Thoma currit'.

2) Item, sciendum quod haec dictio 'praeter' non semper tenetur eodem modo, quia aliquando dicit exceptionem, ut hic: 'Nullus homo praeter Sortem currit', id est, 'Nullus homo excepto Sorte currit'. Aliquando dicit additionem, ut hic: 'Thomas debet solvere duos denarios[162] praeter expensas', id est, 'Thomas debet solvere duos denarios, et cum addendae sunt expensae'. Et aliquando dicit subtractionem, ut hic: 'Decem (14v) praeter quinque sunt quinque', hoc est, 'Decem per subtractionem quinque sunt quinque'.

3) Prima regula: Propositio[163] exceptiva numquam vel raro est

162 Interlinear.
163 In marg.

propria nisi ejus praejacens est universalis. Praejacens vocatur tota propositio quae remanet dempta dictione exceptiva cum suo casuali. Unde praejacens istius: 'Omnis homo praeter Sortem currit' est haec: 'Omnis homo currit'. Tales ergo propositiones sunt improprie: 'Aliquis homo praeter Sortem currit'.

4) Secunda regula: Ad veritatem exceptivae affirmativae requiritur quod praedicatum removeatur a parte extracapta, et quod insit cuilibet contento sub subjecto. Et e contra, requiritur ad veritatem exceptivae negativae [requiritur] quod praedicatum vere affirmetur de parte extracapta, et vere negetur a quolibet contento sub subjecto. Unde exceptiva affirmativa[164] habet duas exponentes, unam affirmativam, etiam aliam negativam, ut dictum est in *Consequentiis*.[165] Pars extracapta vocatur illa res quae excipitur, ut in ista: 'Nullus homo praeter Sortem currit', Sortes est pars extracapta.

5) Tertia regula: Propositio in toto vera vel in toto falsa non potest verificari per exceptionem partis falsae. Et est propositio in toto vera quando est vera pro quolibet ejus singulari, sicut ista: 'Omnis homo est animal'. Et est propositio in toto falsa quando falsificatur pro quolibet[166] supposito, sicut ista: 'Omnis homo[167] est asinus'. Et ideo ista propositio: 'Omnis homo est asinus' non potest verificari per exceptionem istius hominis vel istius asini.[168]

6) Quarta regula: Omnis propositio in parte vera et in parte falsa potest verificari per exceptionem partis falsae. Et est propositio in parte vera et in parte falsa quando est vera pro aliquo supposito et pro alio non, sicut hic[169]: Si aliquis homo curreret et aliquis homo non curreret, tunc est vera: 'Omnis homo currit' pro aliquo homine currente et falsa pro aliquo homine non currente. Item tamen propositio cum sit universalis in parte vera et in parte falsa potest verificari per exceptionem partis falsae. Unde si omnis homo curreret excepto Sorte, tunc posset ista propositio: 'Omnis homo currit' verificari per exceptionem Sortis, sic dicendo: 'Omnis homo praeter Sortem <currit>'. Et sicut illa propositio: 'Omnis homo currit' potest verificari <per> exceptionem unius hominis non currentis, ita etiam potest verificari per exceptionem duorum hominum vel trium non currentium. Hic enim notandum est quod ista propositio: 'Omnis homo currit' non potest verificari per exceptionem duorum hominum non currentium, mediante nota

---

164 Interlinear.
165 *Cons.*, 34.
166 Interlinear.
167 Interlinear.
168 *MS* asinus.
169 Interlinear.

copulationis. Unde ista exceptiva: 'Omnis homo praeter Sortem et Platonem currit' est impossibilis. Probatur, quia ex ista sequitur duo contradictoria, quia sequitur: Omnis homo praeter Sortem et Platonem currit; ergo, nec Sortes currit nec Plato currit. Patet consequentia ab exceptiva ad unam suam expo-(16r) nentem. Et ex alio latere sequitur: Omnis homo praeter Sortem et Platonem currit; ergo, omnis homo alius a Sorte et a Platone currit. Patet consequentia ab exceptiva ad unam suam exponentem. Et tunc arguitur ulterius: Omnis homo alius a Sorte et Platone currit; sed Sortes est alius a Sorte et a Platone; ergo, Sortes currit; et si Sortes currit, Sortes currit vel Plato currit. Et quod Sortes sit alius a Sorte et a Platone patet per exponentes quas habet respectu istius nominis 'alius', quia Sortes est, et Sortes et Plato sunt, et Sortes non est Sortes et Plato; ergo, Sortes est alius a Sorte et a Platone. Et ideo ista propositio: 'Omnis homo currit' non potest verificari per exceptionem duorum hominum non currentium nisi mediante nota disjunctionis. Unde ista propositio exceptiva: 'Omnis homo praeter Sortem vel Platonem currit' est satis possibilis et verificabilis.

7) Notandum tamen quod si subjectum exceptivae affirmativae sit pluralis numeri, sive unum excipiatur sive plura, semper talis exceptiva est impossibilis. Unde haec propositio: 'Omnes homines praeter Sortem currunt', et similiter ista: 'Omnes homines praeter Sortem vel Platonem currunt', et ista: 'Omnes homines praeter Sortem et Platonem currunt' sunt impossibiles. Et causa est quia ex duabus illarum sequuntur duo contradictoria inter se contradicentia. Quod ex prima sequitur contradictio probatur, quia sequitur: Omnes homines praeter Sortem currunt; ergo, omnes homines alii a Sorte currunt; sed illi, demonstrando omnes homines, sunt homines alii a Sorte; ergo, illi, demonstrando omnes homines, currunt. Et ultra: Omnes homines currunt; sed Sortes est homo; ergo, Sortes currit. Et ex alia parte sequitur: Omnes homines praeter Sortem currunt; ergo, Sortes non currit. Patet consequentia ab exceptiva ad unam suam exponentem. Et quod illi, demonstrando omnes homines, sunt omnes homines[170] alii a Sorte patet per exponentes quas habet hujus nominis 'alius' sic, quia isti, demonstrando omnes homines, sunt, et Sortes est, et isti, demonstrando omnes homines, non sunt Sortes; ergo, isti, demonstrando omnes homines, sunt alii a Sorte.

8) Sed hic occurrit dubietas de ista propositione: 'Totus Sortes praeter digitum suum est albus'. Et quod ista sit possibilis probatur, quia staret de possibili quod totus Sortes foret albus excepto digito suo; ergo, staret de possibili quod totus Sortes praeter digitum suum foret

---

170 Omnes homines: interlinear.

albus. Patet consequentia a convertibili ad convertibile. Et quod ista sit impossibilis arguitur, quia illa includit duo contradictoria, videlicet, ista: 'Digitus Sortis est albus' et 'Nullus digitus Sortis est albus'. Ergo, ista propositio est impossibilis. Antecedens probatur, quia sequitur: Totus Sortes praeter digitum suum est albus; ergo, nullus digitus Sortis est albus. Patet consequentia ab exceptiva ad unam suam exponentem. Nam in exceptiva affirmativa illud quod excipitur excipitur pro quolibet significato. Et ex alio latere sequitur (15v): Totus Sortes praeter digitum suum est albus; ergo, quaelibet[171] pars alia a digito Sortis est alba. Patet consequentia ab exceptiva ad primam suam exponentem. Et tunc sic: Quaelibet[172] pars alia a digito Sortis est alba; sed quaelibet[173] pars digiti Sortis est pars alia a digito Sortis; ergo, quaelibet[174] pars digiti Sortis est alba. Et tunc sequitur quod digitus Sortis est albus.

9) Hic dico negando primam propositionem tamquam impossibilis. Et ad probationem illius negatur antecedens. Et si aliquis tunc quaerat quomodo tales propositiones quae sunt in parte verae et in parte falsae possunt verificari per exceptionem partis falsae, ut 'Quilibet pars Sortis est alba', dico quod non possunt verificari per propriam exceptionem, sed per circumlocutionem. Unde ista propositio: 'Quaelibet pars Sortis praeter digitum suum est alba' sic verificatur per exceptionem datam per circumlocutionem: 'Quaelibet pars Sortis quae non est digitus nec pars digiti Sortis est alba, et digitus Sortis non est albus'.

10) Quinta regula et ultima in exceptiva affirmativa est ista: Illud quod excipitur excipitur pro quolibet ejus significato, ut hic: 'Omne animal praeter omnem hominem currit'. Hic excipitur omnis homo. Et ideo sic debet exponi: 'Omne animal aliud ab omni homine currit, et nihil quod est omnis homo currit'. Et sic non est in exceptiva negativa.

EXPLICIUNT EXCEPTIVAE COMPILATAE PER REVERENDUM LAVENHAM.

<TRACTATUS QUI DIFFERT ET ALIUD NUNCUPATUR>

1) Notandum quod 'differt' et 'aliud' eodem modo confundunt terminum in propositione. Et sciendum est quod confundunt terminum subsequentem et non praecedentem. Confundere terminum est dupliciter: uno modo confundere terminum est facere terminum stare confuse et distributive mobiliter. Et terminus stat mobiliter quando

---

171   *MS* quilibet.
172   *MS* quilibet.
173   *MS* quilibet.
174   *MS* quilibet.

potest descendere ad sua singularia copulative, ut 'Sortes differt ab homine'. Alio modo confundere terminum est facere ipsum stare confuse tantum, et hoc immobiliter. Et est stare confuse tantum immobiliter quando terminus non contingit descendere ad sua singularia, neque copulative neque disjunctive, sed per propositionem de disjuncto extremo, ut 'Tu differs ab omni homine'.

2) Et notandum quod, quando arguitur ab inferiori ad suum superius a parte praedicati cum hoc verbo 'differt' aut 'aliud' vel cum aliqua alia dictione habente vim negationis, non valet consequentia. Unde non sequitur: Iste homo differt ab isto homine, demonstrando unum alium a se; et iste homo est aliquis homo; ergo, aliquis homo differt ab aliquo homine. Sed arguendo ab inferiori ad suum superius a parte subjecti cum hac dictione 'differt' vel cum aliqua dictione habente vim negationis est consequentia bona, ut: 'Sortes ab isto homine differt; et iste homo est aliquis homo; ergo, Sortes ab aliquo homine differt'. Et ideo ista consequentia non valet: 'Aliquis homo ab aliquo homine differt; ergo, aliquis homo differt ab aliquo homine', sed est fallacia figurae dictionis, quia arguitur a termino stante mobiliter ad terminum stantem immobiliter, quia haec est falsa: 'Aliquis homo differt ab aliquo homine'. Similiter haec est vera: 'Homo homo non est', et haec est falsa: (16r) 'Homo non est homo'. Quod autem prima sit vera probatur sic, quia iste homo homo non est, demonstrando Sortem, quia iste homo Plato non est; et Plato est homo; ergo, iste homo homo non est. Patet consequentia, quia hic arguitur ab inferiori ad suum superius a parte subjecti cum negatione postposita et cum medio termino. Sed haec est falsa: 'Homo non est homo'. Et tunc quando arguitur: 'Homo homo non est; ergo, homo non est homo', negatur consequentia, quia arguitur a termino stante immobiliter ad terminum stantem mobiliter. Similiter haec est vera: 'Aliquis homo aliquis homo non est', et similiter haec: 'Aliquis homo ab aliquo homine est alius', et similiter haec: 'Aliquis homo homini non est idem'. Et sic a parte subjecti quaelibet illarum est vera, et a parte praedicati quaelibet illarum est falsa. Similiter haec est vera: 'Quilibet homo differt a quolibet homine', quia una est universalis cujus quaelibet singularis est vera. Et habet omnes singulares quas nata est habere, quia iste homo differt a quolibet homine, et iste homo differt a quolibet homine, et sic de singulis, quia iste homo est, et quilibet homo est, et iste homo non est quilibet homo; ergo, iste homo differt a quolibet homine. Sed haec est falsa: 'Quilibet homo a quolibet homine differt', quia est una universalis cujus quaelibet singularis est falsa, quia ista singularis est falsa: 'Iste homo a quolibet homine differt', et per illud quaelibet alia est falsa. Et quod ista sit falsa probatur, quia si iste homo a quolibet homine differt, et ipse est homo, ergo ipse differt a se ipso. Consequentia patet, quia iste

terminus 'homine' supponit confuse et distributive, et contingit descendere ad sua singularia copulative. Et quando arguitur sic: 'Quilibet homo differt a quolibet homine; ergo, quilibet homo a quolibet homine differt', negatur consequentia, quia arguitur a termino stante immobiliter ad terminum stantem mobiliter. Similiter haec est vera: 'Quilibet homo est non idem cuilibet homini'. Sed haec est falsa: 'Quilibet homo cuilibet homini est non idem'. Similiter haec est vera: 'Quodlibet animal differt a quolibet animali'. Sed haec est falsa: 'Quodlibet animal a quolibet animali differt'. Similiter haec est vera: 'Cuilibet homini aliquis homo est non idem', quia isti homini aliquis homo est non idem, demonstrando unum alium, et isti homini aliquis homo est non idem, et sic de singulis; ergo, cuilibet homini aliquis homo est non idem. Similiter haec est vera: 'Tu differs ab omni homine'. Sed haec est falsa: 'Tu differs ab aliquo homine'. Et quando sic arguitur: 'Tu differs ab omni homine; et omnis homo est aliquis homo; ergo, tu differs ab aliquo homine', negatur consequentia, quia arguitur a termino stante immobiliter ad terminum stantem mobiliter.

3) Et sciendum est quod haec propositio: 'Aliquis homo differt ab omni homine' debet sic exponi: 'Aliquis homo est, et omnis homo est, et aliquis homo non est omnis homo; ergo, aliquis homo differt ab omni homine'. Similiter haec est vera: 'Tu differs a me et a te', et sic debet exponi: 'Tu es, et ego et tu sumus, et tu non es ego et tu; ergo'. Et tamen haec est falsa: 'A me et a te differs', quia debet sic resolvi: 'Ab hoc differs, et hoc est ego et tu', et hoc est falsum. Haec etiam est vera: 'A me vel a te differs'. Et tamen haec est falsa: 'Tu differs a me vel a te'. Similiter haec est vera: 'Omnis homo est aliud ab omni homine et non aliud ab homine', quia haec est una universalis cujus quaelibet singularis est vera, quia iste homo est aliud ab omni homine et non aliud ab homine, (16v) et iste homo est aliud ab omni homine et non aliud ab homine, et sic de singulis; ergo, omnis homo est aliud ab omni homine et non aliud ab homine. Patet consequentia a singularibus sufficienter numeratis[175] ad eorum universale, et totum antecedens est verum; igitur.

4) Forte tamen quis respondet negando primam consequentiam, et dicendo quod non debet sic exponi per singularia, quia non est universalis sed hypothetica; et si est hypothetica, non est alicujus qualitatis nec quantitatis; et si sic non est consequentia. Si etiam sit hypothetica, tunc oportet quod sit copulativa. Et tunc est una copulativa cujus utraque pars est vera, videlicet, 'Omnis homo est aliud ab omni homine et omnis homo est non aliud ab [omni] homine'. Et sic sequitur omnino quod illa

---

175 *MS* numeratus.

propositio sit vera. Ideo dicendum est quod illa sit vera, et est universalis, quia nulla propositio de copulato extremo vel de disjuncto extremo est hypothetica, sed quaelibet talis est categorica, scilicet, universalis, particularis, indefinita vel singularis.

5) Modo restat dicere qualiter 'sicut', 'quam' et comparativus gradus confundunt terminum in propositione. Et sciendum est quod eodem modo confundunt sicut isti termini 'differt', 'aliud' et 'non idem'. Verbi gratia, capiatur ista propositio: 'Sortes est ita sapiens sicut aliquis homo mundi'. Et ista significat quod Sortes est ita sapiens sicut iste homo mundi, et Sortes est ita sapiens sicut iste homo mundi, et sic de singulis, quia ly 'homo' stat mobiliter, et contingit descendere ad sua singularia compulative. Et ideo istae convertuntur: 'Sortes est ita sapiens sicut aliquis homo mundi' et 'Sortes est ita sapiens sicut iste homo mundi et sicut iste homo mundi et sic de singulis'. Et arguendo ab uno convertibili ad reliquum est consequentia bona, quia sequitur: 'Sortes est ita sapiens sicut aliquis homo mundi; ergo, Sortes est ita sapiens sicut iste homo mundi, et sic de singulis', et e contra: 'Sortes est ita sapiens sicut iste homo mundi et sicut iste homo mundi et sic de singulis; ergo, Sortes est ita sapiens sicut aliquis homo mundi'. Et quod haec propositio sit falsa probatur, quia posito quod aliquis homo sit sapientior Sorte, tunc debet [sic] exponi ratione istius termini 'sicut' sic: 'Sortes est sapiens, et aliquis homo est sapiens, et non aliquis homo est sapientior Sorte'. Similiter ista est vera: 'Sortes est ita sapiens sicut omnis homo', posito quod Cicero, Sortes et Plato sunt omnes homines, et quod Plato sit sapientior Sorte, et Sortes sapientior Cicerone. Tunc Sortes est sapiens, et omnis homo est sapiens, et non omnis homo est ita sapiens sicut Sortes; ergo, Sortes est ita sapiens sicut omnis homo. Consequentia patet ab exponentibus ad expositum. Et minor est verum, quia suum aequipollens est verum, scilicet, quod aliquid quod est homo non est sapientior Sorte. Et hoc est verum, quia Cicero non est sapientior Sorte. Et Cicero est aliquis homo; igitur. Similiter ista propositio est vera: 'Sortes, qui est minus sapiens quam Plato, est ita sapiens sicut omnis homo', posito casu praedicto. Probatur sic per exponentes: 'Sortes, qui est minus sapiens quam Plato, est aliqualiter sapiens, et omnis homo est aliqualiter sapiens, (17r) [et non omnis homo est ita sapiens sicut Sortes; ergo, Sortes, qui est minus sapiens quam Plato, est ita sapiens sicut omnis homo'. Patet consequentia ab exponentibus ad expositum. Et minor est vera, quia sua aequipollens est vera, scilicet, quod aliquid quod est homo non est sapientior Sorte. Et hoc est verum, quia Cicero non est sapientior Sorte; et Cicero est homo; ergo. Similiter ista propositio est vera: 'Sortes, qui est minus sapiens quam Plato, est ita sapiens sicut omnis homo', posito casu praedicto. Probatur per exponentes sic: 'Sortes, qui est minus sapiens quam Plato, est aliqualiter

sapiens, et omnis homo est aliqualiter sapiens,][176] et non omnis homo est sapientior Sorte, qui est minus sapiens quam Plato, quia non Cicero; ergo, Sortes, qui est minus sapiens quam Plato, est ita sapiens sicut omnis homo'. Consequentia patet ab exponentibus ad expositum. Sed contra: Si Sortes, qui est minus sapiens quam Plato, est ita sapiens sicut omnis homo, ergo, nullus homo est sapientior Sorte. Hic respondetur negando consequentiam, quia arguitur a termino stante immobiliter ad terminum stantem mobiliter. Similiter haec est vera: 'Debilissimus homo mundi est ita fortis sicut omne animal', posito quod sint plura animalia et aliquod illorum fortius et aliquod debilius. Tunc probatur conclusio sic per exponentes: Debilissimus homo mundi est aliqualiter fortis, et omne animal est aliqualiter forte, et non omne animal est fortius debilissimo homine mundi; ergo, debilissimus homo mundi est ita fortis sicut omne animal. Et sic de aliis.

6) Nunc dicendum est de comparativo gradu et isto termino 'quam'. Et sciendum quod eodem modo confundunt terminum sicut 'differt'. Et primo declarandum est qualiter comparativus gradus confundit terminum in propositione, quia non confundit terminum nisi mediante hoc adverbio 'magis' vel 'quam', ut 'Sortes est albior aliquo homine', id est, 'Sortes est magis albus quam aliquis homo', quia quilibet comparativus gradus debet exponi per illos terminos 'magis' et 'quam'. Et eodem modo significat ista propositio: 'Sortes est albior aliquo homine' sicut ista: 'Sortes est magis albus quam aliquis homo', et e contra. Et istae duae propositiones convertuntur: 'Sortes est fortior aliquo homine' et 'Sortes est magis fortis quam aliquis homo'. Et sic omnes tales convertuntur, et quaelibet illarum est falsa, quia haec est falsa: 'Sortes est sapientior aliquo homine', quia si ista foret vera, sequeretur quod Sortes foret sapientior se ipso, quod est impossibile, quia eodem modo confundunt terminum in propositione sicut 'differt', 'aliud' et 'non idem'. Et quod ista propositio: 'Sortes, qui est sapientior Platone, non est sapientior aliquo homine' sit vera probatur sic. Et ponitur quod Sortes sit sapientior Platone. Isto posito, probatur conclusio sic, quia Sortes est sapientior Platone, et iste idem Sortes non est sapientior aliquo homine; ergo, Sortes, qui est sapientior Platone, non est sapientior aliquo homine, quia si Sortes est sapientior aliquo homine, ergo Sortes est sapientior isto homine, et isto homine, et sic de singulis, quod est falsum, quia Sortes non est sapientior se ipso. Dum in ista propositione: 'Sortes est sapientior aliquo homine' iste terminus 'homine' stat confuse et distributive mobiliter, quia in quacumque <propositione> (17v) terminus sequitur comparativum gradum vel

---

176 Homoeoteleuton.

aliquem dictionem habentem vim negationis, stat confuse et distributive
nisi aliquod signum universale sequatur illam dictionem habentem vim
negationis. Sed si comparativus gradus praecedit, vel dictio habens vim
negationis, et signum universale cum termino communi subsequatur,
tunc talis terminus[177] stat confuse tantum, et hoc immobiliter. Similiter
haec est vera in casu: 'Sortes est sapientior omni homine', posito quod
sint tres homines, scilicet, Sortes, Plato et Cicero, et quod Plato sit
sapientior Sorte, et Sortes sapientior Cicerone. Tunc ista conclusio
probatur per exponentes sic: Sortes est sapiens, et omnis homo est
sapiens, et non omnis homo est ita sapiens sicut Sortes; ergo, Sortes est
sapientior omni homine. Consequentia patet ab exponentibus ab expositum. Et quod illa eadem sit falsa probatur, quia Sortes non est
sapientior Platone; et Plato est aliquis homo; ergo, Sortes non est
sapientior aliquo homine. Et tunc ultra: Sortes non est sapientior aliquo
homine; ergo, aliquis homo est sapientior Sorte; et si aliquis homo sit
sapientior Sorte, ergo Sortes non est sapientior omni homine. Dicendum
est quod prima consequentia non valet, haec, scilicet, 'Sortes non est
sapientior Platone; et Plato est aliquis homo; ergo, Sortes non est
sapientior aliquo homine', quia hic arguitur ab inferiori ad suum
superius a parte praedicati cum comparativo gradu. Similiter haec est
vera: 'Animal quod est debilius musca est fortius omni animali', posito
quod fuit tria animalia, *a b c*. Sit *a* musca et *b* aliquod animal debilius
musca. Sit *c* animal debilius *b*. Isto posito, probatur conclusio sic: *b*
animal debilius musca est aliqualiter forte, et omne animal est
aliqualiter forte, et non omne animal est ita forte sicut *b*. Quod
probatur, quia aequipollet huic: 'Aliquod animal non est ita forte sicut
b animal', et hoc est verum, quia *c* animal non est ita forte sicut *b*
animal. Ergo, conclusio vera. Et quod sit falsa probatur sic: Animal
quod est fortius omni animali est fortius musca; et nihil quod est fortius
musca est debilius musca; ergo, non est ita quod animal quod est fortius
omni animali est debilius musca. Ad hoc dico quod ista consequentia
non valet. Et quando arguitur: 'Animal quod est debilius musca est fortius omni animali', ly 'musca' stat confuse et distributive. Et quando
arguitur: 'Non est ita quod animal quod est fortius omni animali est
debilius musca', ly 'animali' supponit confuse tantum. Et arguendo a
termino stante confuse et distributive ad terminum stantem confuse
tantum non valet consequentia; ergo, etc. Similiter ista: 'Sortes currens
tardius [tardius] Platone currit velocius omni homine' est vera, posito
quod tres homines currant, scilicet, Sortes[178] et Plato et Cicero, et quod

---

177 Interlinear.
178 Interlinear.

Sortes currat tardius Platone et Cicero tardius Sorte. Isto posito, probatur conclusio sicut aliae praecedentes. Et sic possunt probari omnes consimiles.

EXPLICIT TRACTATUS QUI DIFFERT ET ALIUD NUNCUPATUR COMPILATUS PER LAVENHAM.

Indiana University, Bloomington.

HENRY OF HARCLAY'S DISPUTED QUESTION ON THE PLURALITY OF FORMS

Armand Maurer C.S.B.

THE controversy over the unity or plurality of substantial forms in man and other composite substances was one of the most heated in the late thirteenth and early fourteenth centuries.[1] The subject was discussed in the early part of the thirteenth century, particularly in its bearing on the unity of man and the solution of the body-soul problem, but only after 1270, the likely date of the public dispute on the subject between Thomas Aquinas and John Pecham at Paris, did the controversy become acrimonious.[2] The condemnation of the doctrine of the unity of substantial form by Robert Kilwardby, archbishop of Canterbury, in 1277, and by his successor John Pecham in 1286, because of the theological errors to which it allegedly leads, lent fuel to the fire by making the plurality of forms a test of Christian orthodoxy.[3] It also solidified the rift between Oxford and Paris over this issue. As Thomas of Strasbourg wrote:

> In England it is held that in man there are several substantial forms, and the opposite will be condemned as erroneous; but Paris holds entirely the opposite.[4]

---

1 On the problem of the unity of substantial form, as it relates to the present article, see E. Hocedez, *Richard de Middleton, sa vie, ses œuvres, sa doctrine* (Louvain, Paris 1925), pp. 199-204, 389-394, 454-477. R. Zavalloni, *Richard de Mediavilla et la controverse sur la pluralité des formes* (Louvain, 1951). E. Gilson, *History of Christian Philosophy in the Middle Ages* (New York 1955), pp. 416-420. D. A. Callus, *The Condemnation of St. Thomas at Oxford* (Westminster, Maryland, 1946); "The Problem of the Plurality of Forms in the Thirteenth Century. The Thomist Innovation," *L'Homme et son destin (Actes du premier congrès international de philosophie médiévale)* (Louvain, Paris, 1960), 577-585. "The Origins of the Problem of the Unity of Form," *The Thomist* 24 (1961) 121-149. (Reprinted in *The Dignity of Science*, pp. 257-285). A. Pattin, "Documentation concernant la controverse des formes au moyen âge," *Bulletin de philosophie médiévale*, édité par la Société internationale pour l'étude de la philosophie médiévale, 13 (Louvain, 1971), 71-109. This article lists mediaeval writings on the controversy over forms.

2 On the dispute between Thomas Aquinas and Pecham, see E. Gilson, *op. cit.*, p. 417.

3 See D. A. Callus, *The Condemnation of St. Thomas at Oxford*.

4 "In anglia enim tenetur quod in homine sunt plures formae substantiales, et oppositum eius tamquam erroneum condemnabitur; Parisius vero totum oppositum tenet." Thomas of Strasbourg, *In I Sent.*, q. 2, a. 1, ed. 1490, f. 26ra; quoted by A. Pattin, art. cit., 86.

Henry of Harclay's Disputed Question on the Plurality of Forms, written a generation after the condemnations by Kilwardby and Pecham,
shows that during this period the debate had lost none of its relevance.
The Question was a product of Harclay's teaching at Oxford shortly after 1310, the year he became Master of Theology. Two years later he
was elected Chancellor of the University.[5] With these Oxford con-
nections, it is not surprising that he champions the doctrine of the
plurality of forms and recalls the condemnations of the opposing
position by the two archbishops of Canterbury. He is critical of the
Parisian masters, especially Thomas Aquinas and Henry of Ghent, for
upholding the unity of substantial form. Their positions were well
known to him, for he had been a student in theology at Paris around
the turn of the century, reading the *Sentences* under Duns Scotus.

In Harclay's view, Thomas Aquinas stands out as the only master who
held the pure position that there is only one substantial form in man
and in all other composite substances.[6] This is an echo of Pecham's
remark that before the time of St. Thomas "the whole world" held the
doctrine of the plurality of forms. Recent historians have found reason
to temper this judgement: earlier theologians, such as John Blund, have
been found to have taught the unity of substantial form.[7] But the impact of St. Thomas' unequivocal and masterly defense of the unity of
substantial form was so profound at the end of the century that its
earlier defenders appear to have been forgotten.

Against Aquinas, Harclay not only cites the condemnations of his
position by Kilwardby and Pecham, but he finds both theological and
philosophical reasons for denying it. If there were only one substantial
form in Christ, namely his rational soul, how could his body lying in the
tomb be said to be the same flesh that hung upon the cross, as the
Catholic faith holds ? The living and dead flesh of Christ would have no
substantial form in common. So we are compelled to maintain that
there is another substantial form in Christ, a corporeal form, that
remained the same throughout Christ's life and death.[8]

A correct understanding of the eucharist leads to the same conclusion, according to Harclay. The body of Christ, which is the terminus of the eucharistic change of bread, must have a substantial form
different from his rational soul. During the three days of Christ's death

---

5 For Harclay's life, see F. Pelster, "Heinrich von Harclay, Kanzler von Oxford und seine
Quästionen," *Miscellanea Francesco Ehrle*, I (*Studi e Testi* 37) (Rome, 1924), 307-356. A. B. Emden, *A
Biographical Register of the University of Oxford to A. D. 1500*, II (Oxford, 1958), 874ff.

6 See below, p. 129.

7 See *ibid.*, note 1.

8 See below, pp. 137-138.

the consecration of the bread would have terminated in the same body of Christ, even though his rational soul was then separated from it. This shows that, besides his rational soul, Christ's body was endowed with a distinct substantial corporeal form.[9] These and other theological arguments urged by Harclay for the plurality of forms, show how closely this issue was tied up with the theology of the day.

In his philosophical defense of his position, Harclay argues not only that there is a plurality of substantial forms in man, but also that man has in fact two souls, one rational and the other animal. We have in common with brute animals an *anima sensitiva,* which corrupts with the destruction of the body, and also an incorruptible intellectual soul. Incidentally, Harclay in other Disputed Questions criticizes Aquinas for teaching that the intellectual soul of man is immortal by nature; in his view its immortality is a gift of grace.[10]

St. Thomas' strongest and most distinctive demonstration of the unity of substantial form in a substance is based on the principle that through its substantial form a substance is made to be absolutely (*esse simpliciter*), whereas it is made to be such and such (*esse secundum quid*) through an accidental form. It follows that if a substance had several substantial forms it would not be one being absolutely speaking, but a composite of several. In short, it would not be *one* substance, nor absolutely speaking *one* being.[11]

Harclay's reply to Aquinas distinguishes between two meanings of the words *esse simpliciter*. In one sense this phrase designates the being conferred by every substantial form in distinction to the being imparted by an accidental form. In another sense it means the complete and perfect being that a substance has in a given species. Now every substantial form gives *esse simpliciter* in the first sense, but only the final substantial form gives being in the second. A substantial form may impart to a substance an imperfect substantial being, which is then completed by a further substantial form.[12] In other words, Harclay envisages, along with other defenders of the pluralist doctrine of forms,[13] a hierarchy of substantial forms in a composite substance, such as man, each of which

---

9 See below, pp. 138-139.

10 See A. Maurer, "Henry of Harclay's Questions on Immortality," *Mediaeval Studies* 19 (1957), 79-107; "St. Thomas and Henry of Harclay on Created Nature," *III Congresso internazionale de filosofia medioevale* (Milan, 1966), 542-549.

11 See St. Thomas, *Summa theol.* I, 76, 4. On the Thomistic doctrine of the unity of man, see A. C. Pegis, "Some Reflections on *Summa Contra Gentiles* II, 56," *An Etienne Gilson Tribute* (Milwaukee 1959), 169-188; "St. Thomas and the Unity of Man," *Progress in Philosophy* (Milwaukee, 1955), 153-173. E. Gilson, *Le Thomisme*, 6e éd. (Paris, 1965), pp. 248-253.

12 See below, p. 150.

13 See, for example, Richard of Middleton, as reported by E. Hocedez, *op. cit.*, 199-204.

gives the substance a level of substantial being, with only the final form (in man his rational soul) completing the being in its species.

Harclay does not hesitate to draw the inevitable conclusion that a composite substance is in fact made up of several beings : possessing several forms, it is several beings. The unity of the substance comes from the final form that completes and perfects it.[14]

Harclay finds the doctrine of Henry of Ghent more to his liking than that of Thomas Aquinas, for it admits a plurality of substantial forms at least in man: a corporeal form (*forma mixti*) that renders man an organized body, and an intellectual soul that gives him rationality, sensitivity, and life. But Henry of Ghent is at fault, in Harclay's view, for denying that man has several souls, and that brute animals as well as men are endowed with a plurality of substantial forms. Harclay is also critical of Henry of Ghent's contention that man's intellectual soul informs primary matter immediately, and not through man's corporeal form.[15]

Henry of Harclay's Question on forms is significant, not for its originality of doctrine or its theological or philosophical profundity. In these respects it is inferior to his Question on Universals, recently edited by Fr. Gedeon Gál.[16] It is the work of a conservative thinker, anxious to maintain Christian orthodoxy, as this was understood in the ecclesiastical circles in which he moved. His vigorous anti-Thomism, here as elsewhere in his Disputed Questions,[17] is attributable to this mentality. The importance of this Question on forms lies rather in the light it sheds on the continuing fourteenth century debate over this embattled issue, and the additional information it gives us concerning the personal views of a notable, though mediocre, Oxford theologian.

Harclay's Disputed Question on the Plurality of Forms is extant in two manuscripts:

> Cod. Vat. Borghes. 171, fols. 13r-15r.
> Cod. Worcester F. 3, fols. 207v-211r.

F. Pelster has described these manuscripts in his pioneering study of Henry of Harclay: "Heinrich von Harclay, Kanzler von Oxford und seine Quästionen," *Miscellanea Francesco Ehrle*, I (*Studi e Testi* 37) (Rome, 1924), 323-324. The Vatican manuscript is usually more correct than the

---

14   See below, p. 152.

15   See below, p. 148.

16   "Henricus de Harclay: Quaestio de Significato Conceptus Universalis," *Franciscan Studies*, 31 (1971), 178-234.

17   See, for example, Harclay's strong attack on St. Thomas' doctrine of the necessary being of some creatures and the natural immortality of created spiritual substances. A. Maurer, "Henry of Harclay's Questions on Immortality."

Worcester. The latter is marred by many omissions of words and phrases, and its readings are often inferior to those of the Vatican manuscript. I have followed the Vatican manuscript except where it can be improved by the Worcester.

UTRUM IN HOMINE SIT ALIQUA FORMA SUBSTANTIALIS PRAETER INTELLECTIVAM

Quod non. Nam tunc intellectiva adveniret enti in actu. Sed omne quod advenit enti in actu accidens est. Ergo intellectiva accidens est.

Oppositum. Nam si non esset alia forma, illa recedente, non maneret eadem quae prius forma aliqua. Ergo post recessum animae Christi a corpore non fuit aliqua forma quae prius; ergo nec idem corpus vel eadem caro. Consequens falsum: ergo etc.[a]

Hic est duplex opinio: Una quae dicit quod tantum est una forma in homine, puta intellectiva, et similiter in omni composito. Alia dicit quod in solo homine duplex est forma substantialis, et in omni alio est tantum una forma. Prima opinio est tantum[b] fratris Thomae,[1] secunda[c] magistri Henrici de Gandavo.[2] Pro prima opinione arguitur multipliciter, probando quod non est in homine nisi una forma simpliciter, secundo quod specialiter non nisi una anima, puta intellectiva.[d]

< OPINIO FRATRIS THOMAE >

Pro prima opinione:[e]

1. Forma accidentalis in hoc differt a forma substantiali, quod accidentalis dat esse secundum quid, et per consequens advenit enti in actu per formam substantialem.[3] Forma substantialis dat esse sim-

---

a   etc.] antecedens W.
b   *Om.* tantum W.
c   secundo V., .2. W.
d   *Add.* id est anima, puta intellectiva W.
e   *Om.* opinione V.

1   St. Thomas, *Summa theologiae,* I, 76, 3-4. For a list of St. Thomas' writings on this subject, see R. Zavalloni, *Richard de Mediavilla et la controverse sur la pluralité des formes* (Louvain 1951), p. 262, n. 1. Harclay's statement that this was the opinion of "only St. Thomas" is an echo of John Pecham's remark that until the time of St. Thomas "the whole world" held the doctrine of the plurality of forms. See *Registrum epistolarum fratris Johannis Peckham,* ed. C. T. Martin (London, 1885) III, p. 866. D. A. Callus has shown that in fact John Blund and other early Parisian masters held that "in man there is only one single soul which imparts vegetative life, sensitivity and reason." See his "The Origins of the Problem of the Unity of Form," *The Thomist* 24 (1961), p. 143.

2   Henry of Ghent, *Quodlibet* IV, q. 13 (Paris 1518; reprint Louvain 1961), fols. 104v-115r; *Quodl.* X, q. 5, fols. 404v-407v. For a list of Henry of Ghent's *Quodlibets* dealing with this subject, see R. Zavalloni, *ibid.,* p. 287, n. 1.

3   St. Thomas, *Summa theol.* I, 76, 4.

pliciter, et per consequens advenit enti in potentia tantum. Et si dicas quod forma accidentalis advenit enti in actu completo, sed forma substantialis potest advenire enti in actu incompleto, contra: tunc[f] nesciretur[g] distinctio inter formam substantialem et accidentalem. Nam ego dicerem tibi etiam quod forma accidentalis, puta albedo, est forma substantialis, quia licet advenit enti in actu per formam substantialem, non tamen completo, et ita nesciretur[g] utrum esset forma accidentalis vel substantialis.

2. Praeterea,[4] secundo, Aristoteles[h] I *Physicorum*[5] dicit quod antiqui qui[i] ponebant materiam primam esse ens[j] in actu, consequenter debeant[k] dicere quod non differt alteratio a generatione. Sed idem sequitur modo, nam subiectum generationis per te est ens in actu. Ergo generatio non differt ab alteratione.

3. Praeterea, V *Physicorum*[6] probat Aristoteles quod generatio non est motus per argumentum hoc: quod movetur est, quod generatur non est. Sed illud non intelligitur nisi de subiecto generationis et motus. Nam quod generatur, ut terminus generationis, illud est, et per consequens subiectum est generationis non ens simpliciter, sed in potentia tantum.

4. Praeterea, sic Aristoteles[l] ibidem[m], V *Physicorum*[7], probat quod generatio non est motus per hoc argumentum[n]: Quod movetur[o] est in loco, sed[p] quod generatur non est in loco. Ergo generatio non est motus. Sed secundum istam opinionem[q] quod est esse tale est in loco. Ergo secundum istam rationem quod est generationis subiectum est in loco. Nam subiectum generationis[r] est compositum ex materia et forma materiali, quam necessario consequitur quantitas, et omne tale est in loco.

5. Praeterea, omnis res habet entitatem a substantiali forma; ergo et

---

f   *Om.* tunc W.
g   nescitur W.
h   secundo Aristoteles] secundum Aristotelem W.
i   *Om.* qui W.
j   *Om;* ens W.
k   debebant W.
l   *Om.* sic Aristoteles W.
m   *Add.* scilicet W.
n   per hoc argumentum] sic W.
o   motus V.
p   *Om.* sed V.
q   rationem W. quod est ... rationem, *om.* V.
r   *Om.* generationis W.

4   St. Thomas, *ibid.*
5   Aristotle, *Physics,* I, 4, 187a30.
6   *Ibid.,* V, 1, 224b35-225b1.
7   *Ibid.,* 225a30-32.

unitatem. Nam ab eodem est aliquid ens et ens unum. Sed si multae formae substantiales sint in eodem composito, ergo illud compositum simpliciter erit plura entia.

6. Confirmat autem[s] doctor[s] qui facit hoc[t] argumentum secundum Aristotelem III *Metaphysicae*[9] contra Platonem, qui dicit quod si esset alia idea animalis et bipedis, animal et bipes non essent idem.

7. Praeterea, arguitur sic per alium doctorem,[10] qui in hoc concordat quantum ad alia composita ab homine. Una generatio terminatur tantum ad unam formam substantialem. Sed omne aliud ab homine generatur unica generatione. Ergo tantum est ibi una forma terminans generationem.

8. Praeterea, per eundem[11] arguitur sic: Si in materia sit possibilitas ad recipiendum plures formas substantiales simul, aut ergo illae educuntur de eadem potentia materiae[u] aut non. Sed de diversis potentiis, non de eadem, propter duo: primo, proprius actus habet propriam potentiam; secundo, quia Commentator[12] dicit, ut ipse allegat,[13] numerus potentiarum in materia est secundum numerum formarum in illa. Ergo oportet quod educantur de diversis potentiis in materia existentibus. Sed cum illae potentiae sint in materia sine ordine, formae perficerent materiam sine ordine, et per consequens generatum non esset unum ens per se, quia partes eius essentiales ordinem non haberent.

9. Item, specialiter arguit[14] quod non sunt[v] plures animae in homine, per rationes et auctoritates. Primo sic: Praedicata quae sumuntur a diversis formis aut sumuntur a formis quae habent ordinem aut a for-

---

s   istud W.
t   istud W.
u   *Om.* materiae W.
v   sint W.

8   St. Thomas, *Summa theol.* I, 76, 3.
9   Aristotle, *Metaphysics* VII, 6, 1045a14.
10 Giles of Rome was sympathetic to this opinion in his early writings, though he abandoned it in his later *De Gradibus Formarum.* See R. Zavalloni, *ibid.,* pp. 272-278. Godfrey of Fontaines also held this opinion to be probable. See R. Zavalloni, *ibid.,* p. 301. It would seem, however, that Harclay has neither of these men in mind. He is likely thinking of Henry of Ghent, who held this view and defended it with many of the arguments recited by Harclay. Harclay later treats of Henry of Ghent's position at much greater length. See Henry of Ghent, *Quodlibet* IV, q. 13, fols. 113v-115r. Godfrey of Fontaines argues in much the same way as Harclay against Henry of Ghent's doctrine in his *Quodlibet* II, q. 7. See M. de Wulf, A. Pelzer, *Les quatre premiers Quodlibets de Godefroid de Fontaines,* II (*Les philosophes belges*) II (Louvain, 1904), pp. 112ff.
11 Henry of Ghent, *Quodlibet* IV, q. 13, fol. 113vF.
12 Averroes, *In XII Metaph.,* c. 11 (Venice 1576), fol. 297rE.
13 Henry of Ghent, *ibid.*
14 St. Thomas, *Summa contra Gentiles,* II, 58, n. 3-4.

mis quae non habent ordinem. Si primo modo, tunc unum de alio praedicatur per se, sed^w tantum secundo modo. Et ponit exemplum: Cum dicitur superficiatum est coloratum, est praedicatio per se secundo modo, quia superficiatum et coloratum^x accipiuntur a diversis formis ordinem habentibus, sicut sunt superficies et color. Eodem modo si animal acciperetur ab una forma, puta sensitiva, et homo ab alia, animal de homine praedicaretur tantum secundo modo dicendi per se, non primo modo. Si autem illae formae non habent ordinem aliquem, tunc praedicatum quod accipitur ab una praedicatur de subiecto accepto ab alia forma per accidens tantum, ut cum dicitur album est dulce, quia dulcedo et albedo sunt formae existentes sine ordine in subiecto. Ergo cum animal praedicatur de homine neque per accidens neque per se secundo modo, sed primo modo, non sumuntur homo et animal a diversis formis, sed ab una tantum.

10. Praeterea, una operatio animae, cum fuerit intensa, impedit aliam, sicut experimur. Hoc autem nullo [V 13r2] modo esset verum, ut dicit,[15] nisi principium istarum operationum esset aliqua una forma et essentia.

11. Praeterea, per auctoritatem: Augustinus in libro *De Ecclesiasticis Dogmatibus*:[16] "Neque enim duas animas in uno homine dicimus, sicut Jacobus et alii quidam Assiriorum scribunt: unam animalem qua animatur corpus, et immixta sit sanguini, et alteram spiritualem quae rationi^y ministret. Sed dicimus unam esse eandemque animam in homine, quae et corpus sua vivificet societate, et semetipsam sua ratione disponit."

12. Praeterea, Augustinus *De Spiritu et Anima*, c.^z 12:[17] "Anima humana, quae in corpore habet esse, et extra corpus anima pariter et spiritus, est non duae animae, spiritualis et rationalis — una qua homo vivat, altera qua homo sapiat — ut quidam putant, sed una et eadem est anima quae in semetipsa vivit per intellectum et corpori vitam praestat per sensum."

13. Praeterea, hoc arguitur per hoc quod, abscedente anima, non

---

w   sed *erased* W.
x   *Om.* est ... coloratum W.
y   ratione V.
z   c. 12] cur W.

15   *Ibid.*, n. 10.
16   Gennadius, *De Ecclesiasticis Dogmatibus*, c. 15; PL 42, 1216. For Gennadius of Marseilles as the author of this work, see A. Bardenhewer, *Patrology* (St. Louis 1908), p. 609; also C. H. Turner, "The Liber Ecclesiasticorum Dogmatum attributed to Gennadius," *The Journal of Theological Studies*, VII (1905), 78-99; VIII (1906), 103-114.
17   *De Spiritu et Anima*, c. 9; PL 40, 784.

manent partes organicae nisi aequivoce; ergo nec aliqua forma complexionalis, eadem ratione. Antecedens probatur per Aristotelem in multis locis. Dicit enim sic in primo libro *De Partibus Animalium*,[18] qui est undecimus liber, non computando librum *De Progressu Animalium*, nec librum *De Causa Motus Animalium*: "Abscedente anima, non plus [W 208r] animal nec partium aliqua eadem relinguitur, nisi figura solum, vel quemadmodum fabulata in lapides permutari." Ergo non fuit alia forma nisi anima.

14. Praeterea, ad idem I *Politicae*[19] dicit Aristoteles sic: "Interempto toto, non erit pes neque manus, nisi aequivoce, ut si quis dicat lapideam." Et probat hoc sic, dicens:[20] "... corrupta enim erat talis. Omnia enim opere[a] sunt[b] definita et virtute. Quare non iam talia existentia[c] non dicendum est eadem essentia sed aequivoca."

15. Praeterea, idem dicit Aristoteles VII *Metaphysicae*,[21] illo capitulo: *Quoniam vero animalium anima*, "si[d] pars hominis definiatur, non sine opere definietur." Ponit exemplum:[22] "Nam digitus mortui et vivi aequivoce est digitus."

16. Praeterea, IV *Meteororum*,[23] ultimo capitulo: "Omnia terminata sunt opere. Quae enim possunt facere eorum opus, vere sunt unumquodque, puta oculus tuus[e] si videt ; quod autem non potest videre nisi aequivoce, puta mortuus aut lapideus." Et quia tu dicis illud tenet[f] in partibus homoeomeriis,[g] quae sunt non unius naturae in toto et parte, cuiusmodi sunt partes organicae, quia quaelibet pars manus non est manus nec quaelibet pars oculi est oculus, sed non[h] valet de partibus homogeniis, id est unius rationis in toto et in[i] parte, illud excludit Aristoteles ibidem,[24] dicens quod ita est[j] eodem modo in[k] carne

a   opera W.
b   sint V.
c   ex natura W.
d   sed W.
e   *Om.* tuus W.
f   illud tenet] identitatem W.
g   ethimologeniis V, ethre[iis] W.
h   nec W.
i   *Om.* in W.
j   *Om.* est W.
k   de W.

18   Aristotle, *De Partibus Animalium*, I, 1, 641a19-22.
19   Aristotle, *Politics*, I, 2, 1253a20-21.
20   *Ibid.*, 1253a23-25.
21   Aristotle, *Metaph.*, VII, 10, 1035b14.
22   *Ibid.*, 1035b25.
23   Aristotle, *Meteors*, IV, 12, 390a10-13.
24   *Ibid.*, 390a14-22.

et osse, sed non est tam manifestum. Et dat causam quare non est[m] ita manifestum in carne, quia non est facile prospicere diversitatem in illis nisi sit valde deperditum, ita quod appareat quod solae figurae manent. Ergo etc.

17. Praeterea, contra opinionem potest argui universaliter quod non est ponenda alia forma nisi una tantum. Non est ponenda pluralitas sine causa et sine necessitate, nam natura agit breviori modo quo potest, secundum Aristotelem V *Physicorum*.[25] Sed una forma tantum faceret quantum plures. Ergo etc.

Probatio assumpti: Nam forma perfectior continet in se imperfectiorem formam, ita quod potest in eadem operatione in qua potest forma imperfectior, ut forma mixti animati formam mixti inanimati, et in elementis similiter forma perfectior imperfectiorem et forma mixti continet formam elementi, ut sensitiva vegetativam, intellectiva utrumque.

Confirmatur. Aristoteles II *De Anima*[26] dicit quod idem[n] in figuris. Sicut enim trigonum continetur in tetragono, ita vegetativum in sensitivo.

18. Praeterea, in natura est ita quod semper generatio unius est corruptio alterius. Ergo nulla forma potest induci nisi prima corrumpatur, nec una removeri nisi alia inducatur. Ergo, recedente anima, necessario nova forma substantialis inducitur, puta cadaveris; et inducta forma intellectiva, necessario expellitur forma praecedens. Ergo etc.

<Opinio Magistri Henrici de Gandavo>

Alia opinio magistri Henrici[27] tenet quod in homine est duplex forma, et in nullo alio. In homine est anima intellectiva et forma mixtionis corporea. Et tria dicit, ut mihi videtur: primo[o] quod est alia forma praeter intellectivam; secundo quod illa non est sensitiva nec vegetativa, sed forma mixti; tertio quod licet sint diversae formae in homine, tamen intellectiva in homine immediate perficit materiam primam sicut forma[p] mixti.

Primum sic ostendit:[28] Generatio, et universaliter omnis mutatio,

l   vel W.
m   *Om.* est W.
n   sicut W.
o   *Om.* primo W.
p   formam W.

25   Aristotle, *Physics*, I, 6, 189a13-16; VIII, 6, 259a7-13.
26   Aristotle, *De Anima*, II, 3, 414b28-32.
27   Henry of Ghent, *Quodlibet* IV, q. 13, fols. 112vB-115rO.
28   *Ibid.*, fol. 112vB.

capit speciem a termino, V *Physicorum*.[29] Modo homo producitur in esse necessario per duplicem actionem, videlicet agentis naturalis hominis generantis, et Dei causantis intellectivam, quae est ex extrinseco. Ergo huius duplicis actionis oportet esse duplicem terminum formalem. Sed anima intellectiva est terminus creationis; ergo alia forma est terminus actionis naturae.

Praeterea, terminus productionis Dei et terminus productionis naturae generantis hominem aut sunt formae tantum (et hoc est propositum), aut sunt totum compositum, et tunc totus homo producitur per actionem naturae, et totus homo similiter per creationem. Et hoc est inconveniens ex utraque parte. Ille enim non causatur cuius aliqua pars praefuit in rerum natura; ex alia parte illud non producitur a natura cuius forma substantialis non est in potestate naturae. Huiusmodi est intellectiva. Ergo etc.

Si opponatur sibi, sicut ipsemet[30] opponit contra pluralitatem formarum in alio composito ab homine, quod istis distinctis formis correspondet in materia una potentia vel duae, ut supra argutum est, respondet quod distinctis formis educibilibus de potentia materiae correspondent diversae potentiae. Sed duabus formis, quarum una educitur de potentia materiae et alia non, sed ab extrinseco, ut intellectiva, illis non correspondet nisi una potentia in materia. Et ideo illa perficiunt materiam secundum eandem potentiam. Ideo contra istam opinionem de pluralitate formarum in homine non vadit argumentum, sed contra plures formas in alio composito.

Secundo dicit[31] quod alia forma in homine non est vegetativa nec sensitiva. Quod sic probat: Nam intellectivum continet perfective vegetativum et sensitivum, sed tamen intellectivum propter sui immaterialitatem excludit formam mixtionis propter suam impuritatem.[q] Et ideo forma quae est in homine cum intellectiva est forma mixtionis, non sensitiva nec vegetativa.

Dicit[r] tertio[32] quod forma mixti non mediat inter materiam primam et[s] intellectivam formam, ita ut constituat aliquod compositum perfectibile primo ab intellectiva. Immo intellectiva immediate perficit materiam primam, determinatam tamen per formam mixtionis. Sed illa

---

q   puritatem V.
r   De W.
s   *Om.* et ... primam W.

29   Aristotle, *Physics*, V, 1, 224a21-225b9.
30   Henry of Ghent, *Quodlibet* IV, q. 13, fol. 113vF.
31   Henry of Ghent, *Quodlibet* II, q. 3, fol. 31Q; *Quodlibet* III, q. 6, fol. 54BC.
32   Henry of Ghent, *Quodlibet* IV, q. 13, fols. 112vB-113rC.

forma mixtionis mediat inter intellectivam et materiam, non ratione perfectibilis sed ratione dispositionis.

Ulterius dicit in alio *Quolibet* 10[33] quod,[t] licet sit alia forma in homine [V 13v1] quam intellectiva, quia forma mixtionis, tamen recedente intellectiva, non manet eadem forma mixtionis quae prius, quia prius intellectiva[u] non recedit nisi propter corruptionem alicuius formae in homine, et hoc maxime quia corruptio unius est generatio alterius, et e converso. Et ideo recedente intellectiva, introducitur nova forma cadaveris. Sed subdit[34] quod in Christo miraculose conservata fuit eadem forma mixtionis quae prius, et non in aliis hominibus. Unde eadem caro Christi quae fuit in cruce posita fuit in sepulcro, sicut probat[35] per multas auctoritates, sed non in aliis hominibus. Unde ipse non[v] approbat[w] articulum damnatum in Anglia, ut dicit, sextum articulum[x] qui dicit sic:[36] "Corpus cuiuslibet sancti vel hominis mortui, antequam sit[y] per putrifactionem mutatum in auras vel elementa, non esse idem numero cum[z] corpore eius vivo nisi secundum quid et ratione materiae communis, ut illa quae invicem transmutantur, ut caro et vermis." Illud non approbat, ut dicit,[37] nisi quatenus sequitur ex octavo articulo, sicut dicit condemnator.[38] Est autem octavus articulus sic:[39] "Quod in homine est tantum una forma, scilicet anima rationalis, et nulla alia forma substantialis; ex qua < opinione > videntur sequi omnes haereses supradictae." Illud approbat,[40] et dicit quod revera illud est haereticum; et opinio alia sequitur ex illa, non[a] tamen est haeretica, licet forsan falsa, quia ex falso potest sequi verum, sed ex vero non sequitur falsum.

---

t   quod licet sit] quolibet sic W.
u   *Om.* intellectiva W.
v   *Om.* non W.
w   probat W.
x   sextum articulum] scilicet articulus W.
y   antequam sit] aut sic W.
z   in W.

a   *Om.* V, *add. interlin. by later hand* W.

33   Henry of Ghent, *Quodlibet* X, q. 5, fols. 404vC-405rC.
34   *Ibid.*, fol. 405F, 406L.
35   *Ibid.*, fol. 406IK.
36   *Registrum Epistolarum Fratris Johannis Peckham*, ed. C. T. Martin (London, 1885), III, pp. 922-923.
37   Henry of Ghent, *Quodlibet* X, q. 5, fol. 410C.
38   Johannes Peckham, *Registrum Epistolarum*, p. 923.
39   *Ibid.*
40   Henry of Ghent, *Quodlibet* X, q. 5, fol. 410C.

\<Contra Opinionem Fratris Thomae\>

Contra opinionem primam, primo per rationes theologicas, secundo per rationes[b] philosophicas.

\<Per Rationes Theologicas\>

Primo per articulos damnatos. Robertus Cantuariensis dicit [W 208v] sic, articulo septimo:[41] "Omnes formae priores corrumpuntur per adventum ultimae: error." Item, articulus quindecim:[c] "Corpus vivum et corpus[d] mortuum sunt aequivoce dicta."[42] Item, omnes articuli Johannis Cantuariensis[43] sunt contra hoc, et excludit quantum potest omnes circumstantias evasionis.

Praeterea, videtur esse contra illud quod tenemus fide catholica. Ita enim scriptum est:[44] "Sicut anima rationalis et caro unus est homo, ita Deus et homo unus est Christus." Constans est quod distinguit inter carnem et animam, quae sunt duae partes hominis. Quid ergo intelligit per carnem nisi compositum ex forma substantiali et materia? Et habetur propositum, quod forma carnis est alia a forma intellectiva.

Si intelligit materiam primam — contra: Prima materia non plus est caro quam lapis; ergo non plus diceret unum ex anima rationali et carne quam ex anima rationali et lapide. Nec potes dicere quod per carnem intelligit compositum ex materia prima et intellectiva, quia tunc non distingueretur, quia ex anima intellectiva et toto composito non fit unus homo.

Praeterea, Christus fuit[e] univoce homo nobiscum, non est dubium. Ergo in Christo non fuit nisi una forma, scilicet intellectiva. Consequens falsum, quia tunc caro quae iacuit in sepulcro non fuit eadem caro quae pendebat in cruce, quia nulla forma substantialis manet quae prius. Consequens falsum et contra fidem catholicam. Unde Ambrosius

---

b   *Om.* per rationes W.
c   *Om.* articulus quindecim W.
d   *Om.* corpus W.
e   *Om.* fuit W.

41   "7. Item quod intellectiva introducta corrumpitur sensitiva et vegetativa." *Chartularium Universitatis Parisiensis,* ed. H. Denifle and A. Chatelain (Paris, 1889), I, p. 559.

42   "13. Item quod corpus vivum et mortuum est equivoce corpus, et corpus mortuum secundum quod corpus mortuum sit corpus secundum quid." *Ibid.* The editors note that the manuscripts contain different forms of these errors, p. 560.

43   Johannes Peckham, *Registrum,* III, pp. 922-923.

44   Symbolum "Quicunque" ("Athanasianum"); H. Denzinger, A. Schonmetzer, *Enchiridion Symbolorum* (Friburg im Breisgau, etc. 1967), p. 42, n. 76.

in libro *De Sacramentis*,[45] et auctorizatur per ecclesiam, de nono distinctione, capitulo secundo: *Omnia quaecumque*, etc[f].[46] Et Magister ponit in libro quarto, distinctione undecimo:[47] "*Ego sum panis vivus, qui de caelo descendi* (Johannes 6),[48] et iterum:[49] *Panis quem ego dabo caro mea est pro mundi vita.* Ex his duabus sententiis aperte datur intelligi quod panis ille Christus est; et iste non duo, sed unus panis et una caro procul dubio unum efficitur corpus, illud vere, illud sane,[g] quod sumptum est de virgine, quod passum est et sepultum, quod surrexit." (Nota quod in littera Magistri non[h] habetur quod passum est et sepultum, sed in originali habetur).[50] Modo, nihil esset verum de isto, data opinione. Nam si alia est forma omnino substantialis in carne viva et mortua, non fuit eadem caro quae fuit in sepulcro et quae in cruce, non plus quam eadem caro hominis[i] de qua caro Christi fuit generata per alimentum vel caro virginis.

Praeterea, sanguis qui fluxit[j] de latere Christi, ipso mortuo, non fuisset idem, nisi aequivoce, cum sanguine ipsius vivi. Cum ergo sacramenta habent efficaciam a sanguine fluente de latere Christi, sicut omnes dicunt,[51] et habetur *De Consecratione*,[k] distinctio 2,[52] non habuerit[l] efficaciam a Christo nisi per accidens et secundum quid.

Praeterea, terminus conversionis panis in corpus Christi virtute verborum sacramentalium est non materia prima nec anima intellectiva, quia anima intellectiva non est ibi nisi per concomitantiam. Ergo oportet esse aliquod corpus habens substantialem formam praeter intellectivam.

Huic respondetur diversimode. Nam aliqui dicunt quod conversio fit in totum compositum ex anima et materia, ut totum habet esse cor-

---

f   *Om.* etc. W.
g   cane V.
h   *Om.* non W.
i   bovis W.
j   fluit W.
k   Consideratione W.
l   habuit W.

---

45   St. Ambrose, *De Sacramentis*, IV, c. 4; PL 16, 458-462; VI, c. 5, 478-482.
46   *Codex Iuris Canonici*, ed. A. Friedbert; III, d. 2, c. 74 (Leipzig, 1879), I, 1344-1345.
47   Peter Lombard, *Libri IV Sententiarum*, IV, d. ii, c. 2 (Quaracchi, 1916), II, p. 804.
48   John 6 : 51.
49   John 6 : 52.
50   That is, these words are in the *Codex Iuris Canonici* but not in Lombard's text. See *Codex*, 1345.
51   See St. Thomas, *Summa theol.*, III, 64, 2, ad 3m. ; St. Augustine, *Ennaratio in Psalmum cxxxviii*, 2; PL 37, 1785; P. Lombard, *Collectanea in Epist. D. Pauli ad Romanos*, 26; PL 191, 1392.
52   *Corpus Iuris Canonici*, III, d. 2, c. 83; ed. cit., I, 1348.

poreum per animam intellectivam.[m] Alii[53] dicunt quod conversio fit in materiam ut habet esse corporeum ab anima intellectiva.[n]

Contra illud: Quia hoc sacramentum a principio suae institutionis habet eandem rem sacramenti; fuit autem institutum in cena ante passionem. Accipio ergo hostiam consecratam in cena illa. In triduo mortis haberet eandem rem sacramenti quam ante passionem, sed modo post mortem ante resurrectionem non fuit materia habens esse corporeum per intellectivam. Ergo cum manet res sacramenti, illud non est materia habens esse corporeum. Eodem modo, si consecratur hostia in triduo, idem sequitur.

Si dicatur ad argumentum praetactum de identitate corporis mortui et vivi, quod manet idem corpus, sed corpus significat habentem corporeitatem, et idem est habens corporeitatem quia idem est suppositum — contra: Illud non solvit auctoritatem, nam illa dicit quod fuit eadem caro quae prius, quod non potest esse verum de supposito tantum.[o] Item, non plus esset una caro quam si esset conversa in lapidem, quia manet idem suppositum.

Praeterea, impossibile est cadaver uniri verbo divino sine nova assumptione. Sed nova assumptio non fuit ibi. Ergo etc. Probo antecedens, nam assumptio[p] naturae a supposito[q] non est nisi determinatio[r] dependentiae naturae creatae ad suppositum divinum, eo genere quo natura dependet ad suppositum. Modo natura composita ex materia et forma non minus dependet ratione materiae ad suppositum quam ratione formae, immo ratione[s] utriusque. Necesse est enim utrumque suppositum aequaliter. Ergo nulla nova forma fuisset introducta in materia sine nova assumptione. Erroneum est autem dicere quod fuit nova assumptio. Quare etc.

Praeterea, persuasio theologica potest esse. Quare enim magis deberem venerari corpus sancti Petri quam corpus vermis nascentis de cadavere Petri, cum utrobique sit aequalis unitas, quia unitas[t] materiae primae ? Item, et canem et[u] lupum qui comedisset Petrum et fuisset

---

m   per animam intellectivam] vel anima intellectiva W.
n   Om. Alii ... intellectiva W.
o   Om. tantum W.
p   Om. non ... assumptio W.
q   a supposito] assumptae W.
r   terminatio W.
s   Om. ad ... ratione W.
t   Om. quia unitas W.
u   vel V.

53   Giles of Rome, De Gradibus Formarum, III, 2 (Venice, 1502), fol. 212; St. Thomas, Summa theol. III, 75, 6, ad 2.

nutritus de carne Petri deberet venerari, [V 13v2] quia materia prima manet eadem utrobique.

Et hic^v respondet Magister Henricus, 10 *Quolibet*,[54] quod magis cadaver Petri debet venerari quam vermis propter ordinem immediatum ad corpus Petri vivum, quem ordinem non habet vermis vel canis. Nam naturali resolutione corpus Petri dissolvitur in cadaver, et forma cadaveris nata est succedere immediate formae corporis vel carnis in eadem parte materiae, et hoc per resolutionem naturalem.

Contra illud est Augustinus, I *De Civitate Dei*, c. 13.[55] Ostendit^w enim Augustinus^x ex intentione congruitatem curae sepulturae mortuorum, praecipue bonorum hominum. Et dat duas causas: una quia ipsa fuerunt organa quibus usus est Spiritus Sanctus. Alia causa, quia corpora non sunt sicut vestimenta,^y sed sunt pars naturae nostrae. Sed nec cadaver unquam fuit organum Spiritus, nec hoc corpus si sit nova forma, nec hoc pertinebat ad naturam nostram nisi ratione materiae primae, et eodem modo canis vel vermis. Ergo deberem sepelire^a lupum qui manducasset^b patrem meum. Unde verba Augustini:[56] "Nec contemnenda nec abicienda sunt corpora mortuorum, et maxime iustorum, quibus^c tanquam organis et vasis ad omnia bona opera usus est Spiritus Sanctus."

Praeterea, Augustinus fuit quandoque istius opinionis, quod anima dat esse corpori, et quod corpus ea ratione est qua animatur, et postea retractavit. Unde in libro *De Immortalitate Animae,*^d versus finem,[57] dicit sic: "A summa essentia species corpori per animam attribuitur, qua est in quantum^e est. Per animam ergo corpus subsistit, et eo ipso est quo animatur, sive universaliter ut mundus, sive particulariter ut unumquodque animal intra^f mundum^g." Quapropter consequens erat^h ut

---

v   Et hic] Huic W.
w   quoniam W.
x   *Om.* Augustinus W.
y   nescita W.

a   spe^{re} W.
b   manducaret W.
c   qui W.
d   *Om.* Animae W.
e   quacumque W.
f   infra VW.
g   *Om.* mundum W.
h   *Om.* erat W.

54   Henry of Ghent, *Quodlibet* X, q. 6, fol. 414D.
55   St. Augustine, *De Civitate Dei*, I, 13; *CC* XLVII (Turnhold, 1955), p. 14.
56   *Ibid.*, lines 1-4.
57   St. Augustine, *De Immortalitate Animae*, c. 15; PL 32, 1033.

per animam fieret corpus. Certe hic videtur loqui pro unitate formarum. Modo Augustinus libro primo *Retractationum,* c. 5,[58] dicit quod
hoc totum temerarie [W 209r] dictum est.[i] Certum est quod non retrac-
taret, nisi esset falsum. Ergo etc.

Aliqui magni hoc dixerunt, quod Augustinus postea retractavit
retractationem[k] in primo capitulo primi libri *Retractationum.* Unde dicit:[l]
"Illud quod temere[m] putam esse dictum in libro *De Immortalitate Animae,*
non quia[n] hoc falsum esse[o] confirmo, sed quia nec verum esse comprehendo."[59] Contra: Illud non valet; immo falsum accipitur. Nam duo
dixerat[p] in libro *De Immortalitate Animae:*[60] quod[q] anima dat speciem
corpori qua corpus est, et similiter quod animal est mundus. Modo
libro primo *Retractationum,*[61] in[r] rectractando librum[s] *De Immortalitate
Animae,* rectractavit totum, dicens: "Hoc totum temerarie dictum est."
Sed postea, capitulo 10,[62] retractando librum *De Musica,* corrigit retractationem quantum ad unum, scilicet quod animal sit mundus, sed non
quantum ad aliud; immo[t] illud manet simpliciter non retractatum.
Unde ipse dicit sic, capitulo 10:[63] "Animal esse mundum, sicut Plato
sensit[u] aliique philosophi plurimi, nec ratione certa[v] indagare potui, nec
divinarum scripturarum auctoritate persuaderi posse cognovi. Unde
tale aliquid a me dictum, quo illud accipi possit etiam in libro *De Immortalitate Animae,* temere dictum putavi. Non quia hoc[w] falsum esse
confirmo, sed quia nec verum esse comprehendo, quod sit animal mundus." Unde de alio dicto non facit aliquam mentionem, et male fuit allegatum, nec esset recitatione dignum, nisi quia fuit a magno[wa] dictum.

i   *Om.* est W.
k   *Om.* retractationem W.
l   *Om.* dicit W.
m   tenere W.
n   quid V.
o   est W.
p   dixerant W.
q   quia W.
r   *Om.* in W.
s   *Om.* librum W.
t   *Om.* immo W.
u   sentit W.
v   ratione certa] idem dicta W.
w   *Om.* hoc W.
wa magistro W.
58 St. Augustine, *Libri Retractationum,* I, c. 5, n. 3; PL 32, 591.
59 St. Augustine, *Libri Retract.* I, c. 11, n. 4; PL 32, 602.
60 St. Augustine, *De Immortalitate Animae,* c. 15; PL 32, 1033.
61 St. Augustine, *Libri Retract.* I, c. 5, n. 3; PL 32, 591.
62 *Ibid.,* c. 11, n. 4; PL 32, 602.
63 *Ibid.*

Contra eandem primam Opinionem per Rationes Philosophicas

Primo Commentator, tertio libro[x] *Caeli et Mundi*, commento 71:[64] "Necesse est, cum ex elementis generatur una forma, ut corrumpantur formae eorum secundum medietatem. Quoniam si corrumperentur[y] secundum totum, tunc prima materia reciperet primo et essentialiter omnes formas,[z] et non reciperet omnes[a] formas compositorum mediantibus istis corporibus." Ista auctoritas non potest glosari, quoniam si sint simul plures formae in materia, scilicet elementorum, sub esse remisso, et forma mixti, quia formae elementorum non corrumpuntur secundum totum.

Praeterea, contra opinionem magistri Henrici,[65] qua dicitur quod formae duae perficiunt materiam immediate, et non una mediante altera, est ista auctoritas expresse, nam reducit ad hoc inconveniens, quod omnis forma immediate perficeret materiam. Nec valet dicere quod immediatio est duplex, vel causae vel effectus: primo modo perficitur materia per formam elementarem immediate, et deinde per formam mixti, non quod una sit pars perfectibilis ab alia. Sed illud non solvit auctoritatem. Ipse enim arguit sic:[66] Si formae corrumperentur secundum totum, forma mixti immediate ingrediretur materiam primam, et non mediantibus illis. Modo, si forma mixti perficeret immediate materiam primam, istud inconveniens sequeretur, scilicet formae manent sicut et corrumpantur; et nihil valet argumentum commenti, et[b] per consequens quod certum est.

Ideo doctor[67] tenens oppositum positi, scilicet quaestio 76, dicit quod opinio commenti est magis impossibilis quam opinio Avicennae[68] ponentis[c] formas elementorum manere[d] integras in mixto et non remissas. Primo quia formae consistunt in indivisibili, secundum Aristotelem IX *Metaph.*[69] Sunt enim sicut numeri, ubi numero addito vel

---

x   tertio libro] primo W.
y   corrumpentur W.
z   *Om.* formas W.

a   *Om.* omnes W.
b   *Om.* et W.
c   ponit W.
d   manere] in aere W.

64   Averroes, *In III De Caelo et Mundo*, c. 67 (Venice, 1574) V, fol. 227BC.
65   Henry of Ghent, *Quodlibet* IV, q. 13, fols. 107rZ; 112vC.
66   Averroes, *ibid.*
67   St. Thomas, *Summa theol.* I, 76, 4, ad 4.
68   This doctrine is attributed to Avicenna by Averroes, *In I De Generatione et Corruptione*, c. 90 (Venice, 1574) V, fol. 370K. See St. Thomas, *Summa theol.* I, 76, 4, ad 4.
69   Aristotle, *Metaph.* VII, 3, 1044a7-12.

remoto est species variata; et ideo non suscipiunt magis et minus. Nec
< minus >[e] est impossibile aliquid esse medium inter substantiam et ac-
cidens, ut Commentator dicit.[70] Ideo ipse[71] dicit aliter ad argumentum[f]
de mixtione, quod formae elementorum manent in mixto non actu sed
virtute. Et quid est hoc subdicit,[72] quia[g] manent qualitates propriae
elementorum, sed remissae. Et in his est virtus formarum elementarium.
Quidquid sit de hoc, sufficit mihi quod[h] intentio[i] Commentatoris fuerit
in contrarium, et auctoritas sua eadem facilitate contemnitur qua ap-
probatur, nam Commentator respondet faciliter.

Praeterea,[k] probo secundum ipsum quod nunquam erit mixtio, sed
tantum iuxtapositio. Illa quae non possunt[l] misceri nisi[m] prius corrumpantur, illa[n] nunquam miscentur. Sic enim possum dicere quod ignis
posset comburere postquam extinguitur. Sed elementa prius natura
corrumpantur[o] quam misceantur. Per te ergo mixta nunquam[p] miscentur, nisi volueris dicere quod eorum mixtio sit eorum una numero[q]
corruptio. Et tunc possum dicere[r] quod ex quatuor elementis per mix-
tionem consurgit unum elementum, ignis vel[s] aqua. Nam possibile est
ignem consumere aquam et terram, et in materiam illorum inducere[t]
suam formam; nec alio modo generatur mixtum ex eis.

Praeterea, probo quod mixtum animatum[u] est realiter[v] simplicius vel
ita simplex[w] sicut est elementum. Nam illud[x] compositum quod con-

e   See St. Thomas, *Summa theol.* I, 76, 4, ad 4.
f   primum W.
g   quod W.
h   quia W.
i   intentio *deleted* W. unius *in mar.*
k   *Om.* Praeterea W.
l   ponunt W.
m   ut W.
n   iam W.
o   *Om.* corrumpantur W.
p   *Om.* nunquam W.
q   unanimus V. *Om.* mixtio sit eorum W.
r   possum dicere] dicere posse W.
s   sub W.
t   reducere W.
u   diminiatum W.
v   *Om.* realiter W.
w   simplicius vel ita simplex] ita simplex vel simplicius W.
x   *Add.* ad W.

70   Averroes, *In III De Caelo et Mundo*, c. 67 (Venice, 1574) V, fol. 227C.
71   St. Thomas, *Summa theol.* I, 76, 4, ad 4.
72   *Ibid.*

stituitur^y ex forma simpliciori^z et materia aeque simplici^a est compositum magis simplex. Sed compositum ex materia et anima intellectiva, scilicet homo, est^b huiusmodi, nam intellectiva est simplicior^c quam forma ignis, cum non sit extensa, neque per se neque per accidens. Et universaliter forma perfectior est realiter simplicior. Ergo homo est simplicius quam ignis realiter vel lapis, saltem ubi non sunt diversae partes^d [V 14r1] organicae.

Praeterea,^e tu dicis^{73} quod qualitates elementorum manent in mixto, sed remissae. Aut ergo eaedem^f numero quae fuerunt in elementis, quod non est possibile; tunc enim migraret accidens de subiecto in subiectum. Ergo sunt aliae^g de novo generatae, similes qualitatibus elementorum. Ergo nulla mixtio, quia istae qualitates consequuntur unam formam tam simplicem sicut est forma elementi. Ergo in substantia mixti nulla est compositio magis quam in elemento.

Praeterea, probo quod ex uno tantum elemento natum est generari mixtum, sicut ex omnibus; immo superfluit^h omnia praeter unum. Passo existente summe disposito, et agente approximato, consurgit actio. Sed materia prima existens^i sub forma ignis ex parte sui est summe disposita ad receptionem formae mixti, dum tamen sit spoliata forma quam^j habet. Ergo agens illud^k naturale quod habet in potestate sua activa potest producere formam lapidis, potest de igne pure facere lapidem vel asinum.

Praeterea, omnis dispositio quam induceret agens naturale ante inductionem^l ultimae formae non esset nisi remotio prohibentis, sicut divellens calumnam respectu generationis. Nam materia est de se apta nata perfici immediate per omnem formam, nec requiritur nisi remotio

---

y   *Om.* quod constituitur W.
z   simpliciter W.

a   simpliciter W.
b   et W.
c   simpliciter W.
d   *Om.* quam ... partes W.
e   *Om.* Praeterea W.
f   eodem W.
g   animae W.
h   superflua W.
i   exequens W.
j   sua W.
k   idem W.
l   individuum W.

73   *Ibid.*

prohibentis. Ergo[m] accidit generationi cuiuscumque rei naturalis quod praecedat talis vel talis dispositio. Ideo quodcumque agens, removens formam praecedentem, sufficeret pro dispositione. Ergo non est ordo essentialis in generatione rei naturalis.

Praeterea, Aristoteles I *Caeli et Mundi*[74] dicit quod mixtum movetur secundum naturam elementi praedominantis in eo. Sed si elementum non manet in mixto realiter, illud non esset[n] verum.

Praeterea, arguo ex parte nutritionis. Nam per virtutem nutritivam corrumpitur forma alimenti,[o] scilicet panis, et materia induit[p] formam membri vel carnis, secundum processum Aristotelis.[75] Quaero:[q] Quam formam recipit in homine? Non intellectivam certum est. Nam impossibile est quod illud agens in cuius potestate activa non est forma, quod illud[r] informet aliquam materiam per formam illam quae non[s] est in sua potestate activa. Ergo materia panis non acquirit intellectivam virtute nutrimenti;[t] ergo aliam formam, et substantialem, constat. Ergo in homine est alia [W 209v] forma quam forma substantialis.

Praeterea, arguo quod sunt duae animae necessario in homine. Nam si intellectiva contineret in virtute sensitivam, cum illud quod est virtualiter tale est perfectius tale quam illud quod est formaliter tale, intellectiva esset sentiens[u] perfectius quocumque modo sensitivo et quocumque genere sensus.[v] Consequens falsum et contra Aristotelem II *De Anima,* capitulo de odore.[76] Dicit enim quod sensum hunc habemus peiorem multis animalibus; ita est in[w] aliis sensibus multis. Dicit[77] quod hoc est ex dispositione[x] organi vel alicuius alterius praeter intellectivam formam et sensitivam. Contra: Intellectiva, secundum istos,[78] continet in virtute formam mixti complexionalis, sicut continet formam sensitivae.

---

m   sicut W.
n   est W.
o   elementi W.
p   inducit W.
q   quia W.
r   illa W.
s   quae non] qualiter W.
t   mixti W.
u   *blank space* W.
v   sensu W.
w   de W.
x   definitione W.

---

74   Aristotle, *De Caelo,* I, c. 1, 269a2.
75   Aristotle, *De Anima,* II, c. 4, 416a18-416b31.
76   Aristotle, *De Anima* II, 9, 421a10.
77   Aristotle, *ibid.,* 421a23.
78   St. Thomas, *Summa theol.* I, 76, 3.

Ergo complexionem perfectiorem in omni parte corporis causabit quam anima[y] sensitiva bruti.

Praeterea, anima sensitiva est unius rationis in nobis et brutis. Patet per[z] operationes quae sunt unius rationis. Sed sensitiva brutorum est corruptibilis; ergo et nostra. Sed intellectiva non est corruptibilis; ergo alia est intellectiva a sensitiva. Probatio consequentiae, nam si esset una corruptibilis et alia incorruptibilis, differunt genere, ex X *Metaph.*,[79] et non essent unius rationis.

Tu dicis, sicut doctor respondet,[80] quod formae non collocantur in genere sed composita. Unde homo est corruptibilis sicut alia animalia. Contra: Saltem formae sunt alterius rationis a sensitiva in bruto et in homine, quia una corruptibilis et alia incorruptibilis. Sed secundum diversitatem formarum est diversitas actionum et operationum; nam ignis vel aqua habet operationes diversas propter diversitatem formarum.

Praeterea, quod vegetativa in nobis et in brutis etiam sit alia a sensitiva, probo[a]. Nam impossibile est eandem formam esse activam et passivam. Vegetativa est forma activa, secundum Aristotelem II *De Anima*,[81] sensitiva est forma passiva tantum secundum eum.[82] Ergo non sunt eadem forma.

Praeterea, impossibile est quod eadem forma secundum numerum sit extensa et non extensa. Sensitiva est extensa per accidens in toto corpore, quia sensus tactus diffunditur per totum corpus, et tactus non est separatus ab anima sensitiva. Sed intellectiva neque per accidens neque per se extenditur, nec eius potentia, quia[b] est in qualibet parte tota simul, secundum Augustinum in multis locis.[83]

Praeterea, determinatio Aristotelis est in contrarium, ut[c] mihi videtur. II *De Generatione Animalium* probat ex intentione quod sensitiva in nobis non producitur ab extrinseco, et per consequens non est eadem forma cum intellectiva. Arguit enim sic:[84] "Omnis forma quae

---

y   alia V.
z   *Om.* per W.

a   potentia W.
b   quae W.
c   *Om.* ut W.

79 Aristotle, *Metaph.* X, 10, 1058b26-28.
80 St. Thomas, *Summa theol.* I, 76, 3, ad 2.
81 Aristotle, *De Anima*, II, 4, 415a23-416b31.
82 *Ibid.*, 5, 416b32-418a6.
83 St. Augustine, *De Immortalitate Animae*, c. 16; PL 32, 1034. *Epist.* 166, 2, 4; PL 33, 722.
84 Aristotle, *De Generatione Animalium*, II, 3, 736b22-28.

est principium corporalis operationis non potest esse sine corpore, ut
ambulare sine pedibus; quare et huiusmodi de foris ingredi est impossibile, sed sicut inseparabilis existentis. Relinquitur ergo[d] intellectum solum de foris advenire, et divinum esse solum." Modo, certum est quod sensitiva[e] in nobis est[f] principium corporalis operationis,
quia utitur organo corporali. Ergo non est ab extrinseco[g]; ergo
educitur de potentia materiae. Ergo non est eadem cum intellectiva.

\<Contra Opinionem Magistri Henrici de Gandavo\>

Contra secundam opinionem, quae est magistri Henrici, quantum ad
hoc quod habet proprium. Dicit[85] enim quod intellectiva continet sensitivam et vegetativam, sed non formam mixti. Contra hoc potest argui,
ut videtur, sic: Quidquid[h] continet virtualiter causam, continet virtualiter effectum. Modo sensitiva bruti continet formam vegetativi et
formam mixti inanimati, nam aliter in bruto essent plures formae, quod
ipse negat.[86] Sed intellectiva in homine continet sensitivam perfectiorem
quam bruti; ergo[i] et formam mixti nobiliorem quam formam mixti
bruti.

Praeterea, probo[j] quod eadem ratione in bruto sunt plures formae
sicut in homine, per argumentum suum. Duae vel plures generationes
terminantur ad distinctas formas. Sed brutum generatur pluribus
generationibus; nam alia est generatio qua generatur cor in animalibus
a generatione alterius partis. Nam una praecedit aliam tempore, secundum determinationem Aristotelis in libro De Animalibus.[87] Ergo duae
formae.

Praeterea, impossibile est quin formae eiusdem rationis habeant
passiones vel proprietates eiusdem rationis et operationis. Sed
manifestum est quod alia est operatio propria hepatis et cordis et carnis
et sanguinis. Ergo aliae formae substantiales.

Praeterea, contra hoc quod dicit,[88] quod licet in homine sit duplex

---

d Relinquitur ergo] reliquo genere W.
e *Add.* non est W.
f *Om.* est W.
g non est ab extrinseco] est ab intrinseco W.
h quicumque W.
i *Om.* ergo W.
j probando W.

85 Henry of Ghent, *Quodlibet* IV, q. 13, fol. 113D.
86 Henry of Ghent, *Quodlibet* X, q. 5, fol. 407N.
87 Aristotle, *De Generatione Animalium*, II, 1, 735a24; *De Partibus Animalium*, III, 4, 666a10.
88 Henry of Ghent, *Quodlibet* IV, q. 13, fols. 112B-113C.

forma, tamen anima intellectiva immediate perficit materiam primam,
— contra: Ex duobus in actu perficientibus eandem materiam vel idem
susceptivum, quorum neutrum est actus alterius nec perfectio alterius,
non fit unum. Sed sic est in proposito. Nam neutra forma est ordinabilis
ad aliam sicut perfectio ad perfectibile. [V 14r2] Ergo non fit unum ex
eis.

Contra utramque opinionem de forma mixtionis, quod in omni composito sit alia forma mixti et elementi: In omni composito sunt
qualitates elementares, ergo et elementa. Antecedens conceditur ab omnibus. Probatio consequentiae. Impossibile est quod una forma simplex
sit subiectum contrariarum qualitatum formaliter. Dico 'formaliter'
quia effective potest esse una forma principium qualitatum contrariarum per accidens, ut sol constringit lutum et dissolvit glaciem. Sed
quod duae contrariae qualitates, ut album vel nigrum, calidum et
frigidum, naturaliter oriantur ex eadem forma simplici est impossibile,
et probatur sine contradictione. Qualitas apta nata est competere composito ratione formae. Modo una forma simplex non potest esse formalis ratiok contrariorum.

Praeterea, probo quod est impossibile quod una sit forma substantialis sanguinis et ossis. Ex eisdem principiis vel partibus essen-
tialibus non consurgit nisi idem compositum, nam causa eadem semper
facit eundem effectum; et hoc semper est verum de causis intrinsecis,
cuiusmodi sunt materia et forma. Sed per te eadem est forma totius
compositi et omnium partium eius, et eadem materia; ergo compositum
totum et quaelibet pars unius rationis.

Praeterea, Aristoteles, II *De Anima*,[89] dicit quod non est possibile
quod duo corpora tangant se in aere vel inl aqua, nisi medium in-
tercipiatur. Ista propositio non posset probari nisi ex accidentibus, ut
quia est humiditas inter corpora plana tangentia se in aqua; et arguitur
ibi esse aqua quia humiditas est ibi subiective in aqua. Eodem modo
arguam tibi hic: Invenitur qualitas elementaris, ergo et elementum.

Praeterea, Aristoteles in libro *De Sensu et Sensato*[90] dicit quod in oculo
dominatur aqua. Platonici dixerunt quod ignis dominatur.[91] Sed in
libro *Caeli et Mundi*[92] dicit quod terra dominatur, quia omne compositum movetur secundum naturam elementi praedominantis. Modo,
si non essent plures formae, non posset hoc salvari.

---

k   formalis ratio] ratio formaliter W.
l   *Om.* in W.

89   Aristotle, *De Anima*, II, 11, 423a28-b7.
90   Aristotle, *De Sensu et Sensato*, II, 438a5.
91   *Ibid.*, 437a22.
92   Aristotle, *De Caelo*, I, 2, 269a2.

Praeterea, Aristoteles I *De Caelo*[93] arguit numerum corporum simplicium secundum numerum motuum, quia corpus simplex vel[m] movetur sursum vel deorsum vel circa medium; et opponit contra se, quia corpus compositum movetur deorsum. Respondet quod movetur secundum naturam elementi praedominantis in eo. Sed si esset lapis tam simplex sicut ignis, nulla esset ratio quin essent plura corpora quam quatuor habentia [W 210r] determinatum locum ad quem moventur.

Praeterea, Aristoteles II[n] *Caeli et Mundi*,[94] secundum litteram commenti, dicit, commento 39, dans causam quare animalia continue et cito senescunt, quia componuntur ex contrariis rebus diversorum locorum, et nulla pars animalium est in suo loco; quapropter animal cito senescit. Ergo in composito necessario sunt multae formae.

Praeterea, littera nostra habet sic:[95] "Tota consistentia animalium ex his. Et talibus est quae differunt propriis locis. Nullam enim partium habet eam quae ipsius regionem." Et est expressa auctoritas quod in corpore mixto sunt multa quae petunt naturaliter diversas regiones.

Praeterea, Augustinus VII *Super Genesim*, capitulo 4,[96] ostendit in corpore esse quatuor elementa: "Non est contemnendum quod medici non tantum dicunt, sed probare se affirmant. Quamvis omnis caro terrenam soliditatem in promptu gerat,[o] habet tamen in se et aeris aliquid quod pulmonibus continetur et a corde per venas, quas arterias vocant <diffunditur>[p]." Tu dicis: Fuit Platonicus.[q]

Praeterea, Aristoteles VII *Metaph.*, illo capitulo:[97] *Quoniam autem*[r] *definitio ratio est,* dicit quod illa quae concipiuntur cum materia[s] corrumpuntur in materiam et partes materiales. Et ponit exemplum:[98] statua in lutum, sphaera in aes, Callias in carnem et ossa. Ergo caro et os sunt partes materiales hominis.

Praeterea, Aristoteles ibidem, in eodem capitulo:[99] "Palam autem

m   *Om.* vel W.
n   *Add.* De V.
o   generat W.
p   *Add.* etc. V.
q   Phonen' W.
r   *Om.* autem W.
s   *Add.* non W.

93   *Ibid.*, 268b13ff.
94   Aristotle, *De Caelo*, II, 6, 288b15-19. See Averroes, *In II De Caelo et Mundo*, c. 37, fol. 120M.
95   Aristotle, *ibid.*, b16-18.
96   St Augustine, *De Genesi ad Litteram*, VII, 12; PL 34, 362.
97   Aristotle, *Metaph.* VII, 10, 1035a24-31.
98   *Ibid.*, 1035a32.
99   *Ibid.*, 1037a5-6.

quod anima est prima substantia, corpus autem materia, animal autem quod est ex utrisque." Ergo materia perfectibilis per animam est corpus, caro scilicet et os; non ergo materia prima.

<AD RATIONES IN OPPOSITUM>

1. Ad primum in oppositum: Cum dicitur[t]:[100] Forma substantialis dat esse simpliciter, forma accidentalis non, sed[u] tale vel quantum; ergo forma substantialis advenit non enti simpliciter, dico quod ens[v] simpliciter potest dupliciter intelligi: Vel ut simpliciter est distinctum contra ens secundum quid, quod est accidens. Ita accipit Aristoteles ens simpliciter I *Physicorum*,[101] cum dicit[w] aliqua fiunt simpliciter sicut sola substantia; accidentia autem fiunt secundum quid tantum. Et isto modo dat omnis forma substantialis esse simpliciter, et forma accidentalis esse secundum quid. Alio modo accipitur esse simpliciter prout idem est quod esse perfectum et completum in specie, non expectans ulteriorem perfectionem,[x] eo modo materia prima est non ens simpliciter sed secundum quid. Et isto modo dico quod non est necesse quod omnis forma substantialis det esse simpliciter, id est esse completum in specie; immo potest esse in potentia ad ulteriorem perfectionem, et essentialem et substantialem.

Ad formam, tunc dico quod differentia inter formam substantialem et accidentalem attenditur penes dare esse simpliciter et esse secundum quid primo modo, non secundo modo.

2. Ad secundum,[102] cum arguitur:[y] generatio non differret ab alteratione, dico quod differentia inter generationem et alterationem est, secundum Philosophum in loco allegato,[z] I *Physicorum*,[103] in hoc quod generatio est transmutatio simpliciter, alteratio et quaecumque alia mutatio est mutatio secundum quid. Quod sic exponit Commentator, commento 63,[104] quia in generatione res amittit nomen et

---

t   Ad ... dicitur] Ad rationem in oppositum. Ad primum cum dicitur W.
u   *Add*. esse W.
v   *Om*. ens W.
w   enim (*in later hand*) W.
x   *Om*. perfectionem W.
y   dicitur W.
z   est, secundum Philosophum in loco allegato] in libro allegato secundum Philosophum W.

100   See above, # 1.
101   Aristotle, *Physics*, I, 7, 190a32-37.
102   See above, # 2.
103   Aristotle, *Physics*, I, 7, 190a32-37.
104   Averroes, *In I Phys*., c. 63 (Venice, 1562) IV, fol. 37v-38r.

definitionem, in^a alia mutatione non amittit res nomen et definitionem. Modo ego dico quod in omni forma substantiali res amittit nomen et definitionem,^b sive fuerint plures formae sive una.^c Et ideo mutatio subiecti compositi ex forma substantiali et materia prima ad formam substantialem ulteriorem non est alteratio, quia res amittit nomen^d et definitionem.

3. Ad tertium,[105] quod generatur non est, quod movetur est, dico sic: Suppono duo: quod forma substantialis ultima quae constituit rem ultimate et perfecte in specie — illa dat esse simpliciter utroque modo loquendo de esse simpliciter, sive ut distinguitur contra ens secundum quid, quod est accidens, sive ut distinguitur contra ens perfectum et completum. Suppono aliud: quod subiectum mutationis et motus, in quantum movetur et mutatur, privatur termino ad quem movetur et mutatur. Ergo subiectum generationis quae est ad formam completam caret esse simpliciter secundo modo dicto, quia forma ad quam movetur dat sibi^e esse simpliciter, quia forma ad quam movetur dabit sibi esse simpliciter. Ergo in quantum huiusmodi non est simpliciter^f secundo modo, sed illud quod mutatur motu proprie dicto non caret esse simpliciter in quantum tale. Ergo non^g dicit quod ipsum non est; immo in quantum huiusmodi est. Nam forma accidentalis, ad quam est motus proprie dictus, praesupponit in subiecto suo esse simpliciter, utroque modo loquendo de esse simpliciter.

4. Ad quartum,[106] quod movetur est in loco, quod generatur non est in loco, dico^h quod illud quod generatur ideo non dicitur esse in loco, quia in quantum generatur caret loco. Nam licet [V 14v1] quantitas sit in subiecto generationis, qua mediante est in loco, tamen hoc accidit sibi in quantum movetur ad formam substantialem per generationem. Nam quantitas non est pars subiecti generationis, in quantum subiectum est; sed quod movetur, in quantum movetur, est in loco, quia motus praesupponit in subiecto suo quantitatem. Nam quantitas est principium, quo mediante, subiectum occupat locum, qui est terminus motus localis.

---

a   *Om.* est mutatio ... in V.
b   *Om.* Modo ... definitionem W.
c   *Add.* forma W.
d   *Om.* nomen W.
e   *Om.* sibi W.
f   *Om.* simpliciter W.
g   *Om.* non W.
h   dicitur W.

105 See above, # 3.
106 See above, # 4.

Item, quantitas est immediatum subiectum qualitatis, quae qualitas est terminus alterationis. Ideo illud quod movetur, in quantum movetur, est in loco; et illud quod generatur, in quantum generatur, non est in loco. Et ita intendit Aristoteles.[107]

Sed contra: Illud non sufficit. Probatio. Nam per illud non distingueretur generatio ab omni motu. Quia accipio motum ad quantitatem: subiectum motus ad quantitatem in quantum huiusmodi non est quantum nec in loco. Probatio. Nam receptivum denudatur a toto genere recepti in quantum huiusmodi. Etsi enim illud quod movetur ad quantitatem sit sub quantitate, tamen hoc sibi accidit in quantum huiusmodi.[i] Eodem modo sicut hic, illud quod generatur, licet sit sub quantitate et est in loco per consequens,[j] tamen non in quantum generatur. Ergo per hoc non distinguitur motus ad quantitatem a generatione.

Dico quod omne quod movetur est in loco, vel per se vel per praesuppositam formam. Tunc motus, in quantum huiusmodi, vel est in loco per formam ad quam est motus. Primo modo omne quod movetur ad formam accidentalem posteriorem quantitate est in loco in quantum huiusmodi. Secundo modo illud quod praecise movetur ad quantitatem est in loco in quantum huiusmodi. Sed subiectum generationis in quantum huiusmodi non est in loco aliquo, nec uno modo nec alio.

5. Ad quintum,[108] cum arguitur: Res habet unitatem et entitatem a forma substantiali; ergo, si sint plures formae, sunt plura entia, respondeo: Dico quod sicut sunt plures formae, ita in composito sunt plura entia; et hoc est verum in simplici elemento, ubi tantum est[k] forma et materia prima, quia illa non sunt idem ens materia et forma. Eodem modo sunt plura entia simpliciter in composito habente plures formas substantiales, accipiendo ens simpliciter, ut distinguitur contra accidens et formam accidentalem. Sed propter hoc illud compositum non est plura entia per praedicationem,[l] quia partes eius integrales non praedicantur de eo. Sed quia ultima forma dat nomen et speciem, quia illa est unica, ita totum compositum unum ens et[m] non duo entia.

Tu dicis: Formae substantiales sunt sicut numeri: VIII *Metaphy.*,[109]

i   *Om.* Etsi ... huiusmodi W.
j   *Om.* per consequens W.
k   *Om.* est W.
l   praedicationes W.
m   et *erased or blotted out* W.

107   Aristotle, *Physics*, V, 1, 224b35-225b1.
108   See above, # 5.
109   Aristotle, *Metaph.* VIII, 3, 1043b37-1044a1.

minimo addito vel remoto, variatur species. Respondeo. [W 210v] Dico quod non habeo pro inconvenienti quod individuum unius speciei sit pars essentialis alterius individui; verbi gratia, sicut in speciebus accidentium, nam colores extremi sunt pars mediorum colorum, et qualitates tangibiles primae sunt partes qualitatum secundarum, secundum Commentorem V *Physicorum*, commento 19.[110] Eodem modo elementa, quae sunt substantiae, sunt partes integrales manentes in mixto secundum Commentatorem: "Unum corpus generatum est speciei alterius in quantum huiusmodi."[111] Sed individuum speciei talis, quae non est nata perfici perfectione essentiali ab alio, non potest facere unum cum alio. Et ego dico quod non omne individuum compositum ex materia et forma est tale quin potest informari et perfici ulteriori perfectione.

6. Ad illud[n],[112] cum arguitur quod generatio unius est corruptio alterius, dico hic quod aliquando[o] est generatio unius contrarii ex alio contrario, sicut unum elementum generatur ex alio elemento, aliquando est generatio perfecti de imperfecto. Primo modo generatio unius est corruptio alterius, secundo modo non; immo forma praecedens et forma sequens sunt compossibiles. Unde contrarietas est inter formas substantiales primas elementorum, non inter formas mixtorum, secundum Commentatorem, II *Physicorum*, commento 53.[113] Et istud probatur per duplicem auctoritatem. Avicenna VIII *Metaph.*, capitulo 2,[114] dicit quod primus doctor (id est Aristoteles) ponit tantum duos modos quibus aliquid fit ex alio: unus modus quando aliquid fit ex alio sicut ex contrario, ut quando ex aere fit ignis; et tunc illud quod fit non manet, quia aer non manet. Alio modo aliquid fit ex alio ut perfectum ex imperfecto, ut quando de puero fit vir, et tunc manet illud quod fit, nec abicitur nisi privatio, non aliquid positivum.

Illud quod Avicenna allegat de primo doctore, id est Aristotele, habetur expresse II *Metaph.*[115] Dicit enim sic Aristoteles: "Dupliciter fit hoc ex hoc: aut quia[p] hoc post hoc, ut ex isthmiis olympia; aut ex puero

---

n   sextum W.
o   alia W.
p   non, *deleted* V; non *added interl.* W, *deleted after* quia hoc.

---

110   I have not found this text here, as cited in W. V reads: "secundum commentum 10 *Metaphysicae*.

111   I have not found this text. V reads: "secundum commentum. Unde (unum?) corpus complexionatum est alterius speciei quam homo."

112   See above, # 18.

113   I have not found this text here, as cited in W, nor in V *Phys.*, c. 53, as cited in V.

114   Avicenna, *Metaph.*, VIII, 2 (Venice, 1508), fol. 97v. W erroneously cites *Metaph.* II.

115   Aristotle, *Metaph.* II, 2, 994a22-31.

vir, ut ex eo quod perficitur perfectum; aut ut ex aere aqua; et ea quae hoc modo fiunt, alterum corrumpitur." Sententia Aristotelis est talis: Aliquid dicitur fieri ex alio praeter illum modum quo dicitur aliquid fieri ex alio, ut post aliud, ut ex isthmiis (id est, tali festo celebrari) fit olympia, quia post illud fit. Praeter istum modum est duplex modus essendi: unum ex alio per se, scilicet, vel ut ex contrario contrarium, et ibi generatio unius est corruptio alterius; vel ex imperfecto perfectum, ut ex puero vir, ubi non corrumpitur aliquid positivum, sed tantum privatio abicitur, et sic generatio unius non est corruptio alterius.

7. Ad aliud,[116] cum arguebatur quod una forma sufficit, quia imperfectior continetur in perfectiori sicut trigonum in tetragono, absque praeiudicio melioris sententiae, videtur mihi quod non est ad propositum. Aristoteles intendit ibi[117] ostendere quod vegetativum potest inveniri sine sensitivo, et non e contrario, non[q] sensitivum[r] sine vegetativo. Sed de speculativo intellectu[s] altera ratio est. Unde verba Aristotelis sunt: "Similiter autem se habet ei quod de figuris est et quae secundum animam sunt. Semper enim in eo quod est consequenter <est in> potentia quod prius est, in figuris et in animatis, ut in tetragono quidem trigonum est, et in sensitivo vegetativum."

Modo videtur mihi quod non vult plus dicere nisi illud quod est consequenter, id est, illud quod est posterius ordine generationis, ut sensitiva, continet quod prius, ut vegetativam, ita quod non est sensitiva nisi sit vegetativa in eodem, sicut non est tetragonum nisi ubi est trigonum. Et quid est hoc dictum? Numquid non potest esse hic tetragonum nisi sit triangulus habens tres angulos tantum? Nec oportet tetragonum hoc modo continere trigonum, nec alio modo, nisi tu dicas quod[t] ideo continet quia trigonum potest inscribi in tetragono, secundum modum quo loquitur Euclides in quarto libro.[118] Et tunc non continet magis tetragonum trigonum quam e contrario, nam tetragonum potest inscribi intra[u] trigonum sicut e contrario, ut probat Euclides.[119]

---

q nam W.
r *Add.* non W.
s *Om.* intellectu W.
t *Om.* quod W.
u infra VW.

116 See above, # 17.
117 Aristotle, *De Anima,* II, 3, 414b28-32.
118 See *The Elements of Euclid,* Book IV, Definition 1; trans. Sir Thomas L. Heath (London, Toronto 1933), p. 113.
119 Euclid does not offer a formal proof of this, but only the explanation of how one rectilineal figure can be inscribed in another, "when all the angles of the inscribed figure are on the sides of the figure in which it is inscribed, each on each." *Ibid.*

Est autem figuram inscribi in alia quando ea quae inscribitur continet illam in qua inscribitur[v] in omni suo angulo interius. Et hoc modo tetragonum in trigono continetur, sicut e contrario. Nec enim continet tetragonum trigonum quasi[w] haberet eandem virtutem quod triangulus. Hoc est planum impossibile. Ergo verum non potest esse dictum Aristotelis,[120] quod tetragonum continet trigonum, nisi quia quatuor anguli continent tres, et minor numerus continetur in maiori. Et ex hoc non sequitur quod sint una forma sensitiva et vegetativa,[x] sicut nec quatuor sunt tres, licet tres sint[y] [V 14v2] pars quatuor.

8. Ad aliud,[121] cum arguitur de praedicatis acceptis a diversis formis, potest dici quod verum est praedicatum assumptum a forma sensitiva, puta animalis, non praedicatur in quid de forma sumpta a forma intellectiva, puta de rationali, quia hoc est per accidens 'rationale est animal'. Tamen praedicatum sumptum a forma sensitiva, puta animal, potest bene praedicari de subiecto sumpto ab utroque, puta a sensitiva et ab intellectiva, cuiusmodi est homo. Species enim a duobus accipitur, scilicet a genere et a differentia, et genus praedicatur primo modo de specie per se, licet non de differentia.

Alio modo potest dici, concedendo quod genus et differentia accipiantur ex eadem forma; tamen ex hoc non oportet quin sit alia forma in homine praeter illam a qua accipitur genus et differentia. Unde dicerem quod animal accipitur a forma intellectiva sicut rationalis, etiam si non esset nisi forma intellectiva, dum tamen esset perfectio corporis, quia, ut dictum est in Quaestione de[a] Universali[b],[122] genus a quadam similitudine accipitur. Verbi gratia, licet in asino sint[c] vegetativa et sensitiva, tamen ego dico quod intentio generis communis, puta corporis animati, sufficienter accipitur a sensitiva,[d] licet sit alia forma a vegetativa[e] propter similitudinem quam habet cum illo ubi est

---

v scribitur W.
w quod W.
x *Om.* et vegetativa W.
y sunt V.
z de V.

a *Om.* de V.
b quia, ut dictum est in quaestione de universali, *stroked out in* W.
c sit V.
d sensitivo V.
e vegetativo V.

120 Aristotle, *De Anima,* II, 3, 414b32.
121 See above, # 9.
122 See Gedeon Gál, "Henricus de Harclay: Quaestio de Significato Conceptus Universalis," *Franciscan Studies* 31 (1971), n. 73, p. 214; n. 78, p. 216.

vegetativum solum. Unde propter hoc non oportet ponere diversas formas.

9. Ad aliud,[123] cum arguitur quod nisi esset una forma, operatio intensa unius non remitteret aliam, dico quod sic. Talis est enim conformitas istarum formarum in eodem composito quod una condescendit et cooperatur modo suo alteri formae, licet fuerint diversae.

<AD AUCTORITATES>

10. Ad auctoritates. Primo ad auctoritatem[f] de libro[g] *De Spiritu et Anima,*[124] dicendum quod non fuit liber Augustini, sed cuiusdam Cisterciensis,[h] sicut habetur a fratre Thoma, IV *Sententiarum,* dist. 44.[125]

11. Ad aliam *De Ecclesiasticis Dogmatibus,*[126] non fuit liber Augustini, sed Gennadii Massiliensis presbyteri.[127] Praeterea, dico quod ipse intendit quod non sunt plures animae in homine incorruptibiles,[i] ut quidam dixerunt. Et quod ita intendit, licet videatur mirabile, probo. Nam ipse dicit[128] continue quod "Animalium animae non sunt substantiae, sed cum carne ipsa carnis vivacitate nascuntur, et cum carnis[j] morte[k] finiuntur et moriuntur. Ideo nec ratione reguntur, sicut Plato et Alexander putant, sed ad omnia naturae[l] incitamenta ducuntur." Patet [W 211r] ergo quid intendit cum dicit non sunt substantiae, id est, non sunt per se subsistentes sine corporibus, sicut intellectivae; et isto modo non sunt animae plures in homine sed una, quia una sola incorruptibilis.

f   auctoritates W.
g   *Om.* de libro W.
h   *corrupt in* W.
i   incorporales V.
j   carne V.
k   carnis morte] carne illa W.
l   *Om.* naturae W.

123   See above, # 10.
124   See above, # 12.
125   St. Thomas, *In IV Sent.* d. 44, q. 3, a. 3, sol. 1, ad 1; *Opera omnia,* ed. Parma (New York: Musurgia Publishers 1948), VII, p. 1108. The work is by the Cistercian Alcher of Clairvaux. See G. Théry, "L'authenticité du 'De spiritu et anima' dans s. Thomas et Albert le Grand," *Revue des sciences phil. et théol.,* 10 (1921), 373-377.
126   See above, # 11.
127   For Gennadius of Marseilles as the author of this work, see A. Bardenhewer, *Patrology* (St. Louis, 1908), p. 609; also C. H. Turner, "The Liber Ecclesiasticorum Dogmatum attributed to Gennadius," *The Journal of Theological Studies,* VII (1905), 78-99; VIII (1906), 103-114.
128   *De Ecclesiasticis Dogmatibus,* c. 17; PL 42, 1216.

12. Ad auctoritates allegatas de philosophia,[129] ad omnes, tam ad illam de libro *De Animalibus* quam ad illam de libro *Metaphysicae,* et libro *Politicae,* potest responderi quod intendit de partibus organicis, cuiusmodi sunt manus, pes, oculus, et huiusmodi organa sensuum, quae non manent eaedem nisi aequivoce in mortuo et vivo. Cuius ratio est, secundum quod dicit Aristoteles,[130] quia determinata sunt operatione. Et ideo, cum non possint in operationem, non sunt talia nisi aequivoce. Sed non tenet in partibus homogeneis, quae sunt unius rationis in toto et in parte, cuiusmodi sunt caro et os et huiusmodi. Sed illud non sufficit ad librum *Meteororum.*[131] Ipse enim ex intentione dicit quod ita[m] est in carne et in osse sicut in partibus organicis. Et probat quod ita est in carne et in osse sicut in organicis sic: Quando illud cuius gratia fit aliquid cessat, et illud desinit esse. Modo, partes homogeneae sunt gratia partium organicarum. Deinde dat causam quare non apparet in carne sicut in parte organica, dicens[132] "non est facile prospicere nisi sit valde deperditum et figurae solae sint relictae, velut[n] antiquorum corpora."

Posset dici ad illud quod corpora organica sunt in duplici genere. Quaedam sunt quae sunt organa distinctarum operationum, ut manus et organa multorum sensuum. Quaedam sunt organa communium operationum, ut organum nutritivae vel generativae et partis[o] vegetativae, et alicuius sensus, ut tactus. Et hoc secundo modo caro est organum vel medium in tangendo, et virtus nutritiva est in omni parte carnis, id est, conversiva[p] alimenti[q] in substantiam rei alendae, et huiusmodi. Et tunc potest dici quod non manet eadem caro quantum ad hoc quod non potest in operationem tangendi vel nutriendi, sicut prius. Et illud confirmatur per hoc quod Aristoteles dicit,[133] quod partes tales homogeneae sunt propter partes organicas, et ideo quantum ad hoc cessant esse.

Sed illud non solvit secundum. Nam Aristoteles dicit[134] quod in rei

---

m   ut W.
n   valde W.
o   partes V.
p   conservativa W.
q   alimento W.

129   See above, # 13, # 14, # 15, # 16.
130   Aristotle, *Meteors,* IV, 12, 390a10-13.
131   *Ibid.,* 389b29-390a1.
132   *Ibid.,* 390a20.
133   *Ibid.,* 390b10.
134   *Ibid.,* 390a14.

veritate erit tanta transmutatio a parte carnis sicut a parte partis
organicae. Sed non apparet tam cito usquequo fuerit multum deperditum de illo. Et illud non potest referri ad carnem in quantum est
organum aliquod vegetativum, nam statim apparet hoc in carne sicut in
oculo, quod non potest esse organum sentiendi nec vegetandi quantum
ad aliquem actum. Et ideo illud non sufficit.

Quid igitur dicendum ? Dico quod illud non probat unam formam;
immo magis plures probat esse formas. Concedi enim potest. Dico
tamen quod non est verum forte quod non manet eadem caro mortui et
vivi nisi miraculose, ut in Christo vel in aliquo alio sancto forte. Immo
dico quod forma una non potest corrumpi nisi alia corrupta. Verbi
gratia, dico quod omne quod corrumpitur, corrumpitur a suo contrario. Et ideo quia forma mixti, secundum Commentatorem II
Physicorum,[135] commento 53, non habet contrarietatem ad aliam nisi
ratione elementorum existentium in mixto, ideo mixtum corrumpitur
ad corruptionem elementorum in eo existentium, ut puta cum vel[r] a
contrario exteriori remittitur unum elementum vel aliud, vel intenditur
ultra debitum, iam desinit illa mixtura esse proportionata respectu formae mixti. Et hoc modo deficit mixtum per actionem contrarii. Ideo
illud quod neque est elementum neque ex elementis non[s] corrumpitur,
quia contrarium non habet. Eodem modo de vegetativo. Nam forma
vegetativi requirit determinatam formam mixtionis complexionalis, et
determinata forma mixti[t] requirit determinatam proportionem elementorum in mixto. Et non corrumpitur vegetativum nisi alia forma
praecorrupta. Unde argumentum magis videtur concludere oppositum.
Nam cum vegetativum non potest corrumpi nisi dupliciter, vel a contrario agente (et non habet contrarium nec[u] secundum qualitates nec
secundum substantias), vel secundum quod requirit aliud secum in esse
quod corrumpitur a contrario; ergo oportet quod corrumpatur ad
corruptionem alterius formae. Ergo alia forma est in vegetativo praeter
formam vegetativam.

Dices saltem illud Aristotelis[136] videtur esse contra articulum fidei[137]

---

r nihil W.
s *Om.* non W.
t *Om.* mixti W.
u *Om.* nec W.

135 I have not found this text.
136 See above, # 12.
137 See Johannes Peckham, *Registrum,* p. 922.

dicentem quod error est quod[v] non sit idem corpus vivum et mortuum, ita in aliis sicut in Christo. Doctor ille Henricus de Gandavo dicit[138] quod in Christo miraculose mansit idem corpus et caro, sicut fuit allegatum,[139] et in aliis hominibus non. Sed illud videtur mihi irrationabiliter dictum. Christus fuit mortuus naturali processu naturae sicut et alii, et eodem modo sicut alius homo fuisset mortuus naturaliter ex vulnere illato. Et ideo sciendum quod licet vulnus illatum sit violentum, mors tamen inde sequitur naturaliter, et dissoluta [V 15r1] fuit harmonia elementorum in illo sicut in alio. Unde corpus eius fuit resolutum in cadaver sicut corpus alterius. Unde Gregorius XXXI *Moralium*, in fine,[140] exponens illud Job 39 [30] de aquila: *Pulli eius lambent sanguinem, et ubicumque[w] fuerit cadaver, statim adest*, dicit Gregorius, "Et non immerito corpus domini propter casum mortis cadaver vocatur."[x] Et ideo in eo fuit mors et resolutio sicut in aliis.

Quid ergo dicendum? Numquid non fuit eadem caro Christi vivi et mortui? Dicendum est, sine praeiudicio melioris sententiae, quod potest intelligi fuisse[y] eadem caro in eo[z] vivo et in mortuo, et similiter in omni alio dupliciter: vel quia partes materiales manent eaedem quae prius, et non tamen eadem forma; vel quod totum, et forma et materia, sunt idem. Primo modo potest concedi quod manet idem corpus et caro, nam elementa eadem manent non dissoluta, sed unum elementorum est remissum alio modo quam prius. Circa quod est[a] intelligendum quod compositum consistit in quadam harmonia elementorum, ita quod ignis habet determinatum gradum, et similiter alia elementa, quodlibet suum.[b]

Pontifical Institute of Mediaeval Studies.

---

v   *Om.* error est quod W.
w   ubi W.
x   locatur W.
y   *Om.* fuisse W.
z   eodem W.

a   *Om.* est W.
b   quodlibet suum] quidlibet simul W.

138   Henry of Ghent, *Quodlibet* X, q. 5, fols. 405F-406L.
139   See above, # 13.
140   St. Gregory, *Moralium Libri*, XXXI, c. 53, n. 105; PL 76, 631.

GIOVANNI ARGIROPULO
ON THE AGENT INTELLECT:
AN EDITION OF Ms.
MAGLIABECCHI V 42 (ff. 224-228ᵛ)

Virginia Brown

WHEN Giovanni Argiropulo (ca. 1415-1487) began to lecture on the *Nicomachean Ethics* in February 1457 at the Florentine Studio, it was unquestionably an event of some importance. He was the first Greek to teach in Florence since Manuel Chrysoloras who left there in 1400,[1] and he gave a renewed emphasis to Greek studies by his teaching of the language and his discourses on Greek texts. Argiropulo's appointment to the Studio was realized after a campaign engineered and conducted on his behalf chiefly by the Acciaiuoli brothers, Donato and Piero, with the help of Alamanno Rinuccini, Antonio Rossi, Marco Parenti, and Andrea Alamanni. He remained in Florence until 1471, giving public lectures as well as private lessons and attracting a devoted following: among his pupils, in addition to those named above, may be included Lorenzo de' Medici, Pandolfo Pandolfini, Bartolomeo della Fonte, and Angelo Poliziano. In one of his letters Argiropulo writes that he had a passion for Greek philosophy and had spent many years in studying the ancient thinkers.[2] From such learning much activity was naturally to be expected, and his supporters were not disappointed. A series of lessons on the *Physics* of Aristotle (1458) followed his inaugural course on the

1 For the life, teaching, and works of Giovanni Argiropulo see G. Cammelli, *I dotti bizantini e le origini dell' umanesimo,* vol. 2: *Giovanni Argiropulo* (Florence, 1941). A more complete bibliography may be found in M. E. Cosenza, *Biographical and Bibliographical Dictionary of the Italian Humanists,* vol. 1 (Boston, 1962), pp. 295-308. In vol. 1 *Manuele Crisolora* (Florence, 1941) of his *I dotti bizantini.* Cammelli observes (p. 80, n. 5) that 'non si può considerare come vero e proprio insegnamento continuato quello del Trebisonda eletto il 7 marzo 1442 *ad legendum in Studio Poesiam* ... e partito l'anno seguente per Roma al seguito della curia papale.'
2 See Cammelli, *Argiropulo,* p. 10 and n. 1.

Ethics, and these in turn were followed by lectures on the *de Anima* (1460) and *Meteorologica* (1462). He is famous for his numerous Latin translations of Greek philosophical works.

Argiropulo does not seem to have written down any of his lectures, or, if he did, they have not yet come to light.[3] What we know of them we owe to Donato Acciaiuoli, his most faithful student, who in a number of instances carefully recorded the words of his master. One of these *reportationes* contains Argiropulo's lectures on the *de Anima* and is now ms. Magliabecchi V 42 in the Biblioteca Nazionale, Florence. Although the prefatory lecture to this series of lessons has long been known to scholars through the work of K. Muellner,[4] the commentary itself remains unexplored. As a small contribution towards making it better known and more accessible, I give here an edition of that part of the commentary (ff. 224-228ᵛ) which concerns the agent intellect (*de Anima* 3.5 430a10-25), a section especially chosen in view of the ancient and medieval commentators' interest in the problem.[5] I should also like to point out that the *praefatio* to the *de Anima* which Muellner edited from Riccardiana ms. 120 (ff. 27-34) is a shorter and apparently reworked and more polished version of the original preface (ff. 1-11 in ms. Magliabecchi V 42).[6] A comparison of the texts shows that the two *praefationes* are closely related, and the major difference between them lies in a series of questions on knowledge and the soul found only in the Magliabecchi codex.[7]

---

3 A note on a flyleaf of Riccardiana ms. 120, which contains Argiropulo's prefatory lectures to his courses, has this entry: 'In veteri huius codicis tegmine legebatur *Praefationes Iohannis Argyropyli dum Florentiae doceret philosophiam. Est autem codex seculi XV et fortasse autographus.*' To the best of my knowledge, this codex has not been established as an autograph of Argiropulo.

4 *Reden und Briefe italienischer Humanisten* (Munich, 1970 (reprint of Vienna, 1899 edition)), pp. 43-53. Muellner has silently emended passim the manuscript's 'possibil-' to 'passibil-'.

5 For the impressive number of medieval commentaries on the *de Anima*, see A. J. Smet, *Initia commentariorum quaestionum et tractatuum latinorum in Aristotelis libros de Anima saeculis XIII, XIV, XV editorum* (Louvain, 1965) and the lists compiled by J. De Raedemaeker and A. Thirry in *Bulletin de philosophie médiévale* 5 (1963), pp. 149-183, 6 (1964), pp. 119-134, 8-9 (1966-67), pp. 63-87, 87-110, 10-12 (1968-70), pp. 194-211, 13 (1971), pp. 109-128.

6 F. ii of ms. Magliabecchi V 42 has a note 'no. 597. Donati Acciaiuoli expositio super libros de Anima secundum expositionem Ioannis Argiropoli. Originale', and C. H. Lohr has therefore assigned the commentary to Acciaiuoli in his 'Medieval Latin Aristotle Commentaries: Authors A-F', *Traditio* 23 (1967), p. 400. However, the fact that the Riccardiana preface is specifically attributed to Argiropulo indicates that he is the author of the preface and presumably of the commentary in the Magliabecchi codex as well since no other name is read before the commencement of the exposition. Consequently the meaning of the entry on f. ii seems to be that Acciaiuoli is the scribe, not the author, of the commentary. See E. Garin, *Medioevo e rinascimento. Studi e ricerche* (Bari, 1954), p. 262: 'Il corso di lezioni sull'anima, di cui ci parla anche il Rinuccini, e che l'Acciaiuoli ci ha conservato ...' and *La cultura filosofica del rinascimento italiano* (Florence, 1961), p. 104: 'In una nota marginale contenuta nella copia del corso sull'*Anima* stesa da Donato Acciaiuoli ...'.

7 Ms. Magliabecchi V 42, ff. 4-5 'utrum sit scientia de anima', ff. 5-7 'utrum scientia hec sit

Ms. Magliabecchi V 42 measures 298 × 171 mm and consists of 272 paper folios with various water marks (Briquet nos. 11881, 6271, 3370). The commentary proper, which is of the lemmatic type, occupies ff. 11ᵛ through 269ᵛ; there is an index of questions on ff. 270ʳ⁻ᵛ having to do with the chapters of the *de Anima*.[8] Lemmata are underlined and generally occur at the beginning of the line, the commentary following immediately in long lines which vary in number from 29 to 40. The collation of the codex is: ii + 6¹⁸ + 1¹⁶ + 1¹⁸ + 1²⁰ + 1¹⁶ + 1¹⁴ + 1¹⁹ + 1¹⁸ + 2²⁰ + 1³ (the last folio is unnumbered).

The script, which may be described as 'rapid cursive', is of considerable interest since it affords a lengthy specimen of the writing of Donato Acciaiuoli. Vespasiano da Bisticci praises Acciaiuoli as a 'bellissimo iscrittore di lettera corsiva',[9] but our first impression is not so much of the beauty of the script as its difficulty. This is owing, in large measure, to the speed with which Acciaiuoli wrote (a characteristic also mentioned by Vespasiano) and, indeed, rapidity was understandably necessary if he were to take down everything. The result is that certain letters tend to resemble each other (*a* and *e*, *a* and *n*, *a* and *u*, *b* and *h*, *c* and *e*, *c* and *t*, *n* and *u*) and to run together. Surprisingly enough, there is only a fair amount of abbreviation, and when it does occur, it is of the most common kind.[10] The orthography of the manuscript shows Acciaiuoli to have been free of any egregious spelling errors and to have written a type of Latin that conformed in many ways to the 'classical' orthography. For example, *f* is never written for *ph* nor is *h* misplaced or inserted wrongly; the same is true of *c* and *ch*. An occasional doubling or omission of letters ('simi*ll*itudo', 'diffe*re*') may be attributed to the haste of the moment. *e* is always used for *ae* and there are no accents on any words. Acciaiuoli rarely indulges in the separation of words at the end of a line; there is nothing strange, however, in his few instances of word division ('conclusio-nem', 'possibi-lem', 'prestantio-rem'). Punctuation signs include the period, colon, and interrogation sign. Capital letters are usually placed correctly at the beginning of a new sentence, a sign that Argiropulo must have been an unusually well-organized lecturer.

Because the commentary actually consists of classroom notes, we

rationalis', ff. 7-8 'utrum anima sit subiectum huius libri'.

8   They have been edited by E. Garin in his *La cultura filosofica*, pp. 120-121.

9   P. D'Ancona and E. Aeschlimann, ed., *Vespasiano da Bisticci. Vite di uomini illustri del seculo XV* (Milan, 1951), p. 332.

10   For example, q̄ = quae

               p̄hus = philosophus

               n̄a = natura

               a̅i̅a = anima

have some indication of Argiropulo's teaching methods. His chief concern is to get at the meaning of Aristotle himself, an approach in keeping with what he expressed elsewhere as to the way in which Aristotle should be taught.[11] The plain and simple style of the lectures is well suited to the needs of students, and the various stages of the explanation are well defined so as to be grasped more easily. The philosophers and commentators expressly cited either in support of or in opposition to Aristotle's statements are Plato[12] and Averroes. Although he does not name him. Argiropulo also had recourse to Gaetano of Thiene's commentary on the *de Anima*. Furthermore, he must have at least suggested to his students that they read Giles of Rome's exposition on the *de Anima* since a marginal note on f. 226^v contains a quotation from that work. This passage could, of course, have been added by Acciaiuoli at another time.

As a Christian, Argiropulo knew that Averroes' doctrine of a single intellect for all men was untenable, and in the prefatory lecture he refers to this *sententia* as *perniciosissima*, noting the absurd conclusions that follow from it.[13] Consequently this question does not enter at all into his own discussion. If Averroes is included in the general term *expositores*, a second point of disagreement is Argiropulo's insistence that immortality and to be separable, unmixed, and impassive are more properly said of the agent than of the passive intellect (ff. 228, 226). These differences notwithstanding, he does rely quite clearly upon Averroes for other matters concerning the agent intellect, and it should be remembered that he studied at Padua (1441-1444), a center of Averroism. Argiropulo could very well have learned his Averroes from Gaetano of Thiene who occupied the chair of natural philosophy at Padua since 1430 and who composed his commentary on the *de Anima*

11 In the preface to his translation of the *de Interpretatione* Argiropulo says: 'Neminem esse profecto foreque arbitror qui non oratorum quorumvis erudimentis neglectis atque posthabitis ad archana philosophiae sententiasque persubtiles Aristotelis elegantius *explicatas illustratasve* summa cum aviditate proficiscatur.' This preface has been edited by J. E. Seigel in 'The Teaching of Argyropulos and the Rhetoric of the First Humanists', *Action and Conviction in Early Modern Europe. Essays in Memory of E. H. Harbison* (Princeton, 1969), pp. 256-260.

12 See E. Garin, *La cultura filosofica,* pp. 119-120 for a letter of Pier Filippo Pandolfini to Donato Acciaiuoli concerning Argiropulo's teaching of Plato.

13 Ms. Magliabecchi V 42, f. 10r-v and Muellner, *op. cit.,* pp. 51-52: 'At preter hanc (*sc. animam cogitativam*) ponit (*sc. Averroes*) aliam animam unicam et esse ubique et inclinatam, ut approprietur unicuique homini, et esse essentiam quandam compositam, quod est mirabile, ex intellectu agente et possibili ... Et hac anima intellectiua dicit hominem intelligere universale, sua uero et cogitatiua intelligere singulare, producere tamen phantasma, ex quo sumit et abstrahit intellectus ille agens et ponit in intellectu possibili et sic percipit universale ... Hec opinio est Averois et in omni expositione philosophi trahit textum ad hoc propositum. In tertio enim uult philosophum diuidere animam intellectiuam in intellectum possibilem et agentem et ponere non duas potentias sed duas substantias, et intellectum agentem uidetur extollere uehementer. Ex ista sententia multa sequi uidentur absurda ... Prima igitur opinio illorum uestustissimorum ... quia hec perniciosissima Auerois.'

around 1443.[14] More extensive investigation of Argiropulo's lectures may show that he, like Gaetano, also used Albert the Great's commentary on the *de Anima*. In any case, the first three lemmata in Argiropulo's exposition are noticeably close in subject matter and verbal parallels to the corresponding passages in Gaetano's treatise;[15] there is also a marginal note (f. 225) with a passage from Gaetano.

For this edition I have examined and transcribed the manuscript from the original. The orthography has been preserved so as to give an idea of Acciaiuoli's Latin. The sentence structure of the commentary is occasionally abrupt but, in light of the fact that we are dealing with lectures delivered to students, I have preferred to emend as little as possible. Regarding the rather abundant marginalia, it was possible in some cases (thanks to Acciaiuoli's *signes de renvoi*) to place the note in its rightful place in the text; other instances which appear to be afterthoughts or general summaries, and as such lack the *signes,* are relegated to an apparatus, and a letter in the text indicates the word or sentence with which they are most likely connected. The Latin version of the Aristotelian text which precedes Argiropulo's exposition is from ms. Magliabecchi V 41 (f. 50); this is a copy, also written by Donato Acciaiuoli, of Argiropulo's translation of the *de Anima*.[16]

Aristoteles, *de Anima* 3.5 (430a10-25)

50 /Cum autem in omni natura sint quedam quorum alterum quidem unicuique generi materies est, quod id esse patet quod est potentia illa cuncta, alterum uero causa est et efficiens omnia nimirum efficiendo atque agendo, talem subiens uidelicet rationem qualem ars conditionem ad materiam subit, necesse est et in anima differentias has easdem inesse. Atque quidam est intellectus talis ut omnia fiat; quidam talis ut omnia agat atque efficiat, qui quidem habitus est quid..m et perinde ac lumen. Nam et lumen eos colores qui sunt potentia actu colores quodammodo facit. Et is intellectus separabilis est et immixtus

14 See S. Da Valsanzibio, *Vita e dottrina di Gaetano di Thiene* (Verona, 1948), pp. 12, 37. Argiropulo's promoters at Padua were Antonius de Rosellis, Stephanus de Doctoribus, Sigismundus de Polcastris, and Bartholomaeus de S. Sophia, and none of the entries for Argiropulo in J. Brotto and G. Zonta, *Acta graduum accademicorum gymnasii patavini ab anno MCCCVI ad annum MCCCCL* link him in any way with Gaetano. As Da Valsanzibio observes (p. 15), it is natural to assume that Argiropulo was a pupil of Gaetano. The use of Gaetano's commentary by Argiropulo seems to support this supposition although it must be admitted that Argiropulo could have had independent access to the commentary at another time.

15 Similar passages also occur in the commentary on the *de Anima* of Paul of Venice, one of Gaetano's own teachers at Padua (cf. Da Valsanzibio, ibid., pp. 9-10). However, the nature of the resemblance is such as to show clearly that Argiropulo's source was Gaetano.

16 On the two translations see Cammelli, *Argiropulo,* p. 116, n. 1.

passioneque uacat cum sit substantia actus. Semper enim id quod efficit atque agit prestabilius est eo quod patitur, et ipsum principium omnino materia. Scientia autem ea que est actu idem existit cum re; ea uero que est potentia in uno quidem prior est tempore, simpliciter autem neque tempore. Sed nec nunc quidem intelligit, nunc autem non. Cum uero separatus iam est, tum id est solum quod est, atque id solum est immortale perpetuumque. Non autem recordamur quoniam hoc quidem expers est passionis. Intellectus uero passiuus est corruptibilis et sine isto nihil intelligit.

Ioannis Argyropyli in *de Anima* 3.5 (430a10-25) commentarius

/*Cum autem* (430a10). Posteaquam philosophus declarauit naturam in- 224 tellectus possibilis, hoc in capitulo naturam intellectus agentis. Nam due uidentur esse uires uel essentie secundum Aueros[1] quibus constituitur anima intellectiua, scilicet intellectus possibilis et agens. Ostendit[2] autem necessitatem intellectus possibilis quia nunc est potentia, nunc actu. Hoc autem in capitulo declarat quod necesse est in anima humana esse intellectum agentem. Diuiditur in tres partes: in prima declarat quomodo necesse esse <t> ponere intellectum agentem; in secunda conditiones quibus percipitur natura intellectus agentis et quomodo conuenit <et>[a] differt a possibili; in tertia soluit dubitationem. Et prima in parte/ostendendo necessitatem intellectus 224v agentis, ponit talem conclusionem quod preter intellectum possibilem est necesse ponere intellectum agentem. Et probatur: in omni genere nature que nunc est potentia, nunc actu, necessario est aliquid quod potest suscipere omnia illius generis et aliud quod omnia eiusdem generis potest agere; at anima intellectiua est quedam natura; ergo hec duo necessario insunt et alterum est intellectus possibilis, alterum agens. Ergo etc. Maior: non solum naturalibus sed etiam artificialibus. In naturalibus, materia prima que omnia suscipit; que omnia agit, prima intelligentia. In artificialibus, materia que subicitur arti; quod omnia artificialia agit est mens artificis uel potius no<u>s. Minor: nam anima intellectiua nunc actu, nunc potentia. Nam est primo ut tabula rasa et tandem euadit actu. Ergo necesse est non solum esse in natura anime intellectiue intellectum possibilem sed etiam intellectum agentem qui deducat eum de potentia ad actum. Hunc intellectum dicit esse ut habitum et lumen, ac lumen facit actu colores. Sic intellectus facit esse actu, scilicet ut intelligantur que sunt potentia in anima intellectiua. Nota quod in omni genere nature in qua aliquid oritur et oc-

---

a   conuenit ~~et differt et~~ differt *legitur*
1   Aver., *In 3 de Anima*, c. 1 text. 5 (Venetiis, 1574) 6.149ᵛD.
2   Aristot., *de Anima* 3.4 (429a22 ff.).

cidit, necesse est ponere tria: unum quod patitur, aliud quod agit, tertium quod fit atque oritur. Et sic in anima humana inueniuntur tria: intellectus agens, intellectus possibilis, intellectus actu. Nam intellectus primo est potentia talis, id est possibilis. At ut deducatur de potentia ad actum cum < per > se non possit, necesse[b] ponere aliud quod deducat de potentia ad actum, et id est intellectus agens. Et ut ille in genere anime omnia suscipere potest, intellectus agens omnia eadem agere potest. Tertium est habitus et sciens intellectus uel species uel intellectio uel aggregatum ex ea et intellectu possibili. Philosophus posuit illa duo; tertium reliquit quia patebit. Nota quod intellectus possibilis est ille qui omnia suscipit, intellectus agens qui omnia agit, ac secundum theologos non omnia que intellectus possibilis suscipere potest intellectus agens agere potest, propter reuelationes que non aguntur ab intellectu agente. Itaque apud eos non fit conuersio. Nam quicquid intellectus agens agere potest, intellectus possibilis suscipere potest, sed non e contra quia sequeretur quod naturaliter possemus percipere articulos nobis reuelatos et principia fidei nostre. Et sic ea naturaliter philosophi percepissent, quod est absurdum dicere. Quare/bene dixerunt theologi. 225 Fuerunt autem nonnulli philosophorum qui dixerunt intellectum agentem esse deum. Nam ut in natura rerum est materia que omnia suscipere potest, sic quod omnia imprimere potest; sic intellectus possibilis et agens. Theologi autem, ut diximus, sic posuerunt. Ex his inferre possumus quod supernaturaliter et naturaliter articulos habemus et percipimus: supernaturaliter quia deus reuelando imprimit in intellectum possibilem et supplet quasi uicem intellectus agentis; naturaliter quia ab intellectu nostro possibili suscipitur qui[c] est potentia naturalis in nobis. Sententia igitur philosophi intelligenda est naturaliter, quod est circa omnia illa et non de reuelationibus, ut diximus.

Nota quod intellectus agens est philosophi sententia *ut habitus*[d] (430a15) quidam, et per hoc uult philosophus intellectum agentem esse actu et intelligere semper. Nam antequam generetur habitus in intellectu, sine presentia specierum non potest percipere; at non est in potestate sua tunc intelligere cum uult. At cum acquisiuit habitum, potest speculari cum uult, id est non indiget presentia rei.[e] Verum non

---

b   *corr.*

c   *corr.*

d   *in marg.*: Expositores accipiunt ut habitus, id est ut quedam perfectio. (Cf. Aegidius Romanus, *Expositio super libros de anima*, text. 18 (Venetiis, 1496) fol. 71, col. B.)

e   *in marg.*: Sed dominus Ioannes exponit quod est ut habitus; quasi intelligit quando uult, et non indiget presentia phantasmatis aut alicuius exterioris ut intellectus possibilis qui non eo pacto est ut habitus quidam. At in separatis a materia idem est habitus et id cuius est, nec intelligendum quod sit habitus acquisitus, et dicitur habitus ut diceremus 'deus est sapientia'.

ita fit in intellectu agente quia semper est actu et est ut habitus.[f] Auerois[3] dicit quod intellectus agens nihil intelligit eorum que sunt hic. Quam opinionem nonnulli[4] moderantur quod non mouetur ab his sed intelligit per essentiam suam, alii non moderantur sed dicunt quod intelligit tantum se. Est igitur ut quidam habitus quia semper est actu. Nam si esset nunc actu, nunc potentia, tunc rursus quereretur de eo quod est potentia et esset abitio in infinitum. Quare standum. Est igitur ut habitus non quia habens illum nunc speculetur, nunc non, sed quia est talis ut semper se intelligat.

Nota circa illud *perinde ut lumen* (430a15) et addit quod facit actu ut lumen colores. Dupplicem habuimus sententiam[5] de coloribus. Prima est communis quod non requiritur ut deducat colores de potentia ad actum, sed propter dispositionem medii et perspicui. Sine enim perspicuo actu uideri colores non possunt. Secunda, quod lumen requiritur ut colores, qui potentia sunt in tenebris, euadant colores actu. Sunt enim antea ut materia cum dispositionibus quibusdam que suscipit lumen ut formam, et efficiuntur uarie propter uarias dispositiones, id est efficiuntur albedines, nigredines etc./Si igitur 225v teneamus secundam sententiam, procedit optime testus philosophi. Lumen facit actu colores; sic intellectus agens species, que sunt aut in memoria aut in cogitatiua potentia, intelligibiles deducit in actu reponendo lumine suo in intellectu possibili.

Et bene posuit *quodamodo* (430a16) quia non simpliciter facit. Sed antea non poterant mouere cum non essent actu, et postea mouent. Si teneamus secundam sententiam, declarabitur testus philosophi sic ut non teneat omnino simillitudo. Nam ut lumen facit colores actu, id est facit ut mouere possint uisum dispositione medii, sic lumen intellectus agentis requiritur et facit ut species et phantasmata fiant actu intelligibiles et mouere possint intellectum possibilem. Et bene posuit 'quodammodo' quia non simpliciter facit actu sed quantum ad immutationem, et disponit medium ut mouere illi possint.

Nota quod philosophus circa illa,quod *talem subit rationem* (430a12-13), intelligenda est similitudo cum moderatione. Videtur enim prima facie

---

f *in marg.*: ueluti ille qui habet habitum qui intelligit quando uult. Et per hoc quod dicit 'quando uult', non intelligit commentator quod actus uoluntatis semper precedat actum intelligendi habituati intellectus quia tunc in actibus intelligendi procederetur in infinitum; sed 'quando uult', scilicet sine presentia intelligibilis exterioris necessario requisita. (Caietanus de Thienis, *Super libros de Anima*, text. 18 (Venetiis, 1493) fol. 64ᵛ, col. B)

3 Aver., *In 3 de Anima* (430a18), c. 3 text. 19 6.162A.
4 Cf. Caietanus de Thienis, *Super libros de Anima*, text. 19 (Venetiis, 1493), fol. 65, col. B.
5 Cf. Aver., *In 2 de Anima* (418a31-b4), c. 3 text. 67 6.84ᵛD ff.; Caietanus de Thienis, *ibid.*, text. 18, fol. 65, col. A.

quod sicut ars se habet ad materiam, ita intellectus agens ad possibilem; illa imprimit formas, iste species. Verum in arte et materia fit ut ars non indigeat aliquo alio ut imprimat in materiam, sed ex sese, non presupponendo aliquid aliud extra, id est formam quam sumat et imprimat. At non ita euenit in [in] intellectu agente quia est phantasma principium propinquum quod simul cum intellectu agente conoperatur ad hoc, ut intellectus possibilis intelligat, quia nec phantasma est sufficiens nec intellectus agens per se ut intellectus possibilis intelligat. Nam si esset intellectus agens sine phantasmate, nunquam intelligeret intellectus possibilis quia indifferrenter et uniuersaliter se habet intellectus agens ad species intelligibiles; contrahitur et quasi limitatur per phantasma ad hanc uel ad illam speciem. At si esset phantasma per se sufficiens, tunc nihil interesset inter uniuersale et singulare quia phantasmata sunt singularia et sic singulariter representarent[ur]. Si non esset opus intellectu agente, et ex hoc sequeretur quod nihil interesset inter intellectum possibilem et cogitatiuam in eo quod singularia intelligere < n > tur. Et hec secundum Aueroim.[6] At si quis diceret 'instrumentum in arte est ut phantasma', dicendum quod instrume < n > tum nihil sibi simile producit. At phantasma imprimit de natura sua et speciem sibi similem, id est speciem intelligibilem que nihil differt nisi quod est uniuersalis. Quare apellatur agens secundarium ipsum phantasma./   226

At is intellectus (430a17). Secunda pars in qua affert conditiones quibus et conuenit et differt intellectus agens a possibili. Discrepo ab aexpositoribus. Expositores[7] uolunt quod his tribus proprietatibus conuenit cum intellectu possibili. Differt una quod agens est substantia actus. Nos dicimus quod istis tribus proprietatibus que competunt utrique intellectui, scilicet agenti et possibili, isti differrunt quia magis competunt agenti quam possibili illa tria, scilicet esse separabilem, immixtum, et impassibilem, et ratio est quod est substantia actus. Quam rationem expositores[8] accipiunt pro quarta proprietate que facit differre. Tenendum quod affert tales conditiones ut diximus. Primo affert tres conditiones-prima quod iste intellectus est separabilis, secunda quod est immixtus, tertia quod uacat passione-et addit quia est substantia actus. Quod allatum est ut ostendat differre intellectum agentem a possibili, sententia mea, quia superius dicebat[9] possibilem esse

6 Aver., *In 3 de Anima* (430a15), c. 3 text. 18 6.161C.

7 Aver., *ibid.* (430a17-18), c. 3 text. 19 6.162A-B; Caietanus de Thienis, *op. cit.*, text. 19, fol. 65, col. B.

8 Aver., *ibid.* (430a18, 20), c. 3 text. 19 6.162A, C-162ᵛE; Caietanus de Thienis, *op. cit.*, text. 19, fol. 65ᵛ, col. A.

9 Aristot., *de Anima* 3.4 (429b5, 429a18, 15).

separabilem et immixtum et impassibilem; que eadem afferrt nunc de
agente. Quid igitur interest etiam per istam particulam? Solum dicunt
nomen expositores.[10] Mea sententia non est talis sed per hoc differt illis
tribus. Est separabilis agens, et ille quoque, uerum alio modo quia
cadere uidetur medius possibilis inter agentem et formam corpoream,
nam magis coniungitur intellectus possibilis cum corporeis. Nam intellectus possibilis intelligit in nobis, at intellectus agens non intelligit
nobis et non coniungitur corpori nisi hoc pacto cum coniungitur et
copulatur cum possibili. Vlterius differt intellectus agens quia immixtus, et hoc magis competit ei quam possibili. Nam etsi intellectus
possibilis non sit forma in corpore, tamen indiget corporeo et existente
in corpore. Intellectus agens minime; est etiam impassibilis et hoc etiam
differt. Nam etsi intellectus possibilis uacat passione corruptiua, non
tamen uacat perfectiua. Verum intellectus agens penitus est impassibilis
et uacat passione etiam perfectiua quia non perficitur cum sit perfectus.
Atque ut intelligatur quod hec tria magis attribuuntur intellectui agenti
quam possibili, addit 'cum sit substantia actus'. Et equiuoce dici potest
quod illa tria competunt et tribuuntur istis; magis enim intellectui
agenti quia possibilis est in pura potentia. At agens est substantia actus
quia idem est substantia sua et actus suus, id est quasi est essentia
quedam actiua.

Atque addit *semper enim id quod agit* (430a18-19), unde antea
dicebamus quod omne agens in eo quod agit est prestantius patiente in
eo quod patitur, et sic introducenda sententia philosophi. Et hec secundum philosophos et non secundum fidem nostram./Nota quod formare 226v
possumus talem rationem sic: Omne agens est prestabilius eo quod
patitur et omnino principium pre materia. At intellectus agens est quod
agit et ut pri<n>cipium, intellectus possibilis quod patitur et ut
materia. At cum esse immixtum intellectui possibili preclare, preclarius
et excellentius attribuatur agenti quia est substantia actus, et nota quod
in separatis a materia idem est actus cum essentia. At intellectus agens
est separatus a materia secundum philosophos nec indiget corpore nec
coniungitur corpori nisi iungatur cum intellectu possibi<li>. At habet
hoc officium infimum; scilicet <ut> ponat et efficiat phantasmata
species intelligibiles et abst<ra>hat uniuersalia a singularibus. At
principale officium habet se intelligere ut untelligentie que mouent corpora celestia et intelligunt se ipsas. Et hec secundum philosophos. Nota
quod Auerois mordere uidetur Platonem et salua sua pace non in-
tellexit Platonem quia contempnit. Dicit[11] igitur quod compulsus est

---

10   Aver., *In 3 de Anima* (430a18-19), c. 3 text. 19 6.162ᵛD-E.
11   Aver., *ibid.* (430a15), c. 3 text. 18 6.161ᵛF.

Aristoteles ponere intellectum agentem quia uniuersale extra animam non est actu ut Plato dicit. Ille ponebat *** Verum Aristoteles non posuit actu uniuersale sed potentia quod est in singularibus et euadit actu uniuersale per intellectum agentem cum abstrahit. Ista sententia est apparens et bella; non tamen tangit Platonem.[g] Aristoteles coactus est ponere intellectum agentem multis de causis multa sunt officia que non possunt fieri sine intellectu agente, inter que est ista abstrahactio speciei que est representatiua uniuersalis et rationis uniuersalis. At Plato nunquam posuit uniuersalia extra animam ita ut predicentur de pluribus, [id est] sed exemplaria illa ueluti rationem humanam in me<n>te diuina; et ipse etiam Plato ponit intellectum agentem sed alio modo quam Aristoteles. Nam posuit[12] habere innatam scientiam animam humanam, et tunc uidetur habere et non habere quia est media inter illas formas et istas materiales. Et cum ingreditur corpus, impeditur et obliuiscitur et incipit operari infimis potentiis et est in potentia ut reminiscatur et intelligat et excitetur a sensibilibus quousque accedatur ad scientiam. Et sic uertit se ad se, et ut excitat se est agens, ut ab sensibilibus patitur patiens diuersis rationibus. Et postremo hoc addat, quod est materia/que potest omnia suscipere et est 227 agens uniuersale quod omnia agere potest; atque in natura anima [ut] est quod omnia suscipere potest, species et simulacra idearum que sunt in mente diuina, que cum omnibus ideis erit ut agens.

Scientia autem ea (430a20). Posteaquam philosophus declarauit necessitatem intellectus agentis et attulit quasdam proprietates quibus ille uidetur differre a possibili, hac in particula nonnullas alias conditiones quibus idem differt a possibili. Et talis conditio sumitur ex modo scientie. Intellectus enim agens et possibilis sunt tales ut sciant, sed alter est semper actu sciens, possibilis nunc actu sciens, id est habet scientias nunc potentia. Dicit igitur quod scientia que est actu idem est re, id est intellectus agentis scientia, que semper est actu, est idem cum re que intelligitur et scitur, id est idem cum intellectu agente quia se ipsum intelligit. Quare est idem cum essentia sua. At scientia possibilis non est idem re quia oritur et corrumpitur remanente intellectu. At

---

g *in marg.*: Sufficit ad presens intelligere quomodo Plato ponebat quidditates, que erant obiectum intellectus nostri, actu abstractas et per consequens actu intelligibiles. Quod si uerum esset, non indigeremus ponere intellectum agentem. Nam sicut eo quod sensibilia sunt actu sensibilia, non indigemus ponere sensum agentem: ut quia calidum est actu calidum, non indigemus ponere tactum agentem qui faciat potentia sensibilia esse actu. Sicut si quiddi[ti]tates essent actu separate, possent per se immutare intellectum possibilem nec indigeremus agente. Egi(dius). (Aegidius Romanus, *Expositio,* text. 18 fol. 71, col. A)

12 Cf. Plat., *Phaedo* 75C-76D, 82D-83D; praef. in cod. Magliabecchi V 42, fol. 9 et K. Muéllner, *Reden und Briefe italienischer Humanisten,* p. 50.

scientia intellectus agentis que est idem re cum agente non corrumpitur quia si corrumperetur, corrumperetur et intellectus, quod est absurdum. Talem enim conditionem habent que sunt idem re ueluti accliuis et decliue, ascensus et descensus. Scientia igitur intellectus agentis est idem re, et in tali predicatione potest dici quod intellectus est scientia. At scientia intellectus possibilis acquiritur ab eodem et talis est potentia prior scientia que est actu. Nam unum indiuiduum ignorat prius et est in eo potentia scientia et precedit tempore scientiam que est actu in eodem indiuiduo.[h] Simpliciter non est uerum quia simpliciter scientia que est actu semper precedit quia siue per inuentionem siue per doctrinam acquiratur. Nam si per doctrinam, tunc doctor habet scientiam actu qua imprimit in addibentem que habet potentia; si per inuentionem, tunc scientia actu intellectus agentis, qui subit uicem doctoris, precedit scientiam illam que est potentia: ueluti ouum precedit gallinam secundum idem indiuiduum, simpliciter gallina precedit. Quare cum sint duo, semper actus precedit potentiam; in uno et eodem precedit semper potentia actum. Intellectus igitur possibilis nunc habet potentia scientiam, nunc actu. Cum acquisiuit habitum, et in eodem semper precedit potentia scientia scientiam actu. Simpliciter precedit scientia actu non solum tempore sed etiam perfectione. Sic igitur perspicitur differe ex scientie conditione. Dici etiam potest quod intellectus idem possibilis, considerando ut est in diuersis indiuiduis, uidetur precedere se ipsum secundum quod est actu; 'se ipsum', inquam, secundum quod est in potentia in alio indiuiduo. At intellectus agens non precedit se ipsum nec suscipit talem uarietatem/et hec est sententia 227v Auerois.[13] Alii expositores[14] deuiant.

Scientia que est actu (430a20), id est scientia intellectus agentis.

Est idem cum re (430a19-20), id est cum essentia intellectus agentis.

Ea uero que est potentia (430a20-21), id est scientia intellectus possibilis in uno et eodem precedit tempore. Simpliciter non precedit et hoc dupplici expositione ut diximus. Nota quod necessario emergit positio intellectus agentis ex his que dixit philosophus, qui est diuersa uis ab intellectu possibili. Nam intellectus possibilis acquirit scientiam et est primo in potentia; postea euadit actu, at non potest deducere de poten-

---

h *in marg.*: In libro *de Interpretatione* philosophus sic: 'Ex hisce dictis hoc quoque constat quod id quod necessario actu continue est. Quapropter si perpetua priora sunt, actus profecto potentia prior est. Atque eorum que sunt, quedam actu sine potentia sunt ceu prime substantie; quedam una cum potentia sunt que quidem partim priora, partim posteriora uidentur esse, nam quidem priora, tempore uero posteriora; quedam enim nunquam existunt actu sed solum semper potentia sunt.' (Aristot., *de Interpretatione* 13 (23a21-26))

13 Aver., *In 3 de Anima* (430a20-21), c. 3 text. 20 6.163ᵛE ff.
14 Cf. Aver., *ibid.* (430a20-21), c. 3 text. 20 6.163A ff.

tia ad actum se ipsum. Ergo est aliud et id non potest esse nisi intellectus agens qui habet actu scientiam. Qui enim fieri potest ut potentia homo euadat homo actu nisi per hominem actu, et hoc aut specie
aut ui? Primum dico propter hominem genera <n> tem uirum propter
sob <ol> em, sic intellectus possibilis aut per doctorem docentem aut
per inuentionem ui intellectus agentis qui habet actu scientiam. Verum
scientia intellectus agentis differt ratione ab scientia intellectus
possibilis, nam in possibili dicitur formaliter, in agente ui scientie et ef-
fectiue.

   Sed nec (430a22). Alia differentia qua differt possibilis ab agente et
seruat ordinem pulcrum. Primum attulit tres illas conditiones, deinde
aliam de scientia quod intellectus agens habet semper scientiam,
possibilis nunc habet, nunc non habet. Et sic loquebatur de primo actu;
nunc aliam affert que est de secundo actu. Nam agens non nunc intelligit, nunc non intelligit, sed semper. At possibilis nunc intelligit,
nunc non intelligit ueluti cum dormit. At in intellectu agente
coniungitur semper secundus actus cum primo. Itaque intellectus
possibilis, ut antea dicebatur, nunc non habet habitum scientie,[i] nunc
habet. Preterea posteaquam habet, nunc operatur, id est intelligit, nunc
non operatur et non intelligit. At intellectus agens et semper habet
scientiam et semper intelligit. Nota quod ista conditio ualde seiungit
intellectum agentem ab possibili et ostendit esse longe prestantiorem.
Nam scientia in intellectu possibili et dependet a phantasmatibus et
cum acquirit scientiam et deinde cum uult operari. Unde oportet in-
telligentem phantasma speculari quoquomodo quia semper per
cogitatiuam fit aditus; ueluti si deum intelligimus opificem uniuersi, oc-
curit nobis species uniuersi.[j] Preterea non semper operatur intellectus
possibilis quia interdum homo aliis uiribus operatur. At intellectus
agens nec acquirit scientiam nec dependet ab aliquo corporeo, quare
228 semper intelligit./

   Cum uero (430a22). Alia distinctio talis est inter eosdem. Dicit enim
quod separabilis est intellectus agens, et hoc est commune cum possibili
etsi uario modo. At cum est separatus, tunc est id quod est, et hoc non
est commune possibili quia si possibilis separatur, non est id quod est.
Quia erat sciens in illo indiuiduo, nunc in isto alio non est quia amisit
quod acquisiuit in illo indiuiduo. Et hec dicuntur secundum Aueroim.[15]
At intellectus agens est id quod est. Nam est intellectus cum est

---

   i   *corr.*
   j   *in marg.*: Semper habet scientiam actu agens. Prima differentia: non semper habet scientiam
actu possibilis. Semper intelligit agens. Alia differentia: non semper intelligit possibilis.

   15 Cf. Aver., *ibid.* (430a22), c. 3 text. 20 6.163A ff.

separatus quia non dependet a corpore nisi secundum suam infimam operationem quia exhaurit a corpore, id est a phantasmatibus. Et cum sit separabilis, tamen non semper est separatus. At cum est separatus ab hoc uel illo indiuiduo, tunc est id quod est cum sit in sua suprema operatione, id est intelligendo se, sicut imaginari de intelligentiis possumus que coniunguntur secundum infimam operationem suam, id est mouendo corpora. At si imaginemur seiungi, tunc remanent in suo esse nobilissimo; sic de intellectu agente dici potest. Coniungitur enim cum corpore ut perficiat, non ut acquirat aliquid.

Cum est separatus (430a22), scilicet quando est separatus cum sit separabilis.

Tum est id solum quod est (430a22-23), id est remanet in suo esse intelligendo se.

Atque id solum (430a23). Alia conditio: intellectus agens est quoddam immortale.[k] At hoc competit possibili, verum non equo discrimine. Nam deus habet immortalitatem, anima immortalitatem; verum deus ex se, anima a deo. Quare cum dicitur aliquid immortale, tamen non sequitur quod eodem modo. Nam materia prima a philosophis dicitur immortalis et deus, uerum deus alio modo et supremo et magis est immortalis. Eodem modo intellectus possibilis qui subit uicem materie. Etsi sit immortalis, tamen agenti magis competit immortalitas, et magis proprie eodem modo perpetuitas. Expositores[16] dicunt philosophum loqui hic de intellectu possibili; mi uidetur quod philosophus dicat eum esse solum immortalem, scilicet intellectum agentem, non quod excludat possibilem sed magis proprie hoc tribuat agenti. Nota quod merito intellectus agens dicitur proprie immortalis quia illud proprie dicitur tale quod nullam mutationem suscipit in sua nobilissima operatione. Semper enim est actu talis, quare proprie ei competit immortalitas. Verum non eodem modo competit possibili etsi immortalis sit secundum essentiam. Verum nunc habet scientiam, nunc non habet considerando in uno indiuiduo. Item indiget corporeo ut acquirat talem perfectionem et nunquam habet eandem numero perfectionem etsi specie conuenie<n>tem quia aliam in hoc, aliam in illo numero. Tale igitur cum nunc acquirat, nunc amittat, non ita proprie dicitur immortalis quia intellectus sciens corrumpitur; non aut intellectus, sicut Socrates albus, non Socrates. Quare proprie attribuetur intellectui agenti./Quare cum sint sensus qui penitus extinguantur et intellectus 228v

---

k   *in marg.*: In primo huius philosophus sic: 'Intellectus autem aduenire uidetur corpori substantia quedam existens, et non corrumpi. Nam ab ea maxime que in senectute fit obfuscatione corrumperetur. Nunc autem perinde fit', et reliqua uide ibi etc. (Aristot., *de Anima* 1.4 (408b18-20))

16   Cf. Aver., *ibid.* (430a20-25), c. 3 text. 20 6.163A ff.

agens qui omnino remaneat, medium tenet possibilis qui remanet
secundum essentiam; corru <m> pitur scientia eius in hoc et in illo.

Non autem recordamur (430a23-24). Mouet dubitationem et soluit. Hec
adduci duppliciter potest. Ex duabus iis essentiis que sunt perpetue
constituitur anime essentia. Cur igitur, cum sint perpetue, non recordamur? Remanent intelle[lle]ctus agens et possibilis quibus constituitur
essentia anime, et secundum talem positionem cur non eorum recordamur? Si enim sit intellectus qui erat in geometre et nunc geometre
extinto in morta <li> tate, cur non recordamur? Soluit philosophus
difficillime dicendo 'non recordamur quia hoc, id est intellectus, scilicet
agens cum possibili, non est passiuus'. Intellectus uero passiuus est
corruptibilis, quare nota quod intellectus agens et possibilis uaca <n> t
passione, etsi diuerso modo, tamen uacant quia non corrumpuntur
secundum essentiam. Intellectus vero passiuus, id est cogitatiua que
deducitur de potentia materie et extenditur extensione subiecti, etsi per
accidens extendatur, dicitur corruptibilis. Que cum subministret immediate intellectui possibili merito dicitur intellectus, et est intellectus
singularis, et est suprema uis organica, et nullo modo percipit uniuersale; et hoc non solum patet in homine sed etiam in brutis. Quare talis
uis que est in homine subministrans intellectui dicitur intellectus et est
passiuus passione corruptiua; intellectus uero agens et possibilis nullo
modo. At sine isto, scilicet intellectu possibili, non potest anima intelligere cum sit minister eius. His dictis patet solutio: permanent illi
duo intellectus ut diximus, at est alius qui est corruptibilis, quo
corrupto non possumus recordari. Quia etiam in uita si homo sciens of-
fendatur in cogitatiua, non recordatur, unde ista uerba correspondent
illis cum dixit[17] 'alio intus corrupto' etc. Non igitur recordamur quia
† consimus et intellectus agens et possibilis est impassibilis †. At cum sit
alius intellectus passiuus, id est cogitatiua, sina qua [cum] intellectus intelligere non possit, et corrumpatur illa, non recordamur. Alio modo
introduci potest dubitatio: quasi cum attribuatur nobis intellectus qui
perpetuo intelligit, cur non recordamur? Respondere possumus quod
hoc fit quia intellectus agens uacat passione; nihil enim a nobis patitur
et suscipit. At est alius intellectus, id est passiuus, id est intellectus
possibilis qui corrumpitur non secundum essentiam suam, sed secundum scie <n> tiam que corrumpitur in hoc aut in illo. Et cum dicit
'sine isto', id est sine agente intellectu nihil intelligit, et ad quod
propositum possibilis non intelligit sine isto agente. Ergo non recordamur. Hoc dicitur quia possibilis non potest sine agente et agens post
mortem non potest exhaurire a phantasmatibus et reponere in possibili,

---

17 Aristot., *de Anima* 1.4 (408b24-25).

quo fut eius intellectio et recordatio. Et intelligendum quod, ut antea dicebamus, album dicitur corrumpi, et musicum, non quia Aristoxenus corrumpatur sed Aristoxenus musicus, ut in primo *Phisicorum*[18] dicit philosophus 'musicus corrumpitur in immusicum' etc. Sic intellectus possibilis passiuus sciens corrumpitur, non intellectus. Unde cum dixit 'communis intellectui agenti et possibili', si sumatur, igitur sic primo modo; si secundo, tunc communis sumatur intellectus possibilis ut sciens. Prima igitur dubitatione sumitur intellectus passiuus pro cogitatiua ui; secunda sumitur pro intellectu possibili sciente qui ut sciens dici potest corruptibilis, non secundum essentiam suam.

Intellectum passiuum (430a24-25). Exponunt isti pro cogitatiua ui. Lege in *Ethicis*[19] ubi dicit 'singularium est sensus'. Is autem est intellectus.

Pontifical Institute of Mediaeval Studies.

---

18 Aristot., *Phys.* 1.7 (189b34-190a12).
19 Aristot., *Nic. Eth.* 7.3 (1147a25-26).

THE *EXORTACIO* AGAINST PETER ABELARD'S *DIALOGUS INTER PHILOSOPHUM, IUDAEUM ET CHRISTIANUM**

Edward A. Synan

PETER Abelard's account of how he imagined a Jew and a Christian might have debated the ultimate goal of human life with an unbelieving philosopher has been called traditionally a *Dialogus inter Philosophum, Judaeum et Christianum*. This title is not without manuscript support, but some scribes adverted to its internal division: an introductory section and two conferences, the first between a philosopher and a Jew, the second, between the same philosopher and a Christian; their headings invite us to call the work Abelard's *Collationes*.[1] The three significant manuscripts of the work present it in what seems to be a first version (Vienna, Nationalbibliotek 819 ff. 1ʳ-59ᵛ) and in a later redaction which includes certain expansions (Oxford, Balliol College 296 ff. 161ʳ-189ᵛ and London, British Museum Royal XI.A.5, ff. 99ʳ-109ᵛ).[2] In the Vienna codex alone, Abelard's unfinished work is followed immediately by an anonymous critique, styled by its author an *opusculum de inquisicione summi boni* (l. 39) and by the scribe, if not by the author, *Exortacio magistri ad discipulum de inquisicione summi boni* (ll. 1-2).

An edition of the *Dialogus* with the *Exortacio* was published by F. H.

* The Nationalbibliotek, Vienna, Austria, has supplied me with a microfilm of their MS 819 and with permission to publish through the Monastic Manuscript Microfilm Library of Saint John's University, Collegeville, Minnesota, U.S.A.

1 For the title: *Dialogus,* Vienna, Oesterreichische Nationalbibliotek, MS 819, fol. 1ʳ: Dialogus petri Baiolardi; in the same codex, the *Exortacio* edited here, fol. 6oʳ, lines 10-11; for the title: *Collationes,* Oxford, Balliol College MS 296, fol. 161ʳ: Incipit prefacio in collacionibus petri abaelardi; fol. 161ᵛ: Explicit prefacio. Incipit prima collacio, philosophi scilicet cum iudeo; fol. 170 bisᵛ: Explicit collacio prima philosophi cum iudeo. Icipit secunda eiusdem cum xpistiano; finally, fol. 189ᵛ: Explicit collacio phylosophi cum xpistiano.

2 That the Balliol codex presents a recension of the work as it is found in the Vienna codex has been argued persuasively by E. M. Buytaert, "Abelard's Collationes," *Antonianum,* 44 (1969), 18-39, especially 32: "... *W*, then, represents the first draft, *O* the revision. It is difficult to assign a place to *L*, because the codex is deficient where the main developments of *O* occur."

Rheinwald in 1831 and this is the text reprinted by Migne.[3] The recent
Textkritische Edition of the *Dialogus* by R. Thomas,[4] however, does not include the text of the *Exortacio*. Since the Rheinwald-Migne edition is not
without flaws, it seems worthwhile to re-edit this short but interesting
reaction against Abelard's *Dialogus* and to provide some notes toward its
understanding. At least two scribes are responsible for the text of the
Exortacio. The first is the man who had written the Vienna text of the
Dialogus and he brought that of the *Exortacio* to the seventh line of folio
60ᵛ. At that point, he, or another scribe using a finer pen and a more
elegant hand wrote two lines of verse. Following these, yet another
scribe completed the text. This last section is very tightly abbreviated,
the lines are crowded, and the hand may well be later than that of the
Dialogus scribe. The spellings of the two (three) sections of text have
been preserved, but modern punctuation has been employed. References to the text in this Introduction are by marginal numbers enclosed
within parentheses.

The fundamental complaint made by the unnamed critic is that,
although a reader will find "something investigated" in Master Peter's
work, he will not find "sufficiently elucidated what the Highest Good
may be, nor where It may be, nor by what path one might most directly
approach It" (37-38). Abelard, of course, was much given to revising
and expanding this works,[5] but it is not impossible that his later redaction of this one represents an effort to meet such criticism as that of the
Exortacio.

Short though it is, the *Exortacio* falls into two parts, approximately
equal in length; these are divided or joined by two lines of verse in dac-
tylic hexameter (46-47). Here it may be mentioned parenthetically that
the Master's lines of verse pose a peculiar problem. In his 1835 edition
Rheinwald cited a *cultor Abaelardi* who had applied two exceedingly apt
lines by Propertius to his calamitous hero:

> At mihi quod vivo detraxerat invida turba,
> Post obitum duplici fenore reddet honor.

---

3   F. H. Rheinwald, *Anecdota ad historiam ecclesiasticam pertinentia*, Particula I, (Berlin, 1831), PL 178.
1611-1684.

4   *Petrus Abaelardus. Dialogus inter Philosophum, Iudaeum et Christianum*. Textkritische Edition. Ed.
Rudolf Thomas, (Stuttgart-Bad Canstatt, 1970).

5   Thus there are three redactions of the *Theologia Christiana*: E. M. Buytaert, *Theologia Christiana*,
in: *Petri Abaelardi opera theologica* ii, (Turnhout, 1969) 28-41 [Corpus Christianorum, Continuatio
mediaeualis XII]; four redactions of the *Theologia Scholarium*, ibidem 53; "one redaction, slightly
enlarged twice" of the *Commentaria in epistolam Pavli ad Romanos*, ibid., i, 24; of *Sic et non* the same
scholar has observed: "... seemingly more forms (or redactions?) of the work have survived than
was believed ...", "The Greek Fathers in Abelard's 'Sic et Non'," *Antonianum*, 41 (1965) 452.

Now Rheinwald's *cultor Abaelardi* was Nicholas Brulart de Sillery, (1544-1624) who supplied an *Apologetica praefatio pro Petro Abaelardo* for the edition of certain works of Abelard that François Ambroise published at Paris in 1616.[6] The second of the two lines included by the Master in his *Exortacio* suggests imitation of the second line from Propertius:

> Lecta sat eximia presens hec phylosophia
> Doctrine triplicem cuiuis prestabit honorem.

If the Roman poet could claim that posthumous *honor* will be rendered with doubled interest, the mediaeval line promises that philosophy will proffer the honorium of a threefold teaching. Was the line of Propertius applied to Abelard in his own lifetime, or is the similarity — *honor (honos),* future promise, the numerically calculated recompense, the metre — mere coincidence? Like the identity of the man who wrote the *Exortacio,* the puzzle resists solution.

In his first section, however, the anonymous author discloses something of what he was. Certainly he was a Master who has presided over the formation in Christian wisdom of a number of disciples, not a few of whom had been disappointingly unfaithful, not only to their academic training, but to what is named their *professio* as well (23-28). The technical term *professio* was used regularly by mediaevals to designate the act of taking monastic vows, or to designate the record of that act.[7] This might suggest that the *Exortacio* is a monk's rebuttal of Abelardian doctrine, but the inference is far from certain. Abelard, himself a monk, who elsewhere employed the term in precisely that sense,[8] had used it in the opening lines of the *Dialogus* with a more general application. There the term *professio* refers to (1) the commitment of the Christian (of whom Abelard says nothing that would in-

6 Propertius, *Elegiarum* 3, 1, 21-22; F. H. Rheinwald, *Anecdota ad historiam ecclesiasticam pertinentia,* Particula II, (Berlin, 1835); PL 178. 71-104 is a reprint of the *Apologetica praefatio* by de Sillery as found in the *Petri Abaelardi filosophi et theologi abbatis Ruyensis ... opera,* ed. F. Ambroesius, (Paris, 1616).

7 See, s.v. *Revised Medieval Latin Word-List,* R. E. Latham, (London, 1965); also, citation by J. Leclercq, *Analecta Monastica,* deuxième série, (Rome, 1953) 130 [Studia Anselmiana, fasc. xxxi], Odo of Canterbury: "Siquidem una est professio quam faciunt et christianus suscepturus baptismum et monachus suscepturus cucullam ... Non enim altius aliquid profitetur monachus quam promiserat christianus, sed prorsus eamdem professionem repetit ..."

8 Thus, recounting his own entry into the monastic life, "Abelard's Letter of Consolation to a Friend (*Historia Calamitatum*)," ed. J. T. Muckle, *Mediaeval Studies,* 12 (1950) 191, Abelard employed the term *professio*: "... quod professioni meae convenientius erat ..." and he had used the same term in the same passage for the entry of Heloise into religious life: "... et se professioni monasticae coram omnibus alligavit;" this usage is to be found also in the second redaction of his *Theologia* "*Scholarium,*" ed. cit. 402: "Addunt etiam nostrae iam aetati ac professioni conuenire ut sicut mores et habitum ita commutem et studium et humanis diuina praeferam uolumina ..."

dicate he was also a monk) to his faith in the New Covenant; (2) the faith of the Jew in his Hebrew Scriptures which constitute, along with rabbinic forward defenses, his "Law;" and (3) the dependence of the philosopher on "natural law."[9] Apart from confirmatory evidence, it would be audacious to conclude that the Master, who has echoed a term used in so broad a sense in the *Dialogus,* meant any more than that some of his students had violated their profession of the Christian Faith, victims cut down, as he put it, by the sword of Antichrist (21-22).

The Master represented himself further as a teacher who esteemed in his students a capacity for independent research and reflection; the *Exortacio* is explicitly directed to just such a disciple. *Studium* is the term the Master chose to express the dedication of his student to learning (3, 105) and here, too, he echoed Abelard: Peter had put this word on the lips of the philosopher in order to designate Christian concern with both the "Old" and the "New" Testaments: *utriusque lectioni maximum impendat studium.*[10] Academic zeal is witnessed, according to the Master, by reading, *legendo,* and by the goal of reading, *intelligendo* (4). "Reading," of course, must be taken in its strong mediaeval sense, for reading of a high order was the scholastic highroad to understanding[11] and the Disciple is praised for his initiatives in the preliminary as well as in the culminating stage of the academic process.

No doubt the Master had been severe in the training he had provided, for not only did he think it right to note that the schoolmaster's rod can be defended, he provided a defense: Although it might crush the weak, the rod stimulates those with talent to advance (6). Was the Master conscious that he was open to the strictures with which Horace has made odious the name of Orbilius?[12] Had he caused

---

9 Abelard represented himself as posing the question: "cuius sint professionis" at the outset of the *Dialogus,* evoking the response: "Unus quippe nostrum gentilis ex his quos phylosophos appellant, naturali lege contentus est. Alii duo vero scripturas habent, quorum alter Iudeus, alter dicitur Xpistianus ..." ed. cit. 11. 7-10; the "phylosophus" held that natural law is "first" in dignity when compared to written laws: "... que prima est ... Lex vero naturalis, id est scientia morum, quam ethicam dicimus, in solis consistit documentis moralibus," ibidem ll. 81-86 whereas the Jew held, in an echo of *Aboth* 1, 1, that: "... circumcisione aut ceteris legis scripte carnalibus observantiis, non tamen hec ideo superflua adiuncta esse concedendum est, sed plurimum utilitatis habere ad amplificandam vel tutius muniendam religionem ..." ibidem ll. 570-574, and, an even more exact echo of the Talmudic formula: "... Unde legalibus observantiis quasi maceria quadam interpositis eorum ritus ita disiungere, ut nulla conservationis vel familiaritatis coniungerentur societate ..." ibidem ll. 591-594.

10 *Dialogus,* ed. cit. ll. 34-37.

11 To the classic exposition of mediaeval *lectio* by M.-D. Chenu, *Introduction à l'étude de Saint Thomas d'Aquin,* (Paris, 2e éd. 1954), ch. 2, may be added the shrewd observations of E. Dimnet, *L'art de penser,* (Paris, 1930) 102-112 on what reading has been and ought to be.

12 Horace, *Epistolae* 2.1.71: "memini quae plagosum mihi parvo Orbilium dictare ..."

school-boy terrors of the sort to which Augustine ascribed his own
revulsion for the tales in Greek that he read willingly in Latin?[13] The
Master's defense of the rod certainly implies that he had used it freely.
At any rate, he was pleased by the results attained with this Disciple.
Having passed through elementary studies, the Disciple was now
capable of working on his own and this accomplishment inspired his
Master to exhibit some exegetical sleight-of-hand.

Scripture, to be sure, has often used the advance of children from a
diet of milk to one of solid food as a figure for the advance of believers
from elementary to advanced instruction in divine wisdom. Our Master
had out-distanced Holy Writ in the freedom with which he has
manipulated this image. No longer breast-fed or, worse yet, nourished
by disgusting gobbets of food pre-chewed by nurse or midwife (7-10),
the Disciple is represented as raising inquiries that testify to his independence and maturity. Rejoicing now in his own teeth, the Disciple
tastes the savor of wisdom garnered at first hand (10-16). The Master
saw an analogy between a child who has been weaned, who does his
own chewing because his teeth have appeared, and the disciples of Jesus
who on a Sabbath-day has plucked and rubbed ears of corn to éat as
they made their way through fields of ripe grain (12-13). Read
"historically" or "according to the letter," the gospel incident makes a
point about Sabbath observance; the master used it to express his views
on scholarly initiative.

This free reading he supplemented unexpectedly with an off-hand
reference to the banquet with which Abraham celebrated the weaning
of Isaac, as if the Patriarch had mounted a kind of academic graduation
ceremony for his son (16-18). Furthermore, according to this untrammeled exegete, the mothers of the Holy Innocents wept, not merely
because their sons had been massacred, but precisely because this had
occurred before they could be weaned (18-20)!

To make excised fragments of gospel text do the work he wanted
them to do, the Master did not hesitate to change the verb *(non) sunt*
from what the scholastics — following Aristotle — called the *secundo
adiacens* usage to its *tertio adiacens* role.[14] For Matthew, (citing the
Prophet Jeremiah), had written: Rachel lamented her children and "she
would not be conforted, because they are not" (*Mtt.* 2 : 16-18; *noluit con-*

---

13 Augustine, *Confessiones* 1.9. 14-15: "Nam et Homerus peritus texere tales fabellas, et
dulcissime vanus est, et mihi tamen amarus erat puero. Credo etiam graecis pueris Virgilius ita sit,
cum eum sic discere cognuntur, ut ego illum ..." and, ibidem, l. 14. 23: "Cur ego graecam etiam
grammaticam oderam talis cantantem? ... saevis terroribus ac poenis ut nossem instabatur mihi
vehementer ..."

14 Aristotle, *Peri ermeneias* 10; 19[b] 20: "... hotan de to esti triton ..."

solari, quia non sunt). Thus, in the phrase of the Latin Vulgate Bible, *sunt* exercises its full existential force and the Master's adjustment of this weakens the verb to the function of a copula only: *non uult consolari quia non sunt ablactati* (20-21). *Non sunt*, in Scripture a pronouncement of non-being, has become uœder the pen of the Master no more than a negative copula, "dividing" the predicate *ablactati* from its subject, thus "lying in the third place" between the two extreme terms.

Students who had come to a bad end take the place of the blameless Bethlehem boys, the Church replaces the weeping Rachel, and Antichirst is pre-figured by King Herod. When heretics, serving the turn of Antichrist, slaughter immature students, the Church laments their destruction because they were not given the chance to reach their *bimatum*; the "two years" of the Innocents has become the twin goal of education, "that pair: understanding and doing" (21-23).

So too, the Book of Revelations (*Apoc.* 3 : 16) speaks ill of those who are neither hot nor cold but tepid, and monks knew well that tepidity in religious observance might well be brought under that scriptural condemnation.[15] "Hot" and "cold" are not metaphors for moral failure in this passage; only the "tepid" hearer of the Word is blamed. The Master, however, was ready to improve upon this pericope as well. Some of his own disciples had become tepid and this meant that they are "childish", even "animal" (23-25), that is, bereft of the rationality that marks the adult.[16] He extended the notion of becoming tepid to that of cooling beyond the point of tepidity to that of extreme cold, and to be cold in the religious and moral sphere is the Master's figure for those who positively persecute those things wich "are of the Spirit of God" (25-26).

As the Master seems to have echoed Abelard's use in the *Dialogus* of the terms *professio* and *studium,* so he seems to have chosen deliberately the term *estimacio* is order to evoke the contentious Abelardian *existimacio.* For Peter Abelard has started a covey of accusations of heresy when he paraphrased *Hebrews* 11 : 1 by defining faith as an

---

15 J. Leclercq, op. cit. 167: "Sed, quod gemens profero, fervor illae primitiuae religionis uersus est in teporem, ut iam terribilem illam de Apocalypsi Ioannis comminationem nostri temporis monachis ueraciter adscribere ualeamus: *Quia lepidus es et nec frigidus nec calidus, incipiam te euomere ex ore meo* (Apoc 3 : 15)."

16 Presumably the common deficiency of human children and brute animals is their inability to reason; the anonymous author may have read the line of Anselm, "Qui enim dubitat quod in natura sua ligno melior sit equus, et equo praestantior homo, is profecto non est dicendus homo," *Monologion* 4; *Sancti Anselmi ... Opera omnia,* ed. F. S. Schmitt (Seccovii, 1938) I, 17 in which Anselm clearly intends that irrational talk and judgments are incompatible with humanity, rational by essence; our critic arraigns his disappointing students as "children," that is, not yet rational, or as "animals," essentially irrational.

existimacio rerum non apparentium.[17] This offered the Master an op-
portunity to allude to yet another standard complaint against Abelard,
namely, that he diminished the mystery of faith by pretending to give
dialectical elucidations of the most profound enigmas of faith.[18] That
Peter's elucidation of the Highest Good in his *Dialogus* seemed in-
sufficient did not tempt the Master to fall into the same courses; he
would not attempt to express the Ineffable (42-44). A good scholastic,
the Master distinguished between the *rei estimacio* and what the *legentis et
inquirentis esuricio* might be; his modest aspiration was to meet the
demands of the second, to renounce the blasphemous enterprise of
taking the measure of the first, for that Reality is beyond our telling —
res ipsa est ineffabilis, except, of course, insofar as we may receive Its help
to speak of It (44-45).

Phylosophia in the Master's verse retains its traditional amplitude as a
Christian love of all wisdoms that stem from Wisdom Itself and here,
once more, Abelard is under indirect attack. In the interest of a
precision that was destined to carry the future, Peter had named the
study of divinity, as distinguished from exclusively rational studies,
theologia,[19] thus giving a new and Christian significance to an old pagan
label. Bernard's annoyance at this innovation did not leave him at a loss
for a memorable retort: "His 'theology,'" thundered the Abbot of
Clairvaux "is more accurately 'fool-ology'."[20]

Thomas of Morigny, should we prefer his vituperative ingenuity,

---

17   See the redaction materials of the *Theologia "Scholarium"* as edited by E. M. Buytaert, ed. cit.
404, ll. 114-115; *existimatio* and *estimacio* are not uncommon in Abelard's writing: *Commentaria ... ad
Romanos,* ed. cit. 102, ll. 207-209: Quorum, scilicet nos blasphemantium, id est non tam pro
existimacione sua quam propter nos blasphemandos id dicentium..." *Expositio Symboli Apostolorum,*
PL 178. 623 B: "... ita Deus vel Dominus sola est dicenda, ut nullatenus res alia Dominus sit
existimanda ..."; *In Symbolum Athanasii,* PL 178. 631 C: "... nonulla est quaestio. Quidquid tamen de
hoc aestimemus ..."; *Problemata Heloissae* 33, PL 178. 715 D: "Quantum aestimo ..."; *Sermo* 18 In die
Pentecostes, PL 178. 509 D: "Repentinus sonitus iste fuit, quia super humanam existimationem
hujus inspirationis gratia crevit."; *Sermo* 32, PL 178. 578 B: "Hanc eamdem portam aestimo, qua et
Christus ad crucifigendum egressus est ..."

18   To Saint Bernard it appeared that Abelard, "Magister Petrus in libris suis profanas vocum
novitates inducit et sensum: disputans de fide contra fidem, verbis legis legem impugnat. Nihil videt
per speculum et in aenigmate; sed facie ad faciem omnia intuetur, ambulans in magnis et in
mirabilibus super se." (1 Corinthians 13 : 12); *Epistola* 92, PL 182. 358 C, D.

19   J. Leclercq, *L'amour des lettres et le désir de Dieu,* (Paris, 1957) 99: "... les mots *theologia, theologus,*
chez un Jean de Fécamp et d'autres, gardaient toute leur saveur antique, et n'avaient pas la nuance
speculative qu'ils recevront en Occident à partir d'Abélard. Un autre terme grec auquel on con-
serve son antique signification est *philosophia*;" yet Abelard on occasion spoke in the pre-Abelardian
accent: "Hinc illud est in laude Christianae philosophiae, hoc est monasticae praerogativae ..."
Epistola vii ad Heloissam, PL 178. 234 B.

20   Bernard, *Tractatus de erroribus Abaelardi,* 4, 9: "... in primo limine Theologiae, vel potius
Stultilogiae suae fidem definit aestimationem ..." PL 182. 1061 B, C.

went a step farther: for him, Abelard's doctrine was "devil-ology."[21] For the older tradition dominated by Augustine — and we shall see how much an Augustinian the Master was — the Christian sage has spoiled the philosophical Egyptians; his "love of wisdom" is a formation, at once moral and intellectual, that embraces the natural law of which the pagan spoke, the Hebrew Scriptures, and the New Covenant to which the Church subscribes (107-111). But it would be an error to think the Master's "threefold honorarium of doctrine" alien to be thought of Abelard. Not only has Abelard used *philosophia* in the wider and more traditional sense,[22] but in the *Dialogus* he has taken the census of the threefold honorarium: the devout reading of the book of nature which is *physica*, the cultivation of Christian reason in a world that embodies truth, *logica*, and in the summit position Abelard did not contest, the moral doctrine, *ethica*, by which a free Christian man, anticipated and supported by grace to be sure, lives the truth he believes and, to a point, understands.[23]

The *Exortacio* presents its positive doctrine on the Highest Good in the first instance as a homiletic echo of Augustine and of Scripture on the incomprehensibility of the Lord. The Bishop of Hippo had developed

21 Thomas of Morigny: "Haec autem eodem ordine verbis eisdem, licet locis diversis, sicut hic posita sunt, ab antiquo serpente per eum in diabologia illa evomita sunt ..." PL 180. 284 A-285 A, *Disputatio ... adversus dogmata Petri Abaelardi.*

22 To the text adduced above, note 19 (*Epistola vii ad Heloissam*) may be added: *Sermo* 32: "Quod diligenter maximus ille Christianorum philosophus Origenes attendens ..." PL 178. 571 B, (cf. PL 178. 207 B; *Sermo* 33: "Ab his duobus tanquam ducibus nostri propositi, seu principibus hujus philosophiae christianae tam in veteri quam in novo populo ..." PL 178. 585 B; ibidem: "Propterea in eremo philosophatur, et reservat se in adventum Christi ... Non vult cum hominibus conversari, in eremo cum angelis philosophatur ..." 585 D; ibidem: "Ut autem nunc documenta sanctorum omittam, gentilium saltem philosophorum exempla nostrae cupiditatis impudentiam remprimant ..." 591 C; ibidem: "Quia si de philosophis ad apostolis, imo ad ipsam sophiam Christum, quasi a minimis ad maxima conscendere velimus ..." 592 B; *Epistola* xiii: "... Cujus etiam amatores tanto verius appellantur philosophi, quanto veriores sint illius sophiae superioris amatores ... nos ab amore mundi in amorem converteret sui; profecto nos pariter Christianos et veros efficit philosophos." PL 178. 355 C.

23 In the *Dialogus*, Abelard has put on the lips of the philosopher the words: "Nostrorum itaque scolis diu intentus et tam ipsorum rationibus quam auctoritatibus eruditus ad moralem tandem me contuli philosophiam, que omnium finis est disciplinarum, et propter quam cetera omnia prelibanda iudicavi ..." ed. cit. ll. 18-22; in the *Theologia Christiana* ii, 33, he has written in his own name: "Vnde et propter ipsam quoque physicam uel cuiuslibet philosophiae perceptionem, quae nonnisi in discussione occultarum causarum consistunt, primum purgandae bonis moribus uitae censebat instandum, ac si ethicam in omni philosophia primum praefigeret gradum, ut quos amore Dei ad uitae honestatem allicere non posset, saltem cupiditate philosophiae aliquatenus ad hoc eos initiaret ..." ed. cit. 145, ll. 439-445; Abelard held that philosophical understanding was salvific for the pagan: *Commentaria ... ad Romanos*: "Nulla itaque ratione cogendi videmur, ut de salute talium diffidamus gentilium qui ante adventum redemptoris nullo legis scripto instructi, naturaliter, iuxta Apostolum, *ea quae legis sunt* facientes, *ipsi sibi lex* erant ..." ed. cit. 141, ll. 285-290.

his views at adequate length in his "little work on the Highest Good" (48-49), the *De natura boni*[24] and the anonymous critic of Abelard knew that behind the *Proslogion* formula of Anselm lies that of Augustine:[25] God is not only that than Whom "nothing better can be thought," He is "indeed better than can be thought by any creature" (51-52). Biblical proof-texts on the divine incomprehensibility are easy to find and the Master found what he needed: 1 *Timothy* 6 : 16, *Jeremiah* 32 : 19, *Romans* 11 : 33, 1 *Corinthians* 13 : 9, 12. To the Augustinian atmosphere engendered by his appeal to the formula that Augustine may have read in Seneca[26] before he bequeathed it to Anselm, the Master added the Augustinian correlation *utor-fruor*:[27] by "using" well created goods we shall come to "enjoy" their Creator, the Highest Good (66-72). Finally, at the end of the critique, the Master borrowed once more from the Augustinian lexicon. Grace leads us to our *patria*,[28] an image for the goal of our wayfaring that Augustine almost certainly found in Plotinus, who had likened to the voyaging of Odysseus our ascent from the allurements of corporeal beauty to Primal Good and Primal Beauty.[29]

No one is less likely than the Bishop of Hippo to divert the theologian from the text of Scripture; our Master had yet another exegetical ploy to unveil, this time, on a term with strong monastic over-tones. This world, he held, is the marketplace of the parable where the Lord of the vineyard finds unemployed laborers — *ociosi pagani* — but also *negociantes ivdei* (oo-oo). Now *negocior* is the negation of *otior*, yet both are clearly

---

24   Augustine, *De Natvra Boni Liber*, recensvit Ios. Zycha (Vienna etc., 1892), [Corpus scriptorum ecclesiasticorum latinorum 25, 855-889].

25   "Aliquid quo nihil maius cogitari possit" of Anselm (*Proslogion* 2) is matched by Augustine's "quo nullus est superior" or "quo nihil superius esse constiterit" found in his *De libero arbitrio* 2, 6, 14, PL 32. 1248; "Quid enim eligamus, quod praecipue diligamus, nisi quo nihil melius invenimus? ... Tanto enim nobis melius est, quanto magis in illum imus, quo nihil melius est ..." *Epistola* 155, 4, 13; PL 33. 672; "Nam cum ille unus cogitatur Deus, ab his etiam qui alios et suspicantur et vocant et colunt deos sive in coelo sive in terra, ita cogitatur ut aliquid quo melius sit atque sublimius illa cogitatio conetur attingere ... Omnes, tamen certatim pro excellentia Dei dimicant; nec quisquam inveniri potest quo hoc Deum credat esse quo melius aliquid est ..." *De doctrina christiana* 1, 7, 7; PL 34. 22.

26   L. Annaei Senecae ad Lucillium *naturalium quaestionum libri VII*, ed. F. Haase, (Leipzig, 1893) I, prol. 159: "... sic demum magnitudo sua illi redditur, qua nihil maius excogitari potest ..."

27   Augustine, *De doctrina christiana* 1, 4, 4; PL 34. 20: "Frui autem est amore alicui rei inhaerere propter seipsam. Uti autem, quod in usum venerit ad id quod amas obtinendum referre, si tamen amandum est ..."

28   Augustine, *Confessiones* 7, 21.27; PL 32. 747: "... Et aliud est de silvestri cacumine videre patriam pacis, et iter ad eam non invenire, et frustra conari per invia, circum obsidentibus et insidiantibus fugitivis desertoribus, cum principe suo leone et dracone: et aliud tenere viam illuc ducentem curia coelestis Imperatoris munitam ..."

29   Plotinos, *Ennead* 1.6.8.

intended to be taken here in a pejorative sense. The "philosophizing pagan" (81) does, and indeed can do, nothing toward the salvation which the Master will describe in thoroughly Augustinian terms as at all points the work of grace. For grace "excites and strengthens our will, illumines our reason, precedes and follows decision, leads us on our road" (117-120). Thus the practical inactivity and the theoretically ineluctable incapacity of Abelard's philosopher on the matter of salvation puts him among the *ociosi* of the parable. *Otium*, however, has a favorable meaning, well-known in the monasteries, and grounded in the usage of Cicero.[30] Jews are pilloried for negating *otium*, even though the disbelieving philosophers have been excoriated as *ociosi*. The *negociantes ivdei* fail, presumably because they are too much occupied with the business of this world and, in fact, with that business in its worst form. Abelard had put on the lips of the Jew in the *Dialogus* a complaint that the only livelihood open to a Jew in Christendom was that of money-lender, a trade especially calculated to provoke resentment on the part of the Jew's debtors.[31] The air of antisemitism that hangs over this phrase is deepened by the Master's somewhat pleonastic reference to the *ebreum ivdaizantem*[32] as companion to the *paganum philosophantem* (81). Saint Bernard had made the same association[33] and Saint Bonaventure would prolong it:[34] neither philosopher nor Jew accepts the cosmic role of Christ. But the Master knew a group he adjudged to be worse than either pagans or Jews; these were the "fraudulent Christians" — *illis peiores, falsi christiani* (73-74). A condemnation of a sub-set of his own community reduces the impression of anti-semitism and anti-intellectualism on the part of the Master, as does a parallel observation by Saint Bernard:

> Jewish disbelief is a night, the ignorance of pagans is a night, the

---

30 An instance of this is the aphorism Cicero ascribed to Scipio on the testimony of Cato: "... Scipionem ... dicere solitum scripsit Cato ... Numquam se minus otiosum esse quam cum otiosus, nec minus solum quam cum solus esset ..." *De officiis* 3.1.1; see J. Leclercq, *Etudes sur le vocabulaire monastique du moyen âge*, (Rome, 1961) 27-41.

31 "Unde nobis precipue superest lucrum, ut alienigenis fenerantes hinc miseram sustentemus vitam, quod nos quidem maxime ipsis efficit invidiosos, qui se in hoc plurimum arbitrantur gravatos." ed. cit. ll. 288-291.

32 This term does not imply proselytizing by Jews among the Christians; see, s.v. *Revised Medieval Latin Word-List*, cited above.

33 "... verumtamen et Iudaei potestate ipsa premebantur, et philosophi scrutatores maiestatis opprimebantur a gloria. Potestas subiectionem, maiestas exigit admirationem, neutra imitationem." *Sancti Bernardi opera*, Sermones II, edd. J. Leclercq and H. M. Rochais, (Rome, 1966) IV, 245; [Editiones Cistercienses].

34 "Dimissis ergo Philosophorum et Iudaeorum erroribus, credimus medicum nostrum Deum et hominem Iesum Christum ..." *Sancti Bonaventurae Collationes in Hexaemeron et Bonaventuriana Quaedam Selecta ad Fidem Codicum Manuscriptorum*, ed. F. M. Delorme, (Quaracchi, 1934) 102.

wickedness of heretics is a night, and a night too is the fleshy or bestial way of life led by Catholics.[35]

Needless to insist that the Master holds the Hebrew Scriptures and, indeed, the Law of Moses, in the same honor (118) as had Abelard;[36] we might be less prepared to note that the natural law, which Abelard had adduced as the sole resource of his philosopher, is considered by the Master to be part of the teaching of Christ (117). The Master's rejection of pagan and of Jewish wisdom is thus to be qualified: both have a value, to be sure, but no Christian, he thought, need have recourse to those who possess only a part of wisdom, subsumed in Wisdom Itself — Jesus is Messiah and salvation is granted only to adults who work in His vineyard, or to infants who receive His sacraments (75-76).

The rest of the *Exortacio* is no more than a web of scriptural tags applied to Jesus of Nazareth as so many reasons for repeating the Gospel injunction: "Hear him!" *ipsum audite* (*Mtt.* 17 : 5), an injunction that the Master has repeated in his own name so fewer than twenty-two times. Here too, we have reason to think of Saint Bernard, for he has used *Matthew* 17 : 5 in a sermon in order to invoke biblical support for an analysis he had proposed:

> But lest these things we say about this "middle advent" seem to anyone to be contrived, "Hear him: if anyone love me ..."[37]

It is perhaps a measure of the distance that separates our anonymous Master from the towering figure of the Abbot of Clairvaux that a rhetorical device found but once in an imposing volume of sermons by the second has been used twenty-two times by the first on a single page. Like Newman's Oxford paragon whose latinity captivated the elder Mr. Black, the Master used on one page the "flowers which Cicero scatters over a treatise."[38]

Yet even in this scriptural cascade, the last philosophical assumptions of the Master are visible for he read his Bible in a hierarchic cosmos. Lesser goods are such because they participate in the Highest Good (62-68); the moral man participates in that same Highest Good (68-72); ontology and morals are parallel.

None of this permits us to identify the Master. His vocabulary (*professio, otium*) evokes monasticism and twice his turn of phrase can be

---

35   "Nox est Judaica perficia, nox ignorantia paganorum, nox haeretica pravitas, nox etiam Catholicorum carnalis, animalisve conversatio." Bernard, *Sermo* 75, PL 183. 1149.

36   Text cited above, note 10.

37   "Sed ne cui forte inventitia videantur quae de hoc adventu medio dicimus, ipsum audite: SI QUIS DILIGIT ME ..." ed. cit. IV, 189.

38   J. H. Newman, *The Idea of a University*, Elementary Studies, no. 3: Latin Writing.

matched in the works of Bernard. But Abelard too was a monk and Bernard was not the only anti-Abelardian to be found in or, at least, based upon a cloister. To say that there is a high probability that the Master was an unidentifiable monk is as safe as it is nugatory. Let us be content with the conclusion that the Master was a traditionalist Christian who shared the hesitations felt by William of Saint Thierry, Thomas of Morigny, and Bernard of Clairvaux in the presence of Abelard's Philonic openness to Greek as well as to Hebrew wisdom.

To the question of our anonymous critic's identity, we have no plausible suggestion to make; has Abelard read the *Exortacio* and produced the Balliol redaction to meet its criticism? There is no hint in the Balliol expansions that this was Peter's concern. Our results, therefore, are negative, but negative results remain results for all that. The shade of the critic who composed this contentious estimate of Abelard's striking venture in the reconciliation of three wisdoms must rest content with the survival of his text without his name.

Exortacio magistri ad discipulum
de inquisicione summi boni

Fili karissime: studium tuum delectat me, quo sapientum scripta
inuestigas, per te ipsum legendo et intelligendo queque non intelligis a
5 me ceterisque senioribus perquirendo. Etenim scolaris illa exercitacio
— qua sub uirga pauitantes proficiunt ingeniosi, deficiunt hebetes —
bonae indolis adolescentibus uix est pro infantilibus nutrimentis, qualia
sepe uidimus ab obstetricibus uel nutricibus masticata, in ora uagien-
cium puerulorum edentulorum poni, eisdem renitentibus et offas aliena
10 saliua infectas interdum fastidientibus. Vnde, cum primis dentatis
maxillis per se mandere possunt, ab aliis masticata non recipiunt,
immo, cum discipulis domini transeundo per segetes copiosas, uellicant
et fricant manu propria spicas maturas, ex indeque grana elicita per se
manducant et experiendo probant in scolaribus illis exerciciis diligen-
15 tissime lactatos non inuenire saporem sapienciae nisi post tempus ablactacionis suae. Hinc est quod abraham patriarcha "grande," legitur
fecisse "conuiuium in die ablactacionis" ysaac; nimirum, est gaudens
(59ᵛ/60ʳ) paterno affectu profectibus tanti filii. Quo contra, "ploratus et
ululatus multus" est racheli ploranti "filios suos," ante ablactacionis
20 tempus ab herode occisos; ac tum plangit ecclesia et non uult "consolari quia non sunt" ablactati eius illi pueri quos trucidat gladius antichristi pro eo quod sunt infra bimatum, non attingentes ad geminae

---

1   *Exortacio magistri* is written by the hand that wrote the *Dialogus* as the last words of line 10,
folio 59ᵛ; a second hand has added in the left margin: *ad discipulum de inquisicione summi boni.*

7ff   For the scriptural use of eating to represent the learning process, see *Ezechiel* 2 : 8 ff.; for the
shift from milk to solid food, see 1 *Corinthians* 3 : 2: Lac vobis potum dedi non escam; cf; *Hebrews*
5 : 12: ...cum deberetis magistri esse propter tempus, rursum indigetis, ut vos doceamini... facti estis
quibus lacte opus sit non solido cibo. Omnis enim qui lactis est particeps expers est sermonis
iustitiae, parvulus enim est; cf. 1 *Peter* 2 : 1-3.

13   *Luke* 6 : 1: ...transiret per sata, vellebant discipuli eius spicas et manducabant confricantes
manibus; cf. *Matthew* 12 : 1: ...vellere spicas et manducare...; *Mark* 2 : 23: ...vellere spicas...

17   *Genesis* 21 : 8: Crevit igitur puer, et ablactatus est; fectique Abraham grande convivium in die
ablactationis eius.

22   *Matthew* 2 : 16-18: Herodes... mittens occidit omnes pueros, qui erant in Bethlehem et in omnibus finibus eius a bimatu et infra... per Ieremiam prophetam dicentem:

Vox in Rama audita est,
ploratus et ululatus multus:
Rachel plorans filios suos et
noluit consolari, quia non sunt.

The words of *Jeremiah* 31 : 15, according to the Vulgate, are:

Vox in excelso audita est lamentationis,
luctus et flectus.
Rachel plorantis filios suos et
nolentis consolari super eis, quia non sunt.

22   The Master may have read in Gregory I, *XL Homiliarum in Evangelia*, liber 1, hom. 9: Duobus

intelligenciae et operacionis fructum. Me miserum! pro quot paruulis
ita michi abreptis ego plorare habeo quia eos, post exercicia scolaria,
25 uideo uel tepuisse in sensum puerilem et animalem, qui 'non percipit
ea que sunt spiritus dei," uel omnino friguisse in reprobum sensum, ut
non solum faciant que non conueniunt eorum professioni, sed etiam
persequantur ea que sunt spiritus dei. Tu autem, fili dilectissime, ut
spero in dei misericordia, proficies eciam ultra bimatum usque adeo ut
30 formidare non habeas gladium antichristi, qui est hereticorum seu
falsorum fratrum sermo dolosus. Nisi enim sic proficeres, nisi ablactatus iam solidum cibum uehementer esurires, de summo bono, sicut
inquiris, non inquireres.
   Occasio uero huiusce inquisicionis ex inde, ut dicis, oborta est tibi
35 quod, legens "dyalogum" sub disceptacione "christiani et iudei atque
philosophi" a magistro petro digestum de summo bono, illic inuenis
aliquid inuestigatum, sed non satis elucidatum: quid sit uel ubi sit i-
psum summum bonum, quaue ad illud uia sit rectissime gradiendum.
Proinde sic accipe istud opusculum "de inquisicione summi boni" in-
40 titulatum, ut si quid boni de hoc bo —'60'/60ᵛ) — no hic inueneris dictum, de hoc ipso bono unde agimus non dubites aut stillasse, si parum
est, aut emanasse, si satis est. "Satis" dico, non quantum ad rei, que uer-
satur, estimacionem, sed quantum ad legentis et inquirentis
esuricionem. Nam res ipsa est ineffabilis, de qua fari utcunque gestimus
45 prout, ipsa iuuante, poterimus

> Lecta sat eximia presens hec phylosophia
> Doctrine triplicem cuiuis prestabit honorem.

   Puto, autem, si opusculum augustini "de summo bono" intitulatum
bene perspexeris, illic habundanter instrueris esse illud summum
50 bonum ex quo, per quod, in quo, sunt omnia bona — magna, media, et
minima, et ipsum tale est vt nichil melius cogitari possit, immo, melius

---

vero intellectus et operatio designatur (PL 76, 1106), an echo of the distinction drawn by Greek and
Roman philosophers between speculative and practical life, v.g. Cicero, *De finibus* 2.13.40:
...hominem ad duas res, ut ait Aristoteles, ad intelligendum et ad agendum esse natum...

   25   *Revelations* 3 : 16: Sed, quia tepidus es et nec frigidus nec calidus, incipiam te evomere ex ore
meo...

   28   *Galatians* 4 : 29: Sed quomodo tunc is qui secundum carnem natus fuerat persequebatur eum
qui secundum spiritum, ita et nunc...; cf. 1 *Corinthians* 2 : 12: Nos autem non spiritum huius mundi
accepimus, sed Spiritum qui ex Deo est; cf. *ibidem*, v. 14: Homo non percipit ea quae sunt Spiritus
Dei.

   31   2 *Corinthians* 11 : 26: ... periculis in falsis fratribus...

   44   Em. MS: *esuriri* followed by blotted letter, horizontal stroke above it.

   48   *Sancti Avreli Avgvstini De Natvra Boni Liber*, recensvit Iosephvs Zycha (Prague, Vienna, Leipzig,
1892), CSEL 25, sectio vi, pars 2, 853-889.

   51   Ed. cit. p. 855, ll. 3-6: Summum bonum, quo superius non est, deus est; ac per hoc in-
commutabile bonum est; ideo uere aeternum et uere inmortale. cetera omnia bona nonnisi ab illo

est quam ab ulla creatura cogitari possit. Nisi, enim, transcenderet omnem, tam angelorum quam et hominvm, cogitationem, non exuperaret
omnem sensum, nec inhabitaret "lucem inaccessibilem," neque
55 diceretur vere "incomprehensibile" quod quis posset cogitatione vel intellectu attingere et comprehendere. Sensit hoc ille qui dixit: "O
altitudo divitiarum sapientiae et scientiae ... quam incomprehensibilia
sunt iudicia ... et investigabiles viae ... Quis enim cognovit sensum
domini?" Attamen "ex parte" illud summum bonum cognoverunt "et
60 ex parte" inde prophetauerunt hi per quos canonica scriptura veteris
ac noui testamenti amministrata est, in qua uelut "per speculum" et "in
enigmate" apparet pulchritudo summi boni, summe ivsticie, summe
vite, summe potencie, summe leticie, summe caritatis, que omnia eisque
similia, de summo bono predicata, non sunt multa, sed vnum causale ac
65 primordiale principivm seu fundamentum omnivm que per ipsum et
post ipsum bona sunt in ordine rerum. Quae, cum in sui natura sint
omnes bonae, utpote a summo bono habentes, est tamen eis et bene vti
— bonum est, et male vti — malum est. Docet autem sacra scriptura,
maxime autem noui testamenti, quomodo inferioribus bonis homini sit
70 vtendum vt perveniat ad summum bonum cuius fructus eternus
tanquam divrnus denarius illi erit persoluendus, qui bonis inferioribus
bene vtendo laborant in vinea, que est presens et peregrinans ecclesia.
Extra quam stantes in foro huius mundi, ociosi pagani sive negociantes
ivdei, sive — illis peiores — falsi christiani, habere denarivm non po-
75 tvervnt, qui solis bene in vinea laborantibus aut, si tempora laborandi
non habent, vt infantes, christi sacramenta gestantibus, dandum

sunt, sed non de illo; p. 856, l. 11: a quo omnia bona seu magna seu parua; p. 858, l. 18: ...minora et
minima bona...

54   1   *Timothy* 6 : 16: Et lucem inhabitat inaccessibilem.

55   *Jeremiah* 32 : 19: Magnus consilio, et incomprehensibilis cogitatu.

56   *Romans* 11 : 33: O altitudo divitiarum sapientiae et scientiae Dei! Quam incomprehensibilia
sunt judicia ejus, et investigabiles viae ejus! Quis enim cognovit sensum Domini? aut quis consiliarius ejus fuit?

59   1   *Corinthians* 13 : 9: Ex parte enim cognoscimus, et ex parte prophetamus...

61   *Ibidem*, v. 12: Videmus nunc per speculum in aenigmate, tunc autem facie ad faciem. Nunc
cognosco ex parte; tunc autem cognoscam, sicut et cognitus sum.

70   *Matthew* 20 : 1 ff.: ... exiit primo mane conducere operarios in vineam suam. Conventione
autem facta cum operariis ex denario diurno... vidit alios stantes in foro otiosos... Quid hic statis
tota die otiosi? 66 Augustine, *De Natura Boni*, ed. cit. p. 873, ll. 6-8: ...factum ipsum malum est, non
illa natura, qua male utitur peccans.

73   Augustine, *De civitate dei* 19 (PL 41, 647): Otium sanctum quaerit caritas veritatis; negotium
iustum suscipit necessitas caritatis, and Aquinas, *Summa theologiae* II-II, 182, 1, in c. (Utrum vita activa sit potior quam contemplativa), give full value to both *otium* and *Negotium* whereas the Master
finds them both worthy of condemnation.

75   *Ecclesiastes* 3 : 1-9: Omnia tempus habent... Quid habet ampluis homo de labore suo?; *John*
9 : 4: Venit nox quando nemo potest operari.

nouerunt, qui non a philosophis aut (60ᵛ/61ʳ) ivdeis christum ignoran-
tibus aut reprobantibus, sed ex ipso christo, veritatis doctrinam ac-
ceperunt. "Ipsum audite!" ait pater celestis. "Ipsum audite!" aio et ego
80 uobis, quicunque me auditis, discipuli seu filii. Ipsum audite pocius
quam paganum philosophantem et ebreum ivdaizantem. Ipsum audite,
non solum ivsta docentem, sed et impios ivstificantem, non per sapien-
tiam "huius mundi" aut "ex operibus legis," sed per fidem, qua doctrina eius creditur et custoditur, sicut ipse ait: "Beati qui audivnt ver-
85 bum dei et custodivnt illud." In custodiendo illo retribucio multa.
Revera hec retribucio multa est, que non habet finem, sed ipsa est finis,
et consummacio participantivm summo bono, frventium summo
gaudio, sapientivm summa sapientia, que est christus. Ipsum audite!
"Consiliarius" est: ipsum audite! "Preceptor" est: ipsum audite! Si non
90 poteris recipere ipsius consilivm vt abnegantes uos uobis ipsum
sequamini, saltem seruate preceptum et in utroque cognoscendo, ipsum
audite. Primo, si fieri potest, ad conseruanda innocentiam, ipsum
audite. Secundo, ubi amiseritis innocentiam, saltem ad agendam
penitentiam, ipsum audite. Si facultas suppetit ad agendum bona, ipsum
95 audite. Si facultas deest, ad uolandum saltem bona, ipsum audite. Si
vultis scire quid sit summum bonum, vel qua via ad illud progredien-
dum, ipsum audite dicentem: "ego sum via et veritas et vita." Nam via
qua itur, et veritas ac vita quo itur, ipse est: ipsum audite! Si forte in
via hac ambulantes "estis tristes," cum discipulis euntibus emmaus, i-
100 psum audite ambulantem uobiscum et consolantem uos vt, tandem,
"stulti et tardi corde," accendamini et dicatis: "Nonne cor nostrum ardens erat in nobis" de illo "dum loqueretur nobis in via, et aperiret
nobis scripturas?" Ipse est qui scripturas ambulantibus in se — via et
veritate — aperit; ipsum audite! "aperit et nemo claudit:" ipsum

---

79 *Matthew* 17 : 5: Hic est Filius meus dilectus, in quo mihi bene complacui: ipsum audite.

82 1 *Corinthians* 3 : 19: Sapientia enim huius mundi stultitia est.

83 *Romans* 3 : 20: ...quia ex operibus legis non justificabitur omnis caro coram illo; per legem
enim cognitio peccati; *ibidem* 4 : 13: Non enim per legem promissio Abrahae, ... sed per justitiam
fidei.

84 *Luke* 11 : 28: At ille dixit: Quinimmo beati qui audiunt verbum Dei, et custodiunt illud.

89 *Isaiah* 9 : 6: Parvulus enim natus est nobis... et vocabitur nomen eius Admirabilis, Consiliarius, Deus, Fortis, Pater futuri saeculi, Princeps pacis...

Praeceptor is applied to Jesus in the gospel according to *Luke* 5 : 5, 8 : 24, 8 : 45, 9 : 33, 9 : 49, 17 : 13,
21 : 7.

90 *Matthew* 16 : 24: ...abneget semetipsum et tollat crucem suam et sequatur me; cf. *ibidem*
10 : 38; also *Mark* 8 : 34 and *Luke* 9 : 23.

97 *John* 14 : 6: Dicit ei Jesus: Ego sum via, et veritas, et vita.

99 *Luke* 24 : 13-32; v. 17: estis tristes?, v. 25: O stulti et tardi corde... v. 32: Nonne cor nostrum
ardens erat in nobis, dum loqueretur in via et aperiret nobis scripturas?

105 audite! Ambulantibus dicit: bonas facite vias uestras et studia vestra;
ipsum audite! pervenientibus dicit: "habitabo uobiscum;" ipsum
audite! Legem naturalem, quam paganus philosophus defendit, ipse
docet: ipsum audite! Legem moysi venit implere non soluere; ipsum
audite! "Lex," quidem annuncians ac demonstrans languorem, "per
110 moysen data est, gracia," autem, "et veritas" eundem sanans languorem, "per iesum christum facta est;" ipsum audite! Summum
bonum se sequentibus et sibi obedientibus promisit in premio cetera
bona inferiora eisdem concessit ad vtilitatem ita vt "omnia cooperen-
tur" eis "in bonum," per bonum vsum quo, non solum bonis, verum et
115 malis vti, docentur in bonum si, tamen, audiant ipsum. Ergo, ipsum
audite, sitque uobis anathema quicunque alivd docet quam quod habet
verbum doctrine ipsius evangelice plena gracia et veritate, gracia ex-
citante ac roborante uoluntatem, veritate illuminante racionem, gracia
uoluntatem preueniente ac subsequente, veritate racionem dirigente
120 atque ducente in viam pacis ad patriam lucis eterne, in qua clare
videbitur et gustabitur summum bonum, quod est pater et filius et
spiritus sanctus, deus vnus ac trinus: "Ipsi gloria in secula seculorum.
Amen."

Pontifical Institute of Mediaeval Studies.

106 *John* 14 : 23: Si quis diligit me, sermonem meum servabit, et Pater meus diliget eum, et ad eum veniemus et mansionem apud eum faciamus.

108 *Matthew* 4 : 17: Nolite putare quoniam veni solvere legem, aut prophetas: non veni solvere, sed adimplere.

109 *John* 1 : 17: Quia lex per Moysen data est, gratia et veritas per Iesum Christum facta est.

110 1 *Peter* 2 : 24: ...cujus livore sanati estis.

113 *Romans* 8 : 28: Scimus autem quoniam diligentibus Deum omnia cooperantur in bonum.

116 *Galatians* 1 : 8: ...aut angelus de caelo evangelizet vobis praeterquam quod evangelizavimus vobis, anathema sit.

Cf. 1 *Timothy* 1 : 3: ...denuntiares quibusdam ne aliter docerent.

119 Augustine, *De natura et gratia* (PL 44, 264): Praevenit ut sanemur, subsequitur ut sanati vegetemur; praevenit ut vocemur, subsequitur ut glorificemur; (cfr. Aquinas, *Summa theologiae* I-II, 111, 3: Utrum gratia convenienter dividatur in praevenientem et subsequentem).

122 *Romans* 11 : 36: ...ipsi gloria in saecula. Amen.

NUGAE HYGINIANAE

Sister Wilma Fitzgerald

WHILE working with manuscripts of *Hygini De Astronomia,* I have encountered numerous codices which although providing nothing
new or significant toward the establishment of a text, nevertheless, they
do contribute toward an appreciation of Hyginus' treatise in an
historical study of science after the eighth century. From these codices
four, ranging in date from the tenth to the fourteenth century, may be
chosen as especially representing medieval usage of Hyginiana material
separately and distinctly from codices containing the traditional trun-
cated four books.[1] These four manuscripts are well known for their
illuminations, but their texts have, so far as I know, never been
examined in detail.[2]

Extant codices of the entire work, a simple compendium of basic
science *de mundo,* but particularly about the composition and
movements of constellations, planets, sun, and moon, including one
book on their mythology are common from England[3] throughout
mainland Europe[4], Spain and Italy[5]. The tradition of four books as will

1 Bernhard Bunte, *Hygini Astronomica* (Leipzig 1875). The text is incomplete in all manuscripts
known.

2 On illustrations particularly of Hyginus cholia texts cf. F. Saxl and H. Meier, *Verzeichnis
Astrologischer und Mythologischer Illustrierter Handschriften des Lateinischen Mittelalters* III. *Handschriften in
Englischen Bibliotheken* I (London 1953), p. xii-xxxiv.

3 London. British Museum. Harley 2506, ca. 1000 Winchester, and the closely related
manuscripts: British Museum. Royal 12.C.IV, (s. xii), and Cambridge. Trinity College 945 (R.15.32),
(s. xi).

4 Especially noteworthy are: Dresdensis Dc 183, (s. ix-x), the basis of Bunte's text; Paris. Bibl.
Nat. lat. 8663, (s. x-xi), from Fleury; Leiden. Vossianus lat. 8°84, (s. xi), an apograph it seems of
Paris. lat. 8663; Paris. Bibl. Nat. lat. 11127, (s. x), from the monastery of St. Wilibrod d'Epternach;
Brussels. Bibl. Royale 10078-79, (s. xi), probably a manuscript of Sigebert of Gembloux; Monacensis
13084, (s. ix-x), and Montpellier. Faculté de Médecine 334, (s. ix-x). On the Munich and Dresden
manuscripts see M. Manitius, "Aus der Münchner Handschrift (Lat. 13084, ix s.)," *Hermes* 40 (1905),
p. 471-478; "Aus der Dresdener Handschrift", *Hermes* 37 (1902), p. 501-510.

5 Vatican. Reginensis lat. 1260, (s. ix), cf. C. Bursian, "Zur Texteskritik der Astrologie des
Hyginus," *Sitzungsberichte der Bayerischen Akademie der Wissenschaft* 5 (1876), p. 1-57, possibly a Fleury
manuscript whose text is related closely to Hyginus' texts in Vienna 2269, (s. xii); Bern 45, (s. x); and

be evidenced by the exemplar codices was paralleled by other traditions more or less static in form: 1) a simple extracting of relevant passages, 2) an edition including two or three of the customary four books, 3) scholia on the *Phaenomena* of Aratus accompanying either Germanicus Caesar or Cicero's Latin translation.

Before treating the codices chosen, it would be helpful at this point to discuss briefly the background generating *De Astronomia.*

The corpus of natural phaenomena has been an intriguing mystery for men in all ages to examine in itself and in its relationship to man.[6] Alexandrian Greeks after the manner of Aristotle sought information on the world about them through speculation, observation, experiment, conclusion thereby setting foundations for true physical science. Unfortunately their monographs often were not appealing to Romans who like Pliny, Seneca, and later Martianus Capella and Isidore of Seville preferred snipping practical or appealing bits of information for their encyclopedic works.

There was to be sure, in the Greek world, an older way of seeing nature. First in a long series of literary works which profoundly and perhaps disporportionally influenced men of letters and science appeared Hesoid's *Works and Days,* in genre *de natura rerum,* in emulators rich. Lucretius, Vergil, Columella, Martianus Capella, Isidore, Bede follow his initiative, sometimes in verse, sometimes in prose.

Medieval Western man inherited through this twofold source an emasculated Greek physical science clothed in a rich literary heritage. In many instances the men responsible would have been astonished to learn the fate of their scholarly studies. Among them Eudoxus of Cnidos'[7] whose star catalogue Aratus of Soli translated into hexameter verse together with weather prognostica probably drawn from Theophrastos' *Weather Signs.*[8]

Aratus' text, despite its elementary and rhetorical character enjoyed considerable popularity among the Alexandrians; found several un-

---

Vatican. Reginensis lat. 123, (s. x), a computus from the monastery of Santa Maria de Rivipullo, Cataluna. A complete description of the contents in the last is found in F. Saxl, *Verzeichnis Astrologischer und Mythologischer Illustrierter Handschriften des Lateinischen Mittelalters in Römischen Bibliotheken* (Heidelberg 1915), pp. 53-59. Of special interest is the text with longer shorthand sections: Milan. Ambrosianus M.12. sup., (s. vii-x), probably from Corvey. Cf. É. Chatelain and P. Legendre, *Hygini Astronomica. Texte du Manuscrit Tironien de Milan* (Paris 1909). The text has many errors of readings found in Paris. Bibl. Nat. lat. 8663 (s. x-xi) and Leiden Vossianus lat. 8°84 (s. xi).

6   For general modern histories of ancient and medieval science see the series by George Sarton, *Introduction to the History of Science* (Baltimore, Md. 1927); Lynn Thorndike, *History of Magic* and Experimental Science (New York 1929); René Taton, ed., *Histoire Générale des Sciences,* Vol. I-II (Paris 1957).

7   Floruit 367 B.C. Cf. George Sarton, op. cit., Vol. I (Baltimore Md. 1927), p. 117.

8   *Ibid.,* p. 143-157.

sympathetic commentators, among them Hipparchus of Nicaea;[9] and served from its inception as a source book of subjects related to celestial matters. In Roman literary circles the poem circulated widely influencing Callimachus[10] and especially Vergil in *Bucolics* and *Georgics*.[11] Cicero, then a young man,[12] translated the poem. Shortly afterwards, another translation, less famous, was made by Germanicus Caesar.[13]

Aratus limited himself to a brief presentation of the major constellation descriptions; myths related to them were in the form of literary allusions. He did not include an enumeration of the stellar composition of each constellation; the planets he refused to discuss on the argument that the task was beyond his ability.[14] As a consequence, frequent, extensive glosses and supplemental material expanding and interpreting Aratus' casual references and supplying additional information early attached themselves to the text both in Greek and in its Latin counterparts. Two better known collections of Aratea scholia are those last edited by Ernest Maass[15] and Alfred Breysig.[16]

Included in but certainly not exclusively part of the Aratea tradition in Hyginus' *De Astronomia*. Evidence about the identity of Hyginus is extremely limited although he is possibly from as early as the first century B.C.[17] For his treatise, Hyginus relied mainly on Greek authors and his major sources although not limiting himself to them are the Καταστερισμοί[18] of Eratosthenes of Cyrene[19] which is quoted some twenty-one times by name and Aratus *Phaenomena* quoted fourteen times by name. Moreover book IV, chapter XII appears to be a verse by verse translation of *Phaenomena* 568-731.

Hyginus' book II is a concisely related, but copious collection of astral myths, book III indicates numbers and positions of the major

9 Cf. J. P. Migne, *P.G.* 19 (Paris 1857), 1002-1136.

10 Cf. Callimachus fr. 24 and 195. Rudolfus Pfeiffer, *Callimachus* (Oxford 1949).

11 Jérôme Carcopino, *Virgile et le Mystère de la IVe Églogue* (Paris 1943), p. 151; Henri Goelzer, *Virgile Les Géorgiques* (Paris 1926), p. xi.

12 Cic. *De Natura Deorum,* 2.41.

13 Edited by Alfred Breysig, *Germanicus Caesar Aratea* (Leipzig 1899) and *Germanici Caesaris Aratea cum Scholiis* (Hildesheim 1867).

14 Aratus, *Phaenomena* 30-44.

15 Ernestus Maas, *Commentariorum in Aratum Reliquiae* (Berlin 1898).

16 Alfred Breysig, *Germanici Caesaris Aratea cum Scholiis* (Hildesheim 1867).

17 Mention in ancient authors includes: Aulus Gellius, *Noctes Atticae* 1.21; Suetonius, *Gramm.* xx; Hyginus, *Astonomica* II.12 (of himself Hyginus says he once wrote a book of *genealogiae*); Isidor., *De Natura Rerum* xvii.i, xix.i, xlviii.i (Hyginus is quoted a number of times anonomously); Columella, *De Re Rustica* 1.1.13. For modern authors cf.: H. J. Rose, *Hygini Fabulae* (Lyons 1934); A. Tolkiehn, "Hyginus", *Real. Ency. der Class. Altertumswissenschaft* ed. A. F. von Pauly, 10 (1917), 628-651.

18 Carl Robert, *Eratosthenis Catasterismorum Reliquiae* (Berlin 1878); Geofridus Bernhardus, *Eratosthenica* (Berlin 1822).

19 Sarton, *op. cit.,* p. 172-173.

stars in each constellation and locates them with respect to neighboring groups. Books I and III treat of the universe, the circles of heaven, the paths of sun and moon, the rising and setting of the constellations and eclipses.

His text, phrased in simple language and providing rudimentary knowledge of scientific matters together with concise factual knowledge of mythology relating to the heavens, could serve admirably as an elementary textbook in matters *de astronomia, de natura rerum* and *de mythologia*. Style, composition, format, content, the proliferation of copies prepared a way for the treatise to become one book or several, a paragraph, or a commentary, anonymous, or attributed to varied authors; and the medieval practice of excerpting encouraged this division of *De Astronomia*.

A flagrant example of extracting portions of Hyginus' text is found in *De Signis Caeli*[20] in those final two paragraphs[21] on the Milky Way and the Arrow which have a line from Ptolemy's Almagest sandwiched between them. Another edited example is the Pseudo-Bedan composition *De Circulis Sphaerae et Polo*.[22]

In manuscripts, Vatican. Reginensis lat. 123,[23] a computus divided into four books: *de sole, de luna, de natura rerum, de astronomia* arranges all the relevant passages from Pliny, Isidore, Boethius, Hyginus, and Bede under proper titles in these four divisions.

Oxford. Bodleian Library MS. Digby 83

The author of the anonymous composition in four books[24] found in Oxford. Bodleian Library. Digby 83, (s. xii), proposed to write for zealous students a compendium on astronomy and astrology derived from the works of the most learned authors. Hyginus is one. Hyginus'

---

20 Migne, *P.L.* 90.945-950.

21 Hyg. *De Ast.* III.3, III.14.

22 Migne, *P.L.* 90.937-940 (942) = Hyg. *De Ast.* I.1-7. Cf. Bunte's edition p. 22 and Charles W. Jones, *Bedae Pseudepigrapha: Scientific Writings Falsely Attributed to Bede* (Cornell Univ. Press 1939), p. 1-4.

23 Cf. *supra* n. 5 and Patrick McGurk, *Catalogue of Astrological and Mythological Illuminated Manuscripts of the Latin Middle Ages* (London 1966), p. xvii.

24 Other codices related to Oxford. Bodleian Library. Digby 83 (s. xii) are: Breslau Univ. Ac., IV, 8°, 11, (s. xii), of French origin; Erfurt. Ampl. Q, 23, (s. xii), and Hannover IV, 394, (s. xiii). Cf. A. van de Vyver, "Les plus anciennes traductions latines médiévales (x-xi siècles) de traités d'astronomie et d'astrologie," *Osiris* I (1936), p. 690.

25 Cited by A. van de Vyver, *op. cit.*, p. 689-691; Millás Vallicrosa, *Assaig d'historia de les idees fisiques i matemàtiques a la Catalunya medieval*. Vol. I (Barcelona 1931), p. 258-276; F. Saxl and H. Meier, *op. cit.*, p. 345; and L. Thorndike, *History of Magic and Experimental Science*, I (New York 1923), p. 707-709.

excerpts as found between folia 5v and 9v are in conjunction with passages of Isidore's *Etymologiae*. For the sake of continuity or for adding further information the Hyginus' passages may be slightly modified by the editor. For example: Digby 83 (f. 5v) ... spectans boreus siue septemtrionalis uocatur, qui nunquam occidit, alter uero australi, qui nunquam uidetur, et austronothus appellatur. Hyginus: (Bunte's edition) I.3 ... spectans boreus, alter oppositus austronotius est dictus. Here the change is caused by an inflation from Isidore (*Etym*. III.37).

Other variants of the Hyginus' text show definite traces of manuscript relationship:

Digby 83 f. 8v ita ut *UVYvy*[26] Hyg. (page 24.8) ita uti
      f. 9r aquilonalibus *UVYvy*   24.16 aquilonis
      f. 9r hoc circulo finito *Y*   24.24 Hoc circulo facto
      f. 9r centroque poloque *UVYvy* 25.4 centroque poli
      f. 9r quanto autem *UVYvy*   25.8 quanto enim
      f. 9v menses horas *Y*   104.22 menses et horas
      f. 46r hic occidens ... terram   83.5
          om. UVYv, add. U² in marg.
      f. 50r sunt omnes vii *add. post*   87.7 *om.*
          ficti *Y*

Manuscript Digby 83 was written near Winchester, the middle of the twelfth century; its drawings Fritz Saxl[27] finds are similar to a manuscript from St. Swithin's in Winchester. But Cambridge. Trinity College 945 (R. 15.32), (s. xi), (*Y*) also is a Winchester manuscript.[28] It would seem fairly evident from the text errors unique to Digby 83 *UVYvy*, as a group, and unique to Digby 83 and *Y* alone that Cambridge. Trinity College 945 (R.15.32) must be considered the source of the Hyginus passages in the former.

WALTERS ART GALLERY MS. 734

Various fragmentary tracts accompany an incomplete *De Astronomia* text in Walters Art Gallery Ms. 734 (*W*).[29] In fact it appears the scribe of

---

26 The sigla are for codices: London. British Museum. Harley 2506, (ca. 1000), (*U*), Royal 12.C.IV, (s. xii); (*V*); Cambridge. Trinity College 945 (R.15.32), (s. xi), (*Y*); Chartres 498, (s. xii), (*y*); Leiden. Vossianus lat. 4°92, (s. xiii), (*v*). Cf. A. van de Vyver, "Les Oeuvres inedites d'Abbon de Fleury," *Revue Bénédictine* 47 (1935), p. 143 (*U*), p. 140-142 (*Y*). A great similarity of agreement in error indicated these five codices derive their Hyginus' text from a similar source.

27 F. Saxl, *Lectures*, Vol. I (London 1957), p. 106.

28 For the rationale behind this attribution cf. Montague R. James, *The Western Mss in the Library of Trinity College, Cambridge*, Vol. II (Cambridge 1904), p. 365-366.

29 *W* dating from the twelfth century was written in early Gothic minuscule. Style North Italian. Rubricated capitals usually mark the beginning of new sections although several are missing

W either deliberately edited his work or copied from an edited exemplar because of the lack of significant breaks between different passages and the change in concluding or introductory passages which provide some textual continuity. In manuscript Digby 83 Hyginus' passages are incorporated into another text; here Aratea passages are addenda in Hyginus' text. Both practices were common by the twelfth century. Briefly the order of texts in *W* is as follows:

I f. 1-18   Hygini *De Astronomia*

II f. 18r   Duo sunt extremi vertices mundi (Maass, *Comm. in Aratum Reliquiae,* p. 309-312)

III f. 19r   Sub geminis prochon fulgentia lumina pandit (Claudi Caesari Arati *Phaenomena,* vv. 433, 435, 436)

IV f. 19r   Ante canem graio Prochio qui nomine ferunt (Ciceronis *Aratea,* vv. 222-226)

V f. 19r   Septem sunt quae vocantur erratice (cf. F. Saxl, *Verzeichnis astrologischer und mythologischer illustrierter Handschriften* Vol. II (Heidelberg and London 1927), p. 131 for a similar incipit. The text is derived from *Aratus latinus* (Maass, *op. cit.,* p. 272-275) and Hyginus II.42.)

VI f. 20r   Quinque solent stellae simili ratione notari (Ciceronis *Aratea,* vv. 455-460)

VII f. 20r   [A]t stellae via diversa lege feruntur (Claudi Caesari Arati *Phaenomena,* vv. 437-445)

VIII f. 20v   Sidera quae gentile praesepe et asinos vocaverunt (Maass, *op. cit.,* p. 296; Alfred Breysig, *Germanici Caesaris Aratea cum Scholiis,* (Hildesheim 1867), p. 129-130)

IX f. 20v   Si vis scire in quo anno cicli stella Saturni sit fac hoc modo numera quod anni sint ex quo Alexander potitus regno est

X f. 21r   Luna bigam habere dicitur sive propter velocitatem (Maass, *op. cit.,* p. 290; Breysig, *op. cit.,* p. 199.)

XI f. 21v   [S]ol dum per trecentos sexaginta et v dies (Maass, *op. cit.,* p. 292; Breysig, *op. cit.,* p. 292)

XII f. 21v   Sol transiens ab Ariete ad Chelas efficit sex mensium

in the last excerpt in particular. Thirty-eight illustrations of constellation figures with star positions marked accompany Hyginus' third book, an illustration for Aselli and one of Luna are found after excerpt VI and before the final paragraph of excerpt VIII respectively. Excerpts V and VI are written in verse form. For further history and description of the illustrations see Dorothy Miner, "Since De Ricci-Western Illuminated Manuscripts Acquired Since 1934," *The Journal of the Walters Art Gallery* XXXI-XXXII (1968-1969). p. 83-87.

30   For convenience, I have numbered these folia, of which two precede and two follow the Hyginus and Aratea material, A B C D. The recto of A and the verso of D are pasted to the covers. On the life of Julian, Bishop of Toledo cf. *Bibliothecae Sanctorum,* Vol. VI, 1216-1218 and *BBL,* I, p. 675, n. 4554.

               (Hyginus IV, 3 this text is the same as that found on f. 15v)

XIII f. 22r   Virtus est animi habitus naturae modo rationi consentaneus (extracts from M. T. Cicero, *De Inventione* II, 159-166)

XIV f.²⁸ Av   ... Angelos videlicet sanctos quoque electos volens intellegi.

              Quod Viri Velut Femine In Proprio Sexu Resurgent (Juliani Toletani *Prognosticon,* excerpts from III, 6 and III, 24)

      C   ... ardeant corpora dampnatorum (*Ibid.,* excerpts from III, 42 and 20)

XV f. Br   per hibetur mox gignit nubes et grandines (A passage on thunder and lightning based on Pliny and others.)

In *W* the Hyginus text lacks the title: Liber Hygini Periti Magistri de Astronomia Hyginus M Fabio Plurimam Salutem frequently found in other manuscripts.[31] It contains the entire text of book I and the opening paragraph of book II;[32] the myths of book II are lacking. Book III is entire; the first chapter of book IV is missing.[33] The text of book IV beginning with chapter II breaks off in chapter VIII,[34] recommences with chapter XII and ends with the final sentences of chapter XIII.[35] Chapters XXXIX and XL from the otherwise missing second book, relating the fables of Hydra and Ara, with slight modifications, are combined with chapters XXVIII and XXXIX on Hydra and Ara from book III. Chapter XXIX of book III lacks the paragraph on *nodum caelestem.*

Agreements in word error indicate certain lines of manuscript affinity. Rarely, *W* agrees in error with two manuscripts cited by Bunte: Dresdensis Dc 183, (s. ix), (*D*) and Guelferbytanus 3147 (Aug. 18.16), (s. xiii), (*G*). With other of the better known early Hyginus manuscripts: Montepessulanus 334, Monacensis 13084, and Vatican Reginensis lat. 1260 there is only the slightest if any agreement in error. A few instances of agreement between *W* and Leiden. Gronovianus lat. 21, (s. xii), (*C*); Vienna 51, (s. xii), (*j*); Paris. lat. 11127, (s. x), (Z); Brussels. Bibl. Royale 10078-79 (s. x-xi), (*B*); London British Mueum. Royal 12.C.IV

---

31 Cf. Vatican Reginensis lat. 1260, (s. ix); London. British Museum. Royal 12.C.IV, (s. xii); Harley 2506, (ca. 1000); Oxford. D'Orville 145, (s. xi), Montpellier. Faculté de Médecine 334, (s. ix-x) and Monacensis lat. 13084, (s. ix-x).

32 Ending: qui notius vocatur ... Bunte, p. 29.21.

33 Quoniam in initio ... ad inceptum revertamur. p. 98.17-99.20.

34 Ending: exortus et qui occasus. p. 105.25. Leiden. Gronovianus lat. 21, (s. xii) also ends at this point after which begins a work attributed to Gerbertus papa (*sic*) for Pope Sylvester II.

35 Arietis exortu ... et exoriri videntur. p. 109.27-112.9.

(*V*), Harley 2506 (*U*), Chartres 498 (*y*), and Leiden. Vossianus lat. 4°92 (*v*) may be cited: (Page references are to Bunte's edition) 22.3 effecti/effeci *VvyW*; 22.7 et ipsi in quibus/in quibus et ipsi *BZTW*; 23.8 austro alter oppositus/alter oppositus austro *ZTW*; esse rationes/rationes esse *GW*; 26.20 et Virginem transiens/transiens et Virginem *jGW*; 82.13 quod *post* quo *add.* *cBZW*; 82.16 stellam *om.* *cW*; 83.4 ad sinistrum/sinistro *jGcB-ZUW*; 83.14 nonnulli esse/esse nonnulli *UVYvW*; 87.3 exoriri ... occidentibus *om.* *jGcBZTDUVYvW* (cf. Montepessulanus 334); 89.21 unam/tres *jGcTVUvW*; 89.24 genu ac/genua *cBZTW*; 90.22 primoribus *om.* *jBZTW*; 100.4 ex una parte ... ratione *jGcBZTW*, *om. ceteri*; 103.16 χεινὴ ... ἀλλήλοισι *om.* *cTVYvW*.

A number of readings unique to *W*, characterized primarily by word or phrase omissions, include the following: 19.9 desidiae *om.*; 25.7 austri *om.*; 81.6 contendat *om.*; 84.17 item in cubito obscuram I *om.*; 85.27 qua caput ... stellam *om.*; 88.6-17 Hunc Aratus ... perperam est intellectam *om.*; 94.8-16 horum conjunctio ... nodum verum appellaverunt *om.*; 95.16 in capite stellas *om.*; 95.4-7 Hostia autem ... omnino x *om.*; 102.2 praestare ... intelligere *om.*

The text of *De Astronomia* in *W* represents one phase of the textual tradition more commonly found in the twelfth century when the four books were frequently separated or rearranged.

MSS. Gottweig Stiftsbibliothek 146 (190) and London. British Museum. Cotton Tiberius B.V

Codices Gottweig 146 (190), (s. xiv), and Cotton Tiberius B.V, (s. xi), represent a third from of Hyginiana: scholia for Cicero's *Aratea*. It is my conviction that the texts used for scholia were selected certainly by the ninth century and remained approximately identical for each constellation described although the entire corpus of scholia in one manuscript might be varied by including or substituting material from other sources such as Isidore's *Etymologiae*, *Aratus latinus*, Aratea material, or commentaries on Germanicus Caesar's *Phaenomena*. The transmission of this text was separate from the main tradition and derived from a common source.

Both the eleventh and the fourteenth century manuscripts present the scholia in the style best known from British Museum manuscript Harley 647, (s. ix),[36] oldest and best source of Cicero's *Aratea* and one ac-

---

36   Harley 647, (s. ix) is most probably to be associated with Servatus Lupus abbot Ferrierès (848) who sought from Ansbald von Prüm a manuscript *Tullium in Arato* ostensibly for supplementing its lacunae by another text. This may be the Prüm copy or the correcting agent. Cf. F. Saxl, *Lectures. op. cit.,* p. 101; Antonius Traglia, *M. Tulli Ciceronis Poetica Fragmenta* (Rome, 1963), p. 9-11; F. Saxl and H. Meier, *op. cit.,* p. xiii ff.

companied by accounts of the constellations in Hyginus' (books II and III) prose. In Harley 647, much to the delight of W. Young Ottley[37] who concluded the manuscript must date from the second or third century, an imaginative scribe combined Ciceronian text written at the bottom of the page, illustrations and commentary in a clever way by completing only heads and extremities of each figure shown, while filling out the outlined body with writing in *capitalis rustica* style.

Our scribe in Gottweig 146 (190) employed similar technical albeit inferiorly executed style[38] writing the text within outlined figures, in fact, he sacrificed text to illustration and words which complete the phrases begun but did not fit the pre-outlined space he, or his exemplar as it proves to be, cut arbitrarily. Cotton Tiberius B.V has the scholia text written around the constellation illustrations which have similarly shaped but completely executed figures. Here the scribe was not bound by figured spatial restrictions, yet Hyginus' texts of fables: Aries (missing in Gottweig 146 (190), Deltoton, Fides, Olor, Capricornus, Sagitta, Eridanus, and the Planetae[39] have the texts found in the limited spaces of Gottweig 146 (190). Surely in the selection of text, one individual scribe's choice or caprice was judge in choosing what of Hyginus would be wanted to fill up the allotted space. There is no readily discernible pattern in the preference of one myth of the several told by Hyginus and certainly no logical reason for including parts of the enumeration of stars and omitting others as is done in these scholia. The selected text for individual constellations is essentially the same in manuscripts Harley 647, Gottweig 146 (190), and Cotton Tiberius B.V, and must have been considered standard scholia for Cicero's *Aratea* at the time the earliest of these manuscripts was written.

The Hyginus scholia text of Gottweig 146 (190) varies from the normal Hyginus text in several instances:

Hyg. II.29	... tanta vis aquae se de Caelo profuderit ut cataclysmus factus esse diceretur.	... tanta aquae de caelo profusa sit ut cataclysmus fieret.
Hyg. II.27	Itaque pro merita diligentia magnam laudem assecutum.	Itaque pro merita assiduitate magnam laudem assecutum.

---

37   W. Young Ottley, "On a MS of Cicero's Translation of Aratus, Supposed to be of the 2nd or 3rd Century," *Archaeologia* 26 (1836), p. 145-214. The text of Harley 647 reproduced here is that contained in Gottweig 146 (190) except for minor variants.

38   F. Saxl, Lectures, p. 101 notes the magnificent simplicity of the drawings gives Harley 647 an impression of being the "most purely classical manuscript which has survived from Carolingian times". On the illustrations in Gottweig 146 (190) see Saxl and Meier, *op. cit.*, p. xiii ff.

39   The scholia texts for the other constellations are taken from *Aratus latinus* ed. E. Maass, *op. cit.*, p. 224-271.

Hyg. II.17	Hic qua de causa sit inter astra collocatus ... Neptunum, quo tempore voluerit Amphitriten ducere uxorem ... Qui pervagatus insulas, aliquando ad virginem pervenit eique persuasit ut nuberet Neptuno.	Hic de qua causa sit in mundo collocatus ... Neptunus quo tempore Amphitriten voluerit Nerei filiam ducere uxorem ... Qui pervagatus paene omnes insulas ei cum persuasit Neptuno nuberet.
Hyg. II.34	Hunc autem, cum Iovem et Mercurium hospitio recepisset ... Quem collo ferens dicitur ad Solem venisse.	Hic autem cum Iovem et Neptunum et Mercurium hospitio recepisse dicitur ... Quem collo ferens ad solem devenit.
Hyg. II.35	Hic dicitur ab Iove custos Europae adpositus esse et ad Minoa pervenisse quem Procris, Cephali uxor laborantem dicitur sanasse.	Hic dicitur custos Europae positus esse ad Minoa pervenisse quem Procris, Cephali uxor, morbo laborantem dicitur sanasse.
Hyg. II.32	Canopos autem insula flumine alluitur Nilo.	Autem urbs flumine alluitur Nilo.
Hyg. II.39	In hac primum di existimantur sacra et coniurationem fecisse.	In hac primum di existimantur sacrificasse et coniurationem fecisse.
Hyg. II.40	... vidit arbores complures ficorum inmaturas; eas exspectans dum maturescerent in arbore quadam earum consedit.	... vidit in arbore quadam complures ficos inmaturas cum aviditate inductus dum maturescerent consedit.
Hyg. II.42	Itaque cum vehementer amor eum incenderet, rem significans e facto stellam Pyroenta appellavit.	Itaque cum vehementer morsum incenderit purolsese appellatur.

Where these texts vary most noticeably as in the *fabula* Olor (II.8), the text of Cotton Tiberius B.V. has the same variation but its own peculiar variants in spelling and word divisions.

Five peculiar additions to the scholia support a theory of a separate, continued scholia tradition and indicate that possibly at one time the scholia passages used here were taken from an earlier complete Cicero *Aratea* text in which verse and prose commentary were closely united. In the commentaries on Pistrix, Piscis notius, Ara, Procyon and Planetae partial lines from the *Aratea* itself are included in the commentary thus:

Hyg. III.33	... omnino xvii.	Omnino decem et octo. Exinde Orion obliquo corpore nitens//inferiora tenent ... (vv. 102-103) (cf. Cotton. Tiberius C.I)

Hyg. III.40	Sed est stellarum omnino xii.	Id est omnino stellarum. Exinde australem soliti quem dicere Piscem//volvitur inferior Capricorno versus ad austrum. (vv. 167-168)
Hyg. III.38	Omnino iiii.	Omnino stellarum quatuor. De qua Cicero sic dicit: Inde Nepae cernes propter fulgentis acumen//Aram quam flatu spiritus Austri (vv. 183-184)
Hyg. III.35	... stellarum iii.	... stellarum trium. Antecanem, Graio Procyon qui nomine fertur// Haec sunt quae visens nocturno tempore signa (vv. 222-223)
Hyg. II.42	... et Mercurio demonstrasse.	... et Mercurio demonstrasse. Quae stellae planetae sunt dictae. (cf. Cotton. Tiberius B.V.)

In at least one instance (II.42), the same error is found in the scholia of Cotton Tiberius B.V and in another (III.33) in Cotton Tiberius C.I.[40]

Regarding the Ciceronian text *Aratea,* Traglia[41] notes Harley 647 has four apographs: Harley 2506; Cotton Tiberius B.V; Cotton Tiberius C.I and Cambridge. Trinity College 945 (R.15.32). It would be reasonable to suppose the Hyginus scholia in these manuscripts derives from a common source. This is apparently true although the scribe of Cotton Tiberius B.V has varied the scholia sources. Gottweig 146 (190) shows Hyginus scholia which have separative readings from Cotton Tiberius B.V and Harley 647, but which ultimately derive from a common although not identical exemplar. It is noteworthy here that the other Aratea material in codex Gotttweig 146 (190) by reason of a number of omitted lines can be shown to possess an affinity with Aratea material found in codices Sangermanensis 12957, (s. ix), Cologne Bibl. Metrop. 83², (s. ix), and two Sangallenses 250 and 902 (s. x et xi) against others cited by Maass.[42] There would seem then to be at least two group divisions in the Hyginus scholia text tradition. Of these the one is represented by Harley 647 and its satellites, the other by Gottweig 146 (190).

40 Although I have examined the text of Cotton Tiberius B.V in a microfilm copy, my only reference to Cotton Tiberius C.I is through the reproductions in F. Saxl and H. Meier, *op. cit.,* III, 2 (London 1953), plates LXVIII, 169; LXVI, 166 and XIII and Saxl, *Lectures op. cit.,* Vol. ii. plates 55a and 54a.

41 Traglia, *op. cit.,* p. 9-11.

42 Maass, *op. cit.,* p. 102. For Cologne Bibl. Metrop. 83² see also Leslie W. Jones, *The Script of Cologne from Hildebald to Hermann* (Cambridge, Mass. 1932), p. 37-40.

Finally the scholia manuscripts Harley 647, Cotton Tiberius B.V, and Cotton Tiberius C.I without question are to be associated with two entire *De Astronomia* manuscripts in codices Harley 2506 and Cambridge Trinity College 945 (R.15.32) yet the scholia do not evidence errors peculiar to these *De Astronomia* texts just they do not show the errors of other well known early *De Astronomia* manuscripts. It must be concluded that the scholia text tradition is separate from the text tradition.

Matters *de mundo, de caelo, de astronomia* were popular in medieval times, manuscripts containing *Hygini De Astronomia* in whole or part were numerous far beyond their scientific value. An examination of their illustrations alone is a prodigious task which needs further studies. The four manuscripts discussed here with respect to their text indicate major forms Hyginus' treatise enjoyed through centuries nine through fourteen and the relative ease with which it was adapted to suit various medieval editors and functions until it was on the one hand neglected in favor of more scientific monographs and on the other no longer as necessary a commentary.

Pontifical Institute of Mediaeval Studies.

MARRIAGE AND FAMILY IN ENGLISH CONCILIAR AND SYNODAL LEGISLATION

Michael M. Sheehan

IN the chapter of his *Feudal Society* entitled "Character and vicissitudes of the tie of kinship", Marc Bloch quotes a *chanson de geste*: "'Be quiet', is the rough response of Garin le Lorrain to the widow of his murdered brother, who is weeping over the body and bemoaning her lot, 'a noble knight will take you up again ... it is I who must go on deep in mourning'".[1] Most of us will have read this anecdote; some many times. But I, for one, am still pulled up sharply by the glimpse it affords of a world in which a marital relationship could be established and destroyed with such ease, almost with insouciance, a world in which kinship provided the permanent and serious bond.

The element of surprise felt by the modern reader is especially strong in one who has for some time been studying the canonical, pastoral and, to a certain extent, the theological sources touching the history of marriage. In fact, it is in a moment like this, when the historian sees the general tone of that type of source material in perspective, that he realizes how different is its point of view from that of the *chanson de geste* just quoted. Sources for the history of marriage are concerned with relationship of the spouses, often paying little attention to the familial group from which they came and into which they would be drawn, or even to their duties to the children they were expected to bring into the world. No doubt, the broad social context in which this literature was written is to be presumed. But sometimes it is quite clear that it presents a view of marriage that is in conflict with that social context. Marriage, after all, was the key to family recruitment. Christian teaching came, in time, to define marriage and that definition did not

---

1 Marc Bloch, *La société féodale,* L'évolution de l'humanité, 24, 2 vols. (Paris, 1939-40), 2, 212. Cf. Marc Bloch, *Feudal Society,* transl. L. A. Manyon (Chicago, 1961), 136. See *Li roman de Garin le Loherain,* ed. P. Paris, 2 (Paris, 1835), 268.

always fit well with older usages. The question of concern here is to learn how, if at all, the family evolved under that pressure.

On the whole, historians of canon law, even those who have published major studies on marriage, have paid little attention to the family as such. On the other hand, historians of civil institutions and, more recently, anthropologists have turned to early canonical sources in their investigations of family and kinship.[2] I suggest that once the traditional point of view of the historian of marriage is widened he will not only make significant contributions to the study of the family, but he will also deepen his understanding of marriage itself.

Simply stated, the Christian conception of marriage included three complementary sets of ideas. 1) Marriage was seen as a sacred relationship, one that provided the ordinary means to the full Christian life. Because of its importance, the Church came eventually to state and defend the conditions that made marriage possible. 2) The ideal sought in the full Christian life was one in which there would be no erotic activity outside marriage. 3) A viable alternative to marriage in religious life and in the clerical state was elaborated. Each of these ideals had an impact on the evolution of the family. I propose, within the limits possible here, to indicate examples of their influence in England and suggest lines of further investigation. The Church's moral teaching and theological investigations usually moved ahead of its law. Here, however, we shall be content to examine two of the sources of that law, the local council and the synod. Whatever their limitations, they indicate the moment at which one can be reasonably certain that an effort was being made to enforce a given mode of behaviour in society. Marriage directly involved the principals of the nuclear group. The word "family" will be used of them, but will also include the group united by blood though no attempt will be made here to enter the discussion of its effective extent in different parts of England or at different times in English history.[3]

*

* *

Let us begin with a consideration of the impact of the Church's conception of religious life as a viable alternative to marriage. There were to be important refinements and developments over the years, but the

---

2   E.g. Lorrain Lancaster, "Kinship in Anglo-Saxon Society", *British Journal of Sociology*, 9 (1958), 230-250, 359-377; D. A. Bullough, "Early medieval social groupings: the terminology of kinship", *Past and Present*, 45 (1969), 3-18.

3   See Lancaster, *art. cit.*, pp. 373-376.

ideal and the realization of dedicated chastity were already established by the time the missionaries — and they were monks — arrived among the Anglo-Saxons. A brief acquaintance with the insular Penitentials makes it clear that Christian leaders were no less realistic about the possibilities of religious life than they were about marriage. But it is also clear that a powerful movement of teaching and example was launched, one that led to a wide-spread conviction that the former was the superior state.

The implementation of such an ideal had considerable impact on the family. In principle the religious renounced the possibility of establishing a nuclear family and withdrew from the obligations and rights of kinship. The kin had no further rights or duties in his regard. Should a child be born to such a person it was without rights in the kin or in the voluntary association that had replaced the kin. The main stages of this interesting process, a process in which religious and their families slowly came to realize the consequences of a choice that had been made, occurred during the Anglo-Saxon period.

Boniface associated a prohibition of the nun's marriage with a synod in Augustine's time.[4] Such a rule is extant in the report of the legates to Adrian I (787) and the constitutions of archbishop Oda (*ca.* 945).[5] A somewhat different approach is seen in Alfred's law forbidding such marriage without the permission of king or bishop. The kin was ignored in the penalty that was attached; payment was to those whose permission had not been sought.[6] The general prohibition was repeated in the ecclesiastical codes of Ethelred and Cnut. These seem to be the last sets of regulations seeking to establish that nuns could not marry. When Anglo-Norman councils turned to the matter, as in the case of those women who had fled to monasteries during the Norman invasion and the investigation of Matilda's freedom to marry Henry I, the bishops were concerned with questions of fact: were these women bound by vows or not?[7]

As early as the legatine synods of 787 the child of the nun was equated with the child of adultery, in this case, the adultery of her who "se Deo voverit, et ... sponsam Christi vocitare non dubitamus".[8] The

---

4 Ep. 50, *S. Bonifatii et Lulli Epistolae*, ed. M. Tangl, MGH, Epp. Selectae, 1 (1916), 83-84.

5 *Councils and Ecclesiastical Documents relating to Great Britain and Ireland*, eds. A. W. Haddan and W. Stubbs (henceforth: H-S), Vol. 3 (Oxford, 1871), 455 and *Concilia Magnae Britanniae et Hiberniae*, ed. D. Wilkins (henceforth: W), 1 (London, 1737) 213.

6 Af. 8, *Die Gesetze der Angelsachsen*, ed. F. Liebermann (henceforth: *Gesetze*; Liebermann's abbreviations for the codes are used throughout), Vol. 1 (Halle, 1903), 54-55. Cf. 1 Em. 4 (942-946) and Northu. 63 (probably 1020-23), *Gesetze*, 1, 184-185, 384.

7 W. 1, 362 and *Eadmeri Historia*, ed. M. Rule, RS, 81 (London, 1884), 121-125.

8 H-S, 3, 455.

child was denied rights of inheritance. A further consequence is revealed in the law of Alfred mentioned above in which the nun's marriage without permission was forbidden: the child, like his mother, was to have no rights in his father's property and, if he were killed, the king was to have the mother's part of the wergild while the paternal kin received its share.[9]

It is interesting to note that there is no similar set of regulations touching the monk. It seemed to have been understood that the nun, more than the monk, needed to be protected: from herself, no doubt, but especially from the importunate suitor or the pressure from the family that would not forget its old prerogative of arranging the marriages of its daughters. On the other hand VIII Ethelred stated that the monk was not to be involved in the feud since he had left the obligations of kinship when he submitted to the rule.[10]

Literary sources reveal the initial difficulty of the Anglo-Saxons in understanding that the property administered by abbots or abbesses did not pass to their families when they died.[11] On the Continent, councils had been careful to protect ecclesiastical property from alienation and their regulations were probably known in England though they are not to be found there except in general terms.[12]

The process whereby the ties of family weakened before the claims of lordship, its chronology and extent, are among the important problems that require an answer of the historian of the Anglo-Saxons. From the foregoing sketch it should be clear that the intrusion of a way of life that did not include marriage was another force in early medieval English society that required an adjustment of the family's conception of itself and a limitation of its role.

*

*   *

The ideal that there should be no sexual activity outside of marriage was elaborated and refined in theological, moral and pastoral writings throughout the centuries. Aspects of human sexuality that involved more than one person, especially those causing injustice or damage to a

---

9   Af. 8.2, 8.3, *Gesetze*, 1, 54-55. Ine 27 (688-691) awarded the wergild of an unacknowledged child to lord and king: *ibid.*, 1, 100-101.

10   VIII Atr. 25, *ibid.*, 1, 266-267: "he gaeð of his maeglage, þonne he gebihd to regollage".

11   See E. John, "The social and political problems of the early English Church", *Land Church and People, Essays presented to H. P. R. Finberg*, ed. J. Thirsk, *Agriculture History Review*, 18 (1970), suppl., pp. 60-62; and M. M. Sheehan, *The Will in Medieval England*, Studies and Texts, 6 (Toronto, 1963), 91-94.

12   *Ibid.*, 91, n. 6. Cf. Abt. 1, *Gesetze*, 1, 3.

third party, were regulated by canon law and frequently came before the ecclesiastical courts. Some of these matters have had an important part to play in the evolution of the family in the West. By way of illustration, I would like to present one development in England. It should be seen in the context of the remarkable effort at reform that characterized the late 12th and 13th centuries, a movement that was especially strong in the period after IV Lateran Council.

The development in question is to be related to the problem of the couple who were unmarried but who lived together or frequented each other's company to the scandal of all. Perhaps in some cases descriptions of this relationship mask the survival of an older form of inferior union with some analogies to the Roman *contubernium*.[13] That matter need not be pursued here. In the context of reform it was a case of public scandal in that, though the couple was free to marry yet, in spite of their obvious attachment, they refused to do so. It was discussed in Peter Cantor's *Summa de Sacramentis* (ca. 1192) and appeared towards 1216 in England in Thomas of Chobham's *Summa Confessorum*.[14] Discussing sins reserved to the bishop or his penitentiary, Chobham points out that the criteria of reservation are the seriousness and public nature of the actions in question. He indicates that it is customary that those who have a concubine and are free to marry are required to abjure or marry her. The abjuration is more than a simple promise to avoid the woman in question, but it takes the form of a promise that, should there be any further carnal relation, the couple will marry. If having taken such an oath a recidivus refuses to do so he is to be summoned before the bishop and charged, not with fornication, but with perjury.

In less than ten years a developed form of this doctrine in which conditional contract replaced promise appeared in episcopal statutes. Its first statement by Peter des Roches at Winchester allowed for several situations. The layman who publicly lived with a concubine was compelled to betroth her or enter into a conditional contract whereby further sexual union would constitute marriage.[15] In the case of him whose intercourse was public and frequent but casual, both he and the

---

13   There is a serious of references to unacceptable unions through the Anglo-Saxon period: Council of Hertford, c. 10, H-S, 3, 120; *Judicium Clementis*, c. 15, *ibid.*, p. 227; *Dialogue of Egbert*, 13, *ibid.*, p. 409; Constitutiones Odonis, c. 7, W, 1, 213; Wi. 3, 4, 4.1, 5, *Gesetze*, 1, 12; V Atr. 10, *ibid.*, pp. 240-241; VI Atr. 11, *ibid.*, 250-251.

14   *Summa de Sacramentis*, ed. J. Dugauquier, Vol. 2, Analecta Mediaevalia Namurcensia, 7 (Louvain, Lille, 1957), 449. *Thomae de Chobham Summa Confessorum*, ed. F. Broomfield, Analecta Mediaevalia Namurcensia, 25, (Louvain, Paris, 1968) 214.

15   C. 54, *Councils and Synods with Other Documents relating to the English Church*, II A. D. 1205-1313, ed. F. M. Powicke and C. R. Cheney (henceforth, P-C), 1 (Oxford, 1964) 134.

woman were to swear a similar oath before witnesses or, if they refused
to do so, to promise with sureties that they would be subject to a fine if,
henceforth, they were found together.[16] A few years later similar
legislation was included in the Coventry statutes. Here, in a context of
the correction of public mortal sin, it is stated that the fornicator who
has foresworn his paramour then returned to her must face the penalty
of marrying her or paying a large part of his property in fine.[17] In the
second set of Salisbury statutes (1238-44) the legislation was directly
related to the proposition "quod omnis carnalis commixtio inter virum
et mulierem extra legitimum matrimonium mortale peccatum existit".
A developed procedure was outlined: public fornicators and their con-
cubines were to be reported by local clergy to rural deans who would
bring them before the archdeacon. If there were no impediment, the
couple were to be compelled by ecclesiastical censures to swear in each
other's presence that further sexual union would constitute marriage.
The form of the oath was given.[18] The second Winchester statutes took
up the matter once more in 1247. This time, abjuration under penalty
of fine was rejected.[19] An attempt was made to render the procedure
more humane: canon 52 begins with the statement that marriage must
be free and between those capable of contracting it. Clergy with
pastoral charge of a couple involved in an extra-marital relationship
were instructed to inquire as to impediments and, if the couple were
free, to try to induce them to marry. If there were an impediment, they
were to abjure each other with prescription of penance should they fall
again. But if they were free, yet refused to marry, the conditional contract was to be imposed on them.[20] Similar, occasionally more detailed,
rules were to appear in episcopal statutes of the last half of the thirteenth century.[21] They were not without opposition. Professor Cheney
included a gloss in his edition of the second Exeter statutes (1287):
"Nota quod hec constitutio est contra iura et naturalem equitatem,
quia de iure libera debent esse matrimonia et sponsalia ..."[22] Be that as

---

16 C. 58, ibid., 1, 135.

17 C. 15 : "... indicatur talis pena ei si eandem cognoverit, quod eam desponset, vel magnum
portionem substantie sue, secundum quod facultates sue competunt, nobis tribuat sub
sacramento." Ibid., 1, 213.

18 C. 53, ibid., 1, 385.

19 C. 55, ibid., 1, 411. On the date, probably 1247, ibid., 1, 403.

20 C. 52, ibid., 1, 410-411.

21 Wells, 13 (1258?) includes a written account of proceedings, as does 3 Winchester, 29 (1262-
65) and 2 Exeter, 7 (1287); ibid., 1, 598, 707 and 2, 999. The form of the oath is given in 1 London, 3
(1245-59), where it is referred to bishop Roger Niger (1229-41), and in 2 London, 80 (1245-59); ibid.,
1, 631, 650.

22 Ibid., 1, 999, n. 4.

it may, there is sufficient evidence to show that that these statutes were enforced.[23]

Thus, in tracing this development through thirteenth-century statutes we discover an attempt to implement an ideal of sexual activity that obtruded on the more important doctrine of the dignity of marriage — a doctrine that was often stated in these very statutes.[24] The context of this position is entirely different from that of the *chanson de geste* cited above but, from one point of view, the two attitudes are surprisingly similar. Garin le Lorrain implied that the replacement of a husband was a slight matter; one of the statutes, in an unhappy phrase, presented marriage as a penalty for fornication. In the former case the needs of the extended family were dominant. In the case of the statutes it was the protection of the public from scandal and the protection of the couple from sin that mattered. It was the needs of the couple, understood in terms of an ultimate good, and of the wider society rather than those of the family that prevailed. On the other hand, the pressures that would cause a couple to enter a marriage that one at least did not desire,[25] should be related to other, quite different forces, that for centuries have led to the forced marriage. The history of this phenomenon is, to my knowledge, not yet written. When it is, this English legislation of the thirteenth century should have a place there. Finally, if there were a type of imperfect union still extant in English society, this legislation may well have helped lift it to the level of regular marriage, with the permanence and the rights and duties that the notion implies. The long-range consequences might well be very important, but they too remain to be investigated.

*

*   *

Though the direction taken by episcopal statutes in the attempt to support a moral position may, in some ways, have been detrimental to it, marriage was of major importance in the Church's view of human life. A consultation of the statutes in question will remove all doubt on this score. In fact, between the beginning of the twelfth-century revival and the end of the thirteenth century, in an intellectual effort that has

23 See R. H. Helmholz, "Abjuration *sub pena nubendi* in the Church courts of medieval England", *The Jurist,* 32 (1972), 81-90 and M. M. Sheehan, "The formation and stability of marriage in fourteenth-century England", *Mediaeval Studies,* 33 (1971), 253-256.

24 See 1 Salisbury, 83 and derivatives: 2 Canterbury, Durham Peculiars, 50, 1 Chichester, 27; P-C, 1, 87, 116, 443, 456-457.

25 See Sheehan, "The formation", *Mediaeval Studies,* 33 (1971), 254-256, the account of Thomas Barbo and Joan Seustere. Thomas was opposed to the marriage.

probably had no equal in western tradition except possibly today, marriage was examined at all levels of thought from theology, through moral guidance and law, to confessional practice. The ends of marriage, its qualities and the conditions for its validity were discussed and stated in detail. Many aspects of the history of the family in the West must, in my opinion, be related to this process if they are to be understood.

Perhaps the most obvious impact on the evolution of the family came from the Church's conclusions on the persons who were free to marry. As the conceptions of consanguinity, affinity and spiritual relationship were refined, the network of forbidden marriage partners enlarged, then diminished. In spite of a hoary tradition in English historiography that the rules in question provided a convenient bolt-hole for those who sought divorce, the question has not been studied with care, either in itself or in its effect on the kindred. To what extent families were denied the possibility of re-enforcing intergroup ties, to what extent lower-class mobility and the resulting restriction of active kinship were consequences of these developments still need careful examination. Beyond this indication of need, it is not possible to pursue the topic here. I propose, instead, to reflect on a dilemma that was implicit in the Church's theory of consent, indicate the way in which it was resolved and suggest implications of that solution from the point of view of marriage and family.

The effect of the Church's position on the consent of the couple appeared quite late in the legislation of the Anglo-Saxons. Ecclesiastical codes of Ethelred (1008) ruled that a year after the death of her husband a widow could do what she willed.[26] The rule was repeated in II Cnut[27] with the addition that neither widow nor maiden was to be forced to marry a man she disliked.[28] By 1175 a council of Westminster would have carried the requirement of consent much further: "ubi non est consensus utriusque, non est conjugium".[29] By this time, theory had progressed still further, the opinion becoming explicit that neither presence nor consent of anyone other than the couple was required. By 1216 Thomas of Chobham could write: "It is clear however that a man and a woman can contract marriage by themselves, without a priest or anyone else, in any place, so long as they agree to live together

---

26   V Atr. 21.1: "ceose syððan þhat heo sylf wille"; *Gesetze*, 1, 242-243. The text is repeated in VI Atr. 26.1. The Latin paraphrase makes it clear that choice is about marrying or not marrying: "libero utantur arbitrio vel nubendi vel in continentia permanendi"; *ibid.*, 1, 254-255.

27   II Cn. 73; in the *Quadripartitus* it is translated: "elegat postea quem velit", thus transferring the choice from marriage to the person married. *Ibid.*, 1, 360-361.

28   II Cn, 73.4, *ibid.*, Cf. Wif. 1, *ibid.*, 1, 442-443; Liebermann dated the treatise 975-1030, preferring a date towards the end of that period.

29   W. 1, 477. Cf. Gratian, C. 30 q. 2. c. 1.

forever".[30] When this point had been reached the dilemma was clear. The stressing of consent made it all too easy for couples to be ignorant of or to choose to forget impediments that rendered their marriage impossible. Later, discovering the impediment, or becoming dubious about their original intent, or simply unhappy, it would be a simple matter for them to deny their union.[31] Easy marriage, without external controls, meant easy separation. Thus the practical implications of a theory of consent threatened the permanence of marriage.

It is interesting to note that the statutes of the thirteenth century avoided stating the possibility of the clandestine marriage. Thus the first Canterbury statutes (1213-14) and their derivatives forbad such unions and carefully prescribed proper public forms. If the marriage occurred in spite of the prohibition, it was not to be admitted without the special authority of the archbishop.[32] It is unlikely that this ruling denied the validity of the contract but it is clear that the weight of the statute was against such proceedings.[33] It is only with the statutes of Wells (1258?) that it is explicitly stated that the clandestine marriage was valid, a point that would not often be made again.[34]

However, the solution to the problem lay along different lines. The main thrust of legislation was to guarantee permanence by the social control of information. In a long series of rules extending from Hubert Walter's council at Westminster in 1200 to that of John of Stratford in London in 1342 more than thirty sets of canons and statutes dealt with the problem of clandestine marriage. They worked out the well known two-stage system whereby proper marriage required an announcement of intent so that parish information about the suitability of the couple could be consulted, followed by a public exchange of consent to ensure that general knowledge of the event might be preserved. In none of these proceedings was the family as such introduced. In fact, it would be one of the main sources and preservers of information about its members, but it was as part of the parish or the vicinage that it was to

30   "Pater igitur quod vir et mulier possunt contrahere matrimonium per se sine sacerdote et sine omnibus aliis in quocumque loco, dummodo consentiant in perpetuam vite consuetudinem." *Summa Confessorum*, p. 146.

31   On the frequency of marriages invalid by pre-contract as revealed by a small sample in the late fourteenth century, see Sheehan, *art. cit.*, 262-263.

32   1 Canterbury, 54, 1 Salisbury, 85, Constitutiones cuisdam episcopi, 59, and Durham Peculiars, 52; P-C, 1, 34, 88, 190, 444.

33   The text, "Si vero secus factum fuerit, non admittatur in ecclesia nisi de speciali auctoritate domini archiepiscopi", has been interpreted to mean that the marriage was invalid: P-C, 2, 1429, General Index, *s.v.* "Marriage, clandestine, invalidity of". There is no indication that exchange of consent had to be repeated. It would seem, rather, that the text is intended to discourage clandestine marriages, requiring that each case come before the archbishop for judgment and, no doubt, for punishment.

34   C. 11, P-C, 1, 597-598; 2 Exeter, 7 is similar: *ibid.*, 2, 999.

be consulted. Heads of families were not required to give consent or even to be present at the public ceremony. On the other hand, the priest, the head of the parish community, was to play a role: first, seeking, receiving and interpreting information as to the couple's capacity, second, by his presence at the betrothal or at least at the marriage.[35]

Such a solution tended to emphasize the principals of the nuclear family at the expense of the extended group. It neither denied nor limited the emphasis on consent by the couple and, in spite of secular tradition of family controls, did not turn to the kin for a solution to the abuse of this consent. The implications of this approach have taken centuries to unfold, but I suggest that in it is one of the keys to the history of the family in the English-speaking world during the last seven centuries.

Pontifical Institute of Mediaeval Studies.

35 On the replacement of the father in the marriage ceremony by the priest, see the discussion of E. Schillebeeckx, *Marriage Human Reality and Saving Grace,* transl. N. D. Smith (New York, 1965), 272-279.

RIDDLES RELATING TO THE ANGLO-SAXON SCRIPTORIUM

Laurence K. Shook

I

IN this paper I am mainly concerned to offer original and possibly correct solutions to Riddles, 17, 18, 49 and 57 of the Exeter Book of Old English Poetry.[1] I am also trying to give precision to solutions already offered for two or three other riddles, and particularly to no. 26, the well-lnown Book Riddle and to no. 4, the most evasive of all the textually complete OE riddles. It is also my intention to allow the riddles I am dealing with to shed what light they can on activities in the monastic scriptorium of Anglo-Saxon England. Riddles, and especially unsolved ones, may well provide misleading evidence helpful, perhaps, to the student of literature but which the historian must regard as at best dubious. It is evidence, however, that should be examined because, as the great E. A. Lowe, of happy memory, once wrote, "*Probationes pennae* too can be of value. History may lurk in any insignificant scribble, especially if it is a name".[2] If history can lurk in a scribe's doodling, it may also lurk in his comments on, and his jests about, the tools of his trade.

The Exeter Book is one of the four manuscripts preserving the bulk of our Anglo-Saxon poetry. It is a miscellany of largely religious poems in a late 10th-century manuscript donated to Exeter Cathedral by Leofric, the first bishop of Exeter, probably between 1050 when the see was moved from Crediton to Exeter and 1072 when Bishop Leofric died. The Anglo-Saxon riddles constitute a collection and are copied out on 22 of the last 30 or 31 folios of the manuscript. They are about 94 in number ("about" because there is doubt as to how many poems in the collection actually are riddles), and many of the riddles towards the

---

1 The numbers of the riddles and, for the most part, the text of the OE riddles are those found in G. P. Krapp and E. V. K. Dobbie, edd., *The Exeter Book* (New York: Columbia University Press, 1936).

2 E. A. Lowe, ed., *Codices latini antiquiores* 6 (Oxford: Clarendon, 1953) p. ix.

end of the manuscript are incomplete because of damage to the pages. Some of the riddles may date from the 8th century, some from as late as the 10th. It is most unlikely that they are all the work of one man or one period.

Stylistically the Exeter Book riddles vary considerably: some are sophisticated and learned, some are simple and completely ingenuous, some are obscene and others deeply spiritual. Most of them have been satisfactorily solved but not all; and it is mainly with some of the un-solved that I am concerned here, although both solved and unsolved will be drawn on for vignettes of daily activity and concern in the Anglo-Saxon scriptorium.

The riddle itself is very old both in literature and folklore. Poets at whatever level of society have always seen and expressed natural phenomena (wind, rain, sun, moon, ice, eggs, etc.) and human artifacts (organ, book, wine, handmill) as riddles. The riddle or enigma as a mode of expressing human experience cuts right across many areas which are the concern of literature and criticism. It resembles, for example, simile, as when David wrote: "My tongue is nimble as the pen of a scribe (Ps 44 : 1); or metaphor, as Aristotle stated: "Good riddles do, in general, provide us with satisfactory metaphors: for metaphors imply riddles";[3] or allegory, "a trope in which a meaning other than the literal is indicated", as Bede explains;[4] or symbol, as when early Christian iconography designs an ἰχθύς "fish", possibly a cryptogram,[5] to depict Christ; or myth in that it expresses, as a German critic of the Romantic period points out, a commonplace that is true;[6] or analogy because it has "its deepest roots in the perception of the analogies of nature";[7] or, much better, epiphany, because when the riddling question has been asked, and the surprising senses of its nature grasped, there follows that new intense awareness that alone is the core of lyric poetry.[8]

Collections of riddles seem not to have been made until the time of the late Latin poets writing in North Africa, who, led by Martianus Capella, established their own peculiar type of encyclopedic scholar-

---

3 *Rhet.* 3. 2 [1405ᵇ 2-5].

4 *De schematibus et tropis*; ed. C. Halm, *Rhetorici latini minores* (Leipzig, 1863) p. 611; transl. G. H. Tannenhaus in *Quarterly Journal of Speech*, 48 (1962) 244-50.

5 Ἰησοῦς χριστὸς θεοῦ υἱός Σωτήρ "Jesus Christ, Son of God and Saviour". See Michael Gough, *The Origins of Christian Art* (London: Thames and Hudson, 1973) p. 24.

6 Ludwig Uhland, *Schriften zur Geschichte der Dichtung und Sage* 3 (Stuttgart, 1866) 185.

7   E. H. Lindley, "A Study of Puzzles with Special Reference to the Psychology of Mental Adaptation", *American Journal of Psychology*, 8 (1896-7) 484.

8   For something close to this see John F. Adams, "The Anglo-Saxon Riddle as Lyric Mode", *Criticism* (1965) 335-48.

ship. Thus we find our first "century of riddles" in the *Anthologia latina* and it is usually assigned to the almost unknown poet named Symphosius whose distinction, other than authoring the first known collection of riddles, is to have been long mistaken for a book, the lost Symposium of Lactantius mentioned by St. Jerome.[9] This confusion explains why in Migne's Patrology the one hundred riddles of Symphosius are located with the works of Lactantius.[10] The latest text of the riddles of Symphosius are located with the works of Lactantius.[10] The latest text of the riddles of Symphosius is to be found in Part 2 of volume 133 of the *Corpus Christianorum: Series Latina,* still not on their own but appended with all other such Latin collections to the works of Tatwine of Canterbury, who flourished some two hundred years after Symphosius was buried.

I say this as an ironic comment on the vagaries of serious publication, not as criticism of the editors of the *CCL* who had to put the collections of riddles somewhere, and elected, not illogically, to put them all together in volumes 133 and 133A after Tatwine's *Grammar.* With a certain practical wisdom, the editors included along with the texts of these collections of riddles, translations into a modern language because, they said, of the "outlandish" latinity of the riddles which they felt might pose problems to most contemporary readers[11] — a friendly gesture towards ignorance which many a student of medieval vernacular literature will welcome.

The collections gathered together in the two parts of the volume 133 of the *Corpus Christianorum* are those of Symphosius, Aldhelm, the so-called "Tullius", the unidentified author of the Lorsch riddles, Boniface, and Frater Eusebius (otherwise known as Hwætberht). It is not my intention to discuss these Latin collections here, but I want to make three points about them which affect my approach to the Exeter Book riddles. First, the collecting of riddles, begun by Symphosius in North Africa, was much imitated and extended in England. Aldhelm, late 7th century, abbot of Malmesbury and bishop of Sherborne, composed a collection of 100 riddles; Tatwine, early 8th century, said by Bede to come from Mercia, and to have been a priest in the monastery called Bredon and subsequently to have become archbishop of Canterbury, composed a series of 40 riddles, the initial letters of the first lines and the final letters of the first lines, reversed, formed acrostics which can be translated: "Turning forty times under these riddles dif-

9 "De viris inlustribus" c. 80; ed. E. C. Richardson in *Texte und Untersuchungen* 14 (Leipzig, 1896) 42.

10 *PL*, 7: 289-98.

11 "Series latina: Aenigmata", *1954-69 Corpus Christianorum* 1-50 (brochure no. 3, 1969), 3.

ferently, the maker reveals the hidden things in the thread of meters;[12] Eusebius, middle 8th century, probably to be identified with Hwæt-berht abbot of Wearmouth in Northumbria, composed 60 riddles, bringing Tatwine's collection up to 100.[13] With this evidence before us it is not surprising that riddles come to flourish in the English ver-nacular and that a goodly number of them — over 90 — are to be found in *The Exeter Book*.

The second point to be made about the Latin collections is that the riddles of Aldhelm and Tatwine (and possibly of others too) were com-posed to teach Latin hexameters, much as Latin colloquies were written to teach Latin vocabulary and sentence structure. It is doubtful that the vernacular riddles of the Exeter Book were written to teach anything. They are probably to a great extent scribal diversion.

Thirdly, some Latin riddles dealt with writing and with the writing tools employed by scribes in the scriptorium. Symphosius has two such riddles: no. 1 which is solved *graphium* or "stylus" and no. 2 which is solved *harundo* "reed". Aldhelm has three scriptorium-riddles: no. 32 *pugillares* "writing tablets", no. 59 *penna* "pen", no. 88 *arca libraria* "book-case". Aldhelm's riddle no. 30, *elementum* "alphabet" is really a grammatical riddle but it includes a number of the motifs of the riddles of the scriptorium and is worthy of mention in the present context. These six riddles, for convenience, appear below in the Appendix, and will not be analysed here. One can see at once, of course, how con-centrated they are in expression, how polished in language, how studied and formal in figure and imagery. Other riddles of the scriptorium tur-ning up in other Latin collections are: *de membrano* "parchment", *de atramento* "ink", *de scetha* "book wallet", *de atramentorio* "inkhorn" and possibly *de charta* "paper". It is clear that the use of these subjects preceded the compiling of the Exeter Book; but the fact remains that the Exeter Book employs many more such subjects and yet rarely takes over either the motifs or the images of the Latin poems. The reason for this, it seems to me, is that it was the scribes who were composing the Old English riddles, that they were having a lot of fun in doing so, and that they had very little occasion to keep their eye on the older Latin texts.

II

The Exeter Book riddles include very few exact renderings of Latin

---

12 Bede, *Historia ecclesiastica*, 5: 23; see W. F. Bolton, *A History of Anglo-Latin Literature, 597-1066* (Princeton: University Press, 1967) 215 ff.

13 Bede, *Historia abbotum*, c. 19; and Bolton, *op. cit.* 219.

riddles. In fact one of the serious obstacles to fully satisfactory scholarship on the Exeter Book riddles over the years has been the determination of scholars to identify the poems of Symphosius, Aldhelm and the others in their Anglo-Saxon dressing. The results have been disappointing, sometimes even misleading. The Anglo-Saxon riddles, like most Anglo-Saxon poems, display minimal dependence upon Latin models. They do, however, continue to show interest in the scriptorium and in the tools of writing. Perhaps the best known of all the Exeter-Book riddles is the so-called "book" riddle or "bible" (*halig gewrit*) riddle, a subject which Symphosius, a pagan, certainly would not, and which the Christian Aldhelm did not, attempt. This riddle is a classic example of linear, or developing, or "process" structure, describing the story of the making of a bible (or a lectionary) from the slaying of a cow or sheep for its hide until that hide, with writing and illustrations on it, became a medium of God's revelation to man.

Halig Gewrit also contains (lines 15-17) a fine example of a moral problem confronting a gifted monastic illustrator. I cite both text and interpretive translation by way of introducing a more speculative analysis of riddles relating to the scriptorium.

> Mec feonda sum feore besnyþede,
> woruldstrenga binom, wætte siþþan,
> dyfde on wætre, dyde eft þonan,
> sette on sunnan, þær ic swiþe beleas
> herum þam þe ic hæfde. Heard mec siþþan
> snað seaxses ecg, sindrum begrunden;
> fingras feoldan, ond mec fugles wyn
> geond speddropum spyrede geneahhe,
> ofer brunne brerd, beamtelge swealg,
> streames dæle, stop eft on mec,
> siþade sweartlast. Mec siþþan wrah
> hæleð hleobordum, hyde beþenede,
> gierede mec mid golde; forþon me gliwedon
> wrætlic weorc smiþa, wire bifongen.
> Na þa gereno ond se reada telg
> ond þa wuldorgesteald wide mære
> dryhtfolca helm, nales dol wite.
> Gif min bearn were brucan willad,
> hy beoð þy gesundran and þy sigefæstran,
> heortum þy hwætran ond þy hygebliþran,
> ferþe þy fodran, habbaþ freonda þy ma,
> swæsra ond gesibbra, soþra ond godra,
> tilra ond getreowra, þa hyra tyr ond ead
> estum ycað ond hy arstafum
> lissum bilecgað ond hi lufan fæþmum

fæste clyppað. Frige hwæt ic hatte,
niþum to nytte. Nama min is mære,
næleþum gifre ond halig sylf.

Some slaughterer deprived me of life,
took away my vital strength. Next he soaked me;
dipped me in water and took me out again;
placed me in the sun where I soon lost
what hairs I had. Next, after I had been polished with slag,
the hard edge of a knife snipped me
and fingers folded me. The bird's delight
travelled closely over me with its useful drops;
over the stained lip it swallowed a drop of liquid
tree dye, then stepped back on me,
journeying over me with a black track. Next an artisan covered me
with protecting boards, covered me with hide;
and to decorate me with gold he attached to me
wondrous metal clasps held by strands of wire.
Now these ornaments and red lettering
and the illustrations are to celebrate far and wide
the Protector of Men and are not foolish vanity.
If the race of men will use me
they will be the sounder and the more successful,
the bolder in heart and the gladder in thought,
the wiser in mind; they will have the more friends,
the more loved ones, the more true and good ones,
the better and more honest ones. Such by their blessedness
will increase the honours and fortunes of men, will wrap them
tight in love's embraces. Discover what I am called
who am so profitable to men. My name is famous,
useful to men and holy in itself.

III

Halig Gewrit is the classical writing riddle, known to anyone who reads Anglo-Saxon at all, and offers only the slightest problems of interpretation. It was not written to mislead or puzzle; it effectively exploits the Latin riddles and exposes, beautifully and joyfully, how any book containing Scriptures has come to be. It is particularly apt in the present context because part of it (lines 7-11) describe the act of writing: "The bird's delight (a kenning for *feðer* "pen") travelled closely over me with its useful drops; over the stained lip (of the inkpot) it swallowed a drop of liquid tree dye (ink), then stepped back on me, journeying over me with a black track." These lines provide a natural springboard into "writing riddles" the first group of scriptorium riddles to be dealt with here.

Three Exeter Book riddles, nos. 51, 19, 64, deal with the scribe and his act of writing (see Appendix for text and translation of 51 and 19) and they have been solved. Riddle 51 speaks of four wights, which enter into the act of writing. These four wights, turn out to be a pen and the three fingers which guide its journey across the parchment-plain leaving a black track of letters and words behind. The motif is Latin, having turned up in Tatwine, no. 6, *de penna,* and was first recorded by Trautmann in 1905.[14] OE Riddle 51 is just a run-of-the-mill beginning to the subject of Anglo-Saxon writing riddles. Riddles 19 and 64, however, take the theme into an imaginative development which long outwitted the scholars. These two riddles present a scene and an action: it is a hunting scene comprising a horse, a rider, and a hawk, all making a journey together. But the scene is not as obvious as I have just presented it because the three objects are not named in the text but enigmatically described in runes, and not in simple straightforward runes but in runic shorthand in riddle 64 and in runes arranged in reverse order in riddle 19.

Early scholars got almost nowhere with riddle 19 because there was nothing like it in Latin. The best they could do was read the runic letters as "horse", "man", and "hawk". The first intelligent (but wrong) solution was that of Erika von Erhardt-Siebold who said the answer was "falconry".[15] The man on the horse, she said, was carrying the hawk on his wrist and the scene was a hunting scene and the solution of the riddle was "falconry". The difficulty with this solution was that the word "falconry" did not really answer the riddling question: "I saw (the riddle said) a horse, a man and a hawk journeying. *Who am I?*" The word "falconry" is no answer to the question. A clumsy question put by an unlettered riddler, said Mrs. von Erhardt-Siebold, but the riddle, she insisted, was only asking us to identify the most popular sport in the middle ages.

Riddle 19 was first solved as a writing riddle by Norman E. Eliason when he recognized that the horse was a pen, the rider was the three fingers gripping that pen, and the hawk the feather sticking up over the writer's elbow; the journey was that of the group across the parchment.[16] The appropriate answer to the question, "who am I who saw this scene?" is the forgotten man, the scribe himself, dreaming no doubt as he scribbled away that if he were a knight, or an abbot or a prior, he might even at that moment be trying his skill at falconry. The

14 Moritz Trautmann, "Alte und neue Antworten auf altenglische Rätsel", *Bonner Beiträge zur Anglistik,* 19 (1905), 196.

15 Erika von Erhardt-Siebold, "The Old English Hunt Riddles", *PMLA,* 63 (1948) 3-6.

16 "Old English Cryptographic Riddles", *Studies in Philology,* 49 (1952) 553-65.

full answer, I suppose, is "Scribe and Writing" or "Scribe at work" and so my formulation *gewritere ond gewrit* which but spells out in Anglo-Saxon Eliason's "Writing Riddle".

IV

I turn now to four riddles for which I think I have original and correct solutions, three of them (17, 18, 49) dealing with the scribe's tools, one (57) with his musical notation. Each of these riddles contributes its own series of vignettes of day-to-day life in the scriptorium. First among these is Riddle 17. A variety of solutions have been offered for this riddle: Latin *ballista,* that is, a stone-throwing engine, was the solution offered by Dietrich, Lange, Prehn and Wyatt; OE *boga* or "bow" by Grein; OE *bæc-ern* "bake-oven" or *bæc-hus* "bakery" by Trautmann and Holthausen.[17]

The speaker in Riddle 17 provides the following clues about his identity: I am the *mundbora,* that is, the protector or container of my herd; I am held fast by wire; by day I spit out and from time to time swallow battle-darts and poisoned spears; I am useful, and the more useful the fuller I am; and men remember what comes out of my mouth.

There is also an external clue: two runes for B and L (ß beorc, ᛚ lagu) have been written above the poem in the MS. These runes seem to have been offered as real clues and all solutions try to utilize them. That is why the solutions all begin with the letter B: *ballista, burg, boga, bæc-ern.* Strangely enough, none of the solutions offered thus far has any use for the L. Of all the clues, internal and external, the first provided — I am the *mundbora minre heorde* "the container of my herd" — is the most enigmatic.

The solutions offered are credible. A ballista is a *mundbora* because it holds, in its belly, rocks, beams and bolts for offensive warfare; it is also made steady by cords; it spits out its artillery and requires refilling; it is useful to princes and to the proud; and men remember what passes through its mouth. It seems to satisfy all the clues. A bake-oven is equally satisfactory: at first blush, it is perhaps odd to speak of an oven as the container of a "herd", but Trautmann, who offered the solution, felt easy about calling cakes and loaves a "herd" because a later Low-German domestic riddle describes freshly baked loaves of bread as "brown horses"; in this solution, the spear-terrors have to be taken to be the flames of the cooking fire; the loaves which come out through the oven door can certainly be called "useful"; and men can be said to remember them.

17 The detail of these references can be found in Frederick Tupper, *The Riddles of the Exeter Book* (New York, 1910) and Moritz Trautmann, *Die Altenglischen Rätsel* (Heidelberg, 1915).

These and other solutions thus far offered seem to me to be unconvincing. The clues, however, take on a new pertinence once the scriptorium factors are brought to bear on the poem. I take it that the Anglo-Saxon scribe (or poet, as the case may be) has here composed a little riddle about the inkwell — the *blæc-horn*, (Latin *atramentorium*) on his writing desk. The main problem is whether, as in the case of the other solutions, an inkwell can be aptly described as *mundbora heorde* or "container of a herd." What is an inkwell's herd or flock? It is, I suggest, the many useful drops the scribe will dip out of the container as well as all the letters and words which he will form out of those drops as he scratches with his quill across the parchment. This is the mystery of his art. My interpretation is really not extravagant when one remembers that in writing riddles generally, drops of ink are always "useful drops" out of which words are formed. The following translation assumes the validity of this solution:

> I am the keeper of my flock
> fast with restraining wires, filled inside
> with treasures fit for a prince. By day oft
> I spit out spear-venom. My success is the greater
> the fuller I am. The Lord knows
> how battle-darts fly out of my belly.
> From time to time I swallow dark
> brown battle-weapons bitter points
> ugly poisoned spears. What is in me is useful.
> It is a lovely wombhoard dear to proud ones.
> Men remember what passes through my mouth.

Two things make me feel comfortable about this translation and solution. The first is the extraordinary appropriateness imparted to at least three of the poet's expressions: to *dægtidum* line 3b, to *attorsperum* line 9a, and to *wombhord* line 10a. Scribal activity must have been essentially a daylight activity, and hence it is by day that bitter ink is spewed forth; the puzzling hapax legomenon *attorspere* echoes in its first element *attor* the *atra* of Latin *atramentum* and *atramentorium*; and the use of *wombhord* suggesting as it does *wordhord*, is most apt in the context here suggested.

The second factor affording me a certain satisfaction over this solution is that it fully and satisfactorily explains the runic B and L, written over the text in the MS, which now become the first two letters of OE *blæchorn*, the word that solves the riddle.

It seems quite possible that Riddle 17 was originally followed by a second riddle on the same subject. Krapp and Dobbie have this to say about the two and a half lines surviving of Riddle 18: "It is almost certain that a good part of this riddle has been lost after *wombe*, line 3, although no loss is indicated in the manuscript, and it is impossible to be sure of a solution on the basis of what remains. Dietrich (ZfdA, XI, 465) solved as 'leather bottle' which is as good as any" (p. 331). I would prefer to specify Dietrich's 'leather bottle' (of 1859) as a *blæchorn* and translate as follows:

> "I am a wonderful thing. I cannot speak a word
> nor express myself before men. Yet I have a mouth,
> and a wide belly."

Since the Exeter Book scribe sometimes groups his poems by theme, and since the words *muð* and *womb* occur as clues in both riddles, 17 and 18 may both be solved satisfactorily as *blæchorn*.

A second complete riddle which I comfortably describe as a riddle of the scriptorium is no. 49. Riddle 49 is, according to Trautmann, another "oven" riddle. Dietrich solved it first as "cage", then, after noting that Aldhelm (ii, 14: "*de arca libraria*") had said that his bookcase whose viscera were filled with divine words yet learned nothing from them, and that the subject of this riddle was twice (line 1 and lines 10-11) described as "dumb", solved Riddle 49 as "bookcase". Most have accepted this solution. I do not think it to be correct, although even if it is, the riddle can still be associated with the scriptorium. I find, however, that the "book-case" solution does not take into account that the riddle speaks of two unknowns: the *anne* of line 1 and the *opre* of line 5. Again, the solution ought grammatically to be a word of masculine gender and the known forms of OE words for bookcase are feminine or neuter. Also the solution is dependent upon taking the *lacum* of line 3 as an instrumental plural of *lac* "gift" rather than, as I think correct, an instrumental plural of *lacu* "stream or pool". The solution I suggest is *penn* and *atrum*, "pen and ink."

I think it best in this case to let my translation speak for itself, with but one word of explanation about my interpretation of the first clue. This concerns the first unknown, which I take to be "pen" or "quill", probably a reed pen rather than a feather. The first clue, which requires some special pleading in my interpretation, states that the first unknown object stands *eardfast,* that is, "firmly in its place." This place I take to be its pen-rack or pencase (Latin *theca*)[18] its proper place when not in actual use. The phrase might also recall that when this as yet unidentified object was a reed, it could also be said to have been in a fixed place; cp. *frumstapole fæst,* "fixed in my original abode" used of the reed pen in Riddle 60 line 3. I translate Riddle 49 as follows:

---

18 Wilhelm Wattenbach, *Das Schriftwesen im Mittelalter* (Leipzig, 1875) p. 187.

"I know *one thing* standing firmly in its place,
deaf, dumb, which many times a day *swallows*
by a craftsman's hand useful pools.
Sometimes there in that place the dark fellow
black and dirty-nosed sends under its palate
another thing that is dearer than the gold
which noblemen often desire,
kings and queens. I will not describe further
this latter thing that is so useful to them,
and does them so much good, and which this dumb thing here,
a dark unknowing thing swallowed before."

I cannot help thinking that the poem's second and third clues —
"swallowing useful pools by a craftsman's (*gopes*) hand, and, a dirty-
nosed fellow who sends something precious under his palate — almost
clinch my "pen and ink" solution.

Two psychologically significant factors emerge from the two riddles,
blæchorn and *penn ond atrum*, just discussed. One is the imaginative sensitivity and respect of the scribe for his tools: his ink is *til, gifre*, a princely treasure, a radiant wombhoard (17: 3, 10), more precious than the
gold which noblemen, kings and queens long for. The other is his
amused recognition that he and his instruments are somewhat alike:
dubiously knowledgeable mediators and transmitters but providing by
their competence a highly useful service to society.

The third significant scriptorium riddle for which I have an original
solution, is the very lovely Riddle 57, which relates how little black
singing creatures are carried up in groups or clusters over rocky slopes,
and that although they tread cliffs they are nevertheless to be found inside buildings; they also name themselves.

The solutions have been "swallows", "gnats", "starlings", "hail-
stones", "raindrops", "storm clouds". Most in favour with the editors of the Anglo-Saxon Poetic Records, Krapp and Dobbie, are bird
solutions, and especially Brett's "jackdaws" and Holthausen's "crows",
which are species of birds with an onomatopoeic name and can accordingly be said to "name themselves". The best handling of the riddle
to date is that of Erika von Erhardt-Siebold who stays with a bird
solution, accepting Brett's "jackdaw".[19]

I take the riddle in a very different sense, one which hinges upon the
meaning of the opening words of the poem, "*þeos lyft*", which all take to
be the air, and which I take more neutrally to be "this thing which lifts"
and which is not in this case the air but the musical scale, the ledges or
other devices by means of which a scribe records the rise and fall of

musical notes. Accepting this interpretation of *þeos lyft,* the translation comes out as follows:

> This "lift" ("ladder"?) carries little things
> over mounting hills. These things are very black,
> swarthy, dark-coated. Bountiful with song,
> they move in clusters. They cry out loudly.
> They tread steep cliffs, yet are the while inside the home
> of the children of men. They name themselves.

A glance at any early manuscript containing musical notes is enough to convince one of the aptness of this solution. The scribe's imagination sees his little black notes as singing birds climbing up and down the real or imagined ledges on the page in front of him.[20] They do, of course, name themselves — do, re, mi, etc.

There are, in addition to the riddles already dealt with, a few others on which this scriptorium approach may yet throw light, but for which I am much less confident that I have found a correct solution. Riddle 4 is a case in point.

This is a difficult riddle and it has been traditionally solved as "bell" (OE *belle*) or "mill" (OE *mylen*). These solutions seem to have been arrived at by a process of learned peeking: Symphosius had two millstone riddles (nos. 51 and 52) and Aldhelm had one (IV, 12); Symphosius had also a "bell" riddle (no. 80 *tintinnabulum*) and so had Tatwine (no. 7, *de tintinno*). Since a knowledgeable Anglo-Saxon riddler might well have dealt with either one of these subjects used by the Latin masters, mighty efforts have gone into demonstrating that he was actually dealing with one or other of them here in Riddle 4. Unfortunately, only the solutions, not all the clues, connect Riddle 4 with any of the alleged Latin models. Krapp and Dobbie have this to say: "The solutions for this riddle vary widely. Dietrich, ZfdA, 11 (1859) 461 suggested "bell" but decided upon "millstone" as the proper answer. Tupper favoured "bell". Trautmann solved as "flail." Holthausen, *Eng. Stud.* 51 (1917) 185, solved as "lock", but in *Anglia* 44 (1920) 346, approved "handmühle." Bradley, *MLR,* 6 (1911) 433 ff., believed that the riddle "relates to some definite story of necromancy;" that is, the "man or maid" seeks an oracular answer, and causes the dead man to be summoned from his tomb and the oracular collar to be placed upon him. The riddle seems to fit "bell" best, though it may well be that the true solution has not yet been hit upon." To which I say fervently, Amen!

---

20 See, for example, page C of the facsimile edition of the Tollemache Orosius, ed. Alistair Campbell, *Early English Manuscripts in Facsimile. Vol. III* (BM. Additional MS. 47967) Copenhagen, 1953.

Of the two more common suggestions, the solution "bell" is the more attractive. In this solution the speaker is a monastery bell (*a micel belle* or a *campana*) which from its tower, or *belhus,* summons the monks to chapel or refectory when the bellringer (the thegn of line 1) pulls the bell-rope. The poem proceeds in three clearly-marked movements: 1. The bell describes itself as periodically employed (*þragbysig*), held aloft by links (*hringum haefted;* the MS has *hringan haefted*), responding obediently to the bellringer (*þegne minum*), thus disturbing its resting-place (*bed brecan*), and announcing with clamour that its lord has given it a neck-pull (*halswiðan*). The bell then tells how when it is at rest, some man or woman often comes along and "greets" or "plays" it (*gretan,* cp. *haerpan gretan* = play the harp), and how in the cold of winter it responds to this grim creature: the warm limb, says the bell, sometimes breaks its bound collar — an accident to be blamed (*on þonce*) on its thegn, a dull fellow. The bell explains that anyone can recognize it for what it is from these clues (*þáer*) and can in words quickly tell its story.

Weak in this solution is the generalized role of the bellringer which renders pointless the taunting of him as a dullard; and the far-fetched, inept or inexact contrasting of the winter-cold bell and the warm limb. Also weak is that the MS has to be emended in order to provide an essential clue: *hringan hæfted* has become *hringum hæfted.* But the solution is not a bad one.

The second solution, millstone, has been elaborately presented by Erika von Erhardt-Siebold in a detailed, learned but ultimately un-convincing article in PMLA.[21] It is now a millstone that is assumed to be in the fixed position, and it is rotated from time to time by a slave. The apparatus is sometimes broken through the slave's clumsiness, especially in cold weather. Mrs. Erhardt-Siebold interprets the term "ring" (line 2) to mean a journal box or a socket in which the heavy millstone pivots. She accepts with many editors the emendation of *hringan hæfted* (line 2) to *hringum hæfted.* Her solution has, it seems to me, all the weaknesses of the bell solution with none of its charm.

I venture to draw this poem into my scriptorium-family of riddles and solve it, not as "bell" or "millstone" or anything complex but sim-ply as "feðer" or "penna", without emending the text, with increased precision of the clues, and with the whimsicality that ought to attach to the relationship between a scribe and his pens.

The pen I have in mind, the speaker throughout the poem, is a quill with the heavy end cut diagonally with a penknife to form a writing nib and wound about with thread for strength and firm gripping. This kind

21   "Old English Riddle no. 4: *Handmill*", PMLA, 61 (1946) 620-3.

of nib is easily enough broken when the scribe's finger (*lim*, line 7) presses too heavily on the pen as is apt to happen first thing on a cold morning as he begins to work in the scriptorium.

The poem proceeds in three movements: the first four lines describe the scratching sounds made by the pen moving over the parchment; the next five and a half lines teasingly reproach scribes, whether men or women, for breaking their pen nibs; the closing two and a half lines put, in anything but conventional form, the conventional question inviting the answer *"feðer"* or *"penna"*. See Appendix for text and several translations. I translate as follows:

> I must, a busy fellow sometimes,
> make a noise when taken up obey my slave
> interrupt my prayer, announce noisily
> that the "master" has given me a "neck-hold".
> Oft a man or woman has gone to greet me (a sleep-weary one)
> Wintercold, I respond to this grim creature
> His warm "finger" sometimes breaks the bound ring
> This, however, is to be blamed on my "slave",
> a dull fellow. A man can recognize me
> for what I am from that, can in words
> quickly "tell my story".

Although I am still uncomfortable about my solution, especially concerning: 'the difficult syntax of *hringan hæfted* (line 2) which I cannot parallel in OE, and which I don't want to emend; the somewhat forced character of *gebundenne bæg*, "the bound ring" (line 8), which I have taken to refer to the reinforced base of the pen just above the nib; and the ambiguity of the *min bed brecan* (line 3) which can be read "break my bed", "break my rest", or "interrupt my prayer". These problems inhere in all solutions, of course, but I should like to think they are less troubling in mine. Yet I am somewhat attached to my solution because of its overall simplicity, of the appropriateness it imparts to the comments on the pen as holding the scribe in thrall day after day, and of the bemused relevance it gives to the expressions *"þragbysig"* (line 1), and *halswriþan* (line 4). I have to leave Riddle 4 as still "dubiously" solved.

Let me make a hurried conclusion about the significance of these Exeter Book riddles. They proceed out of the tradition established by Symphosius and Aldhelm. They are, for the most part, composed as serious poems, but take on the interests of the scribe more than the poet, and in some cases to such an extent that we are justified even in attributing them to scribes or to a single scribe. This does not reduce their significance for medieval literature generally, as the following lines of the *Anticlaudianus* of Alan of Lille suggest:

"The pen of the author and the ornaments of the poet I beg, lest Clio follow the lead of my indolence and wane in power and the pen lie idle rough with mould. The aged parchment rejoices to renew its youth with fresh writing, smiles in its desire to leave its ancient hiding place and the Muse plays on a slender reed. Drench your poet, Apollo, with the waters of your fountain that the parched mind, watered by your stream, may favour us with sprouts and bring the tended sprouts to their final fruit."[22]

Pontifical Institute of Mediaeval Studies.

22 James J. Sheridan, transl., *Alan of Lille: Anticlaudianus or the Good and Perfect Man* (Toronto: Pontifical Institute of Mediaeval Studies, 1973) p. 43.

APPENDIX

Symphosius. 1, Graphium

De summo planus sed non ego planus in imo
Versor utrimque manu; diverso munere fungor:
Altera pars revocat quidquid pars altera fecit.

Ohl Transl. Stylus

Flat on top but not flat below, I am turned either way
by the hand; different duties I perform: the one part
revokes what the other has done.

Symphosius, 2, Harundo

Dulcis amica dei, ripae vicina profundae,
Suave canens Musis, nigro perfusa colore,
Nuntia sum linguae digitis signata magistris.

Ohl Transl. Reed

Sweet mistress of a god, the steep bank's neighbor, sweetly
singing for the Muses; when drenched with black, I am the
tongue's messenger by guiding fingers pressed.

Aldhelm, 30, Elementum

Nos decem et septem genitae sine voce sorores
Sex alias nothas non dicimus annumerandas.
Nascimur ex ferro rursus ferro moribundae
Necnon et volucris penna volitantis ad aethram;
Terni nos fratres incerta matre crearunt.
Qui cupit instanter sitiens audire docentes,
Tum cito prompta damus rogitanti verba silenter.

Pitman Transl. Alphabet

We seventeen sisters, voiceless all, declare
Six others bastards are, and not of us.
Of iron we are born, and find our death
Again by iron; or at times we come
From pinion of a lofty-flying bird.
Three brothers got us of an unknown mother.
To him who thirsts for instant counsel, we
In silence quickly bring out hoarded words.

Aldhelm, 32, Pugillares

Melligeris apibus mea prima processit origo,
Sed pars exterior crescebat cetera silvis;
Calciamenta mihi tradebant tergora dura.
Nunc ferri stimulus faciem proscindit amoenam
Flexibus et sulcos obliquat adinstar aratri,
Sed semen segiti de caelo ducitur almum,
Quod largos generat millena fruge maniplos.
Heu! tam sancta seges diris extinguitur armis.

Pitman Transl. Writing-Tablets

Of honey-laden bees I first was born,
But in the forest grew my outer coat;
My tough backs came from shoes. An iron point
In artful windings cuts a fair design,
And leaves long, twisted furrows, like a plough.
From heaven unto that field is borne the seed
Or nourishment, which brings forth generous sheaves
A thousandfold. Alas, that such a crop,
A holy harvest, falls before grim war.

Aldhelm, 59, Penna

Me dudum genuit candens onocrotalus albam,
Gutture qui patulo sorbet de gurgite limphas.
Pergo per albentes directo tramite campos
Candentique viae vestigia caerula linquo,
Lucida nigratis fuscans anfractibus arva.
Nec satis est unum per campos pandere callem,
Semita quin potius milleno tramite tendit,
Quae non errantes ad caeli culmina vexit.

Pitman Transl. Pen

The shining pelican, whose yawning throat
Gulps down the waters of the sea, long since
Produced me, white as he. Through snowy fields
I keep a straight road, leaving deep-blue tracks
Upon the gleaming way, and darkening
The fair champaign with black and tortuous paths;
Yet one way through the plain suffices not,
For with a thousand bypaths runs the road,
And them who stray not from it, leads to heaven.

Aldhelm, 89, Arca Libraria

Nunc mea divinis complentur viscera verbis
Totaque sacratos gestant præcordia biblos;
At tamen ex isdem nequeo cognoscere quicquam:
Infelix fato fraudabor munere tali,
Dum tollunt diræ librorum lumina Parcaæ.

Pitman Transl. Bookcase

My inwards overflow with words divine,
And sacred volumes crowd my vital parts,
But from them I can never learn one whit-
Unhappy creature, robbed of such a gift,
By my grim fate denied the light of books.

Exeter Book, 51, Gewritere ond Gewrit

Ic seah wrætlice wuhte feower
samed siþian; swearte wæran lastas,
swaþu blacu. Swift wæs on fore,
fuglum framra; fleag on lyfte,
deaf under yþe. Dreag unstille
winnende wiga se him wegas tæcneþ
ofer fæted gold feower eallum.

51 Translation: Scribe and his Writing

I saw four wondrous creatures
travelling together; dark were their tracks,
their trail very black. Swift it was in journeying,
busier than birds; it flew in the air,
dived under the wave. Restlessly did he suffer,
the struggling warrior who directs all four
on ways more (precious) than rich gold.

Exeter Book, 19, Gewritere ond Gewrit

Ic (on siþe) seah. ᛗᚱᚩ
ᚾ. hygewloncne, heafodbeorhtne,
swiftne ofer sælwong swiþe þrægan.
Hæfde him on hrycge hildeþryþe
.ᚷ ᚩ ᛗ . nægled ne rad
. ᚾᚷᛗᛈ   Widlast ferede
rynestrong on rade rofne. ᚻ ᚩ
ᛈᚠᚾᚾ . For wæs þy beorhtre,
swylcra siþfæt. Saga hwæt ic hatte.

19 Translation: Scribe and his Writing

I saw a horse (ᚢᚱᚠᚻ)
high-spirited, his head bright with ornaments,
run very swiftly over the pleasant plain;
on his back he had warlike strength.
The man (ᚷᛗᛈ), armoured (= "nailed"), rode
never away (ᚾᚷᛗᚹ). Far-wandering,
strong in his riding, he carried a strong hawk
(ᚻᛈᚠᛗᚠᚻ   ). The journey was the brighter
for the riding of such. Say what I am called.

Exeter Book, 17, Blæchorn

Ic eom mundbora minre heorde
eodorwirum fæst innan gefylled
dryhtgestreona dægtidum oft
spæte sperebrogan sped biþ þy mare
fylle minre. Frea þæt bihealdeð
hu me of hrife fleogað hyldepilas
hwilum ic sweartum swelgan onginne
brunum beadowæpnum bitrum ordum
eglum attorsperum is min innað til.
wombhord wlitig wloncum deore
men gemunan þæt me þurh muþ fareð

Riddle 17, Mackie Transl. (EETS): Ballista See text for my translation.

I am a protector of my flock,
fast strengthened with wires, and filled inside
with noble treasures. In the day-time I often
spit forth deadly spears; I have the greater success
the fuller I am. My master beholds
how missiles of war fly from my belly.
Sometimes I begin to swallow black and dusky
weapons of battle, bitter arrows,
spears dreadful and venomous. I have a good stomach,
and within it an excellent treasure, dear to gallant men.
Men remember what passes through my mouth.

Exeter Book, 18, Blæchorn

Ic eom wunderlicu wiht; ne mæg word sprecan,
mældan for monnum, þeah ic muþ hæbbe,
wide wombe
                    *   *   *

Ic wæs on ceole ond mines cnosles ma.

Riddle 18, Mackie Transl. (EETS): ? See text for my translation.

I am a wonderful creature; I cannot speak words
or discourse before men, though I have a mouth
and a large belly
                    *   *   *
I was in a ship with more of my kindred.

Exeter Book, Riddle 49

Ic wat eardfæstne anne standan,
deafne, dumban, se oft dæges swilgeð ·
þurh gopes hond gifrum lacum.
Hwilum on þam wicum se wonna þegan,
sweart ond saloneb, sendeð oþre
under goman him golde dyrran,
þa æþelingas oft wilniað,
cyningas ond cwene. Ic þæt cyn nu gen
nemnan ne wille, þe him to nytte swa
ond to dugþum doþ þæt se dumba her,
eorþ unwita, ær forswilgeð.

Riddle 49, Mackie Transl. (EETS) See text for my translation.

I know of one that stands fixed to the ground,
deaf and dumb, who often during the day swallows
useful gifts from the hand of a servant.
Sometimes in his dwelling the dark thane,
a swarthy blackamoor, sends under his palate
other gifts more precious than gold,
which princes, kings, and queens,
often desire. I will not yet name
the race that prepare for his use and benefit
what here the dumb creature,
a dusky ignoramus, has swallowed.

Exeter Book, Riddle 57

Ðeos lyft byreð lytle wihte
ofer beorghleoþa. Þa sind blace swiþe,
swearte salopade. Sanges rope
heapum ferað, hlude cirmað,
tredað bearonæssas, hwilum burgsalo
niþþa bearna. Nemnað hy sylfe.

Riddle 57, Mackie Transl. (EETS) See text for my translation.

This air carries over the steep hills
little creatures that are very black,
swart, dark-coated. Bountiful of song,
they travel in companies, and chirp loudly.
They tread on the wooded cliffs, sometimes on the strong halls
of the sons of men. Name them.

Exeter Book, Riddle 4 (EETS)
(Anglo-Saxon Text)

Ic sceal þragbysig þegne minum
hringan hæfted hyran georne
min bed brecan breahtme cyþan
þæt me halswriþan hlaford sealde
oft mec slæpwerigne secg oðþe meowle
gretan eode ic him gromheortum
winterceald oncweþe wearm lim ...
gebundenne bæg hwilum bersteð
se þeah biþ on þonce þegne minum
medwisum men me þæt sylfe
þæt wiht wite ond wordum min
on sped mæge spel gesecgan: 7

Riddle 4, Paul F. Baum Transl.

Bound with rings I must readily obey
from time to time my servant and master
and break my rest, make noisily known
that he gave me a band to put on my neck.
Often a man or a woman has come to greet me,
when weary with sleep, wintry-cold, I answer him:
(their hearts were angry): "A warm limb
sometimes bursts the bound ring."
Nonetheless it is pleasant to him, my servant,
a half-witted man, and to me the same,
if one knows aught and can then with words
riddle my riddle successfully.

Riddle 4, Erhardt-Siebold Transl.

Fettered by rings, I am busy at times
and diligently obey my attendant:
I break my bed announcing with clamor
that my lord has put a ring on my neck.
Often, when I am weary with sleep, a man or woman
comes and grips me; to this fierce creature
icy I respond. Occasionally a warm limb
bursts the ring lined to it;
however this pleases my attendant,
that dullard, and likewise it would me,
had I any sense and could in words
skilfully tell my story.

Riddle 4, Proposed Transl.

I must, a busy fellow sometimes,
make a noise when taken up, obey my slave
interrupt my prayer, announce noisily
that the "master" has given me a "neck-hold"

Oft a man or woman has gone to greet me (a sleep-weary one)
Wintercold, I respond to this grim creature
His warm "finger" sometimes breaks the bound ring
This, however, is to be blamed on my "slave",
a dull fellow. A man can recognize me
for what I am from that, can in words
quickly "tell my story".

THE *DE REGNO* AND THE TWO POWERS

by Leonard E. Boyle, O.P.

IN a well-known article of 1958,[1] the late Fr I. T. Eschmann, O.P., discussed the two main texts in the writings of St Thomas which deal with the relations between the 'spiritual' and 'temporal' powers. The first (*S*) is at the end of Book Two of the *Scriptum super sententiis*.[2] The second (*R*) is in Book One, c. 14 of the *opusculum De regno ad regem Cipri*, also called, though less correctly, *De regimine principum*.[3] In Fr Eschmann's opinion, 'The two texts do not present an identity of views nor such a similarity as could easily be synthesized. Rather they are contradictory' (177); 'Texts *S* and *R* are contradictory in doctrine as well as method. They also originate in differing and conflicting schools of thought' (182).

For Eschmann (and he shows this at some length), the *Scriptum* 'recalls to mind the dualistic thesis of some 12th and 13th century canonists' (183). The roots of this thesis lie in a letter of pope Gelasius in 494 to

---

1   I. T. Eschmann, 'St. Thomas Aquinas on the Two Powers', in *Mediaeval Studies* 20 (1958) 177-205. In the present essay page-references to this article are given in brackets immediately after citations from Eschmann.

2   2 D 44, q. 2 a. 3, *expositio textus: S. Thomae Aquinatis Scriptum super sententiis*, II, ed. P. Mandonnet (Paris, 1929), pp. 1135-6.

3   This writing, which is attributed to St Thomas by the earliest catalogues of his works, is incomplete and seems to belong to the years 1265-1267. It is generally agreed that the *De regno* in its incomplete form consisted of 21 chapters, ending at Book Two c. 4 as found in modern editions; the remainder is probably the work of Ptolomy of Lucca (ob. 1327). The 'Vulgate' text of the work, which Eschmann uses, is that in various editions of the *Opera omnia* of St Thomas, e.g., Roman edition, I, pp. 160v-168v; Parma edition, XVI, pp. 225-291; Vivès edition, XXVII, pp. 336-412. The same 'Vulgate' text is also to be found in P. Mandonnet, *Opuscula omnia S. Thomae* (Paris, 1927), I, pp. 312-487; J. Mathis, *S. Thomae Aquinatis De Regimine Principum et De Regimine Judaeorum politica opuscula duo* (Turin, 1948). A fresh, but interim, edition is in *S. Thomae Aquinatis Opuscula Omnia necnon Minora*, ed. J. Perrier, I (Paris, 1949), pp. 221-267. An English translation, with valuable introduction, notes, and textual appendices, is to be found in G. B. Phelan and I. T. Eschmann, *St. Thomas Aquinas On Kingship to the King of Cyprus* (Toronto, 1949).

    The text followed in this essay is the 'Vulgate' text used by Eschmann in his article. The Perrier edition, which uses four Paris MSS., numbers the chapters differently to that of the 'Vulgate' edition. Thus I c. 14 of the 'Vulgate' is I c. 15 in Perrier.

the emperor Anastasius,[4] an extract from which was celebrated in the middle ages as the canon *Duo quippe sunt potestates* in the *Decretum* of Gratian (D96 c10).[5] Broadly speaking, and as described by Fr Eschmann, advocates of the dualistic thesis held that 'spiritual and secular powers are not derivative but original *imperia*. They are like first causes, each autonomous in its own order, the spiritual power in the things belonging to the salvation of souls, the political power in things concerning the civil good' (178). If, in a given case, e.g., the popes of the time of St Thomas, the two powers are found in one person, they still remain 'formally distinct' though 'materially united'. 'Not one but two specifically different competences and jurisdictions are attributed to the pope' in such circumstances, and 'these two are not reduced one to the other' (178-9).

The *De regno*, on the other hand, 'contradicts' the *Scriptum* 'exactly at this point', since it holds, according to Eschmann, that 'the pope has one power only: the spiritual power', which, of its nature, 'includes secular power' (179). In a word, the *De regno*, contrary to the *Scriptum*, 'brings about a formal *reductio ad unum* by formally subsuming secular power under spiritual power, especially the papal power' (ibid.). For the *Scriptum*, 'the pope as pope, i.e. as spiritual sovereign and head of the Church, has no political power whatsoever' (ibid.). For the *De regno*, however, 'supreme political power is given him by reason of his spiritual primacy' (180).

Fr Eschmann, then, sees the *De regno* as a prime example of 'theological Gregorianism', the fundamental principle of which, in Fr Eschmann's words, 'is that both *potestas sacerdotalis* and *potestas saecularis* are found within the one church, which therefore emerges as the one super-comprehensive society' (192). It is, moreover, the only work of St Thomas in which there is 'any trace of that curious theology of the Primacy which includes secular power in its essence and appeals to a certain christological materialism for its support' (189). Having compared the *De regno* text on the two powers with that of the *Scriptum*, Eschmann is inevitably persuaded to question the very authenticity of the *De regno* as a work of St Thomas, because of 'the presence, in works of an author of the stature of St Thomas, of two texts belonging to different worlds' (195).

*

* *

4 *Epistolae Romanorum Pontificum*, ed. A. Thiel, I (Braunsberg, 1868), pp. 349-58.
5 *Corpus iuris canonici*, ed. A Friedberg (Leipzig, 1879-1881), I, cols. 340-1.

Now, in all of this Eschmann confines himself to c. 14 of Book One of *De regno*. He does not use any other chapter, nor does he situate that chapter in relation to the chapters that precede or follow it. Further, he presents the *Scriptum* and *De regno* passages as though they were speaking of precisely the same subject. Yet, unlike the *Scriptum,* where the problem is one of conflicting obediences (spiritual and secular), the subject of c. 14 of *De regno* is the precise limits of secular or royal power. Spiritual or papal power is discussed only in order to establish these limits and to highlight the 'intrinsic end' of secular power or kingship.

In c. 12 of *De regno* the author had outlined the office of kings, ending with the striking statement, 'Hoc igitur officium rex se suscepisse cognoscat, *ut sit in regno sicut in corpore anima et sicut Deus in mundo'*.[6] In c. 13 he explains just what he meant by that statement, saying that a king is like God in that he 'creates', 'produces', 'provides', 'governs'. Does this mean, the author then asks, that, like God, the king has complete power over his kingdom and, in particular, over any and every end of his kingdom? Not at all, he explains in c. 14 (the crucial chapter). For although it is true that 'ad omnes reges pertinet gubernatio et a gubernationis regimine regis nomen accipitur' (c. 13), this only applies to the 'intrinsic end' of the kingdom.

For the kingdom also has an 'extrinsic end': 'Sed est quoddam bonum extrinsecum homini quamdiu mortaliter vivit, scilicet ultima beatitudo quae in fruitione Dei expectatur post mortem'.[7] This 'ultima beatitudo' belongs to Christ. The king's rule does not embrace that 'divine kingdom'. For the office of bringing man to the 'ultima beatitudo' or final end is not confided to kings or princes (that would be to confuse the intrinsic and extrinsic ends of society, the spiritual with the temporal) but rather to the priests, the representatives of Christ. In particular this office is entrusted to the Roman Pontiff in as much as he is, by the authority of Christ, the supreme ruler of the kingdom of Christ and the supreme earthly guardian of the final end of man. Where the ministry of this kingdom of Christ is concerned, even the kings of Christian peoples are subject to the pope as to Christ, and must obey his rule:

> Huius ergo regni [Christi] ministerium, ut a terrenis spiritualia essent distincta, non terrenis regibus sed sacerdotibus est commissum, et praecipue summo sacerdoti, successori Petri, Christi vicario, romano pontifici, cui omnes reges populi christiani oportet esse subditos sicut ipsi Domino Iesu Christo.[8]

---

6 Ed. Perrier, par. 40. Chapters 12-15 in the Vulgate edition are cc. 13-16 in that of Perrier.

7 Perrier, par. 44, reads 'extrinsecum' where the 'Vulgate' and other editions read 'extraneum'.

8 Perrier, par. 46, reads, probably correctly, 'Huiusmodi' for 'Huius'.

In Fr Eschmann's view, this passage in the *De regno* gives 'supreme
political power' to the pope 'precisely by reason of his spiritual
primacy' (180). It is difficult to see how the text can bear this interpretation. For the passage above never suggests that popes have
political power, whether direct or indirect, much less that 'secular
power is subsumed under spiritual power, especially the papal power'
(179). Moreover, it is already clear from c. 13, which Eschmann does not
cite, that temporal well-being (the intrinsic end of a kingdom) is the
preserve of the ruler (secular power) and of no one else. The point that
is made directly in c. 14 of the *De regno,* and precisely in the text above,
is that spiritual power, the 'divine kingdom', does not belong to kings
but to priests: '*Huius* ergo regni ministerium ...'. If the kings of Christendom are said by *De regno* to be subject to the pope as to Christ, this is
only in terms of the spiritual regimen committed by Christ to the
priesthood and, in particular, to the pope. Kings and princes have to
obey the pope and be guided by him whenever there is question of the
relationship of the intrinsic end which they control to the extrinsic end,
salvation, which is not under their control.

A philosophical justification of this conclusion is advanced by the
author of *De regno* immediately after the passage ('Huius ergo regni
ministerium ... sicut ipsi Domino Iesu Christo') quoted above:

> Sic enim ei ad quem finis ultimi cura pertinet subdi debent illi ad quos
> pertinet cura antecedentium finium, et eius imperio dirigi.[9]

For Fr Eschmann, this 'brings about a formal *reductio ad unum* by formally subsuming secular power under spiritual power' (179). He
strongly objects to the principle, as he also does forcefully (197) to
another statement of the same principle in the preceding paragraph of
De regno:

> Semper enim invenitur ille ad quem pertinet ultimus finis imperare
> operantibus ea quae ad ultimum finem ordinantur; sicut gubernator ad
> quem pertinet navigationem disponere imperat ei qui navem constituit
> qualem navem navigationi aptam facere debeat ...[10]

According to Fr Eschmann, the author's practical conclusion from this
principle and the shipbuilding example is that 'all kings in Christendom
must obey the pope' — a conclusion which, Eschmann says, 'begs the
question, for the captain has no authority over the shipbuilder in the

---

9 Perrier, par. 46, has a slightly different word-order for the opening phrase: 'Sic enim ei ad
quem ultimi finis pertinet cura'.

10 Perrier, par. 45, reads 'ea quae in finem ordinantur ultimum' instead of 'ea quae ad ultimum
finem ordinantur'.

sense of what St Thomas would call the *ordo praelationis*, in virtue of which obligation and subjection is constituted' (197).

The only difficulty is that the 'practical conclusion' is Fr Eschmann's, not that of the author of the *De regno*. For the *De regno* does not conclude from the principle invoked that the shipbuilder (king) is 'obliged and subject to' the captain (pope) in an *ordo praelationis,* as though his whole existence sprang from and was 'subsumed under' the authority of the captain. The shipbuilder is subject to the captain precisely in as much as the ship be builds (*finis antecedens*) must be fit for sailing (*finis ultimus*). This in no way makes him dependent upon the captain for his very existence ('reductio ad unum'), no more than it implies that the captain builds ships or 'makes' shipbuilders. Like the captain, the spiritual power (the pope), and no other power, has charge of the final end of man, salvation. Like the shipbuilder, the secular power (kings) has to obey the spiritual power in all that involves that final end. But this leaves kings in complete charge of the well-being of their own kingdoms (antecedent end).

Contrary to what Fr Eschmann proposes, there is nothing of 'Theological Gregorianism' here. Rather there is the simple, unadorned Gelasian 'dualism' which Fr Eschmann finds so clearly in the *Scriptum*. A king, the *De regno* holds, rules over his kingdom as a priest (pope) rules over the kingdom of God; but he is subject to the priest (pope) whenever there is question of the 'dominium et regimen quod administratur per sacerdotis officium' (c. 15), that is, the salvation of souls, the end or good that is extrinsic to that of the secular power. As pope Gelasius put it in his famous letter to the emperor Anastasius in 494:

> Duo quippe sunt, imperator auguste, quibus principaliter mundus hic regitur: auctoritas sacrata pontificum et regalis potestas. In quibus tanto gravius est pondus sacerdotum quanto etiam pro ipsis regibus hominum in divino reddituri sunt examine rationem.
>
> Nosti [etenim, fili clementissime, quod licet praesideas humano generi dignitate, rerum tamen praesulibus divinarum devotus *colla submittis* atque ab eis causas tuae salutis expectas inque sumendis coelestibus sacramentis eisque ut competit disponendis, *subdi te debere cognoscis* religionis ordini *potius quam praeesse,*] itaque inter haec *ex illorum te pendere iudicio* non illos ad tuam velle redigi voluntatem.[11]

If further proof were needed of just how Gelasian the *De regno* is, then

---

11   This is the first part of par. 2 of the letter of Gelasius as edited by Thiel, *op. cit.,* pp. 350-1. The version in Gratian, D96 c10, has the opening sentences, 'Duo quippe sunt ... examine rationem', but then jumps ('Et post pauca') from 'Nosti' to 'itaque inter haec ex illorum te pendere iudicio non illos ad tuam velle redigi voluntatem'. The remainder of the text in Gratian is not that of Gelasius but of Gregory VII.

one can turn to the beginning of the next chapter (c. 15) of the *De regno* and to a passage which Eschmann never quotes. There it is stated clearly, and in the best dualistic tradition, that the spiritual and tem-. poral powers are distinct juridical entities:

> Si igitur, ut dictum est, qui de ultimo fine curam habet *praesse debet* his qui curam habent de ordinatis ad finem et eos *dirigere suo imperio*, manifestum ex dictis fit quod *rex* sicut dominio et regimini quod administratur per sacerdotis officium subdi debet, ita *praeesse debet omnibus humanis officiis et ea imperio sui regiminis ordinare*.[12]

In a word, kings rule as directly over their own kingdoms as priests over the kingdom of God. The two powers, spiritual and temporal, are so in command of their own separate spheres that the same terminology is applied in each case in the *De regno*. If the spiritual power 'praeesse debet' and is entitled to 'dirigere suo imperio', so also the secular power 'praeesse debet' and has the right to 'imperio sui regiminis ordinare'.

Again the principle invoked twice in c. 14 is present in c. 15: 'qui de ultimo fine curam habet praeesse debet his qui curam habent de ordinatis ad finem et eos dirigere suo imperio'. This principle, which Eschmann called 'the cornerstone of the construction' of c. 14, is depicted by Eschmann (182) as formally denoting that the ends of the spiritual and secular powers 'are subordinated *per se*'. Later (197), arguing that the conclusion drawn by *De regno* 'begs the question', he approves of Bellarmine's insight when he 'discreetly suggested that the general notion of *architektonike*, taken from Eth. I, 1894a 10, be replaced by the more specific *politike* of Eth. I, 1094a 27'. For Eschmann, convinced as he was that the *De regno* was using the architectonic principle to bolster an hierocratic argument, 'The all too general idea of an architectonic art will not carry the argument one step ahead ... The Aristotelian polis must first be transformed into the *respublica christiana*, then Aristotelian principles will be applicable. St. Bellarmine has shown with refreshing clarity and vigour how an hierocratic argument should be constructed so as to be at least formally correct' (197-8).[13]

---

12   For 'rex sicut dominio et regimini ... subdi debet', Perrier, par. 48, reads 'rex, sicut Domino, regimini ... subdi debet'. For other readings (e.g. 'rex sicut divino regimini') see Phelan and Eschmann, *Kingship*, p. 88.

13   R. Bellarmine, *De summo pontifice* 5.7, in *Bellarmini Opera omnia*, I (Naples 1856), p. 532 b: 'Prima ratio eiusmodi est. Potestas civilis subjecta est potestati spirituali, quando utraque pars est ejusdem reipublicae christianae; ergo potest princeps spiritualis imperare principibus temporalibus, et disponere de temporalibus rebus ad bonum spirituale: omnis enim superior imperare potest inferiori suo'. While not questioning Eschmann's version of Bellarmine, I must point out that most of the Bellarmine argument here, if it depends in any way on *De regno*, does not reflect *De regno* I.14 but rather Book Three. See next note.

The plain fact is, however, that Bellarmine simply *had* to change from *architectonice* to *politike* so as to turn what the *De regno* I. 14 had to say into a 'hierocratic argument'. For (as Bellarmine seems to have recognized), *De regno* I. 14 is anything but hierocratic. If it were, and if the Aristotelian principle invoked in cc. 14 and 15 were meant to prove an absolute subordination of the secular to the spiritual power, then it is curious that the conclusion from that principle in c. 15 is that the secular power is an independent juridical entity.

In fine, the 'all too general idea of an architectonic art' was used deliberately by the author of the *De regno* for the very good reason that he was not advancing an hierocratic argument. Had he resorted, as Bellarmine did, to the *politike* notion, then of necessity he would have arrived at a conclusion which he did not hold and which, I may venture to suggest, Bellarmine saw that he did not hold and therefore changed, brilliantly perhaps, to suit his own 'hierocratic' purpose.[14]

*

* *

If Bellarmine, unlike Eschmann, saw the real, untheocratic thrust of the architectonic argument as deployed by the *De regno,* so also did John of Paris, that celebrated proponent of dualism at the beginning of the fourteenth century.

Eschmann mentions John of Paris once or twice, but apparently without realizing just how much of cc. 14 and 15 of the *De regno* was taken over by John in his *De potestate regia et papali* (1302-1303).[15] Commenting on the principle invoked by the *De regno,* 'Semper enim invenitur ille ad quem pertinet ultimus finis imperare operantibus ea

---

14 It is surely significant (though Eschmann does not mention it) that when Bellarmine cites *De regno* I.14 and the architectonic argument there, all that he is able to conclude is that the passage teaches a simple dualism: 'Sic igitur loquitur Lib. I. c. 14: Huius ergo regni ... et eius imperio dirigi. *Haec ille. Qui clarissime distinguit regna terrena, quae habent pro fine pacem temporalem, a regno spirituali Christi et eius vicarii, quod pro fine habet vitam aeternam' (De summo pontifice,* 5.5: ed. *cit.,* p. 530a). To support his own moderately theocratic position, Bellarmine turns at once, after this unexceptionable comment, to Book Three of *De regno,* the work, probably, of the ultra-theocrat Ptolomy of Lucca. Citing *De regno* III, cc. 13 and 15, Bellarmine comments: 'Haec ille; quibus verbis significat Christum habuisse quidem dominium temporale totius mundi, sed indirecte; directe autem solum dominium spirituale'. He then goes on to discuss III. c. 19, and to mitigate an ultra-theocratic statement there and in III. c. 10.

15 This work has had two recent editions: J. Leclercq, *Jean de Paris et l'ecclésiologie du XIIIᵉ siècle* (Paris, 1942), pp. 168-260, and F. Bleienstein, *Johannes Quidort von Paris Über königliche und päpstliche Gewalt. Textkritische Edition mit deutschen Uebersetzung* (Stuttgart, 1969), pp. 67-352. There is an English translation by J. Watt, *John of Paris on Royal and Papal Power* (Toronto, 1971). A section in Leclercq's introduction gives most but not all of the borrowings from the *De regno* in John of Paris (pp. 35-6). Bleienstein does not note any borrowings, nor does Watt.

quae ad ultimum finem ordinantur', Eschmann notes (182) that 'imperare' has 'a jurisdictional sense'. Then in a long footnote to 'imperare' (181 n. 18) he states that John of Paris simply suppressed 'the embarrassing authority' of the *De regno* 'on this point', for on 'p. 178.30 of Leclercq's edition' of John of Paris 'a long quotation of *De regno* I.14 is suddenly cut short' just before before the architectonic principle is introduced.

Now it is true that John of Paris breaks off his quotation from the *De regno* I. 14 in c. 2 of the *De potestate* just before the phrase, 'Semper enim invenitur ille ...', which precedes the example of the captain and the shipbuilder. But Eschmann nowhere notes that John of Paris explicitly returns later in c. 5 to that very same 'embarrassing authority':

> Ex praedictis patet de facili quid sit prius dignitate regnum vel sacerdotium ... Et ideo dicimus potestatem sacerdotalem maiorem esse potestate regali et ipsam praecellere dignitate, quia *hoc semper reperimus quod illud ad quod pertinet ultimus finis perfectius est et melius et dirigat illud ad quod pertinet inferior finis.*[16] [*De regno* I.14: 'Semper enim invenitur ille ad quem pertinet ultimus finis imperare operantibus ea quae ad ultimum finem ordinantur'].

Although John of Paris does not reproduce the *De regno* text word for word, it does seem clear that he had the passage in question before him, and has taken over from there the architectonic principle which Eschmann implies he avoided.

It must be admitted, however, that the 'imperare' of *De regno,* which according to Eschmann has a jurisdictional sense, has been replaced by John of Paris with the seemingly milder 'dirigere'. But, in fact, John of Paris is simply following the usage of the *De regno* itself, and for reasons which we shall see later. It is true that the *De regno* uses 'imperare' in the example of the captain and the shipbuilder from which the above quotation ('Semper enim invenitur ...') comes, but when it cites the same principle a few sentences later in relation to the spiritual power and the pope, it uses 'imperio dirigi' instead: 'Sic enim ei ad quem finis ultimi cura pertinet subdi debent illi ad quos pertinet cura antecedentium finium, et eius imperio dirigi'. Again, when in c. 15 the *De regno* speaks of the independent spheres of spiritual and secular power, 'praeesse' and 'imperio dirigere' are used in place of 'imperare' — and, significantly, in respect of both powers: 'Si igitur, ut dictum est, qui de ultimo fine curam habet, *praeesse debet* his qui curam habet de ordinatis ad finem et eos *dirigere suo imperio,* manifestum ex dictis fit quod *rex,* sicut dominio et regimini quod administratur per sacerdotis officium subdi debet, ita *praeesse debet* omnibus humanis officiis *et ea imperio sui regiminis ordinare'.*

16 *De potestate,* c. V: ed. Leclercq, p. 183; ed. Bleienstein, p. 87.

John of Paris, then, by using 'dirigere' instead of 'imperare', is following the terminology employed by the *De regno* itself. Far from rejecting the architectonic principle and its application, as anyone who has read Fr Eschmann might expect of a forthright proponent of the 'dualistic' system, John of Paris accepts it, and indeed uses it to show, as the *De regno* does, that in the spiritual order, where the relationship is that of final end to 'inferior' end, the spiritual power is not only over and above but also directs ('dirigit') the secular power.

As it happens (and this, again, is a point that Fr Eschmann overlooks), it is John of Paris himself who states very clearly what is meant by 'imperare' and 'imperio eius dirigi' and who provides an answer to Fr Eschmann's blank assertion that 'imperare' has a 'jurisdictional sense'. For among the many hierocratic arguments that John of Paris lists ('Nunc videndum est quibus innitantur fundamentis qui dicunt sacerdotes et praecipue papam habere potestatem primariam et ipsam a summo pontifice derivare ad principem'),[17] there is one that arrives at a hierocratic conclusion exactly in the same way that Fr Eschmann draws a hierocratic conclusion from the architectonic argument of the *De regno*:

> [23] Item idem arguunt ex ordine finium. In artibus enim ordinatis ars ad quem pertinet ultimus et principalis finis *imperat* aliis artibus ad quas pertinent fines secundarii. Sed saecularis potestas intendit bonum multitudinis quod est vivere secundum virtutem ad quod pervenire potest virtute naturae et eis quae huic adminiculantur. Potestas autem spiritualis intendit bonum multitudinis supernaturale, scilicet aeternam beatitudinem et in ipsum *dirigit*. Finis autem supernaturalis potior est et principalior quolibet alio fine. Ergo spiritualis potestas quae ministris ecclesiae collata est *superior est* non solum dignitate sed etiam causalitate *saeculari* et *ei praecipit* qualiter debeat operari.[18]

Of course, as was pointed out above, the *De regno* never arrives at a hierocratic conclusion such as this. Again, it was also pointed out above that the architectonic argument, which Eschmann (rightly) felt was too 'limping' to support the hierocratic position with which he credited the *De regno,* was deliberately employed precisely because the author of the *De regno* was *not* establishing a hierocratic thesis. Now John of Paris, who himself had used the architectonic argument earlier, shows in his reply to the hierocratic argument above just how the 'ordo finium' is to be understood, and how one cannot jump from the architectonic principle to a hierocratic conclusion:

17 *Ibid.*, c. XI: ed. Leclercq, p. 201; ed. Bleienstein, p. 118.

18 *Ibid.*, c. IX: ed. Leclercq, p. 204; ed. Bleienstein, p. 121. For 'et *eis* quae huic adminiculantur' Bleienstein reads 'et *ea* quae huic adminiculantur'.

Quod vero dicitur vigesimo tertio de ordine finium, respondeo: multipliciter deficit. Primo, quia ars ad quam pertinet superior finis *movet et imperat* artem ad quam pertinet finis inferior *non quidem simpliciter* sed quantum ei competit ad necessitatem ultimi sui finis, et hoc alignaliter est concessum superius in proposito. Amplius, deficit quia ars illa superior *non semper necessario imperat inferiori movendo per modum auctoritatis et instituendo eam, sed solum ei imperat per modum dirigentis ...*[19]

This, I submit, is sufficient to modify Fr Eschmann's unqualified assertion that 'The word *imperare* [in the *De regno* passage] must be understood in the jurisdictional sense is evident from the text and context where the univocally jurisdictional words: *subdi, esse subjectum, subjacere, obedire, servire, famulari,* are frequently and emphatically used' (182). Certainly it does not bear out his further assertion (181 n. 18) that 'imperare' in the *De regno* passage 'has been so understood [i.e. in a jurisdictional sense] by all ancient commentators'. John of Paris, at least, saw a distinction between 'imperare per modum auctoritatis' and 'imperare per modum dirigentis'.[20]

*
* *

The teaching of the *De regno,* therefore, is not 'Theological Gregorianism' but that of undoubted dualists such as John of Paris (who, indeed, may well have been combating those who, like Fr Eschmann, interpreted the work as hierocratic, or who were adapting it, as Bellarmine would later do, for hierocratic purposes). Further, the *De regno* is no more at variance with the dualistic teaching of the *Scriptum super sententiis* of St Thomas than it is out of harmony with the ('univocally jurisdictional'?) language of that font of dualism, the Gelasian letter, with its 'subdi debere' and, rather startlingly, 'colla submitti'.

What, then, of the *De regno* as an authentic or non-authentic work of St Thomas? In some brilliant pages (195-6 especially), Fr Eschmann advanced the opinion that the *De regno* occasioned 'mistrust', chiefly because *De regno* I.14 'belonged to a different world' than that of the

---

19   *Ibid.,* c. XI: ed. Leclercq, pp. 226-7; ed. Bleienstein, p. 159.

20   It may be noted that in c. 15, when delineating the spheres of the two powers, the *De regno* speaks of the superior (spiritual) power as being in a position to 'dirigere suo imperio' when there is question of the final end of man; and it then goes on to say that the secular power has a similar right to 'imperio sui regiminis ordinare' with respect own, human end. Eschmann does not cite the passage, but had he cited it he would have had to explain why his 'jurisdictional sense' of *imperare* (here 'dirigere, ordinare, suo imperio') is not as applicable to the secular *imperium* as he claims it is to the spiritual *imperium*.

Scriptum. And in concluding his article (204) he entered a resonant plea for the rejection of the *De regno*: 'On the foregoing pages St. Thomas' legacy in the matter of the two powers, its native integrality, its substance and meaning, has been put on trial. The defence submits the plea that the testimony of the *De regno* be rejected, this witness not being reliable'.

The present essay has suggested, on the other hand, that the *De regno* text is as 'dualistic' as the rest of St Thomas' 'legacy on the two powers', and it has called John of Paris, an unimpeachable dualist, to witness for the very passage upon which the case for the 'defence' rested. If it now respectfully submits that the defence's plea be denied forthwith, it also expresses the deepest regret (not unmingled with relief) that Fr Eschmann's massive scholarship is no longer with us to sweep the submission fraternally aside.

Pontifical Institute of Mediaeval Studies.

A MIDDLE ENGLISH CHRISTOLOGICAL POEM[1]

Edmund Colledge O.S.A.

THROUGH an uncharacteristic failure of perception, Carleton Brown misunderstood the poet's intentions and sadly mutilated his work when he reproduced from MS Merton College Oxford 248,[2] f. 242ᵛ, a poem's first two stanzas, treating the third and fourth as a separate work of less merit and interest, and therefore relegating them to the notes;[3] and G. V. Smithers left this blemish in his revision of Brown's first edition.[4]

The volume is a composite, part of which consists of sermons collected or composed by John Sheppey, bishop of Rochester, 1352-1360.[5] The poem occurs in a sermon, inc. f. 242ᵃ: 'Recumbentibus xj discipulis, Marco xvjº. In hoc ewangelio ostendit saluator qualis esse debet qui predicat, quid predicare debet, quibus et propter quem ...' Presently 'propter quem' leads the preacher to consider the Christological mystery, which he seeks to illumine by treating anagogically the four riders of chapter vi of the Apocalypse:

> ... ecce equus albus, et qui sedebat super illum habebat arcum, et data est ei corona, et exivit vincens ut vinceret ... Et exivit alius equus rufus, et qui sedebat super illum, datum est ei ut sumeret pacem de terra, et ut invicem se interficiant, et datus est ei gladius magnus ... Et ecce equus niger, et qui sedebat super illum, habebat stateram in manu sua ... Et ecce equus pallidus, et qui sedebat super eum, nomen illi mors, et infernus sequebatur eum, et data est illi potestas super quatuor partes terrae, interficere gladio, fame et morte et bestiis terrae.

So far, this sermon is written in two columns to the page; but as the

---

1 My thanks are due to the Warden and Fellows of Merton College, Oxford, for their permission to cite their MS 248, and to the Librarian for giving me access to it.

2 Cfr. H. O. Coxe: *Catalogus codicum mss. qui in collegiis aulisque Oxoniensibus hodie adservantur* 1 (Oxford, 1852), 96-97, and F. M. Powicke: *The Medieval Books of Merton College* (Oxford, 1931), 171.
3 *Religious Lyrics of the XIVth Century* (Oxford, 1924), 52-53, 258.
4 Oxford, 1952, 52-53, 258.
5 C. Eubel: *Hierarchia catholica medii aevi* (Münster, 1913), 422.

scribe changes from Latin to English he writes straight across the whole width; and his arrangement gives no indication whatever that what follows is not an integral poem:

I sayh hym wiþ fless al bi sprad   He cam vram est
I sayh hym wiþ blod al by ssad   He cam vram west
I sayh þet manye he wiþ hym brouȝte   He cam vram souȝ
I sayh þet þe world of hym ne rouȝte   He cam vram north

I come vram þe wedlok as a svete spouse   Þet habbe my wif wiþ me i nome
I come vram viȝt a staleworþe knyȝt   Þet myne vo habbe ouercome
I come vram þe cheping as a riche chapman
                   Þet mankynde habbe ibouȝt
I come vram an vncouþe londe as a sely pylegrim
                   Þet ferr habbe i souȝt

     He rod vpon a whit hors in þet   Þet he be cam man for þe
     He rod on a red hors in þet   Þet he was inayled to þe rode tre
     He rod on a blak hors in þet   Þet he þe deuel ouer cam
     He rod on a dun hors in þet   Þet þe cloude hym vp nam

He rod on a white hors *and* hadde a boȝ in his hond
                   In toknyng þet he was skyluol
He þet rod on a red hors hadde a sverd *in* his hond
                   In toknyng þet he was medful
He þat rod on þe blakke hors hadde a weye in his hond
                   In toknyng þet he was riȝtful
He þet rod on þe dunne hors hadde muchel uolk þet hym volwede
                   In toknyng þet he was miȝtful

This mysteriously beautiful composition, so badly treated by its editors, has received scant attention from the critics, chiefly, one may suspect, because they too have not understood it aright. Its four-line stanzas are in a form dictated by the quaternions which inspire it: the four points of the compass, Christ's four manifestations as bridegroom, knight, merchant and pilgrim, and the four riders. This use of the quaternion, so much less popular in mediaeval symbolism than the triad, itself shows how the poet has been influenced by the Apocalypse and, through it, by Ezechiel. In all the stanzas, each line contains an image of Christ, followed, after the caesura, by some extending or explanatory comment. There is a skilful alternation between short and long-line stanzas, leading to the effect of amplification in the last, where the lines are longest and the repetitions, 'he þet rod', 'in his hond', 'in toknyng', most insistent.

In what has gone before, the preacher has introduced a dialogue be-

tween the soul and Christ, who has come to save it: 'Vnde venis? ...
Venio inquit de thalamo, ut sponsus dulcissimus. Venio de prelio, ut
miles strenuissimus. Venio de foro, ut mercator ditissimus. Venio de
longinquo, ut peregrinus extraneus. Et sic a quatuor partibus mundi ad
eos veniebat'.[6] This last phrase suggests the double quaternion of the
first stanza. Christ has come seeking for the soul from the four corners
of the earth. So an anonymous *Song of Love-Longing*, recorded c.A.D.
1400, inspired by and partly translating *Dulcis Iesu Memoria,* in one of its
original apostrophes to the Saviour says:

> Swete Ihesu, berne best,
> Þi loue þou in myn herte fest.
> When I go northe, southe, est or west
> In þe alone fynde I rest.'

The sentiment is Augustine's, but there is the same implication as in the
Merton poem's first stanza: in creation Christ is omnipresent. He is
present to us everywhere as the crucified Saviour, his mangled flesh
scattered abroad, every drop of his blood spilt. He is present as the
leader of the multitude of the redeemed (for the etymology of 'manye',
OE *manig* or OFr *mesniee* are equally possible phonologically; either
gives good sense and makes the same point); he is present everywhere in
a world which cares nothing for him. As the sun rises in the east to give
life to the earth till it declines, so 'mors eius mundum vivificavit'. The
southern climes we associate with fruitfulness, and the fruits of the
Redemption are the redeemed. The north for us signifies winter, 'not so
unkind ... as man's ingratitude'.

The introductory Latin text, we have seen, begins a dialogue with the
question: 'Vnde venies?' This is taken up in the second stanza. The poet
has told us whence Christ came; Christ himself now tells the soul how
he came. To any auditor skilled in Latin verses, it would at this point
become apparent that the poet was experimenting with the *Quis est iste?*
tradition, descending from Psalm 23, with its triumphant repetitions of
the rhetorical 'Quis est iste rex gloriae?' By far the finest composition
of this entire genre is the celebrated *Quis est hic qui pulsat ad ostium?*

> Quis est hic
> qui pulsat ad ostium,[8]
> noctis rumpens somnium?
> Me vocat: O
> virginum pulcherrima,[9]

6   F. 242[b]; cfr. Brown, *XIV* 258.
7   Nita Scudder Baugh: *A Worcestershire Miscellany compiled by John Northwood* (Philadelphia, 1956),
130.
8   Apoc. 3 20: Ecce sto ad ostium et pulso.
9   Cant. 1 7: O pulcherrima inter mulieres; and cfr. 5 9, 5 17.

soror, coniux,[10]
    gemma splendidissima,
cito surgens
    aperi, dulcissima.[11]
Ego sum
summi regis filius,
primus et novissimus[12]
qui de caelis
    in has veni tenebras[13]
liberare
    captivorum animas,
passus mortem
    et multas iniurias.

Mox ego
dereliqui lectulum,[14]
cucurri ad pessulum[15]
ut dilecto
    tota domus pateat
et mens mea
    plenissime videat
quem videre
    maxime desiderat.

At ille
iam inde transierat,
ostium reliquerat.[16]
Quid ergo mi-
    serrima, quid facerem?
Lacrimando
    sum secuta iuvenem
manus cuius
    plasmaverunt hominem.

Vigiles
urbis invenerunt me,[17]

---

10 Cant. 4 9: Soror mea sponsa; and cfr. 4 12, 5 1.
11 Cant. 5 2: Aperi mihi, soror mea, amica mea; Matt. 25 11: Domine, domine, aperi nobis.
12 Apoc. 1 17-18: Ego sum primus et novissimus, et vivus et fui mortuus, et ecce sum vivens in saecula saeculorum, et habeo claves mortis et inferni.
13 Luke 1 79: Illuminare his qui in tenebris sedent.
14 Cant. 5 5: Surrexi ut aperirem dilecto meo.
15 Cant. 5 6: Pessulum ostii mei aperui dilecto meo.
16 Cant. 5 6: At ille declinaverat atque transierat.
17 Cant. 5 7: Invenerunt me custodes qui circumeunt civitatem; percusserunt me et vulnaverunt me, tulerunt pallium meum mihi custodes murorum.

> expoliaverunt me,[18]
> abstulerunt
>   et dederunt pallium,
> cantaverunt
>   mihi novum canticum[19]
> quo in regis
>   inducar palatium.

Numerous critics have helped us to appreciate the subtle and ambiguous charm of this, notably, in recent years, Peter Dronke,[20] Rosemary Woolf[21] and Brian Stock.[22] Its skilful allusions to Scripture serve to heighten its atmosphere of enigma. Just as in the Merton poem, a mysterious stranger appears, nameless but with attributes which mark him as a nonpareil, claiming the soul as his own, and telling of his love which has cost him such bitter pains. In the Latin, he calls himself merely the 'filius regis', but the second English stanza here introduces the next quaternion: the stranger has come wooing as would a bridegroom, a knight, a merchant or a pilgrim.

Another Merton lyric, undoubtedly by the same poet, shows the same preoccupation with the notion of Christ as knight and pilgrim:

> Louerd, þou þat foluest me
> wider ward so i fle,
>   Dauid sone, fair to siȝt,
> haue merci on me
> þat ich may habbe meknesse and sorwe of my sinne.
> Lord, þou þat faȝt for me
> wan myn enemy folewed me ...[23]

But what is there merely implicit is here worked out in detail.

The thought of Christ as a 'svete spouse', leading with him the soul as his bride from their nuptial feast, is common and received. The Scriptural origins and the later developments of *Brauttheologie*, the excesses and the frequent lapses of taste of its exponents, and theories which would derive it from the secular literature of courtly love, are known from innumerable critical works. One recent study deserves special mention for its appositeness to the Merton poem's conjunction of 'bridegroom' and 'knight', that of Rosemary Woolf, who observes that

---

18 Cant. 5 3: Expoliavi me tunica mea.

19 Ps. 39 4: Et immisit in os meum canticum novum.

20 *Medieval Latin and the Rise of the European Love-Lyric* (Oxford, 1965-1966), 1 269-271.

21 *The English Religious Lyric in the Middle Ages* (Oxford, 1968), 51.

22 *Medieval Latin Lyrics translated and introduced* (Boston, Mass., 1971), 12-13, 30-33.

23 F. 66ᵛ, inc.: Ihesu þat al þis world has wroȝt; but not, apart from the first two lines, identical with the long meditation on the Passion in Brown, *Religious Lyrics of the XVth. Century* (Oxford, 1939), 133-136.

the analogy of the lover-knight fighting and dying to win back his bride has a dual ancestry, the nuptial imagery of the Old Testament and the metaphor, common already in patristic times, of battle for the Passion; but 'it did not become a commonplace until it acquired a literary analogue in mediaeval romance'.[24] Later, she justly points to the importance as an 'intermediary ... between Biblical gloss and literary development' of Hugh of St. Victor's *De arrha animae,* citing the passage which begins: 'Sponsum habes, sed nescis. Pulcherrimus est omnium, sed faciem eius non vidisti ...'.[25] The conclusion of this tract acquired great fame and authority in the late Middle Ages:

> Vere ille est dilectus tuus qui visitat te, sed venit invisibilis, venit occultus, venit incomprehensibilis. Venit ut tangat te, non ut videatur a te, venit ut admoneat te, non ut comprehendatur a te, venit non ut totum infundat se sed ut gustandum praebeat se, non ut impleat desiderium sed ut trahat affectum. Primitias quasdam porrigit suae dilectionis, non plenitudinem exhibet perfectae sapietatis. Et hoc est quod maxime ad arrham desponsationis tuae pertinet, quod ille qui in futuro se tibi videndum et perpetuo possidendum dabit, nunc aliquando — ut quam dulcis sit agnoscas — se tibi ad gustandum praebet.[26]

W. M. Thompson may be right in suggesting that the opening of Þe *Wohunge of ure Lauerd,*

> Swetter is munegunge of þe þen mildeu o muðe,[27]

is derived from

> Dulcis Iesu memoria
> dans vera cordis gaudia,
> sed super mel et omnia
> dulcis ejus praesentia;[28]

but Etienne Gilson long ago reminded us how close all the contents of the hymn are to genuine works of Bernard, and that this sentiment is found in *Sermones de diversis* IV 1:

> Bonus es domine animae quaerenti te. Si quaerenti, quanto magis munienti? Si tam dulcis est memoria, qualis erit praesentia? Si mel et lac est sub lingua, quid erit super linguam?[29]

Gilson was not at all concerned to prove that Bernard wrote the

24 *The English Religious Lyric,* 45.
25 *Ibid.,* 59; PL 176 954.
26 PL 176 970.
27 Early English Text Society 241 (1958), 20.
28 F. J. Mone: *Lateinische Hymnen des Mittelalters* 1 (Freiburg i.B., 1853, Aalen, 1964), 329.
29 *Les idées et les lettres* (² Paris, 1955), 'La mystique cistercienne et le Iesu dulcis memoria', 39-57.

hymn, for which he has liking and reverence, merely to show that
Hauréau, who detested it, had no support for his contention that Bernard could not have written it. There is little or nothing in Gilson's
thesis to conflict with that of André Wilmart, based upon a minute
examination of the manuscript tradition, that the author seems most
probably to have been an English Cistercian steeped in Bernard's
writings.[30]

Another theme is announced in the first stanza, more fully explored
in the third:

> Iesu spes poenitentibus
> quam pius es petentibus,
> quam bonus quaerentibus,
> sed quid invenientibus?[31]

Gilson has shown us how faithful is this description of what he calls an
'embrassement ... à la fois délicieux et fugitif'. Later, the hymn tells us

> Tunc amplexus, tunc oscula
> quae vincunt mellis pocula,
> tunc felix Christi copula,
> sed in his brevis morula.[32]

Gilson here recalls some of Bernard's expressions: 'Sed heu, rara hora, et
parua mora',[33] 'o si durasset!',[34] 'o modicum longum!'[35]

This thought is not new in Bernard. It is part of the allegory of *Quis
est hic qui pulsat* —

> At ille
> iam inde transierat
> ostium reliquerat —

and it is more explicitly stated in the conclusion of *De arrha animae*.

We may think that some recent critics have been too bold in announcing that the *Ancrene Riwle* is the first work in English to employ
such spiritual-courtly ideas, that the *Wohunge* and the tracts allied with
it took up these ideas as their authors found them in the *Riwle*. Thompson was commendably cautious; and what he wrote of the *Riwle*-group
may have much wider applications. Such ideas reflect the spirit of their
age, beginning to explore the spiritual implications of courtly letters.

---

30 'Le *Jubilus* sur le nom de Jésus dit de saint Bernard' (*Ephemerides Liturgicae* 57, 1943, 1-285).
31 Mone 1 329.
32 *Ibid.* 330.
33 *Sermo XXIII in Cantica*, PL 183 892.
34 *Ibid.* 893.
35 *Sermo LXXIV, ibid.* 1140.

(By no means does one wish to exclude the possibility that such secular literature itself derives from theological writing). We cannot say, in the instance of the *ludus amoris*, whether Hugh had Bernard in mind or Bernard Hugh. All that we can say is that this is what the soul's search for God seemed like to both men, and that either one, hearing the words of a secular *paraklausithuron*, would be reminded of his own spiritual life and experience. We need not doubt that the Merton poem, when it calls Christ 'svete spouse' and 'staleworþe knyȝt', is appealing to the same experience.

The next simile of this stanza, the 'riche chapman', is at first sight less evident; but Scripture, the liturgy and mediaeval devotional literature will all suggest the associations it could evoke. When Christ teaches that the kingdom of heaven is like 'negotiatori quaerenti bonas margaritas',[36] the exegetes tell us again and again that he is speaking of himself. When he commands his followers, 'negotiamini dum venio',[37] he is comparing their zeal for souls with a merchant's acumen and dedication. The idea of commerce and transaction is implicit in the very word 'redemptor'; Christ is our 'again-buyer', as the Wycliffite translators were careful to render the Latin, in their Scriptural versions and in their English of the pseudo-Augustine *De salutaribus documentis*.[38] The Church calls the Incarnation a 'wonderful bargain': 'O admirabile commercium! Creator generis humani animatum corpus sumens ...'.[39] In the Tenebrae of Holy Thursday is sung: 'Iudas mercator pessimus ... denariorum numero Christum Iudaeis tradidit'.[40] The *Wohunge* makes the soul say to Christ that she is a bad bargain: 'A, deore cheap hefdes tu on me, ne was neauer unwurði þing chepet swa deore'.[41]

One of the conceits of the first stanza, that Christ has sought out the soul from the four corners of the earth, is taken up again in the last line of the second, where he says that he has come from an unknown land like a blessed pilgrim who has searched far and wide. The key text here is in the account, in Luke chapter 24, of the encounter with the unrecognized traveller on the road to Emmaus: 'Tu solus peregrinus es in Jerusalem ...' In a recent and valuable study,[42] F. C. Gardiner has assembled an impressive list of the fathers and later commentators who expounded the spiritual significance of this apparition,[43] emphasizing

---

36 Matt. 13 45.
37 Luke 19 13.
38 S. L. Fristedt: *The Wycliffite Bible* 2 (Stockholm, 1969), 153.
39 R.-J. Hesbert: *Corpus antiphonalium officii* 3 (Rome, 1968), 362. I am indebted to the Revd James Walsh, S.J., for identifying this and the next citation for me.
40 *Breviarium monasticum pars verna* (Malines, 1939), 386.
41 Ed. Thompson, 32.
42 *The Pilgrimage of Desire: a Study of Theme and Genre in Medieval Literature* (Leiden, 1971).
43 *Ibid.*, 17-48.

the hardships and loneliness of the pilgrim's lot and how this accords
with the lineaments of the Suffering Servant. Of special interest to Gardiner is the use of Luke and of the classical exegetes in the Church's
drama. He quotes from Karl Young[44] this rubric from the *Lichfield
Statutes* concerning the presentation of the Easter Monday *Peregrini*: 'And
then two of Christ's disciples, Cleophas and a certain other, dressed in
cowls and capes and with staffs, in the manner of pilgrims, leave the
sacristy ... And then Christ joins them; he has a cape, staff and medium-
sized container of wine in the manner of a pilgrim'.[45] He reminds us
that in the *Coventry Play* Cleophas says:

> Sere, me thynkyth thou art a pore pylgrym
> Here walkynge be thiselfe alone,
> And in the cete of Jerusalem
> Thou knowyst ryght lytyl what ther is done;
> For pylgrymys comyn and gon ryth sone,
> Ryght lytyl whyle pylgrymes do dwelle;
> In alle Jerusalem as thou has gone
> I trowe no tydynges that thou canyst telle.[46]

The notion of 'pilgrimage' as an attribute of Christ worthy of imitation
is fundamental to Franciscan spirituality.[47] In chapter 6 of the *Regula
Secunda* we read:

> Fratres nihil sibi approprient, nec domum nec locum nec aliquam rem.
> Et *tanquam peregrini et advenae*[48] in hoc saeculo in paupertate et humilitate
> Domino famulantes vadant pro eleemosyna confidenter, nec oportet eos
> verecundari, quia Dominus pro nobis se fecit pauperem in hoc mundo.[49]

Among Francis's legends is the following:

> S. Franciscus, cum quadam vice in die Pasch£ moraretur in monasterio,
> nec essent a quibus mendicaret, memor Christi qui discipulis euntibus in
> Emmaus hoc ipso die in specie peregrini apparuit, ab ipsis fratribus
> eleemosynam petiit, ut peregrinus et pauper; quam cum accepisset,
> humiliter sacris eos informavit eloquiis quod transeuntes per mundi deser-
> tum tanquam peregrini et adven£, verique Hebr£i Pascha Domini, hoc est
> transitum ex hoc mundo ad Patrem, in paupertate spiritus continue
> celebrarent. Porro peregrini leges sunt sub alieno tecto colligi, sitire ad
> patriam, pacifice transire.[50]

44 *The Drama of the Medieval Church* (Oxford, 1933), 1 481-482.
45 Gardiner 87.
46 *Ibid.* 133.
47 The Revd Conrad Harkins, O.F.M., has given me helpful information on this topic.
48 I Peter 2 11.
49 *Opuscula sancti patris Francisci Assisiensis* (Quaracchi, 1904), 68.
50 Cornelius a Lapide: *Commentarii* (1859-), 8 857; Luke 24 16.

Like so many other Catholic pieties, this notion survived the Refor-
mation in ballads. In F. J. Child's no. 21, *The Maid and the Palmer*,[51]
Christ appears to Mary Magdalene at the well in pilgrim's guise,
through which presently she sees; but the implication, so clear in the
Merton lyric, that it is a human soul he has come on pilgrimage for, is
wanting.

The narrative of the third and fourth stanzas depends directly upon
the passage, already cited in the Latin of the sermon, from the sixth
chapter of the Apocalypse. Just as in the first stanza a spiritual
significance is extracted from the four points of the compass, in the
third the colours of the four horses are given symbolical meaning: one
horse is white to represent the Nativity, another red for the Crucifixion,
another black to stand for vanquished Satan, the last is pale to signify
the cloud into which Christ ascended.[52] Similarly, the fourth stanza interprets each rider's attribute: the bow betokens skill, the sword mercy
(for *medful,* cfr. NED Metheful adj.') — the allusion here must be to
Curtana, 'the sword of mercy' — the balance justice and the multitude
following the rider on the pale horse power.

This transition, from the presentation of Christ as bridegroom,
knight, merchant and pilgrim to his identification with each of the four
riders, is made with ease; and yet to modern readers it cannot but seem
eccentric. There will be few of my own generation whose reading of
this part of John's vision has not been indelibly coloured by the epoch-
making notion picture made in the early 1920s from Blasco Ibáñez's
novel, for whom the very name, 'The Four Horsemen of the
Apocalypse', does not conjure up terrifying visions of Ezechiel's
scourges, war and famine, plague and ravening beasts.[53] In the long
history of Scriptural exegesis, this has been the commoner view; but it
is not the only one. When we consider the iconography of the
Apocalypse, we find a curious discrepancy. Illuminated manuscripts
which use the commentary of the Franciscan Alexander 'Laicus' follow
the commoner tradition in showing, for example, the third rider as
Titus, holding in his scales the Jews 'whom he sold at thirty for a
penny',[54] but this is not so in most of the illustrated Apocalypse-books
produced in England. Only ignorance or temerity would today en-
courage an amateur to engage in the controversies which concern the
provenance, ancestry and inter-relations of such works;[55] but the ex-

51 *The English and Scottish Popular Ballads* 1 (Cambridge, Mass., 1882).
52 Acts 1 19.
53 Ezechiel 14 12-21.
54 M. R. James: *The Apocalypse in Art* (London, 1931), 67.
55 Cfr. e.g. L. Delisle and P. Meyer: *L'apocalypse en français au xiii⁰ siècle* (Paris, 1901); F. D.
Klingender: 'St. Francis and the Birds of the Apocalypse' (*Journal of the Warburg and Courtauld In-*

perts are all agreed that some of the texts and many of the pictures
derive from the commentary of Berengaudus, that otherwise generally
forgotten interpreter of the Last Things.[56] This is his explanation of the
four riders:

> Equus albus justos qui ante diluvium fuerunt designat, qui propter in-
> nocentiam albi dicuntur. Sessor vero equi Dominus est qui sanctis suis
> aeternaliter praesidet. Per arcum autem qui procul sagittas a se mittit et
> vulnerat vindicta Domini potest designari ... Per equum rufum justi qui
> post diluvium usque ad legem fuerunt designantur ... Sessor vero hujus
> equi Dominus est qui in sanctis suis habitat ... Per equum nigrum doctores
> legis possumus intelligere; nigredo enim equi sive obscuritatem legis quam
> docuerunt sive duritiam designat ... Sessor autem equi Dominus est,
> statera vero aequitatem judicii legis demonstrat ... Videntur haec quae de
> equite quarto dicuntur ad Antichristum pertinere; sed quia superiores tres
> equites in bonam partem interpretati sumus, ut convenirent cum aper-
> tionibus trium sigillorum, ordinis rectitudo cogit ut et istum in bonam
> partem intelligamus, quatenus concordet cum apertione quarti sigilli,
> quam ad prophetas pertinere demonstravimus. Equus igitur pallidus
> prophetas significat ... sessor autem hujus equi Dominus est qui in
> prophetis suis inhabitavit. Sed valde durum videtur quod nomen mortis
> habuisse dicitur ... sed si diligenter Scripturas divinas inspexerimus, in-
> veniemus Dominum nostrum Jesum Christum etiam mortem vocari. Nam
> sicut vita est omnium electorum, quibus quotidie vitam aeternam largitur,
> ita et mors dici potest reproborum, quos pro sceleribus suis quotidie
> morti tradit perpetuae.[57]

However, in the Douce Apocalypse. to take only one example, we find
that these comments are accompanied by pictures which show, certainly, the fourth rider on the pale horse as Christ, nimbed and with a
sword, and, behind the horse, Hell's mouth with the crowned, mitred,
wimpled heads of the damned protruding; but the artist has not
followed Berengaudus in identifying the first three 'in bonam partem'.
They are merely human figures: the first, with a bow, being crowned by
the hand of God, the second, with a sword, wearing a hat, the third,
with the scales, wearing a cap.[58] But the Merton poet does follow
Berengaudus, notably in identifying all four riders with Christ.

What have we so far learned of the poet himself? He seems to be a

stitutes 16, 1953, 13-23; R. Freyhan: 'Joachism and the English Apocalypse' (*ibid.* 18, 1955, 211-244); G.
Henderson: 'Studies in English Manuscript Illumination: II: The English Apocalypse' (*ibid.* 30, 1967,
104-137).

   56 M. R. James: *The Apocalypse in Art*, 45-57.

   57 *Berengaudi Expositio in Apocalypsin* (PL 17), 895-920.

   58 MS Bodleian Douce 180, pp. 13, 14, 15, 16, reproduced in C. St. John Hornby: *The Apocalypse
in Latin and French* (Roxburghe Club; Oxford, 1922).

learned man, probably familiar with Berengaudus's commentary. His fondness for the quadruple images of Ezechiel and the Apocalypse is evidenced in another poem in the same manuscript; he seems to have been given to versifying. It appears that he spoke and wrote in a south-eastern dialect of English; this is shown by such spellings and forms as *fless, ssad, sverd, uol, viȝt, vo, volwede, vram*. It seems reasonable to suppose that he is the author of the Latin sermon and of the English verses, both Christological in content, devotional in tone. We do not know what is the significance of the name 'Stanischaue' written at the head of f. 139ᵃ of the Merton manuscript. Brown called it 'apparently the name of the author from whom the sermon which follows was borrowed',[59] but that is mere conjecture, unverifiable unless another more clearly attributed copy of this sermon or other sermons ascribed to a preacher with such a name be found. It could as well be the name of a scribe or of a place.

If we consider the hypothesis that Sheppey was himself the author, we shall find that it works well. We first hear of him on 2 June, 1332, when, as a monk of Rochester, he was given permission to incept in theology at Oxford ([60]) — that is, to mark the successful conclusion of his studies and his acceptance by his university as a teacher by a public disputation and lecture. Any hopes which he may have had of a career at Oxford were in August of the next year dashed, when John Speldhurst resigned as prior of Rochester and he was elected his successor.[61] But his transfer did not mean that he was relegated to obscurity. In 1337 we find him preaching at Paul's Cross.[62] In 1344 he was to have preached at the funeral of Lady Cobham.[63] In 1345 he was abroad, on royal diplomatic business at Avignon and elsewhere.[64] On that occasion Hamo Hythe, monk and bishop of Rochester, sent a letter of recommendation to Cardinal Peter Gomez in which he says of him:

> ... per dictum monasterium Roffense educatus ac subsequenter, habitu regulari suscepto, ad generale studium destinatus, adeo laudabiliter in sacra theologia profecit, quo infra breve compendium ad honorem tocius ordinis omnes scolasticos actus exercuit et cathedram ascendit magistralem. Et postmodum, ad prioratus assumptus officium, sic vixit et docuit, suumque monasterium prudenter et discrete rexit, quod tam regulares observancias per incuriam presidentum omissas quam defectus temporales grandes et varios in edificiis possessionibus et juribus inventos

59 *XIV* 258.

60 C. Johnson, ed.: *Registrum Hamonis Hethe diocesis Roffensis episcopi A.D. 1319-1352* 1 (Canterbury and York Society 48, 1948), 515.

61 *Ibid.* 1 531-534.

62 W. A. Pantin: *The English Church in the Fourteenth Century* (Cambridge, England, 1955), 158 n. 2.

63 *Ibid.* 255-256.

64 *Ibid.* 12.

inestimabili fortuna pariter et gracia reformavit. Unde quasi speculum et exemplar efficitur religiosorum comprovincialium prelatorum. Regi preterea carus habetur.[65]

Haymo ends by strongly recommending Sheppey as his successor. When he died, 4 May, 1352, this happened.[66] It would seem that Sheppey neither expected nor wished for the succession;[67] not long before, we find him asking the abbots president of the English Congregation for permission to retire, in what would have been very comfortable circumstances, to some academic seat. For appraisals of his learning and piety, one must refer to what C. L. Kingsford,[68] Pantin, Stacpoole and others have written of him. He had gifts as a wit and a satirist; this is shown by his Latin fables, and especially their verses.[69] Finally, an important point when we consider his possible authorship of the Merton poem, seemingly so influenced by Berengaudus, we do not need to speculate whether it was in pictorial form that his interpretations became known to Sheppey. Very probably he had seen, in great abbatial libraries or in some royal or princely collection, one or other of the gorgeous volumes so prized by the collectors of his day. It is, however, unnecessary to build upon this probability, since we know that the library of his own monastery possessed a copy of Berengaudus which has survived.[70] He was himself concerned to enrich the library; MS B.M. Royal 10 C. xii, containing Bonaventure's *Breviloquium* and a commentary on parts of Peter Lombard's *Sentences,* was his gift to the monastery, as also, perhaps, MS Royal 12 D. xiv. Of this second we cannot be sure; the inscription reads merely 'Liber de claustro Roffensi per magistrum Iohannem de Scapeya priorem', and there was another Rochester prior of the same name, 1380-1419.[71] Both were no doubt men of Kent, from the Isle of Sheppey, a few miles down the Medway estuary from Rochester; the dialect characteristics of the Merton poem have already been remarked.

A full-scale study of John Sheppey is long overdue. His piety and his intellectual gifts, the brilliance and fame of his sermons, the part which he played as diplomat and bishop in the great world, all demand at-

65 *Registrum Hamonis Hethe* 1 736-742.

66 *Ibid.* 1 738-739.

67 Art., 'Sheppey, John de', DNB.

68 Cfr. Alberic Stacpoole, art.: 'Jean Sheppey', in the *Dictionnaire de Spiritualité.* I am obliged to Dom Alberic for a sight of the proofs of this before publication.

69 Ed. L. Hervieux: *Les fabulistes latins* 4 (Paris, 1896).

70 Berlin Staatsbibliothek MS. theol. lat. Fol. 224; f. 2ʳ, 'Liber de claustro Roffensi per G. Archi-diaconum'. Cfr. N. R. Ker: *Medieval Libraries of Great Britain* (² London, 1964), 160.

71 W. A. Pantin, ed.: *Documents illustrating the Activities of the General and Provincial Chapters of the English Black Monks, 1215-1540* 3 (London, 1937), 87 n. 2.

tention. When that is accorded, tribute should not be denied to him also as a poet whose work can still impress and charm and move us.[72]

Pontifical Institute of Mediaeval Studies.

---

72   This article had gone to press before I was able to consult, in *The Art of the Middle English Lyric* (University of Georgia Press, Athens, 1972), pp. 117-122, Edmund Reiss's criticisms of this text; but I do not wish at all to modify what I have written on what I still consider (as he does not) an integral poem.

THREE FORGOTTEN MARTYRS OF ANAZARBUS IN CILICIA

Michael R. E. Gough[1]

'A LL animals are equal, but some animals are more equal than others.' So wrote the late George Orwell in his political satire, *Animal Farm*. The proposition is one that applies also to the community of Saints; for while there can be no doubt that there are degrees in holiness, some Saints have certainly sunk into temporal obscurity or, in extreme cases, lost official recognition. (Of these almost discredited Saints, George of Cappadocia, much venerated in Greece and patron of England, is an outstanding example.) It would, of course, be unfair to suggest that their downgrading was to be attributed to the sudden discovery of hitherto unsuspected flaws in their spiritual calibre. It is surely due to the realization that documentary or other evidence for their sanctity (in some cases even their very existence) may be open to question.

Of the martyrdom of Tarachus, Probus, and Andronicus, three men who died for their Christian faith during the Diocletianic persecution, probably in the year 304, no evidence was available until comparatively recently apart from what could be deduced from the long account in the *Acta martyrum*.[2] Like modern newspapers, ancient literary sources are known to err from time to time, and many comparatively recent writers have not hesitated to question this particular account in the *Acta*. It is, therefore, a very agreeable duty to show that archaeology, allied with an intimate knowledge of the topography of the city in which the martyrs died, offers overwhelming support for the truth of an important part of the *Acta,* just as archaeology supported, with a justifiably greater impact, the authenticity of the second-century *memoria* of St. Peter on the Vatican hill.

Until a few centuries ago the account in the *Acta* was received with enthusiasm and apparently without reservations, so that the comments

---

1 This article was unfinished at the time of Professor Gough's death on 25 October 1973; it has been completed by his wife, Mary Gough.

2 T. Ruinart, ed., *Acta martyrum* (Regensburg, 1859), pp. 451-476.

of two comparatively modern sceptics must be presented and dealt with before the suggestion that archaeology is the 'handmaid' not only of history, but also of hagiography, may be briefly presented.

In 1927 H. Delehaye was convinced that the *Acta* were spurious, and in 1940 wrote that many details of the account were purely repetitive and, in fact, fictitious. One of his main objections, which does not bear close scrutiny, is 'que la triple comparution dans trois villes différentes, chère aux hagiographes orientaux, est inexplicable juridiquement.'[3] Now if, as the *Acta* state, Tarachus was a native of Claudiopolis (Mut) in Isauria, Probus of Side in Pamphylia, and Andronicus of Ephesus,[4] is there any valid reason to suppose that all three men might not have been simutaneously at Pompeiopolis in Cilicia? As Christians, they would certainly have been questioned first at Tarsus, metropolis of the western part of the Cilician Plain (Cilicia Prima). That the Governor, Maximus, should have held a second enquiry at Mopsuestia (Misis), an important city on the crossing of the Pyramus (Ceyhan), might be more surprising if it were not for the fact that it lay on the direct route between Tarsus and Anazarbus, metropolis of the eastern Cilician Plain (Cilicia Secunda). Such might well accord very well with the travelling pattern of an energetic Governor, in touch with the many cities of his province. Unfortunately the editors of *Vies des saints* were ill-informed of the historical geography of Cilicia, the birthplace of St. Paul and an area travelled extensively by the Apostle. He will certainly have travelled by the very route mentioned above, and he was very much aware of his Cilician identity. As for the curious identification by the authors of *Vies des saints,* viz. 'Pompeiopolis (aujourd'hui Mezethi)',[5] it can only mislead. The truth is that the stream which passes close to Viransehir, the modern name for Pompeiopolis, is called Mezetli Çay. It is sad, too, to find the same authors so carried away by Delehye's interpretation of the *Acta* that they can write, 'Ce jugement sévère semble définitif et la simple lecture des Actes de Tharacus suffit à se demander comment des critiques ont pu croire à leur authenticité entière.'[6] Of course, not even the present writer believes in the *total* accuracy of the *Acta*; that would be too much to expect of any account of which the parallel Latin and Greek texts are not always in agreement. As the authors of the *Vies* continue, in their unintentionally condescending way, 'Nous nous contenterons de les résumer rapidement à cause de leur célébrité passée et pour sauver la parcelle d'histoire qu'ils contiennent peut-être.'[7]

3   Cf. *Vies des saints et des bienheureux*, 10 (Paris, 1952), p. 348.
4   *Acta martyrum*, cc. 1 (p. 452), 2 (p. 454), 3 (p. 455).
5   *Op. cit.*, p. 349.
6   *Op. cit.*, p. 348.
7   *Op. cit.*, p. 348.

Adolf Harnack, like Delehaye after him, found 'eine Erfindung dieser ermüdenden Wiederholungen und der immer wieder markierten Schläge und Martern weniger glaublich'.[8] He is less sceptical on some details of the account; still, 'dagegen ist die Schilderung der Passio, die in der 1. Person Plural. gehalten ist, ganz unglaubwürdig' (c. 10. 11).[9] This is the point at which Harnack and the present writer part company, since my arguments for the authenticity of the Acta as a whole rest almost entirely on the circumstantial and verifiable evidence provided in those two chapters. (I am, incidentally, confining myself to the Greek text of the Acta, as certainly the language which the supposed eye-witnesses of the martyrdom would have described events to their brethren in Iconium (Konya). To be quite fair, Harnack was not totally sceptical about many of the details of the Passio of our three martyrs. 'Dann erhebt sich doch die Frage', he wrote, 'ob nicht das Ganze von Anfang bis zu Ende eine Fälschung ist aber ich getraue mir nicht, sie mit einem sichern Ja zu beantworten.'[10] In fact, in common with other commentators, he was confused, not least because he never saw even the ruins of Anazarbus, where the martyrdom is reported to have taken place. That was no small disadvantage.

Thus far we have confined ourselves to fairly recent objections to the accuracy of the Acta, though the authors of Vies des saints seem to find an earlier consensus in their authenticity surprising, and suggest that 'il est permis de se demander si cette unanimité est le fruit d'études approfondies', the very type-specimen, it might be said, of the academic backhander. 'Paul Allard (1900), qui n'est pas pourtant très exigeant, n'ose affirmer la parfaite sincérité de la dernière partie.'[11] It is this last part in particular that needs full consideration, for it is exactly that same part that Harnack stigmatized as 'ganz unglaubwürdig'.

In this short paper, the writer is not concerned by the 'repetitious' account of the examination of the accused by Maximus, nor even indeed whether their reported sufferings were 'lifted' from other Acta. Let the hagiographers wrangle as they will, the point at issue is no more than whether (given the bare fact of the examination, torture, and martyrdom of Tarachus, Probus, and Andronicus) the physical geography of Anazarbus and the position of certain buildings in the ancient city, as verified by a four month archaeological survey in 1949 and 1950, bear out the last two chapters of the Passio. If they do, then 11 October may take on an added significance in future editions of the Martyrology.

---

8 Geschichte der altchristlichen Literatur bis Eusebius, 2nd rev. ed., part 2, vol. 2 (reprint Leipzig, 1958), p. 480 (n. 5).
9 Ibid.
10 Ibid.
11 Vies des saints, p. 348.

For a start, we should note that Maximus arranged for the future martyrs to suffer death in the amphitheatre at Anazarbus, and a rough English translation of the relevant passage reads as follows: 'In the morning, the whole city including women and children went out into the stadium, for the place of the spectacle lies a mile or so from the city; and when the amphitheatre was full of people ...'[12]

The writer's article on Anazarbus in *Anatolian Studies* 2 (1952) shows clearly, in a plan of the city, that the stadium was ideally situated for a crowd coming out of the city to foregather before it made its way to a gladiatorial show in the amphitheatre to the south of the city and well outside its limits. For a description of the amphitheatre itself, a direct quotation from the article (p. 100) needs, in the circumstances, no apology.

> 'Some 200 m. east of this stretch of road is the amphitheatre, (2). Judging from the position of two piers which stand erect and the traces of others at ground level, its lower part seems to have consisted of twenty-two evenly spaced piers, with intervening arches, which formed an ellipse measuring 62 m. by 83 m. To the east, where the amphitheatre backed on to the crag, the piers were discontinued and the curve was completed by a concrete structure built on to the face of the rock itself.'

This last sentence is of extra importance, since the crag east of the amphitheatre ascends not only sharply but ruggedly, affording an ideal view point for the spectator who wished to watch unseen the spectacle below. Thus ἡμῶν δὲ παραμενόντων καὶ παρατηρουμένων ἀνυπόπτως τὴν φυλακήν[13] describes exactly the position of the writer's wife in 1950 who hid behind rocks the better to observe his actions in the amphitheatre and to hear his conversation (for the acoustics of this amphitheatre were good).

The account continues with a further circumstantial detail after the three martyrs had been carried in, too weak after torture to move for themselves in the arena: 'Therefore when we saw them being carried in by the soldiers, we went forward up the neighbouring mountain with dispatch ... and kept quiet below the rocks.'[14] All this seems to me in accord with the account. At this point, Maximus had both a bear and a lioness set upon the martyrs, but neither beast would so much as harm Tarachus, Probus, and Andronicus. Further indeed the lioness, when provoked on the orders of Maximus, broke through the barrier and the people not unnaturally shouted 'Open up for the lioness.'[15] This may or may not be true, and indeed it does not much matter.

12   *Acta martyrum*, c. 10 (p. 473).
13   *Ibid.*
14   *Ibid.*
15   *Ibid.*, p. 474.

Chapter 11, however, does matter. It relates how at nightfall
Maximus left ten soldiers to guard the bodies of the martyrs and others
judicially murdered that day and to see that they were so confused as to
be unrecognizable in case the Christians might try to recover the martyrs' bodies. ἦν γὰρ τὸ λοιπὸν σκότος ... ἡμεῖς δὲ ὀλίγον ἀποβάντες ἀπὸ
τοῦ ὄρους ('For it was dark ... and we descending from the mountain a
little ...')[16] What would the frightened Christian spectators of the
tragedy have done but precisely that, under cover of darkness?

Then occurred the events related in Chapter 11 of the *Acta* which
two twentieth-century witnesses who have lived in Anazarbus for four
months can confirm as not only not unlikely, still less miraculous, but a
course of events so credible as to offer no occasion for misgiving. The
writer should explain that this judgement applies only to physical, not
to metaphysical, phenomena which in this case are not especially
relevant. The *Acta* read thus: παραχρῆμα δὲ σεισμοῦ γενομένου οὐ μικροῦ,
βρονταὶ καὶ ἀστραπαὶ τὸν ἀέρα συνήλαυνον ('Suddenly there was a considerable earthquake and thunder and lightning came together').[17] Certainly the thunderstorms at Anazarbus occur with monotonous regular-
ity, and earthquakes of various degrees of severity are not uncommon
in that area: witness the one which destroyed Antioch in 525 and the
other in 1965 that destroyed the Severan triumphal arch at Anazarbus.
There would have been nothing extraordinary, therefore, in a thunderstorm and an earth tremor occurring at the same time. At this point it
should be mentioned that the 'mountain' into which the amphitheatre is
built is a mountain in miniature, craggy, steep, and rock strewn on the
west, (the amphitheatre side), but a gently sloping hill on the eastern
side, the whole never more than about five hundred feet high.

The earth tremor and the thunderstorm frightened off the guards,
thus enabling the Christians hiding behind the rocks to creep down to
the arena.[18] They carried the bodies up the craggy side of the mountain
swiftly enough to escape detection, and it must have been relatively easy
to run down with them on the far side. The actual burial of the Martyrs
must, obviously, have taken place on the far, (the eastern), side, and
must have been done during the night. Notably, there are very few
remains of buildings on that side and the Roman city stopped at the
crag.

The final point on which issue may be taken with the critics who
distrust the *Acta* is on the question as to how the news of the mar-
tyrsdom could have been taken undetected to 'the brethren in Iconium'.

16   *Ibid.*, c. 11 (p. 474).
17   *Ibid.*, p. 475.
18   *Ibid.*

Here again knowledge of the terrain makes this less of a problem. The Ceyhan River, (the Pyramus of antiquity), flows not far to the east of Anazarbus, and to this day, although too swift flowing really to be navigable, its banks are an unofficial high road not only for people but also for news and gossip. Thus it would have been easy for one of the Anazarbene Christians to slip up the river into the Taurus mountains at the northwest corner of the Cilician Plain and over the Saymbelli Pass on to the Anatolian plateau, a frequently followed route by herdsmen, farmers, and travelling villagers today. From there, still avoiding the uncompromising Roman roads and still using age old native tracks, they could have made their way west along the plateau, just north of the Taurus, and ultimately to Konya. Anatolians are great travelers in the sense that they move about constantly for commercial, family, or pastoral reasons over huge but defined areas; the Anazarbene Christians would naturally have been familiar with this route, while the Roman official mind might well have considered that a carrier of news could only have travelled along the proper paved road through the Cilician Gates. The brethren in Iconium could have got the news quite quickly even if it had been carried by one person; if it had been passed on by word of mouth, it would have taken a very few days.

The object of this short article is to try to show that the story of the martyrdom of SS. Tarachus, Probus, and Andronicus was dependent on no miracle; everything that was described could have happened perfectly naturally. Perhaps the only really miraculous thing about the account, indeed, was the transcendent faith and courage of the Martyrs themselves.

Pontifical Institute of Mediaeval Studies.

CHARTRES AND PARIS REVISITED

Nikolaus Häring

THE distance between Chartres and Paris is fifty miles: once a one-day journey on horseback, today an hour's drive by automobile. At the end of the eleventh century scholarship in both cities began to show new vitality in such men as Ivo, bishop of Chartres (1090-1116), and William of Champeaux, bishop of Châlons-sur-Marne (1113-1122). The accuracy of the position assigned to Chartres in the ensuing scholastic movement has recently been questioned by an English historian whose allegations call for a re-examination of the available facts.

In 1970 R. W. Southern published a number of articles under the title: *Medieval Humanism and other Studies*.[1] The fifth study (pp. 61-85) is entitled: "Humanism in the School of Chartres". We learn in the preface that the essay "contains the substance of a paper read at the Ecclesiastical History Society Conference in 1965." It will surprise the reader to discover that, according to Southern, the school of Chartres is a *legend* whose "two great founders were R. L. Poole and A. Clerval."[2] Of A. Clerval the paper states: "Sometimes he was demonstrably wrong; but more often he erred simply by giving Chartres the benefit of every doubt."[3] R. L. Poole is treated with no greater discretion though we learn that he "saw the weakness of some of Clerval's new arguments" after it had been shown that Bernard Silvestris was not the same man as Bernard of Chartres.[4] Southern's analysis of Clerval's motives for creating the "system" ends with the declaration: "I think it has now begun to conflict with some of the facts, and the time has come to take the pieces apart again."[5] In following this advice we shall see that Prof. Southern has greatly facilitated his task by ignoring too many facts or pieces that have come to light since Clerval and Poole wrote about the

---

1 Oxford: B. Blackwell 1970.
2 *Medieval Humanism*, p. 83.
3 *Medieval Humanism*, p. 84.
4 *Medieval Humanism*, p. 84.
5 *Medieval Humanism*, p. 85.

school, facts and pieces which buttress and support their view that, in part, the remarkable surge of French learning in the early century had its beginning at Chartres. The man who inspired it was Bernard of Chartres. There is no doubt, of course, that Abelard and his school added to the movement, but the most powerful drive was launched by one of Bernard's students, Gilbert of Poitiers.

I

Masters at Chartres

When Otto, bishop of Freising (1138-58), wrote his *Gesta Friderici* (1156-58) he chose to include a report on both Abelard and Gilbert of Poitiers. Speaking of Gilbert he stresses the thorough training he received under Hilary of Poitiers,[6] then under Bernard of Chartres, and finally under Anselm of Laon and his brother Ralph.[7] Since Anselm of Laon is known to have died on 15 July 1117, Gilbert must have studied under Bernard of Chartres years before that date. This Bernard is, no doubt, the Master Bernard mentioned in Chartrain documents of the time.

In a charter, dated 29 November 1119 and issued in Chartres by the chancellor, the chartulary of Saint-Jean-en-Vallée in Chartres has recorded the names of "Master Bernard" and Chancellor Vulgrinus: "S(ignum) magistri Bernardi ... Datum Carnoti per manum Vulgrini cancellarii."[8] In an oath sworn and signed by the canons of the cathedral ca. 1121 we again meet the names of "Chancellor Vulgrinus" and Bernard who is described as *scole magister.*[9] According to Prof. Southern this Bernard is the "only man ... for whom there is quite convincing evidence of a teaching career at Chartres."[10] In the opinion of the same critic "he is evidently the master referred to as "Master B." in the letters printed by Merlet".[11] Later, however, we are informed that

---

6 The existence of Master Hilary of Poitiers is well documented. See N. Haring, "Zur Geschichte der Schulen von Poitiers im 12. Jahrhundert," *Archiv für Kulturgesch.* 47 (1965) 23-47.

7 *Gesta Frid.* I, 52; MGH SrG 46, 74: Iste enim ab adolescentia magnorum uirorum discipline se subiciens magisque illorum ponderi quam suo credens ingenio, qualis primo fuit Hylarius Pictauiensis, post Bernhardus Carnotensis, ad ultimum Anshelmus et Radulfus Laudunenses, germani fratres, non leuem ab eis sed grauem doctrinam hauserat, manu non subito ferule subducta.

8 R. Merlet, *Cartulaire de l'Abbaye de Saint-Jean-en-Vallée, Archives d'Eure-et-Loir, Coll. de cartulaires chartrains* 1 (Chartres, 1906) 14.

9 R. Merlet and A. Clerval, *Un manuscrit chartrain du xie siècle* (Chartres, 1893) 196: "Bernardus scole magister."

10 R. W. Southern, *Medieval Humanism and Other Studies* (Oxford, 1970) 68.

11 *Medieval Humanism*, p. 68. The reference is to L. Merlet, "Lettres d'Ives de Chartres et d'autres personnages de son temps," *Bibl. de l'Ecole des Chartes* 16 (1854-55) 443-471, especially 461. They are found in MS Chartres, Bibl. mun. 1029 (H.1.19), f. 142v-157 (s. xii).

"it is very likely that Master B. is Bernard of Chartres."[12] We are also told that "after about 1120, for the next 30 years, the connection of every master or pupil with the school of Chartres is conjectural."[13] The premise for this sweeping dogma is the thesis pronounced in the same address that the appearance of names with the title *magister* in lists of witnesses "is quite unsatisfactory."[14] Prof. Southern declares that "we need more evidence than this for the special distinction of the school of Chartres."[15] But, despite the claim that Clerval and Poole created the legend of Chartres, it is admitted by Southern that, leaving aside for a moment "the minor characters mentioned by Clerval", there are "three men who have done most, after Bernard, to make Chartres famous. They are Thierry, Gilbert de la Porrée, and William of Conches."[16] Although it is not at all established that William of Conches ever taught at Chartres, neither Clerval nor Poole has ever denied that there were also "minor characters" who taught there.

When historians speak of the greatness of the school of Chartres in the first half of the twelfth century, they mean at least three scholars who made a notable impact on the intellectual climate of the period: a certain Thierry, William of Conches, and Gilbert of Poitiers. They are anything but the figments of Clerval's imagination. But before we turn our attention to a closer study of these outstanding scholars we may examine what evidence there is to show the continuity of the cathedral school in Chartres.

It has been emphasized by Southern that "the most important document for Bernard's career as a teacher at Chartres"[17] is the *list of signatures* under an oath taken by the canons of Chartres at some time between 4 November 1119 and 1124.[18] Applying the same criterion to witnesses in other documents we should be permitted to make the same assertions concerning those *magistri* that can be shown to have belonged to the cathedral community of Chartres. R. W. Southern adds that in 1124 Bernard "appears as chancellor in an agreement between the monks of St. Peter of Chartres and those of Nogent."[19] The presence of a chancellor named Bernard is also recorded in a charter dated to 1101-29. Bernard's successor, Gilbert of Poitiers, appears as canon in a char-

12   *Med. Humanism*, p. 70.
13   *Med. Humanism*, p. 68.
14   *Ibid.*, p. 68.
15   *Ibid.*, p. 68.
16   *Ibid.*, p. 68.
17   *Ibid.*, p. 68.
18   Merlet and Clerval, *Un manuscrit*, pp. 195-6.
19   *Med. Humanism*, p. 68, note 1: Ch. Métais, *Saint-Denis de Nogent-le-Rotrou* (Vannes, 1895) 240-243.
20   B. E. Guérard (ed.), *Cartulaire de l'Abbaye de Saint-Père, Collection des cartulaires de France* 2 (Paris, 1849) 306: "Bernardus cancellarius".

ter of 27 November 1126, as chancellor in a document bearing the same date.[21]

A. Clerval[22] refers to a Cartulaire de Saint-Jean, Bibliothèque publique de Chartres, no. 1312, f. 1 and 3, to show that Bernard's name occurs in charters dated 1114, 1115, 1118, and 1119. This document is no longer available and probably perished in 1944. According to the catalogue[23] the manuscript with the pressmark 1312 belonged to the 19th century. Its contents are described as "Notices et documents sur l'abbaye de Saint-Jean-en-Vallée et divers établissements en dépendents. On trouve dans ce recueil quelques notices archéologiques imprimées, avec plans et gravures."

Clerval may have quoted the wrong pressmark. The chartulary of Saint-Jean edited by R. Merlet, in part based on manuscript 1724 of Saint-Jean, records "magister Bernardus" in a charter dated to 1110-15. A charter dated 1115 contains a "(Signum Ber)nardi Pictauiensis sub-diaconi". Another charter, dated 1119, records the "Signum Bernardi archidiaconi", while a charter dated 29 November 1119 lists two Bernards: "Signum Bernardi capicerii" and "Signum magistri Bernardi."[24] Two of these charters show the existence of Master Bernard in Chartres during the second decade.

In this context Clerval slipped by claiming that two charters dated 1119-24 and 1124 attribute the title magister to both Bernard and Thierry. Neither the first charter, the oath mentioned above, nor the second, published in the Cartulaire de Saint-Père,[25] mentions Thierry. The fact that Gilbert of Poitiers appears as chancellor on 27 November 1126 adds probability to the assumption that chancellor Bernard died before 1126 or retired. Master Bernard's name is also found in a collection of letters, first analyzed by W. Wattenbach,[26] where we read: "Carnotum ubi ego sub disciplina domini magistri Bernardi dego ..."[27] Since the collection is dated "ca. 1123"[28] the student's letter to his father is another testimony to the existence of a Master Bernard at Chartres in the early twelfth century.

21 B. E. Ch. Guérard (ed.), Cartulaire de l'Abbaye de Saint-Père 2, 264: "Gislebertus canonicus." (p. 267): "Gilbertus cancellarius."

22 Les écoles de Chartres au moyen âge, Mém. de la Soc. archéol. d'Eure-et-Loir 9 (Chartres, 1895) 160.

23 Cat. gén. 11 (Paris, 1890) 392.

24 R. Merlet, Cartulaire de Saint-Jean-en-Vallée, Archives d'Eure-et-Loir, Coll. de cartulaires chartrains 1 (Chartres 1906) 8-14.

25 B. E. Ch. Guérard, Cartulaire de Saint-Père 2, 469. Chancellor Bernard and Canon Gilbert were present.

26 W. Wattenbach, "Iter Austriacum 1853", Archiv für Kunde österr. Geschichtsquellen 14 (1855) 44.

27 Ms. Vienna, Nationalbibl. 2507, f. 43v-44v (s. xii).

28 Cf. Ch. Homer Haskins, Studies in Mediaeval Culture (Cambridge, Mass., 1929) 181.

In the twenties the name Thierry appears for the first time in the (published) charters of the diocese. About 1127 an archdeacon of Dreux, called Thierry, assisted at the drawing up of a charter: "Assistentibus et attestantibus qui subscripti sunt Teoderico archidiacono Drocensi ..."[29] In a charter dated to 1136-39 Archdeacon Thierry is named among the witnesses to a donation made by Bishop Geoffrey (1116-49) to the Benedictine Priory of Davron: "Huius rei testes sunt Salomon cantor, Hugo subdiaconus, Theodericus archidiaconus ..."[30] Together with Archdeacon Drogo, the same Thierry signed a charter issued, according to Métais, about 1137: "Astantibus et concedentibus Zacharia decano, Salomone cantore, Drogone et Theodorico archidiaconis ..."[31] Because of Dean Zachary's presence A. Clerval[32] dates this charter to 1136-42. Archdeacon Thierry's name does not occur in the charters of the cathedral nor in those of Saint-Père de Chartres. Lucien and René Merlet state that he was succeeded by Goslen.[33]

Since this archdeacon is not described as master, more evidence is required to identify him with Master Thierry who, as we shall see, taught the Liberal Arts in Paris in or about 1134, probably earlier.[34] At the same time it is certain that at an unknown date a certain "Master Thierry" was both archdeacon and chancellor of Notre-Dame de Chartes: "Obiit magister Teodoricus, cancellarius et archidiaconus alme Marie."[35] It is generally assumed that the obituary refers to the period after Thierry's teaching career in Paris. The day of his death was 5 December.

29　Ch. Métais, *Cartulaire de Notre-Dame de Josaphat*, Soc. archéol. d'Eure-et-Loir 1 (Chartres, 1911) 33-34. E. Jeauneau, "Note sur l'école de Chartres", *Studi medievali*, terza serie, V, 2 (1964), 2, n. 6 points to the three signatures in this cartulary as being those of Master Thierry. However, he questions both the accuracy of the dates and of the text edited by Métais.

30　Ch. Métais, *Cartul.* 1, 138. A. Clerval, *Les écoles*, pp. 171-172.

31　Ch. Métais, *Cartul.* 1, 126.

32　*Les écoles*, p. 171.

33　"Dignitaires de l'église de Notre-Dame de Chartres," *Archives du dioc. de Chartres* 5 (Chartres, 1900) 103. On p. 194 Thierry is listed as archdeacon of Dreux from 1134-48. It may here be noted that Parisian charters record a "Teodericus subdiaconus" in 1108, a "Theodericus leuita" in 1117, later a "Theodericus sacerdos" in 1119, "Theodericus presbiter" in 1122, "sacerdos" in 1122, 1124, 1133, and "presbyter" in 1134. See Robert de Lasteyrie, *Cartulaire gén. de Paris* 1 (Paris, 1887) 169, no. 149; 198, no. 174; 204, no. 182; 215, no. 194; 217, no. 195; 223, no. 203; 226, no. 205; 244, no. 239; 253, no. 253.

34　I. Brady, *Prolegomena in Sent. in iv libris distinctas*, Spic. Bonav. 4 (Grottaferrata, 1971) 16, does not hesitate to refer the "S. Gilleberti sacerdotis" and "Theoderici sacerdotis" (1133 and 1134) to Gilbert and Thierry. PL 173, 1423-27. R. de Lasteyrie, *Cartul.* 1, 251-253. At that time Gilbert was still chancellor of Chartres.

35　*Necrologium B. M. Carnutensis;* ed. E. de Lépinois and L. Merlet, *Cartul. de Notre-Dame de Chartres* 3 (Chartres, 1865) 206.

When in 1119 Bishop Geoffrey founded the Abbey Our Lady of Josaphat (near Lèves), Hildebert, then bishop of Le Mans (1096-1125), was present, but only two archdeacons, Goslen and Bernard, were available to witness the charter. This archdeacon may well be Master Bernard who witnessed a charter on 29 November of the same year. As if to complicate the matter, the necrology of Chartres lists a "subdeacon and chancellor" by the name of Bernard.[36]

About the year 1124 Geoffrey made a donation witnessed by four archdeacons: Gauterius, Drogo (also called Paganus), Ansgerius, and Richerius.[37] The fact that in two charters, dated 1124-27, only Gauterius[38] appears has led to the conclusion that he was the archdeacon of the cathedral. Another charter, also dated 1124-27, in which the cathedral chapter declares that the mills of Jouy were to be Josaphat's property, was approved by Archdeacons Gauterius and Paganus, Chancellor Gislebert, chévicier Bernard, and others. Chancellor Gislebert was instructed to put the donation down in writing and to seal the document "with the seal of our church."[39] The chévicier Bernard[40] is not the same person as Chancellor Bernard.[41]

On 27 November 1126, Chancellor Gislebert acted as witness to a *priuilegium* granted by Bishop Geoffrey.[42] On 26 February 1133 Chancellor Gislebert[43] provided a charter with the following specification: "Datum Carnoti, in Capitulo Sancte Marie, per manum Gisleberti cancellarii, IIII° Kalendas marcii, anno ab incarnatione M°C°XXX°III°." We have noted that in 1137 Chancellor Gilbert's presence is recorded in a

36 Ch. Métais, *Cart. de Notre-Dame de Josaphat* 1, 4. Merlet and Clerval, *Un manuscrit*, p. 156: "Obiit Bernardus subdiaconus et cancellarius sancte Marie qui dedit huic ecclesie libros suos."

37 Ch. Métais, *Cartul.* 1, 27. Richer of Blois, archdeacon of Dunois, is known to have decorated the portail royal with a statue of the Madonna painted in gold. Lépinois-Merlet, *Cartul.* 3, 19-20.

38 Ch. Métais, *Cartul.* 1, 28-29.

39 Ch. Métais, *Cartul.* 1, 30: "Hanc donationem factam et concessionem precepimus Gisleberto cancellario per scripta memorie mandare et sigillo ecclesie nostre confirmare ac corroborare. Quod ita factum est in capitulo nostro ... assistentibus et concedentibus ... Galterio archidiacono, Pagano archidiacono ... Gisleberto cancellario, Bernardo capicerio". Cf. Guérard, *Cartul. de Saint-Père* 2, 307. Clerval *Les écoles*, p. 165.

40 The chévicier was the lowest dignitary of the chapter. Chévicier Bernard can be traced back to 1119. L. Merlet, *Cart. de la Sainte-Trinité, Soc. archéol. d'Eure-et-Loir* 1 (Chartres, 1883) 38. R. Merlet, *Cartul. de Saint-Jean-en-Vallée* 1, 14.

41 Lépinois and Merlet, *Cart. de Notre-Dame de Chartres* 2, 469: "Presentibus ... Bernardo cancellario ... Bernardo capicerio." Date: 1124. See also Ch. Métais, *Cartul. de Josaphat* (Chartres, 1911) 30-48.

42 B. E. Ch. Guérard, *Cartul. de l'Abbaye de Saint-Père* 2, 267: "Testes Galterius archidiaconus, Zacharias archidiaconus, Richerius archidiaconus ... Paganus archidiaconus, Zacharias archidiaconus, Richerius archidiaconus ... Paganus archidiaconus ... Gillebertus cancellarius ..." We have noted that in another charter (p. 264) which bears the same date Gilbert is listed as canon.

43 E. de Lépinois and L. Merlet, *Cart. de Notre-Dame de Chartres* 1 (Chartres, 1862) 142.

charter issued by Dean Zachary.[44] During the year 1137 Gilbert seems to have left Chartres, for charters dated 1137 and 1139 show that a certain Guido was given the office.[45] According to R. W. Southern Thierry "became chancellor in 1141."[46] This is only a conjecture, first proposed by A. Clerval,[47] on the assumption that Master Thierry left Paris to replace Gilbert.

In 1133, while Gilbert was chancellor, two masters are named in a charter issued by Geoffrey: Master Odo Piszat and Master William de Modalibus (des Muids).[48] Some four years later (ca. 1137) we meet Master Paganus witnessing a charter with Dean Zachary, Cantor Salomon, Archdeacon Drogo, and Thierry.[49] This Master Paganus is obviously not the Archdeacon Drogo "also called Paganus".[50] But he may well be the Archdeacon Paganus mentioned in a charter dated to 1124-27.[51]

In 1144, a charter again records two masters in the bishop's household: Master Robert Petit (Paruus) and Master William de Modalibus.[52] Master Robert probably replaced Master Odo Piszat who, as we have noted, witnessed a charter in 1133 together with Master William de Modalibus.[53] Master William is described a canonicus in two slightly later documents.[54]

At this time an archdeacon Goslen appears among the witnesses.[55] In 1145 he witnessed a charter with Dean Robert and Master Robert Petit.[56] Two years later (1147) Dean Robert and Master William de

44   Ch. Métais, Cartulaire de Josaphat 1, 127: "Presentibus Salomone cantore, Hugone succentore, Gisleberto cancellario, Bernardo capicerio."

45   Cartul. Saint-Père 2, 384 (Testes: Guido cancellarius) and Cart. de Notre-Dame de Chartres 1, 184 (Guido cancellarius). The obituary lists a "magister Guido diaconus et canonicus sancte Marie" whose mother's name was Agnes. Lépinois and Merlet, Cartul. 3, 137 and 163.

46   Med. Humanism, p. 70: "There is not the slightest evidence of a connection between Thierry and Chartres until he became chancellor in 1141. Nor is there any evidence that he taught at Chartres while he was chancellor."

47   Les écoles, p. 171: "sans doute en 1141."

48   L. Merlet, Cartul. de la Sainte-Trinité de Tiron 1 (Chartres, 1883) 210.

49   Ch. Métais, Cartul. de Josaphat 1, 126-127: "Fratribus nostris astantibus et concedentibus Zacharia decano, Salomone cantore, Drogone et Theodorico archidiaconis ... magistro Pagano."

50   Ch. Métais, Cartul. 1, 27 and 116. Paganus was a relatively common name. There was a Master Paganus of Corbeil whose name appears in numerous glosses on Peter Lombard's Sentences. A. M. Landgraf, "Unters. zur Gelehrtengeschichte des 12. Jahrhunderts," Miscell. Giov. Mercati 2: Studi e Testi (Vatican, 1946) 260-275.

51   Ch. Métais, Cartul. 1, 30.

52   Ch. Métais, Cartul. 1, 162.

53   L. Merlet, Cart. de la Sainte-Trinité de Tiron 1 (Chartres, 1883) 210.

54   Ch. Métais, Cartul. 1, 171 (dated to 1144-45) and 173 (dated to about 1145).

55   Ch. Métais, Cartul. de Notre-Dame de Josaphat 1, 172.

56   Ch. Métais, Cartul. 1, 174.

Modalibus were in Etampes.[57] In the same year the two masters acted together with Archdeacon Goslen as witnesses to a charter at Josaphat.[58]

During this period Master John Sarracen, a native of Poitiers, witnessed a donation at Chartres.[59] His presence is noteworthy in view of the increased interest in Greek writings. It is believed that he wrote a commentary on the *Celestial Hierarchy* about 1140.[60] In 1166 he asked John of Salisbury to compare his translation of (Pseudo-) Denis with that of John Eriugena.[61] In the same year John of Salisbury requested from him a clarification of the word *usia* he had come across in St. Ambrose.[62] A year later Sarracen reported to John that after the translation of the *Angelic Hierarchy* he had to postpone the translation of the *Ecclesiastical Hierarchy*.[63]

There is some evidence, during the years 1140-58, of a Master Garin de Prunoi, described as a canon of Chartres in a charter published by Rotrou, bishop of Evreux (1141-58).[64] Rotrou had been one of Gilbert's students and defended his orthodoxy at the papal consistory held at Paris in 1147. In 1148 Master Thierry of Chartres attended the Council of Reims.[65] About the same time he was with Albero, archbishop of Trier.[66]

Bishop Geoffrey died in 1149 and was succeeded by Goslen (1149-55).[67] On 18 April 1150 Goslen refers to two assisting masters: "magistro Milone presbitero, capellano nostro, et magistro Odone de Braiolo, canonico Sancte Marie Carnotensis."[68] Master Odo de Braiolo signed an

57 Ch. Métais, *Cartul.* 1, 177.

58 Ch. Métais, *Cartul.* 1, 179: "Presentibus ecclesie nostre personis Gausleno archidiacono ... magistro Robert Paruo, magistro Guillelmo de Modalibus." An anniversary for a Master Robert is recorded in *Cartul. de Notre-Dame de Chartres* 3, 105.

59 Ch. Métais, *Cartul.* 1, 191: (testes) "Iohannes Sarracena".

60 G. Théry, "Documents concernants Jean Sarrazin", *Arch. d'hist. doctr. et litt. du moyen âge* 18 (1950) 51. See also G. Théry," "Existe-t-il un commentaire de Jean Sarrazin sur la Hier. céleste?" *Revue des sc. phil. et théol.* 11 (1922) 72-81.

61 *Ep.* 149; PL 199, 143C-144B. ·

62 *Ep.* 159; PL 199, 161C-163B: Ambrose, *Liber de Incarn.* 9, 100; PL 16, 878C.

63 PL 199, 259D-260A. Cf. G. Théry, "Jean Sarrazin, traducteur de Scot Erigène," *Studia Mediaevalia in hon. R. J. Martin* (Bruges, 1948) 359-381.

64 M. Deloche, *Cartul. de l'Abbaye de Beaulieu en Limosin* (Paris 1859) 122. B. E. Ch. Guérard, *Cartulaire de Saint-Père* 2, 619: "interfuerunt ... Guillelmus de Bello Visu, magister Garinus canonici Carnotenses." He may be identical with the presbyter Garinus mentioned in a charter by Dean Geoffrey in 1169. Lépinois and Merlet, *Cartul. de Notre-Dame de Chartres* 1, 180. Clerval, *Les écoles*, p. 284.

65 *Analecta Cist.* 22 (1966) 35.

66 *Gesta Alberonis;* MGH SS 8, 257.

67 Ch. Métais, *Cartul.* 1, 207 contains a charter dated 23 September 1149 and issued at Bonneval by Goslen in the presence of two archdeacons: Richer and Robert. Concerning Goslen see *Gall. chr.* 8 (Paris, 1744) 1141-42.

68 Ch. Métais, *Cartul.* 1, 214.

episcopal document on 23 May 1151.[69] Since on 13 June 1151 Master Robert Petit was with his bishop and Abbot Ernald in Bonneval,[70] we have the names of three contemporaneous masters: Master Milo (the bishop's chaplain), Master Odo, and Master Robert Petit who witnessed a charter in 1145.[71] In the meantime Robert Petit had been appointed *succentor*.[72]

Another charter (30 September 1157) shows "Milo, the bishop's chaplain" and Master Odo as witnesses.[73] In addition to these masters, Bishop Goslen had a *notarius* by the name of *Paganus*.[74] He may be the Master Paganus who witnessed a charter about 1137.[75] This Master Paganus, archdeacon of Notre-Dame, Chartres, as early as 1126,[76] is considered the author of the poem *De falsis heremitis qui uagando discurrunt*.[77] Milo is again mentioned together with Master Odo de Braiolo in 1152 and 1153.[78] Master Odo is now described as *diaconus*.[79]

When, in 1155, Bishop Goslen confirmed the transfer of the mill of Jouy to Josaphat he recalled the presence — at the time of the original declaration made in 1137 — of "magister Gislebertus cancellarius qui postea fuit Pictauensis episcopus."[80] It seems that, in 1156, Master Milo was made an archdeacon by Goslen's successor, Bishop Robert (1156-64). Bishop Robert may have been the former Dean Robert who was replaced in 1156 by Dean Ivo. The latter died in 1165. The new dean's name appears for the first time in a charter 18 October 1156.[81] We shall see that he had studied in Paris under Thierry and Gilbert, and that he was Master Ivo before he became dean of the cathedral community at

---

69 Ch. Métais, *Cartul.* 1, 241: "Magister Odo de Braiolo, ecclesie carnotensis canonicus ss."

70 Ch. Métais, *Cartul.* 1, 242.

71 Ch. Métais, *Cartul.* 1, 174. A "magister Milo de Castellione canonicus huius ecclesie" is found in the obituary. *Cartul. de Notre-Dame de Chartres* 3, 69-70.

72 Ch. Métais, *Cartul.* 1, 242: "Hernaudus Bonnevallensis abbas, magister Robertus Paruus succentor."

73 Ch. Métais, *Cartul.* 1, 246.

74 R. Merlet, *Cartul. de Saint-Jean-en-Vallée* 1 (Chartres 1906) 37: "interfuerunt ... Paganus presbiter et notarius episcopi."

75 Ch. Métais, *Cartul.* 1, 126.

76 B. E. Ch. Guérard, *Cartul. de Saint-Père* 1, 264, no. 4.

77 J. Leclercq, "Le poème de Payen Bolotin contre les faux ermites," *Revue bén.* 68 (1958) 52-84. Southern, *Med. Humanism,* p. 67, seems to consider Payen and Bolotin two distinct persons.

78 Ch. Métais, *Cartul.* 1, 258 (dated 1152): Presentibus ... Milone capellano nostro et magistro Odone de Braioto."

79 Ch. Métais, *Cart.* 1, 259 (dated 1153): "Affuerunt testes ... Milo capellanus noster, magister Odo de Braioto diaconus."

80 Ch. Métais, *Cartul.* 1, 270.

81 Ch. Métais, *Cartul.* 1, 272. In 1159/60 Bishop Robert was with Bishop Peter Lombard. R. de Lastyerie, *Cartul. gén.* 1, 357, no. 410. His obituary is recorded in *Cartul. de Notre-Dame de Chartres* 3, 180.

Chartres. The same document mentions Ernaudus as archdeacon of Dreux.[82] Dean Ivo acted as witness in 1159.[83] A year later Bishop Robert signed a charter: "assistentibus nobiscum clericis nostris Milone archidiacono ... et magistro Pagano."[84] Bishop Robert appointed a chancellor whose name was likewise Robert. Dean Ivo who died in 1165 was replaced by Dean Hugh.[85] In a charter dated 1162, Bishop Robert refers to his chancellor Robert as "our notary".[86] He was still chancellor in January 1169.[87] At an unknown date Bishop Robert appointed a new master: "magister Ernaudus de Poncellis (Poncet)" who witnessed two charters with Archdeacon Ernaudus.[88] In 1159 Ernaudus de Poncellis acted as a witness together with Dean Ivo and others.[89] On 13 March 1164 Bishop Robert published a document: "audientibus et uidentibus ... clericis nostris ... magistro Petro."[90] The text reveals that Master Peter was one of the bishop's clerics.

In a charter published at Chartres in 1170 by William (aux Blanches-Mains) who was at that time both bishop of Chartres[91] and archbishop of Sens we read: "attestantibus Gauterio Dunensi archidiacono, magistro Petro Vindocinensi archidacono, magistro Roberto clerico nostro."[92] According to this description Master Peter whom we met in a document dated 13 March 1164 was archdeacon of Vendôme, one of the five rural archdeaconries in the diocese of Chartres.[93] Master Robert may be identical with Bishop Robert's notary[94] and with Robert the chancellor whose presence in Chartres is recorded in a charter published in 1169 by Dean Geoffrey.[95] In the same year Chancellor

---

82 Ch. Métais, *Cartul. 1*, 276: "Iuo Carnotensis decanus ... Ernaudus Drocensis archidiaconus."

83 Lépinois and Merlet, *Cartul.* 1, 168: "Presente Iuone decano."

84 *Gallia chr.* 8, 336D instr.

85 R. Merlet, *Cartul. de Saint-Jean-en-Vallée* 1 (Chartres, 1906) 43: "astantibus et audientibus Hugone decano, Roberto cancellario, Ernaudo archidiacono." The date (1161) given by Merlet would seem to be too early. The obituary of Chancellor Robert reads: "Obiit Robertus beate dei genitricis Marie leuita et cancellarius." *Cartul. de Notre-Dame de Chartres* 3, 187. His anniversary is found on p. 176.

86 Ch. Métais, *Cartul.* 1, 283: "Roberto notario nostro."

87 R. Merlet, *Cartulaire de Saint-Jean* 1, 46 (testes): "Robertus cancellarius."

88 Ch. Métais, *Cartul.* 1, 286 and 287 (dated to 1155-64). A. Clerval, *Les écoles*, p. 285.

89 Lépinois and Merlet, *Cartul. de Notre-Dame de Chartres* 1, 168.

90 Ch. Métais, *Cartul.* 1, 291.

91 Cf. *Gallia chr.* 8, 1145D. Consecrated archbishop of Sens on 22 December 1168, he administered the diocese of Chartres for eight years. When John of Salisbury (1176-80) was elected, he was consecrated at Sens by Maurice of Sully, then bishop of Paris (1160-96). Bishop John bequeathed his library to the cathedral. Lépinois and Merlet, *Cartul. de Notre-Dame de Chartres* 3, 201-202. *Gallia chr.* 8, 1148E.

92 Ch. Métais, *Cartul.* 1, 303.

93 Chartres had five rural archdeaconries: Pinserais, Blois, Vendôme, Dunois, and Dreux.

94 Ch. Métais, *Cartul.* 1, 283.

95 Lépinois and Merlet, *Cartul.* 1, 180.

Robert witnessed a charter together with archdeacons Milo and Ernald.[96] Robert still held this position in 1173.[97] It is doubtful whether
Chancellor Bucardus who wrote a charter for Dean Geoffrey in 1179
belonged to the cathedral community.[98]

Within a span of about 30 years (1133-64) we have met a respectable
number of masters: Odo Piszat and William de Modalibus (1133),
Paganus (ab. 1137), Robert Petit (1144), Milo (the bishop's chaplain) and
Odo de Braioto (1150), Garin of Prunoi (1140-58), Chancellor Robert,
Bishop Robert's notary (1166), Ernaudus de Poncellis (1155-64), and
Peter, archdeacon of Vendôme. We know that until 1137 Gilbert of
Poitiers taught at Chartres and that the necrology of Chartres lists
Master Thierry, chancellor and archdeacon of the cathedral.[99]

To Gilbert and Thierry we can add Dean Ivo (1156-65) whom both
Geoffrey of Auxerre[100] and the chronicler Robert Abolant[101] call
"Master Ivo." The fact that Master Ivo left Paris for Chartres is highly
noteworthy, for many historians tend to dramatize the exodus from
Chartres to Paris. It is also generally accepted that Master Thierry had
also left Paris for Chartres at a time when Paris had become a focal
point of higher learning. And we shall see that a Master Bernard the
Breton who died as bishop of Cornouailles (1159-1167) likewise taught
in Paris before he became chancellor in Chartres.

The survey of masters shows that, at least during the period under
consideration, the cathedral employed a number of teachers. We may
also assume that the chancellor or the dean did a certain amount of
teaching. A twelfth-century chancery hardly employed the ad-
ministrative staff of a modern bureaucracy. During Gilbert's chancellorship (1124-1137) only two charters reveal the chancellor's

---

96 Lépinois and Merlet, Cartul. 1, 183: "Attestantibus personis Carnutensis ecclesie ... Milone archidiacono, Roberto cancellario, Ernaldo archidiacono."

97 Métais, Cartul. 1, 305: "Robertus cancellarius." It seems that, at least toward the end of the
century, Saint-Jean-en-Vallée had its own magister. R. Merlet (Cartul. 1, p. xi) shows evidence of
"magister Gilo Teher, sacerdos et canonicus sancti Iohannis de Valeia" who died during the period
from 1197-1212. A charter drawn up by Abbot Robert of Saint-Jean, dated to 1174-84, reveals the
presence of a "magister Paganus" who apparently belonged to the community of Saint-Jean. A.
Clerval (Les écoles, pp. 175-177) also connects with Saint-Jean a certain Master Hugh whom Hugh
Metel (d. ca. 1157) consults in a letter. Hugues d'Estival, Sacrae antiquitatis monumenta (Saint-Dié,
1731) 374: Ep. 34. Hist. litt. 12, 503. R. Merlet, "Lettres d'Ives de Chartres," Bibl. de l'Ecole des Chartes
16 (1854-55) 459-460.

98 Lépinois and Merlet, Cartul. 1, 202: "Data per manum Bucardi cancellarii ... Actum in
capitulo nostro" (= Chartres). A Clerval, Les écoles, p. 283.

99 Lépinois and Merlet, Cartul. 3, 206. R. W. Southern, Med. Humanism, pp. 67-88, belittles Clerval's "long list of masters." By dividing Payen and Bolotin Prof. Southern made it even larger.

100 Geoffrey of Auxerre, Ep. ad Albinum 2, 11; ed. N. Haring, Analecta Cist. 22 (1966) 71 or PL
185, 588C.

101 Chronicon; MGH SS 26, 237. In both cases the point of reference is 1147.

presence.[102] The ratio is no better for the rest of the period we have examined.[103] We have seen that an archdeacon's duties did not prevent him from being a *magister*.[104] A historian will readily agree that most Chartrain masters listed above were "minor characters". But are we to assume that the number of "minor characters" in Paris was smaller in proportion?

Master Thierry

In 1890 B. Hauréau[1] edited a letter written by Clarembald, archdeacon of Arras, to a noble lady.[2] The archdeacon sent her two short tractates on the opening chapters of Genesis: one written by "magister Theodoricus, meus doctor"[3] and one by Clarembald himself.[4] A compilation of texts preserved in MS Heiligenkreuz, Stiftsbibl. 153, f. 110v (s. xii) attributes a passage from Thierry's tractate to "magister Tirricus."[5] The attribution to Thierry is important because in all extant manuscripts the text is anonymous. Clarembald notes that Thierry's tractate was already found in the Roman archives and that his teacher was "totius Europe philosophorum precipuus."[6]

102 Lépinois and Merlet, *Cartul.* 1, 142 (26 February 1134). Ch. Métais, *Cartul.* 1, 30 (dated to 1124-27) and 1, 127 (dated 1137).

103 R. W. Southern, *Med. Humanism*, p. 66, writes: "We may be sure that the chancellor of the cathedral had a general responsibility for the school — that is he probably appointed a school master." Prof. Southern shows no reason why at Chartres the appointment was made by the chancellor rather than by the bishop himself. The city of Poitiers had two, perhaps three, schools in the twelfth century. But the bishop had no chancellor. His *magister scole (scolarum)* looked after at least some of his correspondence. The appointment was obviously made by the bishop. See N. M. Haring, "Zur Geschichte der Schulen von Poitiers," *Archiv für Kulturgesch.* 47 (1965) 23-47. Southern's description of the chancellor's "many duties" (p. 67) in Chartres lacks confirmation and is not made more convincing by the remark that among other duties the chancellor had "to live as befitted a dignitary of the church" (p. 67). By thus multiplying the chancellor's «duties» Prof. Southern hopes to disprove Clerval's (p. 164) claim that Gilbert taught while he was chancellor in Chartres. We shall see that Gilbert did teach there.

104 Another example is "magister Frumoldus Ostreuadensis archdiaconus" mentioned in a charter issued in 1161 by Andrew, bishop of Arras (1161-73). Cf. N. Haring, *Life and Works of Clarembald of Arras, Studies and Texts* 10 (Toronto, 1965) 10. Master Clarembald was archdeacon of Arras. At Poitiers, Master Arnold Qui-non-ridet was archdeacon of Brioux. See N. Haring, "Bischof Gilbert II. von Poitiers und seine Erzdiakone," *Deutsches Archiv* 21 (1965) 150-172.

1 *Notices et extr.* 1 (Paris, 1890) 49-50.

2 The latest edition is found in N. M. Haring, *Life and Works of Clarembald of Arras* pp. 225-226.

3 Latest edition in N. M. Haring, *Commentaries on Boethius by Thierry of Chartres and his School, Texts and Studies* 20 (Toronto, 1971) 556-575.

4 Latest edition in N. M. Haring, *Life and Works*, pp. 226-249.

5 Haring, *Commentaries*, pp. 46 and 558.

6 Haring, *Life and Works*, p. 226. The reason for sending the book to Rome is not indicated. Presumably it was a sort of voluntary censorship. Cf. G. B. Flahiff, "Ecclesiastical Censorship of Books in the Twelfth Century," *MS* 4 (1942) 1-22.

In his commentary on Boethius, *De Trinitate,* Clarembald mentions two "venerable teachers" who had taught him: Hugh of Saint-Victor (d. 1141) and Theodoricus Brito both of whom tried to answer his "obstinate" questions concerning the precise meaning of *doctrinalis* and *disciplinalis.*[7] In the letter[8] to his friend Odo, Clarembald confesses that he would not have dared to write the commentary, had he not been able to rely on the lectures of Theodoricus Brito and Hugh of Saint-Victor under both of whom he had studied the work with intensity: "apud quos in hoc opere uehementem operam dedi."[9]

These remarks show that he attended Hugh's lectures at Paris before 1141, the year of Hugh's death. He seems to have attended Thierry's lectures at the same time and in the same city. Clarembald's treatise on the Trinity contains certain passages found in Thierry's *Commentum* although he does not openly attribute these passages to Thierry.[10] This allows us to conclude that the author of the *Commentum* was the same Theodoricus Brito. More recently it has been shown that Clarembald copied a passage from Thierry's lectures on Boethius, *Contra Eutychen* when he wrote his *Tractatulus* on Genesis.[11]

For Clarembald Thierry is *doctor meus*: "Ad huius obscuritatis elucidationem doctor meus multa philosophica induxit."[12] Thierry and Hugh are *doctores mei* or *nostri doctores.*[14] Clarembald also attended lectures delivered by both these teachers on Boethius, *De Hebdomadibus.* He tells us that both held that the term *enunciatio* in Boethius was to be understood *complexiue,*[15] and that the word *bonum* at the end of the treatise was to be interpreted as *bonum ordinatum*: "Et hoc quidem modo tam mihi quam meis doctoribus uisum est hoc loco bonum accipi debere."[16]

The works we have shown to have been written by Clarembald's teacher Theodoricus Brito[17] are all anonymous, though a passage preserved in MS Heiligenkreuz, Stiftsb. 153, f. 110, is explicitly assigned

7 Clarembald, *De Trin.,* introd. 10; ed. Haring 69.

8 Clarembald, *Ep. ad Odonem* 3; ed. Haring 64. This letter submits the commentary to Odo for approval.

9 *Ibid.*

10 See *Life and Works;* ed. Haring 28-33.

11 *Commentaries on Boethius by Thierry of Chartres and His School;* ed. Haring, *Studies and Texts* 20 (1971) 31.

12 *De Trin.* 2, 25; ed. Haring 117.

13 *Life and Works,* pp. 69, 88 (meis doctoribus uisum est), 97, 198, 221.

14 *Life and Works,* pp. 95 and 129.

15 *De Hebdomadibus* 15; ed. Haring 198: "Et secundum quidem meos doctores enunciationis uocabulum hoc loco complexiue legendum est."

16 *De Hebdomadibus* 47; ed. Haring 221.

17 *Commentum in Boethii lib. de Trinitate. Lectiones in Boethii lib. de Trinitate* and *Contra Eutychen. Abbreuiatio Monacensis. De sex dierum operibus.*

to "magister Tirricus". In addition, the *Commentarius Victorinus* contains a strong indication that its author's name was Thierry on the strength of a marginal note on f. 95 of MS Paris, Bibl. nat. 14489, where the writer denounces "the heresy of the old hags who swear by the three parts of God." The marginal note entered on f. 95 by the same hand reads: "Theodericus an sint tres partes in deo."[18] Since Thierry's name does not occur in the text, the remark must have been entered by an annotator who considered or knew Thierry to be the author. And since the manuscript itself dates back to about 1160-70, the scribe responsible for the marginal annotation was Thierry's contemporary who took it for granted that readers would know Thierry without further identification. Obviously, for him as for others there was but one Thierry.

It has been common knowledge for almost a century[19] that a certain Theodoricus Brito wrote a commentary on Cicero's *De inuentione*. Thierry's *Lectiones* contains a remark which could be interpreted as a reference to a work on logic: "Sed in logica de hoc satis diximus."[20] Although this "logica" — if it means a written work — has not yet been identified, a recent discovery by K. M. Fredborg[21] establishes Thierry as the author of a fragmentary commentary on the *Ad Herennium*. It is found MS Berlin, Staatsb. lat. oct. 161 (Phillipps 9672), f. 36v-75v (s. xii), which also contains Thierry's commentary on the *De inuentione* (f. 1-36v). The author refers to this work in his introduction to the *Ad Herennium* by saying: "In superiori commentario que super primam rethoricam (= *De inuentione*), conscripsimus ..."[22] This means that Theodoricus Brito also wrote the commentary on the *Ad Herennium*. John of Salisbury notes that he attended lectures on rhetoric given by Master Thierry.[23] He recalls that Master Thierry occasionally lectured on Aristotle's *Topics*.[24]

In his commentary on the *De inuentione* Thierry casts a stone at certain "scolastice disputationis histriones" (heavy-fisted clowns) who set up camp outside his palace only to vilify him: "ut in partibus suis studio pellacie Theodoricum mentiantur."[25] This seems to mean that students

---

18 *Commentaries on Boethius*; ed. Haring 41.

19 See the paper by P. Thomas in *Mél. Ch. Graux* (Paris, 1884) 42.

20 *Lectiones de Trin.* 4, 44; ed. Haring 201. The *Abbreuiatio Monacensis* (p. 377) reads: "Sed in logica satis dicitur."

21 K. M. Fredborg, "The Commentary of Thierry of Chartres on Cicero's De inuentione," *Univ. de Copenhague: Cahiers de l'Institut du moyen âge grec et latin* 7 (1972) 1-36. The *accessus* to this work has been edited by N. Haring in MS 26 (1964) 281-286.

22 K. M. Fredborg, p. 8. In the transcript on p. 9, line 3, the word namque should be divided into nam que.

23 *Metal.* II, 10; p. 80.

24 *Metal.* II, 10; ed. Webb, p. 91: "Magister Theodericus, ut memini, Topica non Aristotilis sed Trecasini Drogonis irridebat. Eadem tamen quandoque docuit."

25 Transcribed by P. Thomas in *Mél. Ch. Graux* (Paris, 1884) 41-42: "scolastice disputationis histriones inanium uerborum pugnis armati tales quidem mea castra secuntur sed extra palatium

attracted "only by the bright light of his name" — *sola nominis aura* —
attended the lectures of "clowns" who capitalized on his presence. This
Thierry, as we have noted, calls himself Theodoricus Brito, said to be "a
man of an uncivilized nation who garbles his words and is disorderly in
both mind and body."[26] In an autobiographical aside the commentator
tells us that "Envy" says these things about him and "Rumour" (*fama*)
spreads them: "Theodoricum ubique accusat, ignominiosis nominibus
appellat."[27] Among ordinary people they defame him as "Boetum
crasso in aere natum."[28] Among religious people they call him a
necromancer or heretic, among scholars a man who corrupts the young
by offering lectures only to more advanced students.[29]

We have thus established an author by the name of Theodoricus
(Theodericus, Terricus, Therricus) Brito. The epithet Brito means that
he was a Breton, a man born in Brittany. He wrote a commentary on
Cicero's *De inuentione* and the *Ad Herennium*, both still extant, the former
in seven manuscripts.[30] At a certain point of time he turned to theology
and authored such works as the *Commentum* on Boethius, *De Trinitate*[31]
and a tractate on the opening chapters of *Genesis*.[32] His lectures on three
Opuscula Sacra have survived in original[33] and abbreviated form.[34] We
have seen that the *Commentarius Victorinus*[35] is attributed to Thierry by a
contemporary scribe.

The progression from the Liberal Arts to theology was nothing
unusual. Abelard, for example, returned from Brittany to "France"
(*Francia*) mainly to "devote himself to theology."[36] Gilbert of Poitiers is
likewise known to have been active in both fields.[37] In a similar fashion
Thierry's first love was the study of the seven liberal arts. A somewhat

---

quos sola nominis aura hinc detulit ut in partibus suis studio pellacie Theodoricum mentiantur."
The term "camp" is also used by Abelard, *Hist. cal.*; ed. J. Monfrin, *Bibl. des textes philos.* (Paris, 1962)
66: "Extra ciuitatem in monte Sancte Genovefe scolarum castra posui."

26   P. Thomas, p. 42: "Ecce Theodoricus Brito, homo barbarice nationis, uerbis insulsus, corpore ac mente incompositus."

27   Thomas, p. 42.

28   *Ibid.*

29   *Ibid.*

30   They are listed by K. M. Fredborg (p. 1) who credits Prof. J. O. Ward (Univ. of Sydney) with
the discovery of MS London, B. M. Harl. 5060 (s. xv).

31   N. M. Haring (ed.), *Commentaries on Boethius,* pp. 57-116.

32   *Ibid.*, pp. 555-575.

33   *Ibid.*, pp. 125-256.

34   *Ibid.*, pp. 317-477.

35   *Ibid.*, pp. 481-528.

36   *Hist. cal.* ed. Monfrin, p. 67: "reuersus sum in Franciam, maxime ut de diuinitate ad-
discerem."

37   *Metal.* II, 10; ed. Webb, p. 32: "Repperi magistrum Gilebertum ipsumque audiui in logicis et
diuinis."

apocryphical story tells us that Abelard, who admits that he was "completely ignorant" of mathematics,[38] secretly attended lectures on
mathematics delivered by "magister Tirricus".[39] Here again the
narrator must have taken it for granted that his readers knew who this
Master Tirricus was. After all, as Clarembald puts it, Thierry the Breton
was "the foremost philosopher of all Europe."

He was the object of enormous admiration. The translator from
Arab into Latin of Ptolemy's *Planisphere,* dedicated to Thierry in 1143,
addresses his former teacher as follows: "Tibi, inquam, diligentissime
preceptor Theodorice,[40] quem haut equidem ambigam Platonis animam
celitus mortalibus accommodatam. Quo factum est principaliter ut ...
unum te latini studii patrem astronomie primitiis donandum
iudicarim."[41] The student hails his former master as "primam sum-
mamque hoc tempore philosophie sedem atque inmobiliter fixam uaria
tempestate fluitantium studiorum anchoram."[42] A critic may, of course,
question the identity. It is his burden to prove that this *latini studii pater*
is not Thierry the Breton. On the strength of the dedication it appears
that in 1143 Thierry was still considered the "seat of philosophy" rather
than of theology.

Another student, the future Archbishop Adalbert of Mainz (1137-41),
studied under "Thedricus" in the early thirties. Adalbert's biographer
states that Thierry's reputation was based on his courses of the triuium:

> Cepit ei dici uirtus et fama Thedrici
> Qui fuit orator et rethor et artis amator
> Gramatice logice uitam ducendo pudice
> Cuius erat genitrix Britannia, Francia nutrix.
> Huius ut audiuit famam non sequitur iuit
> Visere doctorem ...[43]

The poet repeats that Adalbert studied rhetoric, grammar, and logic under Thierry. He makes no mention of theology:

> Discipulus dici dignatur et esse Thedrici
> Rethoricos flores uariosque legendi colores
> Gramaticus fieri 'logicusque laborat haberi:
> His tribus intentus set non ad singula lentus.[44]

38 Abelard, *Dialectica* II, 2; ed. L. M. de Rijk (Assen, 1956) 59.

39 B. Pez, *Thes. anecd. novus* 3 (Augsburg 1721) p. xxii. R. L. Poole, *Illustrations of the Hist. of
Mediaeval Thought and Learning* (London, 1920) 315.

40 Abelard, *Hist. cal.* ed. Monfrin, pp. 64-65) calls William of Champeaux "preceptor meus".

41 J. L. Heiberg (ed.), *Claudii Ptolomaei opera astron. minora* (Leipzig, 1907), p. clxxxvi.

42 *Ibid.*

43 *Vita Adalberti*; ed. Ph. Jaffé, *Mon. Moguntina: Bibl. rer. Germ.* 3 (Berlin, 1866) 589, vv. 686-691.
Before going to Paris Adalbert had studied in Reims.

44 *Vita Adalberti*, vv. 709-712; ed. Jaffé, p. 590.

Bernard Silvestris dedicated to Thierry the philosophical poem entitled *Cosmographia*, composed at Tours during the reign of Pope Eugene III (1145-53): "Bernardus Siluestris Terrico salutem. Terrico ueris scientiarum titulis doctori famosissimo Bernardus Siluestris opus suum."[45]

In a work against Abelard, written about 1140-42, Abbot Thomas of Morigny mentions that he wrote a *Tractatus de rebus uniuersalibus ad magistrum Theodoricum*.[46] The dedications we have quoted contain no reference to Paris or Chartres. But a rubric to the *Cosmographia* reads: "Incipit magistri Bernardi *Megacosmos* editus ad uirum litteratissimum et philosophantium amantissimum magistrum Therricum Carnotensis ecclesie cancellarium et archidiaconum."[47] The note shows that, at least in the eyes of the annotator, this *doctor famosissimus* was a chancellor and archdeacon of the cathedral of Chartres.

Thierry's association with Chartres is confirmed by the chronicler Master Balderic of Trier who has recorded a pompous voyage from Trier to Frankfort made by Archbishop Albero (1131-52) to attend an Imperial Curia convoked by Conrad III (1093-1152). The date was either March 1147 or August 1149. Forty barges were involved and in the archbishop's company were Master Gerland of Besançon and Master Thierry of Chartres: "Magistrum quoque Iarlandum Bisintinum et magistrum Teodericum Carnotensem — duos fama et gloria doctores nostri temporis excellentissimos — secum in sua ducens nauali cammenata in illorum disputatione et collatione delectatus est et a curia domum reuersus decentibus donis largiter honoratos ad propria letos remisit."[48]

Are we to assume that "the foremost philosopher of Europe", Thierry the Breton, was different from Albero's companion, Master Thierry of Chartres, who is described as a teacher "most excellent in both fame and glory in our day" (Balderic) or different from the scholar whom the *incipit* quoted above presents as "uirum litteratissimum et philosophantium amantissimum magistrum Therricum Carnotensis ecclesie cancellarium"? We know but one Thierry the Breton who wrote works dealing with both the liberal arts and theology. By calling him "magistrum Teodericum Carnotensem" Master Balderic indicates the place where he lived at the time, just as "Hugo

45 C. S. Barach and J. Wrobel (edd.), *Bernardus Silvestris, De mundi uniuersitate* (Cosmographia), *Bibl. phil. med. aetatis* 1 (Innsbruck, 1876) 5.

46 *Disputatio anon. abbatis*; PL 180, 321A.

47 Transcribed from MS London, B.M. Royal 15. A XXXII, f. 3 (s. xiii) by A. Vernet, "Une épitaphe inédite de Thierry de Chartres," *Receuil de Travaux offert à M. Clovis Brunel: Mém. et doc. publ. par la Soc. de l'Ecole des Chartes* 12, 2 (Paris, 1955) 663.

48 Balderic, *Gesta Alberonis* 26; MGH SS 8, 257. Concerning the identity of Master Gerland see L. M. de Rijk, *Garlandus compotista. Dialectica. Wijsgerige Teksten en Studies* 3 (Assen, 1959) pp. ix-xi.

Parisiensis" means Hugh of Saint-Victor.[49] For the same reason they referred to Robert of Melun who was born in England.

The theologian Master Thierry of Chartres made such a name for himself that, together with Peter Lombard, Adam of Petit-Pont, and others, he was chosen to attend the papal consistory held in 1148 after the council of Reims.[50] Present at the trial was Master Walter of Mortagne, later bishop of Laon (1155-74) who is the author of a letter addressed to Master Thierry: "Magistro Theoderico Gualterus salutem. Peruenit ad nos quod dicere soleatis essentiam dei non ubique adesse. Quod de uobis credere non potui ..."[51] Since Walter does not call himself bishop it is thought that he wrote the letter before 1155. He had no written evidence and could not believe that Thierry would teach such a doctrine. It is obvious that Walter thought highly of Thierry's competence in theology.

Much less impressed is R. W. Southern who goes as far as to state: "Thierry was not a theologian."[52] Southern's equally mistaken claim that Thierry "has left nothing that is not a record of his lectures"[53] belongs to the same category of inaccuracies.

Thierry's connection with Chartres was also known to the author of the *Metamorphosis Golie* who saw Thierry in Paris and was struck by the sharpness of his tongue:

> Ibi doctor cernitur ille Carnotensis
> Cuius lingua uehemens truncat uelut ensis.[54]

Thierry's sarcastic tongue is also evidenced by a remark made by John of Salisbury: "Master Thierry, I remember, ridiculed the *Topics* as being the work not of Aristotle but of Drogo of Troyes."[55] John of Cornwall, who could recall the christological debates between Master Peter Lom-

---

49 Wibald, *Ep.* 167; ed. Ph. Jaffé, *Mon. Corbeiensia: Bibl. rer. Germ.* 1 (Berlin, 1864) 278: "Vidimus Anselmum Laudunensem (d. 1117), Wilhelmum Parisiensem (d. 1121), Albericum Remensem (d. 1141), Hugonem Parisiensem (d. 1141) et alios plurimos."

50 Geoffrey of Auxerre, *Scriptura* 28; ed. Haring, *Analecta Cist.* 22 (1966) 35. For other masters in attendance see N. Haring, "Notes on the Council and the Consistory of Reims (1148)," MS 28 (1966) 39-59.

51 L. d'Achéry, *Spicil.* 3 (Paris 1723) 522. Cf. L. Ott, *Unters. zur theol. Briefliteratur der Frühscholastik,* Beiträge 34 (1937) 188-213.

52 *Med. Humanism,* p. 81.

53 *Ibid.*

54 Thomas Wright, *The Latin Poems Commonly attributed to Walter Mapes* (London 1841) 28, vv. 189-190. R. B. Huygens, "Mitteilungen aus Handschriften," *Studi medievali,* serie terza 3 (1962) 771.

55 *Metal.* IV, 24; p. 191. An Archdeacon of Troyes called Drogo witnessed charters in 1104 and 1114. *Gall. chr.* 12, 252E and 257E. He witnessed as "Drogo magister" in 1100 (or later). Ch. Lalore, *Catul. de l'Abbaye de Saint-Loup de Troyes, Coll. des principaux cartul. du dioc. de Troyes* 1 (Paris, 1875) 13, no. 3. In the following charter (p. 13), dated 2 April 1103, his name Drogo appears without any title.

bard and his two opponents Robert of Melun, later bishop of Hereford (1163-67), and Maurice of Sully, later bishop of Paris (1160-96),[56] could also remember a typical remark of his Master Thierry: "Scio enim non nullos insolentes ... quos magister meus Thiodericus tum uero nomine pharaones tum ironice fratres suos appellare consueuit."[57] It may well be that he was the "scolaris magister Terricus" who, as Abelard relates,[58] spoke up at the Council of Soissons in 1121 when the papal legate Conon, cardinal of Preneste (1111-23), blundered in a point of theology.[59] When Abelard wrote his *Historia*, ca. 1135, he was in all likelihood not very familiar with this "Terricus quidam scolaris magister" who had stood up for him in 1121. But it is worth recalling that not long after the council Abelard withdrew to a solitude in the neighbourhood of Troyes.[60] About the year 1125 he became abbot of Saint-Gildas where he spent some six to eight years.[61] Since he did not return to Paris until about 1136, it is understandable that he had lost touch with events in Paris for a decade and a half.

When William of Tyre after some twenty years of study in France and Italy (1145-1165) returned to his native land, he remembered with gratitude a number of teachers under whom he had studied the liberal arts: Master Bernard the Breton (later bishop of Cornouailles), Master Peter Helias of Poitiers, and Master Ivo of Chartres.[62] These masters, we learn, had all been students of Master Thierry *for a long time*: "Hi omnes magistri Theoderici senioris uiri litteratissimi per multa tempora auditores fuerunt."[63] Thierry is qualified as *senior* to indicate that he was advanced in years. The comparative *senior* is generally considered to denote a person between forty-five and sixty years of age.[64] The expression is not used to distinguish Master Thierry from another but younger Thierry. In a similar manner Peter Abelard is described as *iunior* to denote that he was then between twenty and forty years of age.[65]

56 *Eulogium ad Alex. papam tertium*; ed. Haring, MS 13 (1951) 268.

57 C. Greith, *Spicil. Vaticanum* (Frauenfeld, 1838) 99.

58 *Hist. calamitatum*; ed. Monfrin, p. 88.

59 *Ibid.*, p. 88. Jean Châtillon, "Les écoles de Chartres et de Saint-Victor", *Settimane di studio del Centro italiano di studi sull'alto medioevo* 19 (Spoleto, 1972) 800, comes to the conclusion: "Le *Terricus* de l'*Historia calamitatum* est donc certainement un maître chartrain."

60 *Hist. calamitatum*; ed. Monfrin, p. 92.

61 R. L. Poole, *Illustrations*, p. 135.

62 *Hist. hieros.* XIX, 12; ed. R. B. C. Huygens, "Guillaume de Tyr", *Latomus* 21 (1962) 822: "Fuerunt autem nobis ... in liberalibus artibus doctores precipui uiri uenerabiles et pia recordatione digni ... magister Bernardus Brito ... magister Petrus Helie ... magister Iuo".

63 *Hist. hieros.* XIX, 12; ed. Huygens, p. 822.

64 "An elderly person".

65 *Glossa in Porphyrium*; ed. V. Cousin, *Ouvrages inédits d'Abélard* (Paris, 1836) 553, or Mario dal Pra, *Pietro Abelardo. Scritti filosofici* (Rome, 1954) 3: MS Paris, Bibl. nat. Lat. 13368, f. 156.

Considering that, in 1145, William met a generation of scholars trained *for a long time* by Master Thierry we may reach the conclusion that Thierry taught in Paris as early as the late twenties. William's account also suggests that in 1145 Thierry was no longer in Paris. We have seen that in 1148 Geoffrey of Auxerre listed him as "magister Theodoricus Carnotensis." At Chartres he became chancellor and archdeacon of the cathedral: "Obiit magister Teodoricus cancellarius et archidiaconus Alme Marie."[66] He bequeathed his library to the cathedral, including his *Eptatheucon (Bibliotheca septem liberalium artium)*, such books of Roman Law as Justinian's *Institute,* the *Novellae,* the *Digest,* and fifty-five other volumes.[67] The *Eptatheucon* whose prologue identifies Thierry as its author ("Incipit prologus Theoderici in Eptatheucon") is a collection of texts (in two volumes) to be used as basic writings for the study of the liberal arts.[68] It perished during a bombardment on 26 May 1944 but has survived on microfilm (MSS Chartres, Bibl. mun. 497 and 498).

The *Epitaphium Theodorici,* edited by W. Wattenbach from a manuscript which belonged to Saint-Pierre of Hautmont (OSB) near Maubeuge, arr. Avesnes, Nord, implies that Thierry died at Chartres:

> Emicuit nato Britannia, risit alumpno
> Gallia, Carnotis corpore, queque suo.[69]

Alexander Neckam (1157-1217) calls him a monk in a context referring to Gilbert of Poitiers, Alberic, Abelard, and Gualo:

---

66 E. de Lépinois and L. Merlet, *Cartul. de Notre-Dame de Chartres* 3 (Chartres, 1862) 206. The death of a Master Thierry was also registered at Sainte-Geneviève (Paris): "Obiit magister Terricus, canonicus noster ad succurrendum" (December 6).

67 *Cartul.* 3, 206. Legal studies are also reflected in Clarembald's *Tractatulus* where he claims that the books of Roman Law are an imitation of the first five books of the Old Testament. *Tractatulus* 5; ed. Haring, p. 228. Legal studies are indicated in the legal volumes donated to the Abbey of Bec by Bishop Philip of Bayeux (1142-62), probably one of Gilbert's students. See PL 150, 780D: "Decreta Gratiani, Codex, Tres Partes et Digesta noua, Digesta uetera, Inforciata et Liber autenticorum, Liber Institutionum et tres libri Codicis, Instituta Iustiniani Minora". Works of Roman Law at Poitiers in the 9th century are still preserved in MS Paris, Bibl. nat. Lat. 4505: "In hoc uolumine ecclesie beatissimi Hilarii Maioris Pictauiensis continentur: Sexdecim libri et leges Theodosii Imperatoris, quattuor Nouell., Titus Gaius. Pauli Sententie, Leges Gregoriane" (f. 1). Ivo, dean of Chartres (d. 1165), donated his books to Saint-Jean-en Vallée. A chancellor called Bernard donated 24 volumes to the cathedral of Chartres: "Obiit Bernardus subdiaconus et cancellarius sancte Marie qui dedit huic ecclesie xxiiii uolumina librorum". We do not know what happened to Gilbert's library.

68 The prologue has been edited by E. Jeauneau, "Note sur l'école de Chartres," *Studi medievali,* terza serie, V, 2 (1964) 34-35. It was first analyzed by A. Clerval, *Les écoles,* pp. 220-248. See also *Cat. gén.* 11 (Paris, 1890) 211-214. G. Lacombe, *Aristoteles latinus* (Rome, 1932) 467-468. L. Minio-Paluello, *Twelfth Century Logic* 2 (Rome, 1958) pp. xxxii-xxxv.

69 "Beschreibung einer Handschrift mittelalterl. Gedichte," *Sitzungsb.* Berlin (1895) 149.

En Porretanus, Albricus, Petrus Alardi,
Terricus monachus, Gualo sophista potens.[70]

Gualo is also associated with Thierry by another poet who confesses
that "Terricus" inspired his philosophy:

Carmina Guallo mihi, Terricus philosofiam
Inspirat. Nostrum pectus utrumque capit.
Lingua diserta sonat Terrici philosophiam
Gualonis redolent carmina nostra stilum.[71]

Unfortunately, we know too little about Gualo "sophista potens" to
draw any conclusion from this association. It has been suggested that
part of Alexander Neckam's information rests on a commentary by
Thierry on Martianus Capella. Proposing various interpretations of the
word *Cibele* Neckam notes: "Vel secundum magistrum Theodoricum
mater deorum i.e. planetarum Cibele i.e. terra dicitur."[72] The question
is then raised whether one strikes fire from a flint. Alexander tells us
that on this matter Master Thierry had a theory of his own: "Magister
autem Theodoricus dicit ignem non de silice prouenire sed aera inter
duos lapides clausum nimio impetu concurrentes in igneam naturam
uersum esse."[73] The present tense *dicit* is a strong indication that
Neckam, who studied in Paris before 1186, used a written source. We
also learn from Neckam that concerning the Milky Way Thierry
proposed his own explanation: "Magister autem Theodoricus
altissimam partem celi eam esse et ideo uideri nobis stellas sine in-
teruallo coniunctas et multum lumen reddere."[74] Thierry's keen interest
in cosmology is well known through his *Tractatus de sex dierum operibus*.

It has even been suggested that Walter Burleigh (1275-1337) has
recorded Thierry's view on Socrates: "Hic (= Socrates), ut ait
Theodoricus, cum esset disciplina omnium philosophorum summus,
adeo studiosus fuit quod neque a mulieribus discere quid utile opinatus
fuerit philosophie indignum. Vnde et Diotimam non erubuit appellare
magistram."[75]

A long epitaph, published by A. Vernet,[76] celebrates Thierry as "the

70 A. Vernet, "Une épitaphe", p. 666, transcribed from MS Paris, Bibl. nat. Lat. 11867, f. 230v.
71 A. Vernet, "Une épitaphe", p. 662.
72 Transcribed by E. Jeauneau, "Note sur l'école de Chartres," p. 11, from Neckam's commentary on the *De nuptiis Mercurii* in MS Oxford, Bodl. Digby 221 (SC 1822) and MS Cambridge,
Trin. Coll. 883 (R. 14. 9), f. 38-63 (s. xiv). The idea that the earth is the mother of the planets is
based on Thierry's view that the stars were made from the water of the earth. *Tractatus de sex dierum
operibus* 28; ed. Haring 567.
73 E. Jeauneau, "Note sur l'école," p. 12.
74 E. Jeauneau, p. 13.
75 W. Burleigh, *Liber de vita et moribus philosophorum* 30; ed. H. Knust (Tübingen, 1886) 120-122.
76 "Une épitaphe," pp. 669-670.

worthy successor of Aristotle,[77] as the first scholar to comment on the (Prior) *Analytics* and the *Elenchi*.[78] The poet then insinuates that Thierry withdrew to a monastery where he "learned that he knew nothing" and where he forgot that he used to be addressed as *doctor*. With a true flair for Chartrain nomenclature the poet concludes:

> Doctorem, protholeuitam simul et logothetem
> Hunc habuit Cartis uix habitura parem.[79]

Vernet's suggestion that Thierry whom Neckam calls a monk became a Cistercian[80] is strengthened by the fact that the Cistercian Helinand of Froidmont (d. ca. 1229) incorporated almost the entire *Tractatus de sex dierum operibus* in his *World Chronicle*.[81] He was obviously so impressed that he made use of it in a Christmas sermon.[82] A relatively high proportion of the extant manuscripts containing works by Thierry were kept in Cistercian libraries.[83]

An early expression of disapproval of Thierry's *Tractatus* on Genesis has been suspected in the *Tractatus de operibus sex dierum*[84] by the Benedictine Abbot Ernald of Bonneval (d. after 1156) whom we met with Master Robert Petit on 13 June 1151.[85] However, speaking of the divine *unitas* Ernald gives Thierry's derivation: "unitas quasi *onitas* i.e. entitas siue essentialitas. Vnde et apud Graecos *on* i.e. substantialis".[86] He also

---

77   "Dignus Aristotilis successor Teodericus."

78   "Une épitaphe," p. 670. The text of the *Prior Analytics* found in Thierry's *Eptatheucon* (MS Chartres, Bibl. mun. 497, f. 296-318 and 498, f. 1-11) has been shown to agree with a passage quoted by Abelard. L. Minio-Paluello, *Twelfth-Century Logic* 2 (Rome, 1958) p. xxxv. Alexander Neckam confirms Thierry's use of the *Elenchi*. See the excerpts from his *Corrogationes Promethei* edited by P. Meyer, *Not. et extr.* 35, 2 (Paris 1897) 677. See also L. Minio-Paluello, "The Ars disserendi of Adam of Balsham," *Med. and Ren. Studies* 3 (1954) 119 and 161. A. Vernet, "Une épitaphe," p. 665. Both works are represented in Thierry's *Eptatheucon*. A. Clerval, *Les écoles,* p. 222.

79   "Une épitaphe," p. 670, vv. 57-58. At Chartres a subdecanus was a ypodecanus, a subcantor a ypocantor. Cf. L. and R. Merlet, "Dignitaires de l'église de Notre-Dame de Chartres," *Archives du dioc. de Chartres* 5 (Paris, 1900) 47 and 71.

80   "Une épitaphe," p. 668. Vernet proposes Vaux-de-Cernay, arr. Rambouillet, dioc. of Paris. Cf. *Gallia chr.* 7 (Paris, 1744) 885-898. Founded in 1118, it adopted the Cistercian rule on 17 September 1147.

81   MS London, B.M. Cotton Claudius B. IX., f. 1-10v (s. xv) and MS Vat. Reg. Lat. 535, f. 2-12 (s. xiii). See N. Haring, *Commentaries on Boethius*, pp. 50-52.

82   *Sermo* 2; PL 212, 489D-490D. Helinand's use in this sermon of Thierry's *Tractatus* was first pointed out by M.-D. Chenu, "Une définition pythagoricienne de la vérité au moyen âge," *Archives d'hist. doctr. et litt. du moyen âge* 28 (1961) 7-13.

83- *Commentaries on Boethius;* ed. N. Haring, pp. 25-34.

84   PL 189, 1515A.

85   Ch. Métais, *Cartul. de Notre-Dame de Josaphat* 1 (Chartres, 1911) 242. During the reign of Bishop Robert (1156-64) he was with Dean Ivo. Métais, *Cartul.* 1, 276.

86   *Comm. in Ps.* 132; PL 189, 1572A. Compare Thierry, *Commentum* II, 22; ed. Haring 75: "Unitas quasi *onitas* ab on Greco i.e. entitas." *Lectiones de Trin.* II, 48 (p. 170): "Unde et unitas dicitur i.e. *onitas* quasi entitas omnium rerum." *Glosa* V, 18 (p. 297): "Unitas enim ipsa est *onitas* atque entitas.

uses Thierry's *intellectibilitas*, found in Thierry's lectures.[87]

We have already mentioned that the compiler of the *Sententie* preserved in MS Heiligenkreuz, Stiftsb. 153, f. 109-132 (s. xii), includes an excerpt (f. 110v) from Thierry's *Tractatus de sex dierum operibus*. The author of the *Liber de solis affectibus* copied a chapter from the same tractate to show that the stars are made of water.[88] It seems that the writer of the *De septem septenis* is the first witness to Thierry's *Commentum* by quoting the sentence: "Ab hac igitur sancta et summa Trinitate descendit quedam perpetuorum trinitas".[89]

P. Duhem[90] discusses an author who lived in Marseille in the middle of the 12th century. In 1140 he began to write a work on astronomy which in view of the numerous astronomical tables (tabulae) Duhem calls "Les tables de Marseille". Like Thierry, the writer holds that the Holy Spirit is the World Soul and the soul of the seven planets. He adds that David (Ps 32, 6) had already expressed this thought. The same author wrote a tract entitled *De compositione astrolabii*. P. Duhem suggests that there was a link between him and Thierry of Chartres. P. Courcelle,[91] on the other hand, thinks that the author knew the commentary on the *De consolatione* written by William of Conches. In a letter of the Chartres collection edited by Merlet reference is made to "Tabulas a uobis quesitas a domino Guillelmo promissas irrequietus ab eo quesiui ..."[92]

Here it may be noted in passing that P. Duhem[93] was the first historian to discover that Cardinal Nicholas of Cusa (d. 1464) used Thierry's *Tractatus de sex dierum operibus* in his *De docta ignorantia*. Later it was found that the cardinal made use of Thierry's gloss on the *De Trinitate* of Boethius.[94]

The question whether Thierry received his first training in Chartres is

---

87   *Comm. in Ps.* 132, hom. 5; PL 189, 1585A. Thierry, *Lect. de Trin.* II, 30 and 32; ed. Haring, p. 164.

88   *Liber de solis affectibus* 49; PL 172, 114D-116A: Thierry, *De sex dierum operibus* 12; ed. Haring, p. 560. The identity was first noticed by E. Jeauneau, "Note sur l'école", p. 19.

89   *Commentum* II, 39; ed. Haring, p. 80: *De septem septenis* 7; PL 199, 961C. Cf. J. A. Robilliard, "Hughes de Saint-Victor", *Revue des sc. phil. et théol.* 43 (1959) 629-630.

90   *Le système du monde* 3 (Paris 1915) 201-215: MS Paris, Bibl. nat. Lat. 14704(I), f. 110-135 (s. xii).

91   "Les commentaires de la Consolation de Boèce", *Arch. d'hist. doctr. et litt. du moyen âge* 14 (1939) 92-94. See also Tullio Gregory, *Anima mundi* (Florence 1955) 135.

92   *Bibl. de l'Ecole des chartes* 16 (1845/5) 463.

93   "Thierry de Chartres et Nicolas de Cues", *Rech. des sc. phil. et théol.* 3 (1909) 525-530.

94   Nicholas of Cusa, *De docta ignorantia;* ed. E. Hoffmann and R. Klibansky, *Nicolai de Cusa opera omnia* 1 (Leipzig, 1932) 14ff. See *Commentaries on Boethius*; ed. Haring, p. 587, *s.v.* N. de Cusa. Although there is no evidence that Thierry wrote Poetry, the possibility cannot be denied. For that reason attention is drawn here to a poem by a Master Thierry whose *incipit* reads: "Vnus dona gerens", preserved in MS Beauvais, Bibl. mun. 11 (3015), f. 167 (s. xii).

an open one. There is no written evidence to show that he studied or taught there before he taught in Paris. The fact that, in the forties, he left Paris for Chartres could be interpreted as a return. There is less uncertainty concerning the study years of Thierry's contemporary, William of Conches, whose keen interest in cosmology seems to flow from the same source.

An examination of Thierry's library does not yield a great deal of information. The necrology of Chartres reads: "Obiit magister Theodoricus, cancellarius et archidiaconus alme Marie, qui dedit huic ecclesie Bibliothecam septem liberalium artium et de legibus Romanis librum Institutionum Iustiniani librum Nouellarum Constitutionem eiusdem et librum Digestorum et preter hec quadraginta quinque uolumina librorum".[95]

This means that he donated some 50-55 volumes to the cathedral, a rather modest number of books according to modern standards. In Thierry's time the place to look for or buy books was not Paris. A. Franklin writes: "La bibliothèque du cloître Notre-Dame du se former lentement par une multitude de petites donations particulières".[96] Such donations were gratefully recorded. On 8 January 1157 bishop Theobald (1144-58) donated three liturgical books. On 3 May 1160 Bishop Peter Lombard bequeathed to the cathedral: "Omnes libros eius glossatos", his *Sentences* and Gratian's *Decretum*. In 1170 a certain Albert left nine liturgical works. Twelve years later Dean Barbedaurus made a similar donation. It is also on record that on 13 July 1208 Bishop Odo Sully (1196-1208) donated a missal and a psalter. Franklin then notes: "Il est probable qu'à l'époque de cette dernière donation, on avait commencé à organizer une bibliothèque dans le cloître".[97] The cathedral library was obviously not the place for Thierry to consult books.

After raising the question whether the abbey of Sainte-Geneviève had a library in Abelard's time Franklin replies: "Tout porte à le croire, mais nous n'en avons aucune preuve positive".[98] Concerning the abbey of Saint-Victor, which received the royal charter in 1113, the same author notes: "Les religieux songèrent presque aussitôt à se créer une bibliothèque".[99] Considering these facts it is extremely unlikely that Thierry should have received his early training in Paris. We know that this is also true of Abelard of whose early education more is known.

---

95 E. de Lépinois and L. Merlet, *Cart. de Notre-Dame de Chartres* 3 (Chartres, 1865) 206.
96 A. Franklin, *Les bibl. anciennes de Paris* 1 (Paris, 1867) 4.
97 Franklin, *Les bibliothèques*, p. 5.
98 *Ibid.*, p. 72.
99 *Ibid.*, p. 137.
100 J. W. Thompson, *The Medieval Library* (Chicago, 1939) 234-235.

But the fact that in the forties Thierry left Paris for Chartres strongly suggests that the ecclesiastical authorities had not forgotten him.

Thanks to the initiative of Bishop Fulbert (1007-29) conditions in Chartres were much more favorable to a scholar. J. W. Thompson holds that "the greatest French cathedral collection of the eleventh century was at Chartres". We find Fulbert sending copies of Cyprian, Porphyry, *Vitas patrum cum psalterio,*[101] Priscian and Donatus to Hildegaire in Poitiers.[102] Fulbert compiled a manual of philosophy including Donatus, Porphyry, and Aristotle's *Categories.*[103] This manual may have inspired Thierry to compose his *Eptatheucon,* still extant in two volumes with a total of 595 folios, which begins with Donatus and Priscian and ends with Ptolemy.[104] There was, as we have seen, no place in Paris where he could have found the 45 works from which he made extracts to present a manual of the liberal arts. The nearest library to find and consult such books was at Chartres. It seems that the libraries of Bec (founded in 1034) and Reims were also well equipped[105] but Thierry is not known to have visited them. Ivo's canonical collections could not have originated in Paris. But it shows the enormous resources of the Chartrian library. The necrology of Chartres mentions that Gilbert of Poitiers took special care of the books kept in the *armarium.*[106] To the flourishing library of the cathedral we should add the remarkable collection in Saint-Père-en-Vallée.[107]

Before we consider William of Conches we may be permitted to transcribe two interesting autobiographical texts from Thierry's commentary on Cicero's *De inuentione.*[108] The introduction[109] reads:

"Vt ait Petronius, nos magistri in scolis relinquemur soli nisi multos palpemus et insidias auribus fecerimus. Ego uero non ita. Nam medius fidius paucorum gratia multis mea prostitui. Sic tamen meum consilium contraxi ut uulgus profanum et farraginem scole petulcans excluderem.

Nam simulatores ingenii exsecrando studium et professores domestici studii dissimulando magistrum tum etiam scolastice disputationis

---

101   *Epist.* 63; PL 141, 232C.

102   Thompson, p. 236.

103   Thompson, p. 235.

104   Clerval, *Les écoles* 222-223.

105   Thompson, p. 233.

106   Lépinois-Merlet, *Cartulaire de Notre-Dame de Chartres* 3 (Chartres, 1865) 168: "librosque armarii diligenter emendatos modis pluribus meliorauit".

107   L. Merlet, "Catal. des livres de l'abbaye de Sainte-Père de Chartres", *Bibl. de l'Ecole des chartes* 15 (1853/4) 263-270. The catalogue dates back to the eleventh century and lists 100 items.

108   Transcriptions of this introduction are found in *Mélanges Charles Graux* (Paris, 1884) 4, by P. Thomas, in *The Journal of Philology* 9 (1880) 6, by R. Ellis, and in H. Suringar, *Hist. crit. scholiastarum* 1 (Leiden 1834) 213.

histriones inanium uerborum pugnis armati tales quidem mea castra
secuntur sed extra palatium quos sola nominis aura hinc detulit ut in
partibus suis studio pellacie Theodoricum mentiantur. Sed, ut ait Persius (4,21): Esto dum non deterius sapiat pannucia Baucis.

Atque hec hactenus ne, cui prefacio incumbit, is eam prolixitatis
arguens forte rescindat ..."

At the end of the first book of Cicero's *De inuentione* Thierry suddenly
interrupts his commentary to insert a passage in which *Inuidia* addresses
Fama.[109] The story Envy has to tell is not a pleasing one:

"Inuidia falso uultu dyaletice subornata Famam sic alloquitur et
fallacibus uerbis, ut solet, aggreditur:

Diua potens! Notum est cunctis quantum rerum in te consistat
momentum. Nam — ut taceam quod auctoritate tui iudicii rerum
humanarum pretium libretur — illud singulare tuum totus predicat or-
bis quod celitum gestamina uicissim assumas: Saturni falcem, fulmen
Iouis, Archadis alas, Gradiui frameam, tum spicula ceca Dione tum
Phebi citharam tum spicula certe Diane.[110]

Te omnes poete ac oratores sequuntur. Te quidam ex sectatoribus
meis summum bonum esse reputant. Te mundus omnis timet offendere.
Te etiam ego ipsa ueneror tum propter antiquam familiaritatem et
amicitiam tum presertim quia sine te scola nostra tapesceret. Cum
igitur et in diuinis et in humanis tam potens appareas, quid est quod
tam patienter opprobria sustines?

Ecce Theodoricus Brito, homo barbarice nationis, uerbis insulsus,
corpore ac mente incompositus, mendacem de se te uocat quod ei
nomen meum super omnes non scribas. Idcirco igitur te uerbis tur-
pissimis persequitur ille superbus inuidus detractor, inimicis supplex,
amicis contumeliosus, sicut etiam sui discipuli de eo adtestantur. Quare
ergo et quod maxime de tuis bonis appetit aut meretur, illud ei sub-
trahe ut ne promeruisse uideatur.

Talibus Inuidie uerbis Fama permota alas concutit, sonos multiplicat,
urbes et nationes duce Inuidia peragrat, rumoribus implet,
Theodoricum ubique accusat, ignominiosis nominibus appellat. Cum
uero rudibus et indiscretis loquitur, Boetum crasso tunc iurat in aere
natum.[111] Quando uero religiosis tunc nicromanticum uel hereticum
uocat. At inter conscios ueritatis tacet. Et si de eo mentio fiat, aliam
hystoriam inceptat.

In scolis uero et scolarium conuentibus mentes conmutat ut
ignominiam eius lucretur. Platonem ei concedit ut rethoricam auferat.

---

109 Six manuscripts have been collated but no variants noted in view of the critical edition
prepared by K. M. Fredborg.

110 Prof. J. Sheridan of St. Michael's University has informed me that the seven *gestamina* sym-
bolize the seven planets: Saturn, Juppiter, Mercury, Mars, Venus, Sun and Moon.

111 Horace, *Ep.* II, 1, 244: "Boeotum in crasso iurares aere natum".

Rethoricam uero uel gramaticam quasi per ypothesim donat ut dyaleticam surripiat. Quidlibet uero potius quam dyaleticam tum mores eius improbos tum negligentiam in studio tum longas interpositiones inculcat. Ad ultimum, cum cetera deficiunt, obicit eum legere prouectis ut nouos detineat uel potius corrumpat ut ulterius non possint apud eum proficere.

> Hactenus Inuidie respondi."

Scholars do not agree on the interpretation or significance of these autobiographical digressions.

William of Conches

John of Salisbury's teacher, William of Conches, must have received his training under Bernard of Chartres. About 1124 he wrote his *Philosophia mundi*[1] which he re-wrote between 1144 and 1149 in the form of a dialogue called *Dragmaticon*.[2] The wide range of his learning is also manifest in his commentaries on Plato's *Timaeus*,[3] on Boethius, *De consolatione*,[4] on Priscian (extant in two redactions),[5] on Juvenal,[6] and Macrobius.[7] There is some uncertainty concerning the *Moralium dogma*,[8] often attributed to William.

The influence of his *Philosophia mundi* has been detected in the works of Helinand of Froidmont (*World Chronicle*), Vincent of Beauvais, Thomas of Cantimpré (*De natura rerum*), Conrad of Megenberg (d. 1374), Radulfus de Longo Campo (Comm. on the *Anticlaudianus*, *Cornicula*), Bartholomew of Parma (*Liber philosophie Boethii*), and the *Cosmographia* preserved in MS Munich *clm* 331, f. 2-9 (s. xiii).[9]

William's writings reveal the sort of interest in cosmology that is

---

1 PL 90, 1127-78 and PL 172, 41-102. See L. M. de Rijk, *Logica modernorum* II, 1 (Assen, 1967) 221-228. A list of 67 manuscripts is found in A. Vernet, "Un remaniement de la *Philosophia* de Guillaume de Conches," *Scriptorium* 1 (1947) 252-255.

2 Edited by G. Gratarolus (Strasbourg, 1567). A. Vernet, "Une remaniement," pp. 255-258 lists almost 70 manuscripts of the work.

3 Edited by E. Jeauneau in *Textes philos. du moyen âge* 13 (Paris, 1965).

4 Excerpts edited by J. M. Parent, *La doctrine de la création dans l'école de Chartres* (Paris-Ottawa, 1938) 122-136.

5 E. Jeauneau, "Deux rédactions des gloses de G. de Conches sur Priscien," *Rech. de théol. anc. et méd.* 27 (1960) 212-247.

6 Excerpts are found in P. O. Kristeller, *Catalogus translat.* 1 (Washington, 1960) 192-195.

7 E. Jeauneau, "Gloses de G. de Conches sur Macrobe," *Archives d'hist. doctr. et litt. du moyen âge* 27 (1960) 17-23.

8 Edited by J. Holmberg (Uppsala, 1929).

9 See E. Jeauneau's article on William in *Lexikon für Theol. und Kirche* 10 (1965) 1131-32. M. Grabmann, *Handschriftliche Forschungen und Mitt. zum Schrifttum des W. von Conches, Sitzungsb. Munich* (1935) 31-54.

characteristic of Thierry's *Tractatus de sex dierum operibus*. Although they must have known each other's writings the common root of their speculations was probably Chartres. William's teaching career seems to have begun in the twenties, for in his *Dragmaticon,* written between 1144 and 1149, he mentions that he had "taught others for twenty years and more."[10] He and Richard the Bishop "used Bernard's method in training their students until they were overwhelmed by the onslaught of the ignorant and gave up", as John of Salisbury words it.[11] Whether he taught in Chartres or Paris or in both cities is a debated question. In William's Commentary on Priscian E. Jeauneau has discovered references to both the Seine and Chartres. His conclusion reads: "l'examen des glosses de Guillaume de Conches sur Priscien faît plutôt pencher la balance en faveur de Chartres."[12]

We have noted that William left Paris (or Chartres) to join the household of Geoffrey the Fair, Count of Anjou (d. 1151).[13] He is thought to have died in 1154. Judging by the number of manuscripts still extant William's popularity surpassed Thierry's by far. In the epitaph attributed to Philip of Harvengt (d. 1183) it is implied that he died in Paris:

> Eius preclaret natu Normantia, uictu
> Gallia, Parisius corpore, mente polus.[14]

Master Bernard

During the period under consideration the name Bernard was very common. It is, for that reason, not always easy to distinguish one Bernard from another. A case in point is Bernard Silvestris whom historians once identified with Bernard of Chartres. Another question may be raised: Was Thierry the brother of Bernard of Chartres?[1] After posing this question R. W. Southern states: "Apart from this relationship he (= Bernard) would scarcely have begun to have a place in the early history of the school."[2] In other words, we are told that "Bernard of Chartres" owes most of his renown to his *brother* Thierry. It would, however, be much more accurate to say that Bernard of Chartres owes most of his present-day reputation as a scholar to John of Salisbury. Ac-

---

10 *Dragmaticon* IV; p. 210: "per uiginti annos et eo amplius alios docui."
11 *Metal.* I, 24; ed. Webb, pp. 57-58.
12 E. Jeauneau, "Deux rédactions," p. 232.
13 T. Gregory, *Anima mundi* (Florence, 1955) 7, n. 5.
14 PL 203, 1393.
1   *Medieval Humanism,* p. 69.
2   *Ibid.*

cording to Southern the *only* evidence for Bernard and Thierry being brothers comes from Otto of Freising.[3] Considering Otto's renown in the field of historiography this evidence should be regarded as quite sufficient.

Otto points to three learned Bretons in his day: Abelard and the two brothers Thierry and Bernard, men of great learning.[4] Without hesitation R. W. Southern declares: "It is certain that the Thierry referred to here was the later chancellor of Chartres."[5] Yet Otto makes no reference to Chartres. For the moment we may agree with Southern's addition that "it is pure hypothesis to say that his brother Bernard was Bernard of Chartres."[6] For Southern, the Bernard mentioned by Otto is the Bernard of Chartres so amply described by John of Salisbury who does not insinuate that Bernard had a brother by the name of Thierry. Although an *argumentum ex silentio* has considerable shortcomings, the fact that Otto calls two Bretons, Thierry and Bernard, men of great learning is undeniable. Hence they were not obscure but well-known men. This can definitely be said of Thierry the Breton whom Clarembald calls "the foremost philosopher of all Europe." Since Otto studied in Paris in the late twenties, the other well-known Breton by the name of Bernard should be associated with the first two decades of the century. We know through John of Salisbury that one of the leading intellectuals in that period was a man known as Bernard of Chartres. No other Bernard is known to have impressed his contemporaries at such an early date. It is, therefore, not unreasonable to assume that Otto had this Bernard in mind when he spoke of the two learned brothers from Brittany.

In this context it may be noted that according to Southern the two brothers denounced by Abelard were Thierry and Bernard of Chartres.[7] But on the same page we are told that it is "pure hypothesis" to say that Thierry's brother was Bernard of Chartres. Abelard neither reveals any names nor does he call them Bretons. He states simply: "Nouimus et duos fratres qui se inter summos connumerant magistros."[8] Southern[9] holds that Abelard "describes Thierry's brother as a very incompetent theologian with an absurd view of the efficacy of

---

3 *Ibid.*

4 *Gesta Frid.* I, 49; MGH SrG 46 (1912) 68: "duo fratres Bernhardus et Theodericus, uiri doctissimi." R. L. Poole, *Studies in Chronology and History* (Oxford, 1934) 242.

5 *Medieval Humanism*, p. 69.

6 *Ibid.*

7 *Ibid.*

8 *Theol. christ.* iv, 80; CCLm 12, 302 (PL 178, 1286A).

9 *Med. Humanism*, p. 69.

the words of consecration in the Mass." But Abelard really finds fault not just with one but with *both* brothers: one who claimed that even a woman could consecrate the Eucharist if the proper words were used, and one who taught that God was "not prior to the world."[10]

In order to evaluate Southern's unfounded claim it should, first of all, be pointed out that in Abelard's day Bernard and Thierry were certainly not the only brothers in the priesthood and that the date of Abelard's reference cannot be disregarded. The first redaction of Abelard's *Theologia christiana,* in which he speaks of the two brothers, is dated to 1122-25. We have seen that in 1135 Abelard could still recall a certain Master Thierry at Soissons. But to say that in 1122-25 Abelard had Thierry of Chartres in mind conflicts with the fact that at that time Thierry was not a theologian but still the "artium studiosissimus inuestigator".[11] In addition, there is nothing to prove that Bernard of Chartres ever taught theology.

We have seen that about the year 1145 William, the future bishop of Tyre, began his studies in Paris. Among those who taught him the liberal arts was "magister Bernardus Brito qui postea in patria unde ortus fuerat episcopus fuit Cornualensis."[12] Just as Master Peter Helias of Poitiers and Master Ivo of Chartres, Bernard the Breton had studied "a long time" (*per multa tempora*) under Master Thierry.[13] This Bernard who studied under Thierry "for a long time" was hardly Thierry's brother, although the possibility cannot be ruled out entirely.

Bernard the Breton, as William notes, later returned to Brittany to become bishop of Cornouailles (*Cornu Galliae*), afterwards called Quimper-Corentin (préf. du Finisterre), today known as Quimper. According to the well-known chronicler Robert de Monte (1154-86) the promotion took place in 1159. Abbot Robert adds that this Bernard had been chancellor of Chartres: "Magister Bernardus Brito, cancellarius ecclesie Carnotensis, factus est episcopus Cornubie in Minori Britannia."[14] He died at Quimper on 2 August 1167.[15] That Bernard the Breton, a native of Moëlan (arr. Quimperlé, Finisterre) was chancellor at Chartres is confirmed by the chronicle of Quimperlé,[16] and by the necrology of

10   *Theol. christ.* iv, 80; CCLm 12, 302 (PL 178, 1286AB).
11   John of Salisbury, *Metal.* I, 5; ed. Webb, p. 16.
12   William of Tyre, *Hist. hieros.* xix, 12; ed. Huygens, p. 822.
13   *Ibid.*
14   *Chronica*; MGH SS 6, 510.
15   P. B. Gams, *Series episcoporum,* p. 605.
16   *Gallia chr.* 14 (Paris, 1856) 877D: "Bernardus, Moelan natus, in Corisopitensi territorio, Carnotensis tamen ecclesie cancellarius, anno 1159 ordinatur e superlaudato Chronico (Kimperlegiensi) ..." L. Maitre and P. de Berthov, *Cartul. de l'Abbaye de Sainte-Croix de Quimperlé, Bibl. Bret. Amoricaine* 4 (Rennes-Paris, 1904) 107-108.

Chartres and of Saint-Denis at Nogent.[17]

William of Tyre met Bernard the Breton in Paris about 1145. Schooled by Thierry Bernard taught the liberal arts. For William he was one of the "scientiarum uasa, thesauri disciplinarum" worthy to be remembered forever.[18]

Although Master Bernard's presence at Paris is thus sufficiently established, it is difficult to distinguish him from another Master and Archdeacon Bernard in Paris whose death is recorded in the obituary: "De domo sancte Marie obiit magister Bernardus sacerdos et archidiaconus qui dedit nóbis ..."[19] The signature of an archdeacon Bernard is found under a charter issued by Bishop Stephen (1124-42), dated to about 1142.[20] During the period from about 1142-46/7 Archdeacon Bernard signed five charters issued by Dean Bartholomew.[21] The name occurs in a charter witnessed in 1144 or 1145 in the palace of King Louis VII.[22] After 1148 Archdeacon Bernard was asked by St. Bernard (1153) to act as a witness.[23] In this document he is called "Magister Bernardus Parisiensis archidiaconus".[24] About the year 1150 he published a statement concerning the Abbey of Saint-Victor[25] and signed a charter drawn up by Gilduin, abbot of the same abbey.[26] In 1154/5 he witnessed a concession made by Adèle, abbess of Montmartre.[27] On 4 September 1154 he was at Saint-Denis together with Master Peter Lombard, Master Walter, Master Manerius, and others.[28] We shall see that Ivo of Chartres whom William of Tyre also mentions was likewise an archdeacon in Paris during this period (1144-1156).

Since Goslen of Lèves, bishop of Chartres (1149-55) died on 2 February 1155, it is not unreasonable to suggest that both Bernard the

17   *Cartul. de Notre-Dame de Chartres* 3, 148: "(Obiit) et Bernardus primo huius ecclesie canonicus deinde cancellarius nouissime uero Corizopitensis ecclesie episcopus." The necrology of Saint-Denis at Nogent is quoted by L. and R. Merlet, "Dignitaires," p. 104: "Bernardus Corisopitensis qui fuit cancellarius Carnotensis."

18   *Hist. hieros.* xix, 12; ed. Huygens, p. 822.

19   B. Guérard, *Cartulaire* 4, 193-194.

20   R. de Lasteyrie, *Cart. gén. de Paris* 1 (Paris, 1887) 280, no. 290.

21   Lasteyrie, *Cartul.* 1, 281, no. 291, with masters Walter and Albert (dated to ca. 1142). *Cartul.* 1, 296 with Master Simon the deacon (dated to 1145-46). *Cartul.* 1, 298 (dated to ca. 1145). *Cartul.* 301 and 302 (dated to 1146-47) with masters Simon the Deacon and Hugh of Champfleury.

22   Lastyerie, *Cartul.* 1, 291, no. 311.

23   Lasteyrie, *Cartul.* 1, 319, no. 353: "magister Bernardus Parisiensis archidiaconus."

24   *S. Bernadi chartae* IV; PL 182, 720B: the same charter.

25   Lasteyrie, *Cartul.* 1, 326: "Magister Gauterus, canonicus Parisiensis" is likewise mentioned in the charter.

26   Lasteyrie, *Cartul.* 1, 331, no. 370.

27   Lasteyrie, *Cartul.* 1, 339, no. 384.

28   J. Ramackers, *Papsturkunden in Frankreich, Abh. der Gesellsch. der Wiss. zu Göttingen*, philos.-hist. Klasse III, 21 (1937) 146.

Breton and Ivo of Chartres were appointed by Bishop Robert (1156-1164). Dean Ivo died in 1165 while Chancellor Bernard was elected bishop of Quimper in 1159 and died there in 1167.

This Bernard cannot be the *senex Carnotensis*[29] described by John of Salisbury. Considering that William of Conches and Richard surnamed the bishop (d. 1182), both John's teachers in grammar, followed the teaching methods adopted by Bernard of Chartres,[30] it is safe to conclude that they had learned those demanding teaching methods at Chartres from "Bernardus Carnotensis, exundantissimus modernis temporibus fons litterarum in Gallia."[31]

John of Salisbury has given a vivid and well-known description of Bernard's *consuetudo*.[32] A letter written by a student to his father stresses Bernard's *disciplina* in the sentence: "Carnotum ubi ego *sub disciplina* domini magistri Bernardi dego."[33] An outstanding student of this *dominus magister Bernardus* was Gilbert of Poitiers.

Gilbert of Poitiers (d. 1154)

Gilbert or rather Gislebert was born in Poitiers. After studying under Master Hilary in his native town[1] he went first to Chartres where he attended lectures given by Master Bernard. Gilbert then turned to Anselm of Laon (d. 1117) and Anselm's brother Ralph (d. 1136) in order to study theology. In 1121 he was a canon in Poitiers where he signed a document.[3] Three years later, in 1124, he was a canon at Chartres.[4] The obituary of Chartres confirms that he was a canon before becoming chancellor.[5]

---

29 *Metal.* I, 11; ed. Webb, p. 29.

30 *Metal.* I, 24; ed. Webb, p. 59.

31 *Metal.* I, 24; ed. Webb, p. 55.

32 *Metal.* I, 24; ed. Webb, pp. 53-58.

33 MS Vienna, Nationalbibl. 2507, f. 43v-44v (s. xiii): in a collection of letters analyzed by W. Wattenbach, "Iter austriacum 1853," *Archiv für Kunde österr. Geschichtsquellen* 14 (1855) 39-51. The collection is thought to have been compiled ca. 1132. Cf. Ch. H. Haskins, *Studies in Med. Culture* (Cambridge, Mass., 1929) 181.

1 *Gesta Frid.* I, 52; MGH SrG 46, 74. Concerning Master Hilary of Poitiers see N. Haring, "Zur Geschichte der Schulen von Poitiers im 12. Jahrhundert," *Archiv für Kulturgesch.* 47 (1965) 23-47.

2 *Gesta Frid.* I, 52; p. 74.

3 N. Haring, "Bishof Gilbert und seine Erzdiakone," *Deutsches Archiv* 21 (1965) 133: P. Marchegay, *Cartul. s. Mauri, Archives d'Anjou* 1 (Angers, 1843) 366, no. 24.

4 B. Guérard, *Cartul. de Saint-Père* 2 (Paris, 1840) 469.

5 Lépinois and Merlet, *Cartul. de Notre-Dame de Chartres* 3, 167: "Obiit Gislebertus primum canonicus huius ecclesie, postea cancellarius litteratissimus, postea uenerabilis Pictauorum episcopus qui huic ecclesie duos sciphos argenteos, preciosos et ponderis octo marcarum, ad cotidianum usum altaris dedit et ne ab eodem usu remouerentur sub anathemate firmari fecit, librosque armarii diligenter emendatos modis pluribus meliorauit et omnes clericos huius ecclesie tam canonicos quam non-canonicos ubiqumque potuit honorauit."

One may wonder why he returned to Chartres. In a collection of 36 letters edited by L. Merlet[6] there is one addressed to "Desiderantissimo atque karissimo domino magistro suo B., G. eius semper et ubique discipulus familiaris."[7] In view of its contents L. Merlet has placed the collection in the time of Ivo, bishop of Chartres (1090-1116). After interpreting B. as Bernard and G. as Gilbert, Merlet proposes his conclusion: "Cette lettre nous semble pouvoir être attribuée avec certitude au célèbre Gilbert de la Poirée."[8]

The conjecture is justifiable as long as no better interpretation is presented. The former student of Master B. was the head of a school in Aquitaine, a part of France in which the diocese of Poitiers is located. The writer of the letter missed his former teacher despite his own good fortunes in Aquitaine.[9] He ends the praise of his former master with the words: "Quicquid sum, tibi post deum attribuo."[10]

According to R. W. Southern the author of the letter was "a raving young admirer of Master B." who "expresses the wildest enthusiasm for his master" and "continues to sigh" for him. This characterization is not intended to be complimentary although the same critic finds no fault with the admiration bestowed on Thierry "with that exaggerated admiration which is the supreme reward of the teacher."[11]

It is difficult to fathom what Southern hoped to accomplish by degrading the writer's sentiments or by defining him as young. Supposing the writer was Gilbert, the definition does not apply. In 1148 Gilbert was some 65-70 years old, as is indicated in the remark made by John of Salisbury to the effect that in 1148 Gilbert had spent some 60 years *in tritura litterarum*.[12] Assuming that he began school at the tender age of five, he was born in 1083, a conservative estimate. Hence he was over 40 years old when he was a canon of Notre Dame in Chartres (1124). Being the head of a school in Aquitaine, the writer, no matter who he was, can hardly be belittled as "a raving young admirer of Master B." We are told by Prof. Southern that "on a cool view the identification of Gilbert de la Porrée with this young admirer of Master B. is quite unlikely."[13] But the future development at Chartres increases the

6 L. Merlet, "Lettres d'Ives de Chartres," *Bibl. de l'Ecole des Chartes* 16 (1854-55) 443-471: MS Chartres, Bibl. mun. 1029 (H. 1. 19), f. 142v-157 (s. xii).

7 L. Merlet, p. 461.

8 L. Merlet, p. 461.

9 L. Merlet, p. 461: "Quamuis etenim mihi in Aquitanie partibus scolas regenti hilari uultu fortuna irrideat ..."

10 L. Merlet, p. 461.

11 *Med. Humanism*, pp. 70-71 and 82.

12 *Hist. pontif.* 8; ed. Poole, p. 17.

13 *Med. Humanism*, p. 71.

credibility of Merlet's conjecture, for in 1124 Gilbert was a canon at Chartres. He was obviously appointed by Bishop Geoffrey (1116-49) who probably remembered Gilbert as a student at the cathedral. It is not unlikely that Master Bernard of Chartres had something to do with the appointment. Whether he died or retired about 1124, Bernard must have paved the way for his successor who appears as Chancellor Gilbert on 27 November 1126.[14] The last record of Gilbert's chancellorship at Chartres is dated 1137.[15]

While Gilbert was chancellor he noticed a new trend and regretted the increasing number of those students who had only one concern: "Make money by fair means, if possible, but otherwise in any way at all."[16] His sentiments were shared by Master Thierry, William of Conches, and Abelard.[17] To reach this goal the study of law and medicine was the most promising branch of learning. Hence shorter courses in the liberal arts were demanded — and provided. As John of Salisbury puts it, Master Gilbert "was wont to deride or deplore, I am not sure which, the insanity of his time." He used to predict that those students "would end up as bakers."[18]

A good characterization of Gilbert is provided by Otto of Freising (d. 1158) in connection with his account of Gilbert's trials in Paris (1147) and in Reims (1148): "There was in those days in French Aquitaine, in the city of Poitiers, a bishop named Gillebert. He was born in the same city and from his youth to extreme old age pursued the study of philosophy in various places in Gaul. In fact as well as in name he had performed the function of a teacher and shortly before these days had been elevated to the dignity of bishop (1142) in the aforesaid city. He was accustomed by virtue of his exceedingly subtle intellect and acute powers of reason to say many things in a way different from what people were commonly used to."[19]

Otto stresses that Gilbert relied less on his own genius than on the authority of those who taught him.[20] According to Otto Gilbert's conduct was in accord with his learning.[21] Despite a certain aloofness

14   B. Guérard, *Cartul. de l'Abbaye de Saint-Père* 2 (Paris, 1840) 267: "Testes Galterius archidiaconus ... Gillebertus cancellarius ... Bernardus notarius."
15   Ch. Métais, *Cartul. de Notre-Dame de Josaphat* 1, 127.
16   John of Salisbury, *Metal.* I, 4; ed. Webb (Oxford, 1929) 15. D. D. McGarry (tr.), *The Metalogicon* (Berkeley, 1962) 19.
17   *Metal.* I, 5; ed. Webb, p. 16.
18   *Ibid.*
19   Otto of Freising, *Gesta Frid.* I, 48; MGH SrG 46 (1912) 67. Ch. Christopher Mierow (tr.), *The Deeds of Frederick Barbarossa, Records of Civ.* 49 (New York, 1953) 82.
20   *Gesta Friderici* I, 52; p. 74 (Mierow, p. 88).
21   *Ibid.*

Gilbert did not ignore the possible consequences of misunderstandings, especially in matters theological. He did not underrate the importance of diplomacy. When on the first day of his trial at Reims (1148) the consistory was adjourned, he "spent the remainder of the day and the following evening with those cardinals who were his friends — and there were many such." John of Salisbury narrates that there was one thing Gilbert would never dismiss from his mind, namely that people who did not know enough theology to distinguish heresy from heresy had left no stone unturned to brand him a heretic.[23] Otto refuses to decide the question whether or not Gilbert "escaped the condemnation of the Church by shrewdly concealing his view."[24] A similar view concerning Gilbert's sincerity has been recorded by John of Salisbury.[25]

Even in secular learning, it was believed, Gilbert had no equal.[26] John of Salisbury could not recall that anyone at the trial in Reims boasted of having read anything Gilbert had not read.[27] As to Gilbert's theology Pope Eugene III (1145-53) declared at the end of the trial in Reims that Gilbert had been found "orthodox on all points and faithful to apostolic teaching."[28]

The reader will recall that in 1137 Gilbert was still chancellor in Chartres.[29] Before 1141 he must have left Chartres, for in 1141 John of Salibury found him in Paris and studied logic and theology under him.[30] In the first half of the previous year (1140) Gilbert attended the Synod of Sens convened to examine Abelard's orthodoxy.[31] Gilbert is known to have lectured on Priscian.[32] Everard of Ypres heard his lectures at Paris *in aula episcopi.*[33] Prof. Southern makes the unfounded

---

22 *Gesta Frid.* I, 58; p. 83 (Mierow, p. 96). Geoffrey of Auxerre, *Ep. ad Albinum* 3, 17; ed. N. Haring, *Analecta Cist.* 22 (1966) 77, confirms this by saying that the "cardinales principales" sided with Gilbert.

23 *Hist. pontif.* 13; ed. Poole, p. 29.

24 *Gesta Frid.* I, 61; p. 87 (Mierow, p. 101). Cf. Geoffrey of Auxerre, *Libellus* 1, 9; ed. N. Haring, *Anal. Cist.* 22 (1966) 37.

25 *Hist. pontif.* 12; p. 28. See the catalogue of authors ed. N. Haring, *Franciscan Studies* 26 (1966) 210: "Gillebertus cognomento Porrata primum scolasticus Parisiensis, post Pictauensis episcopus, seculari scientia clarus, spiritualis etiam studii feruore nichilo minus emicuit."

27 *Hist. pontif.* 10; p. 22.

28 *Hist. pontif.* 10; p. 24. John did not complete his *Historia* until 1164. He dedicated it to Peter of Celle at whose suggestion he had written it. Peter had seen but never heard Gilbert: "quem te uidisse gaudes et doles non audisse" (*Hist. pontif.* 15; p. 41). Peter, it seems, refers to Master Gilbert's writings in a letter to a monk of Saint-Bertin: "Si noua placent, ecce magistri Hugonis, ecce S. Bernardi, ecce magistri Gillberti et magistri Petri scripta". *Ep.* 167; PL 202, 610B.

29 Ch. Métais, *Cartul. de Notre-Dame de Josaphat* 1, 127: "Presentibus ... Gisleberto cancellario ..."

30 *Metal.* II, 10; ed. Webb, p. 16.

31 Geoffrey of Auxerre, *S. Bernardi vita prima* III, 5, 15; PL 185, 312A.

32 R. W. Hunt, "Studies on Priscian II", *Med. and Ren. Studies* 3 (1954) 41-42.

33 *Dialogus;* ed. Haring, MS 15 (1953) 252.

claim that John of Salisbury[34] heard him lecturing on "Mount S. Geneviève." Gilbert died in 1154 as bishop of his native city.[35]

Among his theological writings three were generally received well by his contemporaries: his commentaries on the Psalms, St. Paul, and the *Opuscula sacra*. However, as early as 1141 his commentary on St. Paul was attacked by Gerhoch of Reichersberg[36] who began to use Gilbert's commentary on the Psalms in 1144.[37] It is believed that Gilbert read his *Glosatura super psalterium* in the presence of Master Anselm of Laon (d. 1117).[38] His commentary on Boethius caused Pope Eugene III to test Gilbert's orthodoxy. In 1146 Gilbert's doctrine on the Trinity as laid down in his commentary on Boethius[39] was denounced by two of his archdeacons. When, in April 1147, Pope Eugene held a consistory in Paris, not a single copy of his commentary on Boethius which was said to contain the erroneous teaching was availabe.[40] The commentary is no easy reading and it happened that even some of his students misinterpreted his doctrine.

34   *Med. Humanism*, p. 67.

35   See N. Haring, "Epitaphs and Necrologies on Gilbert II of Poitiers", *Archives d'hist. doctr. et litt. du moyen âge* 36 (1969) 57-87. Gilbert's followers were known as "Porretani", an epithet occasionally attached to Gilbert's name. It may be worth noting here that A. Berty and L. M. Tisserand, *Hist. gén. de Paris. Topographie hist. du vieux Paris* (Paris, 1897) 372-373, speak of "rues des Poirrées" (vicus Poretarum; vicus ad Porretas) in the central region of the university. Hence the epithet "Porretanus" probably denotes the street where Gilbert was known to have resided or taught, at least temporarily. Presumably for the same reason Alan of Lille is occasionally called "Porretanus". Cf. MS Tours, Bibl. mun. 247, f. 484. The street name connotes *porrus* or *porrum*, meaning a leek or scallion. This is what Geoffrey of Saint-Victor had in mind in verse 261 of his *Fons Philosophiae*: "Ex his quidam temperant porri condimenta" (ed. P. Michaud-Quantin, p. 44). The context shows that Geoffrey had the Porretans in mind. Cf. E. A. Synan (tr.) *The Fountain of Philosophy, vv.* 261-264 (Toronto, 1972) 49.

36   P. Classen, *Gerhoch von Reichersberg* (Wiesbaden, 1960) 94. Fr. Stegmüller, *Rep. bibl. med. aevi* 2 (Madrid, 1950) 345-346.

37   P. Classen, *Gerhoch*, p. 96. Stegmüller, *Rep. bibl.* 2, 346-350.

38   The view is based on the *explicit* of MS Oxford, Balliol Coll. 36, f. 145v, quoted by R. A. B. Mynors, *Cat. of the Manuscripts of Balliol College, Oxford* (Oxford, 1963) 26: "Explicit glosatura magistri Gilliberti Porretani super psalterium quam ipse recitauit coram suo magistro Anselmo causa emendationis".

39   Latest edition by N. M. Haring, *Studies and Texts* 13 (Toronto, 1966).

40   N. M. Haring, "Das Pariser Konsistorium Eugens III. vom April 1947", *Studia Gratiana* 11 (1967) 91-118. Gilbert's recently discovered treatise on the Trinity has been published in *Rech. de théol. anc. et médiév.* 39 (1972) 14-50. The attribution to Gilbert of the *De discretione animae, spiritus et mentis*, ed. Haring, MS 22 (1960) 173-191, has been contested by J. Châtillon, "Achard de Saint-Victor et le De discretione animae, spiritus et mentis", *Arch. d'hist. doctr. et litt. du moyen âge* 31 (1964) 7-35. See also J. Châtillon, *Théologie, spiritualité et métaphysique dans l'œuvre oratoire d'Achard de Saint-Victor, Etudes de philos. med.* 58 (Paris, 1969) 129-135. The commentary on the *Quicumque*, published in MS 27 (1965) 23-53, is attributed to Gilbert in the manuscript (MS Klosterneuburg, Stiftsb. 815, f. 145). L. Minio-Paluello, *Studi Medievali* 6 (1965) 123-151, has finally disposed of the opinion that Gilbert wrote the *Liber de sex principiis*. In the 13th century Gilbert was still the object of anecdotes. See, for instance, A. Lecoy de la Marche (ed.), *Anecdotes historiques ... tirés du recueil inédit d'Etienne de*

At the consistory held at Reims in the spring of 1148 Gilbert singled out two of his former students for misrepresenting his thought: "one who is still living in France and another no less hot-brained who has crossed over to England."[41] Two future bishops are known to have studied under Gilbert: the "rather rich" Rotrou, bishop of Evreux (1139-1165), later archbishop of Rouen (1165-83),[42] and Hugh de la Rochefoucauld, bishop of Angoulême (1148-59).[43] Both P. Gams and P. Piolin assign the year 1139 to Bishop Rotrou's installation in Evreux.[44] Before his election he had been an archdeacon at Rouen.[45] Since in 1137 Gilbert was still in Chartres, Rotrou must have studied theology under him in that city rather than in Paris. On the other hand, Hugh de la Rochefoucauld, bishop of Angoulême (1148-59), who also studied theology under Gilbert was elected in 1148/9. Before his election he had been a canon since 1117, an archdeacon (1130-33) and chanter (ca. 1140).[46] When bishop Hugh died in 1159, he was "uix sexagenarius".[47] Hence, born ca. 1099, he was ca. 38/9 years of age when Gilbert left Chartres (1137/8). In view of his age, Hugh must have studied at Chartres in the twenties.

Speaking of Gilbert's life at Chartres Prof. Southern wonders whether Gilbert ever taught while he was there: "He may have taught there but there is a striking absence of pupils who can be shown to have studied under him during those years".[48] We have just shown that both Rotrou and Hugh de la Rochefoucauld must have studied under Gilbert at Chartres. Everard of Ypres states explicitly that he studied in Chartres under Gilbert in a class of four, in Paris in a class of almost three hundred students seated *in aula episcopi*. He stayed with Gilbert in Poitiers until the bishop's death (1154).[49] It seems that Gilbert's classes at Char-

---

Bourbon (Paris, 1877) 212, no. 249. The Dominican Stephen of Bourbon died ca. 1261. Another anecdote is told by Thomas of Chobham, *Summa Confessorum* 4, 5, 5; ed. F. Broomfield, *Analecta med. Namurcensia* 25 (1968) 125. An anecdote told by Stephen Langton (d. 1228) has been published by B. Smally, "La glossa ordinaria. Quelques prédécesseurs d'Anselm de Laon", *Rech. de théol. anc. et méd.* 9 (1937) 370.

41 John of Salisbury, *Hist. pontif.* 10; ed. Poole, p. 23.

42 Geoffrey of Auxerre, *Ep. ad Albinum* 2, 11; ed. Haring, p. 77.

43 *Hist. pontif. et com. Engolismensium* 38; ed. J. Boussard (Paris, 1957) 44: "Qui liberalibus imbutus artibus magistro Gisleberto in Galliis adherens illum maxime in theologia sequutus est." *Recueil des hist.* 12, 399D.

44 P. Gams, *Series episcoporum* (p. 550) and P. Piolin, *Gallia chr.* 11 (Paris, 1874) 576. Robert de Monte, *Chronica* (MGH SS 6, 494) records his promotion under the year 1140: "Successit Rotrodus uir religiosus, bonis ornatus moribus, dilectus ab omnibus, filius Henrici comitis de Warwic."

45 *Gallia chr.* 11, 567B.

46 J. Nanglard, *Cartul. de l'église d'Angoulême* (Angoulême, 1900).

47 *Hist. pont. et com.* 38; ed. Boussard, p. 46.

48 *Med. Humanism*, p. 71.

49 Everard, *Dialogus Ratii*; ed. N. Haring, MS 15 (1953) 252: "Cui Carnotis quartus in lectionem, Parisius in aula episcopi fere tercentesimus assedi. Et ipsi episcopo Pictauis adhesi usque ad ipsius obitum." It should be noted that this information has been available since 1953.

tres were not large, but it is inaccurate to speak of "a striking absence" of pupils.

It is equally inaccurate to discredit Clerval's reference[50] to five students: Rotrou, Ivo (omitted by Southern), Jordan Fantosme, John Beleth, and Nicholas of Amiens. Prof. Southern declares: "For these assertions no evidence is offered."[51] If the critic had continued his reading, he would have found the evidence on pp. 185-186, based on Martène-Durand, *Voyage littéraire* III, 99, or rather (Second) *Voyage littéraire* (Paris 1724) pp. 99-101. In a copy of Gilbert's commentary on Boethius, then preserved at Saint-Amand, now at Valenciennes (Bibl. mun. 197, f. 4v), the two Benedictines found the miniatures and names of three disciples: "Iordanus Fantasma, Iuo Carnotensis decanus, Iohannes Beleth."[52] On f. 5 the drawing of a fourth disciple represents Nicholas whom historians hold to be Nicholas of Amiens. A photographic reproduction of f. 4v has been in print since 1962.[53] It must have escaped Prof. Southern that on p. 177 Clerval points out that Rotrou witnessed in Gilbert's favour at the consistory of Paris (1147). The evidence provided by Geoffrey of Auxerre[54] has been available since 1690 when J. Mabillon published Geoffrey's letter to Cardinal Albinus.

The scholars mentioned on f. 4v and 5 of MS Valenciennes 197 are not entirely unknown.[55] In a letter to Pope Hadrian IV (1154-59) by John of Salisbury[56] Master Jordan Fantasma is described as a cleric of the bishop of Winchester.[57] He objected to the fact that Master John Joichel taught in Winchester. The case was transferred to Canterbury. After examining the *instrumenta* it was decided that Master John could not teach at Winchester against Master Jordan's will. When Master John opposed this decision, Jordan appealed to Rome. On 10 April 1160 at Farnham Master Jordan Fantasma witnessed a charter as "clericus episcopi Wintonensis".[58] Jordan is the author of a French poem describing the war (1173-74) between the English and the Scots.[59] A

---

50   *Les écoles,* p. 164: "Rotrou, Ive, Jordan Fantosme, Jean Beleth et Nicolas d'Amiens".

51   *Med. Humanism,* p 70.

52   See N. M. Haring, *The Commentaries on Boethius by Gilbert of Poitiers, Texts and Studies* 13 (Toronto, 1966) 29.

53   R. B. C. Huygens, "Guillaume de Tyr, étudiant," *Latomus* 21 (1962) 826.

54   *Ep. ad Albinum* 2, 11; ed. N. Haring 7: "discipulos suos ... Rotuldum ... et magistrum Iuonem Carnotensem." (PL 185, 588C).

55   A full transcription is found in *Commentaries on Boethius by Gilbert of Poitiers;* ed. N. Haring, pp. 29-30.

56   *Ep.* 19; PL 199, 13A. C. E. Du Boulay, *Hist. Univ. Par.* 2 (Paris, 1665) 279.

57   Henry of Blois (1129-1171).

58   Fr. Palgrave, *The Rise and Progress of the English Commonwealth* 2 (London, 1832) p. lxxviii.

59   *Chronique de la guerre entre les Anglois et les Ecossois en 1173 et 1174;* ed. R. Howlett, RS 82, 3 (London, 1886) 202-376: with English translation. Earlier edition by F. Michel, *Surtees Society* (1840) 3-95.

manuscript preserved at Vienna contains a *Rithmus Jordanis Fantasmatis*.[60]

Ivo whose name is likewise recorded in MS Valenciennes 197 studied under Gilbert in Paris after attending the lectures offered by Thierry. We shall have more to say about him in the course of this article.

John Beleth is the author of a once very popular *Summa de ecclesiasticis (diuinis) officiis*,[61] written in 1160-64. About 1135 John Beleth witnessed a donation acknowledged by Geoffrey, bishop of Chartres (1116-49).[62] At that time Gilbert was chancellor of the cathedral. In 1164 John was at Frontenay and witnessed a charter as "magister Johannes Beleth".[63] The chronicler Alberic of Trois-Fontaines writes *ad ann.* 1182: "Floruit magister Johannes Beleth in ecclesia Ambianensi. Qui scripsit librum de diuinis officiis."[64] Cardinal Stephen Langton (d. 1228) was one of his students in Paris.[65] His *Summa* must have filled a real need. Among the books John of Salisbury bequeathed to the library of Notre-Dame in Chartres there was a *Liber de diuinis officiis*, presumably the work authored by John Beleth.[66] Arnulph of Lisieux sent a *Liber de diuinis officiis* to Richard, archdeacon of Poitiers.[67] It is known that Garnier of Rochefort, Peter of Poitiers, Sichard of Cremona, Prepositinus, and William of Auxerre borrowed freely from Beleth's *Summa*.[68] There is some evidence that he wrote a work called *Expositiones difficilium prologorum et librorum ueteris et noui testamenti*.[69] The catalogue of Affligem, compiled ca. 1270-73, recommends his *Summa*: "Magister Iohannes Beleth et ipse theologice scole rector Parisius scripsit *Summam de diuinis officiis* de personis et temporibus et multis aliis rebus lectori utilia continentem."[70]

Little is known about the fourth disciple named in MS Valenciennes 197. He seems to have interpreted Gilbert's doctrine with special skill:

Excerpts are found in MGH SS 27, 53-59: MS Durham, Cath. C. IV. 27, f. 138-166v (ca. 1200) and MS Lincoln, Chapter A. 4. 12, f. 158-189 (s. xiii); *Hist. litt.* 23 (Paris, 1895) 345-367.

60 Edited by M. Denis, *Codd. manuscr. theologici* 1 (Vienna, 1793) 354.

61 PL 202, 13-166. Cf. J. F. Maurel, "Jean Beleth et la Summa de eccl. officiis," *Ecole des Chartes: pos. des thèses* (1953) 77-80. He, too, must have studied under Gilbert at Chartres.

62 L. Merlet, *Cartul. de l'Abbaye de la Sainte-Trinité de Tiron* (Chartres, 1883) 226.

63 P. de Monsabert, *Chartes de l'Abbaye de Nouaillé, Arch. hist. du Poitou* 49 (1936) 19.

64 MGH SS 23, 857.

65 G. Lacombe, "Studies on the Comm. of Card. Stephen Langton," *Archives d'hist. doctr. et litt. du moyen âge* 5 (1930) 19. Idem, "The Authenticity of the Summa of Cardinal Stephen Langton," *The New Scholasticism* 4 (1930) 107: MS Paris, Bibl. nat. Lat. 14414, f. 117.

66 Lépinois and Merlet, *Cartul. de Notre-Dame de Chartres* 3, 202 (PL 199, col. xii).

67 *Ep.* 73; PL 201, 103B.

68 See Cl. Baeumker in *Beiträge* 24, 5 (1926) pp. l-liv (Garnerius) and V. L. Kennedy in MS 5 (1943) 9 and 26.

69 Fr. Stegmüller, *Rep. bibl.* 4234.

70 Edited by N. Haring in *Rev. bén.* 80 (1970) 81.

"Nicholaus qui pro dignitate sua archanis Pictauensis episcopi sententiis, ut digni introducantur ad eas, lucem plene expositionis effudit."[71] H. Denifle identifies him with Nicholas of Amiens who according to the *Histoire littéraire*[72] wrote a commentary (then preserved at Saint-Omer, now considered lost) on Gilbert's gloss on the Psalms. Part of this commentary is still extant.[73]

The *Biblionomia* of Richard of Fournival lists two works attributed to Nicholas of Amiens: a *Liber de articulis fidei ad Clementem papam*[74] (= Clement III: 1187-91) and a *Liber annalium* whose preface has been edited by M. T. d'Alverny.[75] However, the chronicler Nicholas of Amiens states that he was born in 1147[76] and that at Reims Pope Eugene "condemned some novelties that Gilbert, *motus subtilitate*, had indulged in."[77] This is not the kind of language Gilbert's disciples used to describe their master.

This may be the place to recall the writings of the Cistercian Everard of Ypres who defended Gilbert against St. Bernard in a fictitious dialogue between a Greek called Ratius and a Cistercian called Everard.[78] He wrote it during the reign of Celestine III (1191-98) in whose entourage the author had been while the future pope was a delegate in France. At an earlier date, Everard addressed himself to Pope Urban III (1185-87) to induce him to examine certain christological theories that were being circulated in Paris.[79] Everard is also the author of a short work dealing with canon law.[80] We have pointed out that he studied under Gilbert at Chartres, Paris, and Poitiers.[81]

---

71 MS Valenciennes, Bibl. mun. 197 (189), f. 5 transcribed in full by N. Haring, *The Commentaries on Boethius by Gilbert of Poitiers* 29-30 with references to earlier sources.

72 H. Denifle, *Die abendl. Schriftausleger, Luther und Luthertum* I, 1 (Mainz, 1905) 345. *Hist. litt.* 12, 473.

73 Fr. Stegmüller, *Rep. bibl.* 5669: MS Alençon, Bibl. mun. 22, f. 1-80, and Vat. Ottob. Lat. 863, f. 1-55.

74 Edited as a work of Alan of Lille: PL 210, 595-618 from B. Pez, *Thes. anecd. nov.* I, 1 (Augsburg, 1721). See P. Glorieux, "Etudes sur la Biblionomia de Richard de Fournival," *Rech. de théol. anc. et méd.* 30 (1963) 227.

75 *Alain de Lille, Etudes de philos. médiévale* 52 (Paris, 1965) 320-322: MS Vat. Reg. Lat. 454, f. 1-83 (s. xiii).

76 (f. 80v): Nicholaus ambianensis nascitur qui hanc seriem cronicorum digessit." A. Wilmart, *Codd. Reg. Lat.* 2 (Vatican, 1945) 76.

77 *Recueil des hist.* 14 (Paris 1806) 22B transcribed from MS Vat. Reg. Lat. 454.

78 N. Haring, "A Latin Dialogue on the Doctrine of Gilbert of Poitiers," MS 15 (1953) 243-389.

79 N. Haring, "The Cistercian Everard of Ypres and His Appraisal of the Conflict between St. Bernard and Gilbert of Poitiers," MS 17 (1955) 143-172.

80 *Summula decretalium questionum*: MS Reims, Bibl. mun. 689, f. 1-74v (s. xii). St. Kuttner, *Rep. der Kanonistik, Studi e testi* 71 (Vatican, 1937) 187-190.

81 *Dialogus*; ed. Haring, p. 252.

The author of the *Liber de uera philosophia*,[82] a work written to vin-
dicate Gilbert, speaks of a "certain Master A(dhemar), canon of Saint-
Ruf (Valence), a man advanced in years but more advanced in wisdom,
religion, and dignity" who spent some thirty years (1148-78) collecting
patristic texts in the libraries "of Gaul, Spain, Italy, and Greece" to
prove that Gilbert was not a heretic.[83] Master Adhemar donated one
copy of this collection to Pope Alexander III (1159-81) who "received it
very gratefully." Another copy went to Maguelone, one to Saint-Ruf
(Valence), a fourth copy to *Alemannia* (Alsace), a fifth to the Benedictines of Psalmodi. A sixth copy, donated to the author of the *Liber de
uera philosophia*, was left behind in Jerusalem when the Knights Templars
were forced to evacuate the city (1187). The collection has not yet been
found, but an abbreviation of it, extant in at least four manuscripts, has
been discovered in Austria.[84]

In addition, Adhemar wrote a *Tractatus de Trinitate*[85] preserved in MS
Vat. Lat. 561, f. 171-282 (s. xii), edited in 1964, in which he fulminates
against those "excelsis clamoribus tonantes magistrum Gislebertum
scripsisse contra fidem."[86] In this treatise Adhemar comments on
Boethius (*De Trinitate*) mainly by providing patristic quotations
elucidating the text.

Adhemar's influence was considerable. The author of the *Liber de uera
philosophia*, a compilation of enormous size, borrowed from Adhemar's
collection. Adhemar's influence can be seen in the *Summa* preserved in
MS Vat. Ross. Lat. 212, f. 96-151 (s. xii) and in the *Introductiones breues ad
fidem sancte Trinitatis pro rudibus instruendis*, preserved in MS Paris, Bibl.
nat. Lat. 2802, f. 78-108v (s. xiii). Both tracts follow the division adopted
by Adhemar: Trinity, Incarnation, and the Eucharist. Neither Everard
nor Adhemar is mentioned by Southern.

The question whether the so-called *Sententie diuinitatis* was condemned
at Reims (1148) has not yet been settled. But there is no doubt that the
author made use of Gilbert's commentary on Boethius.[87]

A word should also be said of three more scholars not mentioned by

---

82   MS Grenoble, Bibl. publ. 290 (1085), f. 3-110 (s. xii).

83   See P. Fournier, *Etudes sur Joachim de Flore* (Paris, 1909) 62-63.

84   N. Haring, "Die Vätersammlung des Adhemar von Saint-Ruf in Valence," *Scholastik* 38 (1963)
407-420. Idem, "Eine Zwettler Abkürzung der Vätersammlung Adhemars von Saint-Ruf," *Theologie
und Phil.* 1 (1966) 30-53. Idem, "In Search of Adhemar's Collection," *MS* 28 (1966) 336-346. Idem,
"Texts concerning G. of Poitiers," *Archives d'hist. doctr. et litt. du moyen âge* 37 (1970) 187-188.

85   Edited by N.Haring in *Archives d'hist. doctr. et litt. du moyen âge* 31 (1964) 111-206. The
manuscript once belonged to the Knights Templars in Paris.

86   *De Trin.* 45, pref.; ed. Haring, p. 126.

87   Edited by B. Geyer, *Beiträge* 7, 2-3 (1909, rpt. 1967): MS Munich *clm* 18918, f. 81-108 (s. xii),
and *clm* 16063, f. 1-78 (s. xiii).

Southern who took up Gilbert's cause: Hugh of Honau, Peter of Vienna, and Hugh of Pisa, called Etherian. Master Hugh of Honau, like Adhemar a canon regular, was "a deacon of the Sacred Palace" at the court of Frederick Barbarossa (1152-91). As Barbarossa's delegate to Manuel I (1143-80) he went to Constantinople on two occasions. On his first mission, ca. 1171, he asked Hugh of Pisa for translations of texts in which Greek Fathers speak of a distinction between nature and person in God. His wish was fulfilled on his second mission to Constantinople.

Hugh of Honau wrote a large work under the title: *Liber de homoysion et homoeysion,* edited in 1967,[88] and another work whose title reads: *Liber de diuersitate nature et persone,* edited in 1962.[89] In his *Liber de homoysion* Hugh refers to Gilbert as his teacher: "teste preceptore nostro Giselberto Pictauiensi episcopo."[90] He knew Gilbert personally, for in his *Liber de diuersitate* he points to the fact that Gilbert often "read Latin versions of the writings of Theodoret, Sophronius, and most of all Athanasius."[91] Hugh is probably the author of the *Liber de ignorantia,* preserved in the same manuscript as the other two works. It was edited in 1963.[92]

The work which Hugh of Pisa composed for his friends Peter of Vienna and Hugh of Honau bears the title: *Liber de differentia nature et persone.*[93] Hugh of Honau also received Hugh Etherian's *De immortali deo.*[94] On his return from Constantinople Hugh of Honau showed his "treasure of books" to Peter of Pavia, then cardinal of Frascati, who was at the time (1180-81) with Barbarossa as papal legate. We learn from Hugh that the cardinal was amazed to see how closely Gilbert's teaching coincided with the doctrine of the Greek Fathers. This is an indication that the cardinal was familiar with Gilbert's writings. Other cardinals showed an interest in the controversy caused by Gilbert. When they were in Constantinople as papal legates, three cardinals: Hubald of Ostia, later Pope Lucius III (1181-85), Bernard of Porto and John, titular cardinal of Saints John and Paul, had encouraged Hugh of Pisa to write his *De immortali deo.* Both Hubald and Bernard were at the Council of Reims (1148).

88   MS Cambridge, Univ. 1824, f. 2-129 (s. xii): ed. N. Haring, *Archives d'hist. doctr. et litt. du moyen âge* 34 (1967) 129-253 and 35 (1968) 211-295.

89   MS Cambridge, Univ. 1824, f. 130-177v (s. xii): ed. N. Haring, *Archives d'hist. doctr. et litt. du moyen âge* 29 (1962) 163-216.

90   *De homoysion* II, 2, 4; ed. N. Haring, p. 184.

91   *Liber de diuers. nature* I, 8; ed. N. Haring, p. 122.

92   MS Cambridge, Univ. 1824, f. 178-188: ed. N. Haring, MS 25 (1963) 209-230.

93   Edited by N. Haring, MS 24 (1962) 21-34. It is dedicated to Hugh of Honau and Peter of Vienna.

94   Hugh of Honau, *Liber de diuers. nature* I, 6-7; ed. Haring, pp. 121-122. Cf. N. Haring, "The Porretans and the Greek Fathers," MS 24 (1962) 181-209.

We still have two letters by Hugh of Honau addressed to Hugh of Pisa in Constantinople.[95] They reveal his deep desire to procure a translation from the Greek of texts that deal with the Trinity. He admits that Latin authors are sufficiently clear, but he wishes to consult the very source of Latin thinking, the Greeks: "quia a Grecis sapientie totius fons emanauit."

On his way to Constantinople Hugh of Honau visited Master Peter of Vienna whom he calls "tui nominis diligentissimus propagator" in his letter to Hugh of Pisa.[96] Peter was born and educated in France. He had likewise asked Hugh of Pisa for a translation of pertinent texts. It is quite possible that Hugh of Honau and Peter met while they studied under Gilbert. Peter went from France to Austria before 1155 and soon became involved in controversies with Gerhoch of Reichersberg (d. 1169) who had been attacking the "novel" doctrines of some French schools since 1141.

Peter's name appears under a charter issued in 1158 by Bishop Conrad of Passau. In a later document (1161) he is called a "member of the Order of Chaplains" (de ordine cappelanorum). He is probably the author of the so-called Summa Zwettlensis,[97] an outstanding example of the sort of theological reasoning practiced in Gilbert's school.

In a letter to Hugh of Pisa Peter highly recommends his friend Hugh of Honau.[98] A letter by Master Peter to Otto of Freising is still extant.[99] So are two letters to Master Peter by Gerhoch of Reichersberg.[100] Letters to Peter by Rudiger of Reichersberg and Haimo have also survived.[101] It is believed that Peter's death is recorded in the annals of Zwettl under the year 1183: "Petrus magister, uir adprime eruditus, obiit."[102] While Gerhoch was very critical of Gilbert, his brother and successor Arno (d. 1175) calls him a "great and renowned master."[103]

Hugh of Honau tells us that Hugh of Pisa had studied dialectica under

---

95 MS 24 (1962) 16-19.

96 See Hugh of Honau, Liber de diuers. nature I, 6 (pp. 121-122) and the letter to Hugh of Pisa, MS 24 (1962) 19. Concerning Master Peter see the basic study by H. Fichtenau, "Ein franz. Frühscholastiker in Wien," Jahrb. für Landesk. von Niederösterr. NF 29 (1944) 118-130. Idem, "Magister Petrus von Wien," Mitt. des Inst. für österr. Geschichtsforschung 63 (1955) 283-297. P. Classen, Gerhoch von Reichersberg (Wiesbaden, 1960).

97 MSS Zwettl, Stiftsb. 109, f. 3-81v (s. xii) and Admont, Stiftsb. 593, f. 9-55v (s. xii): "Religio est debiti finis rectitudo."

98 MS Colmar, Bibl. mun. 188, f. 35-35v (s. xii): ed. N. Haring, MS 24 (1962) 19-21.

99 Edited by H. Weisweiler, Scholastik 13 (1938) 231-246.

100 Edited by H. Weisweiler, Scholastik 13 (1938) 48. P. Classen in Gerhohi opera inedita, Spicil. pont. Athen. Anton. 8 (Rome, 1955) 357-366: "Magno et nouo philosopho P(etro) fr(ater) G(erhochus)."

101 Edited by H. Weisweiler, Scholastik 14 (1939) 41-46 and 47-49.

102 MGH SS 9, 459.

103 Apologeticus contra Folmarum; ed. C. Weichert (Leipzig, 1888) 11.

Alberic and that in his studies of theology he followed the "run-of-the-mill theologians", not Gilbert. But when he began to read and translate Greek Fathers he changed his mind in favour of Gilbert's views.[104] Of his numerous writings the work entitled *De immortali deo*[105] was the most popular. Hugh Etherian died in 1182 after Pope Lucius III (1181-1185) had made him a cardinal.

Another cardinal, Master Laborans, was likewise one of Gilbert's followers. He was born at Pontormo near Florence and died about 1191 as cardinal-priest of Santa Maria in Trastevere. A. Landgraf holds that Laborans studied under Gilbert.[106] According to St. Kuttner he was "trained in France."[107]

It took Laborans twenty years (1162-82) to write his *Compilatio decretorum*.[108] His *Tractatus de iustitia* is dated to 1154-60, his *De uera libertate* to 1144-61. His *Secte Sabellianorum* and *Persone predicatio relatiua est*, both very short tracts, have not been dated.[109]

A close follower, if perhaps not a direct student of Gilbert's was Simon of Tournai (d. 1201) whom Stephen of Tournai (d. 1203) recommended to William, archbishop of Reims (1176-1202), as a man "outstanding among scholars."[110] He is the author of such works as the *Institutiones in sacram paginam*, 102 *Disputationes*, commentaries on the Apostles' Creed and the Pseudo-Athanasian Creed.[111]

Similarly linked to Gilbert is Alan of Lille (d. 1202) of whose student years M. T. d'Alverny writes: "il a fort bien pu étudier avec Thierry."[112] Thierry's influence can be seen in Alan's *Anticlaudianus*. But Alan also borrowed from Gilbert's commentary on Boethius. In fact, he mentions Gilbert's name while discussing "Master Gilbert's" definition of eternity.[113] Since about 1138-42 both Gilbert and Thierry were active in Paris, the latter some years earlier and probably a few years longer, Alan may have attended lectures offered by both scholars. However, there is no written evidence to substantiate this view. Glorieux un-

---

104 Hugh of Honau, *Liber de diuers. nature* I, 7; ed. Haring, p. 122.

105 PL 202, 227-396 under the title *De hersibus*.

106 *Laborantis Cardinalis opuscula*; ed. A. Landgraf, *Floril. patr.* 32 (Bonn, 1932) 1: MS Vatican, Archivio S. Pietro C. 110, f. 1-243v (s. xii).

107 St. Kuttner, *Rep. der Kanonistik, Studi e testi* 71 (Vatican, 1937) 175.

108 A. Theiner, *Disquisitio critica* (Rome, 1836): PL 204, 869-914.

109 The four tracts have been edited by A. Landgraf, *Floril. patr.* 32, 6-66.

110 Stephen of Tournai, *Ep.* 60; PL 211, 353A. Cf. N. Haring, "Simon of Tournai and Gilbert of Poitiers," *MS* 27 (1965) 325-330. L. Hödl, *Die Gesch. der schol. Literatur, Beiträge* 38, 4 (1960) 229-231.

111 A. Landgraf, *Introducción a la historia de la literatura teológica de la escolástica incipiente* (Barcelona, 1956) 140-142.

112 *Alain de Lille, Etudes de philos. médiévale* 52 (Paris, 1965) 20.

113 *Summa 'Quoniam homines'*; ed. P. Glorieux, *Archives d'hist. doctr. et litt; du moyen âge* 20 (1953) 162.

derstates Gilbert's influence when he says: "On sent l'influence ... de Gilbert."[114] The catalogue of Affligem has considerable praise for both Master Simon of Tournai and Master Alan of Lille.[115]

A report on Gilbert's school would not be complete without a note on Radulphus Ardens and Master Martin. The latter compiled a theological *Summa* (dated ca. 1195) with numerous borrowings from Peter of Poitiers, Simon of Tournai, Alan of Lille, Odo of Ourscamp, and others.[116] Radulphus Ardens who died ca. 1200 is the author of more than 200 homilies of considerable doctrinal value.[117] His *Speculum Uniuersale*, dated 1193-1200, is the largest encyclopedia of Christian faith and morals written in the 12th century.[118]

A number of works that emanated from Gilbert's school are anonymous. We have mentioned two in connection with Adhemar of Saint-Ruf. Anonymous also is the *Summa* preserved in MS Bamberg, Staatl. Bibl. Patr. 136 (Q. VI. 50) f. 1-98v (s. xiii) wrongly attributed to Stephen Langton: "Breues dies hominis sunt et numerus mensium ..." A commentary on 1 Cor 1-12, 4 which originated in Gilbert's school has been edited by A. Landgraf[119] who holds that it was written about 1150. The Vallicelliana in Rome owns a manuscript containing a commentary on Romans produced in Gilbert's school.[120] Another such gloss with the same background is preserved in MS Paris, Bibl. nat. Lat. 686, f. 33-70 (s. xiii): "Sicut legis ita et euangelii ..." Marginal glosses from Gilbert's commentary on St. Paul have been encountered in Lombard's commentary on St. Paul's letters.[121] An extremely well written gloss on Gilbert's commentary on St. Paul (with the same incipit) is preserved in

---

114   *Ibid.*, p. 116.

115   *Catalogus uirorum illustrium* 21 and 24; ed. N. Haring, *Revue bén.* 80 (1970) 82: "Magister Alanus Insulis oriundus liberalium artium peritus Parisius ecclesiastice scole prefuit ingenii sui monimenta relinquens. Scripsit Summam ad predicationis officium utilem ..." (p. 83): "Magister Symon Tornaci oriundus. Ex dyalectico subtilissimo ymmo omnium liberalium artium fere sui temporis peritissimo theologice etiam scole Parisius cathedram meruit ascendere magistralem in qua plurimos habuit auditores ..."

116   M. Grabmann, *Geschichte der schol. Methode* 2 (Freiburg i. B., 1911) 524-31. Six manuscripts are listed by A. Landgraf, *Introducción*, p. 153. See L. Hödl, *Die Geschichte*, pp. 247-253. D. Van den Eynde, *Antonianum* 29 (1954) 136-141. The *Summa* attributed to Master Martin de Fugeriis in MS Paris, Bibl. nat. Lat. 3116, f. 1-78v (s. xiii) is the *Sentences* of Peter of Poitiers, as has been shown by Ph. S. Moore, *The Works of Peter of Poitiers, Publ. in Medieval Studies* 1 (Notre Dame, 1936) 30.

117   PL 155, 1301-1626; 1667-2118.

118   J. Gründel, *Das Speculum uniuersale des R. Ardens* (Munich 1961). Eight manuscripts are known to exist. B. Geyer established the dates in *Theol. Quartalschr.* 93 (1911) 63-69.

119   *Studi e testi* 117 (Vatican, 1945) 1-211: MS Paris, Arsenal 1116. f. 57-79v (s. xiii) and MS Leipzig, Univ. 427, f. 29v-48v (s. xiii).

120   Rome, Bibl. Vallicelliana C. 57, f. 152-159v: "Quatuor autem capitulis ..."

121   MS Vat. Ottob. Lat. 86, f. 1-? (s. xiii). A. Landgraf, "Neue Funde zur Porretanerschule," *Coll. Franc.* 6 (1936) 353-365.

MS Boulogne-sur-Mer, Bibl. mun. 24, f. 136v-210v (s. xii), from Saint-Bertin.

· A great number of Gilbert's students were unknown to Clerval when he wrote of Thierry and Gilbert: "Des maîtres aussi fameux que ceux dont nous venons de tracer la biographie ne pouvaient manquer d'élèves."[122] We have every reason to call Gilbert a member of the school of Chartres and to consider his students members of the same school. Its impact on 12th-century thought is so far-reaching that many more years of research will be needed to fix its boundries. Prof. Southern has nothing at all to say about Gilbert's students. Ignoring all the evidence that has come to light after Clerval and Poole published their findings, taking it as a proven fact that Thierry did not study at Chartres, he came to the conclusion that Clerval and Poole founded a legend.

Thierry and Gilbert inspired their students in different fields. It is hardly by chance that the translation of Ptolemy's *Planisphere* was done by an admirer of Thierry's. Gilbert, on the other hand, turned his students to a closer study of the Greek Fathers (Adhemar, Peter of Vienna, Hugh of Honau), of the liturgy (John Beleth), and of canon law (Everard of Ypres, Cardinal Laborans). Gilbert's role in the history of moral theology and sacramentology has not been studied in full detail.

Master Ivo of Chartres (d. 1165)

Master Ivo is one of the four students singled out in MS Valenciennes 197, f. 4v, as students deserving to be remembered forever. We have seen that, together with Rotrou, then bishop of Evreux (1141-65), Master Ivo, later dean of Chartres, spoke in favour of Gilbert's orthodoxy at the papal consistory held at Paris in 1147.[1] While Geoffrey calls him "Master Ivo of Chartres", the Valenciennes manuscript names him "Ivo dean of Chartres".[2] The *Metamorphosis Golie* mentions him in the following context:

> Celebrem theologum uidimus Lumbardum
> Cum Iuone Helyam Petrum et Bernardum.[3]

---

122 *Les écoles*, p. 179.

1 Geoffrey of Auxerre, *Ep. ad Albinum* 1, 11; ed. N. Haring, *Analecta Cist.* 22 (1966) 71: "Et amplius quid faciens discipulos suos episcopum quendam Ebroicensem, generosum satis, Rotomagensem archiepiscopum post futurum, Rotoldum nomine, et magistrum Iuonem Carnotensem testes produxit."

2 *The Commentaries on Boethius by Gilbert of Poitiers*; ed. N. Haring, *Studies and Texts* 13 (Toronto, 1966) 29.

3 *Metamorphosis Golie*, vv. 197-198; ed. R. B. C. Huygens, "Mitt. aus Handschriften," *Studi medievali*, terza serie, 32 (1962) 771. Th. Wright, *The Latin Poems commonly attributed to Walter Mapes* (London, 1840) 28.

Master Ivo was "genere et natione Carnotenssis" as William of Tyre phrases it.[4] With Bernard the Breton and Peter Helias he had first studied under Thierry "for a long time."[5] It is probably not just by accident that the same three names (Ivo, Peter Helias, Bernard) are associated in the *Metamorphosis*. After attending Thierry's lectures, Ivo studied under Gilbert whose "doctrine he professed."[6]

The statement that he was a follower of Master Gilbert is confirmed by the chronicler Robert of Auxerre who writes *ad ann.* 1153: "Inter magistros Frantie opinatissimi habentur Petrus Lumbardus, Odo Suessionensis, Iuo Carnotensis, quondam Gisleberti discipulus."[7] Like Bernard the Breton, Master Ivo was an archdeacon at Notre-Dame in Paris at least from 1144 to 1155/6. In 1156 he was back in his native Chartres. A charter, dated 1144, states: "interfuerunt magister Robertus Pullanus, Iuo Parisiensis archidiaconus, magister Gauterus canonicus ..."[8] The "Signum Iuonis archidiaconi" is found under charters dated to ca. 1145,[9] and 1146/7.[10] On one occasion (1146/7) he signed with Master Simon (deacon) and Master Hugh of Champfleury.[11] The latter opposed Gilbert at the papal consistory at Paris[12] in April 1147 together with Adam of Petit-Pont. It may be added here that Hugh of Champfleury became the chancellor of Louis VII in 1152 and died as bishop of Soissons (1153-75). The last Parisian charter signed by Archdeacon Ivo is dated 1156/7.[13] This charter does not contain the name of Archdeacon Bernard who signed several times in company with him. If Archdeacon Ivo is identical with Ivo the Deacon, he was in Paris as early as 1124.[14] Before 18 October 1156 Ivo went to Chartres and became dean of the cathedral chapter. As such he signed a document on 18 October 1156 with Robert, bishop of Chartres (1156-64): "Ego Robertus dei gratia Carnotensis episcopus ... Ego Iuo decanus ..."[15] Bishop Robert was presumably instrumental in the transfer of both

---

4 *Hist. hieros.* XIX, 12; ed. Huygens, p. 822.

5 *Ibid.*, p. 822.

6 *Ibid.*: "Horum tamen nouissimus, magister Iuo, magistri Gilliberti Porrea Pictauenssis episcopi, quem post magistrum Theodericum audierat, doctrinam profitebatur."

7 MGH SS 26, 237.

8 Robert de Lasteyrie, *Cartul. gén. de Paris: Hist. gén. de Paris* 1 (Paris 1887) 293, no. 313.

9 R. de Lasteyrie, *Cartul.* 1, 298, no. 321: with Archd. Bernard.

10 R. de Lasteyrie, *Cartul.* 1, 301, no. 325: with Archd. Bernard.

11 R. de Lasteyrie, *Cartul.* 1, 302, no. 327: with Archd. Bernard.

12 Otto of Freising, *Gesta Frid.* I, 53; p. 75. Concerning other masters involved in Gilbert's trial see N. Haring, "Das Pariser Konsistorium Eugens III. vom April 1147," *Studia Gratiana* 11 (Bologna, 1967) 93-117. Idem, "Notes on the Council and the Consistory of Reims (1148)," MS 28 (1966) 39-59.

13 R. de Lasteyrie, *Cartul.* 1, 348, no. 394.

14 R. de Lasteyrie, *Cartul.* 1, 226, no. 205: with S(ignum) Teoderici sacerdotis.

15 Ch. Métais, *Cartul. de Notre-Dame de Josaphat*, p. 276.

Bernard the Breton and Ivo. Another charter signed by Dean Ivo under Bishop Robert is dated to 1155-59.[16] During the same period he witnessed a sale[17] and, in 1159, a donation.[18] Ivo's death is recorded in the necrology of Saint-Jean-en-Vallée: "XVIII cal. Septembris apud Ermansum obiit Iuo Carnotensis ecclesie decanus, uir multa scientia et honestate preditus, qui ecclesiam istam Sancti Iohannis in Valleia, quanto affectu uiuens dilexit moriens indicauit cui xxxvi librorum suorum uolumina dereliquit."[19] Dean Ivo died on 15 August. On 16 August 1165 Pope Alexander III celebrated Mass at Vézelay "pro anima Iuonis Carnotensis ecclesie decani."[20]

Ivo wrote a long commentary on the Psalms.[21] Already in Ivo's life time Prior Laurence (1149-53) donated a *Psalterium glossatum secundum magistrum Iuonem* to Durham Library.[22] At that time Ivo was still in Paris. Ivo is also considered the author of a commentary on six Old Testament canticles.[23]

According to Peter Cantor (d. 1197) Ivo's respect for the *Book of Decretals* was not very high: "Ex indignatione magister Iuo Carnotensis librum decretorum ad pedes suos proiecit quasi uilem et inutilem."[24] A passage in Cantor's *Summa de sacramentis* attributes to Ivo a certain doctrine on the effect of perfect love: "Hec sentiebat magister Yuo Carnodensis".[25] A marginal note in MS London, Lambeth Palace 142, f. 110v, cites a christological view held by Ivo.[26] He is quoted by Prepositinus, chancellor of Paris (1206-10), as denying the existence of *proprietates* in God.[27]

In view of the fact that Ivo taught in Paris, it may be worthwhile drawing attention to a letter preserved in MS Bamberg, Staatl. Bibl.

---

16 Lépinois and Merlet, *Cartulaire ... de Chartres* 1, 162.

17 Lépinois and Merlet, *Cartul.* 1, 164: "his coram positis Iuone decano."

18 *Ibid.*, p. 167: "presente Iuone decano." The name of his successor was John (p. 173).

19 *Gallia chr.* 8, 1200B.

20 MGH SS 26, 150: "Ascendit sanctissimus et uniuersalis pontifex Alexander catholicus papa ad altare ut sacram et uiuificam uictimam deo offerret pro anima Iuonis Carnotensis ecclesie decani."

21 B. Smally, "Master Ivo of Chartres," *The Engl. Hist. Review* 50 (1935) 680-686. Fr. Stegmüller, *Rep. bibl.* 5337-40. A. Clerval, *Les écoles*, p. 177.

22 C. H. Turner, "The Earliest List of Durham Manuscripts," *Journal of Theol. Studies* 19 (1928) 121.

23 Fr. Stegmüller, *Rep. bibl.* 5338.

24 *Verbum abbr.* 53; PL 205, 164C.

25 *Summa de sacramentis*; ed. J. A. Dugauquier, *Anal. med. Namurcensia* 7 (Louvain, 1957) 76.

26 B. Smalley, p. 685.

27 A. Landgraf, "Some Unknown Writings of the Early Scholastic Period," *The New Scholast.* 4 (1930) 14. Idem, "Unters. zur Gelehrtengeschichte des 12. Jahrhunderts," *Studi e testi* 122 (Vatican, 1946) 281: "Mag. Iuo Carnotensis dicebat quod huiusmodi relaxationes sunt pius dolus pastorum ecclesie".

Patr. 48 (Q. VI. 31), f. 23-25 (s. xii), partly transcribed by the cataloguers F. Leitschuh and H. Fischer.[28] The full text has been published by B. Barth[29] and by G. Morin.[30] The writer states that he is living in Paris. He concludes the letter to his teacher with the words: "Salutat uos magister Robertus prepositus scole magistri Iuonis." P. Glorieux[31] suggests that the *dominus Luitoldus* referred to at the end of the letter may be Lutolph of Novara, a compatriot of Peter Lombard, who advocated the condemnation of Abelard at Soissons (1121). The comment on Lutolph who taught in Reims is no flattery: "Dominus Luitoldus ueniens Parisius, omissa nostra doctrina, astronomie et nicromantie experimentis operam dedit."[32] In point of time the writer's reference to Ivo may well be a confirmation of William's[33] report that Ivo was one of his teachers in Paris. The identity of Master Robert is more difficult to establish, for in the forties there were at least four masters by that name in Paris.

In this context it should be noted that there was a Master Ivo in the cathedral chapter of Le Mans. A notification published by William of Passavant, bishop of Le Mans (1143-87), and dated to 1143-55, shows that Abbot Matthew of Saint-Florence (Saumur) and "Iuo magister scolarum" acted as witnesses.[34] Incidentally, Abbot Matthew, later bishop of Angers (1155-62), once consulted Gilbert of Poitiers on some theological problems.[35] A settlement arranged by Bishop William, dated to 1164-70, also notes Ivo's presence: "Iuone magistro scolarum."[36] In 1178 the same Ivo witnessed a charter together with two other masters attached to the cathedral: "Huic compositioni interfuerunt de clericis nostris Iuo magister scolarum, magister Hernaudus, magister Girardus de Carcere."[37] About 1180 his presence is recorded again: "Interfuerunt Tigaretus capellanus, Iuo magister scolarum ... magister Ernaldus ... magister Alanus de Buays."[38]

28 *Katalog der Handschr. der k. Bibl. zu Bamberg* 1 (Bamberg, 1895-1906) 412.

29 "Ein neues Dokument zur Geschichte der frühscholastischen Theologie," *Theol. Quartalschrift* 101 (Tübingen, 1920) 409-415.

30 "Lettre inédite d'un étudiant en théol. de l'univ. de Paris vers la fin du xiie siècle," *Rech. de théol. anc. et méd.* 6 (1934) 412-416.

31 "Autour d'une lettre," *Rech de théol. anc. et méd.* 21 (1954) 143.

32 B. Barth, p. 415. G. Morin, p. 416. Abelard, *Hist. cal.*; ed. J. Monfrin, p. 69: "Lutulfus Lumbardus."

33 *Hist. hieros.* xix, 12; ed. Huygens, p. 822.

34 P. Marchegay, *Chartes mancelles de l'Abbaye de Saint-Florence, Revue hist. et archéol. du Maine* 3 (1878) 360-361.

35 "Placuit uobis nostram consulere paruitatem ..." ed. L. d'Achéry in 1651 (= PL 156, 1023-24), then Martène and Durand, *Thes. nov. Anecd.* 1 (Paris, 1717) 427, and again J. Mabillon, *Annal. Ben.* 6 (Paris, 1739) 316: all used a Grandmont manuscript now lost.

36 P. de Farcy, *Cartul. de Saint-Victor au Mans. Prieuré de l'Abbaye de Mont-Saint-Michel* (Paris, 1895) 25.

37 P. Marchegay, *Chartes,* pp. 366-367.

38 L. Delisle and E. Berger, *Recueil des acts de Henri II* (Paris, 1920) II, 136-137.

In conclusion it can be said that in the middle of the century three masters left Paris for Chartres: Thierry the Breton, Bernard the Breton, and Ivo of Chartres. Bernard and Ivo studied under Thierry. It is not known at present where Thierry received his schooling. We shall see that during the same period Peter Helias returned to Poitiers and William of Conches joined the court of Geoffrey, count of Normandy, while Richard surnamed the bishop went to Coutance. Unfortunately, the reasons for this exodus are unknown.

II

Masters in Paris

Paris benefitted greatly from masters schooled in Chartres, but a number of Parisian masters received their training elsewhere. We need not enlarge here on the two well-known masters and antagonists William of Champeaux (d. 1121) and Peter Abelard (d. 1142). They are not associated with Chartres. While Abelard was at Soissons (1121), he encountered two masters he considered his staunchest opponents: Master Alberic of Reims, who died as Archbishop of Bourges (1136-41), and Master Lotulph (Luitolph, Letald, Leutold) of Novara.[1]

Master Alberic of Reims is not to be confused with the Master Alberic whose lectures on *dialectica* were attended "in Francia" by Hugh of Pisa.[2] He taught on Mont Sainte-Geneviève and his followers were known as *Montani*[3] or *Albrici*.[4] This Master Alberic who is not otherwise known as a theologian objected to making any distinction between nature and person in God,[5] a view not shared by Gilbert of Poitiers and his followers.[6] One of them, Hugh of Honau, voices his solemn thanks to Cyril of Alexandria, John Damascene, Basil and Gregory (Nazianzen) who convinced him that in God nature and person are not the same and that the personal *proprietates* are not the same as the persons and essence in God.[7]

Master Alberic seems to have acted as chancellor at Sainte-Geneviève

---

1 Abelard, *Hist. cal.*; ed. J. Monfrin, p. 83. Otto of Freising, *Gesta Frid.* I, 49; MGH SrG 46 (1912) 69. Gerhoch of Reichersberg, *Ep.* 21; PL 193, 367C. Lino Cassiani, "La scuola di Novara ai tempi di Pier Lombardo," *Miscell. Lombardiana* (Novara, 1957) 367. D. Van den Eynde, "Du nouveau sur deux maîtres lombards contemporains du Maître des Sentences," *Pier Lombardo* 1 (1953) 6-9. J. R. Williams, "The Cathedral School of Reims in the Time of Master Alberic," *Traditio* 20 (1964) 93-114.

2 Hugh of Honau, *Liber de diuers. nature* I, 7; ed. N. Haring, p. 122.

3 L. M. de Rijk, "Some New Evidence on Twelfth-Century Logic," *Vivarium* 4 (1966) 1-57.

4 R. W. Hunt, "Studies on Priscian I," *Med. and Ren. Studies* 2 (1950) 50.

5 Hugh of Honau, *Liber de diuers.* I, 7; ed. N. Haring, p. 122.

6 Cf. N. Haring, "The Porretans and the Greek Fathers," *MS* 24 (1962) 189.

7 Hugh of Honau, *Liber de diuersitate* I, 9; ed. Haring, p. 123.

in 1135.[8] He still held this position in 1140/1.[9] During this period, probably about 1136, Abelard resumed his lectures on logic which were attended "for near two whole years" by John of Salisbury. When Abelard left, John continued under Alberic and Master Robert of Melun.[10] John praises Alberic as "opinatissimus dialecticus". A commentator on Priscian tells the story that Master Alberic once attended lectures on Priscian delivered by Gilbert who taught in Paris from about 1137-42. Master Alberic was accompanied by the grammarian Master Garnerus who aroused Gilbert's anger by disregarding a rule he had just explained.[11] At an unknown date Alberic took up studies in Bologna, "unlearned that which he had taught," and returned to Paris where he "untaught the same."[12] Robert, on the other hand, "went on to the study of divine letters."[13] He died in 1167 as bishop of Hereford. Of his theological orthodoxy John of Cornwall assured Pope Alexander III: "In theologia nichil hereticum docuisse certissimum est."[14] Both Robert and Master Maurice of Sully, later bishop of Paris (1161-96), argued in lectures and debates against Peter Lombard's christology.[15] In the presence of Master Achard of Saint-Victor, later bishop of Avranches (1161-71), and Robert of Melun (d. 1167) Robert Cricklade publicly denounced Lombard as a heretic.[16] Robert's followers were called *Melidunenses* or *Meludinenses*.[17]

8 R. de Lasteyrie, *Cartul.* 1, 258, no. 259: "Albericus cancellarius scripsit" (charter of Sainte-Geneviève).

9 R. de Lasteyrie, *Cartul.* 1, 258, no. 259: "Albericus cancellarius scripsit" (charter of Sainte-Geneviève). *Cartul.* 1, 273, no. 282: "Ego Aubericus cancellarius subscripsi" (charter of Sainte-Geneviève).

10 *Metal.* II, 10; ed. Webb, p. 78. The schools of both Alberic and Robert are mentioned by Geoffrey of Sant-Victor, *Fons Philosophiae*, vv. 265 and 269; ed. P. Michaud-Quantin, *Analecta med. Namurcensia* 8 (Namur, 1956) 44. E. A. Synan (tr.) *The Fountain of Philosophy* (Toronto, 1972) 49. Like Peter Lombard, Robert of Melun stayed at Saint-Victor for a while. Concerning the masters of this school see Jean Châtillon," Les écoles de Chartres et de Saint-Victor", *Settimane di studio del Centro italiano di studi sull'alto medioevo* 19 (Spoleto, 1972) 818. Châtillon lists Hugh (d. 1141), Abbot Achard (d. 1170 or 1171), Andrew (d. 1175), Prior Richard (d. 1173), Geoffrey (d. after 1197), and Thomas Gallus (d. 1246).

11 R. W. Hunt, "Studies on Priscian II," *Med. and Ren. Studies* 2 (1950) 42.

12 *Metal.* II, 10; ed. Webb, p. 79.

13 *Ibid.* Robert attended the Council of Reims in 1148. John of Salisbury, *Hist. pontif.* 8; ed. Poole, p. 17.

14 *Eulogium ad Alexandrum papam tertium* 4; ed. N. Haring, MS 13 (1951) 268. Concerning Robert's writings see R. Martin, "L'œuvre théol. de Robert de Melun," *Revue d'hist. eccl.* 15 (1920) 456-489. (1) *Questiones de diuina pagina*; ed. R. Martin, *Spicil. s. Lov.* 13 (Louvain, 1932). (2) *Questiones de epistolis Pauli*; ed. R. Martin, *Spicil. s. Lov.* 18 (1938). (3) *Sententie*; ed. R. Martin, *Spicil. s. Lov.* 21 (1947) and 25 (1952).

15 *Eulogium* 4; ed. Haring, p. 268.

16 Robert Cricklade, *Speculum fidei* III, 5; ed. R. W. Hunt, "English Learning in the Late Twelfth Century," *Transactions of the Royal Hist. Society* IV, 19 (1936) 37-38. See the article in *Dict. of Nat. Biography* 16, 1254-55. The *Speculum* is preserved in MS Cambridge, CCC 380, f. 1-132v (s. xii): "Fidei catholice qua unus deus creditur ..."

17 Jocelin de Brakelonde, *Chronica*; ed. Th. Arnold, RS 96, 1 (London, 1890) 240.

On the advice of his preceptors John resorted to "the grammarian of Conches" and heard his teaching for the space of three years.[18] In the meantime he did some teaching of his own to make ends meet and took courses conducted by Richard surnamed the bishop.[19] In 1159 Richard appears as an archdeacon of Coutances. A letter is still extant in which John asks Master Richard for the works of Aristotle.[20] In 1171 Richard was elected bishop of Avranches to succeed Master Achard. He died there in 1182.[21] John calls him "hominem fere nullius doctrine expertem".[22] Richard is one of the scholars that left Paris in the middle of the century.

John of Salisbury mentions that, while studying subjects pertaining to the quadruvium, he "had for some time followed both the German Hardwin" and Master Thierry for whose course he has very little praise.[23] He found the lectures on rhetoric by Master Peter Helias much more satisfactory.[24] This Master Peter Helias (or Helie) was *natione Pictauiensis*, to adopt the phrase used by William of Tyre who lists him among the "doctores precipui" of the liberal arts in Paris.[25] Like Master Bernard the Breton and Master Ivo of Chartres Peter began his studies in Paris under Master Thierry.

The author of the *Metamorphosis Golie* saw Peter Helias together with Bernard and Ivo.[26] In the fifties Peter must have returned to his native Poitiers, for in 1156 he witnessed a charter issued by Gilbert's successor Calo, bishop of Poitiers.[27] It may be worth recalling that Master Bernard, Master Ivo and Master Richard the Bishop left Paris at about the same time. It seems that Peter Helias signed a charter drawn up by Bernard, bishop of Saintes, at the monastery Saint-Florence, near Niort, in the diocese of Poitiers. It is dated 1159: Datum apud Sanctum Florentium iuxta Niortum ... Ego Petrus Helie canonicus concessi et subscripsi."[28]

---

18 *Metal.* II, 10; ed. Webb, p. 80.

19 *Metal.* I, 24; ed. Webb, p. 57.

20 *Ep.* 211; PL 199, 234C.

21 *Gallia chr.* 11 (Paris, 1874) 481.

22 *Metal.* II, 10; ed. Webb, p. 80. According to the chronicler Robert de Monte Richard was "uir magne literature tam secularis quam diuine." *Chronicon*; ed. R. Howlett, RS 82, 4 (London, 1889) 304.

23 *Metal.* II, 10; ed. Webb, p. 80.

24 *Ibid.*

25 *Hist. hieros.* XIX, 12; ed. Huygens, p. 822.

26 *Metamorphosis Golie*, v. 198; ed. Huygens, p. 771.

27 B. Ledain, *Cartulaires et chartes de l'Abbaye de l'Absie*, Archives hist. du Poitou 25 (1895) 90-92: "Huius rei testes magister Arnaudus Pictauensis, ecclesie Briocensis diaconus, Petrus Helias eiusdem ecclesie capicerius." Concerning Master Arnald see N. Haring, "Bischof Gilbert II. von Poitiers und seine Erzdiakone," *Deutsches Archiv* 21 (1965) 150-171.

28 *Gallia chr.* 2, 460E and 461A instr.

According to C. Oudin[29] Peter resorted to litigation with Isaac of Stella about a piece of forest land, and Gilbert of Poitiers (1142-54) intervened. This view is shared by F. Bliemetzrieder[30] but rejected by J. Debray[31] who maintains "sans doute" that the litigant was a certain Pierre Hélie of Chauvigny.[32] Arnulph, bishop of Lisieux (1141-81), addressed a letter to Master "Petrus Helye" requesting the return from school of a young canon whose conduct was unsatisfactory.[33] John of Salisbury refers to Master Peter Helias in a letter addressed, in 1166, to Richard, archdeacon of Poitiers. John wrote on behalf of Master Walter in Reims who was anxious to recover the books Peter Helias had borrowed from him.[34] This may indicate that Master Peter Helias had died. A gloss quoted by Ch. Thurot records the rumour that Peter was a chancellor: "Dominus Petrus Helye qui fuit cancellarius ut quidam dicunt."[35] The *Cronica abbreuiata* preserved in MS Paris, Bibl. nat. Lat. 15009 calls him dean: "Fuit etiam in Pictauensi ecclesia decanus Petrus Helias in scientia litterarum secularium magnus philosophus (f. 77)." Accordingly, Peter was no theologian although a commentary on Boethius, *De Trinitate*, has been attributed to him.[36]

Peter Helias is best known as the author of the *Sumna super Priscianum*.[37] R. W. Hunt notes that "in its own line" the *Summa* could

---

29 *Comm. de script. eccl.* 2 (Leipzig, 1722) 1485. *Hist. litt.* 12, 486 and 13, 303.

30 "Isaak von Stella", *Jahrb. für Philosophie und spekul. Theologie* 18 (1904) 10.

31 "Biographie d'Isaac de Stella," *Cîteaux* 10 (1959) 188. There was a "Petrus Elie leuita" at Angoulême according to a charter dated to 1117-33. J. Nanglard, *Cartul. de l'église d'Angoulême* (1899) 132. no. 138.

32 Listed in Beauchette-Filleau, *Dict. hist. biogr. et gén. des familles de l'ancien Poitou* 2 (Poitiers, 1891) 352.

33 *Ep.* 14; PL 201, 29A, or *Ep.* 22; ed. F. Barlow, *The Letters of Arnulph of Lisieux, Camden Third Series* 61 (London, 1939) 29. The date (ca. 1159) given by Barlow is quite uncertain. The letter seems to belong to a time when Peter was in Paris.

34 *Ep.* 168; PL 199, 159A: "Negotium magistri Galteri, clerici domini Remensis, pro recuperandis libris quos idem Galterus magistro Petro Elie commendauerat".

35 Ch. Thurot, *Extraits de divers mss. latins pour servir à l'hist. des doctr. gramm. au moyen âge, Notices et extr.* 22, 2 (Paris, 1869) 18.

36 See N. Haring, *Comm. on Boethius by Thierry of Chartres and His School, Texts and Studies* 20 (Toronto, 1971) 20-22. For the numerous writings attributed to Peter see M. Manitius, *Gesch. der lat. Lit.* 3 (Munich, 1931) 186-187. The authenticity of a versification of the *Canticle* attributed to Peter Helias in one of the two extant manuscripts has not yet been examined. See Fr. Stegmüller, *Rep. bibl.* 4 (Madrid, 1954) 314, no. 6615.

37 Manuscripts are listed by Jan Pinborg, *Die Entwicklung der Sprachtheorie im Mittelalter, Beiträge* 42, 2 (1967) 324. Pinborg (p. 23) holds that it was written ca. 1150. The relationship between Peter and William of Conches is still a matter of speculation.

not be improved upon.[38] J. Pinborg considers it "the most important achievement" among 12th-century commentators.[39] The authenticity of the commentary on Cicero's *De inuentione,* attributed to Peter Helias in MS Vat. Ottob. Lat. 2993 (s. xv) is still to be examined. The library of Bruges owns a volume containing what is called *Absoluta Petri Helye.*[40] Another volume contains the *Commentum Petri Helye super maius uolumen Prisciani.*[41] Peter's followers were called *Heliste.*[42]

R. W. Hunt has shown that Huguccio of Ferrara (d. 1210) borrowed from Peter Helias.[43] His *Summa super Priscianum maiorem* was incorporated in the *Speculum doctrinale* of Vincent of Beauvais (d. ca. 1264).[44] *Ad ann.* 1237 a chronicler has recorded the instruction: "ut ... Priscianum maiorem et minorem et Petrum Heliam ... conscriberet."[45]

John of Salisbury also recalls Master Adam (of Petit-Pont), an Englishman and a "man of exceeding sharp wits."[46] But "not for a day" was John his disciple.[47] Together with Hugh of Champfleury (d. 1175) Adam testified against Gilbert at the Parisian consistory in 1147.[48] In the following year he attended a meeting convoked by St. Bernard after the Council of Reims.[49] The view that he became bishop of St. Asaph has been discredited by L. Minio-Paluello.[50] Adam had many followers[51] known as *Paruipontani.*[52]

Alexander Neckam (d. 1217) praises Adam as a star still brilliant in his own time, whereas Gilbert, Alberic, Abelard, and Thierry had only been like earthly lights. John notes that Adam wrote a work entitled *Ars disserendi*[54] whose style he deplores while praising its contents: "utinam

38 "Studies on Priscian II," *Med. and Ren. Studies* 2 (1950) 39.

39 *Die Entwicklung,* p. 23. See also L. M. de Rijk, *Logica modernorum* II, 1 (Assen, 1967) 221-228.

40 MS Bruges, Bibl. mun. 544, f. 94-117v (s. xiii).

41 MS Bruges, Bibl. mun. 535, f. 1-63 (s. xiv). See also MS Bruges, Bibl. mun. 536, f. 1-79 (s. xiii): "Questiones super maius uolumen Prisciani ..."

42 R. W. Hunt, "Studies on Priscian II," *Med. and Ren. Studies* 2 (1950) 17.

43 "Hugutio and Petrus Helias," *ibid.,* pp. 174-78.

44 *Speculum doctrinale* II, 8 ff.; ed. Douai (1624) 86 ff.

45 MGH SS 23, 524.

46 *Metal.* II, 10; ed. Webb, p. 81.

47 *Metal.* III, 3; ed. Webb, p. 134.

48 Otto fo Freising, *Gesta Frid.* I, 53; p. 75.

49 Geoffrey of Auxerre, *Scriptura;* ed. N. Haring, *Anal. Cist.* 22 (1966) 35: "Adam de Paruo Ponte."

50 "The Ars disserendi of Adam of Balsham," *Med. and Ren. Studies* 3 (1954) 116-169.

51 *Metal.* III, 3; ed. Webb, p. 134: "Noster ille Anglus Peripateticus Adam cuius uestigia sequuntur multi."

52 R. W. Hunt, "Studies on Priscian II," pp. 54-55.

53 *Twelfth-Century Logic* 1 (Rome, 1956) p. xxii. A. Vernet, "Une épitaphe de Thierry de Chartres," *Recueil de travaux offert à M. Clovis Brunel: Mém. et documents* 12 (Paris, 1855) 666. Alexander Neckam, *Suppl. defectuum operis* II, 151: MS Paris, Bibl. nat. Lat. 11867, f. 230v.

54 It is also known as *Dyaletica (Alexandri),* dated to 1132. The *Ars disserendi* has been edited by L. Minio-Paluello, *Twelfth-Century Logic* 1 (Rome, 1956) 3-111. The second recension of this work con-

bene dixisset bona que dixit."[55] He also wrote a work called *De uten-silibus* or *Phaletolum* of which thirteen manuscripts are known to have survived.[56] There is evidence that Adam was also a competent theologian.[57] He seems to have been an able textual critic. Neckam relates that where Thierry read *plunula* in Aristotle's *Elenchi* Master Adam corrected it to *lunula*.[58] The necrology of Le Val (dioc. of Bayeux) has recorded Adam's death on 6 August: "Obiit magister Adam de Paruo Ponte."[59] Both the year and the place are unknown.

"Returning after the expiration of three years" John found Master Gilbert and heard him in logic and theology.[60] But Gilbert, as John puts it, was removed too quickly (1142). His successor was Master Robert Pulleyn (d. 1146). In a charter, dated 1144, Master Robert Pulleyn is recorded as witness together with Archdeacon Ivo and Master Walter: "Hec sunt nomina clericorum qui interfuerunt: magister Robertus Pullanus, Iuo Parisiensis archidiaconus, magister Gauterus."[61] When Bishop Ascelin of Rochester (1142-48) requested Robert's return to his diocese, St. Bernard asked him to let Master Robert stay in Paris "ob sanam doctrinam."[62] In 1144 Robert was made a cardinal-priest by Lucius II (1144-45), then chancellor of the Roman curia.[63] While Robert was in Paris, he wrote his *Sententiarum libri octo*.[64]

After Robert had left for Rome (1144), John of Salisbury continued his study of theology under Simon of Poissy, "a trusty lecturer, but dull in disputation."[65] Simon of Poissy (near Versailles), who had a brother called Osmund,[66] is mentioned in the chronicle of Morigny as being in

tains certain sigla (B. H. T.) which L. Minio-Paluello interprets as indicating quotations from B(er-nard), H(elias), and T(hierry).

55 *Metal.* IV, 3; ed. Webb, p. 167.

56 L. Minio-Paluello, *The Ars disserendi,* p. 118.

57 L. Minio-Paluello, *The Ars disserendi,* pp. 168-169. The magister R. Polanus named in the same text is Master Robert Pulleyn (1146).

58 *Corrog. Promethei*; ed. P. Meyer, *Notices et extr.* 35, 2 (Paris, 1897) 677: "Ubi Terricus legit · plunulas antequam iste (liber) uenisset in manus magistri Ade Parui Pontis."

59 A. Molinier, *Recueil des hist. de la France: Obituaires de la Prov. de Sens* I, 1 (Paris, 1902) 630.

60 *Metal.* II, 10; ed. Webb, p. 82.

61 R. de Lasteyrie, *Cartul. gén. de Paris* 1, 293, nos. 313-314. J. Dépoin, *Recueil des chartes et docum. de Saint-Martin-des-Champs* 2: *Archives de la France monast.* 16 (Paris 1913) 144, no. 277. I. Brady, "Peter Lombard: Canon of Notre-Dame," *Rech. de théol. anc. et méd.* 32 (1965) 284.

62 *Ep.* 205; PL 182, 372A. L. Hödl, *Die Geschichte der schol. Literatur, Beiträge* 38, 4 (1960) 96-102.

63 F. Courtney, *Card. Robert Pullen, Anal. Gregoriana* 64 (Rome 1954) 11-17. His name appears un-der a decretal dated 14 February 1145. Jaffé-Loewenfeld, *Reg.* 8713.

64 PL 186, 639-1010 (ed. H. Mathoud). Only two manuscripts are known to be extant: London, B.M. Royal 10.B.V., f. 1-113 (s. xii) and Troyes 459, f. 1-142c (s. xii-xiii). Fr. Pelster, in *Scholastik* 12 (1937) 239.

65 *Metal.* II, 10; ed. Webb, p. 82.

66 R. de Lasteyrie, *Cartul.* 1, 381, no. 450 (dated 1164). He is not to be confused with the "nobleman" Simon of Poissy recorded in *Archives de l'Hôtel Dieu de Paris* (Paris, 1894) 14, no. 33 (1189) and 18, no. 41 (1193).

the king's service: "Qui acceptis regalibus litteris, comitantibus secum Petro capellano et magistro Simone de Pissiaco ..."[67] In 1178 "magister Symon de Pissiaco" made a donation to Saint-Denis du Pas.[68] Simon died in Paris: "De domo sancte Marie obiit magister Symon de Pissiaco qui oratorium Beati Dionisii de Passu reparauit."[69] He is not known to have published anything.

John refers to Hugh of Saint-Victor (d. 1141)[70] but makes no mention of Peter Lombard. After almost 12 years of studies the English scholar joined the papal court where, in 1148, he witnessed the trial of Gilbert of Poitiers.[71] He died as bishop of Chartres (1176-80).

We are now in a better position to appreciate the verses of the *Metamorphosis Golie* dealing with the masters of Paris in the forties. The author describes a dream in which he saw the "doctor Carnotensis", the bishop of Poitiers, the inhabitant of Petit-Pont, the famous theologian Lombard with Ivo, Peter Helias, and Bernard. Most of them, we are told, followed Abelard. He also saw Reginald the monk, Robert the theologian, Bartholomew, Robert Amiclas, and Héloise in search of Abelard. The poet identifies some masters without giving their names. Thus he describes Thierry as "that teacher from Chartres", Gilbert as the man from Poitiers, Adam as the "inhabitant of Petit-Pont". The section that interests us here reads:

> Ibi doctor cernitur ille Carnotensis
> Cuius lingua uehemens truncat uelut ensis
> Et hic presul presulum stat Pictauiensis
> Proprius nubencium miles et castrensis.
>
> Inter hos et alios in parte remota
> Parui Pontis incola, non loquor ignota,
> Disputabat digitis directis in iota.
> Et quecumque dixerat erant per se nota.
>
> Celebrem theologum uidimus Lumbardum
> Cum Iuone Helyam Petrum et Bernardum
> Quorum opobalsamum spirat os et nardum
> Et professi plurimi sunt Abaielardum.[72]

67 *Chron. Maurin.* III; PL 180, 172.
68 R. de Lasteyrie, *Cartul.* 1, 456, no. 559.
69 B. Guérard, *Cartul. de Notre-Dame de Paris* 4 (Paris, 1841) 201, no. 353.
70 *Metal.* I, 5; ed. Webb, p. 19.
71 *Hist. pontif.* 8; ed. Poole, pp. 16-40.
72 *Metamorphosis Golie,* vv. 189-200; ed. Huygens, p. 771. Th. Wright, *The Latin Poems* (London, 1841) 28-29. The variant Ernaldum for Bernardum is proven wrong by the next line. See the *Alloquium ad S. Bernardum,* ed. J. Leclercq, *Receuil d'études. Storia e letteratura* 114 (Rome, 1969) 336: "Nardus tua calida, humilis et odorifica, et tuum ber quod puteus ..."

The poem describes the scene after Gilbert's election to the see of Poitiers (1142). Bernard who is associated with Ivo (d. 1165) and Peter Helias must be Bernard the Breton who was successively archdeacon of Paris, chancellor of Chartres, and bishop of Quimperlé (1159-67). It is not unlikely that he left Paris (ca. 1156) to replace Thierry of Chartres. The statement that most of those scholars "professed Abelard" comes somewhat as a surprise. Unfortunately we are not told in what respect they followed Abelard. We do know that Peter Lombard used and followed Abelard's *Theologia,* as we learn from John of Cornwall.[73] But it is difficult to establish to what extent the other masters "professed" Abelard who taught theology in Paris from ca. 1136 until shortly before his death in 1142. The ever-increasing redactions of the *Theologia* were available since 1120.[74] The poem continues:

> Reginaldus monachus clamose contendit
> Et obliquis singulos uerbis reprehendit
> Qui nostrum Porphirium laqueo suspendit.
>
> Robertus theologus corde uiuens mundo
> Adest et Manerius quem nulli secundo
> Alto loquens spiritu et ore profundo
> Quo quidem subtilior nullus est in mundo.
>
> Hinc et Bartholomeus, faciem acutus,
> Retor, dyaleticus sermone astutus
> Et Robertus Amiclas simile secutus
> Cum hiis quos pretereo populus minutus
>
> Nupta querit ubi sit suus Palatinus.[75]

The poet names thirteen scholars, including Abelard, some of whom have not been identified. The identity of Reginald the monk and Bartholomew is still uncertain. Reginald the monk is hardly identical with the Parisian Archdeacon Reginald whose signatures date from 1094-1119.[76] Robert the theologian may be Robert of Melun or Robert Pulleyn. Master Robert Amiclas received a donation (dated ca. 1175) from a certain Walterius de Barut (who at the time of the donation was a "magister in Francia") and from his brother Eustachius: "Notum facimus presentibus et futuris quod magistro Roberto Amicle et eius heredibus donauimus ..."[77] We know a little more about Master

73 *Eulogium* 3; ed. N. Haring, MS 13 (1951) 265.
74 *Theologia Summi Boni;* ed. H. Ostlender, *Beiträge* 35, 2-3 (1935).
75 *Metamorphosis Golie,* vv. 201-217; ed. Huygens 771.
76 R. Lasteyrie, *Cartul. gén.* 1, 138-204.
77 R. de Lasteyrie, *Cartul.* 1, 437, no. 533. Cf. PL 205, 934B.

Manerius (Mainerius). On 4 September 1154 he witnessed a charter drawn up by Abbot Odo of Deuil (1151-62) at Saint-Denis together with the Archdeacon Bernard (d. 1167), Master Peter Lombard, and other masters: "Huic siquidem nostre executioni interfuerunt Odo abbas Sancti Dionisii, magister Bernardus archidiaconus Parisiensis, magister Petrus Longobardus, magister Galterus canonicus, magister Manerius, Hugo cancellarius Nouiomensis (Noyon), magister Remigius, magister Guillelmus Prior sancte Marie de Gorneio ..."[78]

The presence of so many schoolmen witnessing a document is an eloquent testimony to William of Tyre's remark that he had to adjust his lessons according to the availability of his teachers: "Hos alternatim secundum quod eorum negocia presentes eos permittebant uel absentes, annis audiuimus circiter decem."[79] A notification by Peter Lombard, bishop of Paris (1159-60), includes Master Manerius and Master Anselm among the witnesses.[80] His presence is recorded in a document concerning the Hôtel-Dieu of Paris, dated 1164.[81] In 1171 Master Manerius signed a charter in Paris.[82] Three years later Pope Alexander III refers to him in a letter to the dean and the chapter of Paris, dated 28 October 1174.[83]

Gerald of Wales who studied under Manerius in Paris confirms his allegiance to Abelard: "Magistrum Meinerium, principalem Petri Abelardi discipulum et rethorem incomparabiliter eximium, in auditorio suo Parisius coram multitudine scolarium recitantem audiuimus."[84] He heard Master Manerius complain about the evils of his day: "Magistrum Mainerium in auditorio scole sue Parisius dicentem et damna sui temporis plangentem audiui." He is undoubtedly the Master "Mananerius" quoted in a gloss on Priscian.[86]

We have frequently made reference to William of Tyre's account of his study years which may likewise be presented in full. It depicts the Parisian scene about 1145-1160: "Fuerunt autem nobis hoc medio tempore, quo in partibus transmarinis nostram in disciplinis transegimus

78 J. Ramackers, *Papsturkunden in Frankreich. Abh. der Gesellsch. der Wiss. zu Göttingen,* phil. hist. Klasse III, 21 (1937) 146. Notre Dame de Gournaye-sur-Marne was a foundation of Saint-Martin-des-Champs. See *Gallia chr.* 7 (Paris, 1744) 50 instr.

79 "Guillaume de Tyr," *Latomus* 21 (1962) 822.

80 R. de Lasteyrie, *Cartul.* 1, 362, no. 415: "astantibus ... magistro Manerio ... magistro Anselmo."

81 E. Coyecque, *Archives de l'Hôtel-Dieu de Paris* (Paris, 1844) 2, no. 2.

82 PL 205, 900B. R. de Lasteyrie, *Cartul.* 1, 413, no. 496: "Interfuerunt magister Manerius ..."

83 *Ep.* 1146; PL 200, 998B. Ph. Jaffé, *Reg. Pont.* 12395. *Chartul. Univ. Parisiensis* 1 (Paris, 1889) 7: "dilecto filio nostro magistro Mainerio ..."

84 *Spec. ecclesie,* dist. I; ed. J. S. Brewer, RS 21, 4 (London, 1873) 7.

85 *Gemma ecclesie* II, 37; ed. Brewer, RS 21, 2 (London, 1962) 349.

86 R. W. Hunt, "Studies on Priscian II," p. 16.

adolescentiam (et) in paupertate uoluntaria litterarum studiis etatis nostros dedicauimus dies, in liberalibus artibus doctores precipui uiri uenerabiles et pia recordatione digni, scientiarum uasa, thesauri disciplinarum, magister Bernardus Brito, qui postea (fuit) in patria unde ortus fuerat episcopus Cornualenssis, magister Petrus Helie, natione Pictauenssis, magister Iuo, genere et natione Carnotenssis.

Hi omnes magistri Theoderici senioris, uiri litteratissimi, per multa tempora auditores fuerunt. Horum tamen nouissimus, magister Iuo, magistri Gilleberti Porrea Pictauenssis episcopi, quem post magistrum Theodericum audierat, doctrinam profitebatur. Hos alternatim, secundum quod eorum negocia presentes eos nobis permittebant uel absentes, annis audiuimus circiter decem."[87]

In addition to these "doctores precipui" William heard others, though less frequently and mainly for the sake of debates:

"Audiuimus et alios etsi non assidue, tamen sepius et maxime disputationis gratia, uiros eximios et omni laude prosequendos: magistrum Albericum de Monte, magistrum Robertum de Meleuduno, magistrum Mainerium, Robertum Amiclas, magistrum de Paruo Ponte, qui uidebantur quasi maiora luminaria.[88] These masters, it seems, taught him the liberal arts. In theology William heard Peter Lombard for six years (ca. 1153-59) and quite frequently Master Maurice of Sully:

"In theologia autem uirum in ea scientia singularem, cuius opera que extant prudentum chorus cum ueneratione amplectitur et colit cum reuerentia, uirum sana doctrina per omnia commendabilem, magistrum uidelicet Petrum Lonbardum, qui postea fuit Parisienssis episcopus, annis sex continuis diligenter audiuimus. Magistrum quoque Mauricium, qui ei postmodum in eodem episcopatu successit, sepius audiuimus".[89]

William then went to Bologna where he studied civil law under Hugolinus de Porta Ravennate and Bulgarus. He also heard Martin and James, but less regularly. William then adds that Hilary of Orleans, advanced in years, taught him "in auctorum expositione" while William of Soissons taught him geometry, especially Euclid.[90] It was John of Salisbury who taught William of Soissons the rudiments of logic.[91]

We have already seen that Robert of Melun and Master Maurice disagreed with the Lombard's christology.[92] William, it seems, found nothing wrong with his teaching. He calls him "uirum sana doctrina per omnia commendabilem."

---

87 *Hist. hieros.* XIX, 12; ed. Huygens, p. 822.
88 *Hist. hieros.* XIX, 12; ed. Huygens, pp. 822-823.
89 *Hist. hieros.* XIX, 12; ed. Huygens, p. 823.
90 *Ibid.*
91 *Metal.* II, 10; ed. Webb, p. 81.
92 John of Cornwall, *Eulogium* 4; ed. Haring 268.

In addition to the Parisian masters listed by William of Tyre it should be noted that about 1150 "magister Gauterus canonicus Parisiensis" acted as guarantor.[93] About the same time he acted as witness.[94] He is probably identical with "magister Walterus sacerdos" who is listed with "magister Albertus subdiaconus" about 1142[95] and identical with "magister Gauterus canonicus" listed in 1144.[96]

There was also Master Hugh of Champfleury,[97] mentioned neither by William nor in the *Metamorphosis*. In 1151 Hugh became the king's chancellor. The bishop's chancellor at that time was still Algrinus. In 1160 Master Anselm witnessed a charter with Master Manerius.[98] About the same year Master Odo became chancellor and wrote down a charter signed by Master Galterus and others. Master Galterus was still living in 1164,[100] perhaps as late as 1174[101] and 1175.[102] Both Peter Lombard and Maurice continued to call themselves "masters" after they had been elected to the episcopal see of Paris.[103]

The question may be raised: where did these masters live and teach? Everard of Ypres tells us that Gilbert taught *in aula episcopi*, while Gerard of Wales speaks of the *auditorium* in which he heard Master Manerius.[104] Master Ivo, as we have noted, had his *scola* and his *prepositus*: "Salutat uos magister Robertus prepositus scole magistri Iuonis."[105] Many masters retired to the *domus* attached to Notre-Dame. Hence we read: "De domo sancte Marie obiit magister Symon de Pissiaco," or at a later date: "Eodem die de domo sancte Marie obiit Aubertus, domini pape notarius."[106] Master "Guimundus Carnotensis" also died there: "De domo sancte Marie obiit magister Guimundus Carnotensis concanonicus noster."[107]

Bishop Peter Lombard had his *domus* as is stated in a document of the

93 R. de Lasteyrie, *Cartul.* 1, 326, no. 360.

94 R. de Lasteyrie, *Cartul.* 1, 328, no. 368.

95 R. de Lasteyrie, *Cartul.* 1, 281, no. 359. See also p. 280, no. 290: "Gauterus sacerdos" (date 1142).

96 R. de Lasteyrie, *Cartul.* 1, 293, no. 313.

97 R. de Lasteyrie, *Cartul.* 1, 323, no. 359.

98 R. de Lasteyrie, *Cartul.* 1, 362, no. 415.

99 R. de Lasteyrie, *Cartul.* 1, 361, no. 451.

100 R. de Lasteyrie, *Cartul.* 1, 383, no. 451.

101 R. de Lasteyrie, *Cartul.* 1, 430, no. 521: "Signum magistri Galteri presbiteri."

102 PL 205, 910D "Signum magistri Galteri presbiteri."

103 R. de Lasteyrie, *Cartul.* 1, 370, no. 426: dated to 1161-68. See also "sigill. magistri Petri Parisiensis episcopi." I. Brady, *Prolegomena in Sententias. Spicil. Bonav.* 4 (Grottaferrata, 1971) 36*.

104 *Dialogus Ratii*; ed. N. Haring, MS 15 (1953) 252. Gerald of Wales, *Spec. eccl.* d. I and *Gemma eccl.* II, 37; ed. J. S. Brewer RS 21, 4 (p. 7) and 21, 2 (p. 349).

105 *Theol. Quartalschrift* 100 (Tübingen, 1919) 415.

106 B. Guérard, *Cartul. de Notre-Dame de Paris* 4, 201 and 181, no. 314.

107 B. Guérard, *Cartul.* 4, 8, no. 14.

year 1160: "Actum publice Parisius in domo nostra ..." Other
documents of the period state: "Actum publice Parisius in capitulo
beate Marie."[108] Master Hugh of Novara owned a house in Paris, confirmed (1166/7) by Hugh, abbot of Saint-Germain *in domo episcopali*,[109] in
the presence of Bishop Maurice. Master Manerius was also a house-
owner.[110] Master Hugh of Champfleury "once bishop of Soissons (d.
1175) and the king's chancellor" owned not one but several houses in
Paris.[111] He bought one from a certain Alelmus as we know through
Chancellor Odo.[112] This Chancellor may be Odo of Ourscamp who
complains to Alexander III of the fate of one of his students "qui
prepositus meus in scolis fuerat mihique successit in scolis."[113] The
prepositus was competent enough to teach, especially during the master's
absence. Master Adam of Petit-Pont had a prepositus by the name of
Peter.[114] Another clear example is Peter of Poitiers, chancellor from
1168-78, who had been "prepositus scolarum Petri Comestoris."[115] A
letter by Cardinal Peter of S. Crisogono to Alexander III reveals that a
certain Master Bernard of Pisa was likewise Peter Manducator's
prepositus.[116]

At the third Lateran Council (1179) one Adam of Wales, bishop of St.
Asaph (1175-81), rose in defence of Peter Lombard's christology saying:
"Domine papa, ego et clericus et prepositus olim scolarum eius defen-
dam sententias magistri."[117] Master Roger of Hoveden calls him Master
Adam.[118] According to Ralph of Diceto he was a "canonicus Parisien-
sis."[119]

As to the number of masters Pope Lucius III (1184-85) established the
principle: "ut magistrum scolarum unum in musica et alium in aliis

---

108 R. de Lasteyrie, *Cartul.* 1, 362, no. 415, and 181, no. 314.

109 R. de Lasteyrie, *Cartul.* 1, 391, no. 462. He died in Paris. Guérard, *Cartul.* 4, 13.

110 B. Guérard, *Cartul.* 4, 23, no. 56: "que pertinent ad domum magistri Manerii."

111 R. de Lasteyrie, *Cartul.* 1, 441, no. 536: in domibus magistri Hugonis quondam episcopi
Suessionensis et regis cancellarii."

112 Lasteyrie, *Cartul.* 1, 391, no. 462 (dated to 1166/7): reuera magister Hugo domum illam ab
Alelmo, patre Petri, emerat ... Odo cancellarius.

113 *Ep.* 1; ed. J. B. Pitra, *Anal. nov. Spic. Solesmensis. Altera continuatio* (Paris 1888), p. xxxix.

114 In Ms Leipzig, Univ. 172, f. 102 (s. xii) the *explicit* of Adam's *De utensilibus* reads: "Explicit
expositio super faletholum magistri ade a petro preposito suo laboriose conquisita."

115 Walter of Saint-Victor, *Contra quatuor lab. Francie* IV, 8; ed. P. Glorieux, *Archives d'hist. doctr.
et litt. du moyen âge* 19 (1952) 274; 304.

116 C. E. Du Boulay, *Hist. Univ. Par.* 2 (Paris 1665) 667. PL 200, 1370: "Literaturam et
honestatem magistri Petri Manducatoris decani Trecensis uos non credimus ignorare. Magister
autem Bernardus Pisanus, quondam prepositus eius, tante literature ..."

117 *Contra quatuor lab. Francie*; ed. Glorieux, p. 201. Adam's attendance is recorded in Mansi 22,
217 and 467.

118 *Chronica* (ad ann. 1175); ed. W. Stubbs, RS 51, 2 (London, 1869) 78.

119 *Ymag. historiarum (ad ann.* 1175); ed. Wm. Stubbs, RS 68, 1 (London, 1876) 402.

disciplinis sine contradictione habeatis."[120] In 1207 Innocent III (1198-1216), who had studied theology in Paris under Peter of Corbeil, restricted the number of Parisian masters of theology to eight: "Firmiter inhibemus ut Parisius magistrorum theologie numerus octonarium non transcendat."[121]

The great enthusiasm for learning which Europe witnessed in the 12th century was not without its critics. In the fifties Peter of Blois (d. ca. 1204) wrote to Master Ralph of Beauvais: "Priscian and Tully, Lucan and Persius, those are your gods."[122] And Philip Harvengt (d. 1183) who once met Gilbert in Paris,[123] recalled that he had studied under Anselm, but, he continues, "beatus homo non qui magistrum Ansellum audiuit, non qui Laudunum uel Parisius requisiuit sed qui ..."[124] However, at the same time St. Bernard paved the way for Peter Lombard[125] and turned to the bishop of Rochester asking him to allow Master Robert Pulleyn to stay on in Paris.[126]

It has not been this writer's intention to examine the doctrinal views of all these masters. After outlining or rather sketching the work done by Bernard of Chartres, William of Conches, and Thierry, Prof. Southern arrives at the amazing conclusion: "All their thoughts were old thoughts".[127] One may wonder why Gilbert of Poitiers was not included. He was, after all, the most brilliant and most influential scholar Chartres had produced. And if we consider that the canonical collections compiled by Ivo, bishop of Chartres (1090-1116), set the stage for Gratian, it is even more obvious that, far from being a legend, the school of Chartres was the most powerful intellectual force of the twelfth century.

Pontifical Institute of Mediaeval Studies.

---

120   *Ep.* 185; PL 201, 1316C.

121   B. E. Ch. Guérard, *Cartul. de Notre-Dame de Paris* 1, 68, no. 68. Date: 14 November 1207. A. Potthast, *Reg.* 3218. PL 215, 1248.

122   *Ep.* 6; PL 207, 18A: Priscianus et Tullius, Lucanus et Persius, isti sunt dii uestri. Concerning Master Ralph and his school see R. W. Hunt, "Studies on Priscian," *Med. and Ren. Studies* 3 (1954) 1-39.

123   *Ep.* 5; PL 203, 45C.

124   *Ep.* 7; PL 203, 58C.

125   *Ep.* 410; PL 142, 618.

126   *Ep.* 205; PL 182, 372C.

127   *Med. Humanism*, p. 83. In preparing this paper I lost sight, unfortunately, of a fine article by Peter Dronke, "New Approaches to the School of Chartres," *Anuario de estudios medievales* 6 (1969) 117-140.

GREEK *RECENTIORES*, (Ps.) BASIL, *ADVERSUS EUNOMIUM*, IV-V

Walter Hayes

From almost the time of St. Basil himself all men have recognized this Greek text's importance. For them, it has been an ever ready mine of polemic against Eunomius' extreme brand of Arianism.

However, problems of authorship (and ultimately, of interpretation) have plagued ancient and modern scholars. Perhaps to their time-honored techniques we can add some modern refinements with a computer-based literary analysis of this text and writings of major contenders for honor of author.[1]

But before such analysis, we should be in a position to recognize how this text comes to us, how to evaluate a true and false reading, contamination, conjecture — and know why.

For this purpose, therefore, we have addressed problems of text history, mutual interrelationship of extant manuscripts. And, with publication last year of *The Greek Manuscript Tradition of (Ps.) Basil's Adversus Eunomium IV-V* our task is half done.[2]

Now, only *recentiores* still remain to be studied and reported on. Wherefore, this account of their story will complete *Adversus Eunomium* Book IV-V text history and allow us to proceed securely to a critical edition.

We now ask which manuscripts are these *recentiores* ? What relation do they have to manuscripts from which they have been copied ? How much second hand correction have they sustained ? How much *contaminatio* have they undergone ?

As we have seen, fifteen oldest Greek manuscripts fall into two (family) traditions and four intermediate recensions.

---

1 I have already made a preliminary text study: word count, occurrence averages, alphabetical index in context for *Adversus Eunomium* Books IV-V. Word length, for example, in Books IV-V differs significantly from that in Books I-III.

2 For pre-fourteenth century manuscripts see my *The Greek Manuscript Tradition of (Ps.) Basil's Adversus Eunomium Books IV-V* (Leiden, Brill, 1972).

Alpha Family[3]

We have charted relationships of one group (alpha) thus :[4]

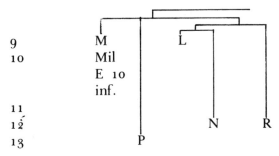

9
10

M
Mil
E 10
inf.

L

11
12́
13

N   R

P

RECENTIORES:

MS h. Paris.[5] Bibliothèque Nationale. Supplément Grec 1325. Fifteenth century (1479 A.D.). Full text of Book IV (fol. 118v-126v) and

3   MS M: Biblioteca Nazionale Marciana 58. MS Mil. E 10 inf.: Milan. Biblioteca Ambrosiana E 10 inf. (olim O 153). MS P: Paris. Bibliothèque Nationale 1301. MS L: Florence. Biblioteca Medicea-Laurenziana IV 27. MS N: Paris. Bibliothèque Nationale 500. MS R: Paris. Bibliothèque Nationale 966. Cf. *(Ps.) Basil.* Appendix I, pp. 158-159.

4   *(Ps.) Basil,* p. 81, I pointed to a close relationship between LNR and LR. Now, however, reading of *recentiores* MSS h and d leads me to re-examine MS N. Significance of N's correcting hand now becomes clear.

A more accurate sub-group is LN. They have 13 readings in common against all other manuscripts:

	LN		All Others
PG 29.676.36	οὐδ᾽		οὐδέ
PG 29.697.6	αὐτοῦ	add	om
	ἑαυτοῦ	om	add
PG 29.704.19	ἑαυτόν		αὐτόν
PG 29.705.29	ἀντιστολάς		ἀντιδιαστολάς

There are another 69 variants of L alone, where N has been erased and changed. These surely represent 69 more readings introduced by scribe-sources of LN, where N has been corrected by a second hand.

Symbol, for example, P (P²), means scribe of MS P performs an action (i.e. adds a word) and a second hand corrector reverses his action (i.e. somehow deletes the word).

The word "add", "omit", "no addition", "no omission" indicate that manuscripts add to or omit words found in Migne *textus receptus,* which simply is taken as normal as a basis for comparison. Cf. *(Ps.) Basil,* p. 78, n. 1.

In these stemma-charts ascending vertical lines do not meet horizontal sub-family lines. This indicates graphically that we do not know how many scribe copies come between autograph, archetype, family, hyparchetype, and extant manuscript.

5   Charles Astruc, Marie-Louise Concasty, *Bibliothèque Nationale. Département des Manuscrits. Catalogue des Manuscrits Grecs. Troisième Partie. Le Supplément Grec,* (Paris, Bibliothèque Nationale, 1960), p. 626. Cf. *(Ps) Basil,* Appendix I, 22, p. 159.

Book V (fol. 126v-142). Single column, 25 lines to page. Signature numbers are missing, but on each quire, last folio, verso, bottom, initial words (*reclamantes*) of subsequent text appear: fol. 124v γενέσθαι (PG 29 701.15), fol. 134v τῆς ζωῆς (PG 29 745.8).

Manuscript dating is quite accurate. Fol. 142 (end of Book V) MS h scribe tells us:

> ἐγράφη ἡ παροῦσα βύβλος ἐν τῇ τῶν Λοκρῶν ἐπιζεφυρέων πόλει ἣ νῦν καλεῖται Ἱέραξ παρὰ Ἀθανασίου κωνσταντινουπολίτου ἐπισκόπου Ἱέρακος καὶ Ὀπίου, ἐν ἔτει μὲν ἀπὸ κτίσεως κόσμου ἑξακισχιλιοστῷ ἐνακοσιοστῷ ὀγδοηκοστῷ ἑβδόμῳ τῆς δὲ ἐνσάρκου οἰκονομίας τοῦ θεοῦ λόγου χιλιοστῷ τετρακοσιοστῷ ἑβδομηκοστῷ ἐνάτῳ.

In Gerace, therefore, Athanasius[6] has copied an ancient codex (now lost) exemplar of our MS h. He assures us that any (second hands) who might wish to place Basil on their side in disputes about procession, relations, and Holy Spirit have not tampered with this ancient text.[7]

Thereupon, for 300 years our copy, MS h, remained in South Italy:

> Ce manuscrit faisait partie de la belle collection des livres rares et recherchés appartenant à la famille des Comtes Guidi de Naples. Il fut enlevé dans le pillage qui eut lieu en 1799 à la sortie des Français de cette ville et fut rendu au Comte Sébastien des Guidi en 1804.[8]

A further note tells us that Count Sébastien donated MS h to Cardinal de Bonnald, archbishop of Lyon for diocesan library use.[9]

Fifty years later Bibliothèque Nationale acquired MS ḥ from archdiocesan sources in Lyon, between 1891 and 1910.[10]

For its part, MS h clearly belongs with alpha family manuscripts. In 160 differences between manuscript families it always agrees with alpha.

Since it shares no readings introduced by M, Pkq, LNRd, or LN, it represents alpha family's purest form.

---

6 Astruc and concasty, *loc. cit.*, identify him as Athanasius Chalkeopoulos, bishop of Gerace (1461-1472) and, then, of Gerace and Oppido (1472-1497). Of course, he himself tells us he was bishop, in 1479, of Ἱέρακος καὶ Ὀπίου.

7 Athanasius is not more specific. In any case, he had no way of knowing author, archetype, manuscript tradition — what additions, subtractions, changes have actually been made, by whom, and why.

It must be said, however, that he refers to second hand changes (visible to his eye and ours) not to *contaminatio*. Further, he refers more particularly to *Adversus Eunomium* I-III, than to IV-V.

8 Paris, Supplément Grec 1325, fol. 143.

9 Paris, Supplément Grec 1325, fol. 143. Note dated Lyon, February, 1853.

10 Henri Omont, *Nouvelles Acquisitions du Département des Manuscrits pendant les années 1891-1910*, (Paris, Leroux, 1912), p. lxx.

However, MS h (scribe) has visibly corrected his own errors 16 times. In another 16 instances a marginal second hand cites what seems to be corrections. But neither alpha nor beta is source. Some additions are marked for inclusion, presumably, as new text, for example:

PG 29.673.27 ἢ add
PG 29.685.39 οὐσία add
PG 29.696.3 αἴτιος add

Again, other marginalia appear to be variant readings:

PG 29.700.22 ἄλλως : ἡ γὰρ κτίσεως φύσις καὶ ἡ κτιστὴ τῇ δεσποτικῇ καὶ θεικῇ εἰς ἓν καὶ ταὐτὸν οὐ συμβαίνουσιν.
PG 29.712.25 ἄλλως : εἰ γὰρ ἀγγέλων ἁμαρτησάντων ὁ θεὸς οὐκ ἐφείσατο.
PG 29.724.27 ἄλλως : ἐναπομαχθεῖσα.

However, these marginalia show their true nature — they are all scholia:

PG 29.692.17 καὶ ὁ υἱὸς ἑαυτὸν ἔχειν ὀφείλει.
PG 29.712.33 τὸ γεννητὸν δὲ μεταλαμβάνει.
PG 29.713.22 ἰδοὺ μία χείρ post ἐστερεώθησαν add.

Nonetheless this hand does provide another dozen variants from beta sources:

PG 29.689.26 λεγοίμεθα G B D
PG 29.689.32 οὖν s u
PG 29.708.23 τοῦ q x VC s t
PG 29.736.28 υἱοῦ s u

Another eight corrections from beta sources appear between text lines. For example:

PG 29.689.9 τῷ u
PG 29.692.19 οὖ P² k u
PG 29.705.10 ἐγένετο m t ἐγένου alpha γενοῦ beta
PG 29.721.14 αὐτούς E F

We see, accordingly, that our scribe corrects himself, a second hand reports readings from unknown sources and from beta. But in every case marginal and interlinear additions are clearly recognizable and in no way affect textual integrity.[11]

---

11 Nor need we postulate a particular beta source, unless, *per impossibile*, additions at PG 29.688.9 and PG 29.692.19 were taken from MS u (Paris, Greek 956) in the last few years (since 1896) by some vandal in Bibliothèque Nationale itself. Athanasius, scribe of MS h, introduced an additional 31 spelling errors which neither he nor his corrector has mended.

Surprisingly, MS h shares 19 readings with beta against MPLNRd:

	MS h, Beta		MPLNRd
PG 29.673.36	ἄρα	add	no addition
PG 29.700.22	οὕτω		οὕτως
PG 29.701.27	δέ	add	no addition
PG 29.701.45	ἀνάγκη		ἀνάγκης
PG 29.705.13	ἐγενήθη		ἐγεννήθη
PG 29.712.18	ἥ	add	no addition
PG 29.712.34	ἄξιον		ἄξιος
PG 29.720.41	τυγχάνειν		τυγχάνει
PG 29.724.13	διαστήσωσι		διαστήσουσι
PG 29.748.28	ὄντα		ὄντος
PG 29.749.45	εὐσεβῶς		εὐσεβῶν
PG 29.757.6	τε	omit	no omission
PG 29.772.39	οὕτω	add	no addition
PG 29.773.39	αὐτῷ ἡ δόξα	add beta	
	ᾧ ἡ δόξα	add MS h	no addition

In addition, MS h agrees with beta and R alone:[12]

	MS h, R, Beta		MPLNd
PG 29.680.30	μου	omit	no omission
PG 29.713.34	τόν	add	no addition
PG 29.717.31	ἀφέωνται		ἀφέονται
PG 29.764.28	οὕτω		οὕτως

And once MS h agrees with beta and P aloné[13]

	MS h, P, Beta		
PG 29.745.28	τῆς ...		
PG 29.745.29	μετά	add	no addition

Thus, we surmise, a scribe (one or many) of alpha (MSS hMPLNRd) copied his exemplar (archetype). After his work there were 121 differences between his copy and that of beta. An ancient scribal predecessor of MS h copied this (121 difference) alpha text. He added (his

---

12 Where R reads by some sort of contamination. This is a necessary consequence of R's relation to LNRd.

13 MSS h and P could each be a form of alpha before MLNR. Quite unlikely. There is no other evidence of any reading shared by MS h, P, and beta. Nor is there any evidence of P and h vagaries shared against all others. Nor, just for the record, is there any evidence of common origin of M, P, and h, as there is for LNRd. Nor do M, P, or LNRd share any (beta) readings which would indicate they are forms of alpha prior to MPLNRd.

own) 31 changes against MPLNRd and beta.[14] Scribe of MPLNRd also copied this (121 differences) alpha text and introduced 19 changes (against MS h and beta).[15]

Conclusion: MS h is clearly an alpha text. Nineteen readings with beta suggest it is a form of alpha prior to that of MPLNRd.[16]

MS k. Paris.[17] Bibliothèque Nationale. Greek 1258. Full text, Book IV, fol. 238-244v and fol. 221-227. Book V, fol. 205-220v and 245-249. Codex quires have not been bound correctly, so Latin marginal notes direct puzzled readers to proper folios. However, this comprises almost all second hand activity. Other marginalia are those of MS k scribe correcting himself.

P shows 58 errors in his text, different from all other manuscripts. MS k has all 58, for example:

	P, MS k	All Others
PG 29.701.9	Παῦλος	ἀπόστολος
PG 29.737.31	κατοπριζόμενος	κατοπτριζόμενοι
PG 29.745.5	τρία	τριάδα
PG 29.772.17	τὸ τῆς καυστικῆς	τοῖς καυστικοῖς

14 Changes here are errors, surely. For example:

	MS h	All Others
PG 29.688.17	εὐήργεσθαι	εὐρεθήσεται
PG 29.689.47	ἐπαγαγαγών	ἐπαγαγών
PG 29.733.39	ἐζιέναι	ἐξιέναι
PG 29.760-8	ἀκοούντων	ἀκουόντων

One MS h reading, however, deserves notice. At PG 29.700.23 beta (rightly enough) reads κτιστική. Alpha shows some kind of misunderstanding. M reads κτίστος. P reads κτίστις. (Both readings are non-words.) LNRd reads κτιστή, which is quite wrong. (κτιστός in this author — PG 29.712.31, PG 29.724.16 or PG 29.749.35 means "created.")

MS h reads ἄκτιστος which must be someone's conjecture, trying to solve a problem like κτίστις. ἄκτιστος is quite correct enough, but less appropriate in context. This reading, ἄκτιστος, also appears in two fourteenth century Paris manuscripts, 956 and 969. But there similarity ceases.

15 In 19 examples of MS h and beta collaboration, thirteen are such that we can actually judge they are grammatically, etc., correct and their opposite (alpha reading) is an "error." In these thirteen instances MS h and beta have the correct reading: PG 29.673.36, PG 29.680.30, PG 29.701.27, PG 29.701.45, PG 29.705.13, PG 29.712.18, PG 29.712.34, PG 29.717.31, PG 29.724.13, PG 740.40, PG 29.745.28, PG 29.748.28, and PG 29.749.45.

16 All we can say for sure: 1. MS h is completely alpha. 2. It shares 19 beta readings against MPLNRd. 3. The opposite of 13 of these readings is an error. Opposite of the other six could also be correct.

It is more economical to assume that MPLNRd changed 19 (correct) readings than that MS h borrowed them by contamination or chanced on them by coincidence.

17 Henri Omont, *Inventaire sommaire des Manuscrits Grecs de la Bibliothèque Nationale et des autres Bibliothèques de Paris et des Départements*, I. *Ancien fonds grec: Theologie*, (Paris, Leroux, 1886), p. 278. Cf. (Ps.) Basil, Appendix I, 20, p. 159.

In addition MS k has 28 beta readings, but only those provided by second hand in P, for example:

Beta, P², MS k
PG 29.716.5   καὶ ὁ ἄγγελος τῇ Μαρίᾳ add
PG 29.729.34   θεὸς αὐτοὺς οὐ δι' αὐτῶν ἐργάζεται add
PG 29.737.40   εἰ δὲ οὐ μετὰ πατρὸς καὶ υἱοῦ add

Moreover, 22 times actual readings in MS k result from misunderstanding of his almost illegible P-P² exemplar:

PG 29.680.32 ἑτεροουσίων P ἑτεροουσίων P² ἑτερουσίων k
PG 29.693.4   δημιουργου (end line) μένων P δημιουργῶν μένων P²k
PG 29.693.20 εἰς P
               πρὸς ἄλλως P² (i.e. πρός is a variant)
               πρὸς ἀλλ' εἰς k
PG 29.697.11 ζῶν P ζῆν sscr. P² ζωήν k
PG 29.740.9   ἀνακόπτων P διά sscr. P² ἀναδιακόπτων k
PG 29.748.22 ὅπως P ὄντως P² ὁ ὄντος πως k
PG 29.749.20 μήτε ... PG 29.749.21 ἐνυπάρχουσαν οὐσίαν.
     P² add the lines in margin, but concludes with ὑπάρχουσαν οὐσίαν.
     MS k copies the addition (also in the margin — he does not know exactly
     where it fits into the text) exactly as in P (same letter shapes, abbreviations) with his version of ὑπάρχουσαν οὐσίαν (error of P² alone)[18].
PG 29.764.45 ἀφέωνται P ἀφίενται sscr. P² ἀφιενωνται MS k.

Conclusion: MS k is clearly from alpha traditions. It derives many readings from the P and P² codex version. Indeed it appears to be a copy of P.

MS q. Paris.[19] Bibliothèque Nationale. Greek 503, formerly Regius 2286 and 1472. Fifteenth century.[20] Full text, fol. 41-44v (Book IV) and fol. 44v-51 (Book V), 51 lines to single column page. Four hands are discernible, scribe, rubricator, and two scholiasts. Scholiast I assures us, for example:

PG 29.684.22 (εἰ τὸ ἀγέννητος)
             τὰ παρὰ ἀχώριστα συμβεβηκότα τρόποι τινές εἰσιν τῶν οἷς
             συμβέβηκασι.
PG 29.684.28 (τί ὁ θεός ἐστιν)
             καὶ ὁ θεόλογος τοῦτο λέγει τὸ θεώρημα.
PG 29.741.39 (ἑπτὰ ὀφθαλμούς)
             ὅτι τὸ πνεῦμα ἑπτὰ ἐνεργείας ἔχει.

---

18   As a matter of fact MS k writes ὑπαρουσίαν, but this is his error alone.
19   Omont, *Inventaire Sommaire*, I, p. 63. Cf. *(Ps.) Basil*, Appendix I, 17, p. 159.
20   Omont, I, p. 63 dates it 14th century.

For his part, scholiast II observes:

PG 29.717.23 τοῦτο ὁ Χρυσόστομος περὶ τοῦ ἀνέμου εἴρηκε λεχθέντα (sic) καὶ τοῦτο εἰς τὸν ἅγιον Ἰωάννην λόγος κϛ΄.

As for its text, MS q agrees with only one of 72 readings which originate with beta manuscripts:

	Beta, MS q		All Others
PG 29.721.22	τὸ ἅγιον	add	no addition

However, MS q agrees with all 85 readings which originate here from alpha manuscripts. In addition, three times, MS q agrees with P^2 and beta, three times with N^2 and beta, three times with N^2P^2 and beta. These may, of course, be coincidence.

Conclusion: MS q is clearly of alpha origin. It seems to reflect text traditions of P and N and shares beta readings afforded by their second hands.

MS b. Vienna.[21] Oesterreichische Nationalbibliothek. Philosophical Greek 224. Dated 1547-1548. Folios 165-170 which interest us are from 1548, single column, 22 lines to page. Large colon separates arguments and text sub-divisions. No second hand interferes with text.

MS b provides 300 (Migne) lines of Book IV text: PG 29.672.1-PG 29.685.22; PG 29.688.25-PG 29.688.36; PG 29.693.40-PG 29.696.14; and PG 29.701.24-PG 29.701.45.

Basil's text is among excerpts from many sources: Macarius of Ancyra, Thomas Aquinas, and Gregory of Nyssa. Mathusalas Macheir (scribe) titles our Basil excerpts:

τοῦ αὐτοῦ ἀντιρρητικὰ κατὰ Εὐνομίου ἀπορίαι καὶ λύσεις ἐκ τῶν θεοπνεύστων γραφῶν εἰς τὰ ἀντιλεγόμενα περὶ τοῦ υἱοῦ ἐν τῇ καινῇ καὶ παλαιᾷ διαθήκῃ : τοῦ μεγάλου Βασιλείου.

For itself, text (PG 29.672.1-PG 29.685.22) runs continuous (fol. 165-169v). Three short excerpts follow, fol. 169v-170. First of these deals with definition of definition, genus, species, and (logical) property, beginning PG 29.688.25 τὸ ἀγέννητος οὔτε ὅρος ἐστὶ θεοῦ οὔτε ἴδιον. At PG 29.688.29 Macheir repeats καὶ εἴ τι ζῷον λογικὸν θνητὸν νοῦ καὶ ἐπιστήμης δεκτικὸν ἄνθρωπος τοῦτο. He crosses it out, himself.

However, at PG 29.688.36 MS b adds (with all Greek manuscripts) the lines PG 29.685.25 εἰ δέ ... PG 29.685.31 σώζηται which was, surely in his

21 Herbert Hunger, *Katalog der Griechischen Handschriften der Oesterreichischen Nationalbibliothek*, I, *Codices Historici, Codices Philosophi et Philologici*, (Wien, Prachner, 1961), p. 355. Cf. *(Ps.) Basil*, Appendix I, 23, p. 159.

exemplar.[22] Further, at PG 29.673.40 MS b shows a tradition title εἰς τὸ πατήρ μου μείζων μού ἐστιν. Finally, fol. 170, bottom, Macheir ends this excerpt with the word ὥστε (PG 29.701.45) abruptly in mid-sentence. He thereupon begins Basil's *Contra Sabellianos*, fol. 170v.

For itself this 300 lines of Migne text in MS b never agrees with any positive beta reading. But it does agree with alpha, for example:

	Alpha and MS b		Beta
PG 29.672.4	οὖν	add	no addition
PG 29.680.42	ἀγέννητον		ἀγέννητος
PG 29.681.10	οὐσία		οὐσίαι

Conclusion: Text of MS b is clearly in alpha tradition.

MS y. Vienna.[23] Oesterreichische Nationalbibliothek. Philosophical Greek 181. Sixteenth century, 25-28 lines to single column page. Purchased by Ioannes Sambucus. Codex content is quite similar to that of MS b. For example, each codex has Basil's *Against Sabellians, Letter 38, Homily* (three) *On Paradise*, and *Against Eunomius*. Mathusalas Macheir is scribe again and provides us with 207 (Migne) lines of *Adversus Eunomium* text of Book IV, PG 29.672.1-PG 29.681.20 corresponding to MS b's first excerpt.[24] There is no second hand interference.

We are interested in manuscript item 12, a selection (fol. 200-204) from Basil's κατὰ Σαβελλιανῶν and (fol. 204-206v) his Κατὰ Εὐνομίου. It ends, fol. 206v, after six lines of handwriting, at PG 29.681.20 in midsentence. Remainder of fol. 206v is blank.

Macheir's title:

τοῦ αὐτοῦ σοφοῦ καὶ θεοφόρου πατρὸς ἡμῶν Βασιλείου τοῦ ὡς ἀληθῶς οὐρανοφάντορος καὶ οἰκουμενικοῦ διδασκάλου καὶ μεγάλου φωστῆρος κατ᾽ Εὐνομίου ἀπορίαι καὶ λύσεις ἐκ τῶν θεοπνεύστων γραφῶν εἰς τὰ ἀντιλεγόμενα περὶ τοῦ υἱοῦ ἐν τῇ καινῇ καὶ παλαιᾷ διαθήκῃ.

This title differs from that of MS b, but text itself scarcely differs at all, for MS y never agrees with any of 35 readings which originate among beta manuscripts.

---

22 Only Syriac manuscript Oriental 8606 (British Museum) excludes this text. This (correct, of course) exclusion may have been the work of his Greek exemplar. These Museum holdings still lack printed catalogues. Cf. *(Ps.) Basil*, p. 4.

23 Hunger, *op. cit.*, p. 289. Cf. *(Ps.) Basil*, Appendix I, 24, p. 160.

24 Even without his autograph we would recognize Macheir's hand, a large, bold, brush-like stroke. It is interesting to note, however, that at PG 29.680.26 (in both MSS b and y) τὸ μετὰ τὸ γενέσθαι περὶ ὧν προέγνω τέλος ἔχει. Macheir uses seven forms of epsilon. He happens to match epsilon form and position-sequence in both manuscripts four times. Three times he does not.

Further, MS y agrees with these text irregularities of MS b:

	MSS b y		All Others
PG 29.672.13	υἱὸν προυπάρχειν		προυπάρχειν υἱόν
PG 29.673.20	τοῦ εἶναι καὶ ἡμῖν		καὶ ἡμῖν τοῦ εἶναι
PG 29.676.2	εἰ	add	no addition
PG 29.676.6	πατρυιοῦ καὶ πατρός		πατρὸς καὶ υἱοῦ
PG 29.676.44	μέν	omit	no omission
PG 29.677.4	λέγει	add	no addition
PG 29.677.12	λέγει πατέρα	omit	no omission
PG 29.681.13	δυνηθείη		δυνήσεται

Yet MS b does not derive directly from MS y, for it does not show these vagaries of MS y alone:

	MS y		All Others
PG 29.673.24	ῥηθήσεται		εἰρήσεται
PG 29.680.18	τοῦ εἶναι	omit	no omission

Conclusion: MS y is of alpha origin.[25] It originates from an exemplar quite similar to that of MS b.

MS j. Naples.[26] Biblioteca Nationale II C 32. Quarto, 372 fols. Fifteenth century, 32 lines to single column page. Scarcely any marginal activity appears. At PG 29.725.13, to cite but one instance, scribe omitted τοῦ ἀνέμου κύριος οὐδὲ τὸ πνεῦμα. He added it himself.

MS j requires special preliminary attention. Item 1 (fol. 1-28) contains Old Testament selections. Item 2 (fol. 28-44) deserves our efforts.[27]

Cirillo, in 1826, described Item 2 as "excerpta ex tribus sermonibus incerti. Videntur excerpta ex tribus S. Basilii *Contra Eunomium* de Trinitate."[28] Pierleoni described them as "ex incerti tribus sermonibus in Eunomium."[29]

It is now possible for us to remove the uncertainness and identify the excerpts:

Excerpts from *Adversus Eunomium*, Book I.

fol. 28.1	λανθάνουσα ... βλαβερωτέρα	PG 29.504B
fol. 28.1	οἱ γάρ ... δοκεῖ	PG 29.515B

---

25 No doubt Macheir copied them both from a common (third) copy. MS y could be copied from MS b, of course.

26 Gino Pierleoni, *Catalogus Codicum Graecorum Bibliothecae Nationalis Neapolitanae*, I (Rome, Instituto Poligrafico dello Stato, 1962), 100, p. 274. Cf. *(Ps.) Basil*, Appendix I, 18, p. 159.

27 We are dealing with quires five (fol. 28-35v) and six (fol. 36-43v). These two signatures must be from a previous codex. Our first excerpt, for example, must be last line of a previous excerpt.

28 Salvatore Cirillo, *Codices Graeci Manuscripti Regiae Bibliothecae Borbonicae descripti atque illustrati*. (Neapoli, Regia typographia, 1826-1832), II, p. 5 *et sqq.*

29 Pierleoni, *loc. cit.*

fol. 28.7	εἰ ... δηλωτικήν	PG 29.536C
fol. 28.10	ἐγώ ... οὐσίαν	PG 29.537A
fol. 28.11	διόπερ ... ἀφροσύνην	PG 29.537B
fol. 28.13	ἐγώ ... δυναμένου	PG 29.541C
fol. 28.15	διά ... ἐκμανθάνωμεν	PG 29.556C
fol. 28.17	τοῦ ... προστρίβονται	PG 29.564B
fol. 28.21	ὁ ... σημαντική	PG 29.564D
fol. 28.27	τοιοῦτον ... ἀπολείπεται	PG 29.569D
fol. 28.30	Rubric: ταῦτα τοῦ πρώτου λόγου.	

Excerpts from *Adversus Eunomium*, Book II.

fol. 28.30	οἱ ... ἀποστερεῖν	PG 29.608B
fol. 28v.8	εἰ ... διαγγέλλων	PG 29.609B
fol. 28v.19	τοῖς ... ἐφέλκεται	PG 29.637A
fol. 29.20	πλήν ... θεοῦ	PG 29.645A
fol. 29v.1	Rubric: ταῦτα εἰσὶ τοῦ δευτέρου λόγου.	

Excerpts from *Adversus Eunomium*, Book III.

fol. 29v.2	ἄρα ... μου	PG 29.653B
fol. 29v.24	ἀρχαί ... κτίσεως	PG 29.660A
fol. 30.8	ἐγώ ... ἀποδιδόναι	PG 29.668A
fol. 30.27	τί ... θεοῦ	PG 29.668C
fol. 30.30	Rubric: τέλος τῶν τριῶν λόγων.	

Excerpts from *Adversus Eunomium*, Book IV.

fol. 30.31	εἰ ... σῴζηται	PG 29.685.22-PG 29.685.31
fol. 30v.5	εἰ ... εἴρηκεν	PG 29.685.31-PG 20.685.36
fol. 30v.8	τό ... κτίσις	PG 29.692.28-PG 29.692.31
fol. 30v.10	εἰ ... εἶναι	PG 29.692.31-PG 29.692.39
fol. 30v.16	εἰς ... λέγηται	PG 29.693.40-PG 29.696.14
fol. 30v.29	τοῦ (Migne ὁ δέ) ... οὐρανοῦ	PG 29.709.29

Excerpts from *Adversus Eunomium*, Book V.

fol. 30v.31	πῶς ... ἁγιάζεται	PG 29.725.3-PG 29.725.41
fol. 31.23	ὅτι ... περιεργάζεται	PG 29.732.4-PG 29.732.15
fol. 31.30	διά ... πληρωτικόν	PG 29.732.16-PG 29.732.28
fol. 31v.6	μή ... ὑπογράφων	PG 29.736.27-PG 29.737.10
fol. 31v.20	οὐκοῦν ... ὑμῶν	PG 29.760.42-PG 29.761.10

Excerpts from *De Spiritu Sancto ad Amphilochium*.

fol. 31v.32	γενόμενος ... γυναικός	PG 32.85B
fol. 32.3	ἤδη ... γενέσθαι	PG 32.108A
fol. 32v.21	ἐν ... ἁμαρτάνειν	PG 32.132A
fol. 33.1	ἁγιασμός ... ζωή	PG 32.136D
fol. 33.15	ἀλλ' ... παραδραμεῖν	PG 32.144D
fol. 33.21	ἀλλ' ... οἰκειότητα	PG 32.148D
fol. 33v.28	τίς ... περισπούδαστον	PG 32.188B
fol. 34.25	ὑψώσατε ... ἐφίκησθε	PG 32.200A
fol. 34.27	ὁ ... πνεύματος	PG 32.205A
fol. 34v.1	αὐτός ... πνεύματος	PG 32.209B

Texts which follow (to fol. 44) are clearly identified. They begin with fol. 36v.21 Excerpts from Basil's *Eulogy on Gordion Martyr*. PG 31.493A, fol. 36v.29 Excerpts from Basil's *Sermon on Isaiah*. PG 30.117A.

MS j, therefore, provides us with eight passages (11 excerpts) 152 (Migne) lines of text from Books IV and V: (fol. 30-30v) (Book IV) PG 29.685.22-PG 29.685.36; PG 29.692.28-PG 29.692.39; PG 29.693.40-PG 29.696.14; PG 29.709.27-PG 29.709.29; (fol. 30v-31v) (Book V) PG 29.725.3-PG 29.725.41; PG 29.732.4-PG 29.732.28; PG 29.736.27-PG 29.737.10; and PG 29.760.42-PG 29.761.10.

For itself, then, in 152 (Migne) lines of *Adversus Eunomium* IV-V text MS j agrees with alpha readings 75 times, but only four times with any beta manuscripts:

	MS j		All Others
PG 29.725.20	Χριστόν	MS u	Χριστοῦ
PG 29.725.31	καί	omit MS Bc	no omission
PG 29.725.35	οὐδέ	MS e	οὐ δή
PG 29.761.9	καὶ πατρός	add MS V Bc s	no addition

These must be coincidence for they assume that MS j has at least three independent beta sources for his selection of four (surely inconsequential) readings.

Furthermore, among 75 alpha readings, three, perhaps, shows MS j's source:[30]

	MSS k j		All Others
PG 29.732.4	ὁ	add	no addition
PG 29.737.3	ἀποδίδωσιν	P	ἀποδιδῶ
PG 29.737.6	γενομένην		γινομένην

Our excerpter (MS j), however, is quite capable of changing text himself. His text differs from all other manuscripts in these readings:

	MS j		All Others
PG 29.685.29	πάντες	omit	no omission
PG 29.685.30	λέγειν ἀγέννητον		ἀγέννητον λέγειν
PG 29.692.32	τῷ	omit	no omission

---

30 Yet MS j can not derive from Mss Pk alone:

PG 29.685.26	ἐπεὶ μή	MLNRj	εἰ τιμή	M² h
			ἐπεί	P
			ἐπεὶ τιμή	P²
			ἐπειὸν τιμή	k
			εἰ δὲ τιμή	beta
PG 29.732.11	ἐνεργῶν	Pk	ἐνεργόν	All Others
PG 29.732.23	ἐχρήσατο	Pk	ἐχρήσω	All Others
PG 760.48	συναϊδίῳ	Pk	καὶ ἀϊδίῳ	All Others

PG 29.725.23 κτίσμα ἢ κτῆμα   κτῆμα ἢ κτίσμα
PG 29.725.41 πνεύματα   τά
PG 29.732.8   θεοῦ   υἱοῦ
PG 29.732.11 καί   μή
PG 29.736.30 τοῦ   omit   no omission
PG 29.736.10 εἴη   add   no addition

Conclusion: MS j shows a predominately alpha text, with some similarity to traditions of MSS P and k.[31]

MS z. Leiden.[32] Bibliotheek der Rijksuniversiteit, Vossi Quarto 54. Fifteenth century, single column, 21-23 lines to page. Eleven excerpts, 127 (Migne) lines of text (fol. 90v-93v) titled τοῦ τετάρτου λόγου. All eleven, however, came from what we call Book V: PG 29.713.16-PG 29.713.43; PG 29.716.41-PG 29.717.2; PF 29.724.38-PG 29.724.44; PG 29.732.35-PG 732.39; PG 29.733.11-PG 29.733.35; PG 29.733.39-PG 29.733.44; PG 29.736.1-PG 29.736.37; PG 29.737.1-PG 29.737.3; PG 29.737.18-PG 29.737.27; PG 29.768.22-PG 29.768.26; PG 29.772.46-PG 29.772.49.

A few times MS z's scribe makes interlinear corrections of his own errors. No second hand introduces changes. At PG 29.724.38 εἰκὼν μὲν θεοῦ Χριστός a scholiast recalls:[33] λέγεται εἰκὼν θεοῦ ὁ ἄνθρωπος τρόπον ἕτερον.

In text areas reported by MS z (135 folio lines, 127 Migne lines) there are 59 readings which originate with alpha manuscripts. MS z agrees with beta only four times:

	MS z		All Others
PG 29.733.41	αὐτοῦ	VC	τοῦ θεοῦ
PG 29.733.43	οὐδέ	DGB	οὐδ'
PG 29.733.43	ἠ	omit MS u	no omission
PG 29.737.18	πιστεύεις	beta	πιστεύῃς

Such concurrence is unsystematic and probably arises from coincidence.

However, MS z incorporates alpha readings some 55 times, especially with R, for example, where it is clear that LN also agrees with R and z, twice:

	R MS z		All Others
PG 29.716.41	δέ	omit	no omission
PG 29.716.42	Μωυσέος	P² k	Μωσέως

31 Other possibilities: 1. MS j borrowed beta readings from beta sources. 2. He derived his excerpts from diverse sources, e.g. ten excerpts from a source like MS N-N² and one other (PG 29.732.16-PG 29.732.28) from a source like P-P².

32 Karel A. de Meyïer, *Bibliothecae Universitatis Leidensis, VI, Codices Vossiani Graeci et Miscellanei,* (Leiden, Bibliotheca Universitatis, 1955), pp. 166-167. Cf. *(Ps.) Basil,* Appendix I, 19, p. 159.

33 Vossi Quarto 54, fol. 91v.

PG 29.724.41	προέγνωκεν		προέγνω
PG 29.736.1	ταύτην		ταύτῃ
PG 29.736.27	δέ	LN	δή
PG 29.737.3	ἀποδίδωσιν	P² k	ἀποδιδῷ
PG 29.772.48	ἐχαρίσατο οὐκ ἐποίησεν	omit LND	no omission

Conclusion: MS z shows clear alpha provenance. In particular we look to text traditions of LNR, and particularly, to that of R as best source for MS z readings.

MS d. Vienna.[34] Oesterreichische Nationalbibliothek. Theological Greek 18. Fourteenth century. Full text. Book IV (fol. 120v-127v) and Book V (127v-136v). Folios have 33/34 lines in single column. Purchased by Auger von Busbecke.

No book division derives from Greek scribes, but a Latin (Western) marginal hand gives Book titles:

fol. 120v Initium Libri Quarti Contra Eunomium.
fol. 127v Hic incipit Liber Quintus Contra Eunomium.

There may indeed be two Greek hands. Scribe I himself is responsible for text, most sub-titles and marginal notes. His title (fol. 120v) for Book IV:

Πρὸς Ἀμφιλόχιον ἐπίσκοπον Ἰκονίου τῆς Λυκαόνων περὶ τοῦ ἁγίου πνεύματος ἐν κεφαλαίοις τριάκοντα.

This is, of course, title of a work which begins fol. 136v. Presence on fol. 120v of this false title is scribal error, for it has been crossed out by scribe or corrector, who inserts a (traditional) title: Κατὰ Εὐνομίου συλλογισμοί. Four other errors, all of them inconsequential, of MS d alone are corrected by himself or a second hand.[35]

Thus MS d's text comes to us just as it was copied 600 years ago.

As for MS d's text itself, it clearly is of alpha origin. Indeed it must come from LNR tradition sources, because it agrees with them 21 times against all others. For example:

	LNR MS d		All Others
PG 29.681.3	ἑτέρα	add	no addition
PG 29.681.4	ἐν	add	no addition
PG 29.681.4	ἑτέρα	add	no addition
PG 29.772.41	ἀλλ' ἰδίως		ἀλλ' ἀϊδίως
PG 29.773.3	ὁμολογία		ἀπολογία

---

34 Daniel von Nessel, *Catalogus sive recensio specialis codicum manuscriptorum Graecorum nec non linguarum orientalium Augustissimae Bibliothecae Caesareae Vindobonensis*, I, (Vindobonae, Voigt et Endteri, 1690), p. 37. Cf. *(Ps.) Basil*, Appendix I, 16, p. 159.

35 Despite his vigilance scribe (or corrector) missed another 13 errors. None of them of any import; scribe of MS d performed well.

Another dozen times MS d agrees with R, in conjunction with a random manuscript sampling. Four times, finally, MS d agrees with R alone against all others:

	R MS d		All Others
PG 29.684.35	ξύλον ἢ λίθον		λίθον ἢ ξύλον
PG 29.721.21	δέ	omit	no omission
PG 29.729.43	Παῦλός φησι		φησι Παῦλος
PG 29.740.36	τῷ	add	no addition

Conclusion: MS d text derives from alpha sources, from sub-family LNR, particularly as embodied in R.

MS p. Florence.[36] Biblioteca Medicea-Laurentiana VIII 23. Fifteenth century. Single column, 32 lines to page. Only 74 Migne lines of text: from Book IV, 27 lines; from Book V, 47 lines.[37]

Actually codex VIII 23 forms a kind of "Catena Patrum de Spiritu Sancto." Thus excerpts from Basil are ranged among those of Maximus, Athanasius, Cyril, and Chrysostom. Among these, *Adversus Eunomium* excerpts are simply titled ἐκ τῶν ἀντιρρητικῶν.

Unlike most Greek scribes our copyist (or his sources) is deliberately re-working texts to fit his purposes. In any case he is not striving to preserve his exemplar untrammeled. He himself, indeed, introduces 15 changes into 74 lines of text. Eight of these are, perhaps, errors. But we see a copy editor's deliberate hand in such changes:

	MS p		All Others
PG 29.701.20	ἀλλὰ τοῦτο ἄτοπον, ὥστε		ἄρα
PG 29.701.21	ταῦτα εἰρηκώς		οὖν τὰ τοιαῦτα ... εἰρηκώς
PG 29.769.29	ἐν αὐτῷ	add	no addition
PG 29.769.10	πρότερον		πρὸ τούτου
PG 29.772.14	τὸ πνεῦμα τὸ ἅγιον		ἀλλ' οὐδέ
PG 29.772.42	ἑαυτοῦ		ἑαυτῷ alpha
			ἑαυτό VC
			αὐτόν All Others

Moreover, even when (fol. 85 and fol. 111v) MS p repeats a text (PG 29.772.34-PG 29.772.46) he changes it:

	MS p		All Others
PG 29.772.14	αὔξησιν οὐ ζητεῖ	(fol. 85)	
	omit	(fol. 111v)	οὐδὲ αὔξησιν ζητεῖ alpha
			οὐδὲ αὔξησιν ἐπιζητεῖ beta

---

36 Angelo Bandini, *Catalogus codicum manuscriptorum Bibliothecae Mediceae Laurentianae varia continens opera Graecorum patrum*, I, (Florentiae, Typis Caesareis, 1764), p. 372. Cf. *(Ps.) Basil*, Appendix I, 50, p. 162 (where this manuscript is placed in beta family) and p. 156 (where it is suggested that MS p is a recension).

37 Book IV: (fol. 80) PG 29.676.2-PG 29.676.6; (fol. 103v) PG 29.696.22-PG 29.696.30; (fol. 110v)

He is freely changing text, for when his omission on fol. 111v causes participle ὤν (PG 29.772.35) to be ungrammatical, he simply omits it.

Despite all this, however, MS p clearly favors alpha readings. Altogether 13 beta readings appears in the space of these excerpts. MS p text agrees only once:

	MS p beta	All Others
PG 29.724.12	ἑαυτούς	αὐτούς

Two concurrences, however, suggest a LNR provenance:

	MS p LNR		All Others
PG 29.724.18	τοῦ		τό
PG 29.729.5	τήν	omit	no omission

MS p, on the other hand, happens not to report these LNR readings:

	LNR	All Others
PG 29.728.1	κυρίῳ	θεῷ
PG 29.772.41	ἀλλ' ἰδίως	ἀλλ' ἀϊδίως
PG 29.772.42	ἀλλὰ τό	ἀλλ' αὐτό

Conclusion: MS p's text is of alpha provenance, perhaps from LNR traditions, when variants at PG 29.724.18 and PG 729.5 had been introduced, but before those at PG 29.728.1 and PG 29.772.42.

We have schematized these alpha *recentiores* thus:

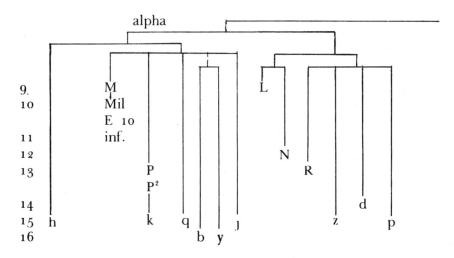

Book V: (fol. 106) PG 29.724.8-PG 29.724.21; PG 29.728.1-PG 29.728.3; PG 29.729.4-PG 29.729.9; PG 29.729.37-PG 29.729.40; (fol. 107) PG 29.769.26-PG 29.769.30; (fol. 85 and fol. 111v) PG 29.772.34-PG 29.772.46; (fol. 108v) PG 29.772.46-PG 29.773.2.

Beta Family

In stemmatics, therefore, if there is an alpha, there must be a beta from which alpha readings differ. Greek manuscripts of (Ps.) Basil, then, have not disappointed us.[38] There is a beta family, whose senior members show this interrelationship:[39]

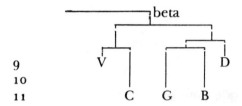

9
10
11

RECENTIORES:

MS n. Vatican.[40] Biblioteca Apostolica Vaticana, Greek 1744. Fifteenth century, single column, 24 lines to page. Fol. 88-99v, 474 Migne lines of text, PG 29.672.1-PG 29.693.19, where text witness itself ends abruptly at πίστις καὶ αὐτός. MS n has lost the next (three) folios — indeed lost them even before the remaining folios received their present number sequencing. Therefore, fol. 100, a new work begins: τοῦ ἐν ἁγίοις πατρὸς ἡμῶν 'Αθανασίου ἀρχιεπισκόπου 'Αλεξανδρείας διαλεκτικὸς ἐν τῇ κατὰ Νίκαιαν συνόδῳ πρὸς "Αρειον.

For itself MS n's *Adversus Eunomium* text (about 2/3 of Book IV) comes to us without scribal or second hand interference. MS n text never agrees with alpha, never with GB or GBD alone, but always agrees with VC, 18 times with VC and one or other manuscript, and 25 times with VC alone.[41] For example:

	VC MS n		All Others
PG 29.673.1	θεοῦ	add	no addition
PG 29.677.15	εὕρηται		εἴρηται
PG 29.685.4	ὁ	add	no addition

38 Cf. *(Ps.) Basil*, p. 93.

39 MS V: Venice. Biblioteca Nazionale Marciana 66; MS C: Paris. Bibliothèque Nationale 965; MS G: Biblioteca Vaticana (Greek) 408 (olim 585); MS B: Oxford. Bodleian Library. Baroccianus 228; MS D: Mount Athos. Monastery of Vatopedi. 68. Cf. *(Ps.) Basil*, Appendix I, pp. 158, 159.

40 Ciro Giannelli and Paul Canart, *Bibliothecae Apostolicae Vaticanae codices manu scripti recensiti iussu Ioannis XXIII Pontificis Maximi, Praeside Eugenio Cardinali Tisserant Episcopo Ostiensi ac Portuensi et S. Rufinae, Sacri Collegii Decano, S.R.E. Bybliothecario et Scriniario. Codices Vaticani Graeci. Codices 1684-1744*, recensuit Cyrus Giannelli. Addenda et Indices curavit Paulus Canart, (Vatican, Biblioteca Apostolica Vaticana, 1961), p. 148. Cf. *(Ps.) Basil*, Appendix I, 49, p. 162.

41 For example λεγόμεθα VC alpha λεγοίμεθα MSS h DGB n and λεγώμεθα RF.

PG 29.685.25   τό   add   no addition
PG 29.689.7   δημιουργός   δημιουργικός
PG 29.689.32   ἐλατρεύσατε   ἐδουλεύσατε
PG 29.692.36   καί   add   no addition
PG 29.693.5   πάντα   πολλά

Four readings suggest that MS n derives from (copied from?) V alone, as opposed to C:

	V MS n		All Others
PG 29.685.6	καί	add	no addition
PG 29.689.47	εἶπεν		εἰπεῖν
PG 29.692.8	γεγεννῆσθαι		γεγενῆσθαι
PG 29.693.10	τοῦ	add	no addition

Conclusion: MS n is clearly a beta manuscript, it derives from VC's tradition, perhaps more immediately from that of V than from that of C.

MS c. Vienna.[42] Österreichische Nationalbibliothek. Theological Greek 113. Full text, Book IV, fol. 195-207, Book V, fol. 207-227v. Single column, 29 lines to page. Nicolaus Patrinus, scribe, finished his work August 27, 1412. A second hand (15th century) corrects a tear in folio 146. A second title for Book V is added by another hand. Andreas Damarius once owned this codex.

Adversus Eunomium text is catalogue item three:

> S. Basilii magni adversus Eunomium haereticum de aequali Patris et Filii et Spiritus Sancti Divinitate sive Deitate Libri Quinque.

As for its text, I have already suggested that MS c is a copy of B.[45] My reasons are both external and internal.[44]
External:
Both codices contain identical works:
1. Basil. *Homilies on Hexaemeron.*
2. Gregory of Nyssa. *De Hominis Opificio.*
3. Basil. *Letters.*
4. *Adversus Eunomium.*
In B *Adversus Eunomium* comes fourth; in MS c, third.

Further, B, as we have it, is a product of at least five hands. 1. Scribe. 2. Scribe or contemporary rubricator. 3. Scribe or contemporary

---

42   von Nessel, *op. cit.,* I, p. 195. Cf. *(Ps.) Basil,* Appendix I, 48, p. 161.

43   *(Ps.) Basil,* p. 90, n. 4.

44   For full description of MS B (Bodleian Baroccianus 228) cf. Henry Coxe, *Catalogi codicum manuscriptorum Bibliothecae Bodleianae, pars prima recensionem codicum Graecorum continens,* (Oxonii, e Typographeo academico, 1853), col. 394.

corrector. 4. Two contemporary scholiasts.[45] 5. Two 14th century scholiasts.[46]

In addition, B has hundreds of para-textual markers (dots, dashes, crosses, daggers, etc.) to mark differences in speakers, arguments, titles *et al.*

Nevertheless MS c (15th century, Nicolaus Patrinus) with one hand shows exactly B's content, marginal corrections and scholia, and para-textual markers.[47]

Internally :

MS c text agrees with that of B in 83 variations against all other manuscripts.[48] For example:

	B MS c		All Others
PG 29.684.31	ἄρα καὶ ὁ υἱὸς		
	καὶ τὰ κτίσματα add		no addition
PG 29.684.37	ἐστί	add	no addition
PG 29.732.15	κατεργάζεται		περιεργάζεται
PG 29.741.2	κτίσιν		κτίσμα
PG 29.745.25	ὑπερῆρηκε		ὑπεξῆρηκε
PG 29.757.21	ἐγένετο	add	no addition
PG 29.765.18	ὁ δέ		καὶ ποτέ
PG 29.765.46	αἵματι		ὀνόματι

Sometimes MS c's scribe accepts corrections by B[2]. For example:[49]

PG 29.680.24	βούλεται	B	βούλονται B[2] MS c All Others
PG 29.688.7	τό	B	τῷ B[2] MS c All Others

But sometimes he does not:

PG 29.692.24	ἀκούει	B MS c	ἀκούσει B[2] All Others

Of course Nicolaus Patrinus (albeit a remarkably faithful scribe) does introduce a few omissions of his own:

PG 29.689.28	ψευδής ...	PG 29.689.29	καί
PG 29.725.12	τὸ σόν ...	PG 29.725.13	τὸ πνεῦμα
PG 29.729.35	ἐν ...	PG 29.729.37	καθάπερ

45 MS B fol. 183 v, 187v; and a second scholiast, fol. 176v, 178, 182.

46 Orange red ink, fol. 166v, 177v, 169, and vermilion red, fol. 175, 177.

47 If MS c is a copy of B, of course, it follows that 18 folios (PG 29.693.12-PG 29.724.8) missing in 11th century B (between fol. 181v-182) were not lost until after 1412.

Nicolaus has an archaizing hand. Were MS c not dated, it would reasonably pass for 12th century or even 11th, and raise the possibility that, were it that early, it might be the ancestor of B.

48 Plus an additional 23 vagaries of B and MS c shared randomly by one or another manuscript.

49 The symbol B(B[2]) indicates that a second hand reverses B's reading.

Conclusion: MS c is clearly a beta text, in B's tradition. Indeed it shows every sign of being an accurate 15th century copy of an 11th century manuscript with its many 14th century marginalia.

MS f. Vatican.[50] Biblioteca Apostolica Vaticana. Greek 1093. Fifteenth century, 31-48 lines to page, single column of varying width. Codex contains excerpts from patristic authors: Basil, John Damascene, Dionysius, Chrysostom, Athanasius.

Two scribal hands are apparent. One script (small, compressed, full of abbreviations) accounts for all but six lines of our text (fol. 30), five excerpts, 24 Migne lines of text: Book IV: PG 29.684.12-PG 29.684.14 (fol. 40); Book V: PG 29.725.10-PG 29.725.11 (fol. 32); PG 29.733.11-PG 29.733.15 (fol. 32); PG 29.733.39-PG 29.733.43 (fol. 25); PG 29.736.17-PG 29.736.27 (fol. 25).

Even in 24 lines our scribe (MS f) or his predecessors has introduced six text changes:

	MS f alone		All Others
PG 29.684.14	ἕτερον		ἂν εἴη
PG 29.725.10	τό	add	no addition
PG 29.733.11	δή	omit	no omission
PG 29.733.11	ταῦτα		τοῦτο
PG 29.733.39	οὐ		οὐδέ
PG 29.733.39	εἰ	add	no addition

However, MS f always agrees with Beta against alpha:

	Beta MS f		All Others
PG 29.725.11	ἴδιον		ἀίδιον
PG 29.733.12	ἐκήρυξεν		ἀνεκήρυξεν
PG 29.733.14	σαφές		σαφῶς
PG 29.733.39	ἐξιέναι		ἔξειν
PG 29.733.41	ἀλλ' ἱκανὸν χαὶ τοῦτο	add	no addition
PG 29.736.24	αὐτοῦ		ἑαυτοῦ
PG 29.736.25	ὁ	add	no addition

In particular, MS f's text tradition seems to reflect a GBD source, not that of VC:

	GBD, MS f		VC
PG 29.733.40	τό	omit	no omission alpha
PG 29.733.41	τοῦ θεοῦ	alpha	αὐτοῦ
PG 29.736.21	σωματικόν	alpha	σωματικῶς
PG 29.736.26	ἄνθρωπος	omit	no omission

---

50   Vatican Library. Handwritten Catalogue, # 323, p. 68. There is no printed catalogue for ·Vatican Greek manuscripts 867-1484 or 1963-2625. Indeed even Vatican's card catalogue does not include manuscripts 2403-2625. Cf. *(Ps.) Basil*, Appendix I, 52, p. 162.

In any case, MS f does not agree with Dgtrewsu:

PG 29.733.40 ὑπάρχειν   MS f VCGBc ὑπάρχον alpha Dgtrewsu

Nor does our scribe agree with errors introduced by MSS Bc:

	MSS Bc	All Others
PG 29.736.24	πράττων	προάγων
PG 29.736.26	αὐτοῦ	ἑαυτοῦ

Conclusion: MS f clearly comes from beta sources. Our scribe favors GBc readings over those of VC or Dgtrewsu. He has not copied from sub-group Bc.

Eight additional manuscripts (MSS gtmrewsu) show texts in close, if complicated, relation to beta traditions, in particular to that witnessed to by D. Before, then, we consider their text and its history, let us first briefly identify and describe each manuscript.

MS g. Mt. Athos.[51] Vatopedi Monastery Library 58. Fourteenth century. Single column, 30-32 lines to page. Full text, Book IV (fol. 119-128) and Book V (fol. 128-144). Original scribe is marginal rubricator.

Four times a corrector repairs errors made by scribe of MS g alone:

	MS g		All Others and g^2
PG 29.717.25	αὐτοῦ λέγοντος		αὐτοῦ τὸ λέγοντος g^2
			αὐτοῦ τοῦτο λέγοντος alpha
			αὐτοῦ τοῦ λέγοντος beta
PG 29.720.2	ἐνεργείας	omit	no omission
PG 29.720.25	πῶς	omit	no omission
PG 29.740.34	ὑμῖν	omit	no omission

Otherwise MS g's text comes to us as its scribe left it.

MS t. Mt. Athos.[52] Iviron Monastery Library 354. Fourteenth century. Single column page, 25 lines. Full text, Book IV (fol. 92-101v) and Book V (fol. 101v-132v).

Second hand (15th century) text changes occur 73 times. We distinguish three types:

---

51 Sophronios Eustratiades and Arcadios (Vatopedinos), "Catalogue of the Greek Manuscripts in the Library of the Monastery of Vatopedi on Mount Athos," *Harvard Theological Studies*, 11, 1924, p. 18.

52 Spyridon Lambros (ὑπὸ Σπυρίδωνος Λάμπρου), *Catalogue of the Greek Manuscripts on Mount Athos*, II, (Cambridge, University Press, 1900), = 4474, p. 95. Cf. *(Ps.) Basil*, Appendix I, 45, p. 161.

1. Interlinear changes (47).

a. Thin line. Corrector derives readings from P tradition:

	Pk MS t²		All Others
PG 29.696.33	πρός		περί
PG 29.752.36	οὕτως		τοιοῦτον
PG 29.757.24	καί	add	no addition
PG 29.765.10	φύσις		κτίσις

b. Middle thickness. Corrector derives readings from G tradition:

	G MS t²		All Others
PG 29.685.37	καθό	add	no addition
PG 29.701.47	γεννηθείς	add	no addition
PG 29.740.9	ὁρῶν	add	no addition

c. Thickest pen stroke. Corrector derives readings from LN:

	LN MS t²	All Others
PG 29.685.8	ὀνόματα	ὄντα

2. Erasure and cramped re-write (20). Here a corrector erases original text and (usually) crams corrections into erased areas. Most errors seem to have been MS t's alone. Three times, however, a correction comes from alpha-VC:

	Alpha VC MS t²		All Others
PG 29.705.18	οὖν	add	no addition
PG 29.748.12	Χριστός	add	no addition
PG 29.749.29	ἢ ποσότητα	add	no addition

Once, this corrector's source can be alpha's tradition alone:

PG 29.744.18	τοῦ	add MS t²	no addition beta

3. Erasure and large scrawl re-write (6). In all six cases errors being corrected must be those of MS t himself.

Finally, 10 times, second hand correctors improperly incorporate change and produce new readings peculiar to this codex alone.

MS m. London.[53] British Museum Arundel 535. Fourteenth century mélange. Third hand[54] on folio 13 affords us two excerpts from Book V, 21 Migne lines: PG 29.725.15-PG 29.725.23 and PG 29.733.11-PG 29.733.24. Scribe's title: τοῦ μεγάλου Βασιλείου.

53 Josiah Forshall, *Catalogue of Manuscripts in the British Museum. New Series. I, part 1, The Arundel Manuscripts,* (London, British Museum, 1834), p. 163. Cf. *(Ps.) Basil,* Appendix I, 47, p. 161.

54 Or, if it is one scribe he surely uses three handwriting styles on fol. 13 — upper 19 lines from hand (style) one, middle five lines from hand (style) two, bottom 12 lines τοῦ μεγάλου Βασιλείου from hand three.

MS r. Vatican.[55] Biblioteca Apostolica Vaticana. Greek 424 (olim 291). Fourteenth century. Double columns, 33-35 lines to page. Full text: Book IV (fol. 34v-42), Book V (fol. 42-54v). At times (e.g. fol. 46v) handwriting style (if not scribal hand) changes, becoming thicker and more erratic.

Moreover, in five instances MS r corrects his own errors, in order to read with (his exemplar and) all others:

PG 29.688.36	τὸν υἱόν	add	
PG 29.689.10	εἰ διά	add	
PG 29.728.33	αὐτοῦ	add	
PG 29.760.49	μόνην μίαν	(scribe)	μίαν μόνην (corrector)
PG 29.769.8	ὄν	add	

MS e. Lesbos.[56] St. John Monastery 6. Fourteenth century. Single column, 26 lines to page. Full text: Book IV (fol. 248-261v), Book V (fol. 261v-284v). Rubricator of 15th century. Two marginal hands, one, a neat contemporary script (cf. fol. 262v, 263); a second, 15th century, larger, more angular (cf. fol. 254v).

Only two instances of second hand interference are relevant:

PG 29.673.16	εἰ	add	MS e² alone
PG 29.713.34	τόν	add	MSS h R VC e²

With such minimal change in text we may be confident that MS e reflects the tradition just as it came from scribe and exemplar.

MS w. Brussels.[57] Bibliothèque Royale 11357. Sixteenth century. Scribe: Christophe Awer. Single column, 20 lines to page. Full text: Book IV (fol. 162v-197), Book V (fol. 197-255).

Former owners have left their marks:

> Iohannes Livineius cathedralis Antverpiensis canonicus et cantor. Redemi ex libris Ioh. Doverini patricii Bruxellensis ac Leodiensis canonici, 1593, Leodii.
> Collegii Societatis Iesu.
> Bibliothèque Nationale de Paris.[58]

---

55 Robert Devreesse, *Bibliothecae Apostolicae Vaticanae Codices Manu Scripti recensiti iussu Pii XI Pontificis Maximi, Praeside Johanne Mercati S. Georgii in Velabro Cardinali Diacono, S.R.E. Bibliothecario et Scriniario. Codices Vaticani Graeci, t. II, Codices 330-603,* (Vatican, Biblioteca Apostolica Vaticana, 1937), p. 141. Cf. *(Ps.) Basil,* Appendix I, 43, p. 161.

56 Athanasios Papadopoulos-Kerameus. Μαυρογορδάτειος βιβλιοθήκη ἤτοι γενικὸς περιγράφικος κατάλογος τῶν ἐν ταῖς ἀνὰ τὴν ἀνατολὴν βιβλιοθήκαις εὑρισκομένων ἑλληνικῶν χειρογράφων καταρτισθεῖσα καὶ συνταχθεῖσα κατ' ἐντολὴν τοῦ ἐν Κωνσταντινουπόλει ἑλληνικοῦ φιλολογικοῦ συλλόγου. Μέρος ά. Κατάλογος τῶν ἐν ταῖς βιβλιοθήκαις τῆς νήσου Λέσβου ἑλληνικῶν χειρογράφων, (Constantinople, S. I. Boutura, [vol. 15-18 Supplement], 1884), p. 147. Papadopoulos-Kerameus dates Mitylene 6 as 12th century. Cf. *(Ps.) Basil,* Appendix I, 44, p. 161.

57 Joseph van den Gheyn, *Catalogue des Manuscrits de la Bibliothèque Royale de Belgique,* II (Bruxelles, Lamertin, 1902), # 938, p. 27. Cf. *(Ps.) Basil,* Appendix I, p. 162.

58 *Ibid.* Cf. MS w, fol. 1 and 128.

Awer himself titles Books I and II correctly. His title for Books III, IV, and V, however is simply λόγος γ΄. He apparently is unaware of book numbers IV and V. This meaning, however, for Book III must be his own error. It is unique in the West and has not been seen since Leontius of Byzantium, *Libri Tres Contra Eutychianos et Nestorianos*, A.D. 543.

Our scribe corrects his own omissions:

PG 29.697.16	δέ	add
PG 29.737.28	καὶ ὁ λόγος συναπιστεῖται	add
PG 29.764.30	ἐάν ... PG 29.764.31 ἐποίησα	add

However, another hand, with an alpha source has effected these changes:

	Beta MS w		Alpha MS w²
PG 29.696.40	τῆς	omit	no omission
PG 29.717.31	ἀφέονται		ἀφέωνται
PG 29.721.16	κύριος	add	no addition
PG 29.744.39	ἔχων		ἔχον

Only these four extraneous readings appear in MS w.

MS s. Paris.[59] Bibliothèque Nationale. Greek 969. Formerly Mazarin-Regius 3430. Fifteenth century, single column, 30 lines to page.[60] Full text: Book IV (fol. 193v-203v) and Book V (fol. 203v-220v).

Scribe and rubricator are probably identical. Three corrector hands. One is MS s scribe himself, where he corrects his own errors — once, at least, incorrectly:

PG 29.760.22	ἀκαμάντως	MS s²	ἀκαμάτως	All Others

Another hand introduces 16 changes. His immediate source is obscure, as in these examples:

			All Others
PG 29.740.4	ἐξ	add MSS q VC Bc s²	no addition
PG 29.741.28	καὶ λέγων	add alpha VC s²	no addition
PG 29.761.9	καὶ πατρός	add N² Bc V s²	no addition

A third hand makes seven corrections from VC sources. For example:

			All Others
PG 29.693.5	πάντα	add VC s²	no addition
PG 29.697.16	τοῦτο	add VC G s²	no addition

---

59 Omont, *Inventaire Sommaire*, I, p. 188. Cf. *(Ps.) Basil*, Appendix I, p. 162.

60 Jean Gribomont, *Introductio, Libri Adversus Eunomium (Basilius, Opera Omnia, Patrologia Graeca*, ed. J. P. Migne, 29), (Turnhout, Brepols, 1959, anastatic reprint), pp. 12-13.

MS u. Paris.[61] Bibliothèque Nationale. Greek 956. Formerly Mediceus Regius 2896. Fifteenth century, single column, 30 lines to page.[62] Full text: Book IV (fol. 193v-203v) and Book V (fol. 203v-220).

We can distinguish three hands. 1. scribe and rubricator 2. contemporary rubricator and 3. contemporary scholiast.

Most marginal activity consists of (traditional) sub-titles. No second hand corrects text errors.

At this point, having identified and described each of these eight manuscripts (MSS gtm rew su) we must accordingly explore their relation to alpha and beta families.

As a group, first of all, these eight manuscripts never agree with any of 107 variations which we call alpha family. These eight agree with 172 instances which we take as peculiar to beta manuscripts.

In point of fact, moreover, these eight function within a larger subset of 12 beta manuscripts (MSS GBcDgtrewsu).

Group GBcDgtmrewsu:

These 12 manuscripts postulate one common source. We see 22 vagaries of this source still present in all 12 manuscripts against alpha and VC.[63]

	GBcDgtmrewsu	Alpha VC
PG 29.673.11	δημιουργηθέντων	δημιουργηθέν
PG 29.696.44	δύναται	λέγεται
PG 29.700.12	γάρ	δέ
PG 29.704.25	ἀπόστολος	Παῦλος
PG 29.744.11	γάρ	δέ
PG 29.756.6	παρὰ κυρίου θεῖον καὶ πῦρ	θεῖον καὶ πῦρ παρὰ Κυρίου
PG 29.768.25	ἄλλοις	ἄλλῳ

Conclusion: There is scribal source responsible for common errors in GBcDgtmrewsu.

Group GBc:

There are, moreover, 26 instances where a scribe of GBc has introduced variations against all other manuscripts. For example:

	GBc		All Others
PG 29.688.2	ἐστίν	add	no addition
PG 29.688.18	αὐτόν	omit	no omission
PG 29.692.24	ἀκούσει		ἀκούει

---

61 Omont, *Inventaire Sommaire*, I, p. 184.

62 Gribomont, *loc. cit.*, concurs with Omont in a 14th century date.

63 There are another 42 variations introduced by this scribe. These are shared (12 of them by P²k alone) by random alpha manuscripts known to have borrowed from this source.

PG 29.732.28	πληρωτικόν		πληρωματικόν
PG 29.733.30	οὖσαν		οὐσίαν
PG 29.748.9	ἕν	omit	no omission
PG 29.757.12	φησιν	add	no addition
PG 29.768.24	τήν	omit	no addition

Conclusion: There is one scribe-source responsible for common errors in GBc.

Group Dgtrewsu:

Furthermore, one source must be responsible for 16 variations still seen in Dgtrewsu against all others. For example:

	Dgtrewsu		All Others
PG 29.677.43	ἐστίν	add	no addition
PG 29.693.22	ὑποτέτακται		ὑποτάσσεται
PG 29.700.29	δέ	add	no addition
PG 29.709.23	πάλιν		ὁ Μωυσῆς
PG 29.713.32	ὁ	add	no addition
PG 29.732.32	τοῦ πνεύματος		τὸ πνεῦμα
PG 29.753.17	γάρ	add	no addition

Conclusion: One scribal source is responsible for common errors in Dgtrewsu.

Group Dgtrew.

Thirteen common vagaries postulate a common source for hyparche-type Dgtrew. For example:

	Dgtrew		All Others
PG 29.672.13	ὥσπερ τά		εἶτα
PG 29.673.28	γε	add	no addition
PG 29.701.29	πρὸ τελευτῆς		προτελευτήσας
PG 29.701.29	ὁ		εἰ
PG 29.737.4	καί	add	no addition
PG 29.744.23	θεοῦ	add	no addition
PG 29.744.24	πνεῦμα	omit	no omission
PG 29.744.24	τό	add	no addition
PG 29.744.41	τό	add	no addition
PG 29.748.28	πῶς		πνεύματος

Conclusion: One source (scribe) is responsible for common errors in Dgtrew.

Group Dgt:

Twelve common variations against all other manuscripts make Dgt a recognizable sub-group and postulate a common source. For example:

	Dgt		All Others
PG 29.737.8	ἐκφυσώμενον		ἐμφυσώμενον
PG 29.744.12	πάντα	omit	no omission
PG 29.748.31	σπουδάζουσιν		σπουδάσωσιν
PG 29.760.10	κτίζοντι		κτίζοντος
PG 29.764.10	τε	omit	no omission
PG 29.764.46	γάρ	omit	no omission

Conclusion: Manuscripts Dgt form a sub-group recognizable in their common errors.

MS g. For its part MS g is a very close kin, if not a direct copy of D. It agress with D four times against MS t and all others:

	Dg	All Others
PG 29.765.30	τό	τοῦ
PG 29.768.9	αὐτῶν	αὐτοῦ
PG 29.772.13	δῆλον ὅτι	δηλονότι
PG 29.772.15	δῆλον ὅτι	δηλονότι

There are, however, eight instances (in three of these D is difficult to read) where MS g is not a letter perfect copy of D. These must be errors of MS g alone. For example:

	MS g		All Others
PG 29.684.11	ἀγνώησεν		ἀγνόησεν
PG 29.693.16	πιστεύητε		πιστεύσητε
PG 29.725.4	τοῦ	add	no addition

However PG 29.720.23 τῆς ... PG 29.720.25 ἐσχηκέναι, missing in D alone, does appear in MS g.[64]

Conclusion: MS g is a close kin of the tradition of D.

MS t. MS t is another close relative of D. It is almost a letter perfect copy of D, except for six instances:[65]

	MS t		
PG 29.692.14	εἰς τὸ πάντα ὅσα ἔχει ὁ πατὴρ		
	ἐμά ἐστιν	add	no addition Dg
PG 29.693.27	τό	omit su	τό D
			ὁ θεός All Others
PG 29.700.29	δέ	omit	no omission Dg su
PG 29.700.30	ἐπί	s u	ἐπεί Dg All Others

---

64 A marker in D indicates that (some) words are missing, but they are not now visible in margin. In any case, scribe of MS g found them in some source.

65 In addition to four Dg alone readings above.

PG 29.705.10 ἐγένετο   γενοῦ D t²
                                                         ἐγένου All Others
PG 29.765.47 Χριστοῦ   add r e w   no addition

Conclusion: MS t is also closely related to text traditions represented by D.

MS m. MS m (two excerpts) affords only 27 Migne lines of text. It does however generate 17 instances of agreement with beta manuscripts, where concurrence with Dgt is a common denominator. For example:

	MS m Beta	All Others
PG 29.725.23	εἰκὼν ὡς	ἱκανῶς
PG 29.733.12	ἐκήρυξεν	ἀνεκήρυξεν
PG 29.733.14	σαφές	σαφῶς
PG 29.733.18	ἵνα εἰς	ἵν᾽ εἰς

Furthermore, MS m does not derive from VC traditions:

	MS m All others		VC
PG 29.725.22	χυρίου πνεῦμα		πνεῦμα χυρίου
PG 29.725.23	χυρίου	add	no addition
PG 29.733.19	ἀϊδίως		ἀΐδιος
PG 29.733.21	ὤν	omit	no omission
PG 29.733.21	θεοῦ	add	no addition
PG 29.733.22	ἅγιον	add	no addition

Nor does MS m derive from GBc:

| PG 29.733.20 | ὁ | add alpha | |
| | | Dgt m | no addition VC GBc |

Nor, indeed, does MS m derive its readings from MSS rew:

	MS m All Others		MSS rew
PG 29.725.16	ἀρτίως		ἄρτι
PG 29.725.20	τοῦ	omit	no omission
PG 29.733.13	τό	add	no addition
PG 29.733.14	διά		δι᾽

Nor does MS m derive from the tradition of MSS su:

	MS m All Others	MSS su
PG 29.733.20	ἀνάρχως	ἄναρχος

Nor, finally, does MS m derive from text tradition of MS t:

	MS m All Others	MS t
PG 29.733.15	Χριστοῦ	θεοῦ

Conclusion: Since in every one of these 17 instances MS m does agree
with DG, it is not unwise to see Arundel 535 as related to and derived
from its tradition. In its full form, then, the sub-group is Dgtm.

Group MSS rew: Further, some sources in MSS rew tradition is
responsible for 119 common variations from all other manuscripts.[66]
For example:

	MSS rew		All Others
PG 29.693.7	εἰπών		εἰ τῶν
PG 29.701.43	πρῶτος καί	add	no addition
PG 29.704.44	ὥσπερ		ὡς γοῦν καί
PG 29.705.3	ὀνομασθείη		νομισθείη
PG 29.724.24	μεταφέρει		μεταφερομένη
PG 29.729.36	ἄνδρασιν		ἀνθρώπου
PG 29.737.14	ἀνερμήνευτα		ἑρμηνεύματα
PG 29.769.34	λειτουργικήν		λογικήν
PG 29.772.9	πνεύματος		τῷ πνεύματι

We are unable to determine a more exact interrelationsyip between
MSS rew. Of course, we recognize a close relationship between MSS r
and e. There are hundreds of para-textual markers and ornamentations
identical in both manuscripts. We know that about half of each codex
contains identical content:

MS r:[67]

1. S. Basilii *Adversus Eunomium* ff. 1-54.
2. S. Gregorii Nysseni *Contra Eunomium*. Praemittuntur ... epistola ad
Petrum Sebastenum. Petri Sebasteni responsum.
3. (fol. 295v) S. Gregorii Nazianzeni *epistola 238* omissis inscriptione et conclusione.
4. (fol. 295v-296) S. Athanasii *epistola ad Iohannem et Antiochum*.
5. S. Gregorii Nysseni *epistola quarta* ... eiusdem *de Deitate* et tribus personis....
1. Iohannis monachi *brevissima de incarnatione*.
Eiusdem *de Carne Christi*
... subicitur Synodi Nicaenae excerptum.
7. S. Gregorii Nysseni *in psalmorum inscriptiones*.
Eiusdem *epistolae* (5-18) ex exemplari mutilo descriptae.

MS e:[68]

1. Βασιλείου Καισαρείας εἰς τὴν Ἑξαήμερον ὁμιλίαι θ'. φ. 95.

---

66 Hyparchetypal scribe is also responsible for another 27 variations (of his own) in concurrence with a random sampling of one or other manuscript.
67 Devreesse, *op. cit.*, pp. 141-142.
68 Papadopoulos-Kerameus, *op. cit.*, p. 147. Ἀνόμιος is adversary of Books I-III as cited by

2. Γρηγορίου Νύσσης ὁμιλίαι β' περὶ τῆς τοῦ ἀνθρώπου κατασκευῆς. φ. 95.

3. τοῦ αὐτοῦ πρὸς Πέτρον τὸν ἴδιον ἀδελφόν· καὶ εἰς τὰ λοιπὰ τῆς Ἑξαημέρου τοῦ ἀδελφοῦ αὐτοῦ Βασιλείου, τουτέστιν εἰς τὴν κατασκεωὴν τοῦ ἀνθρώπου. φ. 117.

4. Βασιλείου Καισαρείας λόγος ἀντιρρητικὸς κατὰ τοῦ δυσσεβοῦς 'Ανομίου. φ. 190.

5. τοῦ αὐτοῦ κατὰ τοῦ δυσσεβοῦς 'Ανομίου ἀντιρρητικὸς β'. φ. 216v.

6. τοῦ αὐτοῦ λόγος ἀντιρρητικὸς κατὰ τοῦ δυσσεβοῦς 'Ανομίου γ'. φ. 246.

7. τοῦ αὐτοῦ κατὰ τοῦ δυσσεβοῦς Εὐνομίου ἀντιρρητικὸς δ'. φ. 251.

8. Γρηγόριος Νύσσης ἐπιστολὴ πρὸς τὸν ἀδελφὸν αὐτοῦ Πέτρον ἐπίσκοπον Σεβαστείας. φ. 288.

9. Πέτρου Σεβαστείας ἐπιστολὴ πρὸς τὸν ἅγιον Γρηγόριον Νύσσης τὸν αὐτοῦ ἀδελφόν. φ. 289v.

10. Γρηγόριος Νύσσης λόγος ἀντιρρητικὸς κατὰ τοῦ δυσσεβοῦς Εὐνομίου εἰς τοὺς ἐκδοθέντας παρ' αὐτοῦ δύο λόγους μετὰ τὴν κοίμησιν τοῦ ἁγίου Βασιλείου.

It is clear, therefore, that codex order and content is remarkably similar. MS r item 1 corresponds to MS e, items 4-7. MS r item 2 corresponds to MS e, items 8-10.

Further, MSS r and e are themselves nearly identical in text. Indeed, they agree in these vagaries alone:

	MSS r e	All Others
PG 29.685.40	ἢ	ἢ
PG 29.696.36	μεταβαλλομένους	μεταβαλομένους
PG 29.713.30	αὐτόν	αὐτό

On the other hand, texts of MS r are almost as intimately connected to those of MS w. MSS r and w agree in six readings against all others:

	MSS r w		All Others
PG 29.673.5	ἄλλο		ἄλλῳ
PG 29.684.5	τό	add	no addition
PG 29.685.41	γάρ		τό
PG 29.689.26	λεγοίμεθα		λεγόμεθα
PG 29.701.35	ὁ	omit	no omission
PG 29.720.33	αὐχέ	MS r	
	ἀδχ'	MS w	ἀδελφέ

Conclusion: One scribal source is responsible for common variants in MSS rew.

Papadopoulos-Kerameus, who (however) identifies the text (*Adversus Eunomium*) in Migne correctly. MS e (Mitylene 6) itself says Εὐνόμιος each time.

Group (MSS) su: Lastly, two manuscripts, s and u, show 14 readings alone. These point to a common scribal source.[69] For example:

		MSS s u		All Others
PG	29.689.6	μεῖζω		μείζονα
PG	29.693.4	δημιουργῶν		δημιουργουμένων
PG	29.713.30	ῥηθέντι		προρρηθέντι
PG	29.724.20	ὁ	add	no addition
PG	29.728.43	γάρ	add	no addition
PG	29.733.20	ἄναρχος		ἀνάρχως
PG	29.740.26	καταφαίνεται		φαίνεται
PG	29.741.9	ὁ		ὡς,
PG	29.748.32	ἀπό		ὑπό
PG	29.761.50	καί	add	no addition

Conclusion: One source is responsible for common variants in MSS s and u. We may schematize our conclusions concerning beta family and *recentiores*:

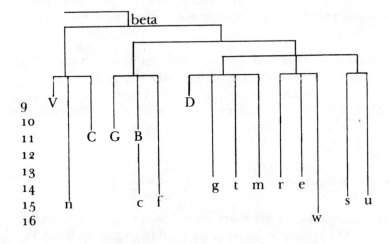

INTERMEDIATE MANUSCRIPTS

In addition to alpha and beta sources other manuscripts provide us with *Adversus Eunomium* text which systematically shares readings of both families. Indeed, choice of readings seems to be deliberate and im-

---

69   There are 79 readings of MS s alone, no more than three of MSS t or u alone. There is no concurrence of MSS t s, t u, or t s u alone. There are no concurrences of VC and MS u alone. There are 44 VC P MS s readings alone, where presumably MS s has adopted (*contaminatio*) 44 VC alone readings. But none of these concurrences affect our identification of the scribe s u.

plies some kind of editorial work.[70] Four such edition-texts exist among older manuscripts. Two of them borrow particularly from LNRd and GBD; two, from LNRd and VC. We schematize their relationship thus:[71]

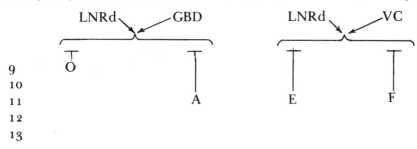

RECENTIORES:

MS x. Modena.[72] Biblioteca Estense 190 (Alpha V.8.14), olim III F 12. Fifteenth century, single column, 32 lines per page. Full text, Book IV, fol. 245v-254v. Book V, fol. 254v-269v. MS x first (of manuscripts we have discussed here) uses commas extensively, besides colon, semicolon, and period.

Book V, indeed, opens without title. In its stead, 13 lines (PG 29.709.38 ὅτι ... PG 29.712.11 τριάς) are written large by rubricator as a kind of book title.[73] This long title is followed (PG 29.712.11) by an added title περὶ τοῦ ἁγίου πνεύματος.

To be sure, MS x's scribe corrects a few of his own errors:

	MS x	Corrected
PG 29.736.33	κτήσεως	κτίσεως
PG 29.772.18	καυστικοῖς	καυστικούς

But a second hand corrector sometimes erases scribal choices (or exemplar readings) to bring in new readings:

	MS x		Second Hand	
PG 29.680.4	ἔχοι	beta	ἔχῃ alpha	
PG 29.744.33	ὥστε	alpha	εἰ N VC F	
PG 29.748.34	ὡς ... PG 29.748.35 ἐκλείψουσι	omit alpha	no omission beta	
PG 29.752.23	φανερά	alpha	φανερόν beta	

---

70 Cf. *(Ps.) Basil*, p. 112 *et sqq.*

71 MS O: Mount Athos. Monastery of Lavra. B 105; MS A: Patmos. Monastery of St. John. Lambda 184; MS E: Vienna. Oesterreichische Nationalbibliothek Historical Greek 35; MS F: Munich Bayerische Staatsbibliothek 466; Cf. *(Ps.) Basil*, Appendix I, p. 160.

72 Christa Samberger. *Catalogi codicum Graecorum qui in minoribus Bibliothecis Italicis asservantur.* (Leipzig, Zentral-Antiquariat der Deutschen Demokratischen Republik, 1965), p. 416. Cf. *(Ps.) Basil*, Appendix I, p. 162.

73 This book title, of course, is unique among manuscripts.

A third (marginal) hand seems to be aware of MS d's tradition:

PG 29.704.39 εἰς τὸ αὐτό   add MSS d and x alone
PG 29.725.15 ὅτι τὸ πνεῦμα τὸ Χριστὸς ὀνομάζεται
                    Comment appears in MSS d and x margins alone.

On the whole, however, MS x's text is an editor's product. At 143 places our editor was given choice (presumably) between an alpha or beta reading. He chose alpha 72 times; he agrees with beta 71 times. But only with difficulty can we point to specific alpha sources. We may surmise that he has a source akin to Pk from these instances:

	Pk and MS x		All Others
PG 29.673.14	οὐχ ὡς	MSS b y	ὡς οὐχ
PG 29.692.5	ὁ	add	no addition
PG 29.693.22	τόν	add	no addition
PG 29.733.19	ἀϊδίως		ἀϊδίῳ
PG 29.744.10	οἰκοῦντος πνεύματος		οἰκοῦντος alpha
			ἐνοικοῦντος πνεύματος
			beta
PG 29.760.26	θεῷ καὶ πατρί	add	no addition
PG 29.760.29	ὡς	add	no addition
PG 29.764.38	τὸ ἅγιον	add	no addition

Or, perhaps, alpha sources for MS x could be LNRd, for example:

	MS x		All Others
PG 29.688.11	τό	N R d	τῷ
PG 29.705.5	εἰς τὸ αὐτό	add	no addition
PG 29.717.13	ἐξεικονίζων	L N	ἐξεικονίζον
PG 29.745.3	τήν	add Nd F	no addition
PG 29.757.28	ἱκανοῖ	N²	ἱκανεῖ alpha
			ἱκανά beta

For their part, beta sources of MS x readings seem to be in VC's tradition:[74]

74 There are hints of an additional GBc source for MS x:

	GBc MS x		All Others
PG 29.676.17	ἄν	omit	no omission
PG 29.724.15	καί	omit F	no omission
PG 28.729.43	φησι Παῦλος	omit	no omission
PG 29.729.44	καὶ πατρός	add rew	no addition
PG 29.761.9	καὶ πατρός	add s²	no addition

There are, in addition, four (seemingly coincidental) concurrences of MS s and x alone:

	MSS s x		All Others
PG 29.689.46	δύναιτ' ἄν		δυνατόν
PG 29.700.32	εἰ μὴ εἰς ὁ θεός	add	no addition
PG 29.728.1	καί	add	no addition
PG 29.744.1	πάντων		πάντα

	VC and MS x		All Others
PG 29.673.22	ὁ	add F	no addition
PG 29.676.21	ὁ	add F	no addition
PG 29.697.2	βούλονται		βούλεται MS s
			θέλουσιν All Others
PG 29.728.17	ἀνακαινίζει	N² F	ἀνασῴζει
PG 29.736.21	σωματικῶς	F	σωματικόν
PG 29.753.24	θεοῦ	F	υἱοῦ
PG 29.773.5	πάντες γάρ	N² F	γάρ alpha
			πάντες All Others

Furthermore, editor of MS x has introduced 102 readings of his own. Some of these (PG 29.760.15 γενῶν for γεννῶν) are simply errors. Some of them represent omissions, additions, transpositions attributable, perhaps, to fatigue. But most changes show a text editor's willingness to change, clarify, and simplify. For example:

	MS x		All Others
PG 29.672.3	ψευδόμενοι		ψευδῶς λεγόμενοι
PG 29.677.5	ἀΐδιος		συναΐδιος
PG 29.680.5	ἀνάγκη	add	no addition
PG 29.685.31	λέγηται		σῴζηται
PG 29.692.21	οὖν	add	no addition
PG 29.728.15	ἀεί		αἰῶνα
PG 29.728.44	θείῳ		ζῶντι
PG 29.732.45	σχέσει		θέσει
PG 29.733.22	ἀληθείας		ἀληθῶς
PG 29.736.27	μετακινοῖτο		μετακίνει
PG 29.737.45	δι'		ἐξ
PG 29.741.4	ἴσον		ἰσάζειν
PG 29.757.4	αὐτῶν τὰς γλώσσας add		no addition
PG 29.757.29	δεῖξαι		διδάξαι

Conclusion: MS x's text is an edition. It borrows from LNRd and VC sources and shows an editor's willingness to introduce alterations.

Of course, F also borrows from LNRd and VC. Do F and MS x show any further similarities to each other?

First of all, however, let it be said that our four recension-type texts — whose of O A E and F — are not copies of each other.[75] They choose among alpha-beta readings, but with no common set pattern.

Nonetheless, remarkably, these recensions do share readings proper to themselves alone, a fact which suggests a common (editorial) source independent of alpha and beta.

75 Cf. (Ps.) Basil, p. 29.

F and MS x, for example, share 14 vagaries alone. (In the instances cited below, E and O appear in parentheses where we lack their text. Where there are no parentheses E and/or O agree with "All Others".)

	F MS x		All Others
PG 29.681.38	εἰ	add (E)	no addition
PG 29.689.10	πατὴρ δυνάμεις	(E)	πατρὸς δύναμις
PG 29.689.15	αὐτοῦ	(E)	ἑαυτοῦ
PG 29.716.46	αὐτοῦ	add (E O)	no addition
PG 29.717.27	ἡμῶν	(E)	ὑμῶν
PG 29.720.47	ὃν προεχειρίσατο	omit (O)	no omission
PG 29.724.12	τῆς	add (O)	no addition
PG 29.724.33	τῶν	add (O)	no addition
PG 29.725.15	Χριστοῦ	(O)	Χριστός
PG 29.725.27	PG 29.725.46 ἐν ... PG 29.725.48 θεοῦ		
		add (O)	no addition

MS x duly repeats this at PG 29.725.46.
F reasonably omits it.

| PG 29.729.38 | οὐδέ | | οὐ |
| PG 29.732.2 | ὁ | add | no addition |

Moreover, eight readings appear, common to E and F alone:

	E F		All Others
PG 29.724.3	τοῦ	omit (O)	no omission
PG 29.724.28	χρυσοῦν	(O)	χρύσεον
PG 29.728.37	οὐδέν	A (O)	οὐδὲ ἕν
PG 29.729.34	θεὸς αὐτοὺς οὐ δι' αὐτῶν	omit (O)	θεὸς αὐτοὺς οὐ δι' αὐτῶν ἐργάζεται omit alpha no omission All Others
PG 29.729.42	γὰρ χάρις	(O)	χάρις γάρ
PG 29.732.35	δή	(O)	δέ
PG 29.748.18	δέ	(O)	δή
PG 29.753.10	σκληροτραχήλῳ	(O)	σκληρῷ τραχήλῳ

A further three readings appear common to E and MS x alone:[76]

	E MS x		All Others
PG 29.721.49	εἶπε	(O)	ἔφη
PG 29.748.21	ἀλλά	(O)	ἀλλ'
PG 29.748.22	ὅν	add	no addition

---

76 For sake of completeness. Evidence for common source for MSS O A:

	MSS O A		All Others
PG 29.681.4	κτίσμα		οὐσία
PG 29.692.33	χατά	MS x	κατ'
PG 29.708.5	ἀλλά		ἀλλ'

Conclusion: These concurrences, surely, point to some common (remote) source, independent of alpha and beta, from which these recensions E and F and MS x derive.

MS W. Moscow.[77] Historical Museum Greek 231. (Formerly Athos, Διονυσίου). Tenth century (932 A.D.), single column, 28 lines to page. Fol. 71-74, 192 Migne lines of text, Book IV, PG 29.672.1-PG 29.681.5.

Whoever prepared this text, Stylianus (Arethas' scribe) or a previous editor, his prime concern was not textual integrity. In 192 lines he introduced 106 novelties against all other manuscripts. At this rate, for a full text, he would introduce 1100 changes. This is about 10 times more than any other Greek text of *Adversus Eunomium*.

To be sure, many of these 106 changes, indeed, could be accidental: 11 simple transpositions, ος misspelled ως six times, three iotacisms, six one-word omissions. But many changes indicate a positive willingness to become involved in text manipulation. For example:

Word changes:

	W (alone)	All Others
PG 29.673.10	δημιουργός	δημιουργεῖ
PG 29.673.24	ὑποδειγμάτων	παραδειγμάτων
PG 29.676.8	καταλαμβάνεται	λαμβάνεται
PG 29.676.9	δύναται	δύνανται
PG 29.676.14	κατὰ πάντα	πάντως
PG 29.676.34	βουληθείς	ἐβουλήθη
PG 29.676.40	ἀδυναμεῖν	ἀδυναμίας

Evidence for common source for MSS A E:

	MSS A E		All Others
PG 29.721.8	αὐτοῖς ἀποφθέγγεσθαι	MSS d x (O)	ἀποφθέγγεσθαι αὐτοῖς
PG 29.733.7	προῆγεν	(O)	προσῆγεν

Common source for MSS A x:

	MSS A x		All Others
PG 724.13	καί ... 14 ἀποστήσωσιν	omit (O)	no omission
PG 29.725.14	ἡμῖν	MS q (O)	ὑμῖν
PG 29.728.10	ἡμῖν	MS q (O)	ὑμῖν

Common source for MSS A F:

	MSS A F		All Others
PG 29.673.31	ἐγέννησεν	(E)	ἐποίησεν
PG 29.689.26	θεοῦ	P²	Χριστοῦ GBD κυρίου All Others

77 Prof. Westerink has just recently called my attention to this text and has loaned me his microfilm. For this I am grateful. For full description of codex, its contents, and Arethas' scholia cf. Leendert Westerink, "Marginalia by Arethas in Moscow Greek Manuscript 231," *Byzantion*, XLII (1972), part I, p. 196-244. Cf. also Archimandrite Vladimir, *Sistematičeskoe Opisanie rukopisej Moskovskoj Sinodal'noj (Patriaršej) Biblioteki, I, Rukopisi grečeskija*, (Moskva, Sinadal'naia Tipografiia, 1894), p. 298.

Phrase Changes:

PG 29.673.5	ἄλλῳ	ἀλλ᾽ ἀνόμοιον
PG 29.673.10	ἂν εἴη	ἄλλο ἢ ἥττων
PG 29.676.26	τυγχάνων	τοῦ πατρὸς ὤν
PG 29.676.42	μήπω	οὐδέπω
PG 29.676.44	πρό	πρίν
PG 29.676.44	πρό	πρίν
PG 29.677.2	πατρὸς ὄντος	πατέρα
PG 29.677.33	τέταρτον	τετράκις
PG 29.680.17	παύεσθαι	τέλος ἔχειν
PG 29.680.18	ἄγγελοι οὖν	οὐκοῦν ἄγγελοι
PG 29.680.39	λείπεται	ἕπεται
PG 29.680.46	γέννημα	γεννητά

Moreover, our editor's clear purpose is to facilitate reader effort with these additions:

PG 29.673.1	καὶ τὸ πνεῦμα τὸ ἅγιον
PG 29.673.3	μονογενής
PG 29.677.2	καὶ πῶς ὀκ ἄτοπον
PG 29.677.39	περὶ τοῦ υἱοῦ
PG 29.677.40	εἰς τοὺς αἰῶνας. Ἀμήν.
PG 29.680.12	οἱ Ἀριανοί (sic)

Furthermore, he fills out cryptic syllogisms, adding ἐστί seven times.

Sometimes, however, our editor does not understand, for he changes text, it seems, just to produce some meaning. For example, PG 29.676.23, instead of an obscure reference to splendor of light εἰ ἀπαύγασμα παντὸς φωτός γεννᾶται μὲν ἐκ τοῦ φωτός..., W changes drastically: εἰ ἀπαύγασμα διὰ παντὸς φωτὸς γεννᾶται ἐκ τοῦ πατρὸς μὲν φωτὸς δέ.... His text is less cryptic, of course, but quite innovative, and theologically ambiguous.

At this point, however, a corrector's hand[78] changes διά to ἐκ and adds οὐκ before ἐκ. His corrected text reads: εἰ ἀπαύγασμα ἐκ παντὸς φωτὸς γεννᾶται οὐκ ἐκ τοῦ πατρὸς μὲν φωτὸς δέ.... At all events, it is clear that this corrector does not produce any known traditional form of text. He recognizes a simple scribal omission of negative and remedies it.[79]

Again, Stylianus' title (for PG 29.672.1-PG 29.680.42) is interesting: τοῦ ἐν ἁγίοις πατρὸς ἡμῶν Βασιλείου ἀρχιεπισκόπου Καισαρείας Καππαδοκίας συλλογιστικοί. Among Greek sources this title best reflects a title used

78 It seems to be Arethas'.
79 Cf. Westerink, op. cit., p. 200, for Arethas' (highhanded) methodology.

300 years before by the (Latin) Lateran Council, 649 A.D.: de *syllogisco Contra Eunomium* facto.[80]

On the other hand, unlike Lateran Council, Stylianus omits mention of Eunomius. Indeed, at PG 29.680.12 he alone among Greeks specifically designates adversaries as οἱ Ἀριανοί (sic).[81] Indeed he writes Ἐρωτῶσιν οἱ Ἀριανοί in large semi-capitals, as though the words were themselves a sub-title among other συλλογιστικοί.

However, 30 lines later, at PG 29.680.42 (first major sub-title) Stylianus (MS W) designates Eunomius by name but seems to imply that a new work begins, with its work-title in large letters: τοῦ αὐτοῦ κατὰ Εὐνομίου ὅτι τὸ ἀγέννητος ὑπάρξεώς τινος δήλωσις καὶ οὐκ οὐσίας.

Nonetheless, despite all this interference — or because of it — Stylianus' text (MS W) appears clearly as an intermediate text. In 14 chances to choose, he show eight alpha readings and six beta readings.[82]

But more importantly what emerges is that F shared this same choice pattern in 13 instances. We are not surprised, then, to see occurrences of W F and MS x together against all others:

	F W	All Others
PG 29.672.6/8	φύσις	φύσει
PG 29.677.32	εὐαγγελίου	εὐαγγελιστοῦ
PG 29.680.18	ἕξει τοῦ εἶναι	τοῦ εἶναι ἕξει
PG 29.680.42	ἐστί	τινος

	W MS x	All Others
PG 29.676.5	εἰ ... ποιεῖ	ἄν ... ποιῇ

This suggestion, then, that F W and MS x may derive from a common (albeit intermediate) text source receives some credibility from an external similarity among these manuscripts. Moscow 231 (alone) actually

---

80 Cf. *(Ps.) Basil*, p. 20.
81 To confirm Stylianus' insight cf. *(Ps.) Basil*, pp. 25 and 33.
82 MS W shares five readings with VC alone:

	MS W VC		All Others
PG 29.676.12	ἡ	omit	no omission
PG 29.676.31	ἀγέννητος		ἀγέννητον
PG 29.676.34	καί	omit	no omission
PG 29.680.13	αὐτόν	omit	no omission
PG 29.680.19	ἀλλά		ἀλλ'

Perhaps coincidence. But in any case W never chooses a GBD reading and shows these alpha readings:

	LNR W		All Others
PG 29.676.17	οὐ μόνον	omit	no omission
PG 29.680.42	ἀγέννητον		ἀγέννητος

numbers all 35 syllogisms between PG 29.672.1-PG 29.680.42.[83] However, for their part, A F and MS x have colon, dash, space, and capital letter for exactly this same set of syllogisms.[84] Only W A F and MS x show this awareness.

Conclusion : We see W as a recension historically related to A F and MS x in a common source.

We may, however, ask one last question of these *Adversus Eunomium* IV-V editors.

Surely they systematically change text by borrowing from abroad, but do they introduce more novelties into their text than scribes do? Do editors emend more than scribes err?

Of course (human condition!) all text transmission is accompanied with progressive accession of error. Yet, although we will never know how many times *Adversus Eunomium* IV-V (2230 Migne lines) has been copied, we do have some 14 hyparchetypes, text tradition check points, at which we can count how many new errors have been added to the tradition.

We can reconstruct very little text history between autograph and archetype. But between archetype and alpha family, for example, by the time alpha family appears, some scribes (or scribe) add 50 textual novelties common to alpha alone. By MPLNRd, add 19; by LNRd, add 21; by LN, add 82.

Moreover, between archetype and family beta scribes (or scribe) add 71 errors. By VC add 130; by GBcDgtrewsu, add 38; by GBc, add 26; by Bc,[85] add 78; by Dgtrewsu, add 16; by Dgtrew, add 13; by Dgt, add 11; by rew, add 119; and by su add 14.

Further, our extant manuscripts also witness to accession of error — between lowest (latest) hyparchetype and actual copy. At extant MS h we see scribes (or scribe) add 31 errors; at M, add 23; at P, add 58; at MS k,[86] add 124; at MS q, add 37; at L, add 29; at N, add 15; at R, add 30; and at MS d, add 49.

Again, among extant beta manuscripts we find that predecessors of V add five new variants; at C, add 10; at G, add 30; at MS c, add 27; at D,

---

83 In point of fact, however, Stylianus misplaces one number.

84 MS x does not use a dash marker. E does not have this text portion. MS O shows no divisions — a fact which confirms us in our supicion that MS O is somewhat removed from text traditions of E F x and, now, W. MSS q d and s have systems of syllogism division, but they divide and sequence their syllogisms quite differently.

85 B is a fragment, MS c is its copy. Where they overlap MS c copies 70 errors introduced by B alone; MS c has eight errors alone.

86 MS k actually introduces 302 of his own errors, 178 ioticisms alone. To be sure, MS k is copied from hard-to-read MS P; but, even granting this, 124 errors is two or three times higher than "average." It is possible that MS k is two or three copies away from P.

add 4; at MS g, add 8; at MS t, add 9; at MS r, add 3; at MS e, add 3; at MS w, add 15; at MS s, add 79; and at MS u, add 8.

Thus we actually have 36 check points.[87] "Added errors" range extends from 3 to 130; average is 36.

It is tempting to suggest, therfore, that each time a scribe copied these 2230 text lines he averaged 36 errors. This would enable us, for example, to surmise that alpha is more than one copy from archetype, and that beta is two copies away. It would suggest that VC is three copies from VCGBD and sub-group rew is two copies from Dgtrew, its immediately preceding hyparchetype.

Be that as it may, however, our *Adversus Eunomium* edition-texts present quite a different picture.[88] F introduces 78 new readings; A, 70; and MS x, 102. "New errors" range is 70 to 102; average is 87.

Thus, to answer our question: It seems that editors of this text not only adopt good readings from both (alpha and beta) sources, but they change text in preparing it more than scribes do in copying it. Thus, indeed, high incidence of innovative change may well be a subsidiary criterion in recognizing an edition.

We may schematize interrelationships of intermediate manuscripts thus:

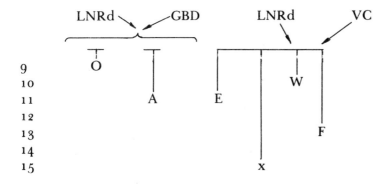

87 Extant alpha manuscripts add many errors. By comparison their hyparchetypes add few. Beta family sources (hyparchetypes and extant manuscripts) act quite oppositely. MS s is an exception.

88 MS E (540 Migne lines) generates 25 (i.e. 125 for full text); W (192 Migne lines) generates 106 (i.e. 1100 for full text); O (875 Migne lines) generates eight (i.e. 20 for full text). This hints that O is not a recension at all and that W is a paraphrase.

Contaminatio

Once, therefore we establish two main lines of manuscript tradition we are able to see how scribes and editors of one group can borrow good readings from another. Among older manuscripts, indeed, we have seen contamination in traditions of P, R, and D:[89]

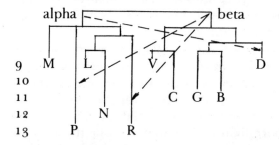

Recentiores:

MS h. Our contention that MS h has the purest form of alpha tradition is confirmed by this that there are only four readings in MS h's text which could originate from beta sub-families:[90]

	MS h		All Others
PG 29.681.4	τὸν κτίστην	Bc	τὴν κτίσιν
PG 29.701.40	οὐκ ἐστί	P s	οὐκέτι
PG 29.733.5	γοῦν	VC rew	οὖν
PG 29.765.18	Μωυσῆς	su	Μωσῆς

Conclusion: This concurrence surely is due to coincidence.

MS P. We have already shown that contamination (28 instances) in P comes in general from beta.[91] But with discovery of sub-group MSS rew we can now point to a specific contamination source. Eight concurrences of P and MSS rew alone show their close interrelationship:

	P MSS rew		All Others
PG 29.688.26	τοῦ	add	no addition
PG 29.729.26	τοῦ	add	no addition
PG 29.740.13	εἰς ἄξιον		ἰσάξιον

89 Cf. (Ps.) Basil, p. 155.

90 Above we dealt with 19 readings of MS h and beta against MPLNR. We asumed they were archetypal readings present before scribe(s) MPLNR added errors. However, here we are dealing with five concurrences of readings developed late, as conjecture or error.

91 Cf. (Ps.) Basil, p. 151.

PG 29.741.3 βιάζει   βιάζῃ
PG 29.752.35 τό   add   no addition
PG 29.756.40 καί   add   no addition
PG 29.761.36 λέγῃ   add   no addition
PG 29.769.34 λειτουργικήν   λογικήν

Conclusion: It is not likely that these are due to coincidence, and we may presume that the other 20 beta readings come from this same source.

MS q. We have seen that MS q is of alpha derivation. It shows only six beta readings. Immediate source of these may well be P's second hand:

	P² MS q Beta		All Others
PG 29.673.30	ἤ ... PG 29.673.32 ὅμοιον	omit M² N²	no omission
PG 29.692.33	βλέπει		βλέψει
PG 29.713.40	καὶ ἐκλείψουσι	add	no addition
PG 29.737.30	πάντες	N²	πάντα
PG 29.748.16	Special seven-line word order		Different word order
PG 29.753.36	θέλει		θέλον

Conclusion: MS q may have acquired some beta readings through P².

MSS b and y. These manuscripts seem to be influenced by a tradition similar to that of P an P² [92].

	P and/or P² MSS b y		All Others
PG 29.673.30-2	ἤ ... ὅμοιον	add	no addition
PG 29.676.28	καὶ πατρός	add DGB	no addition
PG 29.676.37	ὁ	add M	no addition
PG 29.677.16	ἀγέννητον		ἀγέννητος
PG 29.681.6	ὁ	add beta	no addition

Conclusion: MSS b and Y may be related to beta traditions shown by P and second hands in P.

MS j. Again, a few beta readings appear, but only those already borrowed by P². For example

	P² MS j		All Others
PG 29.732.21	καί ... πνεῦμα	add beta	no addition

---

92 MS P² borrows from GB. Cf. *(Ps.) Basil*, p. 152, n. 31.

In three instances, source could N² as well:

	P² N² MS j		All Others
PG 29.732.23	ἰσχυροτάτῳ	R beta	ἰσχυρωτάτῳ
PG 29.737.5	Μωσέος	R rew su	Μωϋσέως alpha
			Μωσέως beta
PG 29.760.46 ἀλλ᾽ ... PG 29.760.48 τριάς	add beta	no addition

Conclusion: MS j may derive its beta readings from traditions of P² or N².

On the other hand, beta family *recentiores* show distinctly alpha readings.

Group Dgtrewsu: Alpha family and sub-group Dgtrewsu concur in 20 readings.[93]

Since Dgtrewsu text contains all distinctive vagaries of VCGB, it derives from a common source. Since it shares 38 errors with GB against alpha and VC, it derives from a source common to GB, and later than VC in beta's tradition.[94]

Yet, now, we realize that Dgtrewsu shares 20 correct readings against VCGB errors.

This presents a decision situation. Is it possible that Dgtrewsu is a form of beta before introduction of VCGB errors? Thus:

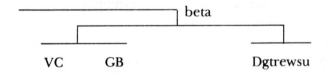

This model indicates that concurrences in error of VCGBDgtrewsu stem from a common source (= beta). Twenty concurrences of alpha Dgtrewsu in correct readings appear as residual archetypal readings where scribe VCGB has introduced additional errors.

SED CONTRA. In this stemma design:

1. We do not explain 38 vagaries common to GBDgtrewsu, except by assuming (a) (possible) that they are beta errors where VC has been contaminated by alpha, or (b) (impossible) that GB instituted readings and they were transferred to Dgtrewsu by textual interference. (*Contaminatio* usually refers to introduction of (presumably) correct readings, since it is usually assumed that no Greek scribe-editor would introduce a series of errors.)

93 Cf. *(Ps.) Basil,* p. 94 and p. 152, n. 32.
94 Cf. *(Ps.) Basil,* p. 93.

2. We appeal to *contaminatio* to explain another 111 concurrences of alpha VC against (separate) error of GB and Dgtrewsu.[95] Furthermore, we find no indication (e.g. VCG, VCB, VGB, CGB, of any further activity of VCGB in error — for example, against errors of alpha and/or Dgtrewsu. This argues against the existence of VCGB as a positive (i.e. error producing) hyparchetype in the tradition.

Therefore, we have proposed a second and much more economical alternative, wherein VC is a form of beta prior to GBDgtrewsu:[96]

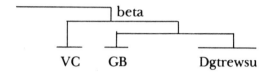

1. Alpha VC concurrences (38) point to an error common to GBDgtrewsu.
2. Alpha VC concurrences (a different 111) point to changes introduced by GBDgtrewsu where one or another manuscript has introduced further changes.
3. GB errors (26) against VCDgtrewsu represent additional errors of GB alone.
4. Concurrences of alpha Dgtrewsu (20) in correct readings appear as *contaminatio*. It happens that errors introduced by beta (not Dgtrewsu) are being corrected.

Many (14) alpha Dgtrewsu concurrences could be coincidence, but six correct readings against a beta error point to a judge, editor, and scribe:

	Alpha Dgtrewsu		VCGB
PG 29.716.25	ὡς ἐνέργεια αὐτοῦ		φυσικῶς
PG 29.720.47	ὃν προεχειρίσατο	add	no addition
PG 29.728.6	θάνατον		ἐκκπςστήν
PG 29.741.40	οὕτω		ἑπτά
PG 29.749.23	ἄρθρου		ἀφθάρτου
PG 29.772.48	ἐχαρίσατο οὐκ ἐποίησεν	add	no addition

Conclusion: Correct readings common to alpha Dgtrewsu are well explained as *contaminatio*.

95 Cf. *(Ps.) Basil*, p. 90.
96 Cf. *(Ps.) Basil*, p. 93. This latter is more reasonable.

Group Dgtrew: Borrowing by hyparchetype scribe Dgtrew may exist, but what evidence we have may be due to coincidence:[97]

	Alpha Dgtrew		VCGB su
PG 29.701.42	σοφέ		σοφοί
PG 29.713.26	τῷ	omit	no omission
PG 29.736.28	οὐ	add	no addition
PG 29.752.10	ἀνομοουσιαστῶν		ἀνομοιουσιαστῶν R GB su
			ἀνομοιοουσιαστῶν VC

	LNR Dgtrew[98]	All Others
PG 29.772.44	ἀλλὰ τό	ἀλλ᾽ αὐτό
PG 29.700.23	κτιστή	κτιστική beta
		ἄκτιστος h d su
		κτίστις M

Conclusion: Scribe-sources Dgtrew may have borrowed alpha readings.

Group Dgt: Scribe Dgt shares readings with VC and a GB source:

	VC Dgt		All Others
PG 29.677.29	γενητός		γεννητός
PG 29.708.40	ἀφιέναι ἐπὶ τῆς γῆς	alpha	ἐπὶ τῆς γῆς ἀφιέναι GB rew su
PG 29.737.23	Μωσῆς	GB	Μωυσῆς alpha rew su

	GB Dgt		All Others
PG 29.757.3	τό		τῷ alpha G rew
			ἐν τῷ VC su
PG 29.769.2	ἑαυτοῦ	Pk	αὐτοῦ alpha VC rew su

Conclusion: These concurrences may be due to coincidence.

Group rew: Hyparchetypal scribe (or sources) rew has 10 alpha readings against beta:

	Alpha rew		Beta
PG 29.692.36	οἷον		οἷος
PG 29.693.27	ὁ θεός		τό G Dg
			omit VC t su
PG 29.705.13	ἐγεννήθη		ἐγενήθη
PG 29.708.41	πᾶσα	add	no addition
PG 29.709.13	ἐξ	omit	no omission

97 These last two readings could be archetypal, where VC, GB, su have (somehow) instituted a common reading.

98 These could be archetype readings, where MSS h, MP, VC, and GB have (independently) originated a common reading.

PG 29.720.19 ὅπερ   ἅπερ
PG 29.737.23 Μωυσῆς   Μωσῆς
PG 29.741.3 Μωυσῇ   Μωυσεῖ Dgt su
                                         Μωσεῖ V Bc
                                         Μωσῇ N C G

Conclusion: These concurrences can be due to coincidence.

At PG 29.765.47 VCGB rew have Χριστοῦ which is omitted by alpha and Dgt su. Either, then, VCGB rew represent an original beta reading, where Dgt and su (independently) omitted it, or, possibly, Dgtrewsu omitted it and scribes in MSS rew tradition then regained Χριστοῦ from VCGB.

Thus, common sense observation tells us that "copy" can contain only what is in its exemplar or what has been added. Thus, if Dgtrewsu was already in error, a correct reading in MS u is adventitious to the tradition. However, this is not sufficient in itself to tell us which reading, if any, was actually in the exemplar.

For example, all Greek text that appears in our manuscripts must be archetypal or be added later. It is possible, to continue the example, that MS u alone has an original reading, when all other manuscripts known to us have added their error — in this case, alpha, VC, GB, Dgt, rew, and MS s. Its presence in MS u assures us that it was in Dgtrewsu, GBDgtrewsu, VCGBDgtrewsu, and archetype: alpha-VCGBDgtrewsu.

Of course, it is possible that every manuscript has lost the original reading and MS u (scribe or predecessors) has regained it by *divinatio*. But this skill, of course, resists standardization and keeps us humble before the testimony of even very young text witnesses.

MS s. Some 35 borrowed VC readings appear in the tradition of MS s. Exact source for these is recognized when we find eight concurrences of V and MS s alone:

	V and MS s		All Others
PG 29.693.10	τοῦ	add	no addition
PG 29.693.13	τῷ		τό
PG 29.708.10	ὁ	add	no addition
PG 29.713.41	αὐτόν		αὐτῶν
PG 29.737.36	διαί		διά
PG 29.740.11	συνκατατάττεις		συγκατατάττεις
PG 29.741.31	ἀναλάβω		ἀναλάβωμαι
PG 29.752.38	ἀπιστεία		ἀπιστίαι

Conclusion: MS s (or its sources) has borrowed VC and V readings from some source in V's tradition.

We may represent this *contaminatio* in *Adversus Eunomium* IV-V text schematically:

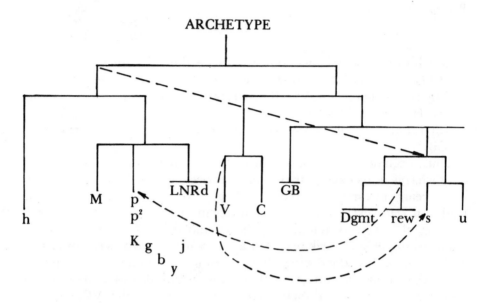

CONCLUSION

What then have *recentiores* added to our knowledge of the text tradition of (PS.) Basil *Adversus Eunomium* IV-V?

1. MS h shows us an early form of alpha. This enables us better to assess readings introduced by MPLNRd. It confirms us in our insight, however, that MPLNRd do represent a positive stage in the transmission.

2. MSS k q b y and j suggest the importance of P and P^2 as source. Or at least, these manuscripts show that P^2 choices from among beta readings enjoyed wide favor, even if P^2 be not their immediate source.

3. MSS z d and p give us some insight into differences of tradition between LN and R.

4. MS n affords a close check on V at all times.

5. MS c reports B's exact form before its folio losses. Thus it has enabled us to establish relationship between G and B.

6. MSS g t and m show changes that developed out of the tradition shown by D, presumably on Mt. Athos.

7. MSS r e w s and u enable us to reconstruct Dgt's form before introduction of specific errors of this sub-group.

8. MS x (and tenth century W) clarifies common editorial origin recognizable among E W F and MS x — even if each has later developed into its own edition.

9. MSS r e and w show us one immedite source for beta contamination into alpha, especially into traditions of P.

10. Beta *recentiores*, especially, by producing greater numbers of subgroups give us some glimpse of how many times a text has been copied.

11. *Recentiores*, by their multitude, give some basis for speculating about average numbers of scribal errors and the mean amount of editorial contamination, wherever it exists.

12. In a word, therefore, since these *recentiores* so clearly form subgroups they point directly to hypothetical scribes and their examplars, whose readings are actually earlier (and often better) than those of extant *vetustissimi*. In every case they put us on firmer ground in attempting to recognize and evaluate ever present textual errors and all the various forms of ancient scholarship: edition, contamination, conjecture, emendation — indeed the whole apparatus of *divinatio*, hand mark of divine Greek scribes.

Pontifical Institute of Mediaeval Studies.

THE PHYSICAL WORLD OF PARMENIDES

Joseph Owens, C.Ss.R.

I

INTEREST in Parmenides has been increasing in recent years. It has been characterized as "immense"[1] in its various aspects, and it tends not only towards considerations of historical and philological moment, but looks even more to the abiding philosophical worth of his thought for all ages. Inevitably a discordant voice will be found minimizing the value of Parmenides' message, and seeing in it a tiring monotone or the purest example of "talking without thinking."[2] The overwhelming trend in the last few decades, however, has been to take Parmenides seriously as a thinker, and to look for profound meaning in the kind of philosophy he introduced into western thought. The widespread influence of his reasoning down the centuries is in fact acknowledged by both friend and foe, and requires explanation in terms that in one way or another rise above the vagaries of historical accident.

After perusing the sizable body of literature devoted to Parmenides in the past years, though, one may still be left in a quandary about the main point involved. That point is what Parmenides meant by being. On this there is no general agreement whatever. The differences among a number of trends of interpretation are radical, and even within the same trend they are significant between one commentator and the next. The recent literature has done marvels in elucidating the text and setting out clearly the often complicated evidence on difficult passages.

1 Alexander P. D. Mourelatos, *The Route of Parmenides* (New Haven and London: Yale University Press, 1970), p. xii. A survey of the present state of the research on Parmenides may be found in Karl Bormann, *Parmenides* (Hamburg: Felix Meiner, 1971), pp. 1-27, with bibliography pp. 253-259.

2 Felix M. Cleve, *The Giants of Pre-Sophistic Greek Philosophy*, 2 v. (The Hague: Martinus Nijhoff, 1965), II, 538. Cf.: "... the source of Parmenides' theory of Being. It is a kind of dividend, the residue or deposit of the spontaneous disintegration of primary matter" — Theodor Gomperz, *Greek Thinkers*, tr. Laurie Magnus, I (London: John Murray, 1906), 171.

But in regard to the main problem at issue, the meaning of the Parmenidean being, there is still much to be desired.[3]

To examine in detail the entire spectrum of these views on the nature of being for Parmenides would of course far exceed the range of a single article. The scope of the present inquiry will accordingly be very restricted. It will confine itself to probing just one of the many understandings of the Parmenidean being that have been given by commentators on the Eleatic thinker. This will be the overall conception of Parmenides' world that Aristotle sketches rapidly in his review of preceding philosophers in the first Book of the *Metaphysics*:

> For, claiming that, besides the existent, nothing non-existent exists, he thinks that of necessity one thing exists, viz. the existent and nothing else (on this we have spoken more clearly in our work on nature), but being forced to follow the observed facts, and supposing the existence of that which is one in definition, but more according to our sensations, he now posits two causes ..." (A 5, 986b28-33; Oxford tr.).

Aristotle's description here follows closely enough the order of the second and third parts of Parmenides' poem as known today from its extant fragments. Only being exists, and it is necessarily one. There is nothing else whatsoever. Yet necessarily also did the "observed facts" (*phainomena*) exert their influence on Parmenides' cognition. What is one according to the reasoned account of the second part of the poem, is taken as multiple from the viewpoint of sensation in the third part, allowing a duality of basic causes. What else can this mean than that the single Parmenidean existent is the world perceived in sensation as multiple and mobile? Does not the passage just quoted assert the *existence* of something that while formally one is more than one "according to our sensations"?

What Aristotle found in the poem of Parmenides was, according to the above presentation, a doctrine in which the single existent is identified with the physical world, the visible and tangible universe. This

---

3 The most thorough and serviceable coverage to date of the literature is found in Leonardo Tarán, *Parmenides* (Princeton, N.J.: Princeton University Press, 1965). Yet the field remains wide open. For instance Mourelatos, p. 254, remarks in regard to one passage: "But the Greek words have a background of associations which Tarán's analysis leaves unexplored." Doctrinally, moreover, the Parmenidean tenet that only being exists becomes for Tarán a razor-edged criterion that guillotines every sensible thing and every human thought out of the real world. It is this strange yet widely accepted conclusion that prompts the present paper to re-examine Aristotle's report. See infra, n. 33. A short summary of the present controversial state of the literature on the Parmenidean being may be found in Leo Sweeney, *Infinity in the Presocratics* (The Hague: M. Nijhoff, 1972), pp. 93-109. On its subject as "what can be talked or thought about," see G. E. L. Owen, "Eleatic Questions," *CQ*, N.S. 10 (1960), 95, and for a survey of the controversy about its subject, see Tarán, pp. 33-36.

world is strictly one and immobile as it is understood in human reasoning, but is multiple and mobile as perceived by the senses. Aristotle does not consider this a consistent doctrine. In describing it he refers back for further discussion on it to the *Physics* (I 3, 186a22-187a11), in which he had argued in the Parmenidean context that "the All" (186b35), consisting as it does of different perceptible things, cannot be a single existent. Though from Aristotle's own viewpoint Parmenides in virtue of his reasoning about being should not be able to have a philosophy of nature, the Stagirite nevertheless treats of him seriously as a physicist.[4] Aristotle throughout regards Parmenides as dealing with an existent physical world, even though from the Aristotelian viewpoint it contradicts the Parmenidean notion of being. No other kind of being than that of the sensible universe is accredited to Parmenides by the Stagirite.[5]

To say that the physical world is the being envisaged in the poem may, however, appear to mean traveling backward on the road of Parmenides. In Aristotle's presentation, the notion of being seems established first, and only afterwards dissipated through sensation into a multiplicity of different things. This would suggest that in understanding Parmenides, being should first of all be probed in complete independence of the sensible world, and only after having been established in its own right should it be confronted with the phenomena of perception. One should not take the physical world as already established and real, and look in it to try to find the being that is described in the second part of the poem. The method indicated, rather, should be the reverse, according to the more or less commonly accepted approach.

This objection from the viewpoint of method overlooks the composition of the whole poem. The poem has three parts, namely the proem, the section on being, and the section on the *doxa*. It does not begin abruptly with the discussion of being. Rather, it commences with Parmenides already in a world of plurality and change, a world peopled by maidens, chariot, mares, gate, threshold, and all their various parts and members. It is a world of multiplicity, vivid sensible appeal,

---

4 *Ph.*, I 2, 184b25-185a13; cf. I 5, 188a20-22. *Cael.*, III 1, 298b14-20. *GC*, I 8, 325a13-23; cf. 3, 318b6-7; II 3, 330b13-15. Tarán, p. 281, finds this puzzling: "It is amazing that Aristotle after having asserted that the Eleatic doctrine does not belong to the inquiry on nature nevertheless goes on to criticize it." Rather, this should indicate that in point of fact Aristotle saw that the object of Parmenides' thought was a real physical world.

5 "... while they were inquiring into the truth of that which is, they thought 'that which is' was identical with the sensible world" — *Metaph.*, I 5, 1010a1-3; Oxford trans. Parmenides had just been included by name among the thinkers to which this statement referred (1009b21). Cf. *Metaph.*, A 3, 984b3-4.

pleasant sounds and flashing motion. Parmenides is being borne upwards from the "dwellings of Night" by the sun maidens to the abode of a goddess from whom he is to learn "all things" (*Fr.* 1.28, DK). The sensible world, the world of plurality and change, is the setting in which the poem commences and in which Parmenides is to learn everything, both the unshakable truth, on the one hand, and on the other the opinions of mortals in which true conviction does not reside (*Fr.* 1.29-31). Chariot, sun maidens and goddess represent poetically a world of plurality and change in which Parmenides finds himself located, and "the opinions of mortals" would seem pretty well to pinpoint the consideration to the world of experience in which and about which those opinions are made. The "dwellings of Night" would seem to express the ignorance under which ordinary mortals labor, while the unshaken heart of Truth means the enlightenment Parmenides is about to receive. The whole project is forged in multiplicity and motion.[6] Without these it could not make its take-off. What is held before the hearer's eyes bristles with plurality and movement, and in this setting the Truth is to be sought. Methodically, therefore, the starting point is the world of perception and imagination. The close links with the other two sections of the poem are assured by the text (*Frs.* 1.28-32; 8.50-52). The thought should accordingly be pursued from the proem through the section on being and into the section on the *doxa*.

Parmenides, then, may be legitimately approached with the question whether the physical world is the single existent with which he is dealing. The question may be detached from its setting in Aristotle and asked just in itself. Is the world of multiplicity and change that men experience in their daily lives the world about whose being Parmenides is inquiring in his poem? Is the universe that appears so variegated and so mobile the one undifferentiated existent to which cogent reasoning concludes? Is Parmenides first and foremost a physicist, focusing his attention primarily on the world that interested the other Presocratics, and concerned with a doctrine of being only insofar as it leads to the truth about the physical world? In a word, is the main thrust of Parmenides' philosophy to be found in the third section of his poem rather than in the second?

---

6 Though the proem is "a literary device," this assessment need not rest upon and accordingly does not imply Tarán's ground that "Parmenides could not have attributed any reality to the goddess because for him there exists only one thing" (p. 31). In the present article's approach that ground has to be left in a problematic state, until the evidence has been examined. What the "literary device" does present, prima facie, is a multiple and changeable world. On the poetry of the proem, see C. M. Bowra, "The Proem of Parmenides," *Class. Philol.*, 32 (1937), 97-112. On the allegorical interpretation of Sextus, and some recent interpretations, see Tarán, pp. 17-30, and on some German studies, Bormann, pp. 56 and 195. At very least the proem makes "the reader feel that he is not embarking on something entirely outside his own experience" — Bowra, p. 112.

The answers to these questions will of course have to be furnished by the fragments remaining from the poem. These are extensive enough and coherent enough to be interpreted in themselves and against the background of fifth century language and archeology. Textual variants may strengthen or weaken a particular philosophical interpretation of a number of lines, but seldom if ever will the choice of a variant have decisive force in determining the philosophical signification of a passage. Later interpretations by commentators, though varying widely, always have to be taken into consideration and carefully weighed. Usually their philosophical background can be isolated and its influence on the interpretation can be gauged. In all cases, however, the final arbiter has to be the text of Parmenides itself. The suggestion taken from Aristotle's assertion is merely that, to grasp Parmenides' notion of being, one must clearly understand the Eleatic's conception of the physical world.

II

Before approaching the text of the poem, though, a preliminary consideration that might radically prejudice the whole issue has to be assessed. It is the widely prevalent notion that for Parmenides the world of sensible experience is nothing but an illusion, and has no real existence at all. This notion is imbibed in one's first acquaintance with Parmenides in text-books. It continues to be ingested and consolidated through further general reading about Greek philosophy. It is defended stoutly by a number of experts on Parmenides in modern times.[7] If accepted as true, it would at once render self-refuting the proposition that for Parmenides the physical world is the existent envisaged in the second part of the poem. If illusory through and through, the physical world could not be this existent or any other existent, since it would be in no way an existent. In probing it to its depths one would never arrive

---

7 E.g.: "The illusions in question include coming to exist and coming to an end, being and not being, shifting place and changing colour: in fact they are presumably all the ordinary manifestations of change and plurality" — Owen, p. 89. "Change of place is also an illusion" — Tarán, p. 138, no. 41; "he denies the existence of the phenomenal or sensible world itself" — p. 198. "... das menschliche Erkennen erreicht das Seiende nicht, sondern entwirft die scheinbare Realität" — Bormann, p. 183. On the other side, however, the illusory character attributed to the Parmenidean *doxa* has been strongly denied, e.g.: "The names that mortal men institute, although false and deceptive, are not mere fancies or illusions of the mind. They are accounts of the one real world" — Leonard Woodbury, "Parmenides on Names," *Harvard Studies in Classical Philology*, 63 (1958), 149. Cf. infra, n. 33. Woodbury's article was reprinted in a slightly revised version, *Essays in Ancient Greek Philosophy*, ed. John P. Anton (Albany, N.Y.: State University of New York Press, 1971), pp. 145-162. Page references in these footnotes are to the original version. The pagination in the reprint differs only slightly.

at anything that could be identical with what Parmenides understands by being. The assertion that as an illusion and utterly non-existent it could be *the* existent patently refutes itself.

Nowhere in the extant fragments of the poem, however, does Parmenides say that the perceptible world is an illusion. The closest to which one may refer for the notion is the description of this "cosmos of my words" as deceptive.[8] But deception does not necessarily imply that the deceptive object is an illusion. Distances are often deceptive, but they are not illusions. Anybody who suffers from misjudging a distance is well aware that he is dealing with something very real. A philosopher who acknowledges spiritual being may regard the materialist as deceived by the unfailing presence of sensible matter in all objects of human perception. This situation is indeed deceptive, for it prompts the judgment that all existents have to be material. The material character of sensible things may in this way be deceptive, but it is far from illusionary. So for Parmenides the perceptible universe may trick ordinary mortals into believing that it is multiple and mobile. But that in no way implies that it is an illusion. It could be just as real and just as existent as perceptible things are for the materialist, even though he be regarded as deceived by them into thinking that the whole of the existent universe is of their kind.

Nowhere do the fragments of the poem assert that perceptible things are non-existent. Rather, these seem understood as things that are absent yet present to the mind (*Fr.* 4.1). Each is regarded as a *being* that is coincident with every other *being* (*Fr.* 4.2), and one *being* is said to draw near to the other (*Fr.* 8.25). The notion is that of existing things coalescing with one another. Each is looked upon first as *a* being, and then as merging in the one whole that is the All. The things that now *are,* from the viewpoint of the *doxa,* and are named by men (*Fr.* 19), are either names of that which exists or refer to that which exists.[9] Existential differences between these things may be banished by the reasoning of Parmenides, but nowhere in the text is there to be found a statement that the perceptible things themselves are non-existent.

Nor is there any indication that people who read the poem in antiquity understood it to mean that the sensible universe is an illusion. The poem was classed as a discourse on nature, that is, on the physical

8 *Fr.* 8.52. See Willem Jacob Verdenius, *Parmenides: Some Comments on his Poem* (Groningen: J. B. Wolters, 1942), p. 59.

9 *Fr.* 8.38-42. On the different interpretations of the last half of line 38, see Woodbury, pp. 147-155; Tarán, pp. 129-144; Mourelatos, pp. 181-188. A discussion of "naming" in the present context may be found in my paper "Naming in Parmenides," to be published in the *Festschrift* now being prepared as a tribute to Cornelia J. De Vogel, ed. J. Mansfeld and L. M. De Rijk, 1974.

world. In the doxographical tradition Parmenides was regularly regarded as a philosopher of nature, even by those who thought it necessary to add that his doctrine of being did away with nature.[10] His notions about heat and cold and sun and moon and sensation were discussed in the same context as those of the other Greek physicists. The third part of his poem was taken to express seriously meant views, views that were understood as those of Parmenides himself. They were not looked upon as collecting or parodying the views of other thinkers. They were dealt with as though they gave a distinctive Parmenidean doctrine about a universe that was as physical and as existent as in any other Greek philosopher.[11]

If anything, the assertion that Parmenides held the physical world to be an illusion would be self-refuting. It would mean that Parmenides who made the statement would himself be an illusion.[12] It would mean that the words in which the doctrine was phrased were illusory. It would mean that the poem and those who heard and discussed it did not exist. There would be nothing that could proclaim the Parmenidean doctrine of being. From what is known of the Greek mentality, moreover, the denial of existence to the perceptible world would ring a jarring note. Even the thoroughgoing Greek Skeptics rejected summarily the idea that they did not believe in the everyday world,[13] and a Sophist like Gorgias could deny being to the world without infringing upon its existence and reality.[14] Rather, the epistemology that followed in the wake of Descartes seems required to consider the physical world as an illusion, and the Greek reaction would probably have been akin to that of Locke[15] had this notion been proposed.

III

Satisfied that the question has been legitimately placed in the Par-

---

10 See testimonia in Diels-Kranz, 28 A, 26; 28-34; 36-48; 51-54.

11 See Karl Reinhardt, *Parmenides und die Geschichte der griechischen Philosophie* (Bonn: F. Cohen, 1916), p. 247; Verdenius, p. 48.

12 See E. D. Phillips, "Parmenides on Thought and Being," *Philosophical Review*, 64 (1955), 558, and similarly for the words "it is," Woodbury, pp. 146-147.

13 See Diogenes Laertius, IX, 103.

14 See account of Gorgias' thinking in Sextus Empiricus, *Adv. Math.*, VII, 81-86, where sensible things are regarded as taken for granted by him while their being, in the meaning of an unchangeable characteristic, is denied.

15 "... for I think nobody can, in earnest, be so sceptical as to be uncertain of the existence of those things which he sees and feels. At least, he that can doubt so far, (whatever he may have with his own thoughts,) will never have any controversy with me; since he can never be sure I say

menidean context and that it is not self-refuting, once may now approach the fragments in search of an answer. These begin with a proem that raises the reader swiftly and joyously to a realm of light (*Fr.* 1.10) where instruction is to be imparted by an unnamed goddess. Imitating Hesiod's introduction (*Theogony,* 1-108) to what is "true" (*Theog.,* 28) about the genesis of the gods, it proposes to give an inspired account both of truth and of the opinions of mortals (*Fr.* 1.28-30). With considerable literary art it presents this ascent as a journey that may be undertaken repeatedly, quite as one applies oneself over and over again to this type of thinking.[16] It ends by explaining why besides truth the opinions of mortals likewise have to be investigated under the inspiration of the goddess, even though in them there is no "true conviction" or "true account" (*Fr.* 1.30-32). About them the goddess is to explain how the appearances or "things that appear" (*ta dokounta*) had to be perpetually and everywhere present in a way that assured their acceptance, or, more strongly, how they all had to exist always in genuine fashion.

Much has been written about this last line of the proem.[17] The text as it stands is clear anough, even though there are two manuscript readings, each well grounded, for the notion that expresses the ubiquitous presence of phenomena. One means that these had to "pervade all things." The other signifies that they had to be "all indeed existent" or "all indeed beings." The overall meaning, at least in this preliminary setting, seems to differ only in degree of forceful expression. The appearances, or things that appear, had to be either perpetually pervading all, or else perpetually being or existent, in a way that made them acceptable or genuinely existent to ordinary human opinion.

The proem, then, intends the inspired message of the goddess to deal with both truth and the *doxa*. Parmenides is to learn about both from the same elevated source. Both will accordingly be the subject matter of his philosophy. The difference between the two is accentuated. Truth is represented as stable. In contrast, the *doxa* does not exhibit the firmness of true conviction or a true account. Yet it is accepted without hesitation by human opinion. How the phenomena had to pervade all in so readily acceptable a way, or how they all had to exist in this ap-

---

anything contrary to his own opinion" — Locke, *An Essay concerning Human Understanding,* IV, 11, 3; ed. Alexander C. Fraser, (Oxford: Clarendon Press, 1894), II, 327.

16 See comments on lines 1-3 and 8, in Tarán, pp. 9-13.

17 See Reinhardt, pp. 5-10; Verdenius, pp. 49-57; Jean Zafiropulo, *L'école Eléate* (Paris: Les Belles Lettres, 1950), pp. 294-297; Jean Beaufret, *Le poème de Parménide* (Paris: Presses universitaires de France, 1955), pp. 23-32; Tarán, pp. 210-216; Mourelatos, pp. 194, n. 1; 203-218; Bormann, pp. 67-69; 200.

parently satisfactory framework, has to be explained on the philosophical level. The doxastic picture of things, even though it contains no truth, has to be accounted for in philosophical terms.

Together truth and the *doxa* are presented as the sum total (*panta-Fr.* 1.28) of the objects of philosophical inquiry. The "opinions of mortals" are readily identifiable as the conceptions men ordinarily have of the visible and tangible world in which they live. For the moment, the object of "truth" is not so clearly pinpointed. "Truth" is merely mentioned as though its significance is familiar to anyone who hears the word. It may be expected, therefore, to carry its usually accepted meaning at the time. It should signify facts and things reported without concealment or obscurity.[18] What the facts or reality now involved are, is not explained in the proem. The only object mentioned in the context is what appears to men. This is the perceptible world of everyday experience. The presumption, until otherwise set aside, is that the visible and tangible universe is the object to be explained from the viewpoint of truth.

The fragment listed next in Diels-Kranz (*Fr.* 2) announces abruptly that only two ways of inquiry can come under consideration. The first is expressed by the verb "is" in a "that" clause. The conjunction and the finite form "is" are the only grammatical components. No subject is mentioned for the verb. In idiomatic English translation the neuter pronoun "it" has to be inserted as the subject. But the pronoun might well be put in parentheses as a reminder that no pronoun was expressed in Parmenides' Greek. The first way, presented in this cryptic fashion, is simply "that (it) is." The only explanations given are that (for it) not to be is not possible, and that this is the road of conviction because it follows on or accompanies truth. Being, in a word, includes its own necessity, and is the stable ground of truth.

The second way is expressed by the negative clause "that (it) is not." It is explained as meaning that (for it) not to be is necessary. It is called "a path entirely void of inquiry, for you could neither know what is not, for that is not achievable, nor could you express it" (*Fr.* 2.7-8). Parallel with the necessity of being, it carries its own impossibility.

What does all this mean? The "inquiry" has to be the one introduced in the proem, the inquiry into "all things" (*Fr.* 1.28). The procedure suggests that one aspect intuited in them is that they exist. This is the aspect of being. It is seen in them all. Whatever lacked it would be notbeing. The dichotomy is devastatingly clear. Being is intuited as an aspect with conceptual content, a content that extends to every other

---

18 See H. Boeder, "Der frühgriechische Wortgebrauch von Logos und Aletheia," *Archiv für Begriffsgeschichte*, 4 (1959), 91-99; Mourelatos, pp. 63-67.

positive aspect. It excludes only non-being. It is accordingly the one path to everything that can be known. Carrying its own necessity, it is not compatible with lack of itself.[19] It thereby offers the stability required by truth, and leaves outside itself only a single alleged way. That is the way of not-being, a way that furnishes no knowledge. But being, wherever it is found, presents that path for inquiry into all things.

So all-embracing is this path of being for Parmenides, then, that it leaves no other approach but that of not-being. He has to limit the ways of inquiry to these two. The being upon which he is focusing attention is understood in a manner that makes it include any positive trait exibited in it. What is understood apart from it can be only the negative not-being, without any positive aspect in which the characteristic of being would manifest itself. So conceived, not-being necessarily lacks all being. But one cannot succeed in bringing an object of this kind before one's mind. One could not know it or express it. The way of not-being is, in consequence, a way that does not inquire at all.

The reason why one could not know not-being is given in *Fr.* 3, suggesting that its place in the poem is in immediate sequence to *Fr.* 2. It may mean either that "thought and being are the same," or that thought is coextensive with being.[20] In either interpretation there has to be being if there is to be thought. A clearer expression of the notion is given later, in the statement that "you will never find thought without that which is, in which it has been expressed."[21] The notion brings forward the observable fact that the object of thought always has to be represented as being. Thought, in a word, always takes place in terms of being. If the object had no being there would be no thought about it. This is apparently the ultimate ground offered by Parmenides for restricting the inspired way of inquiry to the road of being. It is the only way in which one can think, if the notion of thinking is correctly understood. The being in which the thought takes place seems intuited as an object with a conceptual content of its own, a content that leaves only not-being outside its embrace.

Fr. 4 notes that absent things are steadfastly present to the mind, because the mind will not cut off "that which is" from its solidarity with "that which is," whether this be scattered in orderly fashion or brought together. The fragment envisages a multiplicity of things, each

19 This is the ground for the first principle of demonstration, as explained by Aristotle in *Metaph.*, Γ 3, 1005b11-4, 1008a34.

20 For a short survey of the interpretations, see Tarán, pp. 41-44.

21 *Fr.* 8.35-36. A survey of the interpretations may be found in Tarán, pp. 123-128. The paraphrase "You shall not find thinking naked, or deserted by what-is," Mourlatos, p. 170, and his translations, p. 172, bear out even more strongly the thoroughgoing dependence of thought upon being as its only object.

of which may be called "a being." Yet under the mind's eye these different beings coalesce. But originally they appear as arranged in order or *cosmos*.[22] Correspondingly *Fr.* 5 suggests that where one begins does not matter, since it will again be reached. This sentence was quoted in connection with Parmenides' assertion that "that which is" draws near to "that which is" (*Fr.* 8.25), in the sense of different beings coalescing with one another.[23] Again, the presupposition is that of an original multiplicity, allowing one to begin one's reasoning at any part of it with the promise that the reasoning will end up in that same thing.

Fr. 6 repeats the necessity of being for the object of both thought and speech. It mentions a subject for the verb "is," in the form of the neuter present participle and of the present infinitive of the verb "to be." Here the former is best translated in English as "that which is," and the latter as "being." The reasoning is: "that which is" has to be said and thought to be, for being is, while "nothing" is not" (*Fr.* 6.1-2). The subject accordingly is expressed only in terms of being, and the infinitive in Greek as the subject of "is" can stand parallel with "nothing" as the subject of "is not." All goes as though no significant distinction is found between being and its subject. Being, as/expressed by the Greek infinitive, is regarded as more fundamental for the reasoning — because being is, its subject, namely "that which is," is or has being. Being is presented in this way as the basic object of the Parmenidean intuition. It implies immediately that something exists, though the "something" is characterized in no other way than as being.

The fragment goes on to bar Parmenides from the latter "first way" (*Fr.* 6.3), and then from the "way" that mortals travel, for in their wandering mind they regard being and not-being as the same and yet not the same.[24] No examples are given, but the meaning seems clear enough. Mortals in their ordinary way of thinking distinguish being from not-being, as the words attest, but conventionally they give not-being the status of being. If today one seeks examples of this in ordinary

22   On the meaning of this term in the context, see Tarán, pp. 47-48.

23   A discussion of this setting of the fragment and of its interpretations may be found in Tarán, pp. 51-53.

24   *Fr.* 6. There is nothing forced in regarding the way of not-being as a "first way." It and the way of being are equally primitive for Parmenides. In contrast, the way upon which mortals wander is secondary and derivative. Tarán, pp. 60-61, thinks that the goddess is requiring Parmenides to abandon temporarily the way of being. Against this interpretation, see Michael C. Stokes, *One and Many in Presocratic Philosophy* (Washington, D.C.: Center for Hellenic Studies, 1971), pp. 112-115, and Mourelatos, pp. 77, n. 7. There is at least one sense in which the ways of being and of not-being are the *only* ways of inquiry (*Fr.* 2.2), and the notion of two first or primitive ways satisfies this condition. On the other hand, the way actually traveled by mortals is explicitly designated a "way" (*Fr.* 6.3-4 and 9), and is a combination of the two first ones. See also *Fr.* 7.3. On the problems of the three ways, see Bormann, pp. 90-106.

human thinking, one finds them quite readily in the way one says "This is a chair" and "It is not a table." The "is" and the "is not" are given equal status in expressing the truth of the situation. This seems to be the meaning that the words of the poem convey, a meaning that could be expected to appear as obvious without requiring illustration by examples. It is the way that mortals usually think and talk about anything. It is a way actually traveled by men. But it is condemned by Parmenides as wandering and dazed. It coincides quite apparently with the "opinions of mortals," which the proem characterized as lacking the stability of truth (*Fr.* 1.30).

Fr. 7 continues the prohibition to enter either the way according to which not-beings would be, or the habitual way. Rather, the judgment is to be given by reason. *Fr.* 8 gives the reasoning that takes place when one follows the way of being. "That which is" cannot come into being or perish. It is unique and stable, a whole completely together in the present. The reason why it cannot come into being is that there is no not-being from which it could arise, or into which it could develop.[25] This complete homogeneity of being likewise keeps it from any differentiation. Whatever is, is being in the fullness of the notion. If it lacked anything, it would lack everything.[26] It is what is referred to in the names of all things conventionally set up by men, things believed to be genuine, to become and perish, to be and not be, and to change in place or in surface characteristics.[27] As ultimate limit, it is complete from every viewpoint, for there is no not-being to keep it from reaching sameness. Nor is there a being that could be more of a being here and

---

25 *Fr.* 8.1-21. On the meaning of lines 12-13, see Tarán, pp. 95-102; Bormann, pp. 144-145. The construction naturally to be expected is, first, that being cannot arise from not-being, and second, that being cannot come from being. This is the way Simplicius (*In Phys.*, p. 78.25) presents the reasoning, and it had been the situation that confronted Anaxagoras according to Aristotle's (*Ph.*, I 4, 187a32-33) interpretation. It was also the framework used by Gorgias in Sextus' account (*Adv. Math.*, VII, 71), where — though this is denied by Tarán, p. 102 — "what generates" parallels in sufficiently Parmenidean fashion the "need" (Parmenides, *Fr.* 8.9) that would be required to make something come from not-being. But this construction requires emendation in the text. The text as it stands makes both sections of the argument show that being cannot come from not-being, reasoning first that there is no not-being from which anything could be brought forth, and secondly, that anything allegedly brought forth would not be anything other than not-being. The unamended reading is followed by Mourelatos, pp. 100-101, and Charlotte L. Stough, "Parmenides' Way of Truth, B 8.12-13," *Phronesis,* 13 (1968), 91-107.

26 *Fr.* 8.33. On this meaning, see Mourelatos, p. 122, n. 22.

27 *Fr.* 8.38-41. Tarán, p. 137, notes that being and not-being are here bound together closely "as a pair," just as becoming and perishing involve each other. But should not this mean that being "when uttered by mortals" always involves not-being? Cf. "that it is but also is not," Woodbury, p. 150. In human opinion, every perceptible thing *is* itself, and at the same time *is not* the other perceptible objects. Ordinary human opinion certainly does not maintain that a chair both is a chair and is not a chair. But it maintains decidedly that a chair is not a table.

less there. The notion is illustrated by the simile of a perfectly balanced sphere extending from the center with equal force in all directions.[28]

The reasoning is cogent, given the initial intuition of being as a nature with a content. As a nature, being has to absorb all its differences, just as its concept includes them all in one way or another. It leaves only not-being outside itself. Accordingly there is nothing else besides being, nothing from which change could take place or into which it could proceed. No differentiation is possible, for that would mean that something would not be something else. It would involve not-being. Hence the subject in which being is found cannot be in any way different from being. Parmenides is in consequence well served by not having to express a subject for being. At most, he can express it only through the infinitive or participial form of the same finite verb "is." Being is so much a whole and so homogeneous that it cannot have a subject other than itself. Any subject other than itself would have to be not-being. Wherever one finds being, either in change or in any perceptible object of which one says "it is" and "it is not," the identical reasoning holds. As stated in *Fr. 5*, it makes no difference where one begins.

About the physical world, the most illuminating lines in the second part of the poem are those in which all things conventually acknowledged by mortals, with express mention of kinds of change, are called names for being or things named in reference to being (*Fr.* 8.38-41). Of each of them one can in ordinary discourse say that it is as well as it is not. A chair is a chair and is not a table. While from the viewpoint of truth the All is being and nothing else, it had to appear to men as multiple and changing. How can that be?

IV

At this point the goddess states that she has ended her discourse about truth and is going to deal with human opinions (*Fr.* 8.50-52). These words do not imply that she is leaving the *way* of truth. Rather, she still proceeds on the way of truth as she changes the *object* of discussion from truth to *doxa*. She continues leading Parmenides to understand all things.

---

28   *Fr.* 8.42-49. The sphere is expressly offered as an illustration. Being is *"like* the bulk of a well-rounded sphere" (line 43). On the problems and interpretations, see Tarán, pp. 144-160; Mourelatos, pp. 123-130; Bormann, pp. 171-179. Mourelatos, p. 124, considers "simile" as too weak for the relationship between being and the sphere. Yet for him, pp. 126 and 128, it does remain a "comparison." To allow any mathematical differentiation whatever to being would be to play into the refutation given by Plato (*Sph.,* 244E).

Mortals, she declares, have decided conventionally to set up two forms. One of these it is not right to name.[29] In this they have gone astray. The two forms are opposites. The one is characterized by fire, and is gentle, very light in weight, the same as itself in every way and not the same as the other. But also the second is by itself, in contrary fashion unknowing night, thick in body and heavy (*Fr.* 8.53-59). This seems to describe in the doxastic framework the two opposites of the middle part of the poem, being and not-being. The one characterized by fire and flame and perfect self-identity, would coincide with being. The second, characterized as unknowing, night, dense and heavy, would be identical with not-being. As black is a negation for the physicist but a positive color for the artist, designer, or psychologist, so night and earth could be regarded as a mere lack of light. This should not be given positive status. Given it by human convention, however, it provides a positive opposite from which and into which things can change, and by which they can be differentiated. The All now has to appear (*Fr.* 1.31-32) as multiple and changing.

This is confirmed by *Fr.* 9: "But since all things have been named light and night and what (they have been named) in the different cases according to their forces, all is at the same time full of light and invisible night, both equal, since for neither can there be sharing in any way at all." In this fragment the concluding clause has been given widely differing interpretations, interpretations that deeply affect its meaning.[30] The prima facie translation "since nothing with neither" seems

---

29 *Fr.* 8.54. This is the natural interpretation of the Greek, and is followed by the majority of commentators. The objections seem to arise from unwillingness to identify one of the forms (fire) with being. A grammatical objection (Tarán, p. 218) the ἑτέρην would be required does not seem valid, since ἓν μὲν … ἓν δὲ (LSJ, s.v. εἷς, 3) is an alternate construction in cases like this. Also, even the lack of obligation to name one of the two forms could satisfy the meaning here, in the sense that there is no obligation for men to think the way they ordinarily do. On the controversies, see Tarán, pp. 217-225. However, the notion "a unity of which is not necessary" (Tarán, p. 86) is hard to read into the expression "one" in the text, and it is still harder to see that the meaning is "one form, i.e. Being, contains them both" and that "they are identical in this respect" (p. 224). Moreover, other instances suggest that οὐ χρεών ἐστιν conveys a negative injunction rather than absence of necessity — Mourelatos, p. 278. On the "syntactical scramble" in *Fr.* 8.53, see Mourelatos, p. 229, and for *morphai* as "perceptible forms," p. 220. On the relation of "signs" (*Fr.* 8.55) to "capabilities" (*dynameis* — *Fr.* 9.2), see Tarán, p. 162.

30 For the interpretations, see Tarán, pp. 163-164. The reason why the All is filled with light and night is given in the first line of the fragment. Accordingly the ἐπεὶ in line 4 introduces the reason why both are equal. The reason is the one already given in *Fr.* 8.57-58. Each of the two is self-contained, thoroughly the same as itself and not the same as the other. This tenet is referred to briefly by saying that neither is capable of sharing in any way whatever. The required sense emerges in taking μηδέν as an adverb, μέτα (see LSJ, s.v. F) for an impersonal μέτεστι, and οὐδετέρῳ as a dative of advantage. In the accumulation of negatives (Smyth, no. 2761) the second negative confirms the first. If light and night are equated with the being and not-being of the middle part of the poem, they manifest all the sharp difference already established between being and its opposite, namely its negation.

meaningless. The notion of inclusion under or classification under the two forms seems hard to fit into the context, while a denial of participation seems normal here. One form has been emphatically declared not the same as the other (*Fr.* 8.58). This total lack of sharing is now repeated as the reason for their equality in the constitution of the cosmos.[31] The force of neither can be encroached upon by the other. Together they fill the universe.

But what is meant by saying that all things are named "light and night"? This is brought forward as a fact already established. It prompts one to look back to what had been said about naming at *Fr.* 8.38-41. Among the examples was the combination "they are and are not." In the context this combination can hardly be understood in any other sense than the doxastic confusion of being with not-being (*Fr.* 6.8-9). It refers to the things that make the ordinary, everyday world of mortals. Since *Fr.* 9 came shortly after *Fr.* 8 in the poem, and we have no report of what would have been an exceptionally striking statement in the intervening lines, it is scarcely possible that any further explanation why all things are called "light and night" came between the two fragments. *Fr.* 8.53 stated that two forms were named, but the tenet that all things have been named the combination of the two was not established. The assertion seems accordingly to be a restatement in doxastic terms of what had been established, in terms of being, when naming had been earlier discussed. "Light and night," then, would be the doxastic equivalent of "being and not-being." Of everything in the *doxa*, this would mean, men think that it is and it is not, in the sense that it manifests so much light and leaves the rest darkness. That is the general name for each. Specific names are given in accordance with particular characteristics. The listed fragments end with the assertion (*Fr.* 19.3) that men have conventionally posited a distinguishing name for each thing in the *doxa*.

How, though, can a multiple and changing world be set up when reasoning shows that there is only a single undifferentiated being? The difficult *Fr.* 16 explains that thinking takes place for men in accord with the mixture of the much wandering constituents at each moment, for what the nature of the constituents thinks is the same for all men and for each, since the full is the thought.[32] There is little agreement even on

31   On the functional rather than quantitative sense of the equality, see Tarán, p. 163, no. 4, and p. 232.

32   This fragment (*Fr.* 16) has been discussed at great length. See Kurt Riezler, *Parmenides* (Frankfurt: Klostermann, 1934), 65-71 (2nd ed., ed. H.-G. Gadamer, pp. 61-65); Verdenius, pp. 5-30; G. Vlastos, "Parmenides' Theory of Knowledge," *Tr. Am. Philol. Assoc.,* 77 (1946), 66-74; J. Bollack, "Sur deux fragments de Parménide (4 et 16)," *Revue des études grecques,* 70 (1957), 56-71; J. Mansfeld, *Die Offenbarung des Parmenides und die menschliche Welt* (Assen: Van Gorcum, 1964), pp. 175-201; Tarán, pp. 169-170 and 253-268; Mourelatos, pp. 253-259.

the meanings of the key words in this fragment. The overall meaning that emerges is a conception of human thinking as something that varies according to the physical constituents in which it takes place. These vary continually. But they provide a common object of thought for all and each. The reason given is that the full, quite obviously the positive constituent already located in light or being, is what one understands by thought.

This offers an explanation for the continued change and multiplicity in human thinking and its object. It accounts for the common doxastic universe in which all men live, while allowing for individuality in the thinking of each. It permits one to understand Parmenides himself as a unit of thinking that appears in the *doxa*, at a particular time and place.[33] Exploiting the overtones of comparison in the ambiguous Greek word for "full," a comparative force understood by Theophrastus as he quoted these verses, it suggests that as light predominates, thought becomes more intensified, and as light diminishes, thought lessens.[34] Ultimately this would mean that in the ever changing course of events in the *doxa*, death means complete predominance of night, while elevation to the level of the goddess's message means complete predominance of light in understanding everything in terms of being. What is not explained, however, is why the two basic forms should appear with equal force in what is really unique, whole, unchanging and everywhere the same.

V

Careful scrutiny of the fragments themselves, accordingly, bears out Aristotle's assertions that Parmenides was among those who "while they were inquiring into the truth of that which is, ... thought 'that which is' was identical with the sensible world" (*Metaph.*, Γ 5, 1010a1-3; Oxford tr.), that he called being and not-being fire and earth (*GC*, I 3, 318b6-7), that he ranges fire with being and earth with not-being (*Metaph.*, A 5, 986b34-987a2), and that for him the one being "is one in definition, but more than one according to our sensations" (986b31-32), forced in this

___

33 Supra, n. 12. For Tarán, p. 122, to allow existence to a thought "makes thought itself an existent, and this for Parmenides was impossible." Likewise, "the sensible world in which we live can have no existence whatever" (p. 202). Tarán uses this guillotine repeatedly to bring doom to the various objects perceived in the sensible universe. But in Parmenides the conclusion from the premise "Only being exists" should not be "Therefore thought and sensible things do not exist." Rather, it should be "Therefore thought and all sensible things are being, and to that extent they exist."

34 See Theophrastus, *De Sensu*, 3, in Diels, *Dox.*, p. 499 (DK, 28A 46). On the problem of the term "full" in *Fr.* 16, see Tarán, pp. 256-258; Mourelatos, pp. 254-258.

respect to follow the phenomena. The fragments satisfactorily substantiate the tenets that for Parmenides the physical world really exists,
that it is the only existent or being known to Parmenides in his way of
truth, and that he has no rational transition from the cogent reasoning
about its unicity and immobility to its plural appearance in the *doxa*.
The same thing *is* one and changeless, but appears to men as multiple
and incessantly in motion. Once a duality of basic forms in equal status
has been irrationally established, the plurality and change can be explained. But no way of linking this duality with truth can be found.

Is this Parmenidean conception of things coherent in its own
historical setting? The reasoning about being is flawless, provided that
the nature of being is regarded as the object of a human intuition. This
would be normal enough at the time, before the Platonic and
Aristotelian encounters with the puzzling nature of being, and much
before the twentieth century debates whether being is a predicate, and
if so a predicate of an altogether peculiar kind. In the fifth century B.C.
it would appear quite on a par with other notions. It would have a content, and it would be definite and limited as an object of human intuition. It would cogently ground the reasoning of Parmenides in the
middle section of the poem.

The restriction of being to the sensible order is likewise quite in accord with Parmenides' times. On the other hand, the tenet that a
multiple and changing universe can appear in a thoroughly one and
stable being, is an innovation with Parmenides. But this is a situation
that need not have deterred Parmenides any more than it deterred subsequent thinkers who rose above the routine conceptions of their times.
For Plotinus (*En.*, V, 9, 6), the one intelligence is all beings, yet allows
them to be distinct as objects. For Aquinas, subsistent being is unique
and eternally unchangeable in itself, yet in itself it contains the being of
all the multiple and changing things of the sensible universe and allows
all the differentiations and events of the world to be seen in itself. For
Malebranche (*Entretiens*, Préf.; I, 9-10), it is only in God that one sees all
things. For Leibniz (*Monad.*, nos. 56-62), each monad, though completely
self-contained, allows whatever transpires in other monads to be seen in
itself, and for Berkeley the only *esse* of sensible things was their *percipi* in
minds. The situation, therefore, need not be regarded as at all impossible, even though these other thinkers offer philosophical reasons
for the possibility of discerning multiplicity and change within a single
and unchanging entity while the fragments of Parmenides give none.
But against the background of the Eleatic's doctrine of truth, could any
rational justification be asked? Would not that be elevating the *doxa* to
the status of truth, in establishing its possibility by reasoning? Is not
Aristotle correct in saying that here Parmenides was forced by the

phenomena? The Greeks, in spite of their love for form and intelligibility, did not hesitate to acknowledge a radically unintelligible factor at work in the universe, whether necessity for Plato, formless matter for Aristotle, evil for Plotinus. Correspondingly in Parmenides the appearance in being of the two basic doxastic forms would seem to escape the purview of reasoning. Any rational account of their appearing would be self-refuting.

Does this lack of truth in the *doxa* lessen in any way the reality of sensible things? Is the multiple and changing perceptible world any less real to the enlightened Parmenides than to ordinary men?

The answer must be negative. For the Eleatic all sensible things have being, far more being than the ordinary mentality is willing to concede to any one of them. The being of the least of them is all the being of the universe. It lacks nothing that is existent. Only there, in the sensible universe, has Parmenides found being. If the perceptible world did not exist, his reasoning would be deprived of all object.

In a word, sensible things retain for Parmenides their full pristine reality while having it viewed from a different level. A modern example may serve as illustration. Eddington contrasted the solid visible table at which he sat with the mostly-empty-space object he knew as a physicist. Yet the two were the same thing. Moreover, he was aware of the particles-and-space construction through having perceived the visible and tangible things. If the perceptible object were not there, nothing would be there to be known in the physicist's terms. Correspondingly for Parmenides, any denial of the reality of the physical world would do away with the reality of being, and its reduction to an illusory status would make being likewise an illusion. The one stable being and the multiple and changing perceptible world are the same thing, as known respectively through reasoning and through sensation. At least in this instance the fragments show that Aristotle, though in sharp disagreement with the Eleatic's views, correctly analyzed and reported the tenets of a Presocratic thinker.

Pontifical Institute of Mediaeval Studies.